JAMES ANTH

James Anthony Froude remains one of the most commonly referenced and frequently cited of Victorian public intellectuals. Known to intellectual historians as the author of a monumental *History of England* in the sixteenth century and as a key exponent of Victorian religious doubt, he is also noted as the author of a series of scandalously provocative novels and of a hugely controversial biography of Thomas Carlyle. Historians of the British Empire and of Ireland have frequently been compelled to address his sometimes outrageous historical writings. Scholars of mid-Victorian politics have no less often turned to Froude as a typical representative of Victorian fears of democracy, while more recently students of political thought have identified him as an early representative of a new form of Commonwealth civic republicanism.

Yet for all that Froude remains a strangely marginalised, fragmented, and neglected figure. Ciaran Brady now addresses this remarkable gap. Based on a thorough critical examination of all of Froude's published works—many of which have been identified here for the first time—and supplemented by intensive research into Froude's private and widely scattered manuscript materials, he offers the first sustained study of Froude's life and thought. Against the common assumption that Froude's life can be divided along simple lines—the sometime *enfant terrible* who aged into a respectable man of letters—he argues that there was a deeper coherence underlying everything he wrote from the scandalous productions of the 1840s to the orthodox university lectures of the 1890s.

In addition to providing a study of a major but neglected nineteenth century intellectual, Brady offers a critical analysis of the impulses, the aspirations, and the assumptions underlying the Romantic project of personal renovation, and an alternative view of that unique phenomenon known as 'the Victorian sage'.

Ciaran Brady Professor of Early Modern History and Historiography in the School of Histories and Humanities at Trinity College Dublin.

'This book could not be more timely, or more useful in elucidating the roots of a prophetic vocation'

Julia Stapleton, *American Historical Review*

'Brady writes about even the most difficult material with consistent clarity and energy, and with a cool but generous relish for all aspects of Froude's enormous output. Froude's often outré, sometimes absurd and occasionally repellent political opinions and activities are expounded with insight and sympathy, and the portrait of the complex, gifted and exasperating individual that emerges is entirely persuasive'

Eamon Duffy, *Times Literary Supplement*

'a rich slice of intellectual history as well as a memorable portrait of an impressive, if intermittently appalling, personality who left an enduring mark on Irish historiography, Carlylean biography and much else'

Roy Foster, *Times Literary Supplement*

'Brady has mastered not only Froude's own prodigious body of writing but also a vast, demanding literature on Victorian intellectual history. The result is an erudite and absorbing study, a masterclass of scholarly exegesis and lucid analysis … triumphantly renders Froude, the public historian and sage, more intelligible and infinitely more interesting than we may have assumed and, in the process, illumines large swathes of the intellectual landscape of Victorian England'

The Irish Times

'[Froude's] unpublished autobiography should have been called *Disappointment*. There is nothing disappointing, however, in this elegant biography'

Michael Bentley, *History Today*

'With consummate skill and erudition Brady traces the intricate course of Froude's thinking through his work'

Literary Review

'[Froude's] fate is a puzzle, and Brady's exhaustive investigation is the first to give it the attention it deserves'

John Pemble, *London Review of Books*

'Brady ... has written a shrewd, vigilant inquiry into biography and literary ethics'

The Wall Street Journal

'Ciaran Brady's book deserves to be recognised as the definitive biography of the Victorian prophet'

Irish Historical Studies

JAMES ANTHONY FROUDE

AN INTELLECTUAL BIOGRAPHY OF
A VICTORIAN PROPHET

CIARAN BRADY

OXFORD
UNIVERSITY PRESS

OXFORD
UNIVERSITY PRESS

Great Clarendon Street, Oxford, OX2 6DP,
United Kingdom

Oxford University Press is a department of the University of Oxford.
It furthers the University's objective of excellence in research, scholarship,
and education by publishing worldwide. Oxford is a registered trade mark of
Oxford University Press in the UK and in certain other countries

© Ciaran Brady 2013

The moral rights of the authors have been asserted

First published 2013
First published in paperback 2014

Impression: 1

Published in the United States of America by Oxford University Press
198 Madison Avenue, New York, NY 10016, United States of America

British Library Cataloguing in Publication Data

Data available

ISBN 978–0–19–966803–8 (Hbk.)
ISBN 978–0–19–872653–1 (Pbk.)

For Aoife
and
Fiachra and Oisín

Preface

Why write about Froude? Two apparently opposite, but equally unattractive, motives immediately suggest themselves. One lies in the pleasures of retrospective moral censure.

Froude is easy to deplore. His imperialism, his chauvinism, his apparent racism, his unabashed religious bigotry, and his worship of strong men are all attributes so deeply distasteful to modern sensibilities that they readily facilitate reproach. And the fact that he himself divulged evidence of his dark and violent childhood experiences makes it all the more attractive to apply psychological assessment, and to ascribe his ideas to the infections of an abused and pathological mind. Such operations have always been as easy as they are questionable. But even if they were demonstrably valid, their achievement seems to me to be of little benefit, other than satisfying a desire for the moral superiority of hindsight.

Yet an opposite impulse, the wish to exonerate, though it may be slightly more noble, is scarcely of greater value. To assert that Froude was not so bad after all: that he had his good side, that (famously) he abhorred cruelty to animals, that he was kind to the poor, etc.; and to show by highlighting other neglected facets of his life, or by supplying contextual exculpations of his views, that he has been unfairly condemned—is a research investment whose intellectual product, however gratifying it may be to the revisionist writer, is so slight that it too seems hardly sufficient to justify the effort.

In undertaking this study I have been moved neither by a desire to rehabilitate nor condemn, but simply by intellectual curiosity. As an historian of the early modern period with a related theoretical interest in the problems of historical writing and judgement, I have for long been intrigued as to how an individual whose passionate devotion to issues of faith and moral responsibility, and whose deep and conscientious engagement with the practices of historical research were such marked characteristics of his mind should also, and unremittingly, have given free expression to judgements and

opinions which now appear to be so wilful, perverse and often repulsive.
What was Froude he trying to do?

That Froude was a disturbed and disagreeable man was a conventional
estimation from which at the outset I, as an Irishman—a specimen of
humanity which he held in particularly low esteem—had little *prima facie*
grounds to dissent. Now, after several years of studying his writings, actions
and private reflections, I have emerged with an impression of an individual
endowed with far more courage, more intellectual strength, and greater
moral integrity than I had first expected. I have seen too that there is a far
greater coherence in his outlook and purpose than his reputation as a failed
enfant terrible and a lover of self-indulgent paradox ever allowed, and that at
the heart of this consistency was his acute awareness of central moral and
philosophical problems, the importance of which few of us would wish to
deny. But far from dissolving my own discomfort with certain of his opinions, my admiration for Froude's undoubted qualities has simply deepened
my curiosity as to how such apparently profound contradictions arose
between his passionate engagement with the spiritual, ethical and epistemological problems with which many of us continue to be concerned, and his
particular views on politics, religion and race which have so decisively alienated him from us. Put simply, I have sought in what follows to examine
whether the asperities and contradictions which seem to characterise
Froude's work were merely the product of a limited and troubled mind, or
whether they were a symptom of a profound and audacious engagement
with ethical, historical and spiritual questions whose subtlety and complexity we may ourselves have ceased to appreciate.

It is here, however, that a second, more technical question arises: how to
write about Froude? What is the appropriate balance to be set between life
and work, between the public utterances and the private circumstances
which in some degree shaped them? Here Froude presents a particular challenge in that chronologically his life may be sharply divided into two distinct phases. There is the first, running as far as his mid-thirties but
concentrating largely on his twenties, during which his personal life—his
reaction against his father, his dalliance with Newman, his supposed atheism, his scandalous early fictions and his expulsion from Oxford—appears
to embody so much of the troubles of his generation in such a concentrated
form as to command detailed biographical attention. But thereafter, once he
turned to the sedate and conventional modes of writing English history,
secured the editorial chair of the (by then) respectable *Fraser's Magazine*, and

withdrew into a relatively undisturbed, upright private life, the interest of continued biographical study correspondingly declines. Though he had his share of personal achievement and private grief, Froude's public life was—apart from his brief diplomatic mission to South Africa in the mid-1870s—largely uneventful. And such public events or controversies with which he became involved arose primarily from his writings.

Confronted with this pattern, the small band of Froude's biographers have resorted to various strategies. Thus Herbert Paul chose to minimise the depth and significance of his youthful rebelliousness in order to establish greater continuity with his conventional later career. While Julia Markus, building upon the intense personal revelations of his early life, attempted a psychological portrait which, while fascinating, was necessarily of an increasingly speculative character.[1] Waldo Hilary Dunn who, having been given access to materials never seen before (nor since), was in effect Froude's authorised biographer adopted an ingenious strategy, suggested perhaps by Froude's own biography of Carlyle, of publishing his work in two (relatively short) volumes, divided at the point of Froude's turn to history writing.[2]

Froude himself contributed greatly to this bifurcation by means of a manuscript autobiography which he prepared shortly before his death. Confessional, intimate, honest (in so far as any such exercise can be), and far from self-exculpatory, the fragment is also sharply truncated, concluding in the mid-1850s when Froude began to publish the *History of England* which was to transform his reputation and his life. And though there is evidence thereafter that he continued to keep a regular journal which could have formed the basis for a continued autobiography, he seems to have made little effort to do so; while such fragmentary pieces of autobiography that he composed pertaining to this later period are couched in a defensive, apologetic, or consciously manipulative tone far different from the autobiography proper.[3]

Just as there appears to be more deliberation than accident in the shaping of Froude's autobiographical 'remains', so there was also some conscious determination in shaping the actual life which they reflect. For, although it was a crucial one, the abandonment of the confessional voice of the young man in favour of that of the authoritative historian was but one stage in a

1. Herbert Paul, *Life of Froude* (London, 1905); Julia Markus, *J. Anthony Froude: the last undiscovered great Victorian* (New York, 2007).
2. W. H. Dunn, *James Anthony Froude: a Biography* (2 vols Oxford, 1961, 1963).
3. For example, *My Relations with Carlyle* (London, 1903).

lengthy sequence of changing expressive modes which began at least with
Froude's coming to maturity around age twenty, if not years before. At the
heart of this process of mutating ventriloquism was Froude's profoundly felt
sense of his own personal deficiencies. There was nothing overtly deceptive
in this move. For far from seeking to hide or deny his inner weakness, he
converted it into a life principle. The common aim of his several publicly
adopted personae was to demonstrate in his own case the potential of all
human beings to rise above their inherited and accidental characters by a
determined, self-conscious and self-disregarding engagement with the
world. In embarking on such a liberating mission, Froude was doubtless
encouraged by certain key contemporary influences urging a similar leap
from self-doubt to active commitment—Newman, Goethe and, of course,
Carlyle. But the origin of this impulse, and its subsequent management
throughout his life, was Froude's, and Froude's alone. For despite his frequently expressed admiration for each of these powerful figures, especially
Carlyle, it is remarkable how little influence they exerted on the style and
tone of his own distinctive voices. Voices: because, despite its formative
importance, Froude's adoption of the register of the grand narrative historian was not his only resort. Indeed, over the whole of his career he was to
enact an extensive series of different and often contrasting ventriloquisms as
he deemed his audience and the occasion demanded.

In what follows I have sought to reflect this pattern of Froude's own life-
shaping presentations. Thus in the early chapters, where my principal concern has been to describe the circumstances out of which Froude's
consciously constructed life emerged, my approach has been biographical,
contextual, and in some part psychologically speculative. But in later chapters, following his attainment of a firm public persona, I have, except in
those circumstances where events make the presentation of biographical
material requisite, shifted my emphasis from the detail of Froude's private
life to a critical examination of his public expressions. So, for example, while
I have thought it important to provide some account of the social and cultural conditions obtaining in Oxford during Froude's undergraduate days as
being relevant to his crisis of maturation, I have given less attention to the
condition of the university at the time of Froude's brief return to it in the
early 1890s. For the university exerted little further influence on Froude at
that time; nor he on it.

My decision in this matter rests on more than historical or critical con-
venience. For at the core of Froude's life-strategy was a moral conviction

whose force increased as his career developed, and as his sense of the importance of history—as lived and recollected experience—intensified. This was
his belief in the capacity of all human beings to rise above their individual
deficiencies, and to realise the potential which the force of creation planted
within them. This was a liberating, life-enhancing claim. In its implied
acceptance of a fundamental equality between author and reader in a common pursuit of a goal universally attainable, it is moreover, singularly attractive. And in its assumption that the purpose of all imaginative writing, and
history writing in particular, was not for establishment of the superiority of
some particular interpretation over another, or for the aggrandisement of
the author's reputation, but to alert all possible readers to the cluster of
moral challenges that lay before them, it supplies a humbling contrast to the
impoverished way in which so many of us in the academy profess to study
the humanities today.

Yet, for all it sincerity and audacity, Froude's conception of his own prophetic role rested on premises that were beset by moral hazard. One was the
conviction that, notwithstanding the defects inflicted by nature, nurture, and
history, individual humans could unite in a common cause of understanding
their place in the universe which would ultimately resolve their deepest
contentions. This was a claim that Marxists and other social theorists would
find naïve, even self-servingly so. Another risky assumption was the belief
that, having sincerely fought through to his own abnegation of the self,
Froude was in a position to guide other searching souls along the same path:
a claim that Freud and his philosophical precursors would likewise have
found untenable. But finally Froude's presumption that in order to prepare
his audience for the full realisation of their historical potential, he might by
means of rhetorical strategies persuade them to endorse violently hostile
attitudes in regard to the claims for freedom for millions of souls whom he
deemed not yet ready for the privilege, was an attitude which fundamentally threatened the ethical foundations of his entire enterprise.

What then is the point of writing about Froude? It is not only for the
historical and literary interest which a critical review of this strangely
marginalised Victorian may evoke. It lies rather in the present and immediate challenges which his own decisions about the way his life should be
managed present to us. Though all of us now readily assert the right to
express our opinions and our possession of approximate truths, such a claim
entails an equal obligation. This is that in making our public utterances we
must ensure that we are prepared to address the consequences of their

expression which, though ethically inescapable are so often conveniently ignored. For the fundamental condition of all humanity that Froude confronted with such clear-eyed courage has not changed; arbitrarily plunged, as we have been, into the flux of history's forces over which we have little control, our very consciousness still insists that, willingly or not, we humans must assume responsibility for our actions in this world, or else abandon ourselves to meaningless existence. And just as in his time Froude witnessed the falling away of the traditional religious and philosophical protections against this reality, so the palliatives to which subsequent generations have had resort such as empirical science, moral relativism, and material progress have steadily lost their valence. And while we may dissociate ourselves from the means and manner in which he attempted to transcend the historical dilemma as he perceived it in his day, the question of responsibilities which Froude faced, and struggled incessantly to meet, remains obstinately before us.

Acknowledgements

In following Anthony Froude over the many regions on which he has left his trace, I have incurred a debt of unusual extent to archivists and librarians in the United Kingdom, Ireland, Spain, the United States, Australia, and South Africa. And in almost every case I have experienced the benefit of their great professional service and their personal generosity which it is a pleasure to acknowledge now. The role served by these indispensable guardians of cultural life is all the more in need of grateful recognition at a time when, even within our universities, the philistine question as to whether such services are relevant to our needs has now become respectable. But in particular I wish to record my personal indebtedness to the late Gerard Tracey of the Birmingham Oratory and J. R. Madicott of Exeter College, Oxford.

This study was kick-started by an award of Naughton Fellowship at the University of Notre Dame, and I would like to thank the Naughton Fund, and Chris Fox, Jim Smyth, Peter McQuillan and all those at the Keough Institute of Irish Studies who were then and on several occasions since hosts of extraordinary generosity both social and intellectual.

I wish to record my gratitude to my own university, Trinity College Dublin where at all levels, from the Provost, Dr Patrick Prendergast, down, I have been in receipt of continuing confidence, goodwill, and personal support. Trinity's practical assistance freely given throughout this long process has now been capped by a grant in aid of publication by the Grace Lawless Lee Fund. Within my own Department I would like to note the generosity of the real experts in nineteenth-century studies, Bill Vaughan, David Dickson and David Fitzpatrick, toward this interloper from the nether regions, and the support from my early modern colleagues, Jane Ohlmeyer and Micheál Ó Siochrú for this potential traitor in their midst. Though they bear no responsibility for the present enterprise and will doubtless (though in characteristically different ways) find much to criticise in it, I want again to record my gratitude to two inspiring teachers and scholars, Aidan Clarke and Brendan Bradshaw. Throughout all the process of research and writing I have had the inestimable benefit of having a good circle of friends and colleagues within the Department of History and in other disciplines and other universities who have been throughout a constant source of encouragement and inspiration; who patiently put up with my interminable complaints and intolerable enthusiasms; who have read all or part of the work at one stage or another: and whose names it is now a pleasure to record: Robert Armstrong, Eugenio Biagini, Brian Jackson, Helen Kelly, Elizabeth Kingston, Graeme Murdock, John Morrill, Séamas Ó Síocháin, Graham Parry, Eve Patten, and Rory Rapple. Bill McCormack was an unfailing source of stimulating conversation and encouragement. Michael Laffan gave generously of his expertise in modern British and Irish history, and supplied me with a painstaking reading of a late draft which greatly improved it and saved me from many errors and infelicities: my appreciation of his generosity in devoting time , thought and advice to my work is enormous. Some I have imposed on beyond all reason: I wish now to thank my dear friends Michael Quigley, Patrick Geoghegan and Colm Croker. They have lived with Froude for a decade and have been unfailingly generous in the attention which, despite the many pressures on their own time, they have been so willing to offer. At a crucial stage my good friend Jim Murray, who also read the entire book in a critical and constructive way, was a source of reassurance and fortification which I shall never forget. Finally, I must express my special indebtedness to Roy Foster. From the beginnings, when the idea of writing anything about Froude was just a notion, to the very last stages, Roy has been an abiding friend. Without his consistent interest, his generous provision of occasions in which I could try out my ideas, his critical responses, and his shrewd practical advice, I can honestly say this book would never have been brought to completion.

The dedication registers a debt, accrued over many years, which is as deeply felt as it is irredeemable.

Contents

I

Froude's Voices

'The law of man's life is self-annihilation'

James Anthony Froude, 1875

Froude is forgotten. This once unmistakable literary voice which for more than half a century succeeded in stimulating, provoking, and inspiring many thousands of readers, and in scandalising, antagonising, and exasperating at least as many more, has now become submerged in the sedimentary layers of Victorian literary mediocrity. It is, in part, a fate sufficiently deserved. So many of Froude's opinions on politics and society, and on the world in general, now appear so drearily representative of the comfortable middle-class attitudes of his day that there has seemed little reason to retrieve him from the undifferentiated mass of essentially conventional nineteenth-century men of letters.[1] But the extent of this neglect has been neither just nor prudent, and in what follows I shall argue that it has arisen as a result not only of the persistently troublesome and disruptive nature of his voice, but also as a consequence of our own embarrassment in attempting to deal with the intellectual and moral issues which, throughout his career, he insisted on placing before his readers.

I

Froude was more than a domesticated lion of the Victorian literary establishment. He was in several different fields a bold and controversial original.

---

1. On the decline of interest in Froude, compare the contents of Robert Goetzman's *James Anthony Froude: A Bibliography of Studies* (New York, 1977) with the results of an on-line search through Worldcat or the Modern Languages Association International Bibliography.

His early fictional writings were among the first to take on the scandalous and disturbing topics of atheism, adultery, and sexual impotence. A novella he wrote in 1847 contains one of the rarest and most frank depictions of an operating brothel, as well as an experiment in time-shifts and multiple endings which was to be taken up and developed by modernist writers only decades later. In his history writing he was among the very first English historians to found his narrative almost exclusively on manuscript primary sources rather than on standard printed authorities, and he was the very first to extract his evidence from a range of archives across the continent of Europe never before used for the writing of England's history. In regard to the history of Ireland, he was also an innovator, opening up topics in that country's economic and social history which remained part of Irish historians' agenda for almost a century, and questions of England's moral conduct towards its people which remain even now the central preoccupation of some modern scholars.[2] As an observer of contemporary history he was also in some respects prescient. He was among the first English commentators to see that the triumph of the North in the American Civil War presented a fundamental challenge to Britain's international pre-eminence; and he was among the first to advocate a reconstruction of the British Empire as a commonwealth in which power would be shared equally by all members.[3] It was as a biographer, however, that Froude was especially audacious. In his short life of Disraeli which the Tory grandees encouraged him to write shortly after the great man's death, he refused to bow to the pious conventions surrounding such works, and provided instead an account that was not only moderately critical but distinctly modern in its emphasis on its subject's literary talent and psychological temperament. Most notoriously of all, Froude used his position as the official biographer of Carlyle to provide a deeply intimate portrait of Carlyle's relations with his wife Jane which was to be a scandal in its time, and a model for all post-Freudian biographers.[4]

---

2. See the comments by L. M Cullen in W. E. Vaughan (ed.), *A New History of Ireland: vi: The Eighteenth Century*, 123–4; for an example of the continuing relevance of the issues raised by Froude to Irish historians of the sixteenth century, see Vincent Carey, 'John Derricke's *Image of Ireland*, Sir Henry Sidney and the massacre at Mullaghmast', *Irish Historical Studies* (May, 1999).

3. Carl Bodelson, *Studies in Mid-Victorian Imperialism* (Copenhagen, 1924), 172–205.

4. John Clubbe (ed.), *Froude's Life of Carlyle* (Columbia, OH, 1979) is an abridgement with scholarly commentary which includes a discussion of the influence of Froude's work on subsequent approaches to biography in general; the most recent biography, Rosemary Ashton, *Thomas and Jane Carlyle: Portrait of a Marriage* (London, 2002), while offering some qualifications, largely endorses Froude's assessment of Carlyle's conduct in the marriage.

Yet Froude's was also a wilful, unpredictable, and offensive mind. Possessed of a troubled and trouble-making voice from the beginning of his career to its close, he seemed to have made a practice of deliberately provoking enemies and deliberately disappointing friends. At one time or another almost everyone in British public life had good reason to feel mortally offended by Froude. Pious churchman and atheists, radical materialists and idealist Carlyleans, empiricists and mystics, plutocrats and working men, Liberal reformers and High Tories, Irish nationalists and Anglo-Irish landlords, imperialists and colonial separatists were all on occasion infuriated by his public utterances, usually to an intense degree. He even managed to ensure that his two brief intervals of cloistered academic life—the first as Fellow of Exeter College, Oxford, the second as Regius Professor of History at the same university—though separated by fifty years, were infused with controversy.[5]

The persistently uncomfortable nature of Froude's relations with his own intellectual contemporaries should not, however, be seen simply as a sign of his personal eccentricity. It is, rather, a symptom of the complex, and frequently misunderstood, character of the cultural environment in which he worked. That Froude, despite their apparent similarity of interests and life-long friendship, could discount the literary work of Charles Kingsley may not be altogether surprising, but that he should have praised and defended Swinburne and Frank Harris is.[6] That Froude the historian of empire should have reserved his most bitter private comments not for his inveterate public enemy, the Little Englander E. A. Freeman, but for the mild and inoffensive J. R. Green, is similarly unexpected. That he should have deeply admired George Eliot, but loathed her partner G. H. Lewes; that he should have discounted the work of fellow biographer and editor Leslie Stephen, but esteemed that of Stephen's brother Fitzjames; that he should have despised the Church of England establishment, but continued to seek out and even to praise Catholic priests and apologists—these are all seeming incongruities which can be resolved on intellectual rather than psychological grounds. But this very resolution necessarily entails a serious revision of the currents underlying cultural, moral, and political argument in nineteenth-century Britain.

The problem of his 'unclubbability', however, has extended beyond Froude's generation down to our own, for on all those issues which might

5. See chs. 5 and 6; Ian Hesketh, *The Science of History in Victorian Britain: Making the Past Speak* (London, 2011), 153–7.
6. For Froude's admiration of Swinburne, see Froude to Skelton, 15, 19 August 1866, *Table-Talk of Shirley*, 136–7; Frank Harris, *My Life and Loves* (2 vols., London, 1922), ii, ch. viii.

have brought him closer to us, he appears not only to have failed to go far enough for our taste, but actually to have taken off somewhere else. Thus the early fictions' blend of adultery and agnosticism which scandalised his contemporaries we now regard as mild and unsatisfactory, because Froude, we can see, was not an atheist at all, but a passionate believer. Similarly, the great archival discoveries of his books on English and Irish history are obscured for us by the unashamedly polemical interpretations for which he put them to use. His admirable latitudinarianism, his interest in Buddhism, his pleas for a free discussion of religious difference, are spoiled by his repeated attacks on Romanism. His advanced proposals for a British commonwealth are likewise tainted by a strong whiff of racism. And the psychological modernity of his biography of Carlyle is crossed by his own uncritical admiration for the prophet's achievement.

Thus Froude has continued to stand as awkwardly in relation to us as he did to his contemporaries. And in face of our difficulty with taking him whole, we have in general sought to fragment him, calling on his services in several different but always minor ways. As a writer, for instance, he has retained some value for us as a source for some colourful anecdotes concerning the Oxford Movement, or for some characteristic phrase of jingoistic history, or for some enlightened comments on man's cruelty to animals. As an historical figure in his own right he has likewise done some service as a representative victim of Victorian hypocrisy—the burning of his second novel by the sub-rector of Exeter College seems to be the most commonly known fact about him—or of the brutalities of early nineteenth-century childhood. Yet all the while we have preferred to ignore the common source of such different and often contradictory signals: Froude himself. And, as a consequence of his obstinate refusal to be bracketed by us either as a drearily familiar Victorian, or as a harbinger of the modern, he has been condemned to drift toward the margins of our attention, the contradictions and disjunctions that have never been far from the surface of our understanding of his awkward mind attributed lazily to the unstable and perverse nature of his own psychology.

II

Given the frightful conditions of his upbringing, there can be no doubt that his personal psychology exercised a major influence in shaping Froude's public address to the world. But the role that it played was rather more complex than has often been assumed, and the reductionism of our own post-Freudian understanding of motives and conduct has rendered us insensitive to the subtle (and sometimes quite unsubtle) manner in which environment and experience and cultural inheritance conditioned the psychological reflexes of the Victorian mind.

As an early modern historian by training, I have been accustomed not 'to make windows into men's souls', especially when the materials for shining any light inside are rarely present and never adequate. But with Froude, who himself recorded the sufferings of his childhood years with such honesty and dispassion, the obligation at least to acknowledge the operation of psychic forces on the intellect is doubly enforced. Bereft before his third birthday of a mother who had spent most of the years after his birth in a sick-bed, suffering from what was generally believed to have been the consequences of his delivery, Froude's start in life was especially unhappy. The youngest child of seven, he grew up in a household that was, even for its time, remarkably sombre, austere, and dominated by two powerful male figures: his father, Robert Hurrell Froude, the formidable Archdeacon of Totnes, and his eldest brother, the charismatic but mercurial Richard Hurrell Froude.[7] Within this joyless environment—'We were a Spartan family,' Froude records—love was never openly expressed (and perhaps rarely felt). Instead, the young Froude was the victim of sustained physical and psychological abuse. His own memoir records instances of violence and torture with a restrained precision that is impossible to question: his earliest memory was of being whipped for soiling his frock before the age of two; and this late account is given a chilling corroboration through one of the few surviving writings of his mother in the form of a note from her sick-bed begging brother Hurrell to desist from torturing the young Anthony in his cot.[8] In receipt only of intermittent protection and maternal affection from his sister Mary, whose early death he was to record as one of the deepest tragedies of his life, 'poor Att' was designated by Hurrell and his father as a 'sawney'—family-speak for a weakling and a coward, a designation which he himself sorrowfully accepted and took to heart.[9]

---

7. See Piers Brendon, *Hurrell Froude and the Oxford Movement* (London, 1974).
8. Louise Imogen Guiney, *Hurrell Froude: Memoranda and Comments* (London, 1904), 4–7.
9. The *Oxford English Dictionary* records the use of the word as a derisory term for a weakling and a fool as early as 1700.

Amidst this misery, Anthony was possessed of one notable gift. He was intellectually precocious, showing at a very early age a competence in classical languages that was, in this intellectually ambitious and competitive family, a sign that something might be made of the 'sawney' after all. His budding talent, however, was to lead to even further suffering. High-level performance at Westminster Public School led to Anthony's advancement to senior form while still aged twelve. But there, in the jungle anarchy of the unsupervised dormitory, the young 'swot' was exposed to the most brutal forms of maltreatment which not improbably included sexual abuse.[10] Desperate to escape from this 'den of horrors', Anthony ceased to perform; he seems to have embroiled himself in some minor financial scandal, and after three and a half years his father was asked to withdraw him. Two further years of domestic misery followed during which the young Froude was subjected to an intensive regime of censure, interrogations, isolation, and regular flogging by the archdeacon, now infuriated by this apparent confirmation of the sawney's incorrigibility. Until at last, adequate supplications having been made, he was thought ready for sending up to Oxford, though shadowed still by the expectation that he would fail.

The consequences of this endless ordeal will appear to psychoanalytically informed minds to have been utterly predictable. The adult Froude, it may be expected, was deeply marked by his childhood traumas, a prey to all kinds of neuroses, personal dysfunctions, and antisocial impulses. It is easy enough to find evidence for such a familiar prognosis, even if it turns out, on closer examination, to be only of a superficial and quite deceptive kind. Cut loose from his prison, the undergraduate Froude, it has been reported, became dissolute and wayward, and deliberately set out to fail in line with expectations. He drank too much, wasted his father's money, spent his days in idleness, and, most probably, some of his nights in the company of prostitutes.[11] Having established his freedom in this self-destructive manner, he next became aggressive and parricidal, issuing in his first novel, 'The Spirit's Trials' (1847), the most damning indictments of an unloving father fifty years before Samuel Butler and Edmund Gosse, and producing in the second, *The*

---

10. See ch. 2.

11. That Froude had some early personal experience of prostitution may be inferred not only from his account of a brothel in 'The Lieutenant's Daughter', but from his recollections of the common practices of Oxford undergraduates of his day supplied in his essays 'The University Commission', in *Eclectic Review*, 93, June 1851, 699–717, and 'The Oxford Commission', *Westminster Review*, 52 (October 1852), 317–48.

Nemesis of Faith (1849), a plot so scandalous as to compel his mortified father publicly to repudiate him. Only having rid himself of his family demons by this process of abreaction could he properly enter the world of adulthood.[12]

Attractive though such interpretations of the psychic origins of Froude's public persona may be, they remain nonetheless speculative and misleading. Resting largely on the evidence supplied by Froude's autobiographical early fiction, they are at once innocently reductionist in their identification of experience with imagination, and more seriously remiss in overlooking the psychological maturity and control required to transmute the recollections of personal experience into literary art. In the chapters that follow I shall argue that much more ambitious things were going on in Froude's fictions—that his philosophical and literary aspirations were at least as important in their composition as his psychological deficiencies—even if his early literary experimentations were largely unsuccessful.[13] Whatever their contribution to his imaginative creativity, what can actually be said of the effects which the profoundly damaging wounds of childhood worked upon Froude's adult character turns out, in fact, to be surprisingly limited. Despite the repeated crises of his life, both private and public, Froude, it seems, was not a notably unstable figure, marked by impulses of irrationality, and obsession, or tendencies toward self-destruction.

Unlike Edward Fowler—his fictional creation in 'The Spirit's Trials'—Froude as a young man was not a neurasthenic recluse, solitary, and physically fragile. As an undergraduate he was in fact normally gregarious and without even the hint of the consumption that had shadowed his elder siblings. True, he fell in with a set, spent too much on his wine bill in his first year up, went on walking tours in the Lake District, and fell hopelessly in love. At length he reformed his wayward conduct, though too late in the day to take the expected First. But he nonetheless recovered sufficiently from his excesses to take a highly creditable Second and to compose thereafter a prize-winning essay on political economy which put him in line for the junior fellowship at Exeter College that came his way within two years of

12. See Robert Wolff, *Gains and Losses: Novels of Faith and Doubt in Victorian England* (New York, 1978, ch.7); Gertrude Himmelfarb, 'A Forgotten "Worthy"', in *Victorian Minds* (Gloucester, MA, 1975); Basil Willey, 'Froude', in *More Nineteenth Century Studies*; Froude, *The Nemesis of Faith*, edited and with an introduction by Rosemary Ashton (London, 1989). 'The Spirit's Trials' first appeared as the first part of the two part collection *Shadows of the Clouds*, see p.134 below.
13. See ch. 4.

graduation.[14] As a youthful academic performance there was nothing grossly abnormal here.

Once established as a Junior Fellow, Froude, moreover, did not abandon the outgoing, energetic character of his undergraduate days. He made friends easily (he was one of the few Oxford dons to retain acquaintances both among the Newmanites and their opponents), and by his mid-twenties he had established himself at the centre of an energetic and self-confident literary group surrounding the *Oxford and Cambridge Review* which included Charles Kingsley, F. D. Maurice, George Butler, Richard Cowley Powles, and Arthur Hugh Clough.[15] Among other glimpses of his days at Oxford, the journals of Lady Caroline Fox for the early 1840s reveal a young man who was witty, talkative, and charming, offering party tricks in palmistry and graphology to keep his place on the invitation lists; while the recollections of George Butler have Froude leading a reading party in the Lake District, visiting the dissolute Hartley Coleridge, whisky bottle in hand, and taking a kindly but not entirely respectful attitude towards the ageing sage.[16] His correspondence from this time is lively, gamey, and intellectually self-confident, redolent of a man somewhat contemptuous of his elders, and determined to make a mark in the world as a critic and artist—nothing, in short, that can distinguish him from many of the ambitious young dons of his day. Like other young college men of the 1840s, however, he had also become deeply frustrated with the oppressive traditionalism of Oxford, and in particular with the requirement that he take orders in the Established Church as a condition of holding his fellowship. Like many among his circle he planned to escape from Oxford as soon as it was financially feasible, and was researching possible careers in medicine and in teaching abroad even as he was composing his explosive second novel.[17]

The publication in 1849 of *The Nemesis of Faith*, which contained sympathetic treatments of a young man's slide into atheism and a young woman's drift into adultery and ruin, did indeed provoke a crisis in Froude's life. Upon its appearance, Froude was disgraced in Oxford, forced to resign his

14. *The Influence of the Science of Political Economy on the Moral and Social Welfare of a Nation: A Prize Essay read in the Sheldonian Theatre, Oxford, June 8, 1842* (Oxford, 1842), 44 pp.; for a discussion, see ch. 3.
15. See ch. 3.
16. Lady Caroline Fox, *Memories of Old Friends* (2 vols., London 1883), i, 252, 327–8; George Butler, 'Reminiscences of the Lakes in 1844', *Longman's Magazine*, 72 (October 1888), 621–35.
17. See chs. 4 and 5.

fellowship at Exeter, was refused a teaching post in Tasmania to which he had previously been appointed, and was compelled to find a living for himself. Some, though by no means all, of this came as a shock. In regard to his notoriety in Oxford, Froude was quite indifferent. He had long since determined to escape from the university, and the scandal merely facilitated his withdrawal. The withdrawal of the offer of the headmastership of a school in Van Diemen's Land (Tasmania) was mildly discomfiting; but the publicity surrounding it only added to the aura of martyrdom with which in some circles he had been invested. More disappointing, however, was the reaction of his closest friends Kingsley, Clough, Maurice, and Frank Newman, who, though sympathising fully with his intentions in writing the novel, were honestly critical of the manner of its execution.

The reception of *The Nemesis of Faith* by sympathetic friends and ignorant enemies alike served, therefore, as a sharp but salutary lesson. It made clear to Froude that his literary aspirations lay beyond the capacity of his abilities, and convinced him that, since he lacked the skill to voice his message in fiction, other means of expression would have to be explored. Thus, unlike the central figure in the novel, Markham Sutherland, Froude was not plunged into a suicidal despair by this setback. Rather, having defended himself ably against his detractors, he resolved to set out anew. And so, politely refusing the offer to take up a scholarship at Heidelberg and other offers of help, Froude determined instead to strike out on his own. After a short but untroubled courtship he married Charlotte Grenfell, sister-in-law of his friend Kingsley, took up a temporary post as a private tutor in Manchester, and set about purposefully developing an independent career as a critic and essayist.[18]

Thereafter, for those in search of evidence of profound psychological disturbance, the remainder of Froude's personal life is a considerable disappointment, seemingly unperturbed by any further crisis. Though regarded by some in later life as aloof and uncommunicative, others found him immensely charming on first acquaintance.[19] He acquired, moreover, as his substantial

---

18. The offer which Froude politely refused was made by another close friend, the Prussian ambassador Baron Bunsen. Froude also turned down an offer of financial support from Lord Brougham, though he accepted a temporary post as private tutor to a family in Manchester which he held for just over a year while continuing to write for the journals. Upon their marriage in April 1850 Charlotte brought a modest dowry of about £300.

19. See, for example, Wilfrid Scawen Blunt's account of Froude's charm on their first meeting: 'I never was more taken with anyone than with Froude, from the moment he came into the room and spoke, for his voice is the most sympathetic in the world,' *The Land war in Ireland* (London, 1912), diary entry for 1 January 1886, 13, also J.C. Collins's recollections in Dunn, *Froude*, I, 542–5.

surviving correspondence demonstrates, a very large set of acquaintances and a select number of genuinely close friends. His *curriculum vitae*, so to speak, was by modern standards remarkably well-balanced—even boringly so—for in addition to his strenuous literary and editorial occupations, he lived a highly active life. He enjoyed hill-walking, fishing, and especially sailing—a skill at which he was an acknowledged master. He was also in his youth an excellent shot, but gave it up on moral grounds, and his later correspondence contains several instances of his literally disarming attempts to avoid the social obligations of the shoot.[20] He liked cigars, drank moderately, and refused to endorse temperance. He was married twice, and had three children by his first and two children by his second marriage. Bereaved by the death of his first wife Charlotte after a long illness, he married one of her closest friends, Henrietta Warre, possibly with Charlotte's dying blessing, and was devastated when she too died after twelve years of marriage.[21] Unlike those of his friends Carlyle and Ruskin, both unions appear to have been happy—the second more intensely so than the first. And he was, unlike his own father and so many of his contemporaries in the land of Victorian letters, a warm and loving father, fond of family games and private jokes, and not above abasing himself to gain advancement for his sons.[22]

Neither the less than traumatic nature of the crisis of 1849 nor the apparent serenity of the years that were to follow should, however, be seen to endorse the contrary inference that childhood suffering exercised little or no impact on Froude's personality or his outlook on life. Some chronic symptoms of disturbance are indeed demonstrable; and it is precisely because they do not readily yield to the dramatic diagnoses of paperback psychology that the less obvious psychic scars of his youth may be seen to have been all the more persistent, more profound, and even more positive in their effects.

Froude was a lifelong insomniac, troubled on occasion by intense bouts of sleeplessness which drove him to the point of exhaustion.[23] With the sleepless nights came attacks of acute anxiety which afflicted him (and became apparently more painful) even when his position as a respected man

---

20. Froude to Kingsley, 23 March (1863–65?), British Library Add MS 41299 f.III; Froude to Carnarvon, 18 October 1877, Add MS 60799(a) f. 63.
21. Dunn, *Froude*, II, 295, reporting Margaret Froude.
22. See *inter alia* Froude to Margaret Froude, in Dunn, *Froude*, II, 293–4; Henrietta Froude to [unknown], British Library, R.P, f.143; Froude to Lady Derby, 6 April [1883], Derby MSS, Liverpool Public Library, no. 9.
23. See his account of his chronic condition given to the Earl of Carnarvon, British Library Add MS 60997(a) ff.345–7.

of letters had been securely established.[24] And if he was not pathologically depressive, he became in his private life increasingly melancholic.[25] Despite his assertive and combative public persona, he was, as so many acquaintances testified, personally reserved. With close friends, such as John Skelton and George Butler, he could, according to their own testimony, be warm and intimate, but his relations with the majority of the many great political and literary figures with whom he had dealings were generally distant. The nature of his friendship with his closest friends is, moreover, enigmatic. Josephine Butler, fully aware of the disagreements between Froude and her husband on political and educational matters, was once driven by curiosity to eavesdrop on one of their long nights of post-prandial conversation, only to discover the topic that really engaged them: the pleasures and pitfalls of fly fishing.[26] Over time Froude found the demands of social life less and less tolerable. He came to detest residence in London during the season. He loved to withdraw for several months at a time to retreats in Ireland and in Devon; and, in his surviving correspondence, notes that decline invitations to house and dinner parties outnumber acceptances.

Social reservation was accompanied by a form of private repression. In his adult life Froude was afflicted by an abnormal degree of private bereavement and suffering, little of which is registered in his private correspondence or autobiographical writing. Neurasthenic from the outset, his first wife Charlotte became increasingly withdrawn, and, according to Oxford Common Rooms' gossip, fell a victim to narcotic addiction which shortened her life.[27] Froude also experienced the loss of three of his five children. One, Rose May, died shortly after birth: a second, Phyllis, succumbed to the family curse of consumption in her early teens; and a third, Froude's eldest son 'Grenny', died by his own hand.

A source of anxiety since his childhood, Pascoe Grenfell Froude disappointed expectations of following his father to Oxford. At the age of fourteen he secured enrolment as a naval cadet, and after four years training,

---

24. For an example of such anxious thoughts, see the entries in his journal kept while sailing to the West Indies, as extracted in Dunn, *Froude*, II, 550–1.
25. In Froude's private correspondence with close friends such as Ruskin, Charles Butler, and Lord Carnarvon from the later 1870s through to the 1890s the increasing tone of melancholy is unmistakable.
26. Josephine Butler, *Recollections of George Butler* (London, 1894), 45–7, 54.
27. A. L. Rowse, *Froude, the Historian: Victorian Man of Letters* (Sutton, 1994), 12; Charlotte, it has sometimes been suggested, was the model for the neurasthenic Mrs Hale in Elizabeth Gaskell's *North and South*.

which included two periods of punishment for disorderly behaviour, was finally discharged, ostensibly on grounds of ill health. Not without some trouble to himself, Froude found employment for Grenny as private secretary to Sir Maurice Barlow, a middle-ranking colonial administrator in the Cape Colony; and in return the young man almost immediately provoked embarrassment by losing, on the voyage out, a crucial cipher by which Barlow was to communicate with the Colonial Office. To put him on his feet, Froude gifted his son with a lump sum of £5,000 with which he was to purchase a farm in the Cape. But Grenny gambled it away, had himself declared bankrupt, and then, aged twenty-seven, hanged himself.[28]

Grenny's death in 1879, coupled with that of Froude's youngest daughter within the year, doubtless contributed to the darker hues of Froude's later outlook on life. But, in contrast to his response to the death of his second wife, little of this later grieving can be discovered from Froude's own pen. Apart from a mild reference to Grenny's incorrigibility in a letter to his daughter Margaret, a laconic sentence in a letter to Ruskin reporting the first news of his son's death, and a note to his stockbroker explaining the financial consequences of his wasted endowment, the record of the short life of his son must be traced largely in external sources.

Pathological repression should not be attributed to Froude from all this, however. Instead, all that can reasonably be inferred is that when confronted with occasions of private anguish in his later life, Froude resorted to the kind of concealed strategies for survival which had enabled him to withstand with such remarkable success the violent assaults to which he had been subjected in his youth. By definition, the nature of such private techniques defies easy identification, but a number of clues can be found scattered in the surviving evidence of his early years.

Froude's own autobiographical recollections of a young man immersing himself in dissolute ways, carousing with disreputable (but scrupulously anonymous) companions, yet recovering in time to take a respectable degree is, in the first instance, suggestive of a high level of artifice and disguise. More contemporary evidence supports the impression that the young Froude was something of a dandy. John Keble thought him affected as an undergraduate; and Elizabeth Gaskell, who first met him in the months after the scandal of *The Nemesis of Faith*, was at once engaged and irritated by his

---

28. This brief account is derived from sources in the Admiralty papers, National Archives, and the National Archives of South Africa.

mannerisms.[29] His youthful correspondence with Clough is likewise replete with playful affectation.[30] As a Junior Fellow of Exeter he was regarded by some Senior Fellows as disrespectful, and he liked to joke: the trip to Hartley Coleridge was not untouched by a slightly cruel irony, and in 1848 he once hired a band to play the Marseillaise under the windows of the College rector simply to annoy him.[31] Of the darker side of affectation, dissimulation, Froude might also be accused. An early undergraduate letter to Mark Pattison, written in the post-Christmas gloom of the archdeacon's house, supplies unsurprising evidence of adolescent sneakiness: his prodigality having been exposed, Froude is compelled respectfully to suffer his father's reproof, while all the time longing for the fun of term to begin again.[32] Another cringing letter to John Keble has him apologising for his idleness and promising amendment, lest Keble stand in the way of his gaining his fellowship.[33] An innocent recollection of Ralph Waldo Emerson reveals Froude as a young don gesturing theatrically towards the rooms of Edward Pusey (a man whom in reality he had always regarded with little less than contempt) and declaiming 'There is the source from whence all our light has come!'[34] And Froude, of course, did not admit to having been the paymaster of the revolutionary band.

Insignificant in themselves, such instances of youthful masquerade are collectively indicative of a deeper fascination with the contrast between public appearance and private sensibility which appears to have captivated Froude's interest from early on. Initial evidence of this recurrent impulse is supplied by Lady Caroline Fox. Over his several visits she noticed the young man's preoccupation with the gap between an individual's outward persona and his authentic character: thus his fascination with reading personality through handwriting and palms; and thus also his memorable disquisition one evening on the motives and modes of affectation.[35] But Froude's concern with the nature of the self and its relation to the world soon

---

29. Froude to Keble, Keble MSS, Keble College, Oxford; V. A. C. Gattrell (ed.), *The Letters of Elizabeth Gaskell*.

30. F. L. Mulhauser (ed.), *The Correspondence of Arthur Hugh Clough* (2 vols., Oxford, 1957), i, 246–7, 250–1; Froude to Clough, 8 September 1848, Bodleian Library, Oxford, Clough MSS 41032 (Eng. Lett. c190) ff.261–2.

31. Froude's 'autobiographical fragment', printed in Dunn, *Froude*, I.

32. The letter is printed from a private source, in Dunn, *Froude*, I, 102.

33. Froude to Keble, 22 March [1841], Keble MSS, Keble College, Oxford, 162.

34. R. W. Emerson, *Journals and Miscellaneous Notebooks*, ed. Joel Porte (Harvard University Press, 1982), 235.

35. Fox, *Memories*, 328.

extended beyond parlour entertainments and conversation. It exercised a powerful influence over his first literary work, manifesting itself in his critical insterest in the German Gothic, in the work of Ludwig Tieck and the Brothers Grimm, where dual personalities and doppelgängers abound.[36] Less noticeably, but no less significantly, it can be discerned in his early fascination with certain forms of Indian philosophy and with the Zenda Vesta in particular (on the context of whose composition he once planned to write a novel) where the limited personal self is transcended by a vision of the eternal.[37] It can be seen in his intense and continuing interest with the ascetic saints and martyrs of early Christianity whose abnegation of the self in the face of the Christian message of eternal salvation he saw as a variation on the Buddhist insight.[38] Most strikingly it emerged as the dominant theme of his early fiction. It is, for instance, at the core of his portrait of Edward Fowler, the inherently defective weakling of 'The Spirit's Trials' who nonetheless strives to transform himself into a kind of hero; and it is explored from the opposite direction in the character of Markham Sutherland, the anti-hero of *The Nemesis of Faith*, who fritters away his many gifts, intellectual, physical, and material, through lack of resolve.[39]

The critical failure of his fictions did not, however, dispel Froude's preoccupation with the problem of how the blighted and utterly finite self might be made to grasp and to maintain a perception of the vast eternal realities of which it was a tiny but vital part. It remained instead a central preoccupation which was to recur over and again in his writing. It is a central theme of his essays on 'The Lives of the Saints' and on 'England's Forgotten Worthies'; it was, he claimed in an essay of that title, the sole remaining virtue of 'Calvinism'. It was the grounds on which he made his claim for Bunyan's genius; and it was his principal justification for the extraordinarily intimate voice he assumed as Carlyle's biographer. The following passage from an essay on Euripides is merely an example of this recurring Froudian motif:

> Throughout human life, from the first relation of parent and child to the organisation of a nation or a church, in the daily intercourse of common life, in our loves and in our friendships, in our toils and in our amusements ... at every point where one human soul comes into contact with another, there is to be found everywhere, as the condition of right conduct, the obligation to

36. See ch. 5.   37. See chs. 2 and 3.
38. See chs. 2 and 3.   39. See ch. 5.

sacrifice self. . . . The upward sweep of excellence is proportioned, with strictest accuracy, to oblivion of the self which is ascending.[40]

Here was a lofty aspiration indeed. But throughout his career there are indications that even in his private life Froude strove to transform precept into practice. 'I hate myself', he once exclaimed to John Ruskin amidst their intense exchange of letters in the 1870s. But his assertion was made not in a fit of despair or self-disgust; it arose, as he went on to explain, from his conviction that concern with the self was one of the most painful, most futile, and most utterly misguided of human vanities.[41] As in his published writings, this stoical insistence of the vanity of self-consciousness was a recurrent theme in Froude's private correspondence not only with fellow intellectuals, but with politicians and even, oddly enough, with his stockbroker.[42] And it was, by all accounts, more than just an affectation. Major upsets, such as a serious burglary in his isolated farmhouse in Wales when he had little enough to spare, or the destruction of his books and manuscripts by fire, left him relatively unperturbed. To personal criticism, from whatever quarter, he was also in large part indifferent. Though his writings were frequently to embroil him in bitter controversy, he seemed on most occasions to be personally unaffected by hostile criticism, even when, as in the case of the vendetta pursued by Edward Augustus Freeman, it assumed a particularly vicious form.[43] Once established as a distinguished man of letters, moreover, he disdained celebrity: he was indifferent to photographs of himself, and he discouraged autograph hunters (once telling a hopeful applicant that it was his daughter who normally discharged this duty for him).[44] More exasperating was his chronic refusal to supply full dates for his letters—a habit that has presented scholars with frequently insurmountable technical problems, and has ensured that no collected correspondence has ever been produced. This, it appears, was the result which Froude had

40. 'Euripides and sea studies', in *Fraser's Magazine*, NS 11 (May 1875), subsequently reprinted in Froude, *Short Studies on Great Subjects* (London, 1896 edn.), III, 238–9, under the deceptive title 'Sea Studies'; see also similar comments in his *Bunyan*, 54–8.
41. Helen Vilojen, *The Froude–Ruskin Correspondence* (New York, 1966), 38.
42. British Library, Add MSS 6077 A, Carnarvon MSS; Edinburgh University Library, Butler MSS E.87.105.
43. Freeman, who made it his ambition to destroy Froude's reputation as an historian, rarely provoked a response, except on the occasion when he charged that Froude had written his book on Thomas Becket in an act of revenge against his dead brother Hurrell; see 'A few words on Mr Freeman', *Nineteenth Century*, 5 (April, 1879), 618–37.
44. Froude to Mr Knight, 3 April [after 1872], Pierpont Morgan Library, New York, Knight Collection.

intended all along. Late in life he expressed the desire that no official biography be written for him, and in his will he left instructions that all his private papers and correspondence be destroyed.[45] In others also he admired aloofness: a common fortitude in face of the inescapable sufferings of human existence was what underlay his close friendship with the tough-minded Fitzjames Stephen; Dickens, whose talents he fully appreciated, was spoiled for Froude by his need for popular acclaim; the stoic Tacitus was above all others his favourite historian.[46]

The mutation of the youthful dandy into the adult stoic is a type not unfamiliar in British public life, especially among those forced to undergo the rigours of an English public school. In Froude's case the sources for such an attitude towards life can be readily traced to the silent sufferings of the isolated child. But the suggestion that Froude was fundamentally a Victorian stoic is ultimately only a little less simplistic than other psychological explanations, and needs to be qualified by attention to another, equally prominent element in his public character. For Froude was also an inveterate self-writer, intensely engaged with the exploration of his own persona and its presentation before his reading public.

III

No detached and dispassionate commentator, Froude speaks with a distinctive authorial voice that intrudes deeply into all his published work. The strongly autobiographical element in his early fiction has already been alluded to. But a sense of his intrusive individuality as a writer is no less palpable in all his later work. It is there, for instance, in the trenchant, uncompromising, and unapologetic voice of the magisterial narrator of the *History of England*, in the humorous and mildly eccentric middle-aged travel-writer, in the passionate polemical celebrant of 'England's Forgotten Worthies', and in the cool, discriminating memorialist of 'The Oxford Counter-Reformation'. It is a salient characteristic of his biography of Carlyle which so many critics found distasteful, and a similarly personal

---

45. Froude's will, dated July 1894.
46. 'The greatest man who has yet given himself to the recording of human affairs is beyond question Cornelius Tacitus', in 'The Lives of the Saints', *Short Studies on Great Subjects*, I, 555; in the early 1850s Froude proposed to write a history entitled 'The Age of Tacitus'.

presence permeates the elegiac tone of the final sets of lectures delivered by the ageing professor to a new generation of Oxford undergraduates.

And yet the distinctive authorial voice which intrudes itself so strongly in all his work is also a chronically inconsistent one, altering radically from one genre to another. The pious hagiographer is not the historical dogmatist; the dogmatic historian is not the reflective philosopher pleading for a free discussion of theological issues; and the philosopher's serenity is lost in the agonised engagement of the biographer of Carlyle. At once a source of his sustained popularity with the general reading public and of the charges of paradox and insincerity with which he was so often assailed by hostile critics, Froude's ventriloquism—his hiding the actual writer behind the mask of the narrator—became so perfected that it rarely obtruded into the surface of his style. But its mechanisms were revealed through occasional failure. They appear, for example, in the complicated narrative techniques (the introduction of multiple narrators, time-shifts, simultaneous actions, and so on) which he attempted in his early fictions, and which his critics, hot on the scent of autobiographical revelations, have all too often ignored. They can be seen also in the slightly comical case of two essays on Ireland, where he was forced to publish in the second a repudiation of the persona he had assumed in the first under the threat that his deception would be exposed.[47] And, more seriously, the contrivances of authorial affectation are laid bare in his writing on the West Indies where his rhetorical pretences collapse utterly in his attempt to mimic the voice of an innocent traveller while insinuating nonetheless a noxiously racist argument.[48]

In these efforts Froude's failures make his intentions obvious. But the moral purposes and ethical limits of his authorial manipulations were magnificently affirmed in his biography of Carlyle, when Froude, convinced that the only voice which could be adopted to inspire his intended audience was that of his authentic self, rose to face the challenge.[49] Unflinching to the point of self-sacrifice, the narrator's voice in *Thomas Carlyle* is in itself both an abandonment and a vindication of all the authorial guises that had preceded it. The biography of Carlyle represents the greatest practical

47. In 1870, amidst the storm provoked by his anonymous essay 'A Fortnight in Kerry', the threat of exposure forced Froude to confess in a second instalment that he had been assuming the guise of a visitor to Ireland when he had actually been in residence in the area he wrote of for several months of the year over several years: *Fraser's Magazine*, May, September, 1870.
48. Froude, *The Bow of Ulysses: or The English in the West Indies*; for a discussion, see ch. 13.
49. See ch. 12; for an unusually sensitive reading of Froude's intent in the biography, see Christopher Ricks, 'Froude's Carlyle', *Essays in Appreciation* (Oxford, 1996), 146–71.

achievement of Froude's life-long literary endeavour. But the most extended insight into Froude's sense of the relationship of his own self to his public voice that enabled him to write in so many registers is supplied in the remarkable and incomplete autobiographical fragment which he composed in the early 1890s, shortly before his death.

Frequently painful in its content, and resolute in the manner in which it records the sufferings, trials, and failures of his early life, Froude's short auto-biography is one of the most moving pieces of his literary *oeuvre*, and also one of the most problematic. In his decree that no biography be written and his archive destroyed, Froude was by no means alone in the company of eminent Victorians; and likewise in his decision to compose an autobiogra-phy, he was far from unique.[50] Yet when taken together and in conjunction with the persistently assertive voice of his published writings, these moves seem so purposeful as to suggest, to those of us accustomed to the herme-neutics of suspicion, a deliberate attempt not only to suppress information about his character and life, but actually to fabricate it. Misgivings of this kind are easily reinforced by the conduct of his daughter Margaret—a veritable keeper of the flame—who in the years after Froude's death went to extraordinary lengths to see that a biography was actually written based on a portfolio of letters, notes, and, most importantly, on the autobiograph-ical fragment which she had selected and provided to would-be biographers only on the strictest terms.[51] According to these, the autobiography was to form the spine of any biography and was to be inserted into the text as part of its narrative up to the period when it ended (around 1856); it was to be accepted uncritically by the official biographer, whose task it was simply to elaborate on the evidence it supplied from the matter provided in the port-folio.[52] Given these demands, Margaret appears to have had trouble in find-ing a suitable candidate for the commission until she finally settled upon the

---

50. See Trev Lynn Broughton, *Men of Letters: Writing Lives*, a valuable study which, while analysing Leslie Stephen's 'Autobiography' and Froude's *Life of Carlyle* in relation to each other, does not consider Froude's own autobiography
51. On these negotiations, see Dunn MSS, Wooster College Library, Wooster, Ohio; also Sarolea MSS, Edinburgh University Library; after several efforts to find a suitable candidate Margaret appears to have settled finally on Dunn because of a highly sympathetic monograph he had published on *The Froude–Carlyle Controversy* (London, 1930).
52. It is not even clear if the autobiography actually concluded at this point. Margaret had pub-lished an edited version of further autobiographical reflections as J. A Froude, *My Relations with Carlyle* (London, 1903); and to add to the mystery Dunn confesses that he excised some portions relating to Froude's recollections of his relations with Newman because they were made superfluous by what he had written (earlier) in 'The Oxford Counter-Reformation'.

American scholar, Waldo Hilary Dunn. This quasi-official biography finally appeared in the format laid down by Miss Froude, in two volumes in 1961 and 1963; and since then the autobiography, the library, and much of the other material to which Dunn had been given access have, so far as I have been able to ascertain, disappeared.[53]

None of the shenanigans surrounding Froude's archive should be allowed to foster confusion over his own intentions—it was not he, after all, who orchestrated this complicated release of his materials. Yet a writer who persistently professed his belief in the worthlessness of the self while intruding his own striking personality into all his works and then composing an intensely personal autobiography is not easily exonerated from the charge of inconsistency. The light which the autobiography itself sheds on this apparent contradiction is, however, highly revealing. It cannot be said, in the first instance, that, as an account of his early life, it was in any obvious sense grossly self-serving or dishonest. During the course of my research for this book I have found surprisingly few occasions where Froude's personal narrative departs from the externally verifiable record to any considerable degree, and these are generally the result of elision, or confused chronology, rather than positive falsification. Inevitably, they occur; and, as such, they are always significant—the more so because they were probably unintended.[54] But rather more interesting than such unavoidable lapses is the set of organising tropes to which Froude had to resort in reshaping his lived experience as narrative.[55]

The dominant motifs that Froude adopted, knowingly or not, in giving literary shape to his life are readily identified. In his story of childhood suffering, adolescent waywardness, and ultimate redemption Froude is in part following the Augustinian mode, employing the paradigm elaborated by the great classical autobiographer and readily developed in the conversion narratives of English Calvinist tradition of whom Bunyan (a hero of Froude's) was the great exemplar. No doubt this came naturally enough to Froude. In the best Calvinist manner, his mother had enjoined that each of her children should keep a journal of self-examination and auto-criticism.[56] There is

53. Waldo Hilary Dunn, *James Anthony Froude: A Biography* (2 vols., Oxford, 1961, 1963).
54. For one crucial example in regard to his early days at Westminster, see ch. 2.
55. George P. Landow (ed.), *Approaches to Victorian Autobiography* (Ohio, 1979) offers an extremely valuable set of theoretical and empirical studies, though none of the contributors make reference to Froude's fragment; see also the sophisticated discussion in Avrom Fleishman, *Figures of Autobiography: The Language of Self-Writing in Victorian and Modern England* (Berkeley, 1983).
56. See ch. 2.

reason to believe that from his youth Froude had followed the family practice: his early writings and several of his later books and essays show clear
signs of being based upon journals of self-reflection which he kept during
their preparation; and an extensive set of private diaries appear to have been
among the materials which his daughter Margaret dutifully destroyed.

But within this formal framework, Froude's autobiographical narrative is
infused with the language of honestly expressed feeling, with an acknowledgement of suffering and a confession of personal deficiency that runs
against the Augustinian motif of wilful sinfulness and redemption, and is
distinctly Rousseauite in its sensibility. The young Anthony may have been
in Froude's account a weakling and a coward. But if so, he was these things
by nature; and the ordeals which his family had put him through in their
disregard of his nature had merely exacerbated rather than remitted his
faults. His recovery—insofar as it took place at all—had come through
endurance, and through the emergence of better circumstances later on.
A passing reflection on his dead brother Robert encapsulates the profound
ambivalence towards his own self and the circumstances which shaped it
that characterises the memoir:

> I have thought—but perhaps I am too much inclined to lay on circumstance
> the faults of my own character—but anyway I had thought that had Robert
> lived to guide me, my own small career might have been a happier and more
> useful one.[57]

There is a tension at play here and throughout the memoir as a whole
between the Augustinian polarities of redemption or salvation, whose
certitude is based upon a conviction of objective, eternal truth, and a darker
sensibility which perceives that such a truth, if it exists, can be apprehended
only through unstable, deficient, and solitary subject intelligences. 'What is
the meaning of existence? What is the purpose of my presence within it?
What am I to do with what I have been given and with what has befallen
me?' These are the questions posed directly and desperately by Froude's
very first fictional hero, Edward Fowler, in 'The Spirit's Trials' and they are
returned to repeatedly throughout his subsequent writing; and they are
enunciated again, as the defining imperatives of his life in the old man's
autobiography.[58]

---

57. Dunn, *Froude*, I, 10.
58. 'The Spirit's Trials' 110–12; Dunn, *Froude*, I, 126–7, 150–1.

IV

This straining after an understanding of eternal truth within an inescapable web of inherited and acquired subjectivities is not, of course, unique to Froude. In this engagement with the dichotomies of objective knowledge and subjective human perception, of necessity and free will, he was typical of the generation of young intellectuals, scholars, and artists who came of age in the 1840s. He was, it might be said, but another victim of the great crisis in Christian faith which troubled so many of his contemporaries. But such hasty contextualisation answers fewer questions than it may seem; for within this movement Froude trod a singular and almost wilfully individual path.

In their attempts to reconstruct a framework for understanding a world without evidence of a purposeful God, the generation of the 1840s experimented with a spectrum of options which ranged from political radicalism through detached scientific experimentalism to the fideism of the Oxford Movement. Froude, for a period, flirted with each, and even briefly considered in his earliest explorations the possibilities of a Christian political economy.[59] But while several of his contemporaries and companions—and two of his brothers—finally elected for one or other among these, Froude ultimately held himself aloof.[60] Instead, as he grew to maturity he sought enlightenment in the writings of the later German Romantics and the young Hegelians, of Goethe, Schleiermacher, Fichte, and F.W. and A. W. Schlegel. In this also he was not entirely unique; but again only a small minority of his age group were as well-read in contemporary German theology and philosophy as he was, and only an exceptional few acquired the proficiency as a translator which he achieved.[61] Like many also, Froude sought to explore the dilemmas of his generation in fiction. In this he was hardly more successful than most; but few offered so sympathetic an account of the doubters' condition, and none were as audacious in placing questions of sexual morality at the heart of the matter.[62]

In the 1840s and thereafter Froude was within a larger company of those who were profoundly influenced by Carlyle; but few of the prophet's

---

59. *The Influence of the Science of Political Economy* was the title of the prize-winning essay he submitted as part of his campaign for Fellowship in 1842.
60. See chs. 2 and 3.
61. Rosemary Ashton, *The German Idea: Four English Writers and the Influence of German Thought* (Cambridge, 1980).
62. See in general Wolff, *Gains and Losses: Novels of Faith and Doubt in Victorian England* (New York, 1977).

acolytes were to remain so personally loyal to him in his darker days, and none was to be so devastating in the uncompromising assessment of his work. Finally, in the great age of history writing that dawned in the years after 1850, Froude taught himself to become a master historian, an original researcher who worked primarily with archival sources. But for him, historical research always remained a mere means to greater purposes rather than an end in itself, and he repeatedly rejected positivism, empiricism, and any other claims that history might possibly be a science with a decisiveness that rendered him unique and isolated among his fellow historians, and deeply mistrusted by them too.[63]

The cumulative force of such purposefully discriminative choices serves to reinforce the impression that Froude had embarked upon a sustained individual search for a public voice which would at once be comprehensible yet distinctive, familiar, and yet provocative. From the beginning, and throughout his career, Froude found it appropriate to address his public with a variety of different, sometimes recurring rhetorical styles: the pious hagiographer, the sentimental novelist, the polemical essayist, the reasoned philosopher, the authoritative historian, the political dogmatist, the open-minded traveller, the agonised chronicler of flawed lives—all of which were independent of the private self, which was revealed only to a few friends and family, and was regarded by its owner as of no broader significance. Behind this lifelong literary strategy there lay, no doubt, a psychology. In view of the horrors of his childhood and of the manner in which he had striven to overcome them, the adoption of a mask supplied a powerful mode of releasing his creative and expressive energies that had been pent up and repressed by the exigencies of childhood survival. But there was also an aesthetic: Froude's authorial voices were a variation on the multiple masks and guises adopted by so many of the poets and prose-writers of later Romanticism in whose work he had immersed himself, and whose techniques of confession, masquerade, and ventriloquism seemed to have been so useful in their efforts to reveal the eternal world of Creation in the finite world of man. Yet it is impossible at this distance to disentangle the process by which these two forces worked to shape Froude's imagination. It can only be said that Froude was a Romantic not merely from conviction, but from personal necessity as well.

63. See ch 7.

Most importantly of all, there lay also behind this strategy of public presentation an ethic of considerable complexity. As the collapse of faith in the moral and intellectual authority of orthodox Christianity deepened, the generation of the 1840s sought refuge in alternative conceptual frameworks which seemed to hold out the promise of an authority equal to and more durable than the one they had been forced to abandon. Between the various options available—Comtean positivism, Oxford Tractarianism, Romantic radicalism, and Marxist materialism—substantial differences existed. But each, in one form or another, proposed as a solution to the contemporary crisis the recovery of the art of prophecy or, more accurately, the reconceptualisation of thought and perception as instruments for immediately transforming the world. The elevation of the intellectual and the artist as a new kind of prophet provided a powerfully invigorating force to those who had lost faith in traditional forms of belief, and was immensely attractive to Froude's generation for all sorts of reasons, not all of them philosophical or moral.[64] Each was afflicted with its own predictive limitations and its own inherent problems which in the years after the great anticlimax of 1848 would soon make themselves plain.

In the light of the failure of the hopes raised in 1848, Romanticism's peculiar rejection of a scientific basis of one kind or another presented its adherents with problems which were particularly urgent and acute. Having deprived itself of the support of any external, pseudo-objective referent, the force of the Romantic appeal was dependent almost entirely on the individual character, vision, and communicative ability of the prophet alone. The psychological, intellectual, and moral pressures applied by this necessity to function both as a seer and as an agent of the good were immense, and in their different ways many of the movement's great figures suffered under them. In some the fault appeared to lie in their own deficiencies: they had, like Coleridge or Newman, confused the significance of the truth revealed to them, or, like Wordsworth, lost it altogether; or, like the later Carlyle, they had alienated their audience by the obscure and rebarbative nature of their expression. But, more importantly, the general misunderstanding with which their attempt to communicate their vision had been met was itself a

---

64. Other sources of this imperative are considered in general in Stefan Collini, *Public Moralists: Political Thought and Intellectual Life in Britain, 1850–1930* (Oxford, 1991); Jeffrey Von Arx, *Progress and Pessimism: Religion, Politics and History in Late Nineteenth Century Britain* (Cambridge, MA, 1985); T. W. Heyck, *The Transformation of Intellectual Life in Victorian England* (London, 1982); and in a particular case in Noel Annan, *Leslie Stephen: The Godless Victorian* (London, 1984).

symptom of the degree to which contemporary culture was in the process of disintegration. The emergence of this small set of visionaries was, therefore, a profoundly ambivalent phenomenon—an indication that either spiritual transcendence or spiritual decadence was at hand.

Amidst this crisis the addition of simply another prophetic voice, especially one which he regarded as flawed and deficient as his own, would have had little effect other than to make a further contribution to the cultural confusions of the day. But it was precisely on the basis of this modest insight that Froude came to believe that he might play a lesser but not unimportant role in correcting, mediating, and adapting the essence of the great prophets' message for reception by the imperfect and clouded minds of ordinary Englishmen. In the anti-heroes of his early fiction—Edward Fowler and Markham Sutherland—he can be seen presenting case studies of figures who, when confronted by the vision of truth offered by the great prophets, found themselves paralysed and overwhelmed through their own inherent deficiencies: physical and emotional in the case of the former, intellectual and moral in that of the latter. These fictional experiments were far from successful. But even though he abandoned his ambitions as a novelist in the aftermath of his own personal failure in 1849, Froude returned to the problem of how eternal truths might be made intelligible to limited and historically determined human intellects in an early critical essay published in 1852.[65] In this piece on Reynard the Fox Froude followed Goethe in considering the age-old myth of the cunning, disingenuous, but ultimately winning animal as a metaphor for the guises, disguises, and falsehoods which the good man must adopt if he is to act effectively in sustaining justice and truth within the benighted world. The argument Froude developed there provides a rare exposition of the underlying ethical justification for the provocative, exasperating, and carelessly inconsistent literary strategy which he was to adopt throughout the rest of his career.

V

Yet the burden under which the great prophets had eventually buckled bore down with no less force upon their modest follower. In his struggle to tell

---

65. 'Ethical Doubts concerning Reinecke Fuchs', *Fraser's Magazine*, 46 (September 1852), 321–30.

the truth about Carlyle, for example, he can be seen, despite great personal cost, to have succeeded magnificently. But elsewhere, in his writings about South Africa and about the West Indies, his condescending efforts to engage the demos in his particular campaign to transform the Empire produced a nervous, insinuating rhetorical style that was as distasteful in its tone as in its intent.[66] But nowhere did his attempts to use his creative talents to effect a change in popular moral attitudes implicate Froude in a web of aesthetic and ethical problems more than in the case of Ireland.

A frequent visitor to the island from the early 1840s to the early 1870s (in the 1860s he was in the habit of residing annually at Derreen in County Kerry for four months between July and October), he had acquired a rich knowledge of the country even before he began his major work on Irish history. Long before the publication of *The English in Ireland in the Eighteenth Century* (1872–74), Ireland had featured significantly in his *History of England*, his essays, and even in his early fiction. In 1872 he travelled to the United States to deliver a set of lectures on the course of Irish history, and in the late 1880s he returned again to fiction and to Ireland with his *Two Chiefs of Dunboy*.

Yet if Froude's concern with Ireland was deep and sustained, it was far from sympathetic. Though most British intellectuals were opposed to Irish aspirations to independence and were opponents even of Home Rule, few matched Froude in the implacability of his opposition to any attempts at political reform, the virulence of his attacks on the Irish temperament, and his enthusiasm for measures of coercion and repression.[67] Yet on a personal level Froude was popular in those parts of Ireland where he stayed, and counted several Irishmen, including Home Rulers, among his acquaintances. 'It is not true that Froude hated the Irish', remarked T. P. O'Connor, 'except in a metaphorical way.'[68] What O'Connor was hinting at here was the fact that Froude's preoccupation with Ireland was based upon his conviction that the present state of the country and its history represented the greatest single instance of England's failure to discharge the providential role that had been allocated to it at the beginning of the Reformation. Offering

---

66. See chs. 10 and 13.
67. On the hostility of British intellectuals in general to the campaign for Home Rule, see Tom Dunne, 'La trahison des clercs: British Intellectuals and the First Home-Rule Crisis', *Irish Historical Studies*, 23:90 (1982), 134–73; also E. D. Steele, *Irish Land and British Politics: Tenant Right and Nationality, 1865–1870* (Cambridge, 1974).
68. Gerard Lyne, *The Lansdowne estates in kerry*, (Dublin, 2001), 398–400; T. P O'Connor, in *The Sunday Times*, 24 June 1928.

at once an indication that the spiritual and moral regeneration promised at that time had been incomplete, and a warning that, should it fail in its present responsibilities, England might be plunged into an interminable decline, the problem of completing the assimilation of Ireland into the Empire was for Froude as urgent as it was inescapable.[69]

Froude's public utterances on the Irish problem were, therefore, inextricably linked to his essential moral and spiritual imperatives; and it was Ireland consequently that revealed at once the magnificence and the inadequacies of those treasured objectives for which he strove. Whether metaphorical or not, Froude's insistence that the interests of the Irish must forever be subordinate to the metahistorical obligations of the English was wholly unearned: at once historically and morally unsustainable. Insofar as the influence of his Irish writings and of his incessant private lobbying contributed to the obstruction and deferment of a successful resolution of the Irish problem, some portion of responsibility for all the misery, suffering, and disappointment which arose from that failure must be laid at the feet of Froude, moralist.

For it is as a moralist—rather than as an historian, critic, or ideologue—that Froude himself sought above all to be understood, and how he should ultimately be judged. Yet such a judgement is intensely problematic not only in regard to Froude himself, but also in its implications for those of us who choose to make it. Of the sincerity of his aspirations there can be no doubt, nor of the courage and endurance he displayed in attempting to fulfil them. Yet the intrinsic risks of his undertaking are equally clear. Froude's ascetic self-denial permitted him to assume a series of disguises by which to stimulate—or actually to manipulate—different audiences to attend to universal moral issues in their own particular way. That there was craft here, and artistic cunning, is undeniable. But there was also a supreme arrogance. Underpinning it all was an assurance not only that eternal moral principles existed, and not only that Froude himself had been given the gift accurately to apprehend them, but that he also had the capacity to translate such truths into forms more understandable to lesser minds and hearts. This assumption of the absolute superiority of the visionary few over the benighted multitude was in contradiction with the spiritual and moral universalism he had

---

69. Ciaran Brady, 'Offering Offence: James Anthony Froude, Moral Obligation and the Uses of Irish History', in Vincent Carey and Ute Lotz-Heumann (eds.), *Taking Sides: Colonial and Confessional Mentalites in Early Modern Ireland* (Dublin, 2004).

adopted from his youth: a secular version of the vulgar predestinarianism which he had rejected from the beginning. But, more seriously, in permitting him to excuse or ignore the exploitation and repression of such manifestly lesser peoples as the 'kaffirs' of South Africa, the West Indian blacks, and the Irish next door, it was also fraught with the gravest risks for the thing he cared for most: his contemporary and posthumous influence as a moralist.

We know now how utterly Froude failed. In the era of disillusion that followed the Victorian age of doubt, the questions concerning the meaning of the universe, the purpose of our existence and the validity of such concepts as truth, justice, and goodness which he insistently posed, and for which he took so many risks, now seem pathetically naïve in their formulation. Embarrassment with the apparent unsophistication of this particular Victorian's moral struggle, however, should not serve as an excuse for an unwillingness to confront our own moral dilemmas, or for a refusal to face the consequences should we choose to deny their existence altogether. The collapse of Froude's particular enterprise raises broader and more urgent questions regarding the intellectual and academic culture of our own times. Over the last several decades we too have been witnesses to another intellectual and cultural breakdown as so many of the forms of scholarly enquiry established or reconstituted in the closing decades of the nineteenth century have become exposed to fundamental question. The victims at once of successive theoretical challenges and ideological failures, but also of so many careerist or craven surrenders to commercial and institutional pressures, those empirical, analytical, and anti-metaphysical modes of apprehending the world which came into the ascendant as orthodox academic disciplines with the passing of the Romantic moment are themselves now suffering a steady loss of authority. And the capacity of intellectuals (especially those embedded in the academy) to function as independent and effective critics of the prevailing mores of society has at the same time, and for the same reasons, been sharply diminished.

In these circumstances a revisit to the Victorian attempt to regenerate the spiritual and moral basis of society, conducted through an investigation of one of its most versatile, resourceful and committed exponents, is of value not in the interests of antiquarian curiosity, and still less in a spirit of nostalgic reaction. Its aim rather should be to enquire whether Froude's failure to sustain a spirit of independent moral criticism in a secularised world was the result of his own prejudices, defects, and disappointments, or whether it lay fatally at the heart of the entire enterprise.

2

Shadows of the Froudes,
1818–36

I

In seeking access to his earliest conscious years, Froude compels us to attend to his final ones. While independent evidence pertaining to his childhood and youth is exiguous, fragmentary, and scattered, Froude himself, some time in the early 1890s, composed a compact, continuous, and highly informative account of his early life.[1] In this he was far from unique. The composition of memoirs, reminiscences, and straightforward autobiographies was a common practice among leading figures in the late Victorian intellectual and literary world. Many of Froude's acquaintances, including Ruskin, Trollope, Mill, and Spencer, had explored modes of composing subjective accounts of their lives and of their relations with others, while Froude himself was indirectly the cause of one of the most remarkable exercises in the genre—the deeply spiritual account of a life in mid-passage composed by Newman in the *Apologia pro Vita Sua*.[2]

---

1. Retained in manuscript by his daughter and literary trustee, Margaret, Froude's autobiography was supplied to his biographer Waldo Hilary Dunn in the 1930s. In the first volume of his biography Dunn, under an agreement reached with Margaret Froude, published lengthy sections of this text, largely without critical commentary. It remained with Dunn in company with the large file of material left to him by Margaret, but I have been unable to trace its present whereabouts.
2. On Victorian autobiography in general, see George P. Landow (ed.), *Approaches to Victorian Autobiography* (Ohio, 1979); Avrom Fleishman, *Figures of Autobiography: The Language of Self-Writing in Victorian and Modern England* (Berkeley, 1983). Curiously, it was Charles Kingsley's intemperate and irrelevant remarks about Newman in a puffing review of the early volumes of Froude's *History of England*, which Froude had asked Kingsley to write, that gave rise to the *Apologia*. Froude himself was deeply exercised by the *Apologia* when it first appeared; in an important passage in his own autobiography where Froude describes his feelings in recalling his childhood sufferings as an 'infandum dolorem' (unspeakable pain) he is quietly alluding to Newman's extraction of the phrase from the *Aeneid* (Book II, verses 3–6); in a passage in the *Apologia* referring to his agonies in leaving Oxford, see Harold Weatherby, *Cardinal Newman and his Age* (Vanderbilt, 1974), 129–31.

Froude's own exercise in the genre, however, differed from those of his contemporaries in several ways. In the first place no authoritative text exists. The fragment, such as it exists, has come down only through the most curious of circumstances. The original manuscript was given to Froude's authorised biographer, Waldo Hilary Dunn, by Froude's daughter Margaret in the 1930s, under strict conditions concerning how it was to be used in the biography.[3] We do not know if Dunn received the full text, but we do know that he made exclusions from the version he included in his study. What has survived, therefore, is quite possibly a fragment of a fragment. We do know that its original composition was in part the consequence of the storm of personal abuse and innuendo provoked by the appearance of Froude's biography of Carlyle, and might therefore be read in part as an attempt at self-exculpation, though its gestures in this direction are surprisingly modest. Froude did indeed compose a fragment on his 'relations with Carlyle' specifically to justify his biography.[4] But this was conceived and kept separate from his autobiographical exercise, which breaks off roughly in 1856, considerably before he had formed a close association with Carlyle. It was not, moreover, intended for publication. Instead it was addressed to his two surviving children in an effort, perhaps, to reveal to them something about their often absent and usually distant father who had encountered so much controversy and so much hostility in the closing years of his life. In ending abruptly around the time when Froude was aged thirty-eight, it was also something akin to a *Bildungsroman*—an account of the character formation, education, and coming-to-maturity of James Anthony Froude. Finally, in contrast to the major autobiographies of the period, it is resolutely unreflective on the problems of authenticity that are attached to all self-writing. It aims, Froude says at the outset, to supply a plain account of the circumstances and experiences of his early life, to describe 'who we were, from what stock we came and what our life was like'.[5]

This assumption that Froude 'confident in [his] own integrity'[6] could attain such a simple intention was, to say the least, naïve; and like most

---

3. On the conditions imposed by Margaret Froude on Dunn, see Dunn MSS, Wooster College, Wooster, Ohio; neither the fragment nor any of the large body of materials supplied to Dunn by the Froudes is retained in this collection.
4. *My Relations with Carlyle* was not intended for publication during his lifetime; it was published posthumously, and without a clear indication that they were following their father's wishes, by his children Margaret and Ashley in 1903, amidst continuing rancour over the Carlyle biography.
5. Dunn, *Froude*, I, 12.   6. Dunn, *Froude*, I, 12.

autobiographies, Froude's tended to drift toward one of the dominant organising tropes of the genre—in his case, the Augustinian mode.[7] Whether he was conscious of it or not, the dominant myth of Froude's self-representation was that of loss, alienation, and redemption, of the eventual attainment of adult stability and personal integrity by the rejection of self-pity and self-love. Yet the manner in which this Augustinian trope was deployed by Froude was distinctive. Unlike Augustine's, Froude's early life was far from being one of comfort, stability, and love in which the only troubles and anxieties encountered arose from within the mind and the soul. On the contrary, the events detailed in the early pages of Froude's narrative constitute a record of suffering and misfortune which in their duration and their violence far surpass the oppressions remembered by Ruskin and Mill, and even the miseries memorialised in fiction by Butler and Gosse. The successive stages of this protracted ordeal are articulated by Froude in a spare, lapidary voice that, in its meticulous balancing of remembered feeling and distant evaluation, gracefully negotiates between the pitfalls of sentiment and hard-boiled stoicism. 'I have no intention', Froude writes of his schooldays 'of reviving the *infandum dolorem* of my life', while making it plain that 'the unspeakable pain' which he suffered 'left indelible marks on my memory and perhaps on my character.'[8] Froude's redemptive myth is, therefore, a subtly balanced one in which the Augustinian achievement is tempered by a Rousseauite recognition that natural and congenital defects will always make such attainments fragile, conditional, and artificial. Its surrounding contingencies notwithstanding, redemption remained attainable; and in employing it as a central theme of his *memoires d'outre tombe*, Froude was insisting upon the vital formative event of his life: the act of coming to terms with his own sense of his defective self which was also a simultaneous transcendence of that self.

The force of Froude's sustained conviction of the process of his self-formation, for all his acknowledged frailties, challenges his interpreters in many ways. To those of us habitually attuned to critical scepticism the voice of the septuagenarian autobiographer may appear artificial—an attempt to impose a retrospective coherence on a series of accidents, disruptions, and unresolved contradictions—yet it is nonetheless a deliberate artifice, consciously forged in the smithy of the early years toward which it is redirected

7. On the tropology of autobiography, see Fleishman, *Figures of Autobiography*.
8. Fleishman, 32; on the significance of the phrase 'infandum dolorem', see n. 2.

as its most intense focus. The ready conclusion that Froude's self-narrative was a myth—as such exercises usually are—should not obscure the recognition that in the liberating force which it supplied to him, it was also for him the final point of an intensely felt process of living.

Such an observation is all the more relevant in Froude's case because, far from being his only exercise in this form, the late autobiography was merely the last in a series of explorations in remembrance and self-writing with which he experimented throughout his literary career. This repeated concern with the relationship between the constructed recollection of the text and the life actually lived demands that any assessment of Froude's representation of the self must go beyond the familiar attributions of self-serving or exculpatory motive. Critical caution must above all be employed in approaching all his attempts to put shape on his earliest years; for while these were years which continued to preoccupy Froude in his last autobiographical writing, they were also at the core of a series of bold and painful literary experiments which he undertook close to the very beginning of this process of conscious self-refashioning.

Frequently obscure in their expression and clumsy in organisation, Froude's early fictional efforts in autobiographical confession have normally been regarded as naïve expressions of self-pity. Yet for all their imperfections they were also (as will be argued below) assertions of humanity's need to transcend the deficiencies and misfortunes imposed by nature and by environment; and an implied claim on the part of the author that in rewriting his life in this manner, he himself had actually done so. Nothing could have been further from his intentions as a novelist in the later 1840s (and nothing more clearly demonstrated his failings in that art) than that his readers should have understood his intentions to have been so subjective and pathetically self-exculpatory; yet it is as such that his fictions have generally been read by commentators and biographers who have frequently applied materials derived from the fiction as simple autobiographical evidence.

The interpretative challenge posed by Froude's presentation of his self is, therefore, unusually complex, for in addition to the normal suspicion of retrospective reconstruction, it requires also an understanding on the part of the reader that this process of reconstruction had begun to take shape in the earliest phases of Froude's life. The profound and vigorous artificiality of Froude's public persona was, that is, an essential characteristic of his private self. It is with these cautions in mind that I have sought in what follows to disentangle the myths that have come to surround Froude's life and character not in order to lay bare some hidden inner self, but to uncover a powerful and more deeply absorbed myth of personal recon-struction which underpinned his thought and action throughout all of his adult life.

II

> I have been unable to follow our family history beyond my grandfather who died in 1769 at the age of twenty four and lies buried in Avon Gifford churchyard in the South Hams of Devon.[9]

These opening lines in his autobiography represent a curious disclaimer on the part of a writer who had established a reputation as a pioneer explorer in the great untapped treasures of the English manuscript archive; and it was one made all the more peculiar by the fact that, had he cared, he might himself have easily constructed an extensive genealogy of the Froudes along the lines which the enthusiastic amateur genealogist, R. E. Hooppell, was pursuing even as Froude wrote. The origins of the Froude family were, as Hooppell admitted, obscure. Of Norse origin, the name suggests a Viking heritage. But from the twelfth century on, names from which Froude was an obvious derivate began to appear in increasing numbers in south-west England. Their frequency increased to the extent that Hooppell was able to construct an incomplete but continuous genealogical tree of Froudes run-ning through twelve generations down to the historian and his siblings.[10]

Central to Hooppell's genealogical researches were the great lay sub-sidy rolls of the reign of Henry VIII lodged in the Public Record Office, which provided him with a crucial means of identifying, connecting, and differentiating the numerous later Froudes which he found in court and probate records. His success in this makes it all the more strange that the great proponent of the value of underused manuscript sources in bringing a new sense of historical immediacy to contemporary readers and the great apologist of the administrative intrusions of the Henrician state should have himself elected to disregard such a rich resource for original research.

9. Fleishman, *Figures of Autobiograph* 12.
10. R. E. Hooppell, 'The Froudes or Frowdes of Devon', *Transactions of the Devonshire Association*, 24 (1892), 441–57.

Froude's rejection of such an obvious autobiographical starting-point may prompt suspicious minds to speculate that he had something to hide: that he was embarrassed by relatively modest origins, or perhaps that he was anxious to obscure a close family connection with the notorious hard-drinking, hard-riding, and thoroughly disreputable Parson John Froude (celebrated in folklore and song).[11] But more subtle intentions are at play. Parson Froude aside, Froude showed no difficulty about his forebears: they were small landholders, he states, probably worth, by the late eighteenth century, about £500 or £600 a year. And in what was a characteristic strategy of his mature historical style, he found a way of dismissing such tasteless searches for ancestry by means of anecdote. One of his relations (he does not care to specify which one) had been foolish enough to purchase a coat of arms from the Herald's College. It was an embarrassment. Froude's father had hidden it away, and though he may have glimpsed it once, the great historian had no interest whatever 'in such unsuitable vanities', and had never looked for it since.[12] Instead, by rejecting biography's conventional opening trope, by foreshortening his origins and minimising the significance of lineage and place, Froude was able to concentrate his focus on the arena which he himself believed to have the most profound effect on the formation of his character: his own immediate family, his brothers and sisters, and above all his father, who, following his mother's premature death, was to dominate every aspect of Froude's early life.

By the time James Anthony was born in 1818 his father, Robert Hurrell Froude, was, at forty-eight, already a middle-aged man in the midst of a busy clerical career. Economically comfortable and professionally established, he was much respected as a figure of great authority not only within his own parish but as a magistrate in the county of Devon as a whole. By means of Froude's formidable rhetorical skills he has since been preserved in aspic:

> He was a parish priest of the old sort, with strong sense, a practical belief in the doctrines of the Church of England as by law established which no person in his right mind would think of questioning. As a country gentleman and a landowner himself he was looked up to by the tenants and parishioners with affection and reverence. He farmed his own glebe ... He was a magistrate, the most active in the South Hams, and the most rational and just.[13]

11. The parson was Froude's grand-uncle, see S Baring Gould, *Devonshire Characters* (London, 1908), 29–63.
12. Dunn, *Froude*, I, 12.   13. Dunn, *Froude*, I, 13.

This is the historian's deftly sketched portrait of his father. Commonly accepted, its provenance, however, requires some comment. Before it reappeared in the autobiography, it had first been aired in his 1881 essay on 'The Oxford Counter-Reformation', where it served an overtly polemical intent of showing how, even within his own family circle, the character of the English clergyman had declined from the honest-to-God pastors of the late eighteenth century to the effete Newmanites and Puseyites of the Oxford Movement.[14] And though critically informed readers might have noticed the sharp contrast that existed between this benign sketch and the earlier, notorious portrayal of his clergyman father—the cold, hypocritical, and cruel Parson Fowler—in his partly autobiographical first novel 'The Spirit's Trials' the rhetorical effectiveness of the later account lay in its happy familiarity. What Froude was reproducing here is a copy of a comfortingly recognisable type: the pragmatic, moderately religious, moderately Tory clergyman–magistrate, stern and authoritative on the outside but benign and morally sensitive beneath, and happily free of intellectual pretensions withal. Froude, it is true, adds some qualifying touches to this caricature. His father 'had a taste for books ... especially of history and antiquities', and he had a talent for sketching. But the effect of such concessions to complexity is considerably muted by the power of another anecdote through which Robert Hurrell Froude is first introduced:

> He was a fine rider, passionately fond of hunting, and rarely was in a field when he was not the best mounted there. When an undergraduate he leapt the turnpike gate at Abingdon Road with pennies under his seat, pennies between his knees and the saddle, pennies between his feet and the stirrup irons, and carried them all over safely.[15]

An entertaining story which neatly reinforces the impression of the fox-hunting country parson, it served to lead effortlessly to the satisfying conclusion that, as one early reader, surrendering totally to the writer's intent, put it, 'we know the type'.[16]

---

14. 'Our own household was representative of the order. My father was rector of the parish. He was archdeacon. He was justice of the peace. He had a moderate fortune of his own ... and he belonged therefore to "the landed interest". Most of the magistrates work of the neighbourhood passed through his hands ... In his younger days he had been a hard rider across country'; 'The Oxford Counter-Reformation', in *Short Studies on Great Subjects*, IV (1883), 241; the essays were first serialised in the magazine *Good Words* early in 1881.
15. Dunn, *Froude*, I, 13.
16. A laudatory comment made in a review of Herbert Paul's *Froude: A Life*.

There is much in Froude's sketch of his father that is quite verifiable. As is commonly the case, most of the surviving records of Robert Hurrell Froude's public and professional life—ordination lists, episcopal visitations, quarter-session reports and the like—leave only the traces of a featureless functionary of even less interest than Froude's series of stereotyping anecdotes.[17] Yet others suggest a more complex man.

Born in October 1770, Robert Hurrell was the only son of Robert Froude, who had died while his wife Phyllis Hurrell was still pregnant with this their third child. Though young, Robert Froude was a prudent man who had already made careful settlements in regard to his two daughters. The family tragedy thus issued for Robert Hurrell in a surprisingly consoling result as he became sole heir to the Froudes' modest estate. Within a year, moreover, his fortunes improved substantially when on the death of his maternal grandfather he became the principal beneficiary of a substantial Hurrell inheritance which was bequeathed to his mother.[18]

Quite unexpectedly, then, Robert Hurrell Froude became comparatively well off at a very early age. Educated privately, he went up to Oriel College, Oxford, at the age of seventeen in 1788. There he took an ordinary BA, stayed on to take an MA in 1795, took holy orders, and was ordained priest on 10 July 1796. By the time of his ordination he had already secured a curacy which offered a small but for a novice curate a generous stipend of £40 a year. Two years later, in 1798, he was instituted as rector of Denbury, a small country parish with a commensurately small living of £100. But then, in 1799 he attained to the glittering prize of Dartington, made vacant by the death of Francis Yarde, another sporting parson famous for his enthusiastic participation in 'the Dean's Hunt', which at almost £500 per annum was at that time measured as the third most lucrative living in the diocese. Together with Denbury, which he retained for life, this made him one of the most richly beneficed clergymen in the entire see. To that good fortune was added the further benefit of the Dartington parsonage house itself—an opulent, sprawling edifice valued in the early nineteenth century to be among the top 10 per cent of parsonage houses in the diocese, and a substantial glebe farm containing valuable mineral and woodland resources which Parson Froude was to exploit to its utmost throughout his years of

---

17. The records of the diocese of Exeter and the archdeaconry of Totnes held in the Devon Record Office contain a very large amount of information relating to Robert Hurrell Froude's routine activities.
18. Hooppell, 454–5; Dunn, *Froude*, I, 214

tenure. A Justice of the Peace for Devon by 1801, Froude was to serve on the bench at Totnes until his death. In the meantime, in May 1820 he was appointed archdeacon of Totnes—the most senior and by far the most lucrative post among the diocese's archdeaconries.[19]

Aided by substantial inheritances and his own considerable administrative talents, Archdeacon Froude's speedy and easy rise to the higher circles of Devon society was also furthered by the strong and enduring friendship which he formed long before his entry into holy orders with Sir Arthur Champernowne, the lord of Dartington House in whose gift the rectorial living lay. Friends since childhood, as an undergraduate Froude was at the centre of young Champernowne's fashionable social circle in London in the early 1790s. In 1791 Froude accompanied Champernowne on his tour of the ancient piles of England; and Champernowne was Froude's companion on a marathon ride he undertook through the north of England and Scotland in 1796—a record of which, meticulously noting distances covered, natural features encountered, and houses visited, confirms Anthony Froude's testimony to his father's masterly horsemanship. But if he was an excellent rider, the young Rev. Mr Froude was not an enthusiastic huntsman: regarded as something of a scandal, the Dean's Hunt was abolished within four years of his institution at Dartington.[20] Instead, Froude's real passions were antiquarian and artistic. A bibliophile and an enthusiastic visitor of the ruins of early churches, he was also regarded as an artist of considerable technical competence by connoisseurs such as Joseph Farington, Sir William Elford, and the great Sir Edwin Landseer.[21]

19. *Alumni Oxonienses*, s.v; materials pertaining to R. H. Froude's ecclesiastical career and financial standing are to be found in Devon Record Office, Series Z/15; among the most informative are Z/15/33–6, 45; 31/25; Exeter Diocesan Chanters, 310, 341, 523; also the manuscript diocesan Visitation Returns of Bishop Ross (1779) and Bishop Carey (1821); see Arthur Warne, *Church and Society in Eighteenth Century Devon* (Newton Abbott, 1969).

20. On the relations between R. H. Froude and Sir Arthur Champernowne, see C. E. Champernowne, *The Champernowne Family* (privately printed, Exeter, 1954), 270–86; Anthony Emery, *Dartington Hall* (Oxford, 1969), ch. 5; Devon Record Office, Froude's 'Memo concerning Dartington Parsonage', Series Z15/2/12; 'Journal of a Scottish Tour', Houghton Library, Harvard University, MS Eng 1141; *The Diaries of Joseph Farington* (ed. Kenneth Garlick and Angus MacIntyre, 17 vols., New Haven, 1978–98), ii, 314, 340, 369, 514; iii, 783, 787, 792; iv, 1204, 1209; viii, 3089; ix, 3411; x, 3572, 3582; xi, 3852; xii, 3575–6.

21. The surviving sketch-books of Robert Hurrell Froude reveal a highly developed craftsmanship, a steady hand, a fine eye for detail, and an accomplished grasp of perspective, though their choice of subject matter is limited: Devon Record Office, Z/19/2/2, and 'Sketchbook of Robert Hurrell Froude, 1815', Exeter Cathedral Library; *The Diaries of Joseph Farrington* (ed. Kathryn Cave, Kenneth Garlick, and Angus MacIntyre, 16 vols., New Haven, CT, 1959–85), i, 168; ii, 314, 340, 369, 514; iii, 783, 787, 792; iv, 1204, 1209; viii, 3089; ix, 3411; x, 3572, 3582; xi, 3852; xii, 3575–6.

It was during the great northern tour of 1796 that Robert Froude embarked upon his courtship of Margaret Spedding, a sister of one of his close friends at Oriel. Though Miss Spedding was aged twenty-two in 1796, the courtship was conducted at a leisurely pace over six years until, intricate difficulties over the Spedding inheritance having been satisfactorily resolved, the couple were married at Dartington in June 1802.[22]

Children followed soon. Their first child was a boy, Richard Hurrell, born just nine months later on 27 March 1803. Then came Robert Hurrell (19 April 1804), John Spedding (25 January 1807), then two girls, Margaret (16 May 1808) and Phyllis (14 July 1809), and another boy, William (24 November 1810). A short pause relieved this almost continuous series of pregnancies until Mary Isabella was born on 1 August 1814, and after another four years Margaret Froude, then aged forty-four, gave birth to a further and final child in the person of James Anthony, born on St George's Day, 23 April 1818.[23]

Eight children—five boys and three girls—over fifteen years, no infant mortality, and until the arrival of James Anthony, no threat to the robust health of Margaret Spedding Froude. During these years the Froudes moved easily in the highest circles of Devon society, on terms of close familiarity not only with the Champernownes, but also with such grandees of the county as the Bullers and the Aclands, all of whom were frequent visitors to Dartington Rectory.[24]

The archdeacon was undoubtedly a man of influence; but many contemporaries agreed that the real attraction at the rectory was the vivacious personality of Margaret Froude. To the young John Coleridge, son of Samuel Taylor Coleridge, a man not easily impressed, she was 'beautiful in person ... and gifted in intellect with ... genius and imagination'. The saintly Isaac Williams, the scholarly Dean Milman, and the youthful Tom Mozley were equally enchanted by Mrs Froude's spiritual depth, while the worldly Joseph Farington, down on a tour in 1807, was captivated by the wonderful 'Peggy Spedding'.[25]

22. Dunn, *Froude*, 215; for evidence of Margares Spedding's independent intellectual engagements see Paula Woolf (ed.), *Dorothy Wordsworth The Grassmere Journals* (Oxford, 2002), 178-9, 245-7.
23. Devon Record Office, Dartington Parish Registers, Christenings, 1654–1832.
24. 'Memo concerning Dartington parsonage', Devon Record Office, Z15/12/2; for a Critical view of the changes made to the parsonage, see *The Ecclesiologist*, 121 (1861), 284; correspondence between Froude and Sir Anthony Buller, Devon Record Office, 58/3/6,17, and with Sir Thomas Acland, MS 1148m/21(iii).
25. Coleridge, quoted in *A Memoir of the Rev John Keble*, III; *The Autobiography of Isaac Williams* (ed. George Prevost, London, 1892); Dunn, *Froude*, I, 15; Farington, *Diary*, x, 3575.

These two contrasting images of Peggy Spedding and Mrs Froude—the charming social personality and the deeply private soul—are reflected in the small surviving body of correspondence between herself and her eldest children, Hurrell and Robert, while they were away at boarding school. Generally warm and loving, it could suddenly turn demanding and censorious. A letter to little Robert Froude, just ten years old and in his first year away in Eton, begins warmly with 'all we hear of you will make hip hip hurra at home', but turns sharply to a series of injunctions, intellectual and moral, concerning the importance of learning classical languages, and concludes with a hint of eternal retribution:

> ... if you follow your own humour and the example of the world, you will pursue happiness throughout life without ever enjoying it ... such pleasures are 'vanities and vexations of spirit' ... Thus God has decreed only that the virtuous man shall be the happy man.[26]

Hurrell's letters written at the same time indicate that he too had been the object of a similar moral offensive. Intensely competitive and relentlessly self-critical, they record the daily details of his academic progress—'First in Greek, Second in Latin'—and more pitiably, for Hurrell was eleven or twelve at the time, his many deviations from the path of goodness occasioned through such faults as idleness, talking in class, and day-dreaming about boats. And while the other half of the correspondence is missing, Hurrell's repeated apologies indicate that his confessions were met with the expected reproof.[27]

The best-known piece of correspondence between Margaret Froude and her son is not addressed to him at all. This is the remarkable letter composed by Mrs Froude to an anonymous, probably fictional, stranger confessing her complete inability to govern her eldest son.[28] Although as her first-born he has occupied a special place in her affections, and though the delicate nature of his constitution has persuaded her to make so many exceptions for him, she is now compelled to make a terrible indictment. Like an unrestrained animal he is at present ranging about the house, defying and abusing his elders, torturing his younger

26. Margaret Froude to Robert Froude, c.1813, Birmingham Oratory, Froude MSS, folder ii.
27. Harrell Froude to 'Mama', Ang. 1815, Birmingham Oratory, Froude MSS, folder ii.
28. First printed in silently edited form as part of the preface to Hurrell Froude's *Remains*, this same edited version was printed again in Louise Imogen Guiney, *Hurrell Froude: Memoranda and Comments* (London, 1904); the original full text is in Birmingham Oratory, Newman MSS, vol. I (1828–32).

brother (probably William), and frightening the life out of his baby brother Anthony. His conduct is vile: he has recently revived, she knows, 'a dirty practice at his first school and made his brother submit to the disgusting result which all the servants knew and talked of.' And he has persisted in this while his mother lies on her sickbed, looking 'at best a spectre whose days (whether passed in pain or peace) anyone would say are not likely to be many.' To this a final ultimatum is added: 'If he cannot be induced to keep the peace around me, I must leave this house; but what a distress will there be from such a cause—so unfeeling—and such a quarter.'

The mortification likely to be induced by the discovery of such a letter— and Hurrell clearly was meant to discover it—can only be surmised. Carefully preserved among his papers as a memorial of the suffering inflicted by his sinfulness, and printed at the head of his collected writings, *The Remains*, this letter, with its intent to infuse a sense of shame, guilt, and the need for atonement, has generally been seen by commentators on Hurrell Froude as an epitome of his intense and unresolved relationship with his mother, and as a symptom of the manner in which his own passionate but unstable spiritual sensibility was shaped by the force of this incisive, demanding, and ruthlessly judgemental figure.[29]

The dominance exerted by Margaret Froude over her eldest children was not applied in any direct way to her youngest. Immediately after baby Anthony's delivery she suffered a sudden decline in health and became bedridden, and her condition worsened until she died on 16 February 1821. 'She died when I was but two years old,' Froude wrote sparingly and a little inaccurately. 'I seem to remember her voice, but of her appearance, I have no conception ... we had no likeness of her in the family, none at least that I ever saw.' This act of distancing is reinforced by anecdote: his strongest memory regarding her is of her carriage, abandoned and mildewing in the coach house.[30] Whether consciously or not, Anthony Froude had clearly established his distance from his formidable but long-dead mother. But it was by the very fact of her death, and its consequences for her husband and her whole family, that Margaret Froude was to exert a far deeper influence on his young life—one which was to be all the more inescapable because it was indirect.

29. Guiney, *Hurrell Froude*, 4–7; for a more critical view, see Piers Brendon, *Hurrell Froude and the Oxford Movement* (London, 1974), ch. 1.
30. Dunn, *Froude*, I, 15.

III

Margaret Froude's death was the centrepiece in a set of calamities which afflicted the Froudes within four years of the birth of James Anthony. First, in 1819, came the sudden death of Robert Froude's patron and closest friend Sir Arthur Champernowne. This was a deep personal loss; but Champernowne's death also brought more immediate practical problems relating to an encumbered estate, a disputed will, and a large dependent family which were to involve the archdeacon as principal trustee of the estate in a great deal of trouble and litigation for decades to come. Such problems were exacerbated by the deepening of the post-war depression which afflicted not only the Champernowne estate, but Froude's own holding at Dartington. It was in these years that the large modern windows, once boldly introduced into the rectory, were walled up to avoid taxation, and the carriage put away. The depression required not only retrenchment, but charity. In 1820 Robert Froude felt obliged to reduce the yield on his tithes by one fifth; and in 1822, in his role as trustee, he made a similar reduction on the rents of the Champernowne estate. A little later, when Margaret's sister Phyllis provided a substantial sum of money for the erection of a monument in her memory, the archdeacon chose instead to put it toward a scheme of building a set of lodgings for the parochial poor.[31]

These were the general conditions in which, shortly after giving birth to Anthony, Margaret Froude entered upon her terminal decline, her death offering final irrefutable proof that the first, energetic, and adventurous phase of the Froude's family life had come to an end. Suffering the loss of his partner whose name he was incapable even of uttering, the archdeacon took refuge in denial and industry: hard work in his new diocesan position, retrenchment at the rectory, and financial and legal trouble up at Dartington Hall. To the younger members of his bereft family, this made him appear distant, cold, and preoccupied with business. But for the first cohort of the family, Hurrell and Robert—who, as Anthony testified, had developed a special relationship of 'companionship', 'affection', and 'confidence' with their father while their mother was still alive, and which 'especially after my mother's death could not be extended to the rest of us'—more complex

---

31. Materials concerning Froude's administration of the Champernowne estate, Devon Record Office, 58/3/4/9; also Z15/36/1, 10; on rent reductions in the early 1820s, Z 15/33/36/1–2; Z15/33/45; Dunn, *Froude*, I, 15–16; Champernowne, *The Champernowne Family*, 284–6.

problems of adaptation arose; and the principal burden fell upon the eldest, Hurrell.[32]

The extraordinary character of the relationship which developed between Hurrell Froude and the apparently austere and distant archdeacon as revealed by their correspondence through the 1820s and 1830s has frequently been the subject of comment.[33] Jaunty, high-spirited and jocose, Hurrell's letters to his father present a far different spirit to the tortured mind of the 'Private Journal'. Playful and disrespectful of other elders to the point many contemporaries would have regarded as impertinent, they reveal also an affectation of equality which few would have presumed with the formidable senior cleric. Thus, for example, undergraduate Hurrell demands wine, and complains that his father is too busy with such trivial matters as managing the estate to send some off; thus he demands that his father get his best gun rebored or find a better one; thus he apologises for his failure to write, but 'a fellow who neither hunts, sets badgers, or fights dogs has nothing of interest to say'; thus he defies his father's instruction not to visit London before coming home for Christmas, and demands that a good dinner await him when he arrives.[34]

There are, to be sure, discernible notes of strain in this affectation. Occasionally it is clear that Hurrell has overstepped the mark, and an apology is offered; more frequently the gaiety is interspersed with signs of anxiety and self-doubt that is the common currency of the private journal. The divergent forces in Hurrell's personality have given rise to all manner of speculation, and it is possible, as has sometimes been suggested, that in his combination of deeply self-critical introspection and a gregarious and playful public persona, Hurrell was remarkably similar to his mother. Psychological speculation is, however, inconclusive. But, whether it was due to deliberate imitation, or arose from some deep unconscious drives, or was the product simply of sheer genetic inheritance, it is a fact that in the years after Margaret Froude's death, Hurrell began to display to the archdeacon those features of seriousness and play, activity, and reflexivity that were the essential characteristics of his departed companion.

32. Dunn, *Froude* I, 16; for correspondence between the archdeacon and his sons Robert and John, see Devon Record Office, 58/3/4/9.
33. Guiney, *Hurrell Froude*; Brendon, *Hurrell Froude and the Oxford Movement, passim.*; the correspondence between Hurrell and his father is contained in Birmingham Oratory, Froude MSS, folders ii–v.
34. Hurrell to Archdeacon Froude, 8 March, 4 May, 6 September, 11 December 1823; 25 October 1824, Birmingham Oratory, Froude MSS, folder i, nos 3, 6, 17; folder iv, no. 6.

It is also clear that the archdeacon responded powerfully to such a stimulus. He did send the wine; he entertained Hurrell's common-room gossip; and he offered a stream of practical, experienced advice. More importantly, the two debated energetically about matters of ecclesiastical and secular architecture and antiquities. They exchanged drawings of stained-glass windows, of cathedral plans, of ancient ruins. Enthusiastically, the archdeacon made extensive extracts from the old parish records of Exeter diocese for publication by Hurrell in the *British Magazine*. They went on surveying expeditions and travelled abroad together. The archdeacon was a frequent visitor to Oxford, once Hurrell had won his fellowship at Oriel; and Hurrell's friends, Keble, Williams, and Newman among many, were welcomed in the rectory as the archdeacon's own. He engaged passionately with Hurrell in the ecclesiological and political debates of the 1820s, and though he became increasingly concerned about the advanced nature of some of Hurrell's views, he never quarrelled with him. The death of his first son in 1836 was to the archdeacon a blow equal to the loss of his wife.[35]

The impulses which gave rise to this unusually intimate relationship between widowed father and eldest son are not of primary concern here. More pertinent is the rather less happy consequence which Hurrell's adoption of the role vacated by his mother had for the rest of his family. He became their moral censor. Even as they were expressing his own cheekiness or confessing his own anxieties, it is remarkable how so many of Hurrell's letters to his father contained judgements, usually negative, on his siblings. His sisters largely escaped censure: his comments concerning them are sparse, and in the main condescending. But toward his brothers, at school, at home, and in college, he is relentlessly judgemental. Though only a year behind him at Oriel, Robert is reported on to the archdeacon in tones of grave concern. He is not sufficiently committed to his studies, he socialises too much, he keeps bad company, and he has picked up a slangy habit of speech which Hurrell will shortly 'castigate'. John, who did not go up to Oxford but was apprenticed at law in London, did not escape Hurrell's eye. He is extravagant; like Robert, he is easily distracted from his work and is over-impressed by the wrong kind of company.[36]

---

35. Hurrell to Archdeacon Froude, 4 May, 12 August 1823; 1 July, 21 July, 2 August 1825, Birmingham Oratory, Froude MSS, folder i, nos 5, 11; folder iv, nos 10, 11, 14, 15.
36. Hurrell to Archdeacon Froude, 1 February, 8 March, 13 March, 20 April, 22 May 1823, Birmingham Oratory, Froude MSS, folder i, nos 2, 3, 4, 6.

William, though far more studious than the other two, also failed to meet Hurrell's exacting standards. Hurrell's rigour is illustrated by a letter sent to him from Oriel after William, aged seventeen and still at school, had expressed a desire to improve himself. He was glad to learn 'that anything has led you to think more seriously than you used to do of the necessity of exerting yourself and attending to the wishes of my Father.' But he doubted William's resolution, and until he has learned more of the nature and extent of the young man's self-reproach for past failings, whether they extended beyond

> those [things] in which we have always found you deficient [he will reserve judgement]. But one of the things with which we have always found fault has been your great closeness about your pursuits, so that we are quite in the dark about you and hardly know you at all ... the two great things I wish to impress upon you are the necessity of attending more closely to your conduct, and of putting very little confidence in your feelings.[37]

Hurrell was William's coach for entrance into Oxford, and thereafter acted as informal tutor to him at Oriel; and though William worked as hard as anyone could demand, on occasions cramming for up to eighteen hours a day, he earned only Hurrell's qualified approval. He devoted too much time to his favourite subject, mathematics, and neglected classics. His result, a First in the former and a Third in the latter, was deserved, and inferior to Hurrell's Seconds in both.[38]

This was the intensely demanding, judgemental, and studious atmosphere in which the youngest of the Froudes grew up. The very earliest brief mentions of 'Toney' or 'Att', (Hurrell's benign diminutives) in Hurrell's correspondence concern the fact that he is idle and 'not doing much'.[39] But in fact Anthony was an intellectually precocious child. Imaginative, and naturally curious about his environment, his mind was cultivated by stories from early on and later by a liberal attitude toward reading: 'We were allowed to read what we pleased. My own chief delight was in Grimm's *Tales* or *the Seven Champions of Christendom*. The *Arabian Nights*

37. Hurrell Froude to William Froude, 27 April 1828, in G. H. Harper (ed.), *Cardinal Newman and William Froude, FRS: A Correspondence* (Baltimore, 1933), 214–16, and for several letters in a similar tone, 211–18.
38. Hurrell Froude to Archdeacon Froude, 30 January, 18 February, 12 June 1830; Hurrell Froude to Newman, 9 September 1832; *Letters and Diaries of John Henry Newman* (ed. Ian Ker and Thomas Gornall, S. J., Oxford, 1979), iii, 92.
39. Hurrell Froude to Newman, 6 August 1831; *Letters and Diaries of John Henry Newman* (ed. Ian Ker and Thomas Gornall, S. J. (Oxford, 1979), ii, 347.

we revelled in and took into our own souls.' On Sundays, secular literature was put away and the Bible was read, 'as we had good memories we came to know it pretty well', Froude recalled, but, in a manner which distanced him from his elder brothers and from Edward Fowler, the fictional alter-ego with whom he has been too closely identified, 'we were never worried about our spiritual emotions, and in this respect nothing can have been more excellent than our education'.[40]

In other respects, however, his early education proved less happy. He flowered early, developed a flair for classical languages, and before the age of eleven had read the *Odyssey* and the *Iliad* twice in the original. This early promise Froude later came to see as a curse. Considered to be gifted, he was subjected to an extraordinary regime of study: 'I must work, work, work without pause of relief ... the drudgery continued from year's end to year's end ... I was forced like a sickly plant in a hot-house.' There was, moreover, a further even more oppressive dimension to his early education. Whether it was due to his mother's illness, or to a congenital defect, Anthony, it was generally agreed, was afflicted by a weak constitution which needed special attention if it was to improve. Placed in the care of his aunt, Mary Spedding, who had come to nurse her sister and stayed on as a stepmother for the family after Margaret Froude's death, he was subjected by her to a regimen of which the least that can be said is that it was brutal and irresponsible:

> When I was three years old I was supposed to be in need of bracing. I was taken out of bed every morning, and dipped in ice-cold water which ran from a stream into a granite trough ... I didn't die of it, but I didn't grow the stronger.[41]

His earliest memory was of being whipped by her for soiling his frock when he was 'little more than two'.

What Aunt Mary began, brother Hurrell continued with vigour. Regarding Anthony as a 'sawney', he determined, with his father's consent and his brothers' collaboration, to make a man of him through a series of trials and 'experiments' which allowed his own sadistic impulses free rein. In the auto-biography Froude records just a few of these adventures: he remembered being suddenly thrown overboard in deep water to give him a fright; he remembered 'once when I was very little' Hurrell grabbing him by the heels and plunging him headlong into a stream 'stirring the mud at the bottom with my head'; and he recalled Hurrell's psychological tortures even more painfully. From as soon as he learned to walk Anthony enjoyed wandering alone in the fields and lanes around the rectory. Hurrell, whose morbid dislike of other people's privacy was already instanced in the case of William, determined to put a stop to such attempts at independence. Near the rectory was a hollow with a brook, a bridge, and a lonely farmhouse:

> This hollow ... Hurrell tenanted for me with a vague monster with no distinct outline, but more terrible for the want of it, whom he called Peningre, a phantom monstrous and malevolent who might seize me and eat me up. Peningre through my childish years was a frightful reality to me. I learned by degrees that he was an illusion, but the shadow haunted me, long after the substance had departed.[42]

Such were the instances that Froude found it possible to record in his autobiography, but it is clear from the way in which they were presented there that they were but the deepest scars remaining from a childhood of fear and abuse. Throughout his early years, Anthony Froude, identified by his family both as an academic prodigy and as a weakling, was exposed without defence to the 'experiments' of a dominant elder brother whose moral and intellectual authority went unchallenged and whose taste for bullying and cruelty even he himself was compelled to acknowledge.

Though Froude himself readily acknowledged that this prolonged abuse left 'indelible marks' upon him, he never indicated in what manner they did, and so all that remains is speculation. Those who please may find in this childhood trauma the roots of a strange literary sado-masochism which included a servile worship of dominant men, such as Newman and Carlyle, and a concomitant tendency to court outrage and abuse through the provocative stances that he assumed. The obvious nature of such conjectures does little, however, to sanction their authority. Insofar as they are interpretatively attractive, they are also quite untestable, and rest upon an attenuated thread of association upon which it would be unwise to attach any significant weight.

Purely within the context of his childhood, certain inferences supported by the available evidence may be more confidently hazarded. As with all embattled and vulnerable children, young Froude was compelled to resort to his own small resources for survival and defence, though in his case the available resources appear to have been not entirely meagre. Imaginatively

---

42. Dunn, *Froude* I, 18–20.

gifted and endowed with early developed reading skills, he was able to withdraw into an elaborate fantasy, story-telling world of his own devising. But he was also adaptable, capable of finding succour and defence wherever it lay. He formed a close attachment with his sisters, and especially with his nearest sibling, Mary, whose early death extracted from him a deeper expression of grief than for any other of his prematurely deceased siblings. But he worked hard also to win the affection and protection of the second eldest Robert, taking some risk and suffering considerable hardship while learning to ride in order to prove to this less implacable figure that he was not, after all, a 'sawney'.[43] Most importantly, when the opportunity arose, he contrived to get away.

While in the past Hurrell and Robert had been sent away together to elementary school at Otterey, and William had been kept at home until being despatched to Westminster, Anthony, aged nine, happily embraced the chance to go to school at Buckfastleigh parish school in which, though only about five miles away, he was to be a boarder. By the time Anthony went there in the mid-1820s, Buckfastleigh had hardly established a reputation as a school of prestige. Founded in 1813 by the parish priest Matthew Lowndes, 'for the children of the poor', it began with an enrolment of 200, but by the mid-1830s had gone into decline when it became the subject of serious criticism from the diocesan administration.[44] Yet Froude's memories of his first school were almost entirely warm. It was there that his love of the classics was fired by Matthew Lowndes junior, who made up in enthusiasm what he lacked in scholarly proficiency and rigour. Buckfastleigh's principal appeal to the young Froude, however, was not academic, but social. 'In my heart', he confessed, 'I preferred school to being at home.' At Buckfastleigh, despite his physical deficiencies and his academic superiority, he was welcomed by the other pupils and made friends easily. 'Bullying', he was happy to record, 'was by common consent treated as a public crime.' It was punished ceremonially by the pupils themselves by 'buffeting'', a ritual under which the bully was made to kneel bare-backed on the schoolroom floor to receive one blow from each boy with a knotted handkerchief. But even in this, Froude's memory is tinged with tenderness:

43. Dunn, *Froude*, I, 17–20.; 'Poor Att is such a very good-tempered fellow that, in spite of his sawneyness, he is sure to be liked;' Hurrell Froude on Anthony's admission to Buckfastleigh, quoted in Guiney, *Hurrell Froude*, 6.
44. Devon Record Office, Report on Buckfastleigh School, Basket C/25/27.

I can see the poor boy now on his knees with tears in his eyes, suffering more from the shame than the pain of the blows. He had not been very cruel after all, and to me he had been uniformly kind.[45]

In this last, the real charm of Buckfastleigh for young Froude is revealed. His very first memory of the school is of waiting in line with a capful of mazard cherries which he was busy 'devouring and distributing among my new acquaintances'. Later, when he had settled in, 'frequent cakes arrived and baskets of fruit: a sure road to good-will from those among whom such dainties were instantly distributed'. Insecure and conscious of his frailty, Anthony was eager to please and willing to buy popularity when possible, and his efforts to gain acceptance fully succeeded: 'my school fellows were good to me'.[46]

The duration of this pathetic childhood idyll was not long. Within two years it was decided at Dartington that Anthony should follow his brother William to school at Westminster. There then began the most intense phase of Froude's childhood ordeal. Recalled with such poignancy and pain in his autobiography as made his daughter hesitate to allow it to be published, Froude's own account of these days of torment is among the most powerful and moving pieces he ever wrote. Removed from the relative protection of one of the boarding houses which adjoined the school and 'launched' into the dormitory, 'the College' Froude found himself in was a cold, filthy, bare room, devoid of comfort or even furniture. Only the senior boys enjoyed some relief from the drafts, and were allowed some basic amenities, while the juniors, their fags, were condemned to serve each senior 'as his special body servant, bound to wait upon him at all times and for all purposes.' Only the seniors fed well, while the juniors were driven to forage for themselves. Anthony was too weak to do it: 'I was nearly starved.' 'Our washing place, appropriated equally for less savoury purposes, was a long stone trough in an underground vault open to the air ...' and even colder than the dormitory. On his first day, having failed the test of keeping the seniors' fires alight and preparing coffee for them at the same time, he was severely flogged by the older boys—the first of countless beatings he was to receive at their hands.

When my junior year was out I remained the drudge and sport of my stronger contemporaries. No one interfered, it was the rule of the establishment and

45. Dunn, *Froude*, I, 26–30; for Froude's continuing fondness of Buckfastleigh, see the undated (*c.*1862) fragment of a draft letter, Bodleian Library MS 41820 (Eng. Lett., e.48), f.45.
46. Dunn, *Froude*, I, 27–8.

was supposed to be good for me. We wore knee-breeches in those days. I have
had my legs set on fire to make me dance. When I had crawled to bed and to
sleep, I have been woke many times by the hot points of cigars burning holes
in may face. I was made drunk by being forced to swallow brandy-punch. My
health broke down, and I had to be removed for a few months to the boarding
house, but I got little good by it as I was paid off at odd hours for what was
called skulking. When I was sent back to College, it all began again ...[47]

Such independent evidence as is available confirms this terrible testimony—
largely, but with some complication. Under Headmaster Williamson, Westminster was scandalously mismanaged. Younger boys were mixed with
seniors both in classes and in the dormitory without supervision, and the
brutalities and privations suffered by the junior and weaker pupils through
such negligence was the subject of a public enquiry which led to Williamson's
resignation in the mid-1840s. Though it is not explicitly referred to in his
autobiography—except perhaps metaphorically—the probability that
Froude was sexually abused is high. Writing in 1850 in regard to the
Carshalton scandal, Froude was trenchant. Retailing the story of an Eton
boy dying in terror of the damnation which awaited him for his terrible sins
of impurity, Froude added:

> The event in boys' lives at English schools is the incident of sin. They take their
> degree in vice and they are heroes to one another according to the stage to
> which they have descended. I say this is so. I have been at a public school
> myself ... and I am certain that by the mass of boys (I do not say by all) that
> those who have taken the last step are regarded in virtue of it as having passed
> into manhood; they move about in a higher atmosphere, and are looked up to
> with a mysterious awe as belongs to another order of beings.[48]

The decision to introduce the very young but academically advanced
Anthony Froude into classes with older boys and to remove him from the
comparative safety of the boarding house to the snake-pit of the dormitory
was therefore inexcusably neglectful of his welfare.[49]

But there are some indications that the elder Froudes were quite alive to
the dangers and did not come to the decisions lightly. His London-based

47. Dunn, *Froude,* I, 31–4.
48. Froude, 'The Morals of Public Schools', *The Leader,* 19 October 1850, 710.
49. The Clarendon Commission's *Report on Public Schools* (1864) documented in full detail the
    abusive regime of nine public schools, including Westminster, in a manner which fully supports
    Froude's account; see, in general, Christopher Shrosbee, *Public Schools and Private Education: The
    Clarendon Commission and the Public Schools Acts* (Manchester, 1988).

uncle, also Anthony, who acted as an informal guardian for the young boarder, was quite against his leaving the boarding house and joining the senior classes, and both the archdeacon and brother Hurrell were made aware of his reservations. Brother William also expressed misgivings, advising Anthony that he should not seek to go into College at all, 'because it will delay his education'. Hurrell agreed; warning his father that 'it can do him no good to be put with boys of such a different age', and adding characteristically that it showed 'a disposition for display which I do not like'. But ultimately he was prepared to agree with the archdeacon 'in throwing the responsibility on' Anthony himself 'in letting him have his way'. From these stray comments it appears that while the proposal to place the young boy in with the seniors was first rashly made by Williamson, it was Anthony himself who first responded positively to the idea and pressed it upon his more cautious elders, father, brother, and uncle. They did not immediately agree, however. The idea had been floated some time around Christmas 1829, and by April the following year Anthony was still at the boarding house, pressing for the move into College. At that time Hurrell himself visited Westminster in person 'to examine Att's case', and found the evidence less than satisfactory. Williamson had indeed supplied a certificate testifying to young Froude's advanced learning; but he did not regard the certificate as anything 'especial', nor did he stand over such implications as had been drawn from it. 'And I fear', Hurrell concluded, 'Att can hardly be acquitted of having taking on slender evidence what he wished to be true.' The landlady's concerns 'about Att's youth and ill-health' coincided with Uncle Anthony's and his own, and Hurrell was still, at this stage, of the view that his entry into the College be deferred for a year. By June, however, the archdeacon had yielded, young Anthony was permitted to join the big boys in College, and the ordeal began.[50]

Insofar as this small departure from the autobiography reveals anything, it merely confirms the force of the young Froude's determination to grow up, to establish his independence from his austere and oppressive elders. The desperation of the attempt makes the completeness of its failure all the more painful. Froude's later recollection is hardly to be blamed for minimising his own role in this catastrophe of his young life, or in imputing to his family responsibility for a decision of whose dangers they

---

50. Hurrell Froude to Archdeacon Froude, 30 January, 2 April 1830; Birmingham Oratory, Froude MSS, folder vi, nos 3, 9.

were fully conscious, but in which they colluded, if only to teach the impertinent young man a lesson. Three and a half years of unrelieved physical suffering and mental anguish ended finally in complete nervous and physical collapse and minor scandal. On retrieving the clothes and personal property of the broken youth, it was discovered that much had disappeared and much had been destroyed. Rather than accepting Anthony's word that he had been the victim of theft and vandalism, his father concluded that he had pawned or sold his goods, and so immediately upon his arrival home Anthony was severely flogged by the archdeacon under Hurrell's approving eye, and told that the dose would be repeated until he had confessed his fault. He resisted, and was punished until he made a confession of what he himself believed were his real sins. Why the elder Froudes should have been so unfeeling may largely be explained by their inveterate mistrust of 'Att'. But the matter may have been slightly more complicated. Froude acknowledged that he had faults similar to the false charge of pawning; and though he did not indicate what they might have been, the experience of his fictional creation Edward Fowler, whose life so closely parallels Froude's at this time, suggests a possibility. Bullied, tortured, and starved at Westminster, Fowler ran up substantial debts through buying treats to secure relief and protection from his tormentors, and when his cowardly prodigality was discovered he was soundly thrashed by his father. If, as seems likely, Anthony Froude had attempted to apply the techniques of survival that had worked so well at Buckfastleigh, they not only failed him at Westminster but plunged him into deeper suffering at home.

Disowned and, he believed, despised by his father, discounted by Hurrell as an academic failure of whom far too much had once been made, the young Froude was now ostracised at home. Humiliated by not being allowed any new clothes, and being forced to wear altered cast-offs of his family, he was threatened with complete severance from his family by being exiled to factory work in a tannery. It is a dreadful testimony to the extremity of his condition that, aged about fifteen, he did not, once the beatings had stopped, seriously resent these punishments. Threats, intended to shame him, of his despatch to a cheap boarding school in the north did not frighten him, and the tannery did not daunt him, for each still offered a promise of an escape, however dire. And he began to hope for an even greater one: 'the chief consolation that I had was that the consumption which had already proved so deadly in our family . . . was beginning to show itself, and would soon take me away'.[51] In the meantime he found lesser consolations in being allowed to wander alone around the woods and the fields without the fear of encountering Peningre, and more significantly in being allowed to browse unmolested in his father's library. There, though he had for the time lost all interest in studying the ancient languages, he 'read voraciously' and independently, discovering Shakespeare, Spenser and, 'less to my advantage,' Byron.[52] In addition to poetry, he first discovered history: he loved Gibbon, but was even more attracted to Sharon Turner's *History of England.* 'I was thrown into the surprise of an awakening mind.'[53]

This independent intellectual exploration was blighted only when Hurrell returned periodically to tutor Anthony as he had William, but with even less approval of his efforts and hope for his future. Increasingly, however, as Hurrell became engrossed in the great Tractarian campaign which filled his final years, Anthony, who had been allowed by neglect to construct a fragile imaginative independence in private, began to find a more public niche of his own. At first he was put by Hurrell to the dull punitive tasks of copying out and learning off edificatory sermons. But gradually he was advanced to more challenging tests. He was once set to copying a letter concerning Newman's notorious question as to whether Dr Arnold was really a Christian; and when Hurrell began work on a study of Thomas Becket he was directed to supply an English translation of the letters of St John of Salisbury.[54]

The experience of coming to terms with the writings of a graceful medieval Latinist whose idiom and ideas were a world away from the set texts of the public-school exercises was in itself something of an intellectual awakening. But it also kindled a latent interest in theological and philosophical speculation, and so when Hurrell's Tractarian friends came

---

51. Detail in this and the preceding paragraph are derived from Froude's 'Autobiography' in Dunn, *Froude*, I, 39–41.
52. Though later in life Froude lost his youthful enthusiasm for Byron, he was still sufficiently attached to his early idol to write a spirited defence of the poet against some of the more disreputable allegations made against him: 'A Leaf from the Real Life of Byron', *Nineteenth Century*, 14 (August, 1883), 228–42.
53. Dunn, *Froude*, 40.
54. Given the fact that no modern English edition of the letters appeared before 1840, it is probable that in doing so Froude would have had to rely on one of three French editions of John's letters: M. de la Bligne, *Magna Bibliotheca Veterum Patrum et Antiquorum Scriptorum*, xv (Lyon, 1622), repr. *Maxima Bibliotheca Patrum* (1677), vols. x, xiii; C. Lupus, *Epistolae et Vita divi Thomae Martyris et Archiepiscopi Cantuariensis*, 2 vols. (Brussels, 1682), or the section in *Recueil des historiens des Gaules et de la France*, ed. M. Bouquet et al. (xiv–xviii ed. M.-J.-J. Brial), vol. xvi (Paris 1813), 505–625—the latest being the most probable. I am grateful to Professor Anne Duggan for authoritative advice on this matter.

to stay at Dartington, Anthony was permitted to eavesdrop on their intensive discussions. More than sixty years later, and still engaged in his polemic against the Oxford Movement, the autobiographer recalled the manner in which he was scandalised by the opinions he heard expressed in the rectory:

> Everything which I had been taught to believe as a child, everything ... which had touched my imagination, I heard questioned or denied. Transubstantiation, which I had shuddered at the name of, was spoken of as probably true. The Church was the supreme ruler of the world and was sovereign over the State. The reformers, whom I had been taught to look upon as saints, were now to be hated.[55]

The Tractarians' view of history was equally shocking: that Charles I was a saint, that the Revolution of 1688 was a crime, that the Pretender was the rightful monarch, that the non-jurors 'were the true confessors of the English Church'. But while he might not dare challenge their theological authority, here at least Anthony could find grounds for dissent. 'The history which I had been reading seemed to say that ... under the feudal system and the patriarchal sway of the Plantagenets, England had been particularly well skilled in treason.' All this had changed, of course, with the Tudors and the Reformation of the sixteenth century, which had asserted England's independence and laid the foundations of its future greatness. 'I could not but think', says the autobiographer with retrospective satisfaction, 'that there were gaps in my brother's knowledge of his own country.'[56]

Moreover, even as he was working for Hurrell, young Anthony had embarked upon a theological reading course of his own. The results, he records, were mixed. He acquired an early scepticism in regard to theologians 'laying down as certainties what from the very nature of things our limited minds were very imperfectly able to comprehend'. His own observations of the modesty and humanity of a family in the parish whom he had heard denounced in the parsonage as 'atheists' further deepened his scepticism about orthodox authority.[57] But from the earliest sections of John Pearson's seventeenth-century *Exposition of the Creed* he acquired also a conceptual basis for his own intuitive distinction 'between believing and

---

55. Dunn, *Froude*, I, 41–3.   56. Dunn, *Froude*, I, 44.
57. This is a recollection Froude recorded in his 'Science and Theology, Ancient and Modern', *The International Review* (May 1878), 292.

believing *in*' in which personal conviction alone offered a pathway toward certainty in life.[58]

Far more is doubtless being attributed retrospectively here in the 1890s than was actually going on in the mind of the adolescent Froude in the early 1830s, as it is unlikely that the fifteen- or sixteen-year-old, no matter how precocious, should have already adopted such a clear distinction with all its intellectual and moral ramifications. Even allowing for a large element of hindsight, however, it is equally clear that Pearson's insistence on the importance of personal commitment rather than rational acceptance would have registered strongly with an individual struggling for self-identity, and that the first glimmerings of that breakthrough to autonomy in mind and character that had so far been denied to the young man are also being warmly recollected in memory. Through the endurance of long periods of rejection and neglect, through the prospect of imminent death, and through the long and solitary course of study in poetry, history, and theology to which he submitted himself, young Froude had laid the foundations of a proud and vital independence that he was to preserve with uncompromising tenacity throughout his career.

That it was to nurture darker reflexes was also the inevitable consequence of a childhood of lovelessness and abuse: a profound mistrust of human nature (including his own) and a pessimism about its potential and prospects on earth, a scepticism concerning the authority of ideas and opinions which seemed to be based on claims of fact, logic, or plausibility alone, and a preference for those which had been arrived at by personal effort and individual commitment. There may also be discerned here a root of that dubious commitment to the power of conviction over that of demonstration that was so often to be an operating assumption of the later writer's manipulative rhetorical strategy. Finally, related to that preference for the force of belief over its intellectual basis, there was an even more dubious recognition of the value of presentation and appearance over direct statement and open-ended argument which was to be revealed even as the ordeal of Froude's youth was coming to a close.

Though Archdeacon Froude had in fact been preparing for his son's entry to Oxford within months of his withdrawal from Westminster, he had kept it secret from the errant youth. And when at last it was made known to

---

58. First published in London in a small edition in 1659, Pearson's *Exposition of the Creed* has since been issued in many expanded and revised editions.

him, Anthony concluded fully to his satisfaction that his father's relenting was at once highly conditional and discouraging: 'He told me that perhaps I might have another trial, but apparently with unchanged distrust ... he appealed to motives which could not act upon me.'[59]

Notwithstanding this assumption, he went on quietly acquiescing in his father's wishes, resuming the dreary exercises that were now required, and waiting for the time when the independence long refused him but now growing secretly within would finally be achieved. The prisoner now viewing the prospect of a ticket-of-leave would not again make the mistake of a premature break for freedom which had cost him so dear at Westminster. It would come slowly, secretly, and, if necessary, deceptively; and its first stages would be accomplished in his undergraduate years at Oxford.

59. Dunn, *Froude*, I, 43.

3

Independence: Oxford and Ireland, 1836–42

I

Anthony Froude's first years at Oriel College, Oxford, were to be of crucial importance not only in enforcing the drive toward independence and self-knowledge which had only begun to emerge in his adolescent years, but also in shaping the direction it would take. During that time he was to undergo and survive a series of psychological and intellectual crises which, while they were not to issue in any final resolution of his personal and moral problems, were at least to confirm him in the conviction that he had both the means and the strength purposefully to address them.

Ironically, the significance of this formative experience at Oxford has been obscured (perhaps beyond recovery) by the several accounts which he himself provided of it in later years. In addition to the passages in his 'autobiography' he supplied two other narratives: one which could be derived from the early chapters of his autobiographical and sentimental early novel, 'The Spirit's Trials' and a second in sections of his essay sequence on 'The Oxford Counter-Reformation' which he published in the early 1880s.[1] Given the almost complete absence of other sources bearing on his undergraduate career, these accounts have been seized upon by his biographers and pressed into a kind of palimpsest depicting the rich and dramatic story of the ordeal of a young Romantic soul.

---

1. First published in six instalments as 'Reminiscences of the High Church Revival', in *Good Words*, January–June 1881, the essay was reprinted as 'The Oxford Counter-Reformation' in the fourth volume of Froude's *Short Studies on Great Subjects* (1st edn., 1882).

Taken together, these sources offer an account that is in many respects remarkably consistent. But each is also, in its own way, questionable. The autobiography continues in its Augustinian mood:

> I ... found myself suddenly free, surrounded by an agreeable society which was well disposed to be friendly to me. I had a liberal allowance which ... appeared to be boundless. ... The men I lived with were gentleman ... [who] neither intended nor tried to do more than pass without discredit. As they did, I did. I rode and boated and played tennis. I went to wine parties and supper parties...[2]

In this way Froude says he went on 'wasting two years of my already wasted youth'. But all this changed in the summer of 1839 when, while on a reading party in Cumberland, Froude fell in love, with miraculous consequences:

> The sense of being valued by another made me set a value on my own life. I had something to care for, something which made it worth my while to distinguish myself.[3]

With this transformation Froude set to work at his studies. But then disaster struck. The father of the girl who had been the object of his love intervened, and ended the relationship 'through a want of confidence in the stability of my own character'. Froude was driven to despair, and months of idleness followed before he was released from his 'leaden torpor' by yet another epiphany which occurred one winter's night while he was at home in the woods, the scene of so many of his childhood terrors: 'reviewing my past life, observing where I had laid myself open to the enemy, [I] determined to defy him'. He would no longer be 'a slave, a pipe for Fortune's finger to sound what note she pleased upon'. With this resolve the hardened young man set about his studies again; and though it was by then too late to win the hoped-for First, 'I got a fair second and was made to feel that in future competitions I might still recover my place.'[4]

This was the reminiscence of the memorialist of the early 1890s. But more than forty years earlier the principal events in this account had been sketched, though in far sharper relief, in the experience of Froude's fictional alter-ego Edward Fowler. Escaping from a childhood and adolescence every bit as cruel and oppressive as Froude's had been, Fowler immediately went astray in College:

2. Dunn, *Froude*, I, 47.   3. Dunn, *Froude*, I, 51.

4. Dunn, *Froude*, I, 59. The reference to Fortune is from *Hamlet*, act 3, scene 2, line 70; significantly, it continues: 'Give me the man / That is not passion's slave; and I will wear him / In my heart's core.'

Home and College changed places ... At College there was no 'you must' or 'you must not'; at home there was nothing else. Till he went to College ... Edward had never known the idea of amusement ... [at College] Fowler was idle and extravagant. He had been weighed down so heavily, and at College the weight was so completely taken off, that he was a boat without ballast, and he heaved over at every breath of inclination.[5]

Squandering his liberal allowance, Fowler fell hopelessly into debt; and seeking to hide his crime from his father, he was reduced to borrowing secretly from his friends in order to placate Oxford's predatory tradesmen. This not unusual undergraduate trouble was to have even more disastrous consequences when, like Anthony Froude, Fowler fell in love with a young woman whom he had encountered while on a summer's reading party in Wales. Love had the same effect on Fowler as it had on the young Froude. He returned to Oxford determined to make up for lost time, and 'from being the idlest man in College, he grew to be known as a hard worker ... tutors began to change their views ... and higher faces in the university came with good reason to smile on him'.[6]

Crossed from the outset, however, by the rumour that there was a streak of insanity in his inamorata's family, Fowler's affair was suddenly doomed by a series of accidents which issued in his father's refusal of consent.[7]

Heartbroken, Fowler plunged into despair and dissipation; some incidents not specified but which were 'notorious at the university and flung a shadow over him' led to his been 'sent away in disgrace'. 'Disgraced and his disgrace published', he was subjected to the mortification of being flogged by his father.[8] But this last humiliation had at least the effect of distancing the effect of his lover's sorrows, and after a while Fowler stoically and dourly set out again on a journey of recovery, returning to the university and his books to resume the commitment which had been so cruelly broken before. Like Froude, his rehabilitation came too late to win distinction in his finals, 'but he did so partially', and the result was his determination to spend his life as a student.[9]

Given the remarkably close parallels between the autobiography and the fiction, it is hardly surprising that Froude's critics and biographers have

5. 'The Spirit's Trials', in Zeta [Froude], *Shadows of the Clouds*, 46.
6. *Shadows of the Clouds*, 61–2.
7. *Shadows of the Clouds*, 64.
8. *Shadows of the Clouds*, 71–2.
9. *Shadows of the Clouds*, 75–7.

traditionally fused the two into one account—a procedure sanctioned in Waldo Hilary Dunn's authorised biography in which the two are put together as a seamless narrative of Froude's early life. But for all the obvious similarities, significant discrepancies remain not only between the auto-biography and the novel, but also between both and what little may be recovered from the surviving independent evidence of Froude's time at Oxford. Some are minor, some more important.

First, there is little to support the view that Froude spent his first years in college in total idleness or dissolution. Such excesses as he actually confessed to are hardly shocking. In the unreformed Oxford of the 1830s, wine parties and supper parties were mild dissipations, in comparison to other entertainments on offer outside the walls; while rowing, horseback riding, and 'the manly amusement of tennis' were the officially approved undergraduate pastimes, much encouraged by the authorities in contrast to fox-hunting, pugilism, and the ratsbane of billiards—in none of which Froude confessed to have indulged.[10] No scandalous incident appears to have disgraced Froude in the university as a whole; there is no entry under his name in the Proctor's records.[11] Instead, as he himself records, Froude chose to embark on an independent programme of reading in classics, history, and philosophy far broader than what was on offer in the syllabus. Among the moderns he read Gibbon and Sharon Turner; but, enabled by his early linguistic precosity, he was most taken by the Greek origi-nals: Herodotus and Thucydides. 'Aristotle laid hold of me, and Plato's dia-logues opened a new and boundless world.'[12] But it was to the poets and dramatists that he was most attracted. He read Pindar, Aeschylus, and Sophocles. He was particularly taken by the latter's *Philoctetes*: the apparently unrelenting injustice of the poor, despised, deformed but gifted man's suffering suggesting such a parallel with his own experience that he was once reduced to 'crying like a child'—'a solitary experience with me in literature'.[13] His reading was perhaps wayward, as he claims; at any rate it was strategically imprudent, for Froude was to fail his first attempt at Responsions in 1837. But it nonetheless supplied him with a fertile literary foundation on which he was to batten

---

10. See M. C. Curthoys and C. J. Day, 'The Oxford of Mr Verdant Green', in M. G. Brock and M. C. Curthoys (eds.), *The History of the University of Oxford: Nineteenth Century Oxford* (Oxford, 1997), ch. 8.

11. University Archives Oxford, Junior Proctor's Liber Niger.

12. Dunn, *Froude*, I, 48.   13. Dunn, *Froude*, I, 48.

in later life. Froude, it seems, had chosen the life of the scholar some time before Fowler.[14]

That Froude, like Fowler, fell into debt, however, is also clear, from external evidence, even though he makes no reference to it in the autobiography. Despite a relatively generous allowance of between £220 and £240 which the archdeacon, on Newman's advice, had advanced to his son, a letter to Mark Pattison on the last day of 1838 reveals that Froude had developed a serious financial problem, but only, it should be noted, more than two years after his going into residence.[15] Strenuous efforts to clear his debts independently had, not surprisingly, failed, and at Christmas the prodigal had been obliged to confess. By the time he wrote to Pattison, however, Froude's father had relented and agreed, albeit grudgingly, to meet his bills. Thus shriven, Froude resolved never to place himself in such a position again. Nothing survives to say whether or not he was entirely successful in his resolve. But the archdeacon may have increased his allowance somewhat; for years later Froude recorded without a sense of grievance that during his time as an undergraduate his annual expenditure amounted to between £280 and £300 a year, and the silence of the record alone suggests that any further prodigalities were of a lesser order.[16]

But Froude's experience should, in any case, be set in a broader context. It was not difficult for a young man of relatively modest means to fall rapidly and seriously into debt in Oxford in the 1830s and 1840s, and many did so. The profiteering perpetrated upon vulnerable and naïve undergraduates by Oxford's shopkeepers and tradesmen as well as by the college's own servants was notorious. Not only were exorbitant prices charged for luxuries such as wine, fowl, and sweetmeats, but basic food, materials, and services cost far more within the city than anywhere else in the kingdom. The colleges themselves were seen to have connived at this racket, through failure to provide adequate meals and provisions, and through the toleration of private businesses conducted from

14. He passed classics but failed in a part of Euclid. Archdeacon Froude to Keble, 16 February 1837, Keble College, Oxford, Keble MSS 163. The tone of the archdeacon's report of Anthony's failure does not suggest that he was greatly perturbed: 'I trust it will do him good'; Dunn, *Froude*, I, 47–9.

15. Archdeacon Froude to Newman, [?] April 1836, and Newman's reply, 26 April 1836, Birmingham Oratory, Froude MSS, folder vii; Froude to Mark Pattison, 31 December 1838, Bodleian Library, Pattison MSS, 59, fols. 9–10.

16. Froude to [?], 29 January [1865–74], Bodleian Library, Oxford, Eng. Lett. 39101 (Ms Don.d. 137, ff.75–6); there is no indication that Froude, unlike Fowler, suffered corporal punishment at this stage; Fowler's suffering appears to be a fictional repositioning of the punishments actually inflicted on Froude on his withdrawal from Westminster.

their kitchens and butteries. Once imprudent expenditure had taken place, a pernicious system of extended credit which the colleges had allowed to develop among their suppliers ensured that escape from indebtedness would be a very costly matter indeed.[17]

This scandal was a cause of a campaign mounted by several reforming college fellows in the later 1840s seeking the establishment of a parliamentary inquiry. By that time Froude's friends among the dons, including Arthur Hugh Clough and Richard Cowley Powles, were deeply engaged in the campaign. Thus it is proper to see the extended passages on the causes and consequences of Fowler's indebtedness, and the moralisings of the narrator, Arthur, in Froude's novel of 1847 as at least in part a contribution to this intense contemporary debate taking place within the university. As such they are a further reminder that for Froude, autobiographical reflection was at least as much a means of furthering larger moral and social objectives as a self-indulgent end in itself.[18]

On a no less serious matter, it is also true that Froude was personally as profoundly affected as his alter-ego Fowler by the experience of first love. Thanks to the researches of W. H. Dunn the focus of Froude's early love has been identified as Harriet Bush (b.1815), eldest daughter of the Rev James Bush, rector of South Luffenham, Rutland, and holder of a number of other benefices including the curacy of Buttermere, where he was for some time resident.[19] The effect of the affair on Froude is not to be doubted. It not only supplied the central dramatic moment of his first novel, but stayed with him all his life. As late as 1886, while planning a visit to the Lake District, he wrote sentimentally to John Ruskin, remembering 'my autumn love dream of fifty years ago' and planning 'to look about for the pieces of a heart I left broken there forty five years ago'.[20]

In assessing the significance of this undeniably powerful experience, it is important to separate out what can actually be known of it independent of Froude's fictions and reminiscences. It might be noted, for example, that at

17. These abuses, and more, were reported in detail in *Report of the Royal Commission appointed to Inquire into the State ... of the University and Colleges of Oxford*, Parliamentary Papers, 1852 (1482), xxii.
18. That Froude was passionately engaged with the issues during his time as a Fellow in Exeter College is evidenced in an acerbic essay on the university published on the appearance of the Report: Froude, 'The Oxford Commission', in *Westminster Review*, 58, NS 2 (1852), 317–48.
19. Dunn, *Froude*, I, 51–3.
20. Froude to Ruskin, 13 March 1886, in Helen G. Viljoen (ed.), *The Froude–Ruskin Friendship as Represented through Letters* (New York, 1966), 39.

the time that Froude first met Harriet he was, while not yet aged twenty, almost three and a half years her junior; by contrast, Fowler's love, Emma Hardinge, was at most twenty. Moreover, though the scion of a respectable clerical family, Froude was a figure quite unknown to the Bushes: still an undergraduate, a year away from the final university examination which was likely to play a large part in determining his future prospects. Fowler was in a similar position, but he and his family, we are told, had known the Hardinges 'when they had been in Somersetshire. In all he had spent several weeks in their house, and the young ladies had been twice at his father's house at Darling' where he had first fallen in love with Emma. There is nothing to indicate that the Bush family had any previous acquaintance with the Froudes, and Archdeacon Froude would seem to have had no reason to object to the liaison, because he appears not to have known about it at all. But in regard to Mr Bush it seems clear that, given the disparity in age, as well as the uncertainty surrounding the character and prospects of his daughter's suitor, his actions in discouraging the suit were in the context of the risks and responsibilities facing young women at the time, scarcely unwarrantable.[21] Unlike the Hardinges, there is no evidence of insanity in the Bush family, but curiously, among the Froudes' misgivings concerning the proposed marriage of brother William was that there was a history of psychiatric illness in his fiancée's family.[22] So this minor element in the plot seems to have been introduced by the novelist as no more than a mildly malicious joke. Finally, far from instituting a life-crisis, Froude's reconciliation with the Bushes came rather early. In 1844, while on a walking tour in the area, he called on the family with some of his friends and received 'a hearty greeting' from the rector.[23]

The effects of Froude's actual affair appear, therefore, rather less traumatic and certainly less protracted than those which afflicted Fowler. Yet it is also clear both from the autobiography and from independent contemporary evidence that Froude, like Fowler, did indeed suffer an acute personal crisis upon the termination of his brief passion. At some time in the autumn of 1839 he withdrew from Oxford (he was not sent down) and took refuge with his brother William in Bristol. There he announced his intention to

---

21. This is Froude's own assessment as given in the autobiography; Dunn, *Froude*, I, 51.
22. This rumour first surfaced in the 1830, in the context of Sir William Holdsworth's (William Froude's father-in-law) bitter political rivalry with Sir John Henry Seale.
23. See George Butler, who testifies that the meeting was entirely warm and good-humoured; Butler, 'Reminiscences of the Lakes in 1844', *Longman's Magazine*, 72 (October 1888), 621–35.

separate from the family, to move into solitary lodgings in Oxford in order to study 'in the hope of getting a good class' and 'then becoming independent of his family' by taking in students preparing to enter the university. A flurry of attention from William, from his father, and from John Keble, to whom William had written for support, had some effect in softening Anthony's determination. But then there arrived a letter from a friend to whom Anthony had appealed, which instead of sympathising, expressed shock and distaste for his attitude and so jolted him out of his mood of self-pity. The letter may have preceded or coincided with the walk in the night woods reported in the autobiography, but the date of its arrival, as reported to Keble by the much relieved William, indicates that having begun sometime in September or October the crisis was passed by about the middle of November, and the renewal was then under way.[24]

II

The purpose of making such discriminations between life and fiction is not to deny or diminish the significance of Anthony Froude's ordeal, but further to define its character. The compression of autobiography and fiction which has been the conventional way of depicting Froude's early life has not only introduced significant confusions of fact and imagination; it has also obscured the manner in which both texts are themselves the products of an antecedent process of liberation and transcendence in their author's actual life. This is particularly true of the earlier of the narrations, the novel, which is itself an embodiment of the fission between author, narrator, and autobiographical subject which Froude had achieved by the mid-1840s. But the origins of this achievement of independence are to be found not in the novel itself, but in the apparently shared experiences of Fowler and Froude in their years at university during which they irrevocably parted company. For this reason it is necessary not only to indicate the embryonic stages of separation, but also to consider other powerful forces which were central to the life of the author but which were hardly noticed in the account in his fictional creation.

One of such influences excised from the fiction and discounted in the autobiography is fully acknowledged in the third of those exercises in

---

24. William Froude to John Keble, 22 November 1839, Keble MSS 160; William Froude to Archdeacon Froude, 21 November 1839, Lambeth Palace MS 1680, ff.63–4.

reminiscence noted at the start of this chapter: the essays on 'The Oxford Counter-Reformation'. The autobiographical self reproduced here is very different from the nervous, weak-willed Fowler. He is sensitive, to be sure, but also attentive, discriminating, and on the fundamental issues of belief and moral action profoundly serious. The essays contain acutely perceptive sketches of the leading figures of the Oxford Movement, and include a portrait of Newman so rich in observation and anecdote that it has frequently been drawn upon by scholars of Newman and the Tractarians as valuable evidence.[25] In his time in Oxford, Fowler, however, knew little of this religious and intellectual ferment. Indeed, when set against the actual times in which it is supposedly set—the late 1830s—the account of Oxford in 'The Spirit's Trials' is somewhat artificial. Late in his life Fowler confesses that once in the depths of his despair he had secretly visited Newman, who gave him more comfort than any other man. But he had told no one else; he says little more.[26] In the autobiography, however, Froude is almost equally reticent:

> Newman was kind to me for Hurrell's sake. He introduced me to the reading set in the College. I did not much like them, nor they me.[27]

Newman was kind to him, and in return Anthony 'was never shy of him'. But, in contrast to the essays, the autobiography conveys a distinct sense of distance between the young Froude and the Oxford Movement. The older Newman concurred. On reading the 1880s essays he observed, with some surprise, that Froude should have claimed to have known so much about him, given, as he recalled (with verifiable accuracy), that they had rarely been in each other's company.[28]

These remarks suggest, of course, that Froude's 'Counter-Reformation' memoir should be treated with no less critical caution than his novel and autobiography. But the contrast between the presumed knowledge of the essay and the deliberate distancing of the autobiography becomes more significant when related to a further powerful influence operating over Froude's undergraduate life which neither in his novel, his essays on the time, nor in his autobiography he chose to make mention.

'When I went into residence at Oxford', wrote Froude in an assertion of distance which opened the second essay on 'The Oxford Counter-

---

25. 'The Oxford Counter-Reformation', 272-93.
26. 'The Spirit's Trials', 157.   27. Dunn, Froude, I, 47-8.
28. Newman to, R. W. Church, 23 December 1884, C. S. Dessain and T. Gornall, S. J. (eds), *Letters and Diaries of John Henry Newman*, vol. 30, 448-9.

Reformation', 'my brother was no longer alive.'[29] He was, strictly speaking, accurate. Anthony went into residence at Oriel in June 1836, four months after Hurrell's death on 28 February. But he had been in the environs of the university for almost a year before, and plans for his admission into Oriel had been afoot much earlier. As early as June 1834 his father had written anxiously to Newman, asking him to use his influence in securing a place in the college for his youngest son, and seeking his advice in procuring a private tutor to prepare the adolescent for undergraduate life. By November a tutor had been found by Hurrell in the person of the Rev. Hubert Cornish—a dependable High Churchman who ran an expensive finishing school for 'young men of fortune' at Merton village some eight miles out-side Oxford—and Archdeacon Froude was writing to Keble seeking con-firmation of Hurrell's judgement. In July of the following year Hurrell wrote to Newman delicately nudging his memory concerning his agree-ment to enter Anthony's name on the Oriel admission list. Newman duly obliged, and, having been summoned to Oxford to receive final admoni-tions and advice from the fatally ill Hurrell in November 1835, Anthony successfully matriculated from Oriel in the following month.[30]

The family's concern for Anthony did not end there. In March 1836, even as he was reporting to Newman the death of his beloved eldest son, the grief-stricken archdeacon still found strength to plead that Hurrell's old rooms should be given to Anthony when he went up. In April he was happy to report to Keble that his representations had secured the rooms for his youngest son, but he was still badgering Newman about Anthony's future and seeking his advice on an appropriate allowance for a young man. Around this time Anthony was invited to stay with Newman for several days, dining and breakfasting with him, and being introduced, said Newman, 'to some steady men'. In June, notwithstanding the peculiarity that a Freshman should inherit the rooms of a Fellow, it was into Hurrell's rooms that Anthony moved when he finally took up residence in Oriel.[31]

---

29. *Short Studies*, IV, 253.
30. Archdeacon Froude to Newman, 22 June 1834, *Letters and Diaries of John Henry Newman* iv, 285; Archdeacon Froude to Keble, 20 November 1834, Keble College, Oxford, Keble MSS 163; Hurrell Froude to Newman, 30 July 1835, *Letters and Diaries of John Henry Newman*, v, 116–17; Mozley, *Reminiscences*, ii, 32; Dunn, *Froude*, I, 45–6.
31. Archdeacon Froude to Newman, 1 March 1836, *Letters and Diaries of John Henry Newman*, v, 245–6, *Letters and Diaries*, 15 April 1836, v, 277; Archdeacon Froude to Keble, 15 April 1836, Keble College, Oxford, Keble MSS 163; Mozley, *Reminiscences of Oriel and the Oxford Movement*, ii, 27.

That Froude should have elected to pass over the many kindnesses and privileges which fell to him uninvited under the shadow of his deeply lamented older brother is perhaps disappointing. But what is even more surprising is that both in the autobiography and in his detailed memoir of the development of the Oxford Movement he should have neglected to provide any account at all of a crucial event in which his entire surviving family was deeply and emotionally involved for much of his undergraduate career: that is the posthumous publication of his brother's collected essays, papers, and private journals in two sets of two volumes under the title, *The Remains of the Rev Richard Hurrell Froude* (London, 1838–39).[32]

Though it has inevitably been associated with Newman, the origins of the idea that Hurrell's unpublished papers should serve as his memorial can be traced to the Froudes themselves, and to the archdeacon and brother William in particular. The proposal first surfaced in a letter sent by the archdeacon to Newman in March 1836, in which he suggested sending on through his son William the entire corpus of Hurrell's manuscripts for Newman and Keble to do with as they pleased.[33] William Froude, who stayed with Newman for several days, made clear the family's desire that some of the papers at least might be prepared for publication. Newman was doubtful, troubled by the editorial difficulties presented by the unfinished character of several of the essays.[34] In April, however, in the same letter that he asked for advice on Anthony's allowance, Archdeacon Froude not only confirmed William's reports about his desire to publish, but offered to cover all attendant expenses while leaving Newman and Keble in full editorial control.[35] This quickened Newman's enthusiasm, but he remained uncertain as to the form any publication might take. A further instalment of manuscripts containing Hurrell Froude's private journals for the years 1826–27 altered Newman's concept of the publication entirely, not only in size but in character. The *Remains* would now be published not in one but in several volumes in which the journal was to form the leading item of the first issue.[36] The foregrounding of this private and intensely personal

32. For an account of the genesis of this project, see Piers Brendon, 'Newman, Keble and Froude's *Remains*', in *English Historical Review*, 87 (1972), 697–716.
33. Archdeacon Froude to Newman, 7 March 1836, *Letters and Diaries of John Henry Newman*, v, 246.
34. Newman to Archdeacon Froude, 30 March, and to Keble 18 April, *Letters and Diaries*, 168–9, 178–9.
35. Archdeacon Froude to Newman, before 25 April 1836, Birmingham Oratory, Froude MSS, vii; Newman to Archdeacon Froude, 25 April, *Letters and Diaries of John Henry Newman*, v, 283.
36. Newman to Archdeacon Froude, 13 September, *Letters and Diaries of John Henry Newman*, v, 355.

document also fundamentally altered the purpose which the publication was meant to serve. No longer simply a memorial to a lost colleague, the *Remains* would be presented as a revolutionary manifesto, revealing the depth of Hurrell Froude's consciousness of the spiritual malaise afflicting the Established Church, his contempt for the temporising ways of those who regarded the Tractarian critique as a minor diversion, and the intensity of his struggle to bring about a full realisation among his contemporaries of the extent of their fall from grace.[37]

Newman, Keble, and the Froudes fully expected to provoke outrage and controversy with the *Remains*, and when the first volumes appeared in March 1838 the storm they had hoped for duly broke. The liberal secular journals were indignant. 'Oxford Catholicism' was the heading of the *Edinburgh Review*'s notice. 'Treason within the Church' was the title of the predictably alarmist review in *Fraser's Magazine*. Likewise, the organs of Evangelical opinion within the church such as the *Christian Examiner*, *The Eclectic Review*, and the *Christian Guardian* were scandalised. But the more conservative journals, lay and clerical, were also highly critical. *The Times* roundly condemned the editors' decision to publish. The *Church of England Quarterly Review* ignored the editors' defence and charged, like the *Edinburgh* and *Fraser's*, that the volumes were essentially Romish propaganda, while the High Church *British Magazine* and the *Quarterly Review* deplored the editors' folly in seeking to present such an extreme and unstable temperament as Froude's as a model of Christian spirituality. The episcopal bench was moved to condemn: several charges publicly denounced the *Remains*, and by the end of the year the Archbishop of Canterbury, William Howley, had intervened with his own definitive censure. The scandal of the book was soon being discussed in parliament, where Viscount Morpeth cited it as an example of the degeneracy of the unreformed universities, and attempts to defend it by the young Gladstone were roundly shouted down.[38]

There can be no doubt that Newman courted the controversy and was pleased to exploit the opportunity of responding to intemperate and extravagant attacks on Froude with his own reasoned and calmly stated version of

---

37. Newman to Keble, 27 August, 20 November 1837, *Letters and Diaries*, vi, 119–20, 165–8, and to J. W. Bowden, 6 October 1837, *Letters and Diaries*, 145; Keble to Newman, 31 August 1837, Pusey House, Keble MSS.
38. Brendon, 'Newman, Keble and Froude's *Remains*'.

the Tractarian cause.[39] Its effect on the Froude family itself is, however, more difficult to gauge. Archdeacon Froude, whose closeness to Hurrell is evident at several points in the text, must have experienced some embarrassment at his son's forthright criticisms of the current episcopal bench and at the universal condemnation of his son by the bishops, including his own Bishop Phillpotts. The intimate nature of the book also invited attacks of the most personal kind and, amidst the furore, cruel and hurtful things were said. The common imputation that Hurell was of unstable mind and violent tempera-ment must certainly have rankled with those who witnessed the manner in which he bore his sufferings in his last years, especially when the testimony of his own mother was called upon (by the *Edinburgh* reviewer) to prove the case. The archdeacon was particularly disturbed by a strongly worded letter from his friend, the distinguished jurist John Taylor Coleridge, reproving him for his part in a publication which, said Coleridge, could only do dis-honour to his memory and was likely to damage the cause he cherished. Later in 1838 he expressed second thoughts about the publication of the next instalment of Hurrell's writings, which would include his controversial essay on Thomas Becket. But rapid reassurance from Keble and Newman hardened his resolve.[40]

The archdeacon's older children John, Margaret, and William were, moreover, all committed to the cause. William was the most passionately engaged, writing frequently to both Keble and Newman seeking news of developments and reporting his own impressions of the impact of the book; while Margaret maintained a correspondence with Newman reassuring him of her father's continuing good spirits. The publication of the *Remains* and the controversy arising from it appears to have given the family as a whole a focus of unity and a source of energy in coping with the loss both of Hurrell and of his youngest sister Mary which occurred while the first volumes were being prepared for the press.[41]

From all of this, however, Anthony was curiously absent. He appears to have breakfasted and dined with Newman on a few occasions in 1837 and

39. M. R. O'Connell, *The Oxford Conspirators: A History of the Oxford Movement, 1833–45* (New York, 1969), ch. 14; Sheridan Gilley, *Newman and his Age* (London, 1991), 165; Peter Nockles, *The Oxford Movement in Context: Anglican Highchurchmen, 1766–1857* (Cambridge, 1999), 281–3.

40. Newman to Keble, 29 March, 7 November 1838, *Letters and Diaries of John Henry Newman*, vi, 222, 341, and to Pusey, 30 July, 272–3; Keble to Newman, 8 September, Keble College, Oxford, Keble MSS.

41. For the intense engagement of the Froudes with the project, see *Letters and Diaries of John Henry Newman*, vi, *passim*.

1838, but though present in Oxford all this time he played no role in maintaining communications between Hurrell's family and his editors.[42] Anthony's aloofness amidst his family's trials had become by the middle of 1839 a matter of increasing exasperation to William, the family's greatest warrior. When he finally challenged Anthony as to whether he had read Hurrell's works, the younger brother replied cooly that he had indeed read the journal 'some time ago' but that it had had little effect upon him; in fact Anthony appeared to treat the whole matter with such unbecoming indifference that William wrote to Keble complaining of the thoughtless, selfish, and immature disposition of his younger brother, and asking Keble to intervene. The Oxford Professor of Poetry duly wrote the required letter of reproof to the errant undergraduate, who did not deign to reply.[43]

Anthony Froude's contemporary detachment from all this intense and painful family activity is echoed by his later silence on the matter in his fiction, his autobiography, and most remarkably in his essays on the Oxford Movement. Writing years later to another would-be historian of the Movement, Newman said bluntly: 'You cannot, of course, do anything in the way of an account of the Oxford Movement without going to Froude's *Remains*.'[44] The fact that Froude could disregard such an authoritative view should be a warning that his recollections of the 'Oxford Counter-Reformation' were a good deal less detached and more contrived than might appear. But it suggests also that, for all its balance, moderation, and mildly rueful self-criticism, underneath the calm voice of the established man of letters, the defiance of the independent young undergraduate who refused to acknowledge the significance of this family crisis concerning his elder brother still burned. Most importantly, the resonance in the matured voice of the 1880s of the attitudes first struck by the Froude in the 1830s is a further indication that the assertion of intellectual and moral independence had begun long before he himself was publicly to acknowledge it.

Anthony Froude's steely determination to establish his distance from his family amidst their great crisis over the *Remains* is one of the most significant indications of his psychological and intellectual development during his undergraduate years which, because he gave little attention to it in his retrospective writings, has been largely ignored.

42. *Letters and Diaries of John Henry Newman*, vi, 45, 72, 354; ii, *Reminiscences*, 28–31.
43. William Froude to Keble, undated but before 22 November 1839, Keble College, Oxford, Keble MSS, 160.
44. *Letters and Diaries of John Henry Newman*, xiv, 49.

III

There was, moreover, a second, less acute but more pervasive influence which, though it has also been discounted in retrospect, was of equal importance in determining the shape of Froude's drive for independence. This was the structure and character of the academic environment in which he spent his student years. The Oxford into which Anthony entered at the close of 1836 was in some ways similar and in other ways markedly different from that experienced by brother Hurrell during his undergraduate years between 1821 and 1824. Neither was required to take an entrance examination, and both were entered on the Oriel list through their father's influence. Once in residence, undergraduate life for both was dominated by the curricular structures put in place by the great Examination Statute of 1800 and its subsequent developments. Both were required to choose from an extremely narrow curriculum of either Literae Humaniores (Classics) or a combination of Literae Humaniores and Mathematics. Both elected for the former, though in 1834–37 brother William chose the latter. Both studied the same narrow set of books (mostly Greek rather than Latin texts), and both were required to decide whether to present themselves for examination as candidates for an Honours or a Pass degree. Again both chose Honours and so committed themselves to study on an extended reading list of set texts on which they would be examined. Along with every other undergraduate, both took Responsions (or Little-Go) in their second year—an elementary test of their proficiency in the classical languages and logic or geometry. At the time when they presented themselves for final public examination, both, like all undergraduates, were required to undergo a formidable catechetical examination in the Greek Testament, the Thirty-Nine Articles, and that handbook of Anglican apologetics, Butler's *Analogy of Religion*.[45]

By the time Anthony went up, however, important changes had been made to this programme. Whereas Hurrell's final examination had been conducted primarily by *viva voce,* after 1830 the final examination in *Literae Humaniores* was primarily a written test taken over five days on a common set of printed questions. In the 1830s also, the distinctions between Honours men

---

45. M. G. Brock and M. C. Curthoys (eds.), *The History of the University of Oxford: Nineteenth Century Oxford* (Oxford, 1997), ch. 1; for Anthony Froude's undergraduate progress, see William Froude to Keble, 22 November 1839, Keble College, Keble MSS 160.

and Pass men were formalised in advance through separate papers for each group. Divisions among the Honours group had been further refined. The simple division of First Class and Second Class was revised in 1825, and a Third Class formed from a line drawn midway in the merits of the Second Class list. In 1830 a further Fourth Class was instituted.[46]

The effects of these changes on the undergraduate experience were several. Written tests were said to have encouraged sustained argumentation and literary flair; but according to some observers, the provision of a limited number of set questions which could be guessed at and prepared for in advance resulted in a regrettable narrowing of attitudes to reading and study and an over-concentration on the set texts. The reconstruction of the final examination as a formidable, standardised, competitive event with four distinct classes, moreover, had the effect of placing it at the centre of the undergraduates' consciousness from almost the beginning of their university careers.

The new structures intensified the pressure on undergraduate study, and for a few the pressure became too great. By the 1830s anxiety over the forthcoming test was being held accountable for student suicide and nervous collapse. Many more, however, coped with fear of failure by deciding long in advance to take the easy path of the rudimentary Pass paper. These were the men Froude claimed to have known best in his early days, and his sympathy remained with them. 'The idle or dull man', he wrote later of Oxford in his undergraduate days, 'had no education at all. His three or four years were spent in forgetting what he had learned at school. The degree examination was got over by *memoria technica* and three-month's cram with a private tutor.'[47]

Statistics support Froude's point. During his undergraduate years less than a third of the student body took Honours and almost half elected for Pass, while the remaining fifth left without taking a degree at all. In these circumstances, students who determined to take an Honours degree immediately consigned themselves to a distinct minority, committed to a lonely and not very exciting course of study, and exposed at the end to the real possibility of failure and public shame.[48]

---

46. M. G. Brock and M. C. Curthoys (eds.), *The History of the University of Oxford: Nineteenth Century Oxford* (Oxford, 1997), chs. 1 and 8.
47. M. G. Brock and M.C. Curthoys (eds.), *The History of the University of Oxford: Nineteenth Century Oxford* (Oxford, 1997), ch. 8; Froude, 'The Oxford Counter-Reformation', 255–6.
48. M. G. Brock and M.C. Curthoys (eds.), *The History of the University of Oxford: Nineteenth Century Oxford* (Oxford, 1997), ch. 1, esp. 40–3.

The greatest support to the aspiring scholar in facing such daunting challenges was to be found, it was commonly supposed, in the personal tutorships provided by the leading and most successful colleges—notably Balliol and Oriel. By the time Anthony entered Oriel, however, pedagogical conditions there had deteriorated significantly from those prevailing in his brother's time, not least on account of the actions of Hurrell himself. In the early 1820s Oriel enjoyed an undisputed reputation as Oxford's leading seat of learning, largely through a formidable common room of Fellows dubbed outside the college, with somewhat awed derision, as 'the Oriel Noetics', among whom may be counted Edward Copleston (Provost, 1814–28), Richard Whately (the future Archbishop of Dublin), and R. D. Hampden.[49]

Even in their ascendancy the Oriel Noetics had never been a dominant group, and by the time of Hurrell Froude's election as Fellow in 1826 a rising mood of opposition to their relentless rationalism was being fomented by Newman and Keble. In the early 1830s, during the Provostship of the 'noetical' Edward Hawkins, conflict broke out into the open over the crucial issues of the college tutorships. Though tutorships had been central to Oriel's pedagogical success for decades, Keble and Newman had been growing increasingly unhappy with a narrow academic view of the post, which had become marked since the departure in the mid-1820s of Coplestone and Whately. Instead of mere examination cramming, Newman and his followers believed that tutors should exercise a moral and religious influence over their students. This was a laudable aspiration, but in practice it led to what was seen as an unsanctioned accumulation of power and influence over the Honours undergraduates by the four college tutors in opposition to the other Fellows. Resentment was further fuelled by the discovery that Newman and Hurrell Froude had assumed the leadership of the tutors, dividing chambers and promoting candidates to vacant posts without reference to the Provost. When Hawkins found out, he was furious. He demanded that such personal involvement with the students cease; and when Newman and the others refused to comply, he responded simply by refusing to assign any more students to their chambers.[50]

49. M. G. Brock and M.C. Curthoys (eds.), *The History of the University of Oxford: Nineteenth Century Oxford* (Oxford, 1997), 72–6. Though 'the Noetics' were never a coherent group, still less a school, their shared views on the necessity of university and ecclesiastical reform, and their commitment to rigorous logical argument made them appear so to outside observers. Derived from the Greek *noēsis/noētikos*—meaning 'inner wisdom' or 'subjective understanding'—the term had, in its application to the Oriel logicians, a somewhat ironic flavour.
50. O'Connell, *Oxford Conspirators*, chs 4–5.

These were the opening shots in a bitter feud in Oriel which was to grow deeper throughout the 1830s with the struggle over the appointment of R. D. Hampden as Professor of Divinity and the beginnings of the Tractarian agitation. Thus by the time Anthony Froude went into residence in the autumn of 1836, Oriel was already deeply damaged by the ravages of its civil war. It had lost its best tutors, in Newman, Froude, and Wilberforce, and the replacements, handpicked by Hawkins, lacked both their charisma and their pedagogic abilities. The Fellows were now ranged against each other, pro- and anti-Hawkins. College meetings became rancorous and ineffective, and important, formerly agreed-upon reforms, such as the abolition of the privileges of elite undergraduates, the gentlemen commoners, were stalled indefinitely.

This was the divided Oriel of 'the Oxford Movement' remembered with such nostalgia by one of its most partisan Fellows, Thomas Mozley; but it was also the declining and demoralised pedagogic institution recalled more tartly in his memoirs by one of its more sensitive undergraduates, Anthony Froude's contemporary, Mark Pattison.[51] As a result of the struggles of the mid-1830s, Oriel's official historian recounts that 'the college gradually fell from its temporary prominence into the position ... of a respected and even beloved training school for ordinary English gentlemen.' But the decline was rather less gentle. In the early 1820s Oriel was responsible for 15 per cent of all First Class degrees awarded by the university, by the later 1830s it was gaining less than 5 per cent, and by the close of the 1840s, in the carefully calibrated league table constructed by Sir William Hamilton, Oriel was placed decisively in the second division of Oxford's twenty-four colleges.[52]

It is in the context of this divided and declining Oriel, amidst an increasingly demanding university examinations system, that Anthony Froude's supposedly wayward undergraduate career should properly be assessed. Tom Mozley, who acted as his *censor theologicus* in Oriel for a time, could recall nothing more rebellious in his conduct beyond the fact that on one occasion Froude pleaded a knee injury to be relieved of the obligation to attend at one of the mandatory university sermons at St Mary's. Mozley was satisfied of the genuine nature of the excuse, and impressed by the serious

---

51. Compare Mozley, *Reminiscences, passim*, with the *Memoirs of Mark Pattison* (London, 1885), 40, 58, 62–9.

52. D. W. Rannie, *Oriel College* (University of Oxford College Histories) (London, 1900), 155–218; Sir William Hamilton, *Discussions on Philosophy and Literature, Education and University Reform* (London, 1852), app. Iii, c, 651–70.

undergraduate's offer to read any other sermon that Mozley chose to prescribe and to provide him with 'notes' on it; yet Mozley also shrewdly identified what was the defining characteristic of young Froude's undergraduate attitude:

> The fact is that Anthony Froude kept aloof not only from Newman's friends but from most Oriel society. Something had happened to him and he was hardly quite himself throughout his undergraduateship ... a man may live in college and yet be no more of the college than he can become a horse by living in a stable. His habits and amusements were solitary.

He noted also that Froude was less than grateful about having Hurrell's rooms gifted to him.[53]

Mozley's observations need careful reading. Young Froude's remoteness from the broils at Oriel did not entail total isolation from university life. During these years he developed a large number of close friendships with like-minded students, such as Mark Pattison, Frank Newman, and R. W. Church, and it was as a young undergraduate that he first made the acquaintance of one of the closest friends of his adult life, Arthur Hugh Clough.[54] Most of his other friends, it is true, were not to distinguish themselves in later life. But Froude's decision to identify himself with the 'passmen' may, given the contemporary pressure operating in the university, appear now to be less a Promethean revolt than an instance of a general trend of his times.[55]

In any case, as Froude records, he did not abandon the scholarly life. His individually conceived and executed reading programme corresponds closely with the kind of broader reading among the classics and the standard modern histories that would have been expected from someone attempting high Honours in the *viva voce* university examinations of the 1820s, rather than one cramming for the predictable written tests of a decade later. It is

53. Mozley, *Reminiscences*, ii, 34.
54. Froude to Mrs Clough, 30 November 1865, Bodleian Library, Clough MSS 41037 (Eng. Lett. d178), Clough Papers f. 134.
55. At least one of these companions can be identified in the person of Henry Cobbe, later acknowledged by Froude as one of his intimate friends as an undergraduate. Far from being a dissolute, Cobbe took holy orders in 1842, secured livings in the dioceses of Kilmore and Armagh and, in 1866, and was preferred to the rectory of Milton Bryant in Bedfordshire, ending his career as rural dean in the deanery of Ampthill. A direct descendant of an Archbishop of Dublin, Cobbe may have been the friend who secured Froude's first post as tutor in the house of the son of the later Archbishop of Dublin, Dr Eustace Cleaver; Froude to Charles Cobbe, 7 August (1866/70), Huntington Library, San Marino, Cobbe MSS.

evidence, if anything, of a determination to distance himself at once from the idlers, the crammers, and the partisan Tractarians of the Oriel he had entered, and to construct an ideal college from his own imagination. The setback at Responsions may have been caused by this wilfulness. Yet Froude still determined in the inauspicious times of Oriel in the late 1830s to study for Honours. Even amidst the crisis of the autumn of 1839 he believed, over-confidently, that he could take a First.[56]

But the disappointment of taking a Higher Second did not divert him from his plan to continue with a scholarly career by taking in students, and preparing to compete for a college fellowship.[57] He spent the Long Vacation of 1840 leading a reading party of aspiring students in Wales (as did Fowler's tutor, Stemming), and in the autumn he returned to Oxford, taking in more students and returning to his study for a fellowship.[58] In these decisions also, it may be noted, Froude registered further departures from his fictional projection. Fowler did not stay on in college to take students and seek a fellowship. Instead he withdrew into a life of secluded private scholarship on the strength of an inheritance from his conveniently deceased father; and at the time when he was withdrawing into the domestic hermitage of private study, Froude seized on an unexpected opportunity entirely to establish his independence from his family while still preparing for an academic career. He was offered a short-term private tutorship in Ireland.

IV

The place that Ireland was to occupy within Froude's intellectual landscape was immense. Ireland features in his work more centrally than in that of any other Victorian intellectual, and his own contribution to the development of research and interpretation of the island's history has been unique. With the wisdom of post-colonial hindsight it is easy enough to observe that for Froude Ireland represented the 'other' embodying, in its evanescent way, all of the fears, desires, and repressions which the nervous imperialist had need at least to catch a glimpse. It is true also that even as a young man Froude

---

56. William Froude to Keble, before 22 November 1839, Keble College, Keble MSS 160.
57. It may be noted that several of Froude's illustrious contemporaries, including Matthew Arnold and Arthur Hugh Clough, also attained Seconds around this time.
58. Archdeacon Froude to Keble, 19 October 1840, Keble College, Keble MSS 163.

was familiar with the classic representation of such an ambivalent colonialist response in Spenser's *Faerie Queene*.

Yet Ireland was to play a far more complex role in shaping Froude's thought than any simple formula can comprehend. Both as a place and as an historical process Froude's Ireland was an imaginative construction shot through with contradictions, occlusions, and downright misrepresentations. As we shall see later, this imagined Ireland was to serve a crucial organising function in his entire world-view. Throughout his career this conceptualisation of Ireland was to be at once intensely energising and profoundly ambiguous, and these, the central characteristics of his encounter with the country, were to appear quite plainly in his record of his very first experience there in 1841.

In keeping with the master-trope of his pilgrim's memoir, Ireland, for Froude, was a source of revelation, and like the best of such experiences, one that arose quite unexpectedly. Some time in late 1840 or early 1841, while he was still taking students at Oxford, Froude was called upon by the Rev. William Cleaver, an Irish clergyman with a substantial living in Delgany, Co. Wicklow, whose son was preparing for entry into Oxford in the coming year.[59] Cleaver invited Froude to act as tutor for the boy. How the Irishman came by Froude is unclear. In a letter to Keble, Froude reported that the connection was made by an unnamed friend of his who was also a nephew of Cleaver's.[60] At any rate, Froude accepted immediately, and having dutifully sought and received his father's permission, left to take up the post some time in March 1841.

Even before he arrived in Ireland, Cleaver, it seems, had already begun Froude's re-education, for though 'an Evangelical of a marked type' Cleaver's sophisticated bearing seemed so unlike the 'weak, amiable but silly persons' he had been taught to ridicule that Froude became 'eager to know more closely the thoughts and manners of a body who were looked on so unfavourably in the circles in which I moved'. Once in the Cleavers' household, moreover, Froude's education prospered. He had access to books never permitted in his own home, such as Ralph Cudworth's highly metaphysical *True Intellectual*

59. Dunn, *Froude*, I, 63.
60. Froude to Keble, 22 March (1841), Keble College, Keble MSS, 162. Cleaver was a graduate of Christ Church, and may have been a visitor to his old university. It is possible that the friend in question was Froude's undergraduate Irish companion, Henry Cobbe (see n. 55 above). It is also possible that he may have learned of the young Froude through his own archbishop, Whately, who had visited his old college in 1839 and shown a close interest in the character of the undergraduates there.

System of the Universe and, most significantly, Bunyan's *Pilgrim's Progress*: 'I have never ceased to regret that I was deprived when young of a book which, had I known it, would have had a very useful effect.'[61]

His education, however, went beyond books. He discovered for the first time what he perceived to be the plight of the Protestants of Ireland. They were, he came to see, a people under siege, abandoned by their government and by a corrupt and ineffectual Established Church while all around them lurked bitter, seditious Catholics, eager, at the first spark of rebellion, for the opportunity to cut their throats. But the best of them had risen to the challenge:

> Face to face with the old enemy, with the practical effects of Romanism in the midst of the most superstitious, the most imaginative and inflammable people in Europe, the faith of the serious among the Protestants took the shape inevitably of the Protestantism which had fought for the Reformation in the sixteenth and seventeenth centuries.[62]

Life among the embattled but defiant Cleavers was the occasion of yet another epiphany:

> A thousand prejudices dropped off of themselves, the narrowness and silliness of the High Church conception of Evangelicanism among the first of them ... For the first time in my life I was in the presence of a purely spiritual religion, the teaching of the New Testament adopted as a principle of life, and carried into all the details of ordinary thought and action.[63]

But this revelation, as might be expected, was short-lived. 'I had not', says Froude, 'parted with my old admiration for Newman,' and though this devotion had hardly been signalled before, it was apparently sufficient to provoke a fundamental breach with the Cleavers. *Tract 90* appeared in the spring of 1841, and its author was the subject among the Cleavers of severe criticism. Froude rose to the defence, affirming Newman's personal integrity, and supporting his claim that the Thirty-Nine Articles, the foundation stone of the Church of England, were not declarations of dogma, but a magnificent compromise determined by the historical contingencies of their time. This was too much for the evangelical Cleavers, 'and it was decided, though I believe with mutual regret, that we should part'.[64]

61. Dunn, *Froude*, I, 65–6.   62. Dunn, *Froude*, I, 64.
63. Dunn, *Froude*, I, 66.   64. Dunn, *Froude*, I, 66–7.

Thus Froude's account of this further stage in his education as given in the autobiography. The doughty anti-Romanist warrior and the astringent historian of Ireland of later years are all too obvious here. Independent sources pertaining to Froude's further visits to Ireland in 1844, 1845, and 1848, suggest that the preoccupations of the older polemicist were very far from the mind of the enthusiastic young traveller.[65] But since hardly any independent contemporary evidence survives to confirm Froude's memories of his first Irish experience, any attempt to separate out the earliest of the encrusted layers of Froude's recollected Ireland must rely largely on a critical examination of the evidence supplied by the autobiography.

In this regard, Froude's memory was in many ways accurate. A leading light of the Society for the Propagation of Christian Knowledge, the Rev. Mr Cleaver was a preacher of considerable renown, whose passionate evangelicalism is strongly expressed in a set of collected sermons published in 1847.[66] But he was also, as the son of a recent Archbishop of Dublin, a figure of considerable standing within the elite of Irish Protestant society, who was on intimate terms with his father's successors, William Magee and Richard Whately. As Cleaver's position indicates, moreover, Irish evangelicalism was both sociologically and ecclesiologically a phenomenon entirely different from the English version. True evangelical missionaries were, moreover, a minority within the Irish Church, which was becoming increasingly defensive and protectionist in face of the irresistible revival of the Catholic Church. Evangelical rhetoric was frequently an expression of a more inward-looking preoccupation with the reform of the structures, practices, and personnel of the Church which was such a major feature of its history in the early nineteenth century.[67] It was these specifically Irish conditions which appeared to turn figures like Whately, once so disdainful of English evangelicalism, into enthusiastic supporters of the Irish version, and could easily allow the attitude of individuals such as Cleaver to be misconstrued by an uncritical or over-enthusiastic observer such as Froude.

Cleaver, in fact, was a good deal more tolerant of High Church opinion than would be normal among English evangelicals. Himself an Oxford

65. See especially, Froude to Newman, 1 February and 'Wed 29' (May) 1844, Birmingham Oratory, Newman MSS, vol. 25, nos. 15, 73; and to Clough, 15 July, 12 August 1848, Bodleian Library, Clough MSS 41032 (Eng. Lett. c190), fols. 302–8.

66. *Sermons of the Rev. William Cleaver, M.A.* (Dublin and London, 1847), xii, 325.

67. D. H. Akenson, *The Church of Ireland: Ecclesiastical Reform and Revolution, 1800–85* (Newhaven, CT, 1971).

graduate, he was planning to have his son educated there also, and seemed to have no scruple about employing someone with the notorious name of Froude. It was also at his behest that Froude, back for a 'few weeks' visit to his former employers in 1842, arranged for Pusey, then holidaying in nearby Bray, to dine with the Cleavers at Delgany; and though the occasion seemed to have been something of a disaster owing largely to the discourtesies of the redoubtable Dr Daly, the event itself is revealing both of the Cleavers' open attitudes and of Froude's continuing good relations with the family.[68]

The initial parting, in any case, appears to have been far from painful or inimical. Armed with letters of introduction from his well-connected former employers, Froude embarked upon the next stage of his Irish education, undertaking an extensive tour of the island, first travelling inland to the south and then following the western seaboard as far north as Mayo. This Ireland of 1840 is, of course, recalled by Froude through the perspective of the catastrophe that lay imminently ahead. The universal poverty and misery of the Irish peasantry observed in Skibbereen was 'a harvest ready grown for the sickle of hunger and pestilence', and Froude affected to notice also a sharp cultural division:

> Under the hoof of the Protestant, wherever it had been planted, there were decent houses, enclosed fields and farm buildings, with relative signs of prosperity. Outside the Border, the same uniform deformity.[69]

Catholic resentment was everywhere, and rather than improving their lot the peasants were on the point of destroying all in rebellion. Here is the unmistakable voice of the author of *The English in Ireland* of 1872–74; and a striking difference may be noted here with the more contemporary Froude of 1848, who not only hoped for rebellion but was devastated when it failed.[70]

Even in the autobiography residual traces of a more ambiguous sensibility far different from the arbitrary certitudes of the established historian remain. His first overwhelming impressions of the island's natural beauty and antiquity remained with Froude. On his tour in the west he undertook the climb of Croagh Patrick on Pattern Day in July 1841 in the company of thousands of devout pilgrims, 'their bare feet on the sharp stones making me ashamed'. There for the first time he saw 'the remains of the ancient saint's

---

68. Daly, the bishop of Kildare and Leighlin, was pointedly rude to Pusey. Dunn, *Froude*, I, 70–1.
69. Dunn, *Froude*, I, 68–9.
70. Froude to Clough, 15 July, 12 August 1848, Bodleian Library, Clough MSS 41032 (Eng. Lett. c190), fols. 302–8.

chapel; an altar, a bell, a crucifix made of the wood of the true cross.' He was moved by the sight of the rude peasants crawling on their knees to worship these relics, and

> was disgusted when the custodian spurned out of the way a poor fellow whose face was actually beautiful for the rapt devotion which it expressed to show the relics to me a mere unbelieving spectator.[71]

The mood recalled here is far closer to that of the author of 'The Legend of St Neot' (1844) and of slightly later essays in praise of the medieval sanctity than that of the all-knowing historian. But it is also accompanied by a darker recollection of the graveyard of the ancient Irish church at Skibbereen where pressure of space had caused 'each twenty or thirty years' the corpses of the buried to be dug up and thrown aside.

> The bones were collected within the ruin and I walked up the aisle between walls of skulls literally ten or twelve feet high, skulls, the owners of which had not lived out half their natural lives, for the teeth of most of them were white and fresh and perfect. The air was heavy with the smell of half-decayed mortality, and the evil genius of Ireland, the curse which hung over the miserable country was glaring out of these sightless eye-sockets.[72]

Revealed here is the root nerve of Froude's profound sense of the moral and spiritual challenge presented by Ireland to Englishmen which underlay so much of his writing on the country, historical and otherwise. An island where the light of Christianity had burned brightest in its earliest days, and where the remnants of that vision were still to be perceived in a pale and distorted manner, Ireland as it was now, represented an awful witness to centuries of mankind's failure, loss, and evil; and England, which had assumed charge of the country for so much of the time, could claim no exoneration from this terrible degradation.

Such a recognition of moral responsibility and guilt is a central characteristic of Froude's later work. But what is of more immediate significance is the formative influence which this early perception of Ireland exercised over the young Froude's mind. Thus far his search for independence had been largely a negative and inchoate affair, characterised by a refusal to become engaged in the struggles of his family and their friends, and a chronic uncertainty as to alternative possibilities. From early on his independent reading of history had provided some means of establishing a critical distance from the intellectual

71. Dunn, *Froude*, I, 69–70.   72. Dunn, *Froude*, I, 68–9.

dominance exercised by his older brother. Sharon Turner's frankly Protestant *History of England* and Gibbon's monumental exercise in agnostic scepticism had impressed him most, and he had returned to them (with an addition of Hume's English *History*) in his undergraduate days. The effect of such material in diluting the strong medicine of Hurrell and Newman is obvious; yet of itself this was a far from coherent reading programme. How an alternative view of history, different at once from the radical polemic of the Tractarians and the bland progressive confidence of the Whigs, could be constructed, Froude had yet to address.

It was here that Ireland came sharply into focus. An instance both of the promise of providential history, and of that promise's failure, Ireland's fate suggested an entirely different means of perceiving the workings of history's dynamic at large. It was to be through this new perception of history in general, and in the particular illustration which the wretched course of its development in Ireland afforded, that Froude's grasp for intellectual freedom would ultimately be achieved—but not, it must be said, at once.

V

The epiphanies granted to Froude at Delgany, Skibbereen, and Croagh Patrick were neither the final ones which he was to undergo nor the last which Ireland was to offer him. Notwithstanding the deeply etched impressions of the autobiography, more contemporary evidence suggests that this first encounter with Ireland represented a crucial, though yet an early, stage in a process of positive intellectual formation that had only just got under way.

Long before the curious difficulties that had arisen over *Tract 90*, Froude had decided that his stay in Ireland would be brief and that he would return to Oxford to compete for a fellowship and, as the university statutes required, take holy orders. A letter to Keble just weeks after his arrival in Ireland in March 1841 shows him wholly content with his berth among the Cleavers but still planning his return to Oxford to resume his studies, and anxious to secure Keble's goodwill. Self-critical to the point of self-abasement, Froude now apologised to Keble for his coldness during the crisis of the autumn of 1839, but declared that through the experience of doing parish work under the Rev. Mr Cleaver's direction he had begun to outgrow his early deficiencies. With this he announces his intention 'to offer myself as a candidate at

Exeter in June, not however with much hope of success at any rate this year'. He begged Keble to forgive his past neglect and to assist him in his current determination.[73]

Patronage-seeking of this kind was, however, only one element in Froude's career-building campaign, and it was, in any case, ineffective. Perhaps Keble was unmoved, as Froude did not gain (and possibly did not seek) election in June 1841. But he nonetheless returned to Oxford in the autumn to open a different path to academic advance by means of competing for the Chancellor's Prize essay in English—a prestigious competition which offered the winner a means of establishing a reputation in the university as a whole.

The topics addressed in the prize essay competition (founded in 1803) had frequently been concerned with matters of religion and public morality as well as literary appreciation. But the topic set in 1842—'The Influence of the Science of Political Economy on the Moral and Social Welfare of a Nation'—was mildly provocative, coming as it did at a time of increasing debate among the dons as to the value and role of the discipline within the university as a whole. The competition, then, presented an unusual challenge, and it is perhaps a reflection of the young Froude's diplomatic and rhetorical abilities, rather than his intellectual originality, that his entry was regarded by the adjudicators as fully worthy of the award. The prize announced, Froude was invited to read his essay in public in the Sheldonian on 8 June, and in accordance with tradition it was published by the university printer immediately thereafter.

Froude's first published work has been little noticed.[74] He himself never alluded to it, and though he mentions winning the Chancellor's Prize in the autobiography, he does not bother to indicate the topic. Most subsequent commentators have followed his lead. Dunn, his official biographer, ignored it altogether, and many others have acted on the supposition that the essay had not survived or had never appeared in print. But the essay, which was of crucial importance in launching Froude's first career, is nevertheless worthy of attention.

The audience of Froude's essay would have seen it as a contribution to a controversy that had been raging since the endowment by W. H. Drummond

---

73. Froude to Keble, 22 March (1841), Keble College, Keble MSS 162.
74. James A. Froude, *The Influence of the Science of Political Economy on the Moral and Social Welfare of a Nation: A Prize Essay read in the Sheldonian Theatre, Oxford, June 8, 1842* (Oxford, 1842), 44 pp.

of a Chair of Political Economy in Oxford in 1827. Appointments to the Drummond Chair had been the focus of intense argument by prospective candidates and their supporters concerning the intellectual and moral value of the study of political economy. By the time Froude was writing, opinion had already become divided between two poles—one centring on the defence of political economy as a valuable if imperfect study in its own right as advanced in the *Introductory Lectures on Political Economy* published in 1831 by the Chair's second holder, Richard Whately, and another insisting upon the discipline's absolute subordination to Scripture and Revelation as expressed by Newman and the Tractarians.[75]

Froude's essay may be seen in this light as an attempt to tread a path between these two positions. It begins with a critique of some representative texts propagandising the science of political economy published in that leading organ of its promoters, the *Edinburgh Review*. Through their pride in the analytical and deductive powers of their supposed science, the advocates of political economy were guilty of presumption and, more seriously, of moral irresponsibility. Their claims that it could attain to a level of internal coherence and external correspondence equal to, and even surpassing, the other sciences were manifestly falsifiable both through philosophical interrogation and practical observation; while the manner in which they had been led by it to adopt principles and opinions 'in direct contradiction to the wisest and best men of every age, and entirely at variance both with a [*sic*] right reason and revelation' was sufficient in itself to render their general assertions 'false and worthless'.[76]

Having thus condemned the hubristic amorality of the Utilitarians, Froude then proceeded to reconstruct the case for the study of political economy on more modest grounds. It was valuable not merely as a useful set of observations, but more significantly as a means of offering an account of the way in which societies had developed from simple into complex organisms of production and exchange. The faster societies changed and the more complex the social interrelations developed within them, the

75. On the general debate concerning the relationship of political economy to Christian teaching, see A. M. C. Waterman, *Revolution, Economics and Religion* (Cambridge, 1991), Boyd Hilton, *The Age of Atonement* (Oxford, 1988), and specifically for Oxford, Richard Brent, 'God's Providence: Liberal Political Economy as Natural Theology at Oxford, 1825–62', in Michael Bentley (ed.), *Public and Private Doctrine: Essays in British History presented to Maurice Cowling* (Cambridge, 1993), 85–107.
76. *The Influence of the Science of Political Economy*, 10.

more urgent was the need for a science which, for all its epistemological and ethical limitations, could supply an explanation of the origin and character of such developments both to those charged with the government of the state and by extension to the community as a whole. This political economy now promised to do; and what was necessary to remedy its defects was to insure that its conduct and development as a science, and its promotion in the public mind, be placed in the hands of those already charged with the responsibility of maintaining and protecting the country's moral and religious condition in government and in the schools and the universities.

> Desirable as all would confess them [the ends of political economy] to be, if men seek to raise them as a superstructure on any other basis than a sound religious education, either they will not follow at all, or if they do they will prove a curse, and not a blessing.[77]

The contention that political economy was too important to be left to the economists, and should instead be appropriated by the clergy and the dons, can be easily seen as a shrewdly judged appeal to the Chancellor's Prize assessors. But the sources upon which Froude drew to stake out this position are of some interest. There are traces of Coleridge's essay *On the Constitution*, which he had begun to read around this time. And the argument follows Whately's *Introductory Lectures* in accepting that in its everyday operations economics might be permitted the intellectual freedom allowed to the natural sciences, so long as its applications were tempered by its moral monitors. Froude's confidence, moreover, that 'better principles are working in the world' and that under proper tutelage a new intellectual aristocracy of political economists would emerge who would 'extract from the confusion of interests the essential elements of national prosperity', places him closer to the Whatelean camp, and at some considerable distance from the embattled inveighings of the Tractarians.[78]

Equally notable is Froude's attention to the dynamic of historical development toward greater social complexity, and his insistence that the economists' thought should be informed by 'a study of the history of past ages with a humble willingness to listen to the lessons it will give them'. Such a stance suggests the influence of, or at least independent agreement with, the

---

77. *The Influence of the Science of Political Economy*, 42.
78. *The Influence of the Science of Political Economy*, 42–3, 12–14.

views of the recently appointed Professor of Modern History at Oxford, Thomas Arnold, whose inaugural lectures on modern history had been delivered during the term when Froude was preparing his essay and for whom Froude had already expressed great enthusiasm.[79]

This early invocation of history is perhaps an indication of future intellectual preferences, but in the present context it illustrates the young Froude's dissatisfaction with either theological speculation or deductive reasoning alone as supplements to revelation in gaining an understanding of the processes and purposes of Creation. This indirect recognition that the Word of God is in need of further support in the consciousness of man brings to light a further uncertainty which begins to emerge, perhaps unconsciously, toward the close of the essay.

In his anxiety to press the necessity of developing the science of political economy, while recognising its inherent moral and spiritual shortcomings, Froude comes close to suggesting that the real value of religious indoctrination lay precisely in supplying these deficiencies. Having argued himself to the conclusion that 'Political Economy is the body, religion is the soul' of society, he himself expressed the doubt: 'If Political Economy teaches the necessity of religious education, is there not a lurking inclination to Rationalism even in the principles on which it is being conducted?' His answer is disappointingly cautious: 'We trust notwithstanding that there is improvement ... It is enough: let us take comfort.'[80]

These inconclusive closing comments are doubtless a symptom of a desire not to alienate any of the Chancellor's Prize examiners. But they also suggest that, for all his endorsement of Whately and Arnold, Froude had not yet arrived at a settled intellectual position. Having successfully resisted the pressures of family and of his brother's closest friends to join in their great spiritual renewal, and having by independent study, travel, and the cultivation of new associations found a way of establishing his credentials as a scholar in his own right, Froude now discovered that his instruments of liberation offered no conclusive solution to the problems of belief and conduct in the world posed by Newman and his followers.

---

79. *The Influence of the Science of Political Economy*, 17–19. For Froude's early enthusiasm for Arnold's lectures, see the contemporary diary entry of Caroline Fox, 4 October 1842, in Fox, *Memories of Old Friends* (2 vols., London, 1882), I, 327–8; on the impact of Arnold's lectures, see Duncan Forbes, *The Liberal Anglican Idea of History* (Cambridge, 1952), esp. ch. 2.
80. *The Influence of the Science of Political Economy*, 43–4. The analogy of body and soul may be an allusion to Arnold's contemporary comparison of Church and State to soul and body.

In one very practical way, however, his independence had at last been established. In June 1842, the same month as he read his prize essay, Froude gained election to the Exeter fellowship he had coveted. This advancement was, however, clouded: the diocesan testimonials which he supplied were deemed inadequate, and Exeter's Rector was (perhaps deliberately) absent from the college when the Sub-Rector William Sewell, with the support of the other Fellows, deemed the election valid.[81] The dubiety of Froude's position was in some ways fitting, for it reflected the continuing ambivalence of his relationship toward intellectual life in Oxford as a whole. Having successfully asserted his independence from the Tractarians, Froude had discovered that the rational, optimistic alternatives advanced by Arnold and the Anglican economists had proved insufficient to stifle the sombre metaphysical doubts inspired by Newman, and evidenced all too terribly in Ireland. His newly secured position made it not only possible but also urgently necessary that Froude should now voluntarily retrace the path he had taken away from Newman to discover for himself the strengths and the limitations of that demanding but ineluctable presence.

81. Rector Richards to (unknown) and to the editor of the *Oxford Gazette*, undated but *circa* November 1847, Exeter College, Oxford, Froude MSS nos. 15, 49.

4

Newman: St Neot and
St Patrick, 1843–46

The complex nature of Anthony Froude's relationship with John Henry Newman was a cause of some controversy during the lives of both men, and has been a source of continuing confusion ever since. Over time, two related myths concerning their association have grown up, neither of which has been particularly flattering to Froude.

The first suggests that Froude, living under the shadow of his powerful older brother, had always suffered from a passionate but immature attraction to Hurrell's friend and mentor; and that, on entering adulthood, he felt able to express his admiration more openly, becoming one of Newman's acolytes at Littlemore (the hermitage to which Newman had withdrawn from Oxford in 1842) and joining enthusiastically in the great man's project for a series of books on *The Lives of the English Saints*. But upon Newman's going over to Rome in 1845, Froude experienced an intense sense of betrayal (later given vent in the characterisation of Newman in *The Nemesis of Faith*), and that thereafter the disappointed disciple became an implacable Protestant propagandist and scourge of all things Catholic.[1]

The second myth is essentially a variation on the first. It holds that from the outset the young Froude, jealous of his brother, had been infected by a deep resentment toward Newman, and that on his return to Oxford he became a follower of Newman in order to exact revenge. His participation in *The Lives of the English Saints* was a subversive enterprise, its purpose revealed in the satirical scepticism with which he was supposed (erroneously) to have closed his piece, and which, it was said, hurt Newman deeply:

1. Hilaire Belloc, 'Introduction', in Belloc (ed.), *Essays on Literature and History by James Anthony Froude* (London, 1908), ix–xxiii; Augustine Birrell, *Collected Essays and Addresses* (2 vols., London, 1922) ii, 199–212.

'This is all, and perhaps more than all that is known of the life of the blessed St Neot.' His vengeance thus exacted against Newman and his sainted brother, Froude then came into the open in his true Protestant colours.[2]

For both of these myths, Froude himself is partially responsible. In his depiction of the nervous and troubled relationship which his neurasthenic fictional alter-ego Fowler had with Newman, he gave early sustenance to the former; while in his later highly sceptical accounts of the 'The Lives of the saints' project he gave strong support to the latter.[3] But in 'The Oxford Counter-Reformation' and the late autobiography Froude provides a far more nuanced account of his attitude toward Newman which, though it is neither clear nor entirely consistent, is a good deal more persuasive than either of these extremes.

I

Despite the early propagation of both of these myths, it is clear from the recollections of both men that the young Froude had never been close to Newman until the spring of 1843 when his brief and intense engagement with Newman's hagiographical project began.[4] Even then he never became an acolyte, nor was he ever, as another myth affirmed, a novice at Littlemore.[5] It is more accurate to say that while he was determined to maintain his personal independence as an undergraduate, Froude, like so many others,

2. For a clear statement of this point of view, see Kingsbury Badger, 'The Ordeal of James Anthony Froude, Protestant Historian', *Modern Language Quarterly*, 13 (March 1952), 41–55. The canard, repeated by Badger, about the closing lines of Froude's life of *Neot* was given authoritative status in Herbert Paul's early biography, *The Life of Froude* (London, 1903), 34, and broadcast widely through Lytton Strachey's *Eminent Victorians* (London, 1918), 33–4. Froude never wrote these words, nor anything like them; they are in fact a garbled version of the way in which Newman himself concluded a life of St Bettelin: 'And this is all that is known, and more than all—yet nothing to what the angels know—of the life of a servant of God'; 'Life of St Bettelin', in *Lives of the English Saints: Hermit Saints* (London, 1844), 72.
3. Froude, 'The Lives of the Saints', *Eclectic Review*, 95 (February 1852), 147–64 .
4. Dunn, *Froude*, I, 47–8; 'The Oxford Counter-Reformation', 278; *Letters and Diaries of John Henry Newman*.
5. This notion was given currency in C. K. Paul's essay on 'Cardinal Manning' in *The Century Magazine* (May, 1883) 129, where he claimed that Froude was sent by Newman to dismiss Manning at the door of Littlemore when the latter called to see Newman on the point of his defection. Denied by Froude, it was also refuted in E. S. Purcell, *Life of Cardinal Manning* (2 vols., London), I, 249; but an alternative account seems more plausible: forty years later Froude told Wilfrid Scawen Blunt that he travelled with Manning to see Newman at Littlemore when news of his defection emerged, and that *both* of them were refused admission by an unknown novice; Blunt, *Land War in Ireland* (London, 1912), 16.

found it impossible not to admire Newman from afar. In part this was due to Newman's generally acknowledged donnish charisma. Froude recalled Newman not as an austere or grave ascetic, but as a kind, gentle, and witty man who moved easily among the undergraduates at Oriel, impressing them with his reputation as a connoisseur of wine, his impressive knowledge of recent military history, and conversing informally with them on 'the subjects of the day, of literature, of public persons and incidents, of everything which was generally interesting'. No wonder the Oriel undergraduates, Froude says, proudly declaimed *Credo in Newmannum*.[6]

But in addition to these not uncommon features of the charming popular don, Newman impressed the young Froude by the earnestness of his convictions and particularly by the manner in which he expressed them in his public sermons. Belying his image as a dissolute undergraduate, Froude was, in fact, a frequent attender at Newman's Sunday sermons—one of the few undergraduates, Newman later ruefully recalled, who actually did so[7]— and he has left one of the most powerful accounts of the effects of those Sunday afternoon sermons at St Mary's upon his listeners. Having described in chilling detail the sequence of Christ's passion,

> [Newman] then paused. For a few moments there was a breathless silence. Then in a low clear voice of which the faintest vibration was audible in the farthest corner of St Mary's, he said, 'Now I bid you recollect that he to whom these things were done was Almighty God'. It was as if an electric stroke had gone through the church, as if every person present had understood for the first time the meaning of what he had all his life been saying.[8]

Newman's oratory was moving—and distressing. But it was the substance of his message contained in these sermons which on intellectual as well as emotional grounds the young Froude found even more disturbing. In particular Froude recalled two, the first of which had dealt with the awful reality of human predestination.

> [Newman] supposed first two children to be educated together, of similar temperament and under similar conditions, one of whom was baptised and the other unbaptised. He represented them as growing up equally amiable, equally upright, equally reverent and God-fearing, with no outward evidence that one was in a different spiritual condition from the other; yet we

6. 'The Oxford Counter-Reformation', 272–93, esp. 273, 283; Dunn, *Froude*, I, 48.
7. C. S. Dessain and Thomas Gornall, S. J. (eds), *Letters and Diaries of John Henry Newman*, xxix, 342–7, 351–8.
8. 'The Oxford Counter-Reformation', 286., the sermon can be identified as having been delivered on 25 Nov. 1838; see Newman *Sermons delivered on the subjects of the day* (London, 1869), no vi.

were required to believe not only that their condition was totally different, but that one was a child of God, and his companion was not ... Again he drew a sketch of the average men and women who made up society ... They were neither special saints nor special sinners ... None seemed good enough for heaven, none so bad as to deserve to be consigned to the company of evil spirits and to remain in pain and misery forever. Yet all those people were, in fact, divided one from the other by an invisible line of separation. If they were to die on the spot as they actually were, some would be saved, the rest would be lost—the saved to have eternity of happiness, the lost to be with the devils in Hell.[9]

Newman's intent in this sermon, however, had not been to reinforce a bleak Calvinist determinism but rather to develop a case for the crucial importance of the grace-giving sacraments of baptism (and possibly of communion). This was a statement of the sacrament's role stronger than most High Churchmen were willing to allow, for it appeared to grant an equal status to the sacrament as the sole *external* instrument of justification as faith was the sole *internal* instrument, and in this reassertion of the different but equal necessities of baptism and justification it is clear that Newman was attempting some kind of accommodation between traditional Catholic doctrine on the sacrament and the practices of Anglicanism. It was precisely because of this drift toward Roman Catholicism that Newman's admonitory illustration enforcing a terrible distinction between the two very different eternal destinies of two equally good young men presented such a deeply unsettling choice to his hearers, especially to those, like the young Froude, who were struggling with a deep sense of their own deficiency and lack of virtue. The choice that Newman seemed to be putting before them was stark: either they must accept the reality of double predestinarianism with all its arbitrary cruelty, or acknowledge the superiority of traditional Catholic teaching on this topic. But for the young Froude, deep in his struggle for independence from his own family and equally imbued with his own sense of worthlessness, the effect was not inspiring, but paralysing.

Froude's second selection from Newman's sermons was disturbing in a more intellectual manner. In his discourse on 'Faith and Reason Contrasted as Habits of Mind', Newman, Froude recalled, had deployed a clever but deeply disturbing strategy.[10] The logical and empirical arguments advanced

---

9. 'The Oxford Counter-Reformation', 285–6.
10. Sermon X of *Fifteen Sermons delivered before the University of Oxford* (ed. J. D. Earnest and Gerard Tracey, Oxford, 2006), 114–26. The sermon was preached on Epiphany Sunday 1839.

by sceptics such as David Hume against the presence of divine purpose in the world, against miracles, and perhaps even against the existence of God, were, Newman appeared to concede, powerful and often compelling, and attempts to meet them on their own terms were doomed to fail. But it was precisely in its incompatibility with the forms of human reason and empirical enquiry that the real strength of Christian faith lay. Unresponsive to reason's claims, faith was impervious also to its defects. It belonged to a quite different cognitive faculty in the human mind, and was possessed of a coherence and integrity of its own based upon an awareness that the nature of the world was never immediately available to the human mind and could only be inferred by a spirit awakened by the Word of God to the magnitude of the creative design unfolding in their midst.

This was, for Froude, subtle, and possibly even true. But Froude's objection to Newman at this point was not that he was in error and leading other people astray also. It was that in protesting against the cruel caprice of Calvinist predestination, and in subtly exploiting the devastating critiques of the *philosophes*, without having fixed upon a clear idea of the direction in which his own thoughts were leading him, Newman was behaving in an extremely irresponsible manner. He was undermining the confidence of his hearers in the intellectual authority of the teachings of the Established Church, which for them was based largely on the arguments of Paley and Butler, without providing them with anything on which they could rely except blind dependence on Newman's good faith.

> We had all been satisfied about the Gospel History, not a shadow of doubt had crossed the minds of one of us; and though we might not have been able to give a logical reason for our certitude, the certitude was in us, and might well have been let alone ... To remove the foundation of a belief, and to substitute another is like making new foundations to a house—the house itself may easily be overthrown in the process.[11]

There is more uncritical certainty in this retrospective view than may have been the case at the time. For Froude, as we have seen, had been struggling not without success to free himself from the crypto-Catholic sentiments to which he had been exposed at Dartington. But now he found himself confronted with a far more powerful and intellectually sophisticated critique of orthodox Anglican complacency than had hitherto been the case, and young

---

11. 'The Oxford Counter-Reformation', 292.

Froude was as yet without the intellectual equipment sufficient to withstand the force of Newman's subtle attack.

II

Such were the feelings which no doubt contributed to the nervous collapse
which Froude suffered in the autumn of the year in which one of Newman's
most powerful sermons was delivered. But four years on, by the time he
made renewed acquaintance with Newman in 1843, Froude's personal crisis
had long since been overcome. Through his experiences in Ireland, his winning of the Chancellor's Prize, and above all his election as a Fellow of
Exeter College, Froude had at last attained the independence for which he
had been fighting so desperately and uncertainly as an undergraduate. But a
measure of independence having been gained, he could see that the challenges and the doubts which Newman had raised were far too serious both
morally and intellectually to be ignored, 'and out of which some road or
other had now to be looked for.'[12]

Now, however, he was in a position to resume that quest. In addition to
his practical experience, Froude had in the meantime broadened his reading
considerably. He read or reread Wordsworth and Coleridge, and while being
temporarily captured by the latter's *The Friend* and *Aids to Reflection*, soon
found himself valuing the poet over the philosopher.[13] He discovered
Tennyson; and along with so many of his generation he bought and devoured
the anonymously published *Vestiges of the Natural History of Creation*
(1844).[14]

But above all he came to know Carlyle—first through *The French
Revolution* (1837) and then through *On Heroes, Hero Worship and the Heroic
in History* (1841) and *Past and Present* (1843). The influence of Carlyle on
the young Froude was, according to the old memorialist, overwhelming
and enduring. Hitherto all his theological and metaphysical reflections had
been stimulated by books rather than by life. But Carlyle taught him that

---

12. 'The Oxford Counter-Reformation', 311–12.
13. While discounting Coleridge's prose works, Froude in later life continued to profess his admi-
    ration for 'Christabel' and 'The Ancient Mariner'; Dunn, *Froude*, I, 59, 74.
14. Froude's library contained a copy of the first edition (1844). Forty years on he continued to
    profess his admiration for this 'beautiful' book while doubting that anyone as 'dull' as Robert
    Chambers could actually have been its author: Wilfrid Scawen Blunt, *Land War in Ireland*, 16.

problems with which he had been grappling were not to be resolved in books but by engagement with 'present facts, and the world in which I lived and breathed'.

> [In] answer to the sick question of every thinking soul: Why, if God exists, are there no signs of him? Why do the affairs of this world go on as if by natural force, as if there were no God at all? The natural, Carlyle said, was the super-natural, the supernatural, the natural … The question which Carlyle asked of every institution, secular or religious, was not, Is it true, but Is it alive? Life is not truth, but the embodiment in time and in morality of a spiritual or ani-mating principle. Truth can be but one. The animated creation varies in every age and country.[15]

As recollected in this way Carlyle's radical perspective appears as a powerful antidote both to the outmoded orthodoxies of the Established Church and to Newman's speculations, with their troubling implications of a regression to Catholicism. But at the time Carlyle's ascendancy over Froude was far from complete. From Carlyle he was led to Goethe and derived from him an intense conviction of his obligation to take personal responsibility for discovering meaning and value in the real world.[16] From Goethe he moved to the German Romantics, Lessing and Schiller, and also the great German historical theologians, Friedrich Schleiermacher and August Neander.[17] His engagement with the latter suggests that, despite Carlyle, Froude's preoc-cupation with traditional Christian theological speculation remained strong. Indeed,

> Newman interested me more than ever … In spite of my miscellaneous read-ing … I was as yet far from having formed any negative conclusions, and was prepared to be convinced that after all Newman's view might be right as a whole.[18]

And as late as December 1845 he was pleased to note

> how completely they [Newman and Carlyle] both go on the same principle of development, the same principle, though somewhat different indeed when it comes to express itself.[19]

---

15. Dunn, *Froude*, I, 72–4, quotation 73.
16. Dunn, *Froude*, I, 58–9.
17. 'The Oxford Counter-Reformation', 312.
18. Dunn, *Froude*, I, 75–6.
19. Froude to Charles Kingsley, quoted in Dunn, *Froude*, I, 101–2.

When Newman abandoned him for Rome, Froude recalls in his autobiography: 'I could not yet follow Carlyle when he shifted the ground.'[20]

It is against this background of sustained, independent but as yet uncompleted intellectual quest that the nature of Froude's re-engagement with Newman over the *The Lives of the English Saints* is most properly assessed. It was not a sign of his desperate devotion to the great man's mission, nor yet a slyly subversive act. It was instead a genuine attempt to explore ways of moderating Newman's highly charged address to the problems he had so clearly identified (and whose reality Froude fully acknowledged) with approaches alternative to the defeatist historical regression toward which Newman's way seemed to point. Ironically, it was Newman himself, with his grand hagiographical project, who appeared to offer Froude the resolution he was seeking.

III

Conceived in the early months of 1843, Newman's idea for a series of saints' lives was at once clever, ambitious, and insufficiently thought through. Designed as a multi-volume project, he envisaged that the series would eventually encompass the lives of some three hundred saints whose works and words would provide subjects for meditation and veneration throughout the year. The intent of the project, Newman insisted, was 'historical and devotional, but not controversial.'[21] By this it appears he was hoping to appropriate for the Church of England something of the inspirational power associated with the Roman Catholic cult of saintly veneration, while underlining the distinctively historical character of the Anglican tradition. Before long Newman himself was to realise the difficulty of harmonising the opposing impulses of historical reflection and devotional piety, and was in particular to be disillusioned with the hope of keeping the series beyond controversy.[22] But at the outset the immediate effect of his initiative was to attract a remarkably large number of enthusiastic would-be contributors among the Oxford dons, including Anthony Froude.

How and exactly when Froude came to join Newman's team of hagiographers is unclear. In retrospect, Froude declared that it was Newman who

20. Dunn, *Froude*, I, 94.
21. Newman to J. W. Bowden, 3 April 1843, F. J. McGrath and Gerard Tracey (eds), *Letters of John Henry Newman* ix, 312.
22. Ian Ker, *John Henry Newman: A Biography* (Oxford, 1988), 276–82.

first made the proposal, though Newman's contemporary letter of 11 June 1843 suggests that some kind of informal enquiry had first been made by Froude.[23] It is similarly unclear how the subject of St Neot was arrived at. The saint did not feature in the list first proposed by Newman, which included St Grimald, Peter of Blois, and what appears to have been Froude's own first proposal, Walter of Stapledon.[24] Perhaps Newman, with fond memories of his visits to Dartington, felt that the study of the Exeter diocese's oldest and most famous saint would make a suitable topic for a Froude; and perhaps Froude, keen to discover the character of sanctity in the early English church, was happy to accept the challenge.

Though it was among the earliest agreed, Froude's commission was also, however, among the more modest. Newman's 'Prospectus' for the series envisaged two kinds of publication. Where the evidence permitted and the subject was sufficiently important, book-length lives were to be published in separate issues of about 128 pages each. In those cases where the historical evidence was fragmentary, collections of five or six far shorter compositions were to be issued together in one volume. Newman began commissioning authors for the series in May, and it was as a contributor to one of these collections, 'the Hermit saints', rather than as an author of a full-dress life, that Froude was first enlisted. Thus it was envisaged that, initially at least, Froude's contribution to the scheme would be a minor one. But the appearance of his 'Legend of St Neot', published as part of Issue No. 5 early in 1844, indicated that Froude himself had different intentions.[25]

Contributions to the collective issues, it was understood, would be short—a small fraction of the length being allotted to the full lives. Most of the contributors to the collections had worked within the modest proportions suggested in the Prospectus. Thus, of the seven hermits' lives collected in the issue, four extend to considerably less than twenty pages in the collected edition of 1900, one runs to twenty-eight pages, another to thirty.

---

23. Compare Froude's recollections in Dunn, *Froude*, I, 76 and 'The Oxford Counter-Reformation', 316, with Newman: 'I do not know your taste enough to know what to offer you in the series of Lives I am contemplating. I shall set down several names and you can think about them at let me know at your leisure that which you prefer'; Newman to Froude, 11 June 1843, *Letters and Diaries of John Henry Newman*, ix, 243.
24. Stapledon was the reputed founder of Exeter College.
25. For further details, see the editor's very valuable introduction in A. W Hutton (ed.), *The Lives of the English Saints written by Various Hands at the Suggestion of John Henry Newman* (6 vols., London, 1900), and J. Derek Holmes, 'Newman's Reputation and *The Lives of the English Saints*', in *Catholic Historical Review*, 51 (1965–6), 528–38.

But Froude's 'St. Neot', covering sixty pages, is the exception within the whole group. Clearly, despite the minor task that had been assigned to him, Froude had been determined to make the most of his meagre materials in his own distinctive way.

Froude was not the first modern scholar of Neot. At the time that he undertook his commission, exhaustive work on the materials for a life had already been conducted in two antiquarian studies—the Rev. John Whitaker's *Life of St Neot* published in 1809, and a rather more critical review of the evidence included as part of *The History and Antiquities of the Parishes of Eynesbury and St Neot's*, published in London in 1820 by George Gorham (coincidentally the same figure whose views on baptism were to provoke a major crisis in the diocese of Exeter in 1846). Given his extensive antiquarian interests, it seems more than likely that both of these volumes would have found a place in Archdeacon Froude's extensive library. But while it is clear from his text that Froude had used Whitaker, neither there nor in his contemporary correspondence does he give any hint that he used the scholarly and considerably more critical Gorham. Instead, he appears to have relied primarily on a redaction of the fourteenth-century life attributed by scholarly tradition to William Ramsay, Abbot of Glastonbury, the original manuscript of which, housed in Magdalen College, Oxford, had been edited and printed by Whitaker as an appendix to his *Life*.[26]

IV

Froude's 'Legend of St Neot' is written in two distinctly different registers—the first critical and analytical, the second literary and highly rhetorical. It opens with a long introductory section in which, in a thoughtful and dispassionate manner, he reviews the materials of his study and lays out the rationale of his methodology. Of the five extant lives of Neot, none is contemporary. There is a high level of discrepancy between them, and Froude justifies his reliance on Ramsay, because it is the only one which 'proposes to relate *ascertained facts*' [Froude's emphasis], and because it is the only one to avoid 'the grave anachronism of placing St Dunstan at Glastonbury at the

---

26. The various early lives of St Neot had also been discussed in detail in a text which Froude knew intimately: Sharon Turner's *History of the Anglo-Saxons* (5th edn. 3 vols., London, 1828), i, 490–3, 549–73.

time of St Neot's residence there'.[27] Froude's preference for the critical Ramsay over the earlier pietistic lives raised, however, the thorny problem of treating the many other stories that had accumulated around the saint which Ramsay has excluded—most notably the stories concerning the miracles he was supposed to have worked. So Froude felt required to commence upon a discussion of his own methodological approach to the problem.

To dismiss the early hagiographers merely as liars or innocents, as the philosophical historians have done, was, he begins, both arrogant and obtuse. They were far better understood as writers who had been confronted in a particularly acute manner with an epistemological problem shared by all reflective minds at any point in history. This was the sheer difficulty of comprehending and communicating in ordinary language the essential character of extraordinary lives. An indication of the problem could be found in our own practices in everyday life. Each of us, in apprehending and storing important facts, has a tendency 'to forget the real order in which they appear, and rearrange them according to his theory of how they ought to appear.' The more notable the acts, and the more we wish to retain a memory of them, the greater is our tendency to organise them within a suitable conceptual framework, commonly to associate those acts, whether noble, witty, or silly, with individuals who most fully represent in our minds these particular characteristics. In this way we make myths of facts, rearranging them 'in a more conceptual order'; and we make legends out of the lives of our contemporaries. What is true of everyday experience is true of all written history 'which is all more or less fictitious', Froude affirms, 'the facts are related not as they really happened but as they appear to the writer, as they happen to illustrate his views or support his prejudices'. But the process of historical myth-making is no more disingenuous or unnatural than our own innocent practices. Thus fragments of Jewish history find their way into Greek legend, stories from the Greeks are appropriated by the Romans, and so on to our own national histories.[28]

The passage of time under which the absorption and adaptation of legend occurs also, however, introduces important filters of selection and suppression. Just as we clothe the pain and anguish of childhood with a patina of nostalgia, so we select from history according to our desires and our needs.

27. 'St Neot', in *Lives of the English Saints: Hermit Saints* (London, 1844), 74; all subsequent references are to this first edition.
28. *Lives of the English Saints*, 75–6, 78–9.

A principle that has been operative in all ages, it is manifest in our own 'unpoetical times' where scepticism and derision are employed to discount elements of the magical and the mysterious. It was also at work, Froude astutely observes, in the time of the hagiographers themselves, most of whom were writing many centuries after the death of their subjects. Separated as they were from the events which they proposed to relate, and aware also of the meagreness of the materials available to them, it would be shallow to assume that they were quite unconscious of the difficulties facing them in writing any life, let alone that of a saint, and more reasonable to enquire what we would do when confronted with similar conditions. 'Of course we should attempt no more than what we do as it is—if we could not write a Life, we should write a Legend.' Critically approached, then, the hagiographies are not to be read as failed Lives, but 'as myths, edifying stories compiled from tradition and designed not so much to relate facts as to produce a religious impression on the mind of the hearer.' This was the real intent of their work, and our assessment of its value, observes Froude, neatly turning the tables on sceptics, will itself be a reflection of our own spiritual state. The question 'were these things really so?' being thus rendered irrelevant, 'What we should ask ourselves is "Have these things a meaning? Do they teach *us* anything?" If they do, then as far as we are concerned, it is no matter whether they are true or not as facts; if they do not, then let them have all the sensible evidence of the events of yesterday, and they are valueless.'[29]

Despite some highly debatable assumptions this was by far the most considered defence of the hagiographers' work presented in Newman's series. Among Froude's co-writers the strength of the case made for the miraculous nature of the lives they recounted varied considerably. Some, like the author of 'St Bartholomew, Hermit at Farne, AD 1193', were prepared to accept the hagiographers as authoritative, and to defend the miracles and visions they related without hesitation; while others, such as the authors of the lives of St Herbert and St Edelwald, did not feel obliged to justify the stories they recounted at all. J. B. Dalgairns, author of the short sketch of 'St Helier', appeared to be coming close to Froude's position in his observation that 'there is no proof that the writers intended these stories to be believed at all. Many of them may have been merely legends, things worthy of being read for example of life and instruction of manners.' But he balanced this passing

29. *Lives of the English Saints*, 80–1.

concession with the countervailing view that 'We may even be warranted in supposing that God was pleased, for the conversion of the wild population of these islands, to work miracles by the hand of his servant.'[30]

Next to Froude, the most reasoned argument in defence of the hagiographers was advanced by Newman himself in the opening 'A Legend of St Gundleus'. Here Newman was prepared to make the greatest concessions to historical criticism, acknowledging that the evidence of the Lives could not stand up to scrutiny. But the techniques of historical analysis and literary criticism were instruments of the secular mind—sound enough in themselves, perhaps, but of no use to the Christian in his quest to understand the mysteries of Creation. This was a special form of knowledge which mankind had already been taught by the Creator Himself, and was to be apprehended only through prolonged meditation on His works. It was as aids to meditating on the workings of God in the world that the real value of traditional hagiography was to be found. Its address was neither to the scholar or the critic *per se*, but to 'the bulk of Christians'. It did not lay claim to absolute truth, 'but it develops its small portion of true knowledge into something which is like the very truth, though it be not it and which stands for the truth when it is but like it. Its evidence is a legend; its facts are a symbol; its history a representation; its drift is a moral.' Thus Newman could confidently conclude:

> Whether St Gundleus led this life and wrought these very miracles I do not know; but I do know that they are Saints whom the Church so accounts, and I believe that though this account of him cannot be proved, it is a symbol of what he did and what he was, a picture of his saintliness and a specimen of his power.[31]

This was a characteristically Newmanite stance which appeared to gain much by ostensibly conceding much. Given the high demands which it made on personal faith, and the manner in which it cast aside the few evidential supports upon which such a faith might yield, it is doubtful whether Newman could bring 'the bulk of Christians, the multitude' whom he believed he was addressing to appreciate its grandeur. His arguments seemed to abandon those followers who would have preferred a more straightforward defence against external criticism and internal doubt.

30. *Lives of the English Saints*, 11–12.
31. *Lives of the English Saints*, 4, 6; the quotation is from 8.

It is here, however, that the divergence between the purposes of Newman and those of the young Froude becomes clear. Unable to share in Newman's confidence that, through meditation on the symbolic meaning of the life of a saint, the mind of the reader would be illuminated with a sense of the divine, Froude was equally unwilling to engage in indeterminate arguments concerning the actual lives of the saints on the basis of dubious and fragmentary evidence. Instead he wished to emphasise the historical and spiritual significance of the hagiographers themselves. Because it was they who, by their very writings, demonstrated the continuing vitality of the spirituality, piety, and sense of the sacred which they celebrated in their saints. It was they, or rather the form and content of their texts, which provided the necessary conduit, ignored by the lofty Newman, through which the modern mind could be reinvested with a vision of the divine. That this act of communion could not be done directly was plain: history, the passage of time, had ensured that neither in their own words nor in translation could they be comprehended by modern unscholarly minds. If they were to be permitted to work their effects, they must be aided, in turn, by a further mediating channel, a mind attuned to the modern perceptions, but conscious also of the sacred and eternal world which they had inhabited. What was needed, in short, was a modern hagiographer who, in evoking by his language the sense of the invisible world in imaginations deadened by generations of corruption and neglect, would also be a modern prophet.

This was certainly a grand ambition, showing clearly the early influence of Carlyle. But Froude was encouraged in the attempt by the conviction that this universal tendency toward mythification was closely related to that intense but evanescent sense of the eternal and the sublime experienced at some time by most humans. This was an insight best evoked not by philosophers and historians but by the most gifted of poets (he cited a passage from Wordsworth's 'Tintern Abbey' by way of example).[32] But the poet's vision was not granted to ordinary souls, and ordinary souls might often be incapable of sharing the poet's revelations. Thus other means must be found through which such 'vanishing feelings' of the eternal could be given shape and colour. Of these, Carlyle's history and Emerson's prose offered alternatives; but further possibilities were suggested by the legends of magic, mystery, and miracle which were the hagiographer's special province. This was a tall order to meet within the compass of a short legendary Life. But there is

32. *Lives of the English Saints*, 77; the lines are 96–103.

no reason to assume that Froude had set all his store in St Neot alone. The first of several Lives which he planned to write, the immediate aim of this preliminary exercise was to see whether such a project was at all feasible; to test whether even for this moderated version of Newman's aspiration there was an audience prepared to respond, and whether he as a writer was possessed of sufficient powers to attempt it.[33] It cannot be said that on either grounds Froude's experiment was especially successful. But the manner in which he tried to accomplish it, and the lessons which he learned from his failure, certainly bear examination.

V

As indicated above, a sudden change of voice and style takes place when Froude moves from his introductory discourse on method to the opening section of 'St Neot' proper, entitled 'Prince Athelstan'. The very first paragraph—both because it raises all of the text's central themes and because it serves as an epitome of its style—is worth quoting at length:

> The stars shone out on the bay of Sandwich, and the song of revelry and mirth had succeeded to the war-cry and the din of the battle. Twenty thousand Northmen lay dead and dying on the down and on the shore, and the mead and the ale was flowing in the camp of the Saxons. Yet was there one among the victors who found no rest for his weary spirit in the excitement of the banquet; the frantic activities of his fierce countrymen seemed not to him a fit mode of thanksgiving, for deliverance from a rude and heathen foe; and in the calm silence of the night he sought to be alone with his God, to offer praise to him for that day's success. The eagle plume of his bonnet declared him to be of the royal race of Cerdic, and though his person was small, almost diminutive, yet his noble gait and princely bearing seemed to say that he was no degenerate son of that illustrious family; it was Athelstan, the Prince of Kent. Alone he stood upon the battle-field and would have prayed but for the strange tumult of disordered thoughts that pressed upon his spirit. There lay the dead and the dying; and the dull moan of agony, and the sharp cry of the departing soul, mixed harshly with the howl of the gathering wolves and the shrill scream of the eagle and the sea fowl. It seemed to his fevered imagination as if the spirits of hell were flocking there for their prey; for the warriors that lay there were heathen Danes, Odin's sworn slaves,

---

33. While he was at work on St Neot, Froude was eagerly proposing a whole roster of saints to Newman which included St Gribald, King Alfred, and St Patrick.

and bound with a deadly curse to blot out the name of the Christian in Saxon England. Yet was there calm above in the bright Heaven; and the stars that shone so silently, and the peaceful sea, told him that, though man was wild and evil, yet was creation still fair—still offered willing and obedient service to its Maker. The very drunken music of the night banquet became pure in the night air, and fell with softening cadence on his ear. The ripple washed upon the shore in measured intervals; and he felt as he listened that there are powers above which man knows not of; a will serenely working in this world of shadows which is not man's will, as the waves of time roll on, and break upon the shores of eternity.[34]

High-flown, antique, and mannered, the voice Froude adopted here was altogether different from the tone of the rest of the series; for while most of its contributors assumed a tone of piety and reverence toward their subject and their authorities, they also followed Newman's advice in including lengthy extracts from the hagiographies rather than attempting a lofty style of their own.

Froude's authorial voice is in fact a blend of several influences. Newman thought that there was too much of Walter Scott in it, and suggested that the first draft be toned down.[35] But while Froude's style may be reminiscent of Scott in its grandiloquence, its tendency toward rhodomontade, and fondness for pathetic fallacy, other sonorities are also at play. A tone of priestly veneration is certainly audible in several places: 'Holy are the characters of those whom God chooses to do His work on earth' (p. 97); 'In deep faith and generous spirit, heaped he his favour on this holy place' (p. 90). Froude makes clear the link he is seeking to establish between the present narrator and his pious forebears:

> And therefore those good men who gave their labours to commemorate the life of this holy Saint, do properly commence their task at this point ... and that we too who are permitted to labour in the reverential spirit as they laboured, let us join with Abbot Ramsay of Croyland ...[36]

But this, it will be noted, was not how Froude actually began his narrative, which opened on the shores of Sandwich Bay in the wake of the great battle, and everywhere else in his text the undulating register of the pulpit is overlaid

---

34. *Lives of the English Saints*, 84–5.
35. Newman to Froude, 28 November 1843, *Letters and Diaries of John Henry Newman*, x, 35–6; in this letter, which contains comments on Froude's first draft, Newman also suggests a short methodological statement which Froude was to expand to such a degree.
36. *Lives of the English Saints*, 89.

by the sterner tones of the epic. Thus the setting of the battle-wake, with scenes contrasting the exultation of the victorious and the agony of the vanquished, which then moves on to focus on one self-conscious individual, struggling to comprehend the larger meaning of such terrible events, evokes a long tradition of epical visions of the world going back in the Western canon to Homer. The subsequent two sections deal with Neot's novitiate and training at Glastonbury and his establishment of his own hermitage. But even here the outside world of strife intervenes, in the persons of the embattled King Ina, the fierce Cornish prince of Liskeard, whose 'Briton blood boiled with indignation' upon the appearance in his territory of Neot 'his Saxon rival'; and in the reappearance of the young Prince Alfred, still hesitant and fearful of the great destiny that lay before him. The epic mood returns in the last two sections detailing Neot's stiffening of Alfred's courage and his decisive, posthumous intervention in Alfred's great victory over the Danes which provides Froude with the opportunity for another purple passage with which to end his narrative:

> ... there stood Neot once more upon the field of battle in the same terrific majesty as the king had seen him. High he waved the royal standard marshalling the Saxons on to victory. Fierce and fast they followed on their fainting foe and gave no quarter.[37]

The atmosphere of epic is evoked not only by scenes of battle, but by the eternal backdrops against which the action is set. The stars over Sandwich Bay under which the drama commences are answered by the sun, which, observing the final victory over the Danes, 'rolled on through the West that long May day and made no comment', and both are merely representative of the complete set of heavenly bodies which throughout watch over the doings of Neot and his fellow humans.[38]

Its invocations of the eternal and the universal notwithstanding, Froude's miniature epic is a decidedly English one. It is over Sandwich Bay that the heavens watch and it was at Ethendun 'five miles from the village of Iley' that the Danes were finally vanquished, and throughout the text the antiquities, place-names, and natural features of old England are presented with loving (though often spurious) precision. Central to this Anglo-Saxon epic was Froude's controversial identification of Neot with Athelstan which the

37. *Lives of the English Saints*, 128.
38. *Lives of the English Saints*, 128.

opening paragraph asserts—an identification which found no support in the extant early Lives, and had been wholly discredited twenty-five years previously by Gorham. In endowing his subject with royal blood, Froude, it might be surmised, was attempting to magnify his importance. But in fact his representation of Anglo-Saxon England and its rulers is far from roseate: 'England had had warning that if she repented not, she would be delivered into the hands of the heathen; and England had given no credence, but went on still in wickedness', and had indeed 'grown worse instead of better.' Treacherous, tyrannous, and timorous, the Anglo-Saxon princes had reduced their own Christian church to a state of ruin and, having thus disabled it, found themselves powerless to resist the pagan onslaught. The victory at Sandwich Bay gave only temporary respite, and England would remain a prey to rapine by the heathen Danes until Alfred, spurred on by Neot, found the courage to follow his destiny.[39]

Froude, it appears, was more comfortable with Athelstan the man of action than Neot the hermit, and his emphasis on Neot's public actions subsequent to his withdrawal to his hermitage—his establishment of his monastery among the Cornishmen, his visit to Rome to secure aid for the church, his encouragement of Alfred, and his ghostly participation at Ethendun—reinforce the point that action rather than piety lay at the heart of early English sanctity. The sanctity of Neot lay not in his actions alone, but in his inspiration, both in life and posthumously, of other Englishmen, of Alfred, of the Anglo-Saxon warriors at Ethendun, of the medieval hagiographers and their readers, and even now, it might be hoped, of the readers of Froude's rhetorical legend. It was this distinctive perspective that Froude was driven to pose what was for a hagiographer an unusual question:

> If any should ask what earthly work St Neot had done hitherto for England in her many trials and dangers, we answer, that we see not the undercurrents of Providence, and know not *in what way* the mysterious influences of Saints avail, yet we do know ... that ten righteous men would have saved the cities of the plain, and that while just Lot continued to live within their cursed walls, God Himself declared that He could do nothing.[40]

With this reference to the destruction of Sodom and Gomorrah (a terrible instance of divine intervention in human history) it becomes clear that the

---

39. *Lives of the English Saints*, 85–6.
40. *Lives of the English Saints*, 104. Curiously this was a theme that was to resurface in Froude's final intelligible words; see ch. 14, 452.

mould within which Froude was seeking to cast his subject was something other than that of a holy man to be venerated, or of an exemplar of piety to be emulated, or even, as Newman sought, as a revelation of continuing divine intervention in the English Church, but as that of a Carlylean historical hero, continually revealing the supernatural within the events of the natural world.

A Carlylean allusion is made at the very beginning of the 'Life' when the Danes who confronted Athelstan/Neot are described as the slaves of Odin— the first of the heroes selected by Carlyle. Thus in opposing them in life and in his after-life, Neot, this Christian English hero, is being juxtaposed against Carlyle's earliest representative of the hero as an instrument of the divine as his successor. Neot is an alternative *English* version of Carlyle's model of the hero as priest (Luther and Knox), 'he is the warfaring and battling priest who led his people not to quiet faithful labour as in peaceful times, but to faithful valorous conflict in times all violent, dismembered.'[41]

That Neot's times were indeed chronically violent is central to Froude's account; furthermore, his contention that they had become so as a retribution upon the tyranny, corruption, and degeneracy of the English is likewise a Carlylean concept. 'Offences accumulate', says Carlyle in the same lecture, 'till they become insupportable; and are then violently burst through, cleared off as by explosion'. In Froude's account it is the priest/reformer Neot— midway between Odin and Luther—who serves to bring this purgation about.[42]

It was through Carlyle that Froude found the means of investing Newman's project with his broader, less exclusive, and more historically informed commission. By combining the voice of the hagiographer with that of the epic historian, he could ensure that Newman and Carlyle did indeed 'go on the same principle of development'. He could attempt to bring their shared moral vision to a wider group of readers than either had yet reached, by calling upon all Englishmen to recognise the promise of greatness which had once been theirs; and, by revealing to them the loss that had been suffered, provoke them into making it good.

It was this subtle but profound difference in their understanding of the relationship between the historical and the devotional that lay at the root of Froude's increasing divergence from Newman. Soon after he agreed to

---

41. Carlyle, *On Heroes, Hero Worship and the Heroic in History* (London, 1849 edn.), 104.
42. *On Heroes*, 106.

substitute Neot for Alfred, Froude was reporting his intention to follow only St Neot's most critical early biographer, Abbot Ramsay, 'not even mentioning what he does not, beautiful as many of the stories are', and a little later he announced that he would write nothing of miracles at all, saving those in which he himself could believe. By November he professed to have reached a state of total scepticism in regard to any of the accounts of the saint's life.[43] In face of this barrage of letters, Newman maintained his distance. He was slow in replying to Froude's requests, and in addition to voicing disapproval of the Scott-like character of Froude's presentation, appears to have asked for more material on miracles, and also to have been cool about Froude's continuing enthusiasm about writing a life of Alfred for the series.[44]

By early 1844, following the furore caused by the publication of J. B. Dalgairns's *Life of St Stephen Hardinge*, Newman had determined to abort the project, concluding that only those works which were already well advanced should go to the press.[45] Newman's exasperation with Froude, however, remained muted; and for much of 1844 Froude continued on the assumption that his more ambitious project for a Life of St Patrick, with which he had replaced his earlier plan for a life of Alfred, would be welcomed into the series. Early in November 1844, however, as work was progressing on St Patrick, an awkward letter from Froude precipitated a breach. Froude had heard rumours that the purpose of the series had really been to lead readers away from the Church of England. Froude insisted that this had never been his intention, and sought an assurance that no such use would be made of his writings. 'Am I at liberty in what I write to take my own line?', he demanded, 'And am I allowed to regard the question as I have always been taught to regard it? If not I had rather not go on.'[46] This was an impertinence too much even for Newman. He replied immediately in a letter, the draft of which bears unmistakable signs of irritation. 'You brought out your St Neot, I exercised no control over it,' he told Froude. He had read his text neither in draft nor in proofs. 'I let you be then. You have said in what you wrote what you pleased.' In anything else he was to write he

43. Froude to Newman, 21 July, 12, 24, 29 August, 2, 9 November 1843, Birmingham Oratory, Newman MSS, vol. 25, nos. 52, 54, 56, 57, 65, 68.
44. Newman to Froude, 28 November 1843, *Letters and diaries of John Henry Newman*, x, 35–6.
45. Holmes, 'Newman's Reputation and the *Lives of the English Saints*', Newman to Froude, 9 November 1844, Birmingham Oratory, Newman MSS, vol. 25, no. 67.
46. Froude to Newman, 9 November 1844, Birmingham Oratory, Newman MSS, vol. 25, no. 66.

was likewise to say what he pleased. In any case, Newman concluded, 'I think it best that the engagement between us should come to an end.'[47]

And so it did. But the end of their personal relationship did not, for Froude, entail an intellectual breach or a crisis. Newman's dismissal was as much due to his disillusion with the entire project as with Froude's own approach to hagiography; and Froude continued, moreover, both publicly and privately to write respectfully of Newman. On hearing that Newman had been received into the Roman Catholic Church, Froude felt close enough to walk to Littlemore to seek confirmation of the rumour; it was Newman who refused the interview.[48] As late as the winter of 1845–46, long after Newman's conversion to Roman Catholicism had been made public, Froude could still publish a positive review of Newman's *Essay on the Development of Christian Doctrine*, arguing that Newman's subsequent conduct should not be seen to invalidate the force of the book. Most importantly, Froude, despite his scruples, did not abandon his interest in saints' lives. Instead he persisted with his plan to write a life of St Patrick.

VI

This project first took shape early in 1844 while Froude was still at work revising 'St Neot' for publication.[49] In the course of work in the Bodleian Library he had come upon two major works of Irish hagiography compiled by the great Franciscan scholar John Colgan—*Acta Sanctorum Hiberniae* (Louvain, 1645) and *Trias Thaumaturga* (Louvain, 1647)—and found them fascinating. It was, he recalled forty years later, of all the collections of ecclesiastical biographies, the most interesting by far. Colgan's Latin texts gave him an access to a world even more ancient than the Anglo-Saxon world of Neot from which he would otherwise have been linguistically excluded; and his rich selection of Gaelic religious poetry, ranging, Froude believed, from the fifth century to the thirteenth century, offered him the exciting possibility of tracing the development of Irish thought and belief over the whole period from the introduction to the full establishment of Christianity, from the heroic

---

47. Newman to Froude, 9 November 1844, Birmingham Oratory, Newman MSS, vol. 25, no. 67.
48. Froude's recollection as given to Wilfrid Scawen Blunt; see n. 5 above .
49. Froude to Newman, 1 February 1844, Birmingham Oratory, Newman MSS, vol. 25, no. 15. St Patrick appears twice in the 'Legend of Neot', as having spent his last days at Glastonbury, and as a figure whose daily practices in pious mortification were an inspiration to Neot, 90, 101.

age to the Christian.[50] The task he was proposing for himself was formidable, requiring a far greater period of study than Neot. 'The mere story', he explained to Newman while their friendship remained, 'is very long, and to give any effect to it a great deal of the druid worship and Irish history of the times will have to be introduced.' Newman was supportive, lending Froude some materials on Patrick, and arranging to overcome the difficulties of including the 'Irish' saint in a series devoted to English saints.[51]

Behind Froude's enthusiasm lay a confidence in the great heuristic value of the early Irish texts. 'What can be shown to be obviously true among the Gaelic', he explained to Newman, 'would on examination hold equally with the Saxon and other Teuton races.' In addition to the rich literary materials introduced to him by Colgan, his earliest tour around Ireland had convinced him that there were sufficient reliques of the Irish saints' material world surviving relatively unspoiled in the Irish landscape to enable him to reimagine and recapture their experience as well as their consciousness. A return to Ireland to conduct a thorough survey of the known holy places would be an essential part of his research.[52]

Froude began work enthusiastically. Having secured introductions to George Petrie and the scholar and antiquarian James Henthorn Todd, Fellow of Trinity College Dublin, Froude visited Ireland in the summer of 1844 to gather materials, and returned again in the long vacation of 1845 to undertake a detailed survey of the places associated with the life and legends of the saint.[53] By the time of his return to Oxford in the autumn, however, Froude's enthusiasm for the project upon which he had invested so much energy and hope had cooled: 'My two years study had turned the historical ground where I had hoped to find a footing into a bottomless morass.' Despite the evidence gathered and the experiences registered, the Life was abandoned, and though Froude was occasionally to allude to St Patrick and his times in a manner that revealed more than a superficial knowledge, he was never again to attempt a sustained study of early Irish history.[54]

50. Dunn, *Froude*, I, 77; Froude to Newman, 1 February, and 'Wed 29' [May] 1844, Birmingham Oratory, Newman MSS, vol. 25, nos. 15, 73. [May was the only month in 1844 when the 29th occurred on a Wednesday.]
51. Froude to Newman, 2 July 1844; Toovey to Newman, 8 March 1844, Birmingham Oratory, Newman MSS, vol. 25, nos. 50, 27.
52. Froude to Newman, 'Wed 29' [May], 2 July 1844, Birmingham Oratory, Newman MSS, vol. 25, nos. 73, 50.
53. Dunn, *Froude*, I, 86–7.
54. Dunn, *Froude*, I, 93.

What gave rise to this sudden disillusion? The reason much preferred by Froude himself in retrospect was the sheer undependability of the evidence:

> Alas the more I saw and the more I read, the more the individual figure of the great saints of Ireland dissolved into the mist like the sons of Fingal on the rocks of Morven ... the Patrick of legend ... was a title, not an individual ... It was impossible to separate the truth from the wilderness of nonsense. I, at any rate, could make no truth out of it at all, and was obliged to drop my enterprise.[55]

Though it is no doubt true in part, Froude's explanation of his difficulty is a little less plausible than it might appear. For all its interpretative difficulty, the evidence for the existence of an original Patrick (who may or may not have been the first actual missionary to the Irish) was a good deal richer than that available for Neot, and was sufficient to enable a number of Irish scholars, including Todd, to undertake critical historical investigation.[56] Moreover, while the legends and miracles which had become attached to a singular Patrick may indeed have been an accumulation of fact and myth, this was the very process which Froude in the introduction to 'St Neot' had discussed approvingly as evidence of the residual force being exercised by one spiritual individual on later generations.

A second factor contributing to Froude's disillusion is given almost equal prominence in his autobiography. This was his increasing awareness of the emerging crisis in Ireland. 'St Patrick may be a myth', Froude recalled, 'the living Ireland was a reality.' That Froude was deeply affected by the poverty and misery of the Irish peasantry, outraged by the prodigality and irresponsibility of the majority of the Irish landlords, and moved by the bravery and generosity of a small minority among both classes, is clear from so many of his retrospective writings on Ireland. It is important to recall that one of the deepest impressions which Ireland had made upon him from his first experiences there in 1841 was his sense of the existence of two dimensions of reality living in parallel with each other, the wretched conditions prevailing in the tangible material world, and the alternative world of the spirit, intermittently mediated through the piety of the people, their traditions of worship, and the surviving antiquities of early Christian civilisation.[57] It was this

---

55. Dunn, *Froude*, I, 86.
56. J. H Todd, *St Patrick: Apostle of Ireland* (Dublin and London, 1864).
57. See ch. 3, 78–9 above.

sense of the contrast between the beauty of what had first been attempted in the conversion of pagan Ireland, and the misery and degeneration which now prevailed in Christianised Ireland that was one of the strongest forces underlying Froude's desire to write about Patrick. 'I cannot write a life of St Patrick', Froude had warned Newman, 'without at least taking some notice of the present state of the work he has left behind him.'[58] Attentive readers of the 'Legend of St Neot' had not been unaware of the criticism of current moral standards in church and state implicit in his account, and it is likely that, given his indignation about the manner in which Ireland had been so neglected, Froude had in mind a larger and bolder version of this theme.

But if such were his intentions, events were already running well ahead of Froude. The potato blight which was to devastate Irish rural society had only just set in when Froude returned to Oxford from Ireland in the autumn of 1845, and its full effect began to be appreciated in England only in the following two years. There can be little doubt, however, that as the dimensions of the calamity that was rapidly developing in Ireland became apparent, the significance of Froude's proposed intervention was correspondingly diminished, and the attractions of writing an edifying life of Patrick palled.[59]

It is more probable that even before the Irish Famine exercised its full impact, a more personal crisis which Froude underwent while he was still in Ireland was more immediately responsible for his loss of faith in the contemporary value of hagiography. While journeying in the west of Ireland in mid-summer 1845, Froude contracted smallpox and for a week seemed close to death. A doctor misdiagnosed and almost killed him: 'Thanks however to the constant kindness and attention of the good people, I got over it sooner that I looked for.'[60] This near-death experience deeply affected Froude psychologically. It served to confirm the feeling, growing since his time as an undergraduate, that he was not after all destined, like the majority of his siblings, to die young; and in doing so it sharpened his conviction that he must now address himself to the challenge of what he was to do with this

58. Froude to Newman, 9 November 1844, Birmingham Oratory, Newman MSS, vol. 25, no. 66.
59. On Froude's views of the state of famine in Ireland, see Froude to Clough, 15 July, 12 August 1848, Bodleian Library, Clough MSS 41032 (Eng. Lett., c190), fols. 302–9.
60. Dunn, *Froude*, I, 89; Josephine Elizabeth Grey Butler, *Recollections of George Butler* (Bristol, 1909), 45–7.

lease of life that had been gifted to him. The urgency of this looming question was etched with particular sharpness through an hallucination which
he experienced at the pitch of his fever, and which remained with him for
the rest of his life. In thirst-ridden delirium, Froude was visited by a group
of 'airy floating figures ... Though so charitable and very pretty withal, they
did not look like angels, so I supposed that they belonged to the intermediary sphere.' They brought him delicious grapes and promised to satisfy all
his desires.

> 'You can do one thing', I said. 'We are told in our books that you powers of
> the air have a prince over you of some kind or other. Tell me if there is such a
> person.' 'Undoubtedly there is' they answered ... 'he will have the greatest
> pleasure in waiting upon you' ... A sheet seemed to be spread across the garret
> on which was a circle of light like the field of a magic lantern. A figure, so
> I must call it, though it seemed to have none, appeared in focus in the centre,
> but it was without form and void. If anything it resembled a giant lobster,
> remained for a moment, and with the whole phantom vision vanished into
> darkness.[61]

Psychoanalytical conjecture is inevitably inconclusive, though scarcely
avoidable. The erotic ambience in which the vision occurs is obvious, and
Freudians may care to speculate about the terrifying sexual symbolism of
the lobster. That Froude was at this time seeking to grapple with the massive
moral issues presented by human sexuality is a theme which will be developed in the next chapter. But even in regard to the painful questions of
faith and doubt which were then perplexing his conscious mind, the vision
was revealing.[62] The quest for an image of the creating force in terms that
would be familiar and comforting was, it seemed to suggest, futile. There
was no absolute form which could be apprehended by all human imaginations; instead there was nothing other than that which the individual
imagination—including the fevered imagination of the invalid Froude—
must construct for itself from its own resources and experiences.

This was a lesson that carried with it both a liberating promise and a terrible challenge. The promise lay in the possibility that every individual in
every generation might find his own way to an appreciation of that eternal

---

61. Dunn, *Froude*, I, 89.
62. Those interested in speculations alternative to psychological ones might take heed of the fact
    that in Tarot reading the lobster symbolises both a cyclical process of rejuvenation and decay,
    and a sealed, protective shell within which this endless process occurs.

world obscured by the material and the ephemeral, and might be helped in
that quest by the particular prophets of their age. The challenge concerned
the doubt as to whether the roles which Froude had assumed as a hagiographer were indeed the most appropriate for his times. Over the next three
years he would find the challenge more easily accepted than surmounted.

5

Experiments: Critical and Fictional, 1845–49

His abandonment of hagiography did not drive Froude to despair. Instead it merely accelerated his desire to find alternative ways of critically exploring the place of Christianity within the larger history of religious expression and moral consciousness. Over the next four years this same quest, which was to lead Froude through an extended series of experiments in critical and fictional writing, was indeed to issue in the great crisis of his public career: the publication of *The Nemesis of Faith* and its attendant consequences. It is, however, regrettable that it is from the perspective of this notorious event that all of Froude's development over the previous four years has conventionally and simplistically been viewed.

The conventional account of the circumstances leading up to the publication of *The Nemesis of Faith* may be rehearsed briefly. Following his abandonment of hagiography and confronting yet another personal crisis occasioned by Newman's move to Rome, Froude plunged into introspection, digging deep into his own private experience in a desperate attempt to resolve the emotional and intellectual conflicts that had plagued him since youth. The appearance in the spring of 1847 of *Shadows of the Clouds*, a quasi-autobiographical and intensely emotional set of fictions, was an ominous indication of things to come. The book, however, was little noticed, and its effect was further muted when Froude's father, scandalised by what he had read—or rather heard—of its treacherous and unseemly autobiographical nature, sought to buy up the entire edition. But with the publication in February 1849 of his full-length novel, *The Nemesis of Faith*, Froude went altogether too far. The novel's frank discussion of the deficiencies of orthodox belief and of the reasonableness of agnosticism, its sympathetic treatment of sexual, indeed adulterous, passion, and its excoriation of the hypocrisies of the Established Church and its adherents provoked a furore which spilled beyond the polite literary journals into the columns of the popular press. Froude was everywhere anathemised. Reviews (with the notable but marginal exception of a short notice by Mary Anne Evans/George Eliot) were violently hostile.[1] Archdeacon Froude finally disowned his son, the bishop of his home diocese publicly denounced him, and William Sewell, the sub-rector of his own college, Exeter, burned a copy before Fellows and undergraduates in hall.[2] Boycotted by all but a small number of colleagues, and openly attacked in the streets, Froude was forced on threat of expulsion to resign his fellowship and leave Oxford in disgrace.

Much of this is comparatively well known; and insofar as it is remembered at all, it is largely as a brief episode symptomatic of the intellectual and moral crisis of that time and of the repressions and hypocrisies that accompanied it. For this, Froude himself is in some part responsible. After he had become established as a man of letters he seemed frequently to repudiate his brief career as a novelist. *The Nemesis of Faith*, he said, 'had been but a cry of pain',[3] and in 1880 he told his friend John Skelton that he would not allow it to be republished in his lifetime.[4] Such recantations, however, were never unambiguous. In private conversation he continued to assert the righteousness of his actions at the time and the injustice which he had suffered,[5] and even while he was announcing to Skelton his decision not to allow a reprinting, he remained ambivalent: 'As yet I have said No—but why may I not say *Yes* [Froude's italics], and show the world for what slight cause they expelled

---

1. Unlike *Shadows*, *The Nemesis of Faith* was widely reviewed in both the periodical and newspaper press. Among the lengthier hostile reviews are those in the *Christian Observer*, 50 (January 1850), 16–35; *Edinburgh Review*, 90 (October 1849), 293–356; *Fraser's Magazine*, 39 (May 1849), 545–60; *Bentley's Miscellany*, 25 (April 1849), 443–6. George Eliot's exceptionally sympathetic review is in *The Coventry Herald and Observer*, 16 March 1849, np.

2. 'Resolutions in Froude's case', March 1849, Bishop Philpotts to Rector Richards, 1 March 1849, Exeter College, Oxford, Froude MSS, nos. 50–1; Phillpotts published an open letter of condemnation in *The Standard,* 12 March 1849. The 'public burning' of Froude's novel has been sometimes over-dramatised; it was less a public ceremony than an exemplary gesture of condemnation before the Fellows and undergraduates at breakfast in Exeter. The best account of the occasion is supplied by the owner of the burnt copy, Rev Arthur Blomfield, first published as correspondence in the *Daily News* for 2 May 1892, and reprinted in Dunn, *Froude*, I, 227–8.

3. Dunn, *Froude*, I, 148.

4. Froude to Skelton, 19 March 1880, in Skelton (ed.), *The Table-Talk of Shirley* (Edinburgh, 1896), 164.

5. Wilfrid Scawen Blunt, *Land War in Ireland*, 15–16.

from Oxford and half-ruined the now visibly innocent author of the thing?'[6]

It is unfortunate that the initial scandal surrounding Froude's early fictions, coupled with his ambivalent second thoughts, have obscured the intense engagement with religious, ethical, and aesthetic problems out of which they emerged, and so deprived them of independent critical interest. Such a critical investigation of Froude's intellectual development in the later 1840s helps to reveal not only the complex moral and philosophical thought underlying his turn to fiction, but also to show some deeply rooted convictions connecting the passionate hagiographer of the early 1840s with the assured master historian who was to emerge a decade later.

I

His plans for writing a life of St Patrick having been abandoned, Froude threw himself energetically into a programme of reading Germany's new biblical critics, undertaking 'a close and exact criticism' of what they had to say.[7] In this he was by no means exceptional among the intellectual youth of his time.[8] But the effect of this sustained study was to deepen Froude's sense of the acute dilemma now facing him. The Germans did not destroy Froude's faith in Christianity. But they completed his disillusion with such claims for theological and ecclesiastical authority that rested on historical continuity.

> The religion with which we were to direct our lives in this world, and on which we build our hopes for the future, must be a present fact, a reality independent of time ... to be verified, like all other knowledge which we possess,

6. Froude to Skelton, 19 March 1880, in Skelton (ed.), *The Table-Talk of Shirley* (Edinburgh, 1896), 165. In fact, he did say 'yes', in a slightly indirect way. In 1892 his friend Moncure Conway published a North American edition with an introduction strongly defending the aims and achievements of the author, and it was this new edition which Froude's daughter Margaret authorised for publication in England in 1903: *The Nemesis of Faith, or The History of Markham Sutherland by James Anthony Froude, Reprinted from the 2nd edition with an Introduction by Moncure D. Conway* (New York, Dutton, 1892; London, Routledge, 1903). An earlier American reprint of 1879, by D. M. Bennett, appears to have been unauthorised.
7. Dunn, *Froude*, I, 93. It seems likely that Froude had come across Feuerbach, Strauss, and Schleiermacher earlier, through the acquaintance he had formed in the early 1840s with the most important publicist of this group in England, John Sterling (1806–1844).
8. Rosemary Ashton, *The German Idea: Four English Writers and the Influence of German Thought* (Cambridge, 1980).

by living experience, not dependent on whether certain incidents alleged to have happened 1,800 years ago in Palestine could be established by critical enquiries.[9]

This grave obligation to start out again from living experience was, however, made all the more difficult for Froude by two decisions under which he had professed allegiance to traditional authority. In entering upon a don's life in 1842 he had publicly subscribed to the Thirty-Nine Articles, and had confirmed his subscription by taking deacon's orders in 1847. The manner in which these decisions now threatened his capacity to honour the moral obligations he had begun so clearly to see was, moreover, bluntly presented to him on his first attempt to escape from them. Confessing his unfitness for holy orders, Froude proposed to pursue a career in medicine, but discovered to his horror that by law, entry into any of the professions was barred 'to anyone who had so much as dipped his fingers in the ecclesiastical ink.' Froude must either persist in a career for which he believed he had no calling, or resign himself to poverty and ruin. Almost fifty years on, despite all the intervening controversies that were to be a cause of considerable distress, Froude could still recall his decision to take deacon's orders as 'the greatest fault in my life ... soon but too late repented of.'[10] While it inflamed Froude's indignation, the realisation of his imprisonment did not paralyse him, as had his first acquaintance with Newman several years previously. Instead he reacted against it by criticism and argument, and by embarking upon a series of experiments which were to lead him to believe that the best means of resolving his dilemmas lay in the composition of fiction.

Of central importance in this process of critical reconstruction was Froude's involvement in the *Oxford and Cambridge Review*. An inter-university venture—pioneered by William Toogood and F. F. Ivers, with support from Charles Kingsley and F. D. Maurice in Cambridge and by Cowley Powles, Froude's colleague at Exeter—the *Review*, which made its first appearance in July 1845, was intended to be an organ of social and religious speculation and debate.[11] Appearing amid the heated atmosphere of Newman's defection to Rome, it immediately provoked controversy through an essay on the Jesuits, defending them against the calumnies of Eugène Sue, and through

9. Dunn, *Froude*, I, 93.

10. Dunn, *Froude*, I, 94–5.

11. The journal made its position clear in the first article of the first issue, which under the guise of a review of Disraeli's *Sybil* provided a discussion of 'The Politics of the New Generation', *Oxford and Cambridge Review*, 1 (July 1845), 1–11.

some contributions by Edward Pusey which exposed the *Review* to charges of crypto-Romanism. The Oriel Fellow Charles Golightly conducted a vendetta against it both in the Oxford press and through private complaints to the Archbishop of Canterbury.[12] But while he mildly disapproved of the rashness of early editorial policy in certain respects, Froude believed that the controversy in itself was good. 'The more people hate us, the more we rise', he wrote to Kingsley, 'and I cannot but augur well of the abuse ... I think it is better we should go on expressing our sentiments clearly and resolutely, and not minding if we find them alongside their contradictories.'[13]

Froude himself contributed to this combative atmosphere by an approving and sympathetic review of Newman's *Essay on Christian Doctrine* which, in the atmosphere prevailing after Newman's defection, could only be seen as provocative.[14] But his other known contributions indicate that his real interests had moved elsewhere. A review of Carlyle's *Cromwell* is Froude's first published statement on the writer who would be the most important intellectual influence on his life. It is laudatory of Carlyle's style and purpose, but unremarkable except for the approval it gives to Carlyle's justification of Cromwell's actions at Drogheda.[15] Froude's two other contributions are not concerned with history but with philosophy and literature. One of them is an essay on Spinoza.

Though it was unusual, Froude's interest in Spinoza was not entirely exceptional. Coleridge and Carlyle had both pointed to his importance; and in 1843 the critic G. H. Lewes had published a general essay on 'Spinoza's Life and Works' that succeeded in prompting a wider renewal of interest. Spinoza's relevance to the young generation of the 1840s was considerable. As one of the first textual critics of the Old Testament, Spinoza had already confronted the challenges revived by the new critics of the early nineteenth century and claimed to have transcended them. For Spinoza, the undependability of Scripture as the unalloyed Word of God was, given the inescapable fallibility of human nature, only to be expected. Its real value, along with

---

12. Andrew Atherson, *Oxford's Protestant Spy: The Controversial Career of Charles Golightly* (Milton Keynes, 2007); *Dolman's Magazine*, ii (December 1846), 499.
13. Froude to Kingsley, 8 December 1845, quoted in Dunn, *Froude*, I, 101–2.
14. 'An Essay on the Development of Christian Doctrine', *Oxford and Cambridge Review*, 2 (January–June 1846), 135–67. This attribution and the following one is based on Froude to Kingsley, 8 December 1845, quoted in Dunn, *Froude*, I, 101–2.
15. 'Letters and Speeches of Oliver Cromwell', *Oxford and Cambridge Review*, 2 (January–June, 1846), 225–41.

that of other sacred texts, lay in the support it gave to an essentially ontological defence of the existence of God: proof, that is, that the human mind was capable of conceptualising a being greater than all. From this, Spinoza went on to elaborate an intricate metaphysical system which claimed to demonstrate *a priori* the rational necessity of God's existence without regard to human conceptions. In gaining this much, however, Spinoza appeared to some to have surrendered altogether the ground of human free will.

This was the nub of Lewes's reservation. Spinoza's system 'has a logical but not a vital truth'. Through a too heavy reliance on Descartes, he had been misled by metaphor of the mind as 'a mirror of reality'; 'but it is no mirror … it gives no faithful reflection of the world … only a faithful report of its own state as excited by the world.' [16] This was an issue which Froude was to address in a sophisticated theoretical exposition and critique of Spinoza's ethical work which he composed in the early 1850s.[17] In this he would directly confront the determinist implications of Spinoza's thought, and attempt to demonstrate that Spinoza had successfully recovered for humanity the freedom to pursue goodness and truth in the finite world in a manner that can reconcile us with the Creator.

Yet while a rejection of Lewes's notion of Spinoza as a determinist is clear in Froude's earlier essay, his address is less analytical and altogether more modest.[18] 'We have no intention of meddling in this place with the internal character of [Spinoza's] philosophy.' Like Lewes, Froude believes it was Spinoza's misfortune to have worked out his vision of the world within the Cartesian method, 'since it was the prevailing school when he arose'. But 'his philosophy might, if it chose, express itself in the terminology of any or every school', for the essence of 'Spinozism' is to be found not in its methods or its form, but in its aspirations: more than just 'a tendency of the human mind … it is *the tendency* of *the* human mind—what all great philosophies and all great religions have struggled for from the beginning until now.'[19] It was not the

16. G. H. Lewes, 'Spinoza's Life and Works', *Westminster Review*, 39 (1843), 372–407; on the revival of interest in Spinoza in general see Wayne I. Boucher, *Spinoza: eighteenth and nineteenth century discussions* (2 vols., The Hague, 1999).

17. 'Spinoza' *Westminster Review*, OS 64 (July 1855); reprt in *Short Studies* I, 339–400; Froude elsewhere records that the essay was originally accepted for publication in the *Edinburgh Review* by George Cornwall Lewis but was rejected when Henry Reeves took over the editorial chair, see Froude to Sir William Muir, 28 April [1882], Edinburgh University Library, Muir MSS, Dk.2.13.

18. 'The Life of Spinoza', *Oxford and Cambridge Review*, 5 (July–December, 1847) 387–427.

19. 'The Life of Spinoza', 427, Froude's italics.

substance of Spinoza's thought, but the manner in which it developed through self-sacrificing singlemindedness throughout the philosopher's life that commanded admiration; and it was not in his major philosophical and theological works but in his short autobiography that the essence of his greatness was to be found. In the autobiography, which is the focus of Froude's essay, Spinoza records his decision made on the threshold of manhood to give up the pursuit of money, fame, comfort, and pleasure, and to devote himself to the question as to 'whether there was anywhere such a thing as real good which it was possible for me to get at ... whether ... there was anything in the nature of things which, if I could find and get, I should be really and truly happy.' It was this quest for the good at all costs that supplied the original inspiration and underlying passion of a life, with all its public trials and quiet triumphs, that primarily interested Froude.

The public trials were many. Spinoza's successive expulsions from his own community and his school mastering job, his retreat to the hermitage of Rhynberg, his brief period of protection by the De Witt brothers, and his further expulsion from Amsterdam are all detailed in Froude's account. In the midst of all these crises Spinoza suffered also from lesser torments of lesser minds, such as the ingratiating William de Bleyenburg, 'a self-satisfied Protestant ... knowing just enough philosophy to be aware of its difficulties', who exploited Spinoza's generosity in corresponding with him in order to expose the falsity of his philosophy to the world; or the treacherous Albert de Burgh, a former student, now 'sunk under the fascination of Roman Catholicism', who challenged Spinoza with the usual arguments appropriated 'as the exclusive possession of the Church of Rome; apostolical succession, antiquity, saints, martyrs, miracles'.[20] Throughout all this, Spinoza continued living frugally and in obscurity, refusing such protections as would compromise his principles but content withal, his spirit shining forth as one not to be deflected by the vanities, trials, and pettiness of ordinary human life from the primary object of mankind: the quest to know God.

Clearly, what Froude was attempting here was not an essay in intellectual history, but another saint's life. Lacking the qualities of sanctification as required by Newman, Spinoza makes an odd kind of saint. But neither is he simply a secular alternative—a Carlylean hero, changing the world by the sheer energy of his vision. Yet he is, Froude insists, 'a very great man, one of the very greatest

---

20. 'The Life of Spinoza', 420.

men', for though he was in every other respect no different from the mass of humanity, he was 'one of the infinitely small number of men who had followed God with an undivided heart'. Confined by the time and circumstances of his birth and the limitations of his character, he was neither super-historical saint nor historical hero, but merely a sincere and a brave man, honest enough to embrace the insight that had been granted him, and strong enough to live the whole of his life by it. The course of that life deserved recording as an exemplar to the rest of us more or less gifted, more or less strong souls as to what might be done by all of us once the path was made plain.

This notion of the individual human who could be both historically and spiritually significant yet different from Newman's saints and Carlyle's heroes shows considerable confidence on Froude's part. It seems clear that it derives from a reading of Spinoza's philosophy similar to that which he was to make public in his later essay, according to which Spinoza himself is a living example of the possibilities open to individuals who were willing to apply his thought in their own lives. But what is more immediately of interest is the fact that such a reading of Spinoza as a secular saint was made possible for Froude by his contemporaneous engagement with the work of the man whom he then regarded, even more than Carlyle, as the greatest prophet of modern consciousness: Goethe.

Froude had begun reading Goethe (along with Lessing and Schiller) earlier in the decade. At that time the young scholar, struggling to tread an independent path amidst the interminable theological speculations of the time, learned from Goethe a key guiding principle as to how to confront doubt: 'By argument never', Goethe had declared, 'by action always.'[21] Following his engagement with the German theologians, his critical interest in the purpose of Goethe's art became more focused. In his attraction to Goethe, Froude, of course, was typical of his time. By the mid-1840s the defensiveness and embarrassment that had sometimes afflicted Goethe's early advocates in England had been largely dissipated. Most of his major works had been translated, and his reputation as the greatest German poet of his times firmly established.[22]

Yet admiration was not altogether unqualified. Even among Goethe's most enthusiastic proponents, disquiet remained about his apparent moral

---

21. Attributed to Goethe as part of his *Maxims and Reflections*; Dunn, *Froude*, I, 74.
22. On Goethe's reception in nineteenth-century England, see the essays by William Rose and W. H. Bruford, in William Rose (ed.), *Essays on Goethe* (London, 1949).

relativism, about his private life, about the second part of *Faust*, and in particular about the characterisation of the Devil in that play. This continuing unease is clearly evident in an essay on 'The Character and Works of Goethe', published in 1843 by G. H. Lewes—a writer who, after Carlyle, can fairly be described as Goethe's most influential English advocate. Lewes's account of Goethe was generally appreciative, and he was at pains to refute the most hostile criticisms aimed at him. But, as with Spinoza, the vindication was far from total. Goethe's uncompromising individualism, his preoccupation with spiritual and artistic self-development, or 'self-culture', had, according to Lewes, a severely limiting effect, preventing Goethe from attaining an accurate sense of character beyond his own—a defect that was particularly obvious in his depiction of women. It had sustained his highly elitist and conservative view of society and of history, and its effect on the minds of less gifted, less disciplined and less critical admirers had been nothing short of pernicious. For Lewes, then, the commendation of Goethe's strong spirits came accompanied by a clear health warning.[23]

As in the case of Spinoza, Froude's view of Goethe, published in an essay in the *Oxford and Cambridge Review* in January 1846, directly opposed Lewes.[24] Froude's admiration was wholly unqualified. Goethe was 'the most remarkable person the world has seen for centuries', and he is unambiguously modern:

> *Faust* is the poem of this century—the mirror which all thinking men in all countries just at present will receive good from looking into as likely to give them more insight than they will get elsewhere into what is going on inside their own breasts.[25]

What was going on, according to Froude, was a general crisis of faith: 'In this unhealthy modern time, when all is re-examined researched into, questioned and, therefore, supposed possibly to be false ... now every thing is doubted.' But for this universal despondency, Goethe had provided the antidote. Because in his art, especially in *Faust*, he had given dramatic embodiment to his manifesto that the only resolution to metaphysical doubt would be found in an honest, audacious, and ambitious exploration of the world as we find it.

---

23. Lewes, 'The Character and Works of Goethe', *British and Foreign Review*, 14 (1843), 78–135.
24. 'Goethe's *Faust*', *Oxford and Cambridge Review*, 2 (1846) 1–23, unsigned, but the attribution is based on Froude to Kingsley, 8 December 1845, in which he announces that it is to appear in the following January; Dunn, *Froude*, I, 102.
25. 'Goethe's *Faust*', 2.

To teach the extraordinariness of the ordinary everyday life, one might say, is the whole object of all he ever wrote the infinitely pregnant meaning that underlies the meanest action of the meanest men ... he has not scrupled to use the machinery of the Mystery plays ... [but] ... The preternatural machinery of *Faust*, we must never forget is machinery only. He, that individual Faust, is not to be supposed to be introduced into a new element, a new sort of influence different from what surrounds the rest of mankind ... The forms that appear to Faust are about and in every one of us, only in his case the figure assumes a definite outline, by being brought as it were into focus; as he is in his own naked essence, the evil spirit is not and cannot be painted (for who can know what he is) but as he is to us; Mephistopheles is the devil of this age of intellect.[26]

The appearance of the Devil in heaven at the outset of the drama is not, therefore, a mere lapse of taste or an unseemly attempt to shock the pious. It is, in fact, central to Goethe's purpose as a symbolic demonstration that the source of evil lies not in some great passion—pride or defiance—concerning which we humans can evoke a sense of tragedy. It lies rather in something altogether more banal and prosaic—in our own reason. A gift granted by God to aid us in our straining for the good, it was reason, or, more precisely, our uncritical dependence upon the abstract and dispassionate methods of contemporary metaphysical speculation, that was steadily leading us far away from God's purpose.

By representing the troubles of our times in mythologised form, Goethe has not only enabled us, says Froude, to comprehend their deeper significance, but has also shown a way toward a manner of their resolution. For all his weaknesses and vanities, Faust is not intrinsically unregenerate and he is not ultimately damned. This is the central message of *Faust Part II*, which Froude insists has been so grossly misunderstood. But intimations of Goethe's true attitude toward his character are evident much earlier in the 'Prologue in Heaven', and in the scene on Easter morning where, amidst all his disbelief, Faust is for a period redeemed.

Froude never published the promised second article in praise of *Faust, Part II* (or it has not yet been traced),[27] but there is sufficient in what he has

---

26. 'Goethe's *Faust*', 10–11.
27. A translation of sections from the 'Prologue in Heaven' from *Faust* was published in the *Review*, 3 (July–December 1846), 207–17, but the translation there is attributed to Captain Knox. An essay on 'The Three Fausts: Gothe [*sic*], Marlowe and Calderon', which appeared in the *Oxford and Cambridge Review*, 5 (July–December 1847), 51–92, cannot with certainty be attributed to Froude.

written to see that his reading of Goethe had served to develop his philosophical and critical thinking in several ways. First, the congruence with
Spinoza is obvious. In *Dichtung und Warheit* Goethe had acknowledged his
indebtedness to the philosopher in helping make sense of the bewildered
and alienated state in which modern humanity found itself. Many of his
literary inventions can be seen as explorations of the manner in which this
sense of existing within a Creation they could never fully apprehend oper-
ated on individuals, and of the extent to which they succeeded in transcending their benighted condition, with Werther at one end of the spectrum
and Faust at the other. Goethe's success had also helped to reinforce Froude
in the conviction, already apparent in his hagiography, that the best means
of further exploring the causes of the religious and moral disturbances now
afflicting his generation lay in imaginative literature rather than in philosophical, theological, or historical arguments as they were then being conducted. Finally, Goethe's particularly skilful means of deploying magical and
preternatural forms as a metaphor for the real mystery of finite humanity's
relationship to an eternal Creation would have exerted a powerful influence
over a mind already attuned as Froude's was to Carlyle's injunction to
discover the supernatural in the natural.[28]

But for Froude, even more than for Goethe, it was as a metaphor only—
an image imperfectly capturing a reality which it was impossible for us
fully to comprehend. Unlike others of his generation, Froude remained
fixed in the presumption that while the conventional modes of intellectual
discourse were self-limiting, the alternative mystifying modes of certain
poets and novelists, though powerful, were 'mechanical' and ultimately
'subservient' to their philosophical and theological purposes. This tendency
to reduce the magical to the mechanical is an indication perhaps of the
limits of Froude's imaginative powers. Or perhaps such dogged resistance
to the idea of the preternatural as an independent phenomenon may be
seen as necessary to his recovery from the terrors of his youth. Ultimately,
this insensitivity to the possibilities of the magical may also be deemed to
have been partially responsible for his failure in his fiction to represent the
Romantic vision in the form of English realism. For the moment, however,
Froude's confidence in his own critical reading of the Romantics' message
is made abundantly clear in the other notable product of his critical writing

---

28. Among a large body of criticism, see M. H. Abrams, *Natural Supernaturalism: Tradition and
Revolution in Romantic Literature* (New York, 1973).

in the mid-1840s. This was his essay on the Bavarian novelist and fantasist Ludwig Tieck (1773–1853).

By the time Froude came upon him, Tieck was already reasonably well known in English literary circles. Several translations of his selected short stories and full-length novels had appeared since the early 1820s, so that by the middle of the 1840s a fully representative sample of Tieck's work had already been made available in English. Critical reception of Tieck was mixed. Some early enthusiasts had sought to establish a case for him as a bold and distinctive new voice—an ironist who was using the genre of the horror tale and ghost story for critical, even polemical, purposes. But others, discounting the irony or disliking the polemic, simply recommended him as an entertaining purveyor of magical and supernatural tales. The most influential commentary was supplied by Carlyle, who, in scattered comments in review articles and in his own translation of selected *Tales* (1827), offered a mildly sympathetic but far from enthusiastic assessment of Tieck. For Carlyle, Tieck was a genuine poet, but one who was working a curious and limited seam.[29]

This was the rather ambivalent status generally attached to Tieck when Froude, working in collaboration with the well-known Germanist Julius Hare and other unnamed hands, produced late in 1845 a translation of a selection of Tieck's stories drawn mainly from his *Phantasus: eine Sammlung von Mahrchen, Erzahlungen, Schauspielen und Novellen* (1812–16), to which Froude provided a critical introduction. The 1845 edition of the *Phantasus* was considerably shorter than the three-volume original.[30] Lengthy passages of conversation and debate between seven storytellers which Tieck, following Chaucer, Boccaccio, and others, interspersed between his tales were altogether dropped, and no indication given to English readers that they had existed at all. Only seven of the original thirteen tales were included, again without notice of what had been omitted, and three earlier Tieck stories not collected in the *Phantasus* were included, again without indication. The translations are, according to the leading authority on the subject, decidedly uneven. Several are slightly altered versions of earlier translations, some straight copies, and significantly perhaps, only the

29. E. H. Zeydel, *Ludwig Tieck and England: A Study of the Literary Relations of Germany and England during the Early Nineteenth Century* (Princeton, 1931).

30. J. C. Hare and J. A. Froude (eds.), *Tales from the Phantasus of Ludwig Tieck* (London, 1845), reprinted as Ludwig Tieck, *Tales of Fairyland* (London, 1879), without reference to the editors.

three added tales are, according to the same authority, distinctly superior renderings.[31]

The 1845 collection, then, has all the signs of a rushed job. It is, however, in Froude's critical eighteen-page 'Preface' that the principal interest of the volume lies. In the debate on Tieck's status, Froude was unambiguously on the side of the enthusiasts. Unjustly discounted in England, Tieck, Froude insisted, was almost the equal of Goethe himself: '... he is a modern poet in every sense of the word; and that is why we claim so high a place for him.'[32] Tieck's reputation in England as a teller of magical supernatural tales is a gross misrepresentation. 'The wild preternatural spirit which breathes through all his tales forms but a subservient part' of his intent. Rather,

> the first startling feature ... in all the characters in these tales is their terrible reality. In all the circumstances of the wild and wonderful ... instead of finding the persons of the same fantastic character, such as we might naturally expect as harmonising better with the elements in which they work ... instead of saints with power of working miracles, or the ideal heroes of the age of chivalry—we have the very men and women which we ourselves are and such as we see every day around us ... No matter what the conditions be under which he pictures them working, his men are real men, not fantastic ...[33]

This disjunction between the real persons of his tales and the unreal environment in which they are placed by Tieck is merely a literary conceit, a way of representing the ultimate reality 'in which our moral nature hangs; and is, in fact, nothing more than the very element in which we all live, only held in a certain light that we may see it'. Tieck's magical environments, moreover, 'are not so unreal as they seem.' It is only because most of us in our everyday lives have been blinded to all but one of the multiple wonders of Creation that we assume so. The great poets have always been alive to 'the teeming wonders of the world' and 'the world as mirrored in third minds appears transfigured'. But great poets are rare, and those equipped to comprehend and respond to their vision are equally few. So Tieck has sought in his magical *Tales* to employ a metaphor that would be at once more accessible to and more commanding over our own limited imaginations.

Tieck, then, is not a mere fabulist. He is essentially a moral writer concerned with the great moral issues, 'with the nature of man as he finds him,

---

31. Zeydel, *Ludwig Tieck*, ch. 6, esp. 186–8.
32. *Tales from the Phantasus*, v.
33. *Phantasus*, iv–v.

and with the working of the moral laws, the natural tendencies of virtue and vice in the system of the universe'. He has posed the big questions, 'What am I? How came I here? What is my business here?', and having, as his earlier novels bear witness, emerged triumphantly from 'this fearful struggle' himself, he was now exploring less difficult and more attractive means of presenting this experience to a wider readership.[34]

This seems strained; and Froude even conceded that his critical commentary must work against the emotive intentions of the author. But he nevertheless proceeded to offer a strong reading of a selection of the stories. 'Runenberg' is the story of the weak-willed 'Christian', born into a very comfortable life who, feeling a vague dissatisfaction with life, goes in search of meaning. But as he is given some insight to the nature of Creation and the obligations that it entails for him, he flinches, falls into despair 'and is lost forever'. Readers of *The Nemesis of Faith* will find in Christian a model for Markham Sutherland far closer than Froude himself. There is no similar model for Edward Fowler. But Emilius, the central figure in 'The Love-Charm', is

> a dreamer whose power exhausts itself in speculation, and never acts at all except on impulse, without firmness, without will to give oneness of design and consistency to his actions ... this character no matter how pure may be in general its purposes or how lofty its aspirations is exactly the one most open to be laid under the spell of some other force.[35]

So described, he occupies a condition very close to the central character of 'The Spirit's Trials', and it is scarcely an accident that the test which both characters fail emerges out of the moral challenges of sexual attraction.

But while he selects these for special comment, the stories, Froude insists, are not to be read singly, or in separation from each other. 'It is only by the light of the whole that the parts become intelligible', and readers are advised that 'the way to understand them is to try to analyse the feelings left on our mind by the whole.' If the collection is read in this way, then a set of related themes soon becomes apparent. One is the longevity of evil in history: that 'a single sin, unrepented of and unatoned for, becomes a destiny.' There is no escape from moral responsibility. A second is a particularly stern view of the nature of human tragedy, Greek rather than Renaissance in character, which characterises it not as the consequence of an individual's peculiar flaw, but

34. *Phantasus*, iii.   35. *Phantasus*, xiii.

as an external force acting upon all humanity regardless of individuals' weaknesses and strengths. Finally there is the related necessity for all of us, despite our benighted condition, our defects, and our weaknesses both congenital and accidently acquired, to strive to discover the good in each instance in our lives, and to act on it, or else bear the full consequence of inaction.

Froude's reading of the *Phantasus* is undoubtedly polemical. It underplays the author's genuine passion for the preternatural, and overstates the consciously moralising intent of the tales. The interest of the 'Preface', however, lies not in the accuracy of its assessment of Tieck, but in the light it throws on the direction of Froude's own thought at this moment. Coming of age in a time of great religious turmoil in Germany, Tieck, Froude tells us (erroneously), had been born a Roman Catholic but had lost his faith. His work represented a hard-won struggle to reconstruct for himself a foundation for belief in God and the purposes of his Creation. Tieck's escape from the turmoils of religious and moral doubt had been gained, significantly, not by historical and biographical work but by imaginative literature. More significantly still, he had done so by writing about real, ordinary people, and not about 'saints' and 'heroes'.

The relevance of this (rather oversimplified) account for Froude in the Oxford of the mid-1840s is obvious. Rejecting not only the means favoured by Newman as a vehicle for the promotion of spiritual renewal, but also the alternative celebration of the heroic advocated by Carlyle, he would turn instead to fiction. And in Tieck he had discovered a most encouraging example of the manner in which the concern which had moved him to write the lives of saints could be realised in fiction. But if Tieck was an inspiration, he was not to be uncritically emulated. The latter's fascination with the supernatural was something Froude himself regarded as 'a subservient part'. Useful as a technique through which imagination, intuition, and intellect might be bound together, tales of mystery were not essential to the purpose. 'English readers', says Froude, 'will not be contented with the suggestion of allegory.' Instead, an alternative more realist means through which this unity could be demonstrated was suggested in the all too human characters drawn fictionally by Goethe and realised historically in the lived experience of ordinary courageous men such as Spinoza.[36]

36. *Phantasus*, ii,

These were the critical and philosophical influences which, as much as any of the psychological motives that have often been attributed to him, underlay the second major phase in Froude's intellectual development: his transition from hagiography to fiction. Spinoza, Goethe, Tieck—the objects of Froude's early study—were, for all their obvious differences, engaged in the same great undertaking, each seeking a means of conveying to the human mind a true sense of the nature of all Creation and of its own place within it—the former by means of philosophical reflection, the latter two by harnessing the power of fantasy and imagination. But the achievement of each was, for the needs of 'modern Englishmen', insufficient. The preternaturalism which Tieck had conceived of as metaphor had become for too many limited imaginations an end in itself. Likewise, Goethe's great drama had been similarly misunderstood, its audacity too strong for timid English minds, while Spinoza's system had equally lost its power to excite: its Cartesianism, as Lewes suggested, disagreeable to Englishmen's empirical instincts. And so, rather than depending on philosophical argument, Froude would follow Goethe and Tieck in employing an intimate emotionally charged fictional mode to engage his readers' attention. But he would not resort to the occult, the mystical, or the supernatural. His characters would be 'ordinary', instantly recognisable to the university-educated, troubled middle-class English male reader at whom his message was primarily directed, and far from being heroes or saints they would be, like Tieck's characters, flawed by nature or experience. The individual's search for truth was to be represented in fiction as it was in real life, as being repeatedly crossed and confused by the interacting forces of history, contingency, accident, and sheer human deficiency. The enormity of the task being confronted and the corresponding necessity to rise to it would be underlined, as in Tieck's frightening stories, by uncompromising depiction of failure and its consequences. But in emulating a strategy which Goethe had so masterfully deployed both in *Werter* and *Wilhelm Meister*, sensitive readers would be made aware of the possibility of liberation and success by noting the correspondences between the characters who failed and the author who, in creating them, also transcended them.

Here were the seeds of a remarkably ambitious literary enterprise which, far from being the product of a passing psychological impulse of an overwrought mind, was to occupy Froude for more than three years of intense critical and creative activity.

II

Having once committed himself to fiction, some time toward the close of 1845, Froude withdrew from Oxford and established himself in a cottage near Torquay, from where, he informed his friends, he was determined to renounce all communication except with the select few, to abandon on abstract speculation, and give himself over to imagining.[37] Though he was far from wholly absent from Oxford at this time, the two creations that make up *Shadows of the Clouds* were the product of this rustication, and a short story, dealing with themes addressed also in *Shadows*, entitled 'Louisa Varden', which appeared in the *Oxford and Cambridge Review* in June 1846, is very likely from his pen also.[38] Notwithstanding the far from sympathetic reception with which *Shadows* was greeted on its appearance in June 1847, Froude was unabashed. Naughtily, he reviewed the book anonymously and favourably in the *Oxford and Cambridge Review*, and in 1848 he was still proposing a second edition extended by further posthumous essays of its central character.[39] What was to issue as *The Nemesis of Faith* was in progress at Oxford at least as early as October 1847, when Mark Pattison recorded that Froude was well advanced upon a novel.[40] By January 1848 this early draft had been abandoned, and Froude was reporting progress on a second longer version. It was provisionally entitled 'Evelyn Herbert', he told Chapman, and would be twice the length of *Shadows*.[41] It rapidly grew in length: according to Clough, writing three weeks later, it was to be a major three-volume effort which had already been accepted for publication by the great John Bentley.[42] By March, however, this also was proving unsatisfactory.

37. Froude to Cowley Powles, 16 February 1846, Dunn, *Froude*, I, 103–4.
38. 'Louisa Varden', *Oxford and Cambridge Review*, 2 (January–June 1846), 349–66. The identification of Froude as the author of this story is made in 'Out of the Depths', *Universal Review*, 2 (1859), 90. Froude never repudiated the attribution.
39. Froude to Chapman, 7 January (1848), Pierpont Morgan Library, New York, Misc. Eng. MSS, MA 4500; *Oxford and Cambridge Review*, 5 (July–December 1847), 256–60. I have made the attribution on the basis of a close correspondence between the defence mounted here and that of Froude's letter to Joseph Richards, 22 July 1847, Exeter College, Oxford, Froude MSS, no. 25. Froude's continuing confidence in the value of *Shadows* is evident in his private correspondence, Froude to William Long, 1 and 30 January 1848, quoted in Dunn, Froude, I, 110–11; 'Preface', *Nemesis*, 2nd edn., iii–xviii: 'I have written a tragedy; I have been supposed to have written a confession of faith', iii.
40. Diary entry for 14 October 1847, printed in Pattison, *Memoirs*, 215.
41. Froude to Chapman, 7 January (1848), Pierpont Morgan Library, New York, Misc. Eng. MSS, MA 4500.
42. Clough to Tom Arnold, 31 January 1848, F. L. Mulhauser, *Correspondence of A. H. Clough*, I, 200.

Froude had flung the text 'into the darkest corner of my room there to lie till I know better'. Having made 'a clean sweep', Froude was now contemplating an historical novel, 'a great oriental romance', based upon the life of Zoroaster and the ZendaVesta.[43] By May, his enthusiasm for this plan had dissolved: 'Innumerable things have begun to crystallize but they have fallen to pieces again for want of a central idea,' he wrote gloomily to Kingsley. But writing to William Long around the same time, he reported that he was already starting work on a completely new plan, a novel to be called 'The Student's Pilgrimage', and had already written one chapter.[44] In early July, however, he sailed for Ireland, to live 'en communiste with an Irish peasant family' in Spartan conditions in a small lodge on the Killarney estate of Lord Kenmare. He had gone alone and without books, determined only 'to listen to my own music' and to write.[45] Working steadily and in almost complete isolation, Froude made rapid progress, and by 8 September he could report happily to Clough, 'I have this morning finished the last lines of the rough copy of my wicked little novel.'[46] Revision was complete by the end of the year, and in January 1849 Froude was at work on printer's proofs. The book was published on 24 February.

Before then, another composition—a short story entitled 'The Swedenborgian', composed before his stay in Ireland—had appeared in the January issue of *Fraser's Magazine*, and Froude had already produced a small body of poetry which though shown to selected friends was to remain unpublished.[47] During much of 1849 Froude was engaged in a strenuous defence of *The Nemesis of Faith* and in the preparation of a second, corrected edition with its defiant explanatory preface. Even then he had not yet done with fiction as a form of exploring and expressing moral choices, and in 1850, returning to the example of Tieck, he was at work on what was to be his final experiment in fiction: the allegorical moral fable. In speaking retrospectively of *The Nemesis of Faith* as 'a cry', Froude was disregarding the fact that the book was not a sudden explosion of emotion but had issued

43. Froude to Kingsley, 19 March 1848, quoted in Dunn, *Froude*, I, 115–16.
44. Froude to Kingsley, 16 May 1848, and to Long, 18 May 1848, quoted in Dunn, *Froude*, I, 117–19.
45. Froude to Clough, 15 July 1848, Bodleian Library, Oxford, Clough Papers 41032 (Eng. Lett. c190), ff.302–4.
46. Froude to Clough, 8 September 1848, Bodleian Library, Oxford, Clough MSS 41032 (Eng. Lett. c190) ff.261–2.
47. *Fraser's Magazine*, 39 (January 1849), 64–78; F. L. Mulhauser, 'An Unpublished Poem by James Anthony Froude', *English Language Notes*, 12 (1974), 26–30.

only after a long period of gestation and exploration, radical experimentation, and sustained self-criticism.

It is in this context of continuous critical and literary experimentation that Froude's engagement with fiction-writing is most appropriately assessed. That it was to end in failure was a fact which almost everyone, including Froude himself, was to acknowledge; and the apparent completeness of this failure has led even the most sympathetic commentators to conclude that it was a mistake, a psychological crisis, 'a purgation of his emotions' after which he was able to commence on his true vocation as an historian.[48] But whatever its hidden psychological motivations, the abundant evidence concerning the complex origins of his literary enterprise demands a more critical approach to Froude's attempt to transform his moral and philosophical preoccupations into artistic practice.

III

In the light of the critical and ethical investigations from which it arose, it would seem more appropriate to address Froude's corpus of fiction not through a sequential examination of each individual piece, but rather by adopting the method which Froude himself had counselled in his essay on Tieck, and to regard the *oeuvre* as a unified enterprise aimed toward a single end. From this perspective it becomes clear that the distinctive characteristic of the entire work is not its emotional or confessional nature, but its audacious and sustained experimentalism. Within this hugely ambitious attempt to translate moral argument into aesthetic experience, four common features in Froude's several fictions may be discerned: their complex narrative strategies: their fascination with issues of time, contingency, and chance; their insistence upon the undependability of his narrators' and his reader's perspectives; and, notoriously, the unattractively weak nature of most of his central characters.

Ultimately, the demands which Froude's persistent and often playful disruptive literary tactics placed upon his readers were to prove too great for their patience (and perhaps for his own creative capacities). Yet that such

---

48. For a summary of conventional critical views on Froude's early fiction, see Robert Lee Wolff, *Gains and Losses: Novels of Faith and Doubt in Victorian England* (New York, 1977), ch. 7.

failures of apprehension and communication were to reinforce the judgement that Froude's fiction was the product of an unmastered and immature confessional impulse was especially unfortunate. In his exploitation of the autobiographical mode, Froude was by no means exceptional among the fiction writers of his day, and by the time he began to write, the purposes to which confessional autobiography had been put in the hands of the master Goethe had been largely grasped by English readers.[49] In fact it is only as one element within the matrix of experimental narrational techniques which he deployed that Froude's deliberate resort to autobiography—perhaps the least original of his techniques—is most properly understood. Regrettably, however (and partly as a result of his technical and imaginative limitations), the uncritical assumption that Froude's use of autobiography was merely a direct reflection of his own naïve and sentimental character has flourished in a manner that has not only overstated the centrality of its role, but has led also to a serious misunderstanding of the complex function it was intended to serve.

The several similarities between the biography of Edward Fowler, the central figure in 'The Spirit's Trials', and that of his creator have already been indicated. Fowler's oppressive father, his ordeal at public school, his mildly dissolute undergraduate life, and his painful experience of first love all appear to be drawn from Froude's own early experiences. But important divergences obtaining between Froude and his fictional projection have also been indicated, and are no less significant. Recovering from his own undergraduate turmoils, Froude, as we have seen, did not retire to the refuge of home, like Fowler. He went instead to Ireland and returned again to Oxford triumphantly to win a university prize and claim his fellowship. As a Fellow of Exeter he was not at all a reclusive scholar. He made friends easily and soon counted a wide range of Oxford's most promising young men among his acquaintances, including Arthur Hugh Clough, Matthew Arnold, Francis Palgrave, George Butler, Richard Cowley Powles, William Long, later mayor of Bath, A. P. Stanley, later Dean of Westminster, W. F. Donkin, later

49. See in particular, Robert Lee Wolff, *Gains and Losses: Novels of Faith and Doubt in Victorian England* (New York, 1977); Kathleen Tillotson, *Novels of the 1840s* (Oxford, 1956), and several of the essays included in George P. Landow (ed.), *Approaches to Victorian Autobiography* (Athens, OH, 1979). For Froude, the attractions of the autobiographical mode would also have been reinforced by his reading of Goethe; Susanne Howe, *Wilheim Meister and his English Kinsmen: Apprentices to Life* (New York, 1930); O. W. Long, 'English and American Imitations of Goethe's *Werter*', *Modern Philology*, 14 (1916) 193–216.

Professor of Astronomy at Oxford, and the distinguished classicist John Conington.[50] Through his active association with the *Oxford and Cambridge Review* he formed what was to be one of the most important friendships of his adult life with Charles Kingsley. Visiting Oxford in 1848, Ralph Waldo Emerson was especially taken with Froude's warmth and charm, and noted his close friendship with Clough and their combined enthusiasm for the establishment of an ambitious transatlantic literary journal.[51] There is evidence also that, quite unlike Fowler, Froude had become experienced and assured in his dealings with women. Perhaps nowhere is his characteristic attitude more plainly revealed than in a letter written at a time when he was supposedly convulsed by the writing of *The Nemesis of Faith*. 'I have been gadding about the country', he told Clough in a letter written from Killarney in September 1848, 'partly in the society of young ladies which I am still forced to confess my weakness for ... Are you a disciple of Proudhon ... who saith that between the sexes can be no society?'[52]

Autobiographical associations between Froude and Markham Sutherland, the central character of *The Nemesis of Faith*, are altogether more tenuous. Again there are some obvious correspondences. Sutherland went to Oxford, fell heavily under the influence of Newman, and suffered the onset of a deeply troubling scepticism concerning the truth-claims of established religion after Newman's defection. But, as is the case with Fowler, it is the differences rather than the similarities between Froude and his creature that are most revealing. Sutherland did not come from a clerical family, was not the victim of an oppressive father and bullying siblings; rather, he enjoyed a quite cosseted existence as a youngest son, indulged by his father and adored by loving sisters. Where Sutherland, after much agonising, goes on for ordination, Froude immediately regretted taking even deacon's orders, and by the time of writing his novel had found a way of abandoning them altogether.[53] Similarly, the crucial entrapment scene in which Sutherland is tricked by a devious group of his parishioners into declaring his doubts about the authority of the Bible has no parallel in Froude's life. It was

50. Dunn, *Froude*, I, 95–7; Clough to Tom Arnold, 31 January 1848, F. L. Mulhauser (ed.), *Correspondence of Arthur Hugh Clough* (2 vols, Oxford, 1957), I, 166; Froude to P [Palgrave?], [1850?], Pierpont Morgan Library, New York, Misc. Eng. MSS, MA 4500.
51. Ralph L. Rusk (ed.), *Letters of Ralph Waldo Emerson* (10 vols., New York, 1939–92), iv, 48, 56, 60, 62.
52. Froude to Clough, 8 September 1848, Bodleian Library, Oxford, Clough MSS 41032 (Eng. Lett. *c*190), ff.261–2.
53. Froude to Rector Richards, 26 October (1847), Exeter College, Oxford, Froude MSS, no. 18.

derived instead from a similar event in the life of Spinoza, with whom, as we have seen, Froude had become particularly engaged. Froude finally did not go into exile in Switzerland, did not, as far as any of the evidence allows, contract an adulterous affair, was not partly responsible for the drowning of a young child, and did not enter a monastery. Rather, these events in the second half of the novel have very clear echoes of another novel by a writer with whom, along with Spinoza, Froude had become intensely interested: Goethe's *Elective Affinities*. Concerning any autobiographical correspondence between himself and his creation, Froude himself, moreover, could hardly have made a more trenchant denial: 'I have been told by my friends', he wrote at the close of the second edition's preface, 'that I ought to notice a report that my story is autobiographical. I have no objection to the world so believing if it please them. But the report is mythic; and, as I can myself judge about it, wholly and entirely false.'[54]

Correspondences between Froude's experiences and those of his characters are not, of course, to be discounted, particularly in the case of Edward Fowler. But his intermittent use of autobiography, and its combination with other altogether different literary and biographical allusions, suggests that far from being explained as some form of psychological crisis, Froude's own attempt at the genre should be seen as but one component of a complex of narrational devices intended, as Goethe had intended his own explorations in the mode, to evoke a particular response from his readers.

The intended significance of such parallels as Froude had chosen to draw between his own life and that of his sickly, reclusive, or morally weak creations was left entirely, but crucially, unstated. It lay in the fact which attentive readers were expected to grasp for themselves: that in presenting the weaknesses and failings of his youth, the author had already succeeded in transcending them. In representing the thoughts and feelings of an individual whom he once was in part—and might have been in whole—Froude had found a vehicle for exploring what he, along with so many others in the 1840s, regarded as the most urgent challenge of their time. This was the problem of how the weakened, frustrated, and bewildered minds of his generation might be enabled to apprehend the vision of God's Creation once so readily attainable by earlier, simpler, and clearer minds.

---

54. *Nemesis*, 2nd edn., xvi; see also Harriet Martineau's report of Froude's objections to attempts to explain the crisis of faith being experienced by his generation on 'a simple psychological basis'; Martineau to W. J. Fox, 18 July 1849, Valerie Sanders (ed.), *Harriet Martineau: Selected Letters* (Oxford, 1990), 118.

But the task of coming to terms critically with the effect of intermittent and partial autobiography was only one of the several challenges which Froude sought to put to his readers. Given the work of self-criticism and self-liberation that he was setting for them, no less than for himself, it was necessary also that their conventional expectations concerning the representation of experience in fiction should likewise be subverted and disappointed. For this he would turn to a variety of literary devices, inspired by his readings of Goethe and Tieck, and of course Carlyle, which included undependable narrators, improbable plots, apparent accidents, and a variety of written forms including letters, journals, and fragmentary jottings. Yet the application of such technical means were always subordinate to the central purpose of his writing which for Froude, as for his mentors, was nothing less than the moral reinspiration of his readers. But unlike most of his models, and even more audaciously than Goethe himself, Froude was determined that the locus of such transformation should reside not on the lofty grounds of philosophical or historical reflection but on the concrete, everyday incidents of social interaction, and on the central, inescapable, but largely unspoken experience of sexual attraction and desire.

IV

Froude's first fictional publication, *Shadows of the Clouds*, is itself a bold experiment with form. Under this common title he has bound together a novel, 'The Spirit's Trials', and a novella or fantasy, 'The Lieutenant's Daughter'. Though it has been largely ignored by those few who have commented on the work, the idea that the two sections were meant to be read in sequence and in relation to each other is clear enough not only from the common epigraphs which introduce the entire work, but also from Froude's own critical comments on reading Tieck—and his invariable practice of referring collectively to the pieces as *Shadows*—and also from important thematic links which will be indicated below. Yet even in regard to the individual components themselves, some interesting experimental forays are at play.

Although plot summaries of 'The Spirit's Trials' have tended to convey the impression that it is a conventional (if rather poor) *Bildungsroman* unfolding the sufferings of the young Edward Fowler and his gradual achievement of independence, it is worth noting that all these events are recounted neither as autobiography nor through the perspective of the all-seeing author.

Instead, Froude employs the device of an intermediate narrator, Arthur, who, as well as telling the tale, is also a character in the story. Detached and unsentimental, Arthur is wry about the Hardinges (the family among whom Fowler finds his ill-fated love)—sentimentalists who mistake softness and irresponsibility for kindness and tolerance. He is equally superior about Edward's father, Canon Fowler, whom he describes as cold, unimaginative, and with the bad habit 'of always over-saying things and particularly over-threatening [sic]'.[55] He reserves his greatest censures, however, for Fowler himself. Weak, self-pitying and deceitful, Edward's fundamental defect, he tells us, 'was that he was constitutionally a coward'; and his failure to address this congenital fault had intensified the sufferings and misfortunes of early life. Armed with this insight and with his own firmly held, liberal pedagogic views—the need to praise the young, to build upon their own talents, to avoid over-whipping, and so on—Arthur then goes on to demonstrate the case through a detailed account of Fowler's 'earlier history'.[56]

The circumstances through which Arthur (and through Arthur, the reader) becomes aware of these formative experiences are themselves ambiguous. He became friendly with Fowler, he tells us, only around the time of his graduation, at a time when 'I knew nothing about his history, nothing but one or two facts which were notorious at the university.'[57] Arthur, then, came to know about Edward's miseries only relatively late and only through Edward himself. The admission which comes almost halfway through the novel is revealing: used as part of a set of clues provided in the text, it helps date Edward's graduation to around 1836–37, some three or four years in advance of Froude's (and contemporary with his own liberating going up to Oxford). More importantly, it casts doubt on Arthur's own authority as narrator. All those sage pronouncements about the Hardinges, Canon Fowler, and Edward are therefore based on one source, Edward himself, supplemented by his own conventional and right-thinking opinions. That Froude wishes to make us conscious of the conditional nature of his narrator's perspective is suggested by a hint placed far earlier, at the beginning of the autobiographical section, when Arthur concedes:

> He told it me himself long after this, but it appears to me that with him (perhaps more or less with everyone) if early life is made the mirror where the

55. *Shadows of the Clouds* (1847 edn.), 2–3, 32.
56. *Shadows of the Clouds*, 38–40.
57. *Shadows of the Clouds*, 76.

after life is shown, the distortion of each will be found to correspond and correct each other; and so, and so only, can a real image of him as he was be
arrived at ...[58]

This concession opens up a serious problem that threatens the entire structure and narrative sequence of the novel, as well as the perspective of its
authorial voice. If Arthur knows about Fowler only through Fowler, and is
aware that the later Fowler is providing him with the only available evidence about the feelings and experiences of the young Fowler, how can we
trust anything in his account at all? But having raised it, Froude evades it:
'But if this be not so, Fowler's history is remarkable, and without a doubt, I
think, deserves some attention for itself.' This is an awkward move, but for
the sake of the story a necessary one; but the ellipsis, the punctuation, and
the hesitant 'I think' are enough to suggest that doubt is lingering nonetheless; and it is left to the readers, on the basis of their own feelings and experience, to make up their minds as to how they are to receive this splintered
narrative.[59]

The significance of this fracture in the narrator's perspective becomes
more obvious in the final segment of the novel which, beginning with a
declaration to the reader that the years between 1840 and early 1846 have
been utterly passed over, comprises about a third of the entire text. Here a
radical change of form occurs. Instead of short chapters of ten to fifteen
pages each, all written by Arthur, through which the previous section of the
book is organised, the last section is taken up by one large chapter of
seventy-seven pages. This in turn is broken up by a series of devices not
hitherto used. For the first time we hear Fowler himself speak, first in a set
of three dated letters to Arthur, next in a sequence of lengthy reported
direct speech, then in a long passage extracted from Fowler's translation of
a piece on dying by the German mystic Jean-Paul Richter, and finally in the
form of two documents retrieved from Fowler's study after his death—one
a letter in explanation of his participation in *The Lives of the English Saints*,
and the other an incomplete account of a nightmare or vision which had so
troubled Fowler.

The effect of all this is to diminish both the presence and authority of the
narrator. Gone is the voice of the shrewd chronicler of human weakness.
Arthur is reduced to recurring banalities concerning the weather, the terrors

58. *Shadows of the Clouds*, 22.
59. *Shadows of the Clouds*, 22.

of consumption, and the complications of his travel arrangements. In responding to thoughts and beliefs expressed in Fowler's correspondence and
conversation, he is equally at a loss. 'His views I could only half-understand',
he comments 'and not at all sympathise in'; and again, 'What Fowler's faith
exactly was I did not know.' But, 'jarring as his entire method of looking at
things was against all I had been taught to think myself . . . what he would say
had a strange fascination'.[60] Toward the close, Arthur makes one desperate
effort to interrogate Fowler concerning the grounds of his faith, using an
attack on Newman as his opening grounds, and is left even more confused
by Fowler's unexpected defence of the renegade. At one point in their discussions Fowler interrupts Arthur's expressions of concern with a remark
that has clear echoes of the concessions made in the first part of the novel:
'Why Arthur, you know no more of me now than I told you.'[61] At the close
the narrator's voice is altogether silenced, as Fowler's 'Remains' are placed
before Froude's readers without a single interpretative comment.

The narrative voice thus plays a more subtle role in 'The Spirit's Trials'
than might be assumed. It works to unsettle the assumption common to
readers of this type of fiction that they are in the company of a sensible all-
knowing narrator who will eventually reveal the significance of his tale in
terms that they will find comprehensible and satisfying. Arthur's viewpoint,
simple and underinformed from the beginning, is soon troubled and
becomes increasingly confused: and so Froude's readers are required to work
for themselves, eventually leaving Arthur in his perplexities, and obliged, if
they are to comprehend Fowler, to follow him along his own chosen path.
By its very loss of authority, the narrator's voice serves ironically to under-
score Fowler's own contribution to the partial transcendence of his early
ordeals which once more attentive readers are expected to grasp.

Undependable narrators are a feature in Froude's other fiction, though
their function is less subtly worked than in 'The Spirit's Trials'. Like Froude,
but unlike either Arthur or Fowler, the narrator of the 'The Lieutenant's
Daughter' had gone to Ireland, contracted fever there, and had an hallucina-
tory experience 'in a kind of imagined magic lantern show' (recalling
Froude's fevered visions of 1845) which becomes the basis of the tale. The
story, then, is the product of a fevered mind, and is therefore subject to all
the ambiguities of meaning which arise therefrom: are we readers to take it

60. *Shadows of the Clouds*, 122, 143–4.
61. *Shadows of the Clouds*, 138.

as a true vision of a reality otherwise hidden from us in the waking world, or merely a personal psychosis? Even then the phantasmagoria is interrupted in part by long sequences of direct speech, and more so by the provision of letters from one of the characters directly to the reader without comment.[62] And to deepen our troubles the narrator has no control over the final shape and outcome of his involuntary tale, but is himself supplied by the informing genii of his dream with two utterly opposed endings between which he leaves the reader to choose.[63]

The nature of the narrator's undependability in Froude's next fictional exercise, 'The Swedenborgian', is far simpler. Related in the first-person singular, the teller of this short story is a romantic young man in love with the *fiancée* of an older man, the Swedenborgian of the title, and who conducts a secret and irresponsible pursuit only to realise at the close that the wiser old man was aware of his quest from the outset, and, once convinced of its sincerity, was willing not only to withdraw but to support his rival's suit. Here the theme is again the induction of a well-intentioned but limited mind into the workings of the true world—this time by the happy means of a deeper and wiser one. The lightness and brevity of the story is hardly sufficient to support the theme. But in Froude's most ambitious and most worked-over effort, *The Nemesis of Faith*, structural complexity and narrative instability recur, again through the introduction of an intermediating voice named Arthur.

The nomination of Arthur is surely no accident. There is probably an element of playfulness here: Arthur may be an allusion to his close friend and literary confidant Clough, for Clough had partly modelled the character of Arthur in his own *Bothie of Tober-na-Vuolich* (which he completed while Froude was writing *The Nemesis of Faith*) on Froude. But it is also a defiant assertion on Froude's part of his continuing confidence in the value of the narrative character and technique employed in *Shadows*. The Arthur who appears in *The Nemesis of Faith*, however, as the passive recipient of Sutherland's thoughts and reports, resembles more the perplexed figure of the closing section of 'The Spirit's Trials' than the confident, opinionated character readers meet at its beginning. The novel opens with a set of ten letters, which, running for about a third of its length, are addressed to Arthur and received by him without comment. These cover the unfolding of the

62. *Shadows of the Clouds*, 256–62.
63. *Shadows of the Clouds*, 282–7.

plot from Sutherland's unwilling entry into the priesthood, the exposure of his heterodox views, the kindness of the bishop, and his final decision to resign his curacy. A short six-page commentary by Arthur then follows which serves to introduce a large selection of Sutherland's thoughts (apparently extracted out of further undated letters to Arthur). Then Arthur introduces Sutherland's 'Confessions of a Sceptic'—a fragmentary testament found after his death—which takes up the middle section of the novel. Only in the last third of the book does the narrator appear in strength. Here Arthur, the omniscient, recounts the story of the origins and course of Sutherland's fateful liaison with beautiful but married Helen Leonard. Without revealing the source of his information, he reports events in detail, records exact dialogue, and intersperses his right-thinking judgements throughout the text without hesitation. 'Fools, and blind!' he exclaims early in his account of the lovers' self-delusions, and, in contrast to his disappearance in the earlier novel, is present at the close, austerely to clinch the moral of the sorry life of the now deceased Sutherland: 'and no living being was left behind him on earth, who would not mourn over the day which brought life to Markham Sutherland'.[64]

The structural and narrational reversal that has taken place between 'The Spirit's Trials' and *The Nemesis of Faith* is curious. It is possible that it represents a concession on Froude's part to his readers who misunderstood the intent of the former text. But Froude's insistence on continuity of technique through the maintenance of the narrator is an indication that any such concession was highly qualified. In addition, however, to the demands imposed by Froude's unstable narrational strategies, compositional continuity between the two fictions is reinforced by a second feature which, in addition to undependable narrators, is a striking characteristic of Froude's fiction. This is the chronic improbability of his emplotments.

In this regard, 'The Spirit's Trials' is once again typical. The improbalities which riddle the story begin early on when Edward's love for Emma Hardinge is first crossed by the rumour that insanity ran in her family. It happened 'unluckily' that Edward's elder brother had recently been married into such a family, and the good canon was disturbed by the coincidence.[65] More serious mishaps follow. Persuaded that the rumour was without foundation, the canon relents and writes to Edward grudgingly, giving him

64. *The Nemesis of Faith* (2nd edn., 1849), 179, 277.
65. *Shadows of the Clouds*, 20.

permission to marry. Fowler hastens over the moorlands with the letter to announce the joyous news to the Hardinges, but on arrival he discovers to his horror that inexplicably somewhere on his journey he had lost the letter: 'it was gone ... somewhere it was gone and not to be found again.'[66] The loss is not immediately disastrous. The Hardinges take his word. But its gravity becomes clear only in the light of another terrible accident concerning a letter which takes place later in the same year. It happened that Edward, like so many Oxford undergraduates, had fallen into debt in his first years at university. Fearing the canon's wrath, he had sought to conceal it from him by seeking a loan from a fellow student who was willing to help him. The answer to his request was to be sent to Edward during the Christmas vacation at Darling. But: 'Accident detained him a day later than he had expected. His friend's letter arrived before he had arrived to receive it ... Mistake brought it to the canon and it was opened.'[67] This was truly catastrophic. Having brooded on the matter, the canon decides to inform the Hardinges of Edward's improvidence and deceit. Mr Hardinge is horrified, and, concluding that Edward's earlier lost letter was also a part of his contrivance, directs Emma to break off the engagement. Other accidents ensue. Emma, in her disappointment, is distracted by the attentions of a young clergyman, Henry Allen. She appears to consent to marry him, but is then persuaded by her father to accept the suit of another clergyman, the Rev. Mr Barnard. Then, finding that she cannot go through with it, and confessing tearfully to her father on the eve of the wedding, Hardinge relents and agrees that on the morrow Barnard is to be told of her decision by means, as it happens, of another letter. Barnard takes the turn of events surprisingly well:

> He retires; his trial is over; he has been tempted out from his quiet haven upon a sea where vessels of his build commonly find a worse fate than his. Let him go home then once more, and thank God upon his knees that foul weather was not sent too late to escape.[68]

And Emma duly marries Allen.

This improbable little sub-plot is an apparent distraction; but the novel's greatest improbability is saved for the end. Diagnosed with terminal consumption, Fowler has withdrawn to Torquay to contemplate life and peacefully to await death. The serenity of his final days, however, is interrupted by

---

66. *Shadows of the Clouds*, 55.
67. *Shadows of the Clouds*, 64.
68. *Shadows of the Clouds*, 108.

an astonishing coincidence. One day, while walking on the pier, Fowler sees a little boy who has just fallen into the water. On impulse he dives in to save him, and having done so, fatally ruins his own delicate health. But next day, while descending into his final illness, he is visited by the grateful parents, who turn out to be none other than the Rev. Mr and Mrs Henry Allen. On such a slender thread does the final sequence of the novel, including Fowler's reconciliation with Emma and his peaceful demise, depend. There is little reason to wonder why readers have found the story so unsatisfactory.

Froude, however, remained unperturbed by an absence of verisimilitude. Almost by definition the melodramatic plot of 'The Lieutenant's Daughter', which is little more than a sequence of unhappy chances that led Catherine Grey, the unhappy woman of the title, from the peace and tranquillity to disgrace, destitution, and death, is utterly improbable. If her mother had not died at her birth, if her father's savings had not been lost in an insurance company's failure, if he had not died from the shock, if she had not gone to the Carpenters and met the cad Henry there, if she had not encountered the Miss Arthurs and been degraded by them—such are the unnecessary contingencies, the 'five links hung upon a chain', writes Froude pointedly, which collectively determined Catherine's fate. Remove any one of them, as he finally does, and the result would have been different.[69]

Of itself, this seems banal; and combined with the other improbabilities that characterise Froude's fiction as a whole it might be seen as evidence of a chronic inventive incompetence. But in the light of the philosophical and critical studies which accompanied his turn to fiction, this emphasis upon radical contingency can be understood more credibly as a Spinoza-informed understanding of the imperfect grasp which the finite mind necessarily holds over the infinite reality of which it forms only a tiny part. From this perspective, accident, coincidence, contingency, and improbability are more than cognitive concepts shaped by our intellect to take account of and contain the flux of experience. They are symptoms of that intellect's chronic incapacity to apprehend its own true nature and the nature of the universe which surrounds it.

For those willing to follow him, moreover, Froude supplied abundant indications of this ontological and theological standpoint on several occasions throughout his fictions. But the opening of 'The Lieutenant's Daughter' provides the clearest statement of this philosophical position. The

69. *Shadows of the Clouds*, 286.

narrator—and here the 'I' is closest to Froude himself—is 'haunted' by a definition of time loosely attributed to Hooker as 'the measure of the motion of the heavens'. If that be the case, he ponders, then 'if from the interposition of some unknown cause' the speed of the planets' motion were to accelerate or slow down or stop, time itself must follow. He reminds himself, however, that this is merely a matter of our epistemological limitations, not reality: 'We measure time, and indeed all things, not according to the real order of nature as it is in itself, for of that we know nothing, but according to the order in which they present themselves to our senses.' This does not quite suffice, for, Froude proceeds, if it were possible to arrange matters in the world so that 'the visible system should only *seem* to reverse its movement', would not the sensation of reversal be presented to us as a fact? Then, in what might be seen to be something of an Einsteinian anticipation, Froude posits the idea of a railway carriage running along the equinoctial line in the same direction as the earth's motion, but at double the velocity. Would not its passengers undergo the experience of a reversal of time?

> From today we should pass into yesterday, from yesterday into the day before; month before month and year before year, the earth would uncoil its life and with it the lives of all her children with all their doings, fates, and fortunes.[70]

In strict philosophical terms, Froude claims, 'there is nothing *a priori* impossible or even improbable' in such a reversal or of bringing it about in the artificial manner he proposed. But our perplexity in face of this logic is the symptom of our failure to grasp and hold on to the sense of our place in the universe which has been given to us by revelation, by art, by the natural phenomena of nature itself:

> Eternities lie on each side of life, and we are equally ignorant of both. Forward and backward are but modes in which we express our relation to ourselves and things, and there is nothing more unlikely in such a change in fact taking place, or more unnatural in the character of it, than in the tide of a great river turning to ebb again when we have seen it for half a day flowing continuously the other way.[71]

This philosophical foundation having been so clearly stated, Froude then goes on in the story itself to conduct a series of elaborate experiments with splintered vision and temporal dislocation. It begins in the near present with

---

70. *Shadows of the Clouds*, 193–6; the quotation is from 195.
71. *Shadows of the Clouds*, 195.

the narrator's report of his trip to Ireland. Now it moves in a dream sequence only slightly backwards from the death of the disgraced and diseased Catherine Grey on her father's grave. Next it shifts forward to a local newspaper office where commenting on the discovery of the body reporters provide some brief account of Catherine's departure from the region under some scandal about an unsolemnised marriage. The narrative then moves back from this report to a real-time account of Catherine's arrival in London, her abandonment by her supposed husband, and her fall into prostitution at the hands of a pair of madams—the significantly named Miss Arthurs. Another reversal is then enacted by means of extracts from Henry Carpenter's letters which give an account of Catherine's arrival at his aunt's house and his determination to seduce her. It moves still further back as the genii of the narrator's vision tells him the story of the lieutenant's sad life and ruin which caused Catherine to move to the Carpenters in the first place, and finally back further again to an account of how the Carpenters themselves arrived in the area. The entire performance is then completed by the vision's provision of two radically alternative endings—the first as written, the second where, none of these accidents having occurred, Catherine had lived happily ever after. Though it had been employed on occasion in other tales of romance, it can be seen that behind Froude's use of the device of alternative endings there lay more than a fashionable imitation: it was an ultimate demonstration of the experience which he was so anxious to awaken in his readers.[72]

Though they are more disguised elsewhere in his fiction, the same philosophical intent underlying his plots can also be discerned. 'Poor Time!', says Arthur in 'The Spirit's Trials' in a momentary flash of insight, 'the thin abstraction! The fault, if fault it be, lies in ourselves.'[73] But the conditional clause is an indication of Arthur's unwillingness to follow his insight through. The point is made more sharply later on in the novel when, close to death, Edward asks an uncomprehending Arthur to read from his translation of Jean Paul:

72. Phyllis Grosskurth—one of the few critics to have considered 'The Lieutenant's Daughter'—has noted the curious correspondence between the story and the double endings of John Fowles' pseudo-Victorian novel, *The French Lieutenant's Woman*; Fowles denied any influence; Grosskurth, 'The French Lieutenant's Woman', *Victorian Studies*, 16 (September 1972), 130–1. It may be noted further that *Wuthering Heights*—a novel which deployed shifting time sequences and narrative perspectives with far greater dexterity but hardly more popularity—appeared in the same year as *Shadows of the Clouds*.

73. *Shadows of the Clouds*, 60.

> In the hour of darkness rejoice ... that thy life has its dwelling in the great life
> of the Infinite. The earth-dust of the globe is inspired by the breath of the
> great God ... The sea of time glistens like the sea of waters with unnumbered
> beings of light; and death and resurrection are but the flaming valleys and
> flaming mountains of the ever rolling ocean.[74]

Arthur reads, but remains perplexed.

The theme of the human mind's difficulty in grasping and holding on to
a sense of the infinite spirit and its purposes is also central to *The Nemesis of
Faith*, where once more it is ironically introduced through the common-
sense platitudes of Arthur.

> All nature [he assures us] is harmonious, and must and shall be in harmony
> forever ... The wretched only feel their wretchedness: in the universe all is
> beautiful ... Pain and pleasure are but forms of consciousness; we feel them for
> ourselves and for those who are like ourselves. To man alone the doings of
> man are wrong, the evil which is with us dies out beyond us.[75]

All of this is asserted, however, late in the novel, after the tragedy of Helen's
daughter's death and Sutherland's realisation of the recklessness of their
affair. In the midst of all the misery, guilt, and suffering that surrounds him,
even Arthur sees that it is a poor consolation: 'Poor consolers are such
thoughts, for they are but thoughts, and alas! Our pain we feel.' Still, reflecting that they are good enough for him—'Me they console as I think over
in this farce tragedy of a world'—if not for the anguished Markham and
Helen, he presses on with his story.[76]

This pointed satire on Arthur's metaphysical complacency is underlined
by a contrast with Sutherland's response to an earlier experience about
which he sought to trouble Arthur. Walking through the woods one day he
had become entranced by the ruins of an ancient Christian site and imagined that the ruin itself had spoken to him. Denying its own attributed
authority, the ruin lectures him on the evanescence of all human perceptions of truth, the once great potency of paganism, the inevitable decline of
Christianity, and the relativity of all belief-systems, and it concludes with an
ominously prophetic warning:

> Once, once for all, if you would save your heart from breaking, you must learn
> this lesson ... you must cease in this world to believe in the eternity of any

---

74. *Shadows of the Clouds*, 172.
75. *The Nemesis of Faith*, 196.
76. *The Nemesis of Faith*, 196–7.

creed or any form at all. Whatever grows in time is a child of time, and is born and lives and dies at its appointed day like ourselves ... Life is change, to cease to change is to cease to live.[77]

But having been granted this revelation, Sutherland, like most humans, is unable to stay with it on his own, and turns for consolation: 'This is what the old ruin said to me Arthur. Arthur, did the ruin speak true?' Reassured by Arthur that it does not, he makes the fateful decision to take holy orders.[78]

V

It is against the background of these narrative techniques—his employment of unstable narrators, elaborate time-shifts and improbable plots, and recurring reflections on the inadequacy of human cognition, all of which have been deployed to put readers on their mettle—that one further characteristic feature of Froude's fiction, which has commonly been seen as its most salient shortcoming, requires reconsideration. This is the unattractive, defective, and imperfectly realised nature of the characters he conceived as the central figures in his novels. The failings commonly (and understandably) attributed to Froude's central characters, to Edward Fowler and Markham Sutherland in particular, are several. They are weak, both morally and mentally (and in Fowler's case physically). They are self-absorbed and impossibly speculative and intellectual. Afflicted by an overwhelming sense of his own deficiencies, Fowler is unable to overcome a setback in love, indulges deeply in self-pity and self-harm, and withdraws from the world to cultivate his thoughts and feelings without fear of challenge. When that challenge does come, in the guise of the return of the loving Emma, he rejects the opportunity to fight back, and surrenders himself to death.

Sutherland is even less attractive. When he is first presented to us at the very opening of *The Nemesis of Faith*, he is already in the grip of *accidie*—the terrible psychological malaise that inhibits all action because it denies all hope. A kind of English Oblomov (who coincidentally made his first appearance in the same year), Sutherland has been overcome by a heavy torpor which prevents him from discharging even the most modest of social

77. *The Nemesis of Faith*, 33–4
78. *The Nemesis of Faith*, 34.

obligations, even answering the anxious letters of his friends. He feels spiritually and intellectually empty. 'Oh! how I wish I could write,' he exclaims, marking an ironic contrast with his creator, Froude, who is, after all, writing him; but he cannot express himself with sufficient clarity to be an author. 'I can do nothing', he despairs, 'but write to you, dear Arthur.'[79] He is not entirely bereft. Naturally intelligent and sensitive to the force of the theological and social criticisms fashionable in his day, he has become deeply repelled by the moral hypocrisies and social pretensions of the Established Church. He is abreast also with the most radical German thought, and capable, albeit nervously, of playing with it. But his chronic self-doubt has fundamentally disabled him, leading him to wish that all in all it would have been better had he never been born. Out of this, all his troubles (and the troubles he visits on others) follow. His taking of holy orders was not an act of will, but of weakness. His exposure as a doubter is also an accident that he allows to befall him. The affair into which he drifts is also an event over which he exerts little control—a combination of Helen's need for love, favourable occasion, and his own lack of will-power; and its ending is a result of his unwillingness to see matters through by elopement. He cannot follow Helen to a monastery, cannot follow the Newman-like tutor, Frederick Mornington, to Rome. He fails even to commit suicide.

Far from being a symptom of his imaginative limitations, however, the unattractiveness of Froude's main characters which so many of his readers found distasteful is entirely deliberate. 'The author intended to paint Edward Fowler as a natural but quite repulsive character,' Froude told the Rector of Exeter (though without acknowledging responsibility for authorship);[80] and in an anonymous review for the *Oxford and Cambridge Review* he went further:

> Fowler … was never a person with whom we feel inclined to, or were intended to sympathise. Weak and timid at the outset, then shuffling and dishonest, afterwards idle and extravagant, even in the period of his reform hard and self-defended, to the end cold and heartless—how can anyone sympathise with him or assume he was the author's ideal man?[81]

Froude might have expected the deliberately ambiguous nature of his novel's title (trials for or trials set by the spirit?) to alert readers to the obvious *double*

---

79. *The Nemesis of Faith*, 43, 29.
80. Froude to Rector Richards, 22 July (1847), Exeter College, Oxford, Froude MSS, no. 22.
81. *Oxford and Cambridge Review*, 5 (January–June 1847).

entendre of its principal character's name. In its nineteenth-century usage, 'fowler' connoted both a hunter of game and one who spoils or pollutes a chosen path or purpose. Readers might have been expected to derive from this a hint as to the spoiled nature of his character's quest. Clearly they did not. But in Markham Sutherland (and again perhaps there are hints in the name), he attempted to draw a character whose inability to rise to the challenges of life was more abundantly clear.

> The hero is evidently from the introduction a weak if amiable man' [Froude told his long suffering rector, this time wholly admitting authorship], and I wished to paint such a man struggling in the element of scepticism which [is] ... the element in which all young men have moved ... That [Sutherland's] end was disastrous no one will deny, and that it was so because he hesitated between two opinions and [joined] himself heartily to neither, and destroyed his mind then in stuffing it with intellectual difficulties of which the church offered him no resolution.[82]

This intense concern with intellectual and speculative confusion helps illuminate what Froude saw as the urgent contemporary relevance of his characters, but it does not entirely explain why, in contrast, say, to George Eliot, who was exploring similar perplexities, Froude chose to make his characters irredeemably flawed. It was not due to some deep misanthropy; for Froude believed that human natures came in all ranges, good and bad. It arose rather from his perception that whatever their natural capacities, the attitudes and actions of human beings were deeply influenced by the environment in which they were plunged from birth. In this way, nurture as much as nature formed a crucial force through which character was shaped in the world. This was a subtle and understated theme. But some clue to Froude's understanding of this interaction is offered in one of the longest chapters of 'The Spirit's Trials' in which Arthur expounds his views on education.[83]

Arthur's pedagogy is reassuringly liberal, and the fact that it is based upon an account of Fowler's (and Froude's) childhood ordeals has given rise to the understandable conclusion that it is indeed Froude's own. He deplores such cruelty and austerity as prevailed in the Fowler household, but he is equally superior about the opposite practices of the Hardinges, who brought up their children without any attempt at discipline or restraint: 'You never heard a "You shall not" or a "You must not" ... To be sure they

---

82. Froude to Rector Richards, 10 April (1849), Exeter College, Oxford, Froude MSS, no. 46.
83. 'The Spirit's Trials', ch. 2.

were let to do almost anything they pleased that was not wrong.' Against these extremes, Arthur presents his own moderate view. 'With the very large class of boys of a yielding nature', says Arthur without further definition, generous and trusting tutelage will succeed in 'creating and fostering generous impulses' and in keeping 'in check the baser ones'.[84] This seems sensible, in keeping with the more liberal opinions of the time. But gradually a whiff of irony begins to arise from Arthur's *bien pensant* opinions. He apologises for any implied criticism of Fowler's upbringing. 'Whipping is good', he allows:

> God forbid too I should think of blaming Canon Fowler! He was a busy practical man of the world, far too much employed in being of active service to it to be able to spare time in attending minutely to peculiarities in the disposition of his children.[85]

So whatever the general theory, exceptions may be allowed at the discretion of parents. The irony here is Froude's, not Arthur's. Despite their superficial differences, what each of these approaches (including Arthur's sensible middle way) share is a common dependence upon assumptions and prejudices which are merely reflective of the cultural norms dominant at one time or another. As such, they derive from a concept of the human mind and its potential which is necessarily relative and ephemeral. Against these transient notions, Froude then presents Fowler's considerably more profound views of childhood development:

> I cannot believe we are any more answerable for the mistakes of our early life than a young student of painting for his bungling first attempts ... We are started only with faculites and materials, we have to become acquainted with the nature of both, and equally [both] require time and practice to get skill in their use. Certainly what we know of man in fact, proves, if induction can prove anything, that the experimental skill of another is as little transferable in morals as in art.[86]

Fowler's pedagogy is a strongly constructivist one. He accepts that people as they appear are a mixture of good and bad. But he denies the possibility that the human soul, having been created by God, can be fundamentally evil. The fact that the mixture soon appears and evil tendencies take shape must

---

84. *Shadows of the Clouds*, 11, 23
85. *Shadows of the Clouds*, 36–7.
86. *Shadows of the Clouds*, 115–16.

therefore be considered not as an alternative process, but as the symptoms 'of bewildered seekings after what is considered good.'[87]

Here then is the dilemma. Given the nature of Creation and of humanity's special place within it, the primary task of each individual must be to strive toward the discovery of what is truly good over what merely appears to be so. But the finite human mind is a most imperfect instrument for attaining what it most desires. So what is to be done? Precepts, principles, and traditions have their place, but they are inevitably insufficient:

> But at present there are many mistakes which science has failed to understand, and one is obliged to make them to know they are mistaken; one must fall to know what it is to stand ... to be obliged so many times to be taught, and taught the same thing over and over; each time forgetting the meaning of the word, and having to look it out again in the dictionary of suffering.[88]

The individual, that is, must experiment, must undergo trial, and as Fowler came eventually to realise, must actively rebuild his own moral character. 'I have had all my work to do with myself so late', he tells Arthur, 'built downwards too, the foundations last and hardly finished.'[89] But it is a task which no one else could have done for him, and which he could have no more learnt from simply following good instructions than an artist can produce art merely by following the directions of a master. It is an experience every soul, including Froude's readers, must undergo alone.

This, of course, is precisely what Markham Sutherland failed to do. Though deeply conscious of his own congenital defects, he allows himself to be overwhelmed by them. 'I am not strong enough', he confesses, 'without the support of system and position to work my way', and he recognises 'with what absurd childishness one goes on asking people for advice knowing all the while that only *one's self* can judge, and yet shrinking from the responsibility.'[90] The fragmentary records of his repeated attempts to confront his deficiencies provide abundant evidence of his failure of nerve. By turns reflective and sentimental, abstract and autobiographical, Sutherland's ponderings, which take up almost half the length of the novel, have frequently been isolated by commentators from the course of the novel itself, and read as expressions of Froude's own opinions during a time of personal

---

87. *Shadows of the Clouds*, 118.
88. *Shadows of the Clouds*, 117.
89. *Shadows of the Clouds*, 115.
90. *The Nemesis of Faith*, 19.

crisis. But, as was the case in his earlier fictions, closer attention to his text will reveal that Froude's intentions were altogether more complex and ironical.[91]

The most obvious difference between Sutherland's intellectual condition and that of his creator is that his reflections, in contrast to Froude's several combative and varied exercises in criticism and fiction, were inchoate, fragmentary, and private. The eight short pieces which precede the 'Confessions of a Sceptic' do not offer a coherent argument, but are merely a series of signposts to Sutherland's growing doubt. They are all couched in the negative, all incomplete, and even the most sustained exercise in analysis among them ends in irresolution. Beginning with a rather mild curiosity concerning the taboo on critical thinking in regard to theological matters which he perceives to be pervasive in the Established Church, Sutherland gradually probes a little deeper. Contemporary argument concerning the findings of science among scientists themselves makes him doubt the status of scientific argument as a guide to truth and, by implication, the authority of such arguments made on behalf of religion by proponents of natural theology such as Paley. From this he moves to doubt the claims of any formal religion to a monopoly on truth, regarding the Christian, Muslim, Jewish, or Hindu faiths merely as partial and historically relative expressions of mankind's spiritual yearnings. From this relativist position he begins to doubt the validity of the concept of sin. In this, the longest and most crucial segment, Sutherland's mind seems to be at its most incisive. He summarises his argument thus:

> While we find such endless differences between the actions of different men under the same temptations, or of the same men at different times, we shall yet be unable to find any link of the chain undetermined by the action of the outward circumstance on the inner law; or any point where we can say a power lay in the individual will of choosing either of two courses—in other words to discover sin. Actions are governed by motives. The power of motives depends on character, and character on the original faculties and the training which they have received from the *men or things* among which they have been bred. Sin, therefore, as commonly understood, is a chimera.[92]

This being the case, the Christian doctrine of atonement was not only a mistake but an appalling perversion, forcing upon ordinary individuals, who

---

91. These sections occupy pp. 77–163 of the 1849 second edition, and the 'Confessions' occupies pp. 99–163.
92. *The Nemesis of Faith*, 92.

cannot be other than they are or act other than they do, responsibility for the actions of other earlier individuals who were equally incapable of rising above their circumstances. All of this has been required merely to satisfy the wrath of a vengeful God; but for Sutherland the horror of this realisation is tempered by a convenient historical relativism. Following Feuerbach, he asserts that mankind's concept of sin is a reflection of the state of its cultural advance, from primitive fears to the metaphysical philosophers' proof that no force antagonistic to God could exist, and concludes happily: 'The spectre which haunted the conscience is gone. Our failures are errors, not crimes … and as little violations of his [God's] law as the artist's early blunders or ultimate and entire failures.'[93]

Taken out of context, this may seem like another rebellious manifesto of the late 1840s. But readers of the entire novel who have followed the course of Sutherland's career—observing his indolence, his *ennui*, his irresponsibility and the disastrous consequences which his real actions in the world have exerted on those around him—will be struck by the irony of such new-found confidence. Suspicions of this kind are given immediate confirmation by the 'Confessions of a Sceptic', which, though by far the longest of these reflections, remains, like everything in Sutherland's life, a fragment broken off in middle course.

A partial autobiography within a partial biography, this section is further evidence of Froude's persistent interest in exploring multiple and shifting narrative techniques. Like the novel itself, the confession opens with a grand statement of Sutherland's sense of *accidie*. Life for him 'is a kind of Egyptian bondage' where 'we cry for something we cannot find' and where 'we cannot satisfy ourselves with what we do find'.[94] But immediately the narrative turns to an intensely nostalgic recall of the halcyon days of Sutherland's childhood (which in its sweetness and light, incidentally, contrasts so markedly with Froude's upbringing, and echoes that of Tieck's Christian). In this idyllic setting, Markham believes, the true foundations of religious faith lie 'in this early unreasoning reverence … not in authenticities, and evidences and miracles', and Sutherland himself acquired 'the intensest reverence' for 'the mystery of Christianity'.[95] But steadily this idyll was dissolved—first by the interruption of religious controversy into the peaceful household, next by his realisation of

93. *The Nemesis of Faith*, 96.
94. *The Nemesis of Faith*, 99.
95. *The Nemesis of Faith*, 117.

the extent of adult hypocrisy in regard to religion, and then, irrevocably, by his encounter, while an undergraduate at Oxford, with Newman.

Newman, indeed, is the most destructive influence on Sutherland—a nemesis of faith in himself. It was Newman who had deepened the doubts of the younger generation in the authority of the Church of England—first by conceding the force of rationalist critics, next by offering the most pre-posterous arguments in favour of faith over reason (Sutherland cited Newman's sermon on religious doctrine as the most extreme example),[96] and finally by abandoning everyone and going over to Rome. Sutherland did not follow Newman to Rome. But his resistance was not purposeful; it was a consequence merely of his chronic inability to commit. And so, disil-lusioned with all received opinion, attracted to no alternative, and incapable of finding a commitment equal to the cosy, emotional securities of child-hood, he relapsed into a passive scepticism, childlike in origin but capable of generating all kinds of suffering and loss as its consequence.

In several respects, then, Sutherland might be seen as an antithesis to Froude's earlier creation, Fowler. Whereas Sutherland is paralysed by his doubts, Fowler acts: he refuses holy orders, withdraws from Oxford, and devotes himself to the strenuous task of reconstructing his character and his personal belief in Creation. The contrast between the two figures is most clearly revealed in their attitude toward Newman. Though flattered (like Froude) to have been invited by Newman to contribute to the 'Lives of the Saints', Fowler was never an unquestioning acolyte: 'it was impossible I could really feel toward them as he did.'[97] Through his own quest for meaning he was made immune from the specious arguments offered by Newman, and confirming his reservations, Newman's defection merely had the effect of confirming in him a determination to find his own way. The idea, however, that in *The Nemesis of Faith* Froude was simply revisiting the theme of 'The Spirit's Trials' from the opposite direction—scepticism embraced leading to perdition where scepticism overcome had led to salva-tion—is rather too simple; for in both cases Froude was at pains to demon-strate that his characters were profoundly defective.

While Fowler may have been Sutherland's superior in his attempts to overcome his weakness and rebuild his life, his reformation was based largely on his absolute withdrawal from society and a rigorous control of his

---

96. *The Nemesis of Faith*, 157–8.
97. *Shadows of the Clouds*, 184.

circumstances designed to minimise his exposure to life's accidents. But accidents occurred—most fatefully in the form of Emma's son's near-drowning. Although Fowler's instincts were powerful enough to enable him to act courageously, he remained unable to address the unexpected consequence of his action in his renewed connection with the love of his life. But Sutherland, while he is far from being socially phobic, is even more than Fowler an incomplete man. Unable to confront the challenges set by his own deficiencies and the demands of his time, he has relapsed into an insipid relativism, his apparent charm disguising the true danger which he posed to all who sought to be close to him.

In both cases the defects of these incomplete men did not primarily concern matters of religion or philosophy; for Fowler had largely resolved his doubts, while Sutherland had simply abandoned them. Instead, they bore directly on those universal, inescapable, but largely unspoken occasions of social intercourse which one, by his deliberate stance of refusal and omission, and the other, by his careless acts of selfish commission, threatened to convert into experiences of pain and loss for any who touched them, and most particularly for those who loved them.

VI

It is by no means surprising that Froude should have been drawn toward an exploration of the ethics of love and sexual attraction. In this he was hardly alone: having for long been demystified by classicism and rationalism, the metaphysical and mystical qualities of the medieval idea of love had been revived and transformed by Rousseau and the early German Romantics with whom Froude was already familiar.[98] To many of Froude's friends and contemporaries at Oxford in the 1840s, Clough and Arnold among them, questions concerning the ethics of sexual conduct were becoming increasingly pressing,[99] and Goethe, whose treatment of love and desire both in *Faust* and in *Die Wahlverwandtschaften* (*Elective Affinities*) had combined a frankness of statement and a seriousness of purpose, was once more an

---

98. Two classic works are still of relevance: C. S. Lewis, *The Allegory of Love* (Oxford, 1936), and Denis de Rougemont, *Love in the Western World* (2nd edn., New York, 1956).

99. On Clough in particular, see Rupert Christiansen, *The Voice of Victorian Sex: Arthur H. Clough, 1819–61* (London, 2001), and Anthony Kenny, *Arthur Hugh Clough: A Poet's Life* (London, 2005), esp. 82–3, 117–29; also Park Honan, *Mathew Arnold: A Life* (London, 1981), esp. 151–67.

inspiration. There were, however, additional reasons why Froude should have become particularly engaged with the problem. The reality of sexual attraction presented in an especially acute fashion the ethical questions concerning the relationship of natural instincts—were they strengths or defects?—to acquired characteristics—were they necessary or hypocritical?—with which he had been grappling from youth. But it was no less pertinent to the metaphysical problems regarding unexpected contingencies and unpredictable consequences with which he had also been preoccupied. Froude's personal experience of sexual abuse at Westminster, moreover, and his evident awareness of the prevalence of prostitution in Victorian Oxford, cannot be discounted in explaining the strength of his determination to place sexual conduct at the centre of his practical ethics. Yet notwithstanding the potency of its appeal as a subject for ethical consideration, it was also one fraught with risk, hazarding scandal, and outrage; and his decision to place it close to the centre of all his fictions, most overtly in *The Nemesis of Faith*, combined with all the other technical, critical, and philosophical demands he had chosen to make on his readers, was to prove disastrous to his reputation as a novelist and to the purposes he had intended.

Ironically, in view of the scandal it provoked, Froude's address to the problem of sexual conduct is at its simplest in *The Nemesis of Faith*. Paying homage to (or seeking protection from) Goethe in its borrowings of plot from *Elective Affinities*, the final section of *The Nemesis of Faith* recounts a disastrous series of events in which Sutherland, seeking solace on the shores of Lake Como (the setting of Goethe's novel), falls in love with the married but unloved Helen Leonard.[100] Their preoccupation with each other leads to the neglect of Helen's daughter, Annie, who dies from exposure after nearly drowning. Suffused with guilt, Sutherland attempts suicide, from which he is prevented by the appearance of his old Oxford tutor, the Newman-like Frederick Mornington, and is then persuaded to convert to Catholicism and enter a monastery. Failing once more to overcome his doubts, he leaves, and filled with self-pity and self-loathing, dies for want of a will to live.

A suitable end for an adulterer, no doubt. But what gave most offence in this section was Froude's far more sympathetic treatment of Helen. It is Helen who, while nursing Sutherland's mild illness, initiates the love affair, and who, when Sutherland becomes troubled by its development, is con-

---

100. Froude might also have hoped that his readers would catch the allusion in this character's name to two of the central figures of *Faust Part II*.

vinced that in responding to the demands of love she was doing no wrong. She wants to reveal the affair to her husband and beg for release:

> I will throw myself at his feet and ask his forgiveness, not for loving you, but for ever having been his. That was my sin: to promise what I knew not, and what I could not fulfil.[101]

Her daughter's death is regarded by her as punishment 'for my sin in marrying her father'. When Sutherland rejects her—'I never really loved you; a heart like mine was too selfish to love anything but itself'—Helen will not betray her trust. She enters a convent, but 'lived and died unreconciled with the Church', refusing to admit that 'she had sinned in her love for Markham Sutherland' and declaring with her dying breath 'that her sin had been in her marriage, not in her love'.[102]

This is heady; and Froude's frank identification of Helen's love with sexual passion did little to reassure his prudish readers' sensibilities. But even as he seems concerned with a chivalric defence of Helen's purity of motive, Froude is equally concerned with exploring Sutherland's moral irresponsibility which in all ways contrasts with Helen's maturity. At the beginning of the affair Sutherland wants Helen to run away with him and abandon Annie. Helen refuses. When Annie discovers them, Sutherland again wishes to flee: Helen determines to leave Leonard. While Helen remains steadfast in her love, Sutherland renounces his. While Helen remains defiant among the nuns, Sutherland in his monastery now 'as feeble as a child' can only remember her 'in an agony of shame'.[103]

A central theme running through the novel, from his sickly nostalgia for his childhood home, through his time as a parish priest, his affair, and his reduction to total dependence on Mornington, Sutherland's moral and psychological immaturity has one further vital function in the plot. He is sexually inexperienced. All along his life, Arthur tells us, 'he had turned with disgust from every word which was sullied with any breath of impurity; the poetry of voluptuous passion he had loathed'. But Arthur disapproves:

> Alas! It would have been better far for him if it had not been so. He would have had the experience of his fallen nature to warn him by the taste of the fruit which it had borne in others.[104]

101. *The Nemesis of Faith*, 187–8.
102. *The Nemesis of Faith*, 211, 225.
103. *The Nemesis of Faith*, 217, 222.
104. *The Nemesis of Faith*, 171.

This affirmation of the need to acquire sexual knowledge was a bold assertion for an early Victorian novel; but it was more than a casual aside. It
formed indeed a central theme running throughout Froude's fiction. In
'The Swedenborgian', the light story which he composed while struggling
with *The Nemesis*, he again explores the phenomenon of the basically well-
intentioned individual who risks committing grievous wrong through the
character of the youthful narrator, Mr Frankland. Honest, but as the name
also implies, without any sense of obligation to his elders, Frankland is a
more attractive character than Fowler or Sutherland.[105] Intelligent, sceptical
of all mystical and metaphysical speculations and suggestions, he is far from
introspective, and fully confident in his own moderate and rational moral
attitudes. But he is also passionately and innocently in love with the beautiful Georgina de Courcy, who is betrothed to Mr Fenton, the middle-aged
Swedenborgian of the title, and he is entirely reckless of the consequences
of his pursuit if things should go wrong. They almost do: a riding accident
after which Georgina and Frankland are left alone in an abandoned cottage
awaiting help hopelessly compromises her and threatens a scandal that might
have ruined her reputation beyond recovery. He is also willing without
compunction to risk causing untold grief to Mr Fenton, and to Georgina's
widowed mother; but in the end he is saved from the worst consequences
of his irresponsibility by the superior wisdom of Fenton, who, having
become convinced of Frankland's genuine love, gracefully withdraws.

This is a simple and happy tale. Equally simple but far from happy are the
consequences which issue from the conduct of Henry Carey, the libertine
in 'The Lieutenant's Daughter', who in his absolute and active amoralism is
an antithesis to Sutherland, and who wreaks havoc wherever he goes. Yet
'The Lieutenant's Daughter' offers one of the most realistic brothel scenes
in Victorian fiction. The Misses Arthur who run the establishment are well-
realised individuals, neither villainised nor sentimentalised in Froude's
sketch. The naturalness with which they are drawn echoes the matter-of-
fact treatment of the workings of prostitution represented in 'Louisa Varden',
the earlier story published anonymously in the *Oxford and Cambridge Review*.
In this sentimental tale a young woman of good character is seduced by an
Oxford don who then abandons her, and, expelled by her father, she falls
rapidly into prostitution. As in Froude's other tale, the fateful operation of

---

105. In law, a franklin was a freeman who paid no dues to any superior, and frankland was land
     free of feudal dues.

contingency is central: Louisa's affair with the don is discovered by the most unexpected chance. But the moral consequences of such actions are described in the most devastating terms. 'One slip and there is no forgiveness for us women in this world,' says Louisa:

> And the men that bring us to this sigh and lie until they have cheated us of our one treasure—and then degrade us into the filthy instruments of their filthy pleasures—they spurn us, beat us, trample us down, and tread us underfoot in the dungheap of sensual filth they themselves have raised.[106]

Similarities of plot, structure, and language make the contemporary attribution of the story to Froude probable. But more important is the underlying consistency of theme between 'Louisa Varden' and 'The Lieutenant's Daughter'. Both are intended to underline the profundity of the ethical problems raised by the unspoken but everyday availability of sexual commerce. The temptations of sex are all around, and the question is how are they to be dealt with?

Froude's challenge that humans must actively take responsibility for the instincts nature has endowed on them is directed, of course, to men. Froude's women in these stories are victims: 'The life they live is so passive, whether it be of pain or pleasure.'[107] Yet an indication that Froude's perception of the problem is far more subtle than a mere conventional injunction to abstinence is presented in the case of Edward Fowler. Toward the close of the novel, as Fowler lies dying from his exertions in saving Emma's son, Emma for several months maintains a vigil at his bedside, sometimes reading to him, and sometimes speaking to him in a low tone that no one else can hear, for 'what she might have to say to him, she might well shrink from betraying to a stranger's ear'. Arthur finds the pattern perturbing. He has suspicions of Emma's disposition which he finds difficult to confront. At times when Fowler was asleep, he watched her,

> with her clear blue eyes full *set* upon him with an expression so strange and unearthly ... thoughts unworthy alike of her and me, would at times intrude, and I have tried to drive my eyes into her heart to see what was written there; but always I had to ... hang my head ashamed. My nature to sit in judgement on hers![108]

106. 'Louisa Varden', 352, 357–8.
107. 'Louisa Varden', 359.
108. *Shadows of the Clouds*, 151.

Seen through Arthur, this is ambiguous. But Arthur's authority as a narrator has already been compromised, so Froude's readers must make their own response. To aid them, Froude supplies two further pieces of evidence. The first appears when, close to death, Fowler declares that he wishes to receive the sacrament from the hands of Emma's husband, Allen. On entering, Arthur hears Fowler remonstrating with Emma, who is kneeling by his bed: 'Emma, remember. It was wrong, it really was, it might have been a fearful peril.' And with his dying breath he admonishes her:

> If your heart has ever lingered upon me with a thought which should have been his [Allen's], if my form has ever lain as a shadow between you two … take this last scene with you as all the place hereafter I shall hold in your memory. Love him with as warm or warmer love than ever you felt for me.[109]

This is an oddly ungrateful response to one who had shown him such undivided attention over many months. Arthur finds Fowler's coldness in the presence of Emma's unconditional love especially perturbing: 'The most painful feature about him was that he appeared to feel no regret at leaving earth or anyone upon earth.' And when Arthur presses him he is chilled by the response: 'But why should I regret them?', Fowler answers, and dismisses Arthur's sympathy for those left behind: 'What pain they experience they should learn to take as a discipline', as a means of seeing all living things, 'not as they are in themselves, but as they are in God.' Arthur is not convinced. Fowler might have changed his mind, he thinks, 'had mature life been given him'; but Fowler's faith, he fears, 'was peculiarly, and almost necessarily, what a mind arrives at which has neither passion nor prejudices': a mind that is not fully matured as human. It is this final judgement on the inadequacy of a life lived in isolation from the world of real humanity that is confirmed in the last pages of the novel by means of the second piece of evidence which Froude supplies in the form of an account of a waking nightmare which Arthur discovers among Fowler's papers.[110]

Fowler had been in the ante-chapel at Magdalen, entranced by the light of the windows and candles inside, the swelling of the organ, and the singing of the choristers. 'Inside all was so beautiful; all seemed an outpouring from the divinest depths of the purest devotion.' But outside, in the ante-chapel with him, he was aware of 'loose idle dilettante worshippers of the

109. *Shadows of the Clouds*, 165.
110. *Shadows of the Clouds*, 149–50.

beautiful, drawn there by love of sweet sounds, and women with that upon their forehead which seems to say a love less pure than that had brought them to a scene so holy'. Fowler shrank from them: 'loath[ing] the outcasts I was thrown among', and longed to be in the chapel 'where the angels were hymning their praises before the throne of God'. But he was excluded.[111]

> I heard a voice say, such is the penalty of those who seek Heaven their own way and not by the grace of the sanctuary; they shall see the glories they crave, but they shall be taken with their pride and their internal inheritance is with the evil.[112]

The vision began to pall, and as the service ended 'the white worshippers' filed out and began blending with the crowd outside. Then came a horrible realisation:

> Close by me one surpliced figure whispered under a deep overhanging bonnet. I caught the words—they were an assignation.[113]

This is the final line in the novel; and the readers, deprived of any further comment from either Arthur or Froude, are left to come to their own conclusions concerning the pious, passionless Fowler.

VII

In reaching this deliberately inconclusive ending, Froude was aiming for a particularly acute representation of what was the recurring and the essential message of his moral fiction. The great crisis which his generation was undergoing was not, he had come to see, merely a matter of theological speculation and intellectual debate; and concentration on these aspects had deepened rather than alleviated it. Similarly, the efforts of those such as Newman to transcend it by uncovering long but hidden traditions of faith, spirituality, and sainthood had foundered spectacularly. Such traditions were chimerical, and cleaving to them led only to a hopeless obscurantism. While the fundamental questions concerning the existence of Creation and the role of conscious mankind within it were eternal, the manner in which they manifested themselves was, as Carlyle had shown, historically relative and

111. *Shadows of the Clouds*, 187–8
112. *Shadows of the Clouds*, 188.
113. *Shadows of the Clouds*, 189.

transitory. Crises such as that which was presently developing were unique epiphenomena which could never be understood by reference to previous convulsions, but only in themselves through the language, concepts, and feelings prevailing at the time of their occurrence.

Beneath the great forces of inexorable historical change there remained a lower but equally ineluctable plane of unique individual responsibility for actions committed or omitted. Whether this responsibility was perceived through such general phenomena as 'the condition of England' and the catastrophe of Ireland or, on a more personal level, through a loss of faith or a loss of moral standards, it was an issue that remained urgently in need of address. In this insistence that individuals must assume full personal account-ability for their existence in a changing world (or else share in the respon-sibility for all the evils that took place around them), the great Goethe had already led the way; but owing to the scattered and incompetent manner in which his works had been translated or expounded, his message to the young Englishmen of the 1840s had been misconstrued or perverted. As with Carlyle, his perceived contempt for all religious establishments and all orthodox learning had rendered him suspect to Oxford's troubled young men. It was to this particular group, however, whose potential significance was of far greater proportion than its size, that Froude, on account of his own intellectual, psychological, and spiritual pilgrimage, felt particularly capable of addressing.

There was, then, a deep sense in which Froude's fictions were, after all, autobiographical, as he exposed his own experiences and feelings to dis-cover how far they were shared by others of his generation, and explored where they might lead him (and those like him) if they were not tran-scended by the act of imagination and creation which he, as author, was conducting. For this reason it was both artistically and ethically necessary that the act of self-transformation which he was presenting as author should be paralleled by similar efforts at critical self-examination among his readers which he sought to provoke by all those formal, narrational, and textual devices which pepper his fictions. That such a demanding programme of reception and response entailed serious risks was inevitable; it would have had little validity had it not been so. But Froude's further decision to relate the general theological and philosophical dilemmas of his time to one of the most acute ethical problems facing the audience of young men he was pri-marily addressing was an even more audacious step. The decorum with which, for the most part, he dealt with the issue of sexual responsibility, and the profound ambiguity of the characters which he created in order to explore it, may have given him sufficient confidence to believe that the challenge had been met. But if so, Froude miscalculated badly. He was soon to find that, for all his subtlety and ingenuity, the demands which he placed on his readers, coupled with the potential offence of his central theme, provoked a storm of outrage and misconception in which the moral resolution he wished to affirm was altogether lost. It would be some time before he realised that the same blend of authorial demonstration and transformative reading which was so essential to his purpose could be recovered in the altogether more conventional genre of narrative history.

6

The Road to Recovery: From
Philosophy to History, 1849–56

I

The personal consequences suffered by Froude in the wake of the scandal provoked by the appearance of *The Nemesis of Faith* was at once less serious than has been commonly supposed, and at the same time of considerably greater import. Ostracised by his own college following the dramatic book-burning, he was compelled to resign his fellowship to avoid a more humiliating expulsion. He soon became the subject of public outrage as the Oxford papers and the national press joined in the universal condemnation of his 'wicked little book'. The public outcry soon proved personally damaging. In the autumn of 1848, as he was preparing *The Nemesis of Faith* for publication, he had applied for and secured the post of schoolmaster in the recently established grammar school at Hobart in Van Diemen's Land. In the wake of the scandal, however, the board of trustees withdrew the offer; and Froude was now without the prospect of employment. At the same time, his father, already deeply injured by the notoriety of *Shadows of the Clouds*, totally repudiated him, cancelling a sum of £5,000 which he had proposed settling on him. Expelled from Oxford and unemployed, Froude was now also destitute.[1]

Despite such dire circumstances, Froude's mood at the breaking of this crisis was remarkably buoyant. 'I never felt lighter nor happier than in the months which then followed,' he recalled. 'I was not frightened. The worst that could befall me seemed light by the side of the burden which I had got

---

1. Exeter College, Oxford, Froude MSS, nos 16, 28–30, 35, 40, 43, esp 51 'Resolutions in Froude's case'; Dunn, *Froude* I, 130–50, 228–32; for particularly rancorous commentary on Froude and his book, see *Morning Herald*, 6 March 1849, and *The Standard*, 6 and 9 March 1849.

rid of.'[2] For about six months before the appearance of his novel he had actively been seeking means of escape from Oxford: he had announced his intentions to his father and the College Rector as soon as he returned from Ireland in the autumn of 1848, and in addition to pursuing the post in Hobart he was actively investigating the prospects of setting up in business on his own. Not surprisingly, therefore, his correspondence with his closest friends—notably Kingsley, Clough, and William Long—immediately on the outbreak of the scandal, is rueful but unbowed. 'It *is* a bore to see old friends turn their backs on one,' he complained to Clough, only to add that some still stuck to him. He was upset for 'poor old [Cowley] Powles,' his friend at Exeter, who was agonising about the scandal, and he asked Kingsley to write 'to satisfy him that I am not inspired by the Devil; you would be doing *him* a great kindness, and me too'. He regarded the burning of the novel with mild amusement, reflecting that in adding to its notoriety it could only increase sales.[3] On the other hand, his short correspondence with Rector Richards over his resignation and the threat of expulsion was both dignified and warm. 'I should be glad if you would let me shake hands with you before I go,' he wrote on the eve of his departure from Oxford in early March, 'let me say I leave the College with the warmest feelings of gratitude too tight yourself for your long kindness and forbearance'. A month later, when the storm had subsided a little, he wrote a long letter to Richards explaining his aim in writing *The Nemesis of Faith* in full confidence 'that in a few years you will look on the book and its author differently'.[4]

If Froude lost some friends at Oxford, he was confirmed in the friendship of others. The Longs remained loyal, and invited him to take refuge with them in Bath. Arthur Stanley, 'who never failed a heretic in distress, still less a friend', was supportive.[5] Clough was steadfast, F. D. Maurice sympathetic, and Frank Newman, having sent Froude a passionate letter of criticism, withdrew it in a friendly one.[6] But above all it was Kingsley who came to Froude's rescue. Amidst the storm he invited Froude to come stay

2. Dunn, *Froude*, I, 147.
3. Froude to Clough, [28] February 1849, F. L. Mulhauser (ed.), *Correspondence of A. H. Clough*, i, 246; Dunn, *Froude*, I, 147–8; Froude to Elizabeth Long, n.d., 1848, Dunn, *Froude*, I, 127; to Kingsley, 27 February 1849, Dunn, *Froude*, I, 133–4.
4. Exeter College, Oxford, Froude, MSS, Froude to Rector Richards, (March), 10 April 1849, nos. 34, 46.
5. Dunn, *Froude*, I, 147.
6. Froude to Clough, 25 and 28 February, 6 March 1849, F. L. Mulhauser (ed.), *Correspondence of A. H. Clough*, i, 246–7, 215–16.

indefinitely with him and his family in the not so unfamiliar West Country sites of Ilfracombe and Clovelly. There he protected Froude from the very worst of the venomous public statements and poisonous private letters addressed to him, while also dismissing the adverse comments from his own family and friends that came his way. Though he was later to differ significantly from Kingsley in several respects, Froude never forgot the gratitude he owed to Kingsley for this time.[7]

Friends also sought to offer financial support. Despite his disapproval of the novel, Frank Newman worked hard to secure reviewing commissions for him, and even proposed him as editor of the *Manchester Guardian*.[8] A more immediate offer came from a syndicate of well-wishers centring around Baron Bunsen, the Prussian ambassador to the Court of St James, and Richard Monckton Milnes in the form of an invitation to take up a two-year fellowship in theology in the University of Bonn, for which an advance allowance of £100 was sent to Froude in hard cash. Flattered, Froude briefly considered the prospect, and was strongly encouraged to do so by Bunsen. But the author of *The Nemesis of Faith* could not in good faith abandon the world and make a retreat into speculative theology, so he politely declined (and returned the money!). It was then that, quite unexpectedly, he received an offer from Samuel Darbishire, a well-to-do Manchester lawyer of Unitarian leanings and a rare admirer of Froude's writing, to act as tutor to his son Vernon and his daughters Marianne and Louisa for a respectable fee and room and board. Within two months of his departure from Oxford, Froude had found some financial security again.[9]

In another, even more important respect, Froude's life changed dramatically. In tandem with his determination to give up his fellowship, Froude had determined on getting married. Even as *The Nemesis of Faith* was about to appear he was enquiring gamily of his friend Elizabeth Long whether she could 'find a Georgina ready made who will do for me'.[10] His allusion was to the female interest in 'The Swedenborgian' who had ultimately married the narrator and lived happily ever after. She apparently responded positively, for within a month Froude was asking to be remembered to 'my

---

7. Dunn, *Froude*, I, 147; Brenda Colloms, *Charles Kingsley: The Lion of Eversley* (London, 1975), 113–18; Susan Chitty, *The Beast and the Monk: A Life of Charles Kingsley* (New York, 1975), 121–3.
8. Froude to Elizabeth Long, 1 May 1849, Dunn, *Froude*, I, 157–8.
9. Dunn, *Froude*, I, 148–52, 238; James Pope Hennessy, *Moncton Milnes: The Years of Promise, 1809–51* (New York, 1955), 297–8.
10. Froude to William Long, n.d. and 24 February 1849, Dunn, *Froude*, I, 131–2.

volunteered bride'. But soon it was too late. In March, while Froude was in retreat at Clovelly, Kingsley performed a further vital service by introducing him to the younger sister of his wife Fanny, the eighteen-year-old Charlotte Grenfell, youngest daughter of Pascoe Grenfell, MP, wealthy governor of the Royal Assurance Company, and master of an opulent establishment in Belgrave Square.[11]

Froude's first encounter with Charlotte Grenfell was unfortunate: he first met her in March 1849 when, sailing to the Kingsley's cottage at Ilfracombe, Charlotte spent the journey being sick at the bottom of the boat. But the relationship soon blossomed under the encouragement from Charles and Fanny Kingsley, and by the summer Charlotte and Froude were intent on marriage. There were obvious difficulties to the suit. Froude was still without definite prospects, and the wealthy Grenfells were wary. By midsummer Fanny Kingsley had grown cautious, and on learning that her initial enthusiasm was beginning to wane, Froude was sufficiently concerned to issue a stern rebuke:

> My Dear Mrs Kingsley,
>
> You are offended already as I hear from Charlotte. I partly expected it, and yet you are fainting too soon, and it is not reasonable of you. You remember that I warned you that I intended to take my own way in life, doing (as I have always done) in all important matters, just what I should think good at whatever risk of consequences, and taking no other person's opinion when it crossed with my own. Now in this matter I feel certain that the way to save Charlotte most pain is to *shorten* the struggle, and that will be best done by being short, peremptory and decided in allowing no dictation and no interference ... I cannot hold you excused if you withold the sympathy you promised because I do not follow what you advise.[12]

Here is a revelation of the steely Froude, who had already liberated himself from his family, established his distance from Newman, outraged the Oxford common rooms, and scandalised public opinion. It is clear evidence of the strength of his determination to be married as soon as possible (and it is from this time that a tradition of the Darbishire family that Froude might have been willing to transfer his suit to one of his pupils has its origins).

---

11. Froude to Elizabeth Long, 1 May 1849, Dunn, *Froude*, I, 157–8. Pascoe Grenfell had died in 1838, and Charlotte's guardian at the time of the courtship was her eldest brother, the formidable Charles Pascoe Grenfell (1790–1867), MP, and governor of the Bank of England; it was his permission that Froude struggled to secure.
12. Froude to Fanny Kingsley (July) 1849, Dunn, *Froude*, I, 160–1.

Within a month, however, the concerns of the Grenfells had been assuaged, and Froude's engagement was announced without scandal. Also, within a month of taking up his position with the Darbishires Froude had leased a house in Green Leys, a Manchester suburb, and was writing to Fanny Kingsley, seeking advice on household goods and domestic management. A modest settlement granting Charlotte an annuity of £300 had been accepted, and on 3 October she and Froude were married in the Grenfell family church at Eaton Square.[13]

Froude's establishment in Manchester was by then universally acclaimed a success, as both his later recollections and the contemporary letters of one of his pupils, Marianne Darbishire, testify.[14] The happy circumstances reported in the Darbishire correspondence are confirmed, moreover, if in a mildly ironical manner, by a frequent visitor to the Darbishires, Elizabeth Gaskell:

> If anyone under the sun has a magical, magnetic, glamour-like influence, that man has. He's *aut Mephistopheles aut nihil* that's what he is. The DDs [Darbishires] all bend and bow to his will, like reeds before the wind blow whichever way it listeth. He smokes cigars constantly; Père, Robert, Arthur Vernon (nay once even little Francis), smoke constantly. He disbelieves, they disbelieve; he wears shabby garments, they wear shabby garments ... I stand just without the circle of his influence; resisting with all my might, but feeling and seeing the attraction. It's queer![15]

That Froude was immensely happy in these months is also evident from his contemporary correspondence. 'One does not like to say much about one's happiness,' he wrote to his friend Max Müller in late November. 'I looked for very little and I have found a great deal. I should have called myself perfectly happy, only that I should have called myself so a month ago, and I am far happier now than I was then.' 'I married with confined expectations', he confided to Elizabeth Long at the same time, 'and as if in reward they have grown like the grain of mustard ... I do not know by which of my sins ... I have deserved to be as happy as I am.'[16]

13. Froude to Elizabeth Long, 26 August 1849, Dunn, *Froude*, I, 161–2; Froude to Clough, 20 September 1849, F. L. Mulhauser (ed.), *Correspondence of A. H. Clough*, I, 271–2; *Annual Register, 1849*, 1024. On the terms of the marriage settlement, see Froude to Clough, n.d., 1852, Bodleian Library, 41034 (Eng. Lett. d177), Clough Papers, ff.66.
14. Dunn, *Froude* I, 54–7.
15. J. A. V. Chapple and Arthur Pollard (eds.), *The Letters of Mrs Gaskell* (Manchester, 1966), 83–4.
16. Froude to Max Müller, 25 November; Elizabeth Long, 30 November 1849, Dunn, *Froude*, I, 165–6.

At the centre of this unprecedented happiness was the joy that he was now experiencing with Charlotte. Spirited and with strong intellectual interests, Charlotte had infuriated her brother-in-law Kingsley both by her interest in Catholicism and her fondness for Spinoza. Froude liked to boast that he had rescued her from the former, but he was clearly delighted by her interest in the latter. Charlotte was prepared to submit herself as one of her husband's pupils in the early days at Manchester in a manner that Froude found entertaining; but her critical annotations on her copy of *The Nemesis of Faith* suggest that she was far from intellectually docile.[17] They began to write together, and Froude expected in the spring of 1850 that a jointly authored work would shortly appear in print. If Froude was 'master' of studies, moreover, Charlotte, as Froude loved to tell his friends, was mistress of the household. She determined the number of students he was to take, and where they were to be taught. She banished smoking from the house except the study, and she selected which of Froude's friends and acquaintances might call. There was, however, more to Froude's delight than shared intellectual interests and a playful sense of partnership. From the outset of the marriage Froude was eager to father children. As early as November he was, with some rashness and indiscretion, telling friends that this was what he was most looking forward to. He had no cause for impatience: by the beginning of 1850 Charlotte was pregnant, and their first child, Georgina Margaret, was born safely and healthily on 13 September.[18]

The birth of his first child, moreover, helped resolve the final and most painful consequence of Froude's scandal: the breach with his family. Initially indifferent to his estrangement from his father, Froude, it appeared, had seriously underestimated the pain which the public nature of the affair had caused the ageing archdeacon. His own regret deepened in 1850 as early overtures met with stern rebuff, but still he remained stoical. By January 1851, however, his brother William had signalled his forgiveness, and Froude was confident that through his good offices (and those of

---

17. Froude to Clough, 20 September 1849, F. L. Mulhauser (ed.), *Correspondence of A. H. Clough*, 271–2. Waldo Hilary Dunn was in possession of the copy of *Nemesis* annotated by Charlotte, and quotes extracts from it in his biography; but the copy has not surfaced since: Dunn, *Froude*, I, 162–3; Chapple and Pollard (eds.), *Letters of Elizabeth Gaskell*, 86, 91.

18. Froude to Max Müller, 25 November 1849, and to Elizabeth Long, April 1850, when he hints archly, 'and *next September* I shall be happier still [Froude's italics]; Dunn, *Froude*, I, 165, 167, 179. The choice of Georgina as a first name may or may not have been related to the heroine of 'The Swedenborgian'.

William's wife) 'matters are mending slowly but surely.' Disappointment of these hopes during 1851 filled Froude with impatience and irritation rather than grief; but the birth of his second child, Rose Mary, in May 1852 once more accelerated the process of rapprochement which was completed over the summer. At the end of the year Froude and Charlotte spent Christmas at Dartington, and 'all was so well as if it had never been otherwise'.[19]

In so many respects, then, Froude's fortunes had undergone a wonderful improvement in the critical year of 1849. The frustrated and embattled don had now become a truly liberated man, in love, married, and an expectant father. If he had lost friends, he had made several new ones, and more importantly had seen proved the loyalty of his oldest and dearest ones. Though far from well off, he was equally distant from the threat of poverty. In addition to Charlotte's annuity, he was expecting to earn an annual total of £150 from tuition fees, and promises of lucrative writing commissions, he estimated, were already beginning to bear fruit in the amount of £50 or £60. In regard to the future he could afford to be confident. Writing fees were going up, and even if some accident were to befall him personally, he was assured that the Grenfells and the Froudes would insure the welfare of Charlotte and her children. Recalling these circumstances two years later, when Arthur Clough, himself contemplating marriage, asked his advice, Froude could write confidently: 'On £500 a year income only, a man who can do without a horse and a tailor's bill and a lady who can do without a maid may marry with prudence in any part of England.'[20]

II

By the close of 1850, however, despite his popularity and his domestic bliss, Froude was growing restive. In some part this may have been due, as Elizabeth Gaskell surmised, to Charlotte's unhappiness with her new circumstances, her persistent but unidentifiable ill-health, and her refusal to mix in society. But Froude himself advanced different reasons for his dissatisfaction. 'The Unitarians here', he told Max Müller in November, 'partly from dislike of

---

19. Froude to Elizabeth Long, 7 January 1851, 16 December 1852, Dunn, *Froude*, I, 181, 192; Froude to Clough, 16 May 1852, F. L. Mulhauser (ed.), *Correspondence of A. H. Clough*, I, 284.
20. Froude to Clough, n.d., 1852, Bodleian Library, Oxford, Clough MSS 41034 (Eng. Lett. d177), ff.66–8.

my books, and partly from a foolish jealousy of an Oxford man ... show me a cold shoulder and even look coldly on the Darbishires on my account.' By the following April he was even more determined. 'We hate Manchester— Manchester in any form', he told Elizabeth Long, 'Unitarian Manchester most of all ... and when we leave the place, which we shall do in the summer, we shall leave it without breaking any ties except such as one might form with a prison cell.'[21] His plans to move with Charlotte to Wales to a cottage named Plas Gwynant at the foot of Snowden had already crystallised. There was snobbery here—the Unitarians were 'vulgar', 'insolent', and 'graceless'—and also wounded pride: his supply of students soon dried up.[22]

There were more serious problems. His plans to start a great new book were stalled, and a collection of essays which he had started as soon as he left Oxford and had been compiling since was now put away, and the proposed work with Charlotte came to nothing. 'All I have written', he told Elizabeth Long in April 1850, 'looks like winter and is consigned not to the fire but to the closet as a step down to the waste-paper basket.'[23] At the core of this disenchantment and unexpected loss of creative energy there lay, however, a deeper matter concerning which Charlotte's discontent and the vulgar Unitarians were at best a distraction. This was the recognition that, by his own terms, *The Nemesis of Faith* had been a failure.

While he was in the eye of the storm that broke on the publication of his novel, Froude had seemed to revel in the scandal he had provoked. Initial reactions were predictable. The popular dailies were scabrous and personal. The *Morning Herald* and *The Standard* launched a campaign demanding the withdrawal of the teaching appointment in Hobart, making scandalous allegations about his teaching career in Oxford and more verifiable claims about the dubious manner in which he had gained his fellowship in Exeter. Such standard organs of Anglican orthodoxy as *The Church and State Gazette* and the *Christian Observer* issued vituperative denunciations—the former suggesting that its author rather than the book deserved burning. Mainstream secular reviews, such as *Bentley's* and the *Literary Gazette* behaved similarly,

---

21. Froude to Max Müller, 25 November 1849, and to Elizabeth Long, n.d., April 1850, Dunn, *Froude*, I, 165, 167. The feelings may have been mutual, and it is generally agreed that Elizabeth Gaskell's portrait of Mr and Mrs Hale in *North and South* expresses her ambivalent feelings about the Froudes: see J. G. Sharps, *Mrs Gaskell's Observation and Invention* (London, 1970), 220–1 and the sources cited there, and Angus Easson, 'Mr Hale's Doubts in *North and South*', *Review of English Studies*, 31 (1980), 30–40.
22. Froude to Elizabeth Long, n.d., April 1850, Dunn, *Froude*, I, 166–7.
23. Dunn, *Froude*, I, 167.

condemning the book as much for indecency and obscenity as much as for its supposed defence of atheism.[24]

The force of these assaults compelled Froude to reply to such charges. He wrote a spirited letter to *The Standard* defending his integrity, presenting a brief exposition of the origin and purpose of the novel, and demanding an apology. He provided an extended 'Preface' to a second edition of the novel which came out in June 1849 in which he attempted an explication of the philosophical and ethical underpinnings of the book, and reiterated his insistence that Sutherland had never been intended to be perceived in a sympathetic light.[25] For the most part, however, he preferred to remain aloof from controversy, confident that the underlying truth and value of his message would shortly be perceived, if not by the majority of readers, at least by those to whom he most wanted to appeal. 'I may expect a turn of the tide', he wrote confidently to Elizabeth Long in May 1849, as 'public opinion of 1851 will not be the public opinion of 1849. Be sure of it.'[26]

Within a year, however, Froude had less reason to be confident. From *Fraser's Magazine* with which Froude was already associated, Froude expected some support. But none came. Although the chosen reviewer, John Ludlow, was well known in his own right as an outspoken critic of the Anglican establishment and its hypocrisies, his assessment was wholly negative: 'We regret that his book should have been published', he wrote, addressing the author, 'that for its own sake, we dare not recommend its intimate perusal, in short (speaking with awe, and endeavouring to stand in the writer's place for self-examination) that its publication is a *sin* not to be justified or palliated, but to be repented of'. The review in *The Eclectic Review* in relation to which Froude had been similarly expectant was, when it appeared in 1850, equally disappointing, the reviewer likewise regretting that the novel had ever been written and dismissing its case as 'shallow and one-sided'. Around the same time in the *Westminster Review*, Geraldine Jewsbury, another reader from whom Froude had expected support, published her assessment, which,

---

24. *Morning Herald*, 6, 9, 10, and 13 March 1849; *The Standard*, 6, 9, 10, 12, and 13 March 1849; *Church and State Gazette*, 9 March 1849, 150–1; *Christian Observer*, 50 (January 1850), 16–35; *Bentley's Miscellany*, 25 (April 1849), 443–6; *Literary Gazette*, 3 March 1849 (no pagination).

25. Froude to the editor of *The Standard* (letter dated 7 March), 9 March, demanding an apology for his poor reading of the book; *The Nemesis of Faith* (2nd edn., 1849), iii–xvi, denying autobiographical association altogether; and esp. 'I have found nothing to make me doubt the publication of a second edition', xv.

26. Dunn, *Froude*, I, 157–8; see also Froude to Rector Richards, 10 April 1849, Exeter College, Oxford, Froude MSS, no. 46.

though not wholly critical, was equally discouraging. Though Froude had aimed, wrote Jewsbury, to be a voice crying in the wilderness, he had nothing positive to offer by way of prophecy: 'The work is oppressive and painful; it suggests nothing; there is no outlet from it ... His book is constructed like a town in which every street should be a *cul-de-sac*.'[27]

Such public comments echoed the private opinions of his own friends. Kingsley, his protector, remained firm in his view that the book had been a mistake. F. D. Maurice, though prepared to defend Froude against the most vicious charges and to counsel caution in potential reviewers, was himself unwilling to review the book sympathetically, regarding it as a failure which through its own timidity and obscurity had exposed itself to misunderstanding and scandal. The Longs likewise remained unpersuaded. Clough proffered no help, and Jewsbury's review confirmed in public what had already been circulating in rumour—that Carlyle, the focus of all aspiring minds of the day, had not been impressed.[28]

Even more dispiriting than his failure to convert good friends, however, was the unexpected support which Froude garnered from certain unwelcome quarters. As both a critic and a victim of the Anglican establishment, the author of *The Nemesis of Faith* was rapidly identified as a friend by the most radical and avant garde literary circles. G. H. Lewes, whom Froude thought 'a blackguard', tried to provide succour by offering to commission several articles from him at generous rates for his newly reconstituted *Westminster*.[29] Harriet Martineau thought him a martyr, and approached him with a proposal of including *The Nemesis of Faith* in a series of scandalous and suppressed books which she proposed republishing. The young Mary Anne Evans published one of the few fully sympathetic reviews of the book in the *Coventry Herald* which identified him as a harbinger of a radical attack on convention, respectability, and authority; and though flattered by this rare praise, Froude himself felt obliged in a personal letter to the reviewer to dissociate himself from such an identity.[30] Considerably more disturbing was the singular and lavish praise heaped upon the novel by the leading spokesman of London radical opinion, Henry Crabb Robinson, who

27. *Fraser's Magazine*, 39 (May 1850), 545–60; *The Eclectic Review*, 18 (September 1850), 257–83; *Westminster and Foreign Quarterly Review*, 51 (April 1849), 137–8.
28. Kingsley to Max Müller, 10 May 1852, Bodleian Library, Oxford, Max Müller MSS; Frederick Maurice (ed.), *Life of Frederick Denison Maurice*, I, 51619; Dunn, *Froude*, I, 147–50.
29. Froude to Kingsley, 10 November 1849; Dunn, *Froude*, I, 164.
30. *Coventry Herald and Observer*, 16 March 1849; Cross, *George Eliot's Life* (New York, 1970), 109.

transformed the review into an occasion to attack Christianity, orthodox and evangelical, as a whole.[31]

In the face of all this, it was Froude himself who was scandalised. His principal purpose in writing had been neither to undermine authority nor to encourage heterodoxy. He had sought instead to arouse the many well-meaning but confused university-trained men from the perplexed passivity into which they had fallen, to awaken them to the moral and historical perils of their condition, and to inspire them to take responsibility for the course of the world's development, and for their own actions within it, before it was too late. In this, of course, it was rapidly becoming clear that by whatever measure he took, he had failed. *The Nemesis of Faith* had been, as even his kindest critics had suggested, inadequate to its purpose. It had added to the very confusion it had sought to dissolve, it had alienated those it sought to address, attracted those for whom he shared no cause, and, worst of all, it had distorted and adulterated the public voice of its author.

Froude, however, 'could not part with an ambition to recover my clouded reputation, and be of some use to my generation': the prophetic urges that had fired the literary experiments of the 1840s lived on.[32] While he might regret its result, Froude never repudiated the sincerity of the attempt or the continuing importance of the purpose of the undertaking. Yet if he was to recover from the damage that had been done, and resume the mission he had failed to fulfil, he must go beyond this disastrous adventure in fiction, and discover an altogether different voice by which to re-present himself in public and resume this self-appointed mission to his generation. In 1850 the manner in which this new voice would be discovered was still a matter of some uncertainty, as his hesitation over a proposed German translation of his novel, and the abandonment of a set of related essays on which he had been working for over a year indicated.[33] But one decision was settled on early. In addition to Charlotte's unhappiness, the impulses of his own self-selected destiny now convinced him that it was vital that he should give up tutoring, and leave Manchester for the isolated hermitage of Plas Gwynant under the shadow of Snowdon in North Wales.[34]

31. E. S. Arbuckle (ed.), *Harriet Martineau's Letters to Fanny Wedgewood* (Stanford, 1983) 110; *The Christian Reformer*, 5 (May 1849), 270–7.
32. Dunn, *Froude*, I, 153.
33. See Froude to P (Palgrave?), (1850?), Pierpont Morgan Library, New York, Misc. Eng. MSS, MA 4500.
34. An insight into Froude's outlook at this time is given in Froude to Thomas Ballantyne (editor of *The Leader*), 7 June 1850: 'I have a thing which I may sell you if you like ... but as I can sell it elsewhere and cannot afford to work gratis I fear I must ask you whether you pay', Iowa University Library, Froude MSS, 8MsL/F492ba.

The restless but as yet unclear ambition behind this decision, Froude records, is explored in a fable entitled 'The Cat's Pilgrimage', which was one of a series of fables he wrote at this time—some in collaboration with Charlotte—that were published in the weekly newspaper *The Leader*.[35] The fable tells of a female cat who, dissatisfied with her comfortable life in a well-run farmhouse, sets out to find some answers to the same fundamental questions with which Froude had been preoccupied in his more sophisticated fictions: what is the point of life, 'what are we here for', and what is best for us to do. Her enquiries among the other animals are unsatisfactory: her fireside companion, a pet spaniel, offers a simple hedonistic explanation: 'The world was made for dogs … men and women are put in it to take care of dogs … I eat my breakfast and am happy.' Further disappointments follow, as others advance on the dog's simplicity with the maxim—'Do your duty'—but appear to mean something different by it. A blackbird defines doing her duty as looking after her fledgeling and singing over the grave of her lost love. An ox says, like the dog, it is to eat one's dinner, and thinks the cat ungrateful for thinking that insufficient. A bee says it is to make honey, and angrily tells the cat that she should be killed, as bees kill their drones, for failing to find something useful to do. An owl in its wisdom preaches that it is to wonder about the mysteries of the world, but when pressed reveals that the central issue which it has been considering forever is which came first, the owl or the egg, for which she has as yet found no satisfactory answer. They disagree, and the cat is haughtily dismissed:

> Find out!' said the Owl, 'We can never find out. The beauty of the question is that its solution is impossible. What would become of all our delightful reasonings, O unwise Cat, if we were so unhappy as to know.[36]

The owl concludes that the cat is too flippant for philosophy. Next comes a rabbit who, like some of the others, replies that doing one's duty is getting one's dinner and feeding one's young. By now, however, the cat is hungry and suggests that she might do her duty by eating the rabbit. The rabbit

---

35. Originally appearing in four instalments in *The Leader*, 29 June, 6, 13, and 20 July 1850, 'The Cat's Pilgrimage' next appeared in print without acknowledgement in 1867 in the first edition of Froude's *Short Studies on Great Subjects* (2 vols., London), 281–310. It was subsequently republished in a limited and rare edition with illustrations by 'J. B' (Edinburgh: Edmonston and Douglas). For ease of reference, citations here are from the collected Silver Library edition of *Short Studies* (London, 1893–4), I, 630–50. On Froude's plans for a series of such tales, Froude to Elizabeth Long, 1 May 1849, Dunn, *Froude*, I, 157–8.
36. *Short Studies*, I, 639

pleads for its life for the sake of its young, and the cat retires more confused than ever. It is then that she encounters a fox feeding his young on a goose in a cave. A veritable Reynard, who glories in his reputation as a rogue, to the fox the only law in the world is 'that the weakest go to the wall'. That is what the humans practise, and animals who fail to see it are deluding themselves. Duty for the fox is 'to use his wits and enjoy himself ... to eat and not be eaten.' Fox knows that some day he will be caught and hanged by a rope in the farmyard, but until then he is resolved to be happy: he has to hunt and cheat to get his prey. But this is his nature, and like the domesticated dog, he is happy.[37]

Saddened by her experience, the cat returns home to the hearth rug and the complacent spaniel. 'I have learned something', she tells the dog, 'and knowledge is never pleasant.' She has learned that for all their limitations, the creatures she had met were at one with themselves in what they perceived was doing their duty, that the fox, whose knowledge of what was going on in the world, was infinitely superior to theirs, was equally happy in his condition, and that only she herself who had no duty to do and only a nagging curiosity about what she ought to do was the one who was actually unhappy. The only way to be happy, she now realised, 'was to go about one's business like a decent Cat'. But a cat's business was hunting and killing, and this she had not been bred to, she had been bred on the contrary to do nothing, thus: 'I consider myself an unfortunate Cat.' At this point, however, breakfast is served, and while the dog does tricks, 'his penance' to earn its fare, the cat is unmolested, 'and if one might judge by the purring on the hearth rug, the Cat, if not the happiest of the two, at least was not exceedingly miserable'.[38]

Despite its simplicity of form, the purpose and meaning of 'The Cat's Pilgrimage', as its somewhat ambiguous conclusion indicates, is far from self-evident. The fabulist form encourages, of course, the anthropomorphic identification of stereotypes. The animals may in turn be seen to correspond with recognisable sociological types: the cat and dog as members of the privileged leisure class; the ox and bee as labourers, agricultural and industrial; the owl as clergy or dons; the fox as man of affairs; and the cat as a further representation of Fowler/Sutherland, 'the superfluous men'. Simultaneously they can be seen as representations of fundamental human

37. *Short Studies*, I, 645–6.   38. *Short Studies*, I, 650.

characteristics: the selfish (spaniel), the sensual (blackbird), the dull (ox), the deluded (owl), the self-righteous (bee), the weak (rabbit), the cynical (fox), and the hopelessly speculative (cat). Yet the contrast between the apparent contentment of each of these types and the equally obvious deficiency of their characters deepens uncertainty as to what Froude is trying to convey, while the apparently superior place granted to the cynical fox in the cat's estimation of her experience adds substantially to the tale's ambiguity.

There is, moreover, an historical dimension to the story which seems in tension with its fabulist form. The cat's boredom and discontent are not existential. They have arisen from quite specific painful occurrences: the disappearance of her children and the recent death of her 'lover' Tom. The bereavement and grief which provided the impetus of the cat's pilgrimage is echoed at several points in the tale. Most immediately, it is contrasted to the blackbird, who, though like the cat has been deprived of lover and off-spring, nonetheless continues singing on and on as if nothing had happened. The theme recurs in the case of the foolish rabbit whose multiple and highly dependent children are the principal reason for the cat's decision not to eat it. By contrast is the fox, whom the cat encounters in the act of feeding his many young cubs with a goose which 'his eldest cub had the night before brought home', and whose meal she is invited to share. Proud of his wiliness, he is even more pleased by his progeny: elaborating upon his general contentment, 'think of my feelings as a father', he reminds the cat, 'when my dear boy came home with the very young gosling which was marked for the Michaelmas dinner! Old Reineke himself wasn't match for that young fox at his years.'[39]

With the exceptions of the self-sufficient fox and the insufficient rabbit there are no other practising parents in the tale. The ox and the owl are alone in their habitats, and appear always to have been so. The bee, of course, is a neuter whose only passion, aside from work, is the desire to kill the drone, its natural progenitor. And the spaniel indignantly renounces the prospect of parenthood: 'Children indeed! … when I have got men and women. Children are good enough for foxes and wild creatures, refined dogs know better.'[40] Froude's own personal delight in fatherhood at this time is strongly evident in his contemporary correspondence. But more general issues were at stake in the story. For Froude, as we have seen, the

39. *Short Studies*, I, 646.   40. *Short Studies*, I, 648.

natural right and the joy of sexual fulfilment are founded upon an acceptance of responsibility for individual conduct and its consequences.
Inextricably linked to the acceptance of duties toward progeny and posterity is, moreover, an historical obligation toward antecedence—themes that
also arise obliquely in the tale. Early on, the cat recalls that in past times her
ancestors were adored: 'We are going down in the world . . . and that is why
living on in this way is such an unsatisfactory sort of thing.' She reminds the
pet spaniel that he too had had better forebears: 'they [the humans] went
down on their knees to you to ask you to give them good things, just as you
stand on your toes for them now to ask for your breakfast'. The fox, when
reminded by the cat of his likely fate in the hunt, avers to the hounds'
betrayal of their nature and sale of their freedom. And the cat, returned from
her journey, understands that she too is an historical entity bred away from
the natural instincts of her kind.[41]

Notwithstanding all the generalising tendencies of the fable, history still
happens. For all their happy complacency in doing what they believed was
their timeless duty, the animals were part of an ever-changing process
which had first created them and was continuously shaping their destiny—
a process which they could never hope to comprehend and over which
they could exercise no control. All of them, moreover, had experienced
some sense of disappointment and loss, even if, like the spaniel, they had
been reconciled to it, or like the bee railed against it, or like the owl they
had decided to convert defeat into an object of veneration. And sooner or
later, all would experience death. The most acute intelligence among them,
the fox, accepts this and has only a breezy stoicism to offer against it:
'When the farmer catches me I shall be getting old and my brains will be
taking leave of me; so the sooner I go the better, that I may disgrace myself
the less.'[42] For the cat this is too 'sad'. Ultimately, all the fox has to offer is
acceptance of a fate no different than the owl's; and her repudiation of this
outlook determines the cat's decision to return home. Poised midway
between the dull, the vain, and the over-worldly, she rejects the fox, and
resolves with what is left of her nature and with what her breeding has
done to find her own way. This solitary resolution is the distinctly qualified
note with which the story closes.

41. *Short Studies*, I, 633–4.   42. *Short Studies*, I, 647.

These underlying themes, left largely implicit in 'The Cat's Pilgrimage', are more explicitly stated in a series of lesser fables on which Froude and Charlotte were working at the time and which he coupled with his story when finally he allowed it into print.[43] 'The Farmer and the Fox' is a brief tale, clearly intended to follow upon the earlier story, in which the prophecy foretold there is realised, and the fox, despite all his stratagems, is hanged by the farmer by a rope in the yard.[44] 'The Lions and the Oxen' is a condensed world history recounting the decline of the great beasts and the eventual revelation that their claim to a right to eat oxen at their pleasure was no longer enforceable.[45] 'The Parable of the Breadfruit Tree' is a more sophisticated allegory telling the story of a tribe of men who 'after one of those heavy convulsions which have divided era from era and left mankind to start again from the beginning' find succour in an extraordinary life-giving tree and continue to cleave to it generation after generation, long after it has lost its vitality, and long after new sources of life originally spawned by it have appeared elsewhere because of dullness, fear, and the pull of tradition.[46] Finally, 'Compensation' offers a short discussion between a bird, an antelope, a tree, and a rock in which each expresses envy for the other's advantages until the tree concludes in response to the rock's complaint that all of the rest have life: 'Alas! … we have life … we have also what you have not, its shadow—death. My beautiful children which year by year I bring out into being, expand in their loveliness only to die.'[47]

Such gloomy presentments help make clear what, at the end of her pilgrimage, lies at the heart of the cat's hard-earned and ambivalent resolve. Her quest left unsatisfied by the range of opinions and attitudes she has encountered; her sense of alienation deepened by her equidistance from the dull and the quick, she would have to pursue those questions by the few meagre talents left by nature and by breeding, but manifestly surviving in her nonetheless. If 'The Cat's Pilgrimage' was, as Froude later declared, a reflection of his state of mind at the time of his decision to leave Manchester, it represented a restatement rather than a repudiation of the claim for artistic independence that had been asserted, somewhat prematurely, in his fictions.

43. Froude to Max Müller, 25 November 1840, and to Elizabeth Long, n.d., April 1850, Dunn, *Froude*, I, 165, 167.
44. *Short Studies*, I, 653–5.
45. *Short Studies*, I, 651–3.
46. *Short Studies*, I, 656–9.
47. *Short Studies*, I, 660–2.

The quest was to continue. But now, tempered by an awareness of the sorry contemporary state of human consciousness to which the reception of *The Nemesis of Faith* by critics and admirers alike had given rise, its course would be different. In the withdrawal to Plas Gwynant (and the surrender of any return to Oxford) there would be exile, in the abandonment of teaching and in the severe curtailment of the writing commissions which he had initially welcomed there would be a kind of silence, but, as the fox, wiser in the ways of the world than any who claimed to see beyond it, had enjoined, there would also be cunning.

III

Though he had determined in the early 1850s still 'to be of some use to my generation', the actual direction which this new course would take remained uncertain. On the whole, moreover, Froude's thinking about his choices was almost entirely negative. A new edition of *The Nemesis* would not, after all, be published, and a German translation would not go ahead. He would not work for the new journal being founded by 'the blackguard' G. H. Lewes, he would not write for Samuel Lucas's young Tory organ, *The Press*, and he abandoned his plans to publish his fables as 'Tales by Zeta' in *Fraser's*. What he did undertake immediately was translation, relevant, idiomatic, and anonymous.

Some time in 1851 Froude secured from Bohn a contract to supply a translation of at least two of Goethe's novels: *Die Wahlverwandschaften* (on which he imposed the now authoritative English title, *Elective Affinities*) and *The Sorrows of Young Werther* for publication in their Standard Library series. By the spring of 1852 the former was already with the press, and *Werther*, he told his friend Max Müller, was almost ready to go off.[48] In the event, how-ever, Froude's 'Werther', never saw the light of day, and when *Elective Affinities* eventually appeared in 1854, the publisher decreed that the transla-tor should remain anonymous.[49]

48. Froude to Max Müller, 16 May (1852?), British Library, Add MS 46359, f. 77: 'My Dear Müller, Can you tell me in haste what the conventional meaning of "Spanische Dorfen" is ... The Elective Affinities is done and printed. Werther nearly done and not printed. I am well sick of translating.'
49. *Novels and Tales by Goethe ... Translated Chiefly by R. D. Boylan Esq.* (Bohn, London, 1854); a note by 'HGB' (Bohn) states: 'The Elective Affinities has been executed by a gentleman well known in the literary world who does not wish his name to appear', v.

What happened to Froude's 'Werther' is unknown; but the publisher's note attached to *Elective Affinities* made clear Bohn's concern with the remarkable frankness with which Froude rendered the most intimate and controversial sections of the text. When it came to rendering Goethe's novel into English, Froude produced the most uncompromising version of Goethe's words that English would allow. Froude's success in effectively preserving the metaphorical character of the original German has been noted by commentators. But of no less importance for his time was his success in putting before a mid-Victorian readership as frank an account of the sources and character of sexual attraction and conduct as Goethe himself was prepared to give. Nothing could be more indicative of the determination of the author of *The Nemesis of Faith* to confront the complexities of sexual ethics than the frankness with which he rendered the text of *Elective Affinities*.[50]

Translation thus provided an interim and indirect means of vindicating the moral purpose of Froude's misunderstood fiction, but in regard to more direct means of achieving his purpose, Froude was still uncertain. There were 'various projects which I did not like to lay aside. There were moral problems to be faced.' 'Atheistical theories' were again current, which Froude found pernicious. Whatever his doubts about the present state of established religion, it was clear to Froude that philosophy alone had failed 'to restrain the brutal part of human nature', while once, in the form of early Christian piety, religion demonstrably had.[51] At this point Froude was contemplating a large 'philosophical–historical survey of the state of things internal and external from Nero to Trajan' which he entitled 'The Era of Tacitus' and which promised to address this issue.[52] Nothing came of it, however. Instead, under financial pressure and the temptation of the high prices now being paid by the literary journals, Froude turned to reviewing and essay-writing. These were 'desultory efforts', Froude later recalled, but amidst the body of his early journalism a set of essays (several of which he found fit to reprint in his selected essays) trace a path of his turn toward history.

---

50. David J. De Laura, 'Froude's Anonymous Translation of Goethe', *Papers of the Bibliographical Society of America*, 69 (1975), 187–96; R. R. Hare and P. L. Shillingsburg, 'A Note on Froude's Anonymous Translation of Goethe', *Papers of the Bibliographical Society of America*, 71 (1977), 508–12; Susanne Stark, 'A "Monstrous Book" after all": James Anthony Froude and the Reception of Goethe's *Die Wahlverwandtschaften* in Nineteenth Century Britain', *Modern Language Review*, 98 (2003), 102–16. None of these authorities were aware of the letter to Max Müller confirming and dating Froude's translation and his work on *Werther*.
51. Dunn, *Froude*, I, 168.
52. Froude to Clough, 20 September 1849, F. L. Mulhauser (ed.), *Correspondence of A. H. Clough*, I, 271–2; Froude to Elizabeth Long, 30 November 1849, Dunn, *Froude*, I, 167.

One opportunity was provided by a commission from *Fraser's* to review a collaborative work by the scientist and amateur philosopher Henry George Atkinson and the radical feminist and publicist Harriet Martineau, entitled *Letters on the Laws of Man's Nature and Development*.[53] Conceived as an attack on philosophical idealism and religious mysticism, and as a defence of the scientific basis of materialism, the *Letters* had not only relied on rational argument, but sought to strengthen their thesis through Atkinson's meticulously recorded experiments in mesmerism and phrenology. Their methods exposed the authors to ridicule in the higher journals: Martineau's brother James published a devastating attack in the *Prospective Review* which resulted in a permanent rupture of their relationship.[54] By contrast, Froude's approach was mild. Regarding the book as a symptom of the broader cultural and spiritual malaise which he himself had sought to combat with such unsatisfactory results, its effects were deplorable—not because of the intentions of the authors, but because of the unintentional succour which it gave to minds already prepared to surrender all belief in the spiritual and the eternal, and to affirm their desires or their current ways of living as sufficient justification for their existence. The materialist version of the mind/body problem, Froude argued, was necessarily inadequate because the conceptualisation of the problem was itself a human construct and thus a reflection of the problem it seeks to escape. The distinction was in practice beyond the human faculties; and even if it were sustainable by the mind, the alternatives which it presents to the same finite human intelligence are stark: 'Either [matter] was created out of nothing by Almighty God. Or it is eternal. And it is hard to say which alternative is more awful.' For Froude, the regular reformulation of this necessarily intractable problem was itself a symptom of the decline or disappearance of a primal understanding of human consciousness which he unabashedly identifies as reverence for the very fact of Creation and faith in its purpose. Thus the real dichotomy in human existence lay not in such indeterminable speculations concerning mind and matter, but between these futile, enervating conjecturings and the dynamic creative force of faith in a purposive universe.

Froude's essay on 'Materialism' served several polemical purposes at once. It allowed him to make clear that, whatever some of his readers may have assumed, he had no sympathy for atheism nor the scepticism which tolerated

---

53. *Fraser' Magazine*, 43 (April 1851), 418–34.
54. 'Mesmeric Atheism', *Prospective Review*, 7 (April 1851), 224–62.

it. More importantly, it provided him with the opportunity of restating in contemporary terms the ethical historicism which he had first explored in his earlier hagiographical and critical writing, but which his literary efforts had failed adequately to convey as an imminent crisis. Finally, it supplied an occasion for another effort at applying the rhetorical shift that had also been a characteristic of his earlier writings. Surfacing once more in 'Materialism' was that sudden alteration in register between the cool and balanced tone which predominated in the expository and analytical sections of the essay, and the deeply reverent, prophetic language with which it closes. Even if we are indeed on the threshold of some dire epoch of atheism as heralded by the book he has been discussing, Froude concludes in the voice of the Psalmist:

> We will not fear though the earth be moved, and though the hills be carried into the midst of the sea; though the waters rage and swell and though the waters rage at the tempest, the rivers of that very flood—that awful atheist deluge—shall in the end make glad the Holy City, the place of His Tabernacle, and cleanse and fertilize where it threatens to destroy.[55]

The intent of such a dramatic change from the rational and analytical to the millennial and chiliastic can be readily surmised: following on the moderate, reasoned voice of the bulk of the essay, the exalted Old Testament rhetoric of Froude's concluding sentences was designed to emphasise the force of conviction with which the writer himself had been imbued. That it had actually worked such an effect on his readers is, however, open to doubt. Froude himself believed his essay had served only to alienate his radical allies while failing to convince those he wished to address. 'Materialism' was, however, only an early instance of the complex strategy of intellectual and rhetorical reconstruction which he had gradually undertaken in the early 1850s. Five other essays composed around the same time helped advance his quest in a considerably more effective manner.

Of these, an essay entitled 'The Lives of the Saints', though not published until 1852, was among the earliest.[56] Ostensibly a commentary on the work of the Catholic hagiographers, the Bollandists, the essay soon develops into a larger consideration of hagiography in general and the cultural significance

---

55. *Fraser's Magazine*, 43 (April 1851), 434. Froude is quoting loosely from the *Book of Psalms*, 46.
56. Though it appeared first in *The Eclectic Review*, 95 (1852), 147–64, Froude dates it in *Short Studies* as having been written in 1850; references here are to the version printed in *Short Studies*, I, 545–75.

of its disappearance. Acknowledging the failure of the recent attempt to revive the genre of which he had himself had been a part, Froude argues that the fault lay only partly with the naïvety of its participants; it was more importantly a reflection of the present culture's state of religious and moral decline. 'Fact idolators', modern Englishmen, had become enamoured by the clever but essentially negative discoveries of science and philosophy while at the same time growing blind and deaf to the beauties of a spiritual myth; their dismissal of the form of medieval hagiography as childish, disingenuous, or poetic being a sorry indictment of their own benighted condition. 'The superstition of science scoffs at the superstition of faith.' Our loss of sympathy with the extraordinary humans of early Christianity was itself a condemnation of our present condition; for all around us in the natural world, if we cared to look, was the evidence of the living reality of the vision of Creation which the Christian saints had possessed, and of the way they chose to live with it—but to this natural history also we have become blind.

To this recognisably Romantic version of the Fall, Froude adds his own particular emphasis on the character of our moral decline within the material world which he had first essayed with such alarming results in his fiction: our loss of sexual control. The frequently advanced argument that early Christian asceticism and monasticism represented some kind of withdrawal from the world, he asserts, revealed a profound misunderstanding of the true force of the movement: 'Monasticism represented something more positive than a movement against the world'; it was 'the realization of the infinite loveliness and beauty of personal purity.' Having made the claim, Froude next sets it in broad historical terms: the Greeks, despite their piety, their wisdom, and their 'exquisite ... sense of beauty', never 'supposed any part of their duty to the gods to consist in keeping their bodies untainted.' Worse than that:

> With only a few rare exceptions, pollution too detestable to be even named among ourselves, was of familiar even daily occurrence among their great men; was no reproach to philosopher or to statesman.[57]

Under the republic the Romans practised their own form of austere self-discipline. But morality was loved by the Romans not for its own sake but 'for what resulted from it, for the strength and rigid endurance which it

---

57. *Short Studies*, I, 567.

gave.' Thus when, under the empire, the Romans had no further use for personal virtue, Rome became 'a picture of enormous sensuality, of the coarsest animal desire, with means unlimited to gratify it'.[58]

All this had been reversed with the coming of Christianity. Moving beyond the limiting and artificial confines of mere rational philosophy, rejecting the false dualism of mind and spirit espoused by the Manicheans and the Neo-Platonists, the early Christians 'sought to present the body to God as a pure and holy sacrifice, as so much of the material world conquered from the appetites and lusts, and from the devil whose abode they were'. In virtue of their exertions, all humanity has been given an insight into a higher form of life:

> Henceforth we require, not greatness only, but goodness; and not that goodness only which begins and ends in conduct correctly regulated; but that love of goodness, that keen pure feeling for it, which resides in a conscience as sensitive and susceptible as a woman's modesty.[59]

With this we have come a long way from a critical examination of the Bollandists. But Froude's main concern has been to argue once more that our own loss of sensibility in regard to the medieval hagiographers is a symptom of a more general loss of moral compass, the evidence of which lies all around.

This trajectory of Western civilisation's moral and spiritual history is developed further in a pair of essays which explore the topic from opposite sides—one on 'The Homeric Life' and a second on 'The Philosophy of Christianity'.[60] In the former, which is ostensibly a consideration of the debate on the authorship of the *Odyssey* and the *Iliad* (Froude is mildly on the side of single authorship), Froude is again preoccupied with the evidence of evolving human consciousness. In Homer 'the Divine law of justice is conceived as clearly as we in this day can conceive it. The Supreme power is the same immortal lover of justice, and the same hater of iniquity, and justice means what we mean by justice.'[61] Likewise, through the systematic contrasts he makes between Achilles, who believes only in himself, and

---

58. *Short Studies*, I, 568.
59. *Short Studies*, I, 570–1.
60. 'The Homeric Life', *Fraser's Magazine*, 44 (1851), 76–92, reprinted in *Short Studies*, I, 502–44; 'The Philosophy of Christianity', *The Leader* (1851), no pagination, reprinted as 'The Philosophy of Catholicism', *Short Studies*, I, 188–201; reference is made here to the version printed in *Short Studies*.
61. *Short Studies*, I, 514.

Hector, who has faith in the immortal, Homer reveals an ancient Greek perception of divine providence that is no less sophisticated than its Christian successor. The manner in which Homer deals with war offers even clearer evidence of the Greeks' moral refinement. Although struggle, victory, and defeat are dominant themes in the epics, there is no dwelling upon the gore and horror of the battlefield simply for its own sake, either for pleasure, as in the savage scenes in the *Niebelungenlied*, or in despair, as in the modern verse of Byron. Indeed, the only modern who comes close to representing the honour and nobility of defeat in battle is the young German, Lennau [*sic*], whose early descent into insanity is a sign of the fragility of the vision in modern times.[62] In its combination of the highest human virtues of manliness and refinement, 'Homer's age', Froude concludes confidently, 'was cultivated to a degree the like of which the Earth has not witnessed since.'[63]

Such an argument might seem to be at odds both with Froude's general moral historicism and in particular with the repudiation of Greek love included in 'The Lives of the Saints'. But his position is more nuanced. Although he makes no reference to homosexuality, Froude does, however, acknowledge some moral 'discolouration' cast over Homer's age, through the treatment and the position of women. Adultery, prostitution, and female slavery were accepted in Homer's Greece in a way utterly unacceptable to the present or even to the feudal world. But, on the other hand, Homer's high view of the value and purpose of war contrasts with the savage scenes so beloved of warlike epics of feudal times. Froude's conception of a mutating moral consciousness was neither simply progressive nor entirely regressive. It was a broadly cyclical process under which some cultures at times came close to approximating a clear vision of the nature of Creation; but none ever fully attained it. That there was an element of halting progress within this history was, however, suggested in the strength of the medieval saints' perception of the world. In 'The Philosophy of Christianity' Froude offers a brief sketch as to how such progress could take place. In this he argues that the famed asceticism of the medieval saints was a practical result of the blending of Greek idealism and Oriental sensibility which took place by the close of the fifth century with the decline of Manichaeism. Though

62. Froude is referring here to the Austro-Hungarian poet Nikolaus Lenau (Nikolaus Franz Niembsch Edler von Strehlenau, 1802–1850), the author of a number of epic poems, including a 'Faust' and a 'Don Juan'.
63. *Short Studies*, I, 531–2.

distasteful now and incomprehensible to some, it reflected the real strength
of early Christianity as the saints struggled to 'anticipate in life the work of
death in uniting themselves more completely to Christ', and by overcoming
the temptations of the flesh they had proved that the sanctification and salvation of mere humans was a genuine possibility for all.[64] The loss of this
acute consciousness was, however, irrevocable. But the question that now
urgently required an answer was how, given the evidence that a crisis was
well under way in Protestant England, might a means be found which
would be adequate to the challenge?

In the essays so far considered Froude largely left this question unanswered. But in two further essays composed around this time he came closest to a summary statement of his views subsequent to the failure of *The
Nemesis of Faith*. The first was an essay on Emerson's *Representative Men*
(New York, 1850).[65] The opening tone of Froude's 'Representative Men' is,
in contrast to the other essays, distinctly captious. Asserting his new-found
independence from a figure who in the 1840s he regarded to be as significant as Carlyle, Froude objects not merely to Emerson's particular selection
of representative individuals, but to the idea of representivity at all. In the
Homeric age and in the time of the saints, Froude argues, such differentia-
tion would have been inconceivable, for, since greatness was then understood as proximity to timeless ideals, it was their very uniformity—their
'sameness'—which marked them as great. But 'the age of the saints has
passed' Froude acknowledges, and 'they are no longer any service to us'. In
their place there has been nothing but Emerson's men and the empty novels
of Ainsworth and Bulwer. This cultural poverty—'the utter spiritual disintegration into which we have fallen'—is everywhere evident, its reality made
palpable in our failure to comprehend the heroism and piety of earlier ages.
The sources of this decline are several: 'Many of them lie deep down in the
roots of humanity', and many of them the consequences of profound historical forces which 'leave individuals but a limited margin within which
they may determine what they will be'.[66]

But within such narrow confines Froude indicates a number of identifiable causes. One lies in our deep mistrust of the ascetic spirit—of the drive
toward self-abnegation. Another is our mistrust of heroism: 'Courage does

---

64. 'The Philosophy of Catholicism', *Short Studies*, I, 199–200.
65. 'Representative Men', *Eclectic Review*, 95 (1852), 568–82; reprinted in *Short Studies*, I,
576–601.
66. 'Representative Men', in *Short Studies*, I, 587.

not help to make money, and so we have ceased to care about it.' A third is our mistrust of altruism—of good works. All of these impulses, Froude then suggests provocatively, had their origin in the Reformation. A revolt against the decadent hypocrisies of a moribund religion, the Protestant rejection of the empty pretences of Catholic teaching was wholly understandable. But as it has in turn begun to decay, Protestantism is bereft of its own sources of spiritual regeneration:

> The old hero worship has vanished ... but no other has arisen in its stead, and without it we wander in the dark. The commonplaces of morality, the negative commandments, general exhortations to goodness, while neither speaker nor hearer can tell what they mean by goodness—these are all which now remain to us; and thrown into a life more complicated than any which the earth has yet experienced, we are left to wind our way through the labyrinth.[67]

In seeking a resolution for this bleak condition, Froude in this essay has little enough to offer beyond an exhortation to recognise and celebrate the good and the brave in the everyday and the ordinary. But in the second and far more intellectually concentrated essay Froude proceeds to argue that these familiar nostrums are in fact the only ones which have any foundation in philosophy.

Subsequently recognised as an exposition of remarkable quality, Froude's second essay on 'Spinoza' (written around 1852 but not published until 1855) supplies a rare demonstration of his capacity as a philosophical analyst.[68] Far from being wholly admiring, as he was in his earlier essay, Froude now offers a critical account of Spinoza's entire system of thought of considerable subtlety and acuity. Toward the close of his demonstration Froude acknowledges that while Spinoza's message 'is singularly beautiful', it is developed at a level of abstraction that few 'Englishmen' would be prepared to follow it. But

---

67. *Short Studies*, I, 591.
68. 'Spinoza', *Westminster Review*, OS 64 (July 1855); reprinted in *Short Studies*, I, 339–400. Froude elsewhere records that the essay was originally accepted for publication in the *Edinburgh Review* by George Cornewell Lewis, but was rejected when Henry Reeves took over the editorial chair; see Froude to Sir William Muir, 28 April [1882], Edinburgh University Library, Muir MSS, Dk.2.13. The value of Froude's essay was acknowledged by George Eliot; see Gordon Haight (ed.), *The George Letters*, 211, by Robert Willis, author of a major life of *Benedict Spinoza* (London, 1877), 198–200, and in Sir Frederick Pollock's major study, *Spinoza: His Life and Philosophy* (London, 1880): 'In English the best general view is still given by Mr Froude's essay [in] the *Westminster Review*', 26.

even if we cannot believe Spinoza's system taken in its entire completeness, yet we may not blind ourselves to the disinterestedness and calm nobility which pervade his theories of human life and obligation.[69]

This assertion comes, however, after an exposition in which he claims to demonstrate that

Spinoza is, after all, but stating in philosophical language the extreme doctrine of Grace; and St Paul ... may be accused with justice of having the same opinion. If Calvinism be pressed to its logical consequences, it either becomes an intolerable falsehood, or it resolves itself into the philosophy of Spinoza.[70]

This is sly. Spinoza has rescued right-thinking Christians by demonstrating that, despite the damage done by the biblical critics, the essence of the Christian view of the world could be recovered and defended philosophically. Yet he had done so in a way which remains unacceptable to English minds not only because of its abstractions, but because of its questionable *a priori* assumptions. Yet his reconstruction still contained a profound problem that lay also at the heart of Christian—or at least of Pauline—teaching. This was the question of human responsibility for sin: the terrible implication that, as creatures of God, 'we should be without power to obey Him without his free grace, and yet be held responsible for our failures when that grace is withheld'.[71]

'It is idle to call a philosopher sacrilegious', Froude goes on, 'who has but systematized the faith which so many believe, and cleared it of its most hideous features.' Having thus steeped his readers in such a quandary, Froude proceeds to work a way out through an even more detailed analysis of Spinoza's own address to the problem of human freedom in which he shows that in practical terms an active commitment of humans to know the good and to act upon it is a necessary component of the whole divine plan. The human mind, says Froude expounding Spinoza, has been invested with capacity actively to seek out the good through the contemplation of ideas that are 'adequate' (that is, founded upon demonstrable laws of Creation as revealed in Spinoza's system), and the ability to reject 'inadequate' ideas based on our subjective and defective experience. By rigorously pursuing the former and rejecting the latter through continuous and self-conscious discipline, we become free:

69. *Short Studies*, I, 389.   70. *Short Studies*, I, 363.   71. *Short Studies*, I, 364.

> So far ... as we know clearly what we do, as we understand what we are, and
> direct our conduct, not by the passing emotion of the moment, but by grave,
> clear, and constant knowledge of what is really good, so far ... we are ourselves
> the spring of our own activity—we pursue the genuine well-being of our
> entire nature.[72]

To Froude this is inspiring; but it is also a counsel of perfection. He sees, in his
self-consciously 'English' manner, two related objections. The first concerns
the practical inequalities that obtain between different individuals: not all men
can be artists or saints, not all can be held equally responsible for acts of sin,
crime, or folly. Everything depends on contingent matters of inheritance,
opportunity, and experience. This inequality of capacity and opportunity
which is demonstrable throughout humanity's history is discounted by
Spinoza—Froude's second objection—because in his metaphysical preoccupations he has neglected the reality of historical change as it is experienced by
human minds. Although geometric propositions may be stated in present or
future tenses without significant difference, in the sense that 'if two lines in a
circle cut each other, the rectangle under the parts of one *will* equal that under
the parts of the other', the same does not apply to historical propositions.

> Allowing ... as much as we please that the condition of England a hundred
> years hence lies already in embryo in the present in existing causes, it is a para-
> dox to say that such conditions exist already in the sense in which the proper-
> ties of a circle exist.[73]

This is, in fact, Spinoza's position, and though he allows elsewhere that 'for
practical purposes we are obliged to regard the future as contingent, and
ourselves able to influence it', he never really addresses this fundamental
tension in his system.[74]

   Thus, while Spinoza's philosophy may be the best possible approxima-
tion of the nature of divine Creation available to our limited minds, it is
in practice of very limited value to us as we attempt to make sense of our
existence and seek to act properly upon that sense. This is a chasm that
only a contemplation of human history can bridge, for in its recurring
revelation of general human weakness, ignorance, courage, and conviction, in its assessment of the individual sources of such apparent vices and
virtues, and most importantly in the delineation of their consequences in
particular times, places, and circumstances, history fulfils a vital purpose.

72. *Short Studies*, I, 386.   73. *Short Studies*, I, 366.   74. *Short Studies*, I, 394–5.

It is the only true means by which our minds can secure even a fleeting sense of our individual place, and that of our fellow creatures, in the vast schema of Creation.

It was this acute reformulation of the needs of his audience that brought sharply into focus a literary genre alternative to criticism, philosophy, and fiction which even at the time that he was writing on Spinoza was also beginning to attract Froude's attention: the writing of English history.

IV

In his autobiographical fragment and elsewhere Froude recalled that his interest in the history of the English Reformation had first been sparked by the controversies which it had raged around it both at home in Dartington and during his time as an undergraduate at Oxford.[75] But in fact the idea of focusing on the subject as his principal object of study and writing emerged only slowly, and in part by accident. Froude's earliest scholarly interests lay, as we have seen, in early medieval England and Ireland; and in the period immediately following his departure from Oxford his intention had been to concentrate on the emergence of Christianity within the Roman Empire as a means of developing the ideas of changing spiritual consciousness which had for so long engaged him. Moreover, in addition to the frequent references to the early Christian era which were a feature of his essay-writing at this time, the first essay in history which he composed, on King Alfred, was a further revisit to the times and concerns of St Neot.[76] Early in 1852, however, a number of circumstances combined to begin the transformation of the moralising novelist and critic into an historian of the sixteenth century.

The first of these was a commission from the *Westminster Review* to write a review essay on Mignet's recent *Histoire de Marie Stuart*. The French historian's account had been highly sympathetic in the current Romantic vein.[77] But the review offered Froude an unexpected opportunity to rehearse the

---

75. Dunn, *Froude*, I, 40–1.
76. 'King Alfred', *Fraser's Magazine*, 45 (January 1852), 74–87.
77. François Auguste Marie Mignet, *Histoire de Marie Stuart* (2 vols., Paris, 1851). On the image of Mary Stuart in the nineteenth century, see Jayne E. Lewis, *Mary Queen of Scots: Romance and Nation* (London, 1998), chs. 7–8; Helen Smailes and Duncan Thomson, *The Queen's Image: A Celebration of Mary Queen of Scots* (Edinburgh, 1987).

issues of personal morality which had been preoccupying him for so many years—now, however, in rather different terms. Here was an instance of the disastrous consequences of personal irresponsibility in matters of emotional and sexual conduct which far exceeded those of any of his fictional creations; and yet Mary had been exonerated by modern writers, her sins and her crimes diminished by those afflicted with a sentimental urge to defend and celebrate this 'tragic' heroine. In doing so they had done a great violence to the historical record, and an even greater violence to the unchanging moral precepts which historical study was intended to uphold. For Froude, the indictment of contemporary sentimentalist writers—so symptomatic of the loss of moral compass against which he had for so long been warning—was far more important than a revisionist condemnation of the unfortunate Scottish queen. But the extraordinary force of his attack, and the unashamedly anti-French, anti-Scottish, and pro-English ramifications of its central contention, made it seem wonderfully provocative to the *Westminster's* readers.[78]

The essay was very well received, so similar commissions followed. In July he published a stirring essay on the Elizabethan maritime adventurers entitled 'England's Forgotten Worthies'.[79] In the following year he contributed essays on Mary Tudor and John Knox in the January and July issues of the *Westminster* respectively.[80] An essay on Cardinal Wolsey and a critique of John Campbell's *Lives of the Lord Chancellors* appeared in January and July 1854 in the same journal.[81] Thus Froude's reputation spread. For *Fraser's* Froude contributed a two-part article on 'The Morals of Queen Elizabeth' in October and November 1853, and a substantial review of J. H. Burton's *History of Scotland*.[82] This body of writing, along with a series of lesser reviews which he provided both for *Fraser's* and the *Westminster*, confirmed Froude's transformation from a novelist of dubious reputation to an historian of increasing authority.[83]

78. 'Mary Stuart', *Westminster Review*, 57 (January 1852), 96–142.
79. *Westminster Review*, 58 (July 1852), 32–67; reprinted in *Short Studies*, I, 443–501.
80. 'Mary Tudor', 'John Knox', *Westminster Review*, 59 (January 1853), 1–34; 60 (July 1853), 1–50.
81. 'Cardinal Wolsey', 'Lord Campbell', *Westminster Review*, 62 (July 1854), 1–48; 61 (April 1854), 446–79.
82. 'Morals of Queen Elizabeth', *Fraser's Magazine*, 48 (August–October, 1853), 371–87, 489–505; 'Burton's *History of Scotland*', *Fraser's Magazine*, 48 (August–October, 1853), 127–42.
83. For Froude's early determination to devote himself increasingly to history-writing against the advice of friends, see Froude to Clough, 22 November 1853, F. L. Mulhauser (ed.), *Correspondence of A. H. Clough*, I., 466–7.

Several of the principal characteristics of the great history soon to be conceived are first displayed clearly in these preliminary essays. Here Froude's readers first discover the voice of the stern moralising historian, and here also the unquestioning English nationalist. None of these features is surprising when seen from the perspective of the finished grand narrative of the 1860s, but they represent a marked departure from the troubled cosmopolitan intellectual of the 1840s. Most notable of all is their strident reassertion of the Protestant myth, so absent from the early fiction. The Mary Stuart of the essay is the faithless Duessa of *The Faerie Queene*; Mary Tudor the Bloody Mary of Foxe's *Book of Martyrs*; John Knox the Old Testament prophet *redivivus*; and Drake, Hawkins, Gilbert, and Raleigh, celebrated as the 'worthies' in the most influential and remembered of these early essays, are the hero-saints of the great confessional struggle fought out on the high seas.

'England's Forgotten Worthies' has frequently been identified as the epitome of this new chauvinist style, an inspiration for Kingsley's *Westward Ho!* and a host of lesser schoolboy adventures, and for a school of patriotic history paintings in the style of Millais' *The Boyhood of Raleigh* (1870).[84] But the essay itself is a rather more uncertain exercise than the flattery of later imitations might imply. It was highly polemical in tone, opening like his essay on 'Representative Men', in a tone of indignant rejection of the assumptions of the unhappy editors of the Hakluyt Society whose recent set of publications provided the occasion of the essay.[85] In restricting themselves to editing and collating the documentary evidence concerning the lives and times of the great Elizabethan seafarers, the dry-as-dust scholars, Froude charged, had misinterpreted their true historical significance. They were not merely heroes and adventurers; they were the spiritual representatives of their nation, equal to and even more deserving than the statesmen, scholars, and reformers who had filled the pages of collections of 'worthies' from the ur-text Foxe's *Book of Martyrs* to his own time. Moreover, they were martyrs too: 'They were cut off in the flower of their days, and few of them laid their

---

84. A. L Rowse, *Froude*; for a more critical analysis, see J. W. Burrow, *A Liberal Descent: Victorian Historians and the English Past* (Cambridge, 1983), ch. 4.
85. Founded in 1846, the Hakluyt Society sought to publish scholarly editions of accounts of voyages, discoveries, travel journals, navigational achievements, and geographical reports of importance. By the time of Froude's essay it had already issued a dozen substantial volumes. Froude's largely unfair attack on the Society's editorial practices was bitterly resented, and gave rise to much comment in subsequent publications. R. H. Major—one of the editors castigated by Froude, and sometime Honorary Secretary of the society—published a lengthy rebuttal (including correspondence with Froude) in the second edition of his *Selected Letters of Christopher Columbus* (London, 1870), vi–cxlii.

bones in the sepulchres of their fathers ... Life to them ... was a life of sacrifice ... of which the cross was the symbol.'[86] Such assertiveness is strained; and Froude, given the evidence supplied by the Haklyut texts, is compelled to concede their faults. 'They were no ... saints in the modern sentimental sense of that word ... private adventurers as they all were it was natural enough that private rapacity and private badness should be found among them as among other mortals.'[87] Yet 'far below such prudential economies lay a chivalrous enthusiasm which in these dull days we can hardly realise ... the high nature of these men and the high objects they pursued will become visible to us only as we can throw ourselves back into their times and teach our hearts to feel as they felt.'[88] As historical argument this will appear tendentious; but our failure to be convinced, Froude claims, is due neither to the simple strangeness of the past nor to the failings of the historian, but to our own unrealised loss of comprehension.

The strain of such a mode of historicist assertion is further intensified by the quite contradictory attitudes struck in some of the essays. Thus Mignet's apology for Mary Queen of Scots is roundly denounced 'for stereotyping calumny and stimulating a vicious sympathy with wrong', and Lord Campbell is excoriated for uncritically passing on the most scandalous tittle-tattle concerning the lives of great men to the public 'whose appetite for depreciation he has so successfully gratified'. But Froude himself is similarly uncritical in his summary judgements of those of whom he approved and those of whom he disapproved. Thus Mary Tudor died 'knowing that no man or woman left on this earth would waste one regret or shed one tear upon her memory', while Froude devoted two long papers to the purpose of rebutting every slur upon the character of Elizabeth I which 'the mean and base invented [and] the foolish and bigoted ... believed.'[89] Similarly, Froude passed lightly over the faults of Cardinal Wolsey which were not those 'which should weigh with posterity against so much genuine excellence'; for Wolsey had 'accomplished more actual good for England than perhaps any single minister did, except Lord Burghley.'[90] He forthrightly defended the brutal intolerance John Knox had displayed toward the young Mary Stuart and the

86. *Short Studies*, I, 495
87. *Short Studies*, I, 472.
88. *Short Studies*, I, 458.
89. 'Mary Tudor', 34; Morals of Queen Elizabeth, Part I', 374.
90. 'Cardinal Wolsey', 47.

ageing Cardinal Beaton, whose murder Knox had celebrated: 'Beaton was guilty of murder, and whatever punishment is due to such crimes, he must be held to have deserved.'[91]

These are the early appearances of those bold inconsistencies of judgement which were to be such a source of exasperation to critical readers of Froude's later history. They are made all the more disconcerting by those occasions on which Froude reveals that he is himself aware of the complexity of judging moral conduct in history and in politics. 'Except on Machiavelli's principles', asks Froude at the opening of his essay on Mary Stuart, 'who can tell what political morality is?' 'We cannot judge kings and statesmen as we judge each other,' for they must act in emergencies 'and the emergency must pronounce for itself on the right and the wrong ... immutable morality [should not] intrude where it has nothing to say.'[92] In this way Froude can exonerate Elizabeth and Knox and the sea-dogs from the worst of the crimes alleged against them. But why not also Mary Stuart, Cardinal Beaton, and Machiavelli's Prince for that matter? Though he never condescended to offer any justification for his convenient moral calculus either in the essays or, notoriously, in the *History of England*, an indication that there was after all some consistency underlying his apparently wilful incoherence is to be found in two non-historical essays which he composed as he was developing his apprenticeship as an historian.

The first is entitled 'Ethical Doubts concerning Reineke Fuchs'.[93] Drawing upon Goethe's version of the medieval fable, Froude's meditation on 'Reineke' is one of the most playful and disturbing of his moral writings. It begins simply enough with a dismissal of Macaulay's influential essay on Machiavelli which had attempted to rehabilitate the Florentine by accounting for the more deplorable aspects of his political philosophy as merely the result of the peculiar historical influences under which he and his generation suffered. Had Machiavelli lived elsewhere or at a different time, Macaulay had generously concluded, his genius would have been unadulterated by these particular accidents of circumstance.[94]

To Froude this superficial moral relativism was quite unacceptable: Macaulay has struck 'the very lowest stone of our ethical convictions, and declared that the foundation quakes under it'.[95] But just as he is on the point

91. 'John Knox' 5.
92. 'Mary Stuart' 96.
93. *Westminster Review*, 46 (September 1852), 321–30; reprinted in *Short Studies*, I, 602–29.
94. 'Machiavelli', *Edinburgh Review*, 45 (March 1827), 259–95.

of dismissing it, Froude suddenly changes register. Adopting an unusually intimate tone, he confesses to his readers that his conscience has just reminded him of his own secret regard for an even greater reprobate, Reynard the Fox. There follows a mock baring of the soul on the part of the author which, while echoing in its pretences to great perplexity and innocence the trickeries of the mythical fox, nevertheless issues in a number of clear and disturbing assertions. One is the author's belief—based, he says, on enquiry—that most of us hide a secret admiration for Reynard, and exploring this sneaking regard, Froude argues that we admire him because he is above all extraordinarily able: 'That is the very *differentia* of him. An "animal capable".' And being so efficient he is successful in all that he sets out to do. Admiration of the successful is a form of wish-fulfilment—a reflection of what we would like to be. Then the argument makes a surprising shift: if admiration is based on introspection, an analysis of what we admire in ourselves reveals that we do not admire our virtues: 'a man does not praise himself for being good', but rather 'for the face which nature made—the strength which is ours we know not how—our talents, our rank, our possessions'. In short, whether for good or ill, what we admire in ourselves and others are not virtues which we have acquired, 'but *gifts*' (Froude's italics). This, then, is what really lies behind our regard for Reynard: 'He has gifts enough ... and if he lacks the gift to use them in a way which we call good, at least he uses them successfully.'[96]

This is an unsettling conclusion for a self-appointed moralist to reach—all the more so, as he goes on to admit that some of Reynard's actions, such as his eating of the unhappy hare, Lampe, lack any justification whatever. But the essay, like the original tale is, of course, a satire. Its point is not to celebrate the unprincipled fox, but rather to expose the feebleness of the moral standpoint of Macaulay and other liberal-minded historians who like to pretend that his kind do not really exist. The Machiavellian, like Reynard, is not an accidental product of time or place. He is a universal human character confirmed both through mythification and through our own introspection: the man *capable* of exploiting the circumstances in which he finds himself in his own interests regardless of others, of acting in the world and of shaping it as he pleases. To diminish such figures, as Macaulay and his like have done, is not simply to commit a psychological or moral error—serious

95. *Short Studies*, I, 604.   96. *Short Studies*, I, 618, 624.

enough though those errors are. It is also fundamentally to misunderstand the very process by which history works, and the challenge which it poses to moral precept by the way it works. As the exigencies of time and circumstance change in ways which most of us have no comprehension, the Reynards of the world *act* for good or for ill, and we, whether we are geese like Reynard's victims or sovereigns like Noble, the king of Reynard's world, permit them to do so. This is not, of course, to say that they act for the good, or that they are always as perfect in their capability as the mythical fox; but the interaction of these distinct individuals with the particular circumstances prevailing in their day is the true dynamic of history. The manner in which we respond to support or oppose their actions is a moral obligation on us all; and the task of helping us estimate the moral value of these Reynard actions is the proper duty of the historian.

But how is this to be done? 'The mere record of actions', says Froude in a contemporary essay that reveals he is already sensitive to the limitations of historical knowledge, 'will forever lead us astray. They are all embedded, so to say, in a series of circumstances out of which they have arisen, and which no effort of imagination will ever reproduce.'[97] For Froude, the way out of this *impasse* lies in the study of character: of the geese, the lions, the crows, and above all, the Reynards of the world. 'The actions of men form their characters', Froude grants, 'but their characters, again, interpret their actions,' and the only way out of this circularity is by means of a thorough survey of the surviving materials to discover 'the impressions formed of character by such contemporary living persons as were competent to form an opinion'.[98] As a defence of the value of extensive historical research this is mildly encouraging, but the invocation of the judgements of historical figures to defend the legitimacy of the historian's exercise of judgement itself involves a certain circularity which Froude cannot easily escape. Epistemological sceptics will observe that this is merely a way of allowing one generation to select what it finds most congenial from the expressions of another; unless, that is, one accepts that there is a further objective coordinate governing this intergenerational exchange—that there is, for all its mystery and our inability fully to comprehend it, a purpose in the course of historical change

---

97. 'Morals of Queen Elizabeth I', 373.
98. 'Morals of Queen Elizabeth I', 373–4.

which can become increasingly obvious with distance. This was precisely what Froude had in mind.

On the face of it this might seem to be just a further invocation of 'the Whig interpretation of history'. But the very distinctive nature of Froude's historical teleology is evident in the exploration of man's condition in a universe from which we cannot escape and which we cannot hope to understand that he attempted in the second, very different, essay he composed around the same time. 'The Book of Job' was ostensibly an exercise in biblical literary criticism.[99] The text, Froude argued, was best understood as a polemic against the complacent morality of the Jewish patriarchy which taught that the lives of men were watched over by an all-seeing omnipresent God who rewarded the good and punished the evil, not only in the coming life but in this. Job's God, of course, did not conform to this rule, but visited the unfortunate man with a series of sufferings and afflictions that almost broke his spirit, alienated his friends, and lost him the respect of the community. It was with these social or public consequences rather than God's purpose that Job's author was primarily concerned: the repudiation of Job revealed the hypocritical state of a community that had become too complacent about God, too familiar with moral conventions, too sure that it understood the way the world worked. For Froude, the lesson of Job remained pertinent: the same drift toward moral paralysis represented in Job's world threatened once again, Froude argued, to undermine all religious systems, most notably Judaism's successor, Christianity. It was presently observable in a public morality that had converted theological arguments into absolute truths, superficial generalisations into immutable decrees, and served 'as an instant interpreter . . . of any unusual calamity, such as a potato blight, a famine, an epidemic'. The reference to the Irish Famine is obvious, and the impact of this disaster, as we shall see, loomed heavily over Froude's historical thought.[100] But this recent display of moral decadence was merely the latest instance of a process of falling away which was recurrent in human history. The fundamental question was: How could any culture seek to escape from such apparently inexorable moral degeneration?

A partial answer is supplied in Job's painful confrontation with God when, from the depths of anger and despair, he demands an explanation of God's purpose, and has revealed to him in a vision the whole beauty and

---

99. *Westminster Review*, 60 (October 1853), 417–50; reprinted in *Short Studies*, I, 281–338.
100. See ch. 9.

majesty of Creation. In perceiving the magnitude of Creation, he appre-
hends also the proper place of human kind within it, and withdraws, not in
despair but in hope, to the ordinary life, determined to live no longer in
passive obedience of God's laws but in active fulfilment of His purpose. This
is magnificent; yet it is not, Froude recognises, reality, but merely the mas-
terstroke of a poet's imagination. So the question remains, as it did with
Spinoza, as to how, without Job's vision, ordinary men were to gain knowledge of their role in God's purposeful universe. Knowledge in itself was not
enough. What was required instead was that individuals, regardless of their
place in society, should be made aware that they had a responsibility to live
not for themselves but for the sake of the Creator and for the purposes
which Creation had laid down for humanity. And it was necessary also that
individuals' awareness of their communal responsibilities should be expressed
in a manner which went far beyond the negative avoidance of wrong-
doing, and embraced instead an active commitment to doing good in the
world, to making a difference.

How was such a moral awakening to be achieved? The options were few.
Of itself, established religion was inadequate, for it had long ago shown that
it had no means of resisting the drift toward moral ossification that occurred
to all doctrinal positions over time. Provocative and disturbing fiction of the
type initiated by Goethe and imitated by Froude had likewise failed in
England. Carlyle in his early writings had indeed shown the way, but in the
early 1850s his influence, if not his power, was palpably waning. Yet in his
own intensive period of exploration and experimentation, Froude had discovered the potential of another mode of address sufficient at once to
enlighten individuals' minds as to the nature of the world in which they
found themselves, and also to awaken in them the conviction that they must
act purposively within it or bear the consequences of their own inaction. It
lay, he had become convinced, in the fashioning of a distinctive and
deliberately disturbing historical voice.

7

The Promise of England's Past: Writing the *History of England*, 1854–70

'The right understanding of our English History is nothing less than an understanding of the rule under which we are governed by the Almighty Lord of the world; and on the due acknowledgement of which and due submission to its dictates, our happiness, our only highest and true good, depends.'

James Anthony Froude, 1855[1]

Once he had determined upon it, Froude's commitment to his great historical project remained intense, sustained, and unwavering for more than fifteen years. But while it was to issue ultimately in triumph, erasing Froude's reputation as a scandalous novelist and establishing his name in the public mind as an eminent historian, it was not to be without trial, and his success was not to be without qualification either with his audience or within himself.

I

At the outset, even before he began work on the *History*, Froude was obliged to fight bitterly with John Chapman, his former publisher and owner of the *Westminster Review*, to free himself from an informal commitment into

---

1. Froude, 'Suggestions on the Best Means of Teaching History', in *Oxford Essays by Members of the University* (London, 1855), 47–79; quotation from 78–9.

which he had entered in the uncertain days of the early 1850s to provide a brief history of Henrician England based on a selection of state papers made available to Chapman by the Deputy Keeper of Public Records, Sir Francis Palgrave.[2] Having done so, he next worked hard to persuade his new patron, John Parker of *Fraser's Magazine*, to fund a more ambitious project which would cover the entire sixteenth century and would be based upon a far broader range of manuscript and printed sources than had originally been planned. In the end, Parker's offer was a good deal more handsome than Chapman's; for in addition to an advance (which Froude deemed highly satisfactory), he threw in the promise of a steady supply of free books, regular commissions for review, and free accommodation during Froude's research trips to London.[3] Thus in the autumn of 1854 Froude set down to work, and in April 1856, at almost exactly the date of his thirty-eighth birthday, the first two volumes of the *History of England from the Fall of Wolsey to the Death of Elizabeth* appeared, taking the narrative as far as 1540. Two more volumes appeared in March 1858, completing his account of the reign of Henry VIII. Volumes V and VI, covering the reigns of Edward VI and Mary I, were published in the summer of 1860; and steadily, over the next decade, Froude published six volumes on the reign of Elizabeth I in sets of two, appearing in the autumn of 1863, the autumn of 1866, and the spring of 1870.

During this long period of research and composition, several important changes took place both in the circumstances of the author and the character and content of his *History*. At the beginning of the project Froude was a freelance reviewer, writing mainly for the *Westminster* and for *Fraser's*, but also allowing work to appear in other reviews such as the *British Quarterly*, the *Eclectic Review*, and the American journal *Littell's Magazine*. In the later 1850s, however, as his relations with Chapman deteriorated, Froude moved closer to John Parker, and in 1861 he finally declared his allegiance by accepting the editor's chair at *Fraser's*, having acted unofficially in that capacity for several months previously.

His decision to accept the offer was in large part the consequence of personal tragedy. In April 1860, after a long illness, Froude's wife Charlotte

---

2. Froude to Chapman, 14 April 1854, Bodleian Library, Oxford, MS 41815 (Eng. Lett. e28), ff. 110–11; 5 November (1854), Bodleian Library, Oxford, MS 41794 (Eng. Lett. e1), ff. 194–8; Froude to Palgrave, 1 May (1854), Bodleian Library, Oxford, MS 41843 (Eng. Lett. e133), ff. 52–7.
3. Froude to Chapman, 10 August (1860), Bodleian Library, Oxford, MSS 41794 (Eng. Lett. e1), ff. 198–9. Dunn, *Froude*, I, 174–5, 199, 201.

died at their house in Bideford, north Devon, leaving Froude widowed with three young children (aged ten, eight, and six) and without the generous annuity settled on Charlotte which had done so much to cushion the family in the early 1850s.[4] With nothing to keep him in Bideford (where they had moved to be closer to Charlotte's own family), and with an urgent need for a steady income, the offer to move to London to edit *Fraser's* was therefore highly opportune. Thus, having resisted such permanent obligations for all of his adult life, Froude, now aged forty-two, grasped it. By the autumn of 1860 he was already acting as editor in collaboration with John Parker junior; and when the latter died suddenly in January 1861 Froude was officially appointed sole editor. In the following August he moved to London with his family, taking up residence at 6 Clifton Place, Hyde Park.

During this period also the *History* itself changed in size, character, and scope. What had originally been envisaged as a six-volume history (two volumes for Henry VIII, one each for Edward and Mary, and two for Elizabeth I) had already by 1860 outrun its bounds. Now Froude determined, with the agreement of John Parker, who had entered into a business arrangement with Charles Longman, to devote another six volumes of proportionate size to the reign of Elizabeth alone. The range of materials covered would also be enlarged. Hitherto Froude had confined himself primarily to English materials housed in the Rolls Office, the British Museum, and the Bodleian Library. He had also made use of printed editions and calendars of correspondence of the Habsburg and French ambassadors to the early Tudor courts. Now Froude determined to conduct his own original research abroad, and his volumes on Elizabeth were to be considerably enriched by a mass of documents uncovered in the course of two extensive visits to the Spanish archive at Simancas, the Archive Royaume at Brussels, and the Staatsarchiv at Vienna.

But while the new sources added to the depth and complexity of the narrative, they did not change its form. The later chapters were of the same structure, length, and substance as those which they succeeded—though readers' difficulty in coping with them may have been added to by the omission of the running headlines which had facilitated navigation in the earlier volumes. All of the stylistic characteristics of the earlier volumes

---

4. Froude to Kingsley, 20 April 1860, quoted in Dunn, *Froude*, II, 282; Frances Kingsley (ed.), *Charles Kingsley: Letters and Memorials*, ii, 104–9. In addition to Georgina Margaret and Rose Mary, noted earlier, Charlotte gave birth to their third child and first son, Pascoe Grenfell Froude, in February 1854.

which had entranced some readers and exasperated others—the detailed political narrative, the dramatic set-pieces, the unqualified judgements on events and personalities, and the apparently contradictory sets of values alternately invoked—remained present in the Elizabethan volumes as they had been in the first Henrician ones. Despite the size of the operation and the duration of its composition, a powerful uniformity in content, structure, form, and style pervades the entire work, ensuring a consistency of response from readers, from those—mostly critics and historians—who reviled it,[5] to others—large numbers of the reading public—who enthusiastically embraced it.[6] Running through Froude's *History of England* there is a persistent current of provocation, taken by some sympathetic readers as the source of his recurring capacity to surprise and stimulate, and by others of his wilful determination to exasperate and offend. In either case, such responses are a symptom of a characteristic feature of his historical writing: namely, its perennial tendency to provoke readers by raising and then disappointing expectations. It is this defining element that supplies the *History* with its underlying unity and coherence.

II

In retrospect it has become easy to regard this huge twelve-volume survey of the history of England in the sixteenth century as comfortably occupying

5. Reviews of Froude's several volumes were legion, and most are listed in Robert Goetzman, *James Anthony Froude: A Bibliography of Studies* (New York, 1977), 36–40. Among the most influential negative reviews were Goldwin Smith in the *Edinburgh Review*: 'Froude's King Henry VIII', 108 (July 1858), 206–52; 'Froude's History of England, vols. V–VIII', 119 (January 1864), 243–79; and 'Froude's Reply to the Edinburgh Review', 108 (October 1858), 586–94. E. A. Freeman's notorious vendetta was pursued in the *Saturday Review*, 16 January 1864, 80–2; 30 January 1864, 142–4; 27 October 1866, 519–20; 3 November 1866, 550–1; 24 November 1866, 642–4; 1 December 1866, 677–8; 29 January 1870, 116–18; 5 February 1870, 187–8; 12 February 1870, 221–3; 19 March 1870, 374–5; 16 July 1870, 75–6; 23 July 1870, 105–6; and 23 November 1872, 658–9. Other notable positive reviews of segments of the works are by W. B. Donne, *Fraser's Magazine*, 54 (July 1856), 31–46; 58 (July 1858), 15–32; and 62 (July 1860), 1–17; and by F. D. Maurice, in *Macmillan's Magazine*, 2 (August 1860), 276–84. Charles Kingsley' fateful review of vols. VII–VIII appeared in *Macmillan's Magazine*, 9 (January 1864), 211–24.

6. Owing to the loss of the business records of Longman & Co, figures of sales and print runs are no longer available; but the commercial success of the work is evident in the frequency of reprints and cabinet and popular editions announced in newspaper advertisements throughout the years 1860–90, and in the publication of an authorised North American edition by the major New York publishing house, Scribners.

a place amidst the grand narrative histories of high Victorian culture.[7] Here, it seems, is another colossal commemorative monument fitting nicely between Freeman's *History of the Norman Conquest*, Hallam's *Constitutional History of England since the Reign of Henry VII*, and Macaulay's *History of England since the Accession of James II*. Like Freeman's, Hallam's, and Macaulay's, Froude's narrative is indeed an account of the steady unfolding of English liberty, focusing in his case on two major signposts along that highway, the Henrician Reformation and the defeat of the Spanish Armada. Like Freeman and Macaulay also, Froude was pleased to assert that the growth of freedom he was tracing in this particular stretch of history was distinctively English, separate from (and by heavy implication superior to) other nations' development, and rooted in the particular characteristics of the English nation. In addition to his sharing in this celebration of English nationalism, Froude likewise appeared to agree with his fellow historians on the cultural and constitutional mechanisms driving this great historical process. It was through the apprehension of new ideas, the development of new practical skills, and the thirst for new experiences that the young men of the sixteenth century first enabled England to break free from the shackles of the medieval world, and then defended her new-found independence against the forces of Counter-Reformation. Moreover, as with the other good Whigs, the principal vehicle responsible for the initiation, registration, and confirmation of cultural change appears for Froude to have resided in the statute roll of the English parliament. In a programmatic essay published before the appearance of the first instalments of his *History* Froude had argued for a greater use of the statute rolls and of parliamentary history in general as a means of improving the teaching and writing of English history. It was in the statute book, said Froude, that 'the true history of this English nation substantially lies buried'; and in the opening pages of his first volume he repeated the claim.[8]

Yet the very first chapter dispels any notion that Froude can be easily accommodated within the Whig tradition of English historiography. The

---

7. Among the most thoughtful recent critical considerations of Victorian history-writing which contain perceptive analyses of Froude's *History* are J. W. Burrow, *A Liberal Descent: Victorian Historians and the English Past* (Cambridge, 1983); Rosmary Jann, *The Art and Science of Victorian History* (Columbus, OH, 1985); and Jeffrey von Arx, *Progress and Pessimism: Religion, Politics and History in Late Nineteenth Century Britain* (Cambridge, MA, 1985).

8. 'Suggestions on the Best Means of Teaching History', in *Oxford Essays by Members of the University* (London, 1855), 47–79; *History of England*, I, 5–17, 29–38 (hereafter *HoE*). All references are to the Longman cabinet edition of 1870.

History opens with a lengthy survey of the social and economic conditions prevailing in England at the middle of the sixteenth century which appears to echo Macaulay's famous Chapter III. But it is also, in part, a refutation. The sixteenth century was indeed a period of major social upheaval and advance. Population began to grow, towns began to recover, trade began to expand, and a great development in the rural economy began to take place. But the profound and rapid changes of the era are not surveyed by Froude in a spirit of Macaulayesque celebration. There were losses too. The fading feudal order may have produced its tyrants and its over-mighty subjects, but it also maintained a strong sense of community and of shared obligations between all levels of society, and a general sense of public morality, responsibility, and generosity which was all too soon to be replaced by the harsher imperatives of market forces and individual self-interest. In the midst of this, the role played by the English parliaments, notably through the Statute of Liveries (1540), the Statute of Artificers (1563), and the Henrician poor laws, was primarily protective and conservative of all that had been good in the old ways. These efforts for the most part succeeded up to the last quarter of the century: 'The great social revolution was about to occur, but its progress was slow, the duties of property continued to be ... more considered than its rights ... and duty to the state was at all times sufficient to over-ride private interest.'[9]

Froude's perspective here has rightly been seen as representative of that alternative ideological stream of Tory radicalism which stood against the predominant Whig or Liberal progressivism of his day.[10] But this identification should not be pressed too far. Froude's nostalgia for old England was strictly limited. He made no effort to obscure or diminish the defects— political, social, and above all, religious—of the later middle ages; and in pointing up the virtues of the medieval past, his intent was far from sentimental. The very force of the revolutionary changes of the sixteenth century had rendered the principal beneficiaries of that revolution—all subsequent generations of the English people—constitutionally incapable of maintaining a natural sympathy and understanding for the lost world of their forefathers. 'In this alteration of our own character', Froude writes at the very outset of his work, 'we have lost the key by which we can interpret the character of our fathers.'[11] Our complacent belief in the inevitability of

9. *HoE*, I, 10-11.
10. See in particular, Burrow, *Liberal Descent*, ch 4.
11. *HoE*, I, 3.

material and moral progress has led not only to an unjust disregard of the medieval past but, more importantly, to a fundamental misunderstanding of the great upheaval in which it had been washed away. For Froude, 'the revolution of the sixteenth century', as he termed it with heavy Carlylean overtones, was indeed both necessary and irrevocable—not for the eras of material and political progress which it inaugurated, but for the great spiritual conflict which it initiated.[12] The assertion of England's independence from Rome and its establishment as a Protestant nation made the period of the sixteenth century nothing less than an epoch in English history for which, despite all the costs and losses it entailed, every subsequent generation of Englishmen owed a debt of gratitude.

Although it was a cause of some dismay and embarrassment to his liberal and secular readers, the frankly sectarian nature of Froude's narrative, which featured the triumph of Protestantism and the defeat of Catholicism as its central theme, earned him considerable approval in evangelical and militantly Protestant quarters. But here too Froude disappoints. His judgement on Catholicism was indeed severe. An old form of faith which had long since lost its vigour, Catholicism in the sixteenth century was spiritually defunct: it paralysed or perverted those who still clung to it, and maintained its hold on men only through instruments of terror and repression. Protestantism, by contrast, was the real source of spiritual vitality in the world, destined to bring triumph to all those who sincerely embraced its teaching. Yet while Catholicism was degenerate, individual Catholics were not. Froude has much to say about the integrity and courage of Catholic martyrs and victims of persecution; and, in a manner most disturbing to his contemporaries (but now generally accepted by historians), he repeatedly asserts that a kind of quiet Catholicism continued to be the natural disposition of the majority of the right-thinking gentry and yeomanry of the English countryside until close to the end of the sixteenth century.[13]

Conversely, Froude's assessment of Protestantism and Protestants is mixed. Luther, brave pioneer of the revolution, is the subject of unqualified praise, and Knox, the genius of the Scottish Reformation, is the one outstanding hero in the entire *History*. But Calvin is less sympathetically viewed: a narrow dogmatist and speculator in subjects that can allow of no simple resolution, his teachings encouraged fanaticism wherever they took hold, and led to

---

12. *HoE*, 9, 17, 94, 164.   13. *HoE*, I 44–9; VI, 39; VII 29–30.

atrocities smaller in scale but equal in cruelty to those perpetrated by the Catholics.[14] Yet Froude's strictures upon confessional extremists entail no sympathy for the Anglican *via media*. Throughout his text the Established Church is subjected to severe judgement. 'Scandalous dilapidation, destruction of woods, waste of the property of the see ... the incumbent enriching himself and his family at the expense of his successors—this is the substantial history of the Anglican hierarchy,' Froude thunders. Individually, few of the bishops escape censure. They were either weak and corrupt like Parker, hypocritical like Jewel, or ambitious nonentities like Whitgift. Even Cranmer, who is vindicated in Froude's eyes by the noble manner of his death, first appears in the *History* as an ambitious and scheming academic. Froude closes the entire work with the polemical contention that the establishment of the Church of England was the greatest disaster of the history he has surveyed.[15]

Froude's even-handed dismissal of all major forms of organised Christianity may have appealed to the agnostics or the Unitarians in his audience. But believers and unbelievers alike among Froude's readers were shocked by the mode of moral judgement which he himself presented in place of traditional values. Before Froude, traditions of historiographical interpretation concerning the early stages of the English Reformation had been somewhat ambivalent. All good Protestants believed that it had ultimately been a good thing. Since the end of the seventeenth century there had been some unease, at least as to the manner in which it had been initiated, in regard to the role played by Henry VIII, in contrast to the religious reformers themselves, and most particularly in relation to Henry's treatment of his first wife, Catherine of Aragon.[16] In his own account of events Froude brushes all such scruples aside. As the Reformation had been necessary for England, the king's divorce had been necessary too: everything that had been done to achieve that outcome had therefore been perfectly justified, and everything that had sought to resist it, including Catherine's proud but desperate defence of her honour, unworthy of consideration. Froude's unqualified defence of the actions of Henry and his minister Cromwell, his justifications of the illegal treatment of Catherine, the pursuit and execution of More and Fisher, and for all the accompanying oppressions of the 1530s, on the grounds that the outcome legitimated all, provoked such a scandal that Froude felt

14. HoE, IX, 306
15. HoE, XI, 100; XII, 4–9, 24, 553–4.
16. Rosemany O'Day, *The Debate on the English Reformation* (London, 1986), chs. 3–4.

obliged on a number of occasions to explain himself. But it did not inhibit him from further disturbing reversals of the expected moral conventions. Thus his thorough debunking of the 'good' Duke of Somerset and his qualified rehabilitation of the bad Duke of Northumberland;[17] and thus also his uncomfortable reminders that the sea-going saviours of the Protestant nation were also unprincipled slavers who let their human cargo drown, and his remarkable defence of the bloody Duke of Alva:

> He returned to Spain leaving behind him an eternal memory of infamy because he had not succeeded. Those who attempt to extinguish a revolution in blood play for a high stake. If they win, their cruelties pass into history as the necessary severities of a wise and courageous rule. If they fail, they are the ministers of Satan to be forever execrated and abhorred. Yet the difference, after all, may be only in the intellectual appreciation of the circumstances.[18]

Though some full-blooded English nationalists might have found it possible to endorse Froude's defence of Henry VIII on the grounds that it had all turned out for the best in the end, the extension of the same mode of assessment to the hated Alva was a corollary that few were prepared to stomach.

Froude's unwillingness to fit easily into one of several identifiable prearranged modes thus presents a series of provocations to believers and non-believers, Whigs and Tories alike. There remains also a final literal instance which his text disappoints. Having planned from the outset (and regularly published his intention) to bring his narrative down to the end of Elizabeth's reign, readers of the final two volumes were abruptly informed, by a mere change on the title-page, that the author had abandoned his intention and was now concluding the history after the defeat of the Spanish Armada some fifteen years before. Froude's justification of this sudden change of mind, supplied not in a preface but in the closing pages of the work, was perfunctory. He had decided to end his story, he claimed, because all the major themes of his study had come to a close in 1588. The threat of invasion and conquest had transformed the mind of the majority of Englishmen: they ceased to hanker after Catholicism and conformed themselves willingly to Anglicanism. The Reformation was thus vouchsafed in England.[19]

---

17. *HoE*, V, chs. xxiv–xxvi (244–5, Froude's assessment of Somerset's character); ch. xxviii, on the accession of Northumberland, is significantly entitled 'The Reformed Administration'. In this, Froude may be seen to have anticipated more recent reassessments of the two regents, but the agreement is more coincidental than consensual.

18. *HoE*, XI, 17.

19. *HoE*, XII, 530–1.

To readers even superficially acquainted with the closing years of Elizabeth this was hardly persuasive. The threat from Spain remained live for more than a decade, and was to be the occasion of major encounters at sea and on land which Froude was prepared to ignore. Developments in Ireland to which Froude had devoted considerable space in his narrative (and on which he produced remarkably original work) were about to issue in a massive rebellion which almost destroyed English government there and bankrupted the Crown. But despite his steady building toward the promised climacteric of the Nine Years War, this too, in the end, Froude elected to leave aside. Similarly, the 'golden era of prosperity' to which Froude had alluded in his account of the 1570s and 1580s was to turn into a period of sustained depression and discontent of which he had warned at the beginning of the work, but in the event this was to be dismissed in a paragraph as a mild upset that had been promptly dealt with by legislation. The Tudor succession question, which had been the central motif of Froude's entire narrative, remained unresolved, and was to result in the dangerous treason of the favourite, Essex. Finally, in ending his *History* where he did, Froude forfeited also the opportunity of presenting Shakespeare, the figure whom at the very opening of the work he had identified as the representative figure of the great revolution he was about to describe.[20]

Even in the final words summarising the significance of his vast work, Froude seemed determined to underline its inchoate character:

> Many problems ... were left unsettled. Some were disposed of on the scaffold at Whitehall, some in the revolution of 1688; some yet survive to test the courage and ingenuity of modern politicians. But the worst legacy which princes or statesmen could bequeath to their country would be the resolution of all its perplexities, the establishment once and forever of a finished system, which would neither require nor tolerate improvement.[21]

Disappointment of conventional expectation was therefore more than an incidental aspect of Froude's work, an occasional blemish to be regretted or a congenital flaw to be excoriated. It was rather an essential feature of his rhetorical encounter with his readers. Froude, that is, set out to perturb, to upset assumptions about his character and purpose as an historian, and to unsettle comfortable prejudices about history itself. It is the persistently provocative nature of his address that distinguishes Froude from the majority of his contemporary fellow historians whose style—whether dramatic,

20. *HoE*, I, 70–2.   21. *HoE*, XII, 562.

magisterial, polemical, or merely descriptive—was reassuringly predictable in manner. To understand how this distinctive approach to history-writing emerged, and what purpose it was intended to serve, it is necessary to return to the broader contexts, philosophical and historiographical, against which it arose, before attempting a closer analysis of what Froude was actually seeking to achieve within his own text.

III

By the time of the appearance of the first volumes of Froude's *History* sixteenth-century England was by no means a *terra incognita* of historical scholarship. Long before Froude the clerical historian Sharon Turner had produced a four-volume history of the century based largely on printed records.[22] Other scholars, such as P. F. Tytler and Sir Harris Nicolas, were producing substantial histories of shorter periods in the century, scholarly text-editing societies such as the Camden Society and the Hakluyt Society were making a large body of hitherto unknown documentary materials available to the reading public, and more popular works, such as Agnes Strickland's *Lives of the Tudor Queens*, were offering a fresh, scholarly, informed perspective to a more popular audience.[23] But above all, the field of medieval and early modern English history was then dominated by John Lingard's massive *History of England from the First Invasion of the Romans to the Accession of William and Mary*, four of whose volumes were devoted to the sixteenth century.[24] A massive work, based not only on standard printed sources but on materials in the Vatican and in the continental seminaries of the English Catholic mission to which Lingard's Protestant contemporaries had no access, Lingard's *History* was genuinely original in content and carefully restrained in tone. Lingard sought to provide a straightforward narrative of events along the narrow line of high politics with the minimum of commentary. But as a Catholic, Lingard was also engaged on a subtle propagandist campaign of his own, 'to make the Catholic cause respectable in the eyes of the public', and

---

22. Sharon Turner, *History of the Reign of Henry VIII*; *History of the Reigns of Edward VI, Mary I and Elizabeth* (4 vols., London, 1826–9).
23. For a general survey, see G. P. Gooch, *History and Historians in the Nineteenth Century* (London, 1913), ch. xv; Agnes Strickland, *Lives of the Queens of England* (12 vols., 1840–48).
24. John Lingard, *History of England from the First Invasion of the Romans to the Accession of William and Mary* (14 vols., London, 1823–49).

the more his *History* gained in popularity and respect, the more overt his defence of English Catholicism became. While he acknowledged the corruption of the late medieval church, he condemned Henry VIII's assumption of royal supremacy as an usurpation which furthered the spiritual decline of church and people, and while he made no defence of the Marian persecutions, he produced a highly critical portrait of Elizabeth I.[25]

From early on, some of Lingard's critics were alive to his implicit objectives: the radical John Allen, among others, violently attacked him in the pages of the *Edinburgh Review*, and Robert Southey was driven to write his passionately prejudiced *Book of the Church* (1825) in direct opposition to Lingard's insinuations. But Lingard's influence grew steadily and his editions continued to enjoy consistent popularity with the reading public up to the 1850s. He began, moreover, to exercise increasing influence over other English historians by his reasonable and precise defences of his methods. Thus Hallam, for all his suspicion, concurred in Lingard's critical view of Elizabeth, and Sharon Turner, in the preface to the final two volumes of his *History of the Reigns of Edward VI, Mary I and Elizabeth* (1826–29), made reference to the granting of Catholic Emancipation celebrating 'the meridian splendour of such a national phenomenon', and announced that in what was to follow he was determined neither 'to increase enmities nor excite the dissatisfaction' of any readers, whatever their disposition.[26]

It is possible, then, to read the forthrightly Protestant stance of Froude's *History* as a defence against the supposedly insidious ecumenism promoted by Lingard. That this was part of Froude's intention is certainly the case. But it is clear both from the *History* itself and from a series of preliminary and programmatic essays with which he preceded it that Froude's real objectives were greater than a refutation of the dangerously plausible papist. More sinister than Lingard's subtle slanders was the manner in which his style of denigration was adopted and indeed inflated by others who had no idea that they were sharing in his purposes. The modest antiquarian Sir Harris Nicolas and the remarkable woman historian Agnes Strickland were among those singled out by Froude for reproof—the former for swallowing idle gossip about Elizabeth and Sir Christopher Hatton, the latter for allowing her attachment to Mary Queen of Scots to cloud her judgement of Elizabeth.

---

25. For different assessments, see E. Jones, *John Lingard and the Pursuit of Historical Truth* (London, 2001), and Philip Cattermore, *John Lingard: the historian as apologist* (Leicester, 2013) the quotation from Lingard is at p. 101.
26. Turner, *Reigns of Edward VI, Mary I and Elizabeth* (London, 1829) xi.

In addition, Froude pursued a special vendetta against the legal historian Lord Campbell, exposing his interpretative errors and denouncing his penchant for scandal and gossip.[27]

Gullible, sentimental, or sensationalist historians were not the only writers colluding inadvertently in Lingard's corruption of history. Ironically, given Lingard's own view of the type, Froude regarded those he described as 'the philosophical historians' as being even more culpable in this betrayal of history. Between them, the eighteenth-century historians Gibbon, Robertson, and their modern counterparts, among whom he included Macaulay, the Scottish historian J. H. Burton, and above all H. T. Buckle, had been guilty of a profound perversion of the purposes and possibilities of historical writing. In his confident assertion that Machiavelli could be converted into a good nineteenth-century liberal, Macaulay had been irresponsibly naïve. Burton's *History of Scotland* was marred by its unquestioned confidence in 'the progress of the enlightenment, of humanising influences, of large minded toleration &c., &c ... as if the improvement of man's nature was an unquestioned and unquestionable fact.'[28] Buckle has written of the history of man as 'a natural growth as much as the growth of an acorn ... his whole proceedings on this planet ... his good deeds and his bad ... all reducible to laws, and could be made as intelligible as the growth of the chalk cliffs or the coal measures.' Like the others, Buckle 'cared little for individuals ... Great men with him were but larger atoms obeying the same impulses with the rest ... with them or without them the course of things would have been much the same.'[29] To Froude, this attitude toward the study of history was nefarious. It was intellectually smug and politically self-serving. More seriously, in its bland invocation of impersonal laws of development, it constituted a dereliction of moral responsibility:

> Morally, the general opinion seems to be that men keep tolerably near a common standard, of which the lowest scarcely falls short and which the highest but slightly exceeds ... All men have faults, and, therefore, saints and heroes had. These ideal characters have no existence in the practical world; and man has, in all times and all places, been much what we now find him.[30]

27. 'Morals of Queen Elizabeth', *Fraser's Magazine*, 48 (August–October 1853), pt. I. 371–87, pt. II., 489–505; 'Lord Campbell', *Westminster Review*, 61 (April 1854), 446–79.
28. 'History of Scotland' (by J. H. Burton), *Fraser's Magazine*, 48 (August 1853), 127–42.
29. 'The Science of History: Paper delivered at the Royal Institution, 5 February 1864', reprinted in *Short Studies*, I, 1–38, to which reference is made hereafter; quotations from 7–8.
30. 'Morals of Queen Elizabeth, part I', 371.

Such moral *laissez faire* is unacceptable to Froude on many counts. It was psychologically and sociologically naïve, neglecting the force actually exerted over history by the heroes, saints, villains and—most commonly— the Reynards of humanity. It was also historically simplistic. In their 'doctrine of averages', Buckle and Comte may have contented themselves that while they could not determine which individuals might 'cut their throats' at any one time, they might estimate the proportion of the population likely to do so. But this was an illusory consolation, for the averages would change from generation to generation as each generation changed under the forces operating in history, unknown and unpredicted by a form of investigation that saw no need to recognise it.

More serious still, in their methodological confidence the philosophical historians had inadvertently undermined the legitimacy of historical study altogether. If human nature is, after all, no more than the unchanging mixture of virtues and vices, 'if we are all but little beings, the best of us tainted with weakness', what was the point of repeatedly studying this dreary phenomenon through history, when it was more profitable to study 'the meaner organizations—the flower, the bird, and the beast' which might lend us a deeper insight into our own being. Ironically, in their own certainty about the normal mediocrity of humankind, the philosophical historians were hardly different from the medieval hagiographers or the epic poets who in representing their respective subjects, the saint and the hero, postulated a more noble but no less absolute ideal type which lay outside the temporal process of historical consciousness itself. A curious reversion has thus taken place where, for all their pretensions to superiority over their predecessors, 'writers ... who affect to be above party spirit and to take philosophical views of things' have made it easy for us to 'foretell the estimate which they will form of the disputed characters of history, with as much certainty as we can say what Surius or the Benedictines will say of a saint'.[31]

But finally, and most importantly, the philosophical historians had been ethically irresponsible, refusing to confront the central issues of the study of humanity. Referring specifically to Burton, Froude asks:

> What in general does he believe to be the meaning, end, purpose of human life—in what does man's business consist, what are his duties, his proper hopes and fears?[32]

31. 'Morals of Queen Elizabeth, part I', 371–3.
32. 'History of Scotland', 139.

These are the questions which any historian writing history for his fellow men should ask, Froude asserts. But far from confronting them, the philosophical historians have regarded them as redundant. Reducing all such questions to matters of self-interest, enlightened or otherwise, they had not only evaded the problem as to whether this ought to be the case, but had also ignored the countless examples of individuals in history who denied their maxims.

This was a powerful indictment. But Froude's condemnation of the ahistoricity of the polemicists, the sentimentalists and the philosophical historians raised no less serious problems for any proposed alternative. If the historical sociologists' claim to know the patterns of historical development was illusory, how could the historicists claim to have some special dispensation giving them a direct insight into history's meaning? In two essays written while the *History* was being composed, 'History: Its Use and Meaning' and 'The Science of History', Froude sought to confront this difficulty directly.[33] The problem of seeking an historical validation for historical judgement is itself, Froude argues, a philosophical confusion. It arises, he claims, only when we espouse unnecessary and preposterous claims for what historical argument can do; when we claim, for example, that history teaches lessons, that it is possible to establish an objective account, that it is possible to discern certain patterns or laws of development. But none of these claims can be maintained by reference either to logical analysis or to experience. Indeed, the very notion that they can is itself a symptom of the degree to which our own understanding of history has degenerated from what it originally was, and essentially remains. To understand the real purpose of history, we must look to its origins. The historical imagination, Froude asserts, has its origin in the poetic vision, in the epic poem, the tragedy, and the elevated romance of the saint's life.

> In its commencement History was not distinguished from poetry or religion, but all three were one ... and where it has been seen to supersede or destroy them, it has only been that it may once more resolve them into itself.[34]

To the historian as to the artist, the interest of life lies in the study,

> not of institutions, not of progress of the species, not of the development of ideas, or other loud sounding nonentities; but of personal character in conflict

---

33. 'History: Its Use and Meaning', *Westminster Review*, 62 (October 1854), 420–48; 'The Science of History: Paper delivered at the Royal Institution, 5 February 1864', reprinted in *Short Studies*, I, 1–38.
34. 'History: Its Use and Meaning', 449, also 429.

with the circumstances of life, and crushed by them or rising over them triumphant.[35]

The unpopularity of these literary forms in modern times is not a sign of their internal exhaustion but of our own loss of ability to see and comprehend the world through their lenses. This is not a cause for despair, however. This falling away, says Froude, closely allying himself with Wordsworth's central insight, is but a necessary stage in the dialectical encounter of the human spirit with Creation. And, as the poet himself had prophesied, there is more to come, but it is up to all of us to play a part in bringing it forward; and it is up to those who write history in this mode to find a way of escaping the dreary misapprehensions of the purpose of history which have captured its contemporary practitioners, and to discover again a voice through which the historian will perform his proper duty.[36]

The role of the great historian was, therefore, the same as that of the great dramatist or poet. Operating under different rules and accepting different constraints, all were concerned with presenting in manifold forms the same moral challenges which, no matter how they may mutate, humanity must confront as long as consciousness survives. In proportion to the prophetic and transformative effect which their work exercised over their audience, the historian and the artist were equal.[37]

The influence of Carlyle over Froude's historical thought in these essays is unmistakable.[38] His contempt for narrowly partisan perspectives of confessional history, his dismissal of simple ideas of material and intellectual progress, his affirmation that the dynamic of historical consciousness was to be found registered in the thoughts and actions of powerful individuals, his insistence that the duty of the historian like that of the artist was the moral regeneration of his audience, can all be found earlier in Carlyle's writings on history.[39] Froude's indebtedness to the great man is thus clear; but it was also increasingly ambivalent.

---

35. 'History: Its Uses and Meaning', 422.
36. In both 'History: Its Uses and Meaning' and 'The Science of History' Froude quotes from stanza ix of Wordsworth's 'Ode on the Intimations of Immortality' in support of the insight he is trying to rekindle among his readers.
37. 'Science of History', 28–38.
38. Although it makes no direct reference to the book, the essay on 'History: Its Uses and Meaning' was prompted by a reissue of Carlyle's *Past and Present* (originally published in 1843, rprt, 1854).
39. Thomas Carlyle, *Historical Essays*, ed. C. R. Vanden Bossche (Berkeley, CA., 2002), supplies a modern edition of Carlyle's most important theoretical essays with a useful introduction.

For Froude, as for many others of his generation, Carlyle's exemplary masterpiece in historical writing as art and as prophecy was *The French Revolution* (1837). Itself a polemic against orthodox history, *The French Revolution* was a radical experiment in historical style. Writing almost entirely in the historic present, its authorial voice was at once that of witness—urgent, insistent upon the immediacy of the narrated events—and at the same time judgemental and prophetic. Hurried through the streets and scenes of the Revolution by his indefatigable guide, the reader is assailed by sounds, smells, by successive dioramas of magnificent courage and boundless cruelty. But throughout, Carlyle has a moral to teach: his narrative traced the course of a great bursting forth of the human spirit in its quest for liberation and its equally sudden engulfment in the vortex of destructive passions that the breakout unleashed. Carlyle's teaching was not an admonition against freedom; it was rather a warning against its misguided pursuit through the superficial and ephemeral guides of philosophy and ideology. True human freedom was not to be realised through dominance in the external world but in the interior rediscovery of the spirit. Carlyle sought to teach this truth not by argument and demonstration but by enmeshing his readers in an extraordinary experience of simultaneous communion with, and alienation from, the past, through a style which even while it submerged the individuals of the past into a common suffering mass, emphasised the reality of the author's presence in the reader's head. His concluding sentences served to seal the covenant of mutual obligation in this spiritual quest upon which in turning his pages and entering his mind his readers had embarked:

> And so here, O Reader, has the time come for us two to part. Toilsome was our journeying together, not without offence; but it is done. To me thou were as a beloved shade, the disembodied, or not yet embodied spirit of a Brother. To thee I was but as a Voice. Yet was our relation a sacred one ... [for] while the Voice of Man speaks with Man hast thou not there the living fountain out of which all sacredness sprang. Man, by the nature of him, is definable as 'an Incarnated Word'. Ill stands it with me if I have spoke falsely: thine also it was to hear truly.[40]

Here if ever was a manifesto of history writing not only as an art, but as an occasion of prayer for redemption; and it was as such that it was received

---

40. Thomas Carlyle, *The French Revolution: A History* (Modern Library edition, New York, 2002), with a valuable introduction by Jonathan D. Rosenberg. The quotation is at 776.

by all those disillusioned with the moral claims of orthodox religion or fashionable social theory—Froude among them.

The aspiration as declared was enormous, and the possibility of its falling short became more perturbing with each passing year, as the enthusiasm of the reading public began to wane, and more conventional historical voices—Lingard, Strickland, and, most ominously of all, Macaulay—grew in popularity over the 1840s. Even more unsettling was the suspicion that the master's powers were beginning to wane. None of Carlyle's work in the 1840s came near the mastery of *The French Revolution*. In the overtly programmatic *Past and Present* (1843) Carlyle abandoned narrative in favour of a set of contrasting explorations, and the voice he adopted was that of the engaged advocate rather than the prophet historian. What eventually emerged from his much-anticipated study of Cromwell was not a continuous history of this hero of the *English* Revolution but an edition of *Letters and Speeches* where a disturbing sense of editorial intermittency was reinforced by the instability of the author's voice at war with itself through the conflicting alter-egos of the Impatient Poet and Dr Dryasdust. Carlyle's admirers were further disappointed by his announcement that he was abandoning English history altogether to undertake a study of Frederick the Great which would take years to complete. He thus presented his deepest admirers with a dilemma. Despite his acknowledged role as the celebrant of history as a mode of moral philosophy, and his occasional master-demonstrations of writing in that mode, Carlyle's own concerns appeared to be leading him away from the task he had urged, and he was in danger of leaving his audience bereft of their prophet.[41]

It is possible to see some of this mounting concern for his mentor reflected in Froude's essays written before and during the composition of the *History*. Thus the essay on Knox, with whom Carlyle is directly compared, registers amidst its adulation some criticism of its hero's insensitivity to the immediate political circumstances of his day; similarly, in 'Reineke Fuchs' Carlyle is alluded to as a figure gravely misunderstood not entirely through no fault of his own.[42] The essay on 'History' concludes with an overt appeal for Carlyle's return:

---

41. On Carlyle as an historian, see Jonathan D. Rosenberg, *Carlyle and the Burden of History* (Cambridge, MA, 1985); Rosemary Jann, *The Art and Science of Victorian History* (Columbus, OH, 1985); C. R. Vanden Bosche, *Carlyle and the Search for Authority* (Columbus, OH, 1991).
42. 'Ethical Doubts concerning Reineke Fuchs', *Short Studies*, I, 612–14.

Can we hope for such a teacher? ... We cannot tell. It may be all a dream. It may be that he is among us at this hour.[43]

The biblical allusion is obvious, but as Carlyle had now (1855) apparently abandoned English history for the while, and as Froude was already well advanced upon his, it also seemed proper that while the prophet struggled in his wilderness a more modest interim voice might be of service in keeping his desperate and hungry people primed until at length the true bearer of the good news returned.

IV

It is against these overlapping literary and critical contexts that a closer reading of Froude's own *History* is best attempted. As a response to the increasing trivialisations of popular history and the increasing respect for the Catholic Lingard, Froude's revival of the spirit of the sixteenth-century Reformation can be seen as a continuation of his campaign to revitalise the moral fibre of doubting Protestant Englishmen. In its revival of detailed narrative and its eschewal of grand interpretative frameworks, it can likewise be seen as a riposte to the rationalist and positivist forms of history-writing which he had seen as contributing so much to the moral crisis against which he was struggling. In the light of Carlyle's withdrawal from his public, Froude's *History* should also be seen as an interim intervention, undertaken to keep the great man's readers in awareness of the real issues at stake in history while awaiting the prophet's reappearance. Such a perspective on the *History*, which regards it neither as an attempt to imitate Carlyle nor to supersede him, but to prepare the ground for his return, offers a means of understanding the many ambiguities of the book. It helps explain the intermittent nature of his engagement with other historical schools, sectarian and philosophical, which gave rise to such a sense of disappointed expectations on the part of many critics, but it also throws light on the curious nature of his literary relationship to Carlyle, frequently noted but never explained by commentators on his work: that is, its unmistakable differences in form, substance, and style from the work of the master he professed so much to admire.

The literary differences between Carlyle's *French Revolution* and Froude's *History of England* are manifold. The *History* is, of course, far larger: twelve

43. 'History: Its Uses and Meaning', 448.

volumes to Carlyle's three; almost two million words to less than three hundred thousand. The chronological scope is likewise different: fifty years in Froude's case, ten in the case of Carlyle. But the proportional coverage is also significant. In his steadily paced narrative Froude allots with remarkable consistency an average of one hundred pages to each year; Carlyle in his episodic treatment varies from seventy to none at all. Other formal differences are important. With Carlyle, the organising principle of each chapter is the event, the storming of the Bastille, the fall of Robespierre, and so on, which forms the central stages of his narrative. With Froude, although there are several set pieces—the trial of Sir Thomas More, the slaughter of the rebels of 1549, the execution of Mary Queen of Scots—they are invariably embedded in large stretches of complex chronological development to which the reader is redirected as soon as the drama of the event has been concluded.

There are also marked differences of idiom. Carlyle's history is written throughout in the historic present; Froude's is relentlessly in the past tense. Carlyle's rhetorical addresses to the 'Reader' are frequent and urgent; Froude's remarks to his readers are rare and detached. The authorial voices in the two works as a whole are markedly different. Carlyle's is clearly imitative of the Old Testament prophet: literary and symbolic allusions to the Bible abound, his vocabulary is archaic or pseudo-archaic; his cadences frequently echo the Authorised Version. By contrast, Froude's voice is more even and altogether more moderate—quite different from that which he affected in his earlier hagiography, or in the intense language of 'England's Forgotten Worthies'. Hilaire Belloc, in an insightful essay, once described it as an attempt at 'looking at the world from the standpoint of the men around him' that is 'the mass of well-to-do Protestant Englishmen of the reign of Queen Victoria'.[44] There is much in this. Froude's text abounds in observations about men and women and about public affairs in general which would have appeared reassuringly sensible to an educated middle-class readership of his time. But there is in addition a persistent tone of worldly irony, the witty knowingness of the man who had once given rein to strong feelings and has learned to count their cost. There is an echo of the great classical historians whom Froude most admired: Thucydides after the collapse of the Athenian state, and, even more, Tacitus at the end of the

---

44. In his introduction to a selection of Froude's *Essays in Literature and History* (London, 1904), xii–xiv.

Roman Republic. But even so, this prevalent ironic style is occasionally interrupted by flashes of conviction which jolt the reader in the strength and sometimes the perversity of their contention.

Significantly, such sudden disruptions of the conventional narrative tone occur in Froude's treatment of those events which constitute some of the greatest set pieces of the text: the occasions of martyrdom or pseudo-martyrdom. From the early Protestants, to the Catholic victims of Ket's rebellion, to the fires of Smithfield, and the ferocious repression of the Northern Rising, martyrs, Protestant and Catholic, feature regularly in Froude's text. A recurring motif throughout the book, martyrdom consti-tutes an absolute standard by which its central characters are measured. Supposed bigots such as Sir Thomas More, or fanatics like the Anabaptists, or weak-spirited prevaricators like Cranmer, earn Froude's forgiveness by their acceptance of martyrdom. Mary Stuart is excoriated because of her disingenuous assumption of the martyr's pall, and ordinary men and women otherwise unknown to history are raised far above their social betters in Froude's eyes by their sincere and deliberate self-sacrifice. This was more than a mark of respect, for, as he had indicated in his programmatic essays, martyrdom for Froude was by definition a super-historical act—a leap of faith beyond the concerns, interests, conflicts, and contingencies of histor-ical time into the eternal principles of right and wrong. In repeatedly returning to it, Froude was in effect puncturing his narrative with vertical lines of force which, in drawing his readers away from the apparently inexo-rable dynamic of history to the contemplation of the unchanging absolute, served in an immediate and intense manner the same function as his invoca-tions of Wordsworth's moral vision.[45]

The effectiveness of this periodically interruptive narrative technique is more apparent when seen against a further distinctive feature of Froude's chronicle: that is, the extraordinary breadth of the canvas on which he chose to work. Despite his title, this is not simply a history of England. It includes also at regular intervals extensive chapters on Scotland and Ireland (both of which were based on extensive original archival research), and the English narrative is embedded in a wider survey of developments on the European Continent; of the machinations of Rome and the Holy Roman Emperor in the first volumes, of the stratagems of Philip II and the intrigues of the court of Catherine de Medici in the later ones.

45. 'History: Its Uses and Meaning', 426–7; 'Science of History', 22–4.

One of the most impressive achievements of Froude's *History* for which he is still allowed some grudging respect by professional historians is his exploitation of several foreign archives.[46] Froude's industrious research methods should not, however, be misunderstood. In scouring the collections at Brussels, Paris, Vienna, and Simancas, Froude was not simply engaged in an exercise in scientific or empirical thoroughness—a project in which he himself had little confidence. Instead, his multifaceted perspective enabled him to present his readers with a set of contrasting but simultaneous perceptions of the same event or problem which fractured the artificial linearity imposed by retrospect, and reconstructed the thick complexity of actual experience. Characteristically, the main lines of his English narrative are at all times crossed and encumbered by an account of circumstances developing elsewhere, and of perspectives emanating from some other place; and so the forces which caused Henry VIII to act so decisively, Somerset to blunder so disastrously, and Elizabeth to prevaricate so persistently, are explained as the complex product of events and attitudes outside their immediate comprehension and control.

This sense of the complexity of historical development is not only conveyed through the overall stretch of the book; it is incorporated and repeated in each of its individual chapters. The demands of reading a Froude chapter are several. Running at over one hundred pages and filled with detailed historical matter with which even the most cultivated reader would have been wholly unfamiliar, a serious reading of a chapter could take anything between two and three hours—a complete session, in short. Having finished it, the reader, it seems reasonable to presume, was not likely to embark immediately upon another marathon. Thus the mechanism of the book seems designed to enforce a certain mode of reading under which the typical reader is intended to absorb the matter of one chapter separately, and to reflect on it before returning for another session with the chapter next in line. In this, the Froudian reader can be seen to be re-enacting the classical approach to the reading of the Bible—a concentrated session followed by reflection. It is significant in this regard that in his essay on 'History' where he was seeking to reinvigorate the practice of imaginative interactive engagement with

---

46. For a respectful but somewhat misplaced assessment from the perspective of a modern 'professional' historian, see G. R. Elton, 'J. A. Froude and his *History of England*', in Elton, *Studies in Tudor and Stuart Politics and Government*, iii (Cambridge, 1983), 391–412; see also the sensitive but by no means uncritical introduction in Eamon Duffy (ed.), *J. A. Froude's 'The Reign of Mary Tudor'* (London, 2009).

history Froude suggested that it was only in 'the popular feeling of religious persons toward the Bible history' that the kind of reader's response that he wished to cultivate was still to be found.[47]

But the actual experience of such a reading session was, of course, entirely different. In Froude, characteristically, the reader is exposed not simply to the unfolding of one narrative line, but to the interaction of several which, while working separately, converge to produce a new situation whose outcome, in all but the most exceptional circumstances, is left uncertain and deferred to the next chapter. A structural analysis of some chapters, chosen more or less at random from the earlier and later volumes of the *History*, may provide some sense of this kaleidoscopic experience.

Chapter XXII, 'The Reign of Elizabeth', is in many ways typical of those which precede and succeed it.[48] One hundred and four pages long, it covers the chronological period between September 1571 and August 1572. It opens in England with rumours of Catholic conspiracies running rife. But then 'an insignificant accident' enables Cecil to entrap the Duke of Norfolk. The first dozen pages thus cover Norfolk's interrogation. Rapid scene-shifts over the next eighteen pages move the narrative from Alva in Flanders to complex intrigues and negotiations at the French court, to Philip II's strategic calculations from El Escorial. Next there is a return to Westminster for the trial of Norfolk; then a move north to Sheffield to view the circumstances of Mary Queen of Scots. This serves as a prologue to a lengthy account of the progress of civil war in Scotland, and of Elizabeth's prevarications concerning it. 'So the wretched uncertainty drove on', Froude complains, 'nor was Scotland the only scene of her diplomatic eccentricities.' Another long passage on intrigues with France follows until the scene shifts again to London, and a set piece on the execution of Norfolk is supplied. The narrative, however, does not end at this ostensibly suitable terminus; it continues for another twenty pages in which the consequences of the renewal of rebellion in the Lowlands for Spain, France, and England are reviewed. Elizabeth's prevarication is again highlighted; and Froude includes a letter from Cecil addressed to the Huguenot leader Coligny, expressing his frustrations and anxieties which Coligny was not to live to receive. Even so, he will not allow his narrative to conclude on this poignant note, but takes three more pages to describe the circumstances leading up to the execution of the Earl of Northumberland.

47. 'History: Its Uses and Meaning', 431–2.
48. *HoE*, X, 286–389.

Such a synopsis might suggest a lack of authorial control, but Froude's management of the sections is, in fact, quite assured. The scenes are set with great economy and clarity, and the options confronting his actors are succinctly stated and weighed. Writing commonly in plain, single- or double-claused sentences, his narrative moves with remarkable ease and speed. His reader therefore experiences little difficulty in absorbing the significance of the particular events or attitudes being delineated. Yet the cumulative effect of these repeated shifts, returns, and indeterminacies is to instil the reader with a sense of the perplexity and uncertainty of historical change which was the common experience of historical figures themselves, and of all sentient beings when they are *not* reading or writing history. A further demonstration of this authorial strategy may seem superfluous. But if only to echo Froude's first readers' experience of reiteration, and to show that it was consciously at work at the very beginning of his project, one further examination may be allowed.

The fifth chapter in the very first volume of the *History* is entitled 'Marriage of Henry and Anne Boleyn'.[49] One hundred and eighteen pages long, it also begins in a mist of diversity and uncertainty of opinion among clergy and laity, and of the various rumours gathered by government spies. Confusion is everywhere. 'Leaving for the present these disorders to mature themselves', Froude next plunges into the 'very Slough of Despond' and embarks on a survey of European diplomacy in order 'to trace the tortuous course of popes and princes, duping one another with false hopes, saying what they did not mean and meaning what they did not say'. The perspectives and aims of Francis I, Charles V, and Pope Clement are examined in detail, the Turks are brought into play, then affairs in Ireland, then developments in Scotland. But, forty-eight pages in, Henry cuts through the thickets of all of these intrigues and abruptly marries Anne. This marks a high point in the narrative, and Froude spends a few pages in a complex justification of the king's action. But the narrative of diplomacy resumes as the response of the pope and princes is described. At the sixtieth page Froude intervenes: 'From this choking atmosphere we now turn back to England and the English parliament; and the change is from darkness to light, from death to life.' But the break is not entirely clean, for a review of the parliament's proceedings issues in a discussion of the act of appeals against Rome and its deeply inequitable effect when applied retrospectively to Queen

49. *HoE*, I, 371–489.

Catherine. These ambiguities, however, are left hanging, and the narrative shifts briefly to the intricacies of European diplomacy, and back again to the question of the status of Queen Catherine and Princess Mary after the enforced annulment of the royal marriage where, once more, the moral issues on both sides are weighed. Finally, in the closing pages of this chapter Froude introduces the contemporaneous martyrdom of the early Protestants Frith and Hewlitt. Apparently disconnected to and unanticipated in anything that had been said over the previous hundred pages, it is derived from a letter by Cranmer in which 'in the light gossiping tone of easiest content' he is describing his doings in relation to the king's divorce, and tacks on a report of his part in the trial.

The technique of accumulating multiple perspectives, each related to the other only by the drive of narrative sequence which Froude employs here and throughout the *History*, is strongly reminiscent of that developed by the great masters of fictional realism: Balzac, Stendhal, and Tolstoy. Froude, however, is anxious to remind his readers that they *are* in fact reading history; and that as sentient humans they are engaged in a retrospective exercise that is at once clarifying and alienating. Repeatedly, therefore, in the midst of his thickly woven narrative Froude intervenes to present his readers with this dual effect. Thus, in the midst of his dense account of the proceedings surrounding Henry's divorce of Catherine of Aragon, in the chapter just summarised Froude interposes:

> Thus it is that while we regret, we are unable to blame, and we cannot wish undone an act, to have shrunk from which might have spared a single heart, but *might* have wrecked the English nation ... Few thinking persons can suggest any other method in which either the nation or the king could have extricated themselves.[50]

This is special pleading—but of a particular kind which challenges the uncommitted reader either to become complicit in the urgent rationalisations of sixteenth-century policy-makers, or to take up and follow through an entirely different view of England's historical development. In other instances Froude's implication of his readers is more subtle. His account, for example, of the wedding celebrations of Queen Anne is studded with references backwards and forwards, toward the sorry condition of the discarded and repudiated Catherine, and the even more deadly fate that awaits Anne.

50. *HoE*, I, 446.

In history, Froude suggests, there can be no evasion of consequences: what was historically necessary is not necessarily good to individuals; and individuals less than good in their intentions and actions may nonetheless be historically justified.

A more positive lesson is essayed in Froude's treatment of a minor incident in Cranmer's life around the same time. Toward the end of this chapter, as we have seen, Froude introduces Cranmer's breezy account of the martyrdom of the early Protestants which he had added as an afterthought. As with Queen Anne's nuptials, Froude has a moral to point: his readers know well the similar fate that awaits Cranmer himself twenty years on. Here, however, he has more to say by way of historical instruction. The off-hand manner in which the story is related, Froude says, 'is no less suggestive than the story itself':

> The immediate present, however awful its import, will ever seem common and familiar to those who live and breathe in the midst of it. In the days of the September massacre at Paris the theatres were open as usual; men ate and drank, and laughed and cried, and went about their common work, unconscious that those days that were passing by them so much like other days, would remain the *dies nefasti*, accursed in the memory of mankind forever ... It is only when time has done its work, and all which was unimportant has ceased to be remembered that such men and such times stand out in their true significance.[51]

The intended effect upon the readers of this exercise in refractive representation is complex. The Carlylean reference will have been unmistakable to Froude's literate audience, who will also have been expected to reflect independently on the glorious death that lies before Cranmer. But the fact that even Cranmer, sainted martyr, should, like an ordinary man, show no sense at all of the gathering forces which are to issue in his apotheosis is at once a disturbing reminder of the artificiality of our retrospective vantage-point, and a powerful indication of the magnitude of the forces working unseen in his world and, by natural extension, in ours.

The indeterminacy and contingency of events and the ignorance and myopia of individuals are, then, recurring motifs in Froude's narrative. But they are deployed not as ends in themselves in support of some claim that the ways of Providence are mysterious, arbitrary, and unknowable. As in the case of the Greek tragedians, they supply the necessary and inescapable

---

51. *HoE*, I., 486.

atmosphere within which the primary focus of interest in his *History* must be examined: that is, the character and conduct of individual human agents. The cast of characters passing through Froude's volumes is considerably larger and their psychological range considerably more varied than any prejudice about his Carlylean fascination with 'great men' might suggest. Heroes there are, but few: and hardly any are without flaw. The purest of these is John Knox, whose appearances are strangely brief and intermittent in the work, his greatness being more affirmed than demonstrated. Knox died in 1572, and 'the full measure of [his] greatness' could never have been grasped by his contemporaries. 'It is only as we look back over that stormy time and weigh the actors in it one against the other that he stands out in his full proportions.'[52] Froude's other historical hero was problematic in a rather different way. Unlike Knox, whose imperatives were left incomplete in his lifetime, Henry VIII was the very embodiment of will who was prepared to take uncompromisingly radical action once the fundamental realities of his situation became clear to him. Froude's rehabilitation of Henry from the then conventional assessment that he was a brutal despot was among the most controversial elements of his first volumes and attracted the most hostile reaction from reviewers.[53] Seen as a whole, however, Froude's Henry is not without blemish, and as the *History* develops the king is revealed as erratic, domineering, and impulsive, as well as being the saviour of his nation. Even at the beginning, Froude concedes one grave defect in the royal character: 'with women he seemed to be under a fatal necessity of mistake.'[54]

A similar ambivalence also attends his account of those Elizabethan adventurers who first established his name as an historian. The achievement of Hawkins, Drake, and Gilbert in saving England from Spanish invasion and Catholic domination is once again celebrated; but now darker tones are added. Hawkins' and Drake's activities as unscrupulous and ruthless slavers are conscientiously registered, and Gilbert's responsibility for some of the bloodiest atrocities of sixteenth-century Ireland is presented to his readers without any attempt at exculpation or extenuation.[55]

---

52. *HoE*, X, 445–7.
53. This was the burden of Goldwin Smith's review in the *Edinburgh Review*: 'Froude's King Henry VIII', 108 (July 1858), 206–52, and also of the anonymous reviewer in *The Christian Remembrancer*, 32 (July 1856), 64–102. The Catholic *Dublin Review* was, unsurprisingly, very critical on this issue, 41 (December 1856), 307–44.
54. *HoE*, I, 469.
55. *HoE*, VIII, 470–80, X, 506–9.

Consummate villains are as rare in Froude as perfect heroes, and only those who have excelled equally in all vices, such as Sir Thomas Seymour, or Lord Darnley, or the Earl of Leicester, are reserved for special censure. Damning judgements are called forth in Froude only by a special kind of reprobate whose sin appears to approximate to a form of pride. These are the individuals endowed by God with extraordinary gifts who wilfully elect to turn those gifts against the purposes for which they were intended. Reginald, Cardinal Pole was one of such who is given a place in Froude's *History* which seems disproportionate to his actual importance. Stigmatised from his very first appearance, Pole resurfaces frequently in Froude's text as a man who brought suffering and ruin wherever he moved. 'His character was irreproachable', says Froude, 'without spot or stain; and the system to which he had surrendered himself had left to him of the common selfishnesses of mankind his enormous vanity alone. But that system had also extinguished in him the human instincts, the genial emotions by which theological theories stand especially in need to be corrected.' Froude's critics discerned here a veiled caricature of Newman. But though there are interesting similarities—superior intelligence, subtlety, reckless self-determination—Froude's portrait of Pole was designed to fulfil a far more important function within the dramatic structure of the whole work. Pole was a recurring historical type whose force of personality always made an impact on history, and always for the worst:

> He belonged to a class of persons at all times numerous, in whom enthusiasm takes the place of understanding; who are men of an 'idea'; and unable to accept human things as they are . . .[56]

If Pole—Robespierrist or Newmanite ideologue—is the great perverse force of Froude's early volumes, Mary Stuart is the prime villain of the later ones. Froude's portrait of Mary is by no means without nuance. She is intelligent, dexterous, brave, and if fond of luxury, capable also of great endurance and patience. She was possessed of many of the talents necessary in a great sovereign, gifted in many ways not granted to Elizabeth. But she was afflicted nonetheless by one great and irredeemable defect: she was an egoist.

> Mary Stuart was ever her own centre of hope, fear, or interest; she thought of nothing, cared for nothing, except as linked with the gratification of some ambition, some desire, some humour of her own.[57]

56. *HoE*, III, 23–53, VI, 531.   57. *HoE*, VII, 359–60.

In ordinary persons such self-centredness was not very remarkable, but in a sovereign it was a grave defect—even more so in one endowed with so many talents to rule and to sway opinion. In one charged with the responsibilities of rule at a time of great historical and spiritual crisis, however, it was not merely a deplorable weakness: it was an unforgivable sin.

Mary, moreover, compounded the gravity of her offence both in life and in death. In simulating for her own purposes the images of a persecuted victim, and in assuming at her death the mantle of a religious martyr, Mary blasphemed. She polluted the sacred act of martyrdom, so central to Froude's *History*, by her dissimulation, and the evil which she then spawned lived on, the cause of bloodshed through many centuries of Scottish history, and alive still in the blinding, enervating sentimentalism of her popular biographers.

But villainy, like heroism and martyrdom, is an especial quality embodied only by the few. For the most part Froude is concerned to present his readers with a large cast of men and women of affairs—many of them intelligent, all resourceful, and all sincere in their commitment to the tasks to which they have been set. At the pinnacle of these good men of affairs is Elizabeth's first secretary and constant adviser, Cecil. In patiently and routinely coping with the ceaseless intrigues of court politics, the challenges of international diplomacy, the occasional calamities of unexpected misfortune, and, above all, the persistent prevarications and contradictions of his sovereign, it was Cecil who steadily navigated the English state through successive crises in the later sixteenth century, never confident about what might happen next, but always certain that his ultimate purpose was the preservation of the English Reformation. No martyr, no saint, no genius even, Cecil made mistakes, and sometimes soiled his hands with ignoble instruments, but he proved his worth by the tenacity with which he held to the vision of England's historical destiny which had been granted to him, and applied all his skills and talents to make it a reality. He was quintessentially the man capable: a righteous Reynard.[58]

Cecil is the standard by which all other men and women charged with public responsibility are measured in Froude, but such measurement also provides the basis of a moral calculus of considerable sophistication. Thus sympathetic figures, such as the Scottish regent Moray, ultimately fail

---

58. Cecil is first introduced as the single-minded English patriot in *HoE*, V, 303, and reappears in this guise on numerous pages throughout the five volumes pertaining to the reign of Elizabeth.

because, in placing too much confidence in the essential righteousness of
their cause, they could not see that it must be striven for and defended with
all the skills at their disposal; while less morally creditable figures such as
regent Morton are adjudged to have been more successful in the cause of
the Reformation than his predecessor.[59] This balanced assessment of the
moral character of individuals is extended in Froude even to those who are
clearly on the wrong side of the historical struggle for religion. Thus Froude
shows an unexpected sympathy for Alva and Mary of Guise, the French
regent in Scotland who did so much to thwart the advance of the
Reformation. Maitland of Lethington is among Froude's most sympathetic
portraits—a figure whom Froude privately confessed he had found the
most attractive of all his characters. Shrewd, resourceful, cultured, and passionately committed to the cause of a British union of the crowns, Maitland
mistook this means of history's progress as an end in itself, and perished
thereby: Reynard at bay.[60]

Amongst the men of affairs it is not the execution in good faith of *acts*—
however evil they may have been in their consequence—that is the real
cause of censure by Froude. Rather, it is the failure to act at all. It is this that
characterises Philip II's failure as an historical agent. Unlike his father,
Charles V, for whom Froude expressed deep sympathy, Philip was indecisive,
irresolute, slow to heed the advice of his counsellors, and frequently paralysed by his own desire for control.[61] His procrastinations may have severely
damaged the cause of Counter-Reformation which he served, but they
were also the cause of the misunderstandings, false expectations, and exaggerated fears which were to issue in so much unnecessary violence and
suffering. Philip, however, was merely the understudy of the greatest pre-
varicator of them all: Elizabeth I.

Increasingly as the *History* progressed, Froude's attitude toward the last
Tudor sovereign darkened until his mounting attacks on the good queen of
legend were to become as controversial among his critics as his earlier
defence of Henry VIII. Once again, however, his assessment of Elizabeth is
not simple. In addition to acknowledging her many virtues—bravery and
mercy being among his favourites—Froude's analysis of the causes of

59. *HoE*, VII, 267; IX, 222, 581–7; X, 447; XI, 282–301.
60. *HoE*, X, 440, 453, 471–5; for Froude's privately expressed sympathy for Maitland, see Froude
    to David Laing, 13 June, 26 December 1862, 12 December 1864, Edinburgh University Library,
    Laing MSS, La IV 6; and to Skelton, 14 December 1864, *Table-Talk of Shirley*, 134.
61. *HoE*, IX, 312–13.

Elizabeth's refusal to commit is measured. Sometimes it was due to justified uncertainty; sometimes it was shrewd; sometimes it was a response to untoward pressure. But for all that, it was Elizabeth's preferred response to any situation whatever was at stake; and Froude was in no doubt that this perennial characteristic was a direct reflection of her femininity.[62]

That Froude shared in the general male prejudices of his day regarding the fundamental distinctiveness of male and female qualities is beyond dispute, and it is clear also that he accepted without question the common assumption that by nature women were not suited for the responsibilities of public life.[63] It is true, moreover, that such unlucky women as had a public role thrust upon them are generally not well accounted for in his *History*. Catherine of Aragon, Anne Boleyn, Catherine Howard, and Mary Tudor all receive unsympathetic treatment at his hands. But there are also exceptions. Jane Seymour is a saintly creature, Lady Jane Grey, to whom as 'Queen Jane' is given a share in a volume's title, is accorded the respect Froude reserves for martyrs, Mary of Guise is credited for having the courage of her convictions, and even Catherine de Medici is granted some exoneration. Such exceptions indicate merely that Froude was no unqualified misogynist. His indictment of Elizabeth, however, rests on one specific implication of her womanhood. It is that, putting considerations of self and sovereignty before all, she refused all invitations to marry and bear children. Froude's point is not that Elizabeth should have been ready at all times to make herself available to appropriate suitors. It was on occasion right for Elizabeth to prevaricate and dissimulate, as she did with Philip II, for example. But at other times it was not only unjustifiable, it was historically disastrous. Such, for example, was the queen's toying with the unfortunate Duke of Anjou, which merely antagonised the Spaniards and alienated the French at a time when a joint movement might have issued in the triumph of a Protestant League in the Lowlands and in France. In these circumstances, Froude's judgement on Elizabeth is withering:

> If it be supposed that public interest, however great, could not have required the Queen to devote her person and happiness to a union which she disliked, there is no excuse for the false and foolish trifling which exhausted

---

62. *HoE*, XII, 555–61 offers a summary of judgements which Froude has been making in passing throughout the five volumes of the *History* pertaining to the reign of Elizabeth.
63. Rohan Maitzen, 'Plotting Women: Froude and Strickland on Elizabeth I and Mary Queen of Scots', in Lynette Felber (ed.), *Clio's Daughters: British Women Making History, 1790–1889* (Danvers, MA, 2007), 123–52.

the patience and irritated the pride of the Royal family of France, and weakened the already too feeble barriers which were keeping back the tide of Catholic fury.[64]

This is Froude at his harshest, and modern opinion will not only deplore his psychological prejudices, but will also note his gross underestimation of the difficulties of Elizabeth's political, constitutional, and diplomatic situation.[65] While it doubtless rested upon and exploited the conventional prejudices of his time, Froude's intent in developing this motif of Elizabeth's prevarication was not primarily to denigrate the characteristics of her sex. It was there to reinforce his message of the necessity of decisive action in the midst of amorphous change. Henry, hero, did so for the good; Somerset, vainglorious weakling, for ill; Elizabeth is saved from the normal weaknesses of her sex by the quiet but sustained exertions of the accidental hero Cecil. Because of this, the English revolution of religious reformation was saved not completely and not triumphantly, but sufficiently to allow the struggle to continue in times to come. In ending at 1588 Froude's *History* deliberately concludes on a note of achievement, but not of finality.

After all this it is possible to suggest a synopsis of the complex experience which Froude had sought to produce for readers of his *History*, both in each of its chapters and in the compass of the book as a whole. Having first plunged them into an atmosphere of contrasting perspectives, conflicting expectations, and common uncertainties, and having provided them with a virtual sense of immediacy that overrode the misleading certitudes of retrospect, Froude then placed before them a whole theatre of characters where real villains and heroes are few, and martyrs equally exceptional. The vast majority, however, would have been familiar enough to readers of Balzac or Trollope—mediocre in their gifts and moral strength, but confronted by an unending series of events that required of them an action which they made either rightly or wrongly, or not at all. Their responses, whether positive, negative, or neutral, nonetheless contributed to the course of historical development that was in process before them, advancing, retarding, or perverting it as their characters and their powers allowed.

64. *HoE*, X, 305. Froude continued in a sentence summarising his views of the relative standing of the major figures in the latter part of the *History*: 'At home she submitted herself more entirely to Cecil's guidance, and bore herself with a dignity and a wisdom more becoming an English sovereign.'

65. For recent assessments of Elizabeth's conduct in regard to the possibilities and risks of marriage, see Susan Doran, *Monarch and Matrimony: The Courtships of Elizabeth I* (London, 1996).

The intended effect of this rhetorical assault upon his readers' sensibilities was multiple. Through it, Froude sought not only to answer the insinuations of Lingard's subtle polemic, but also to undermine the complacent and illusory certainties constructed by the philosophical and sentimental historians. More importantly, however, by inducting his readers into his own conception of the moral difficulties inherent in being alive and sentient amidst the processes of history, Froude was striving to present them with the real challenge of living in history, shared by all generations, ancient, medieval, and modern, from which no alternative view, whether intellectually sophisticated or emotionally naïve, could offer escape. This was the ineluctable obligation of all conscious humanity: a choice either to be part of, to oppose, or (like the Edward Fowlers and Markham Sutherlands of the world) to remain supine before the forces of change which for good or for ill were inexorably in motion all around them. In this, Froude's *History* constituted a renewal of the original Carlylean challenge which demanded of each reader individually: how were you, in your time, in your benighted circumstances, and with your limited capabilities, how were you going to act now?

V

This was a high ambition, and the extent of his success is partly evident in the remarkable popularity with which his heavy, spiky, and demanding volumes were generally received by the reading public. Readers everywhere hailed Froude as a great modern stylist, without knowing quite why. Without seeing that beneath the deft phrases, vivid descriptions, dramatic turns, ironic reflections, and bursts of passionate conviction which characterised the surface of his text, there lay a rhetorical and compositional strategy of great artistic complexity. But if Froude's popularity among the general reading public is an index of the success of his ambition, the disappointed expectations and hostile reactions that he provoked among a large set of critics is also a measure of its limitations.

Froude expected and even welcomed controversy on the appearance of his first volumes in 1856. His attacks on the Established Church and on the smugness of the philosophical school of historians positively courted critical reactions from the organs of those opposite pillars of orthodoxy: the *Christian Remembrancer* and the *Edinburgh Review*. Ignoring the former, he replied trenchantly to Goldwin Smith's right-thinking critique in the *Edinburgh Review*, and seemed to enjoy the notoriety he had acquired.[66] But as the subsequent instalments appeared in 1858, 1860, 1864, 1866, and 1870, other complications arose. While his popularity remained high in the daily press, the heavyweight monthlies and quarterlies remained cool; and critics in new influential organs such as the *Contemporary Review*, the *National Review*, and *The Academy* were not won over. From 1864 onward, moreover, Froude found himself the object of a malicious vendetta pursued by the medieval historian Edward Augustus Freeman through the pages of the popular *Saturday Review*, where Freeman supplied no less than sixteen reviews of his last six volumes, all of them ferociously hostile. Even worse, Froude's attempt to secure a favourable puff by his friend Charles Kingsley resulted in one of the most notorious *bouleversements* of the time, when Kingsley's unsolicited attack on Newman provoked in response the latter's magnificent *Apologia pro Vita Sua*. The irony that a history which had as one of its objects the final indictment of Catholicism as a spiritually exhausted husk should have brought forth one of the finest specimens of modern Catholic thought was not lost on Froude.

Hostile reviews alone, however, were not sufficient to cause Froude grave concern. At worst they perpetuated his continuing status as a man of controversy, and so distracted attention from the address which he sought to make to his readers. Other problems arising in the course of this sixteen-year undertaking, however, were more serious. As Froude was publishing the middle volumes of his *History*, Carlyle completed his own painful, twelve-year project: his study of *Frederick the Great*. The product of much personal torment, it had exhausted him, and though it sold well, its influence was nothing like *The French Revolution*. 'The English mind', wrote Froude, 'remains insular and is hard to interest…in any history but its own. The tone of *Frederick* nowhere harmonized with popular sentiment among us, and every page contained something to offend.'[67] Then, in 1866, within a year of its completion, Jane Welsh Carlyle died suddenly, plunging Carlyle into a melancholy from which he never recovered. Froude, who was his closest

66. For a list of the most important reviews, see n. 4 above. For later critical reviews in the new magazines, see *Contemporary Review*, 4 (April 1867), 437–72; *National Review*, 3 (July 1865), 107–27; and *The Academy*, 1 (8 January 1870), 108–10. Froude's reply to Goldwin Smith was published anonymously as 'The *Edinburgh Review* and Mr Froude's *History*', in *Fraser's Magazine*, 58 (September 1858) 359–78.
67. Froude, *Thomas Carlyle: His Life in London*, ii, 284–5.

friend at this time, fully realised the effect of his wife's death on Carlyle's imagination: beyond offering attrition for the suffering he believed he had caused her, Carlyle would write no more. The prophet had gone silent, and the acolyte's text was all that his public would receive.

These gathering anxieties were essentially private, but were complemented by a broad range of public issues which, even as his *History* was working its way through his readers' consciousness, Froude was becoming increasingly aware required urgent address. Some of these issues had engaged him to a greater or lesser degree since the early 1840s: the continuing problems of poverty and inadequate education. Ireland also remained as morally troubling as it had been to the young man on the eve of the Famine. But to these recurring preoccupations two other related developments added renewed urgency. The first was the apparently unopposed triumph of the principles and values of Liberal *laissez faire* in English public life and in the domestic and foreign policies of successive governments. The second was the growing acceptance within governing circles of the inevitability of the extension of the arena of political participation through franchise reform. Together these developments posed a particularly acute challenge toward the ethical values and moral responsibilities which Froude was convinced stood so urgently in need of revival. Carlyle had already seen this, but his attempts to warn against it in the splenetic and unbridled *Shooting Niagara* (1867) had been less than effective—a further indication of the prophet's declining powers. By contrast, Froude, whose own public voice had now been established, though in controversial and disturbing terms, was in a unique position to attempt a modified Carlylean address to the broadened but untested audience of his compatriots. He might do so not only because the *History* had for whatever reasons captured the imaginations of so many readers, but also no less importantly because, even as his reputation as an historian of England had been established, he had become editor of one of the most popular and influential organs of English middle-class opinion: *Fraser's Magazine*.

8

The Problems of England's Present: Editing *Fraser's*, Changing Voices, 1860–74

I

Froude's assumption of the editorial chair at *Fraser's* is usually taken as marking his final transformation from *enfant terrible* to stalwart spokesman of the Victorian literary establishment. The fiery young moralist who had scandalised conventional opinion mutated, it appears, over the 1860s into a solid defender of orthodoxy, and a spokesman, even, of reaction. A scourge of Gladstone and Liberalism, he emerged as a strident imperialist who could be found railing at the effects of the modest broadening of the franchise in 1867, the mild Education Act of 1870, and any attempt to respond to the demands of the politically resurgent Irish.

Many standard modes of explanation may be proposed for this sorry but not unfamiliar development. First, psychological ones: having discharged himself of the frustration and rage provoked by his oppressive father and brothers, this scion of a High Tory, High Church family, it may be surmised, simply returned to his natural roots, as soon as his freedom from such pressures had been assured—the old archdeacon having died in 1859. In 1862, moreover, he had recovered sufficiently from the early death of his first wife, Charlotte, to marry her first cousin, Henrietta Warre, thus commencing a union which was by all accounts supremely happy until Henrietta's death twelve years later.[1]

Sociological explanations may also be invoked: as editor of *Fraser's*, Froude received the same generous stipend of £400 that John Parker senior had

---

1. Froude to Elizabeth Long, 12 June 1861, Dunn, *Froude*, II, 294–5, 297–8, 349.

paid to his own son, and when the magazine was taken over by Longman in 1863 he was granted a substantial salary increase in order to stay on. By this point Froude had moved to the centre of London life, enjoying the acquaintance not only of the capital's leading literary and intellectual figures, but also of its most influential politicians, jurists, soldiers, and civil servants. His ascent in social status was reflected in his increasingly fashionable residential addresses. From a modest cottage in Bideford, Devon, he moved to Clifton Place, Hyde Park, and from thence in October 1865 to the recently built and highly fashionable development in Onslow Gardens, Kensington.[2] Some or all of these influences were doubtless at play in Froude's evolution at least to some degree.

The nature and extent of their importance, however, must remain indeterminate. Froude never settled fully into London literary life. He repeatedly professed his abhorrence of 'the Season', delighted in frequent absences from the city, and in 1862, after more than two successful years in the editorial chair at *Fraser's*, he was still showing an interest in applying for an academic post in the form of the newly established Chichele Professorship of Modern History at Oxford.[3]

Political or ideological explanations are more solid. The middle years of Froude's editorship witnessed a further broadening of the franchise and important attendant changes in the character and organisation of the main political parties and in the manner in which political issues arose and developed. It has been argued that Froude, in company with the other leading intellectuals of his time—Matthew Arnold, Leslie Stephen, John Morley, and W. E. H. Lecky—shared in the general disenchantment and pessimism which arose from the disappointing effects of franchise reform, and of the first general election held under its auspices in 1868. Free-thinking moralists who had long been deeply frustrated with the stultifying orthodoxies of the Established Church and of respectable Evangelicalism, they had looked forward eagerly to a regeneration of political and moral debate which, they believed, the broadening of the franchise would bring about. Immediately

---

2. Dunn, *Froude*, II, 326–50. Some entertaining light on Froude's tenancy at Onslow Gardens is thrown on an undated letter of complaint from Froude to the estate agent concerning the breaking of his windows by boys playing cricket and football in the estate's common gardens; Cambridge University Library, Vansittart papers, Thornton correspondence, VNST II/7/5.

3. Dorothy M. Owen, 'The Chichele Professorship of Modern History, 1862', *Historical Research*, 34 (1961), 217–20; Froude's brief letter of application, however, did not persuade the appointments board of the seriousness of his interest in the post.

upon the assembly of the new parliament it became clear that such a renewal was unlikely to take place. Instead, the bulk of the members returned under the new regime turned out to be even more venal, more concerned with immediate advantage, and more susceptible to pressure from vested interests than the unreformed parliament. The continuing power of the paralysing orthodoxies was displayed early on in the failure of the Gladstone government to respond to demands for the disestablishment of the Church of England, and even more powerfully in the concessions made both to Anglicanism and Dissent in the Education Act of 1870.[4]

There is much to be said for this thesis, as a marked change in Froude's attitudes as expressed in his editorial commissions and his own essays can be discerned around the close of the decade. For most of the 1860s Fraser's under Froude's editorship had taken advanced or progressive positions on several issues—most particularly in its defence of free-thinking and religious heterodoxy—and it is only from 1870 that his emergence as a modern Jeremiah issuing uncompromising tirades regarding colonies, Ireland, the bane of party politics in general, and the Liberal administration in particular, begins to take shape. Thus he may appear to fit quite comfortably into the pattern of the disillusioned intellectuals of the mid-Victorian era. But the nature of Froude's move to reaction is more complex, or at least more distinctive than such a simple model might suggest, and a too-ready identification of Froude with this group runs the risk of obscuring some important external forces and some equally important individual developments during his time at Fraser's which were in themselves sufficiently powerful to alter the character and direction of his public concerns and utterances in a unique manner. Of these, the most immediately obvious was the external pressure of competition.

II

Founded in 1830 by the brilliant and mercurial William Maginn, *Fraser's Magazine of Town and Country* was deliberately conceived as a rival to the

---

4. See among others, Jeffrey Von Arx, *Progress and Pessimism: Religion, Politics and History in Late Nineteenth Century Britain* (Cambridge, MA, 1985); Lionel Trilling, *Mathew Arnold* (New York, 1938), esp. chs. 8–9; Christopher Harvie, *The Lights of Liberalism: University Liberals and the Challenge of Democracy, 1860–86* (London, 1976); Asa Briggs, *Victorian People: A Reassessment of Persons and Themes, 1851–67* (2nd edn., London, 1970); Noel Annan, *Leslie Stephen: The Godless Victorian* (London, 1984), esp. ch. 10.

popular Edinburgh-based *Blackwood's Magazine*.[5] Like *Blackwood's*, *Fraser's* was designed to be a secular miscellany, combining samples of contemporary fiction, poetry, *belles lettres*, and literary criticism, with essays on politics, religion, and social affairs. Like *Blackwood's* (and unlike the *Edinburgh* and the *Quarterly* with which it was not intended to be in direct competition), *Fraser's* was a monthly containing something in the region of 130 pages (a little larger than *Blackwood's* average issue), and at 2s 6d per issue it was priced to match its main competitor. Though in its earliest years *Fraser's* was successful in rivalling *Blackwood's* circulation of around 8,000 copies, its figures began to fall steadily in the 1840s, and by the later 1850s, under the editorship of John Parker junior, it had fallen even further behind with a circulation of less than 3,000 per month, against *Blackwood's* 10,000.[6]

Then, in the early years of Froude's editorship, competition in the market for monthlies increased sharply with the appearance of a large number of new journals which were deliberately aimed at taking a share of this expanding middle-class market, and were priced highly competitively at 1s per issue. Most prominent among the new 'shilling monthlies' were *Macmillan's Magazine*, first published in November 1859 under the editorship of David Masson, and the *Cornhill Magazine*, which, under the editorship of William Makepeace Thackeray, made its first appearance in the same month that Froude formally undertook editing *Fraser's*. Incorporating fiction, poetry, travel, and *belles lettres*, but also commissioning serious articles from fresh or distinguished authors on politics, religious and philosophical debate, scientific research, and international developments, the new shilling monthlies presented a serious competitive challenge both to *Blackwood's* and to *Fraser's*. Beginning with a massive sale of 100,000 copies for its first issue, the *Cornhill's* circulation settled at around 30,000 throughout the 1860s before declining to about 20,000 in the 1870s. *Macmillan's* subscription was probably in the region of 8,000 during this period. A challenge of a different kind came from another new entrant into the monthly market. Edited by the flamboyant George Sala, *Temple Bar: A London Magazine of Town and*

5. On the early history of *Fraser's*, see Miriam Thrall, *Rebellious Fraser's* (New York, 1934).
6. For brief histories of the major magazines, see the essays supplied for each in W. E. Houghton (ed.), *The Wellesley Index to Victorian Periodicals, 1824–1900*, 5 vols. (Toronto, 1965–88) (on-line version available through proquest at http://wellesley.chadwyck.co.uk), to which reference is made hereafter. For circulation estimates, see Alvar Ellegärd, *The Readership of the Periodical Press in Mid-Victorian England* (Göteburg, 1957), and W. E. Houghton, 'Periodical Literature and the Articulate Classes', in Joanne Shattock and Michael Wolff (eds.), *The Victorian Periodical Press: Samples and Soundings* (Leicester, 1982), 3–27.

Country was intended to be of considerably lighter tone and content than the other new journals. But, as its subtitle implied, it was also conceived in direct competition with the lighter, *belles-lettrist* aspect of *Fraser's*, featuring easy-going travel essay, *pieces d'occasion*, and the like. While all of the competitors may have hoped to encourage multiple subscriptions from its targeted readership, the pressures which these new organs placed upon the older and more expensive monthlies, as distinct from the quarterlies, were particularly grave.[7]

Anxious about the financial state of the magazine from the beginning, Froude remained deeply concerned about its commercial affairs throughout his period of tenure. But his achievement in this extremely difficult market was substantial. During his time in office he managed to keep the size of the journal at a respectable average of 135 pages, double-columned, which contrasted favourably with *Macmillan's* average of eighty pages, and remained slightly above both *Blackwood's* and the *Cornhill*. In 1863 he successfully persuaded the new owner, Henry Longman, to increase substantially the honorarium paid to contributors in order to match the competition's rates, even though such generosity was accompanied by a rigorous enforcement of word limits, and small economies of production. In 1870 he bowed to pressure from Longman to follow Sala in the undignified practice of having his name printed on the title-page of each issue. But Froude also rose to the challenge. By early 1863 he was proud to tell friends that subscriptions had begun to rise well above the nadir reached in the last days of Parker; and by the later 1860s they may have ascended as high as 8,000. By 1870 sales appeared to have levelled off at a respectable plateau of around 6,000—a situation regarding which, even if it continued to cause concern, Froude could justifiably take credit.[8]

It is against this background of the greatly increased demands of competition that Froude's editorial strategy should be assessed. Compelled to respond to the new topics and fresh perspectives placed on offer by the new magazines, the editor of *Fraser's* was likewise required not to risk forfeiting

---

7. G. J. Worth, *Macmillan's Magazine, 1859–1907: No Flippancy or Abuse Allowed* (Aldershot, 1993), chs. 1–3; *The Cornhill Magazine* (special issue of *Victorian Periodical's Review*, 32, 1999); on *Temple Bar*, G. A. Sala, *The Life and Adventures of George Augustus Sala* (London, 1895); for circulation, the sources cited in n. 4 above.
8. Oscar Maurer Jr, 'Froude and Fraser's Magazine, 1860–1874', *University of Texas Studies in English*, 28 (1949), 213–43; Froude to Skelton, 8 March 1863, *Table-Talk of Shirley*, 128; Froude to Elizabeth Gaskell, October 1863, printed in R. D. Waller (ed.), 'Letters Addressed to Mrs Gaskell by Celebrated Contemporaries', in *Bulletin of the John Rylands Library*, 19 (1935), 160.

his old readership to the more comforting pages of *Blackwood's* and *Temple Bar*. In his management of the journal, therefore, Froude was required to pursue a delicately balanced strategy. Partly because of this, Froude, unlike his predecessors, issued no editorial testament either at the beginning of his tenure of office or thereafter. The essentially conservative premises on which he undertook the task were clearly expressed in two obituaries for the recently deceased Parker, one of which appeared anonymously in the December 1860 issue of *Fraser's*, and a second which Froude himself contributed to the *Gentleman's Magazine* in February 1861. It was Parker's conviction (and by implication his own), wrote Froude in the latter,

> that the cause of truth was best served when the points on which men differed were submitted to the most free discussion, and when the representatives of two different schools of opinion had the fullest opportunity of expressing themselves.[9]

Writing privately to John Skelton some two years into his editorship he assured him:

> On controverted points I approve myself of the practice of the Reformation. When St Paul's Cross pulpit was occupied one Sunday by a Lutheran, the next by a Catholic, the next by a Calvinist, all sides had a hearing, and the preachers knew that they would be pulled up before the same audience for what they might say.[10]

Balance, impartiality, and an editorial policy of strict neutrality seemed therefore to be the ideals which Froude was now to embrace in a mood far removed from the urgent exhortations which had characterised so much of his writing over the previous fifteen years. Amidst the demands of commerce, it may appear, the fires of youth had been finally extinguished.

Froude's apparent conversion to the ways of orthodoxy was made manifest in several practical ways. In the years after 1847 the Parkers had set about transforming 'rebellious *Fraser's*' magazine, which under Maginn had enjoyed such a reputation for lively, irreverent, and frequently scabrous copy, into a journal of sober middle-class and middle-brow opinion. The merciless fusillades, sendups, and hoaxes of the early period disappeared, to be replaced by respectable fiction and verse, mildly humorous pieces, reminiscences, and travel-writing. This was the inheritance which, with some significant departures, Froude was

9. *Gentleman's Magazine*, 55 (February 1861), 221–4.
10. Froude to Skelton, 17 December 1860, in Skelton (ed.) *Table-Talk of Shirley*, 125.

to retain during his fifteen years in the editorial chair. Several of the writers, for example, whom Parker had first recruited in the 1850s—including John Skelton, A. V. Kirwan, A. K. H Boyd, and George Whyte-Melville—continued to place articles in *Fraser's* throughout Froude's tenure of office. In doing so they helped preserve the magazine's conservative, unadventurous tone. Thus, in addition to light fiction and (in the main) even lighter poetry, travel writing, personal reminiscences, and *belle lettres* (along the lines of 'Concerning Disagreeable People', or 'Recreations of a London Recluse') continued to feature in most of the issues to appear under Froude.[11]

Yet the extent of Froude's surrender to cautious conservatism is easily be exaggerated. For at the same time as he was careful not to alienate tradi- tional readers, he strove to meet the intellectual challenge presented by the new monthlies on several fronts. A rough comparative contents analysis reveals some interesting developments in his editorial policy. Despite his reliance on some contributors inherited from Parker in the early years of his editorship, Froude commissioned a large number of new writers over the period. During the 1860s an average of thirty-six writers contributed annu- ally to *Fraser's*, and in the early 1870s the number of writers commissioned by Froude rose substantially to an annual average of forty-eight. These fig- ures did not compete with the average of around fifty-five writers who annually contributed to *Macmillan's*, but they compare well with the less than thirty on whom *Blackwood's* and the less than thirty-five on whom the *Cornhill* normally relied.[12] In contrast to *Blackwood's*, moreover, *Fraser's* list of contributors under Froude exhibited a surprising freshness as the years of his editorship advanced. While it is true that *Macmillan's* may be seen in retrospect to have engaged the flower of the mid-Victorian intellegentsia, *Fraser's* in this period secured several contributions by such notables as Leslie and Fitzjames Stephen, Matthew Arnold, Richard Burton, Francis Newman, Andrew Lang, Edward Dowden, and Theodore Martin, as well as taking credit for the first appearance of such subsequently recognised classics as John Stuart Mill's essays on 'Utilitarianism' and John Ruskin's on 'Political Economy'.[13] In the face of competition from the new journals, Froude was

---

11. These comments are based on a review and analysis of the contents lists and attributions of *Fraser's* provided in the Wellesley Index.
12. Analysed from the lists and attributions for the periodicals in the Wellesley Index.
13. See previous note; Mill's 'Utilitarianism' appeared in *Fraser's*, 64 (October, November, December, 1861), 391–406, 525–34, 659–73; Ruskin's 'Political Economy' appeared in 65 (June, 1862), 784–92; 66 (September, December, 1862), 265–80; 742–56; 67 (April, 1863), 441–62.

also sensitive to what would now be termed 'gender balance'. The Irish-born writer and activist Frances Power Cobbe was one of his most frequent contributors, but several other women authors, including Elizabeth Gaskell, Helen Taylor (Mill's daughter-in-law), Florence Nightingale, Henrietta Keddie, and Margaret Elliott also appeared more than once in its columns.[14]

This substantial extension of *Fraser's* writers' stable reflected a corresponding broadening in the range of issues discussed. In response in particular to pressure from *Macmillan's*, *Fraser's* displayed an increasing attention to contemporary political affairs. The number of essays devoted to domestic and European politics increased markedly over the 1860s, and all of the most significant topics preoccupying public debate in the 1860s and early 1870s—including parliamentary and franchise reform, the state of the army, navy, and colonial office, education, urban decay and development, trades union recognition, India, Ireland, the American Civil War, the Franco-Prussian War, and Italian unification—were given substantial space in the journal.

For all this gain there was an inevitable cost. Under the pressures and constraints of space, some categories of writings had to give way, and by the end of the 1860s Froude, who had become increasingly dissatisfied with the quality of the material he was receiving in that form, decided that it would be fiction. Under the Parkers, fiction, in the form of serialised novels and short stories, had represented almost a third of the magazine's annual content, but under Froude this proportion declined steadily throughout the 1860s, and in his final years in the chair disappeared altogether.[15] A less marked decline also occurred in the genre of travel and light essay writing whose proportion of the magazine's annual output shrank from around a third to a fifth of the magazine's annual output. This decision to meet the challenge of *Macmillan's* rather than that of *Temple Bar* was conscious and not easily made. Longman was not happy. Froude himself appreciated the force of the argument that the magazine was more likely to prosper by becoming more popular in tone, even though, he told Parker, he would resign the chair if such a policy decision were made.[16]

14. The number of contributions are respectively: Cobbe, 28; Gaskell, 5; Taylor, 3; Nightingale, 3; Keddie, 17; Elliot, 2.
15. On Froude's concern about the disappearance of fiction, see Froude to William Allingham, 6 August (1869/70), Beinecke Library, Yale University, Hilles MSS Box 9, Froude files.
16. Froude to Francis Power Cobbe, 4 February (1863/4), Huntington Library, San Marino, Cobbe Papers, 7.

The need to match the more serious of the new monthlies also heavily influenced the intellectual and ideological tone of the magazine's address to leading issues. In contrast to the competition, Froude pursued a deliberately neutral editorial line on several major issues. Thus he published Francis Newman's and Fitzjames Stephen's greatly opposed views on the reform of the government of India.[17] On the American Civil War he published John Stuart Mill's and Moncure Conway's defences of the North, but also other contributions by 'A White Republican' (Hiram Fuller) which took a strongly pro-Southern view.[18] A dialogue setting out the cases for and against the granting of women's suffrage, but offering no conclusion, was typical of *Fraser's* editorial position on this emerging question; though in 1870 Froude commissioned a review of Mill's *On the Subjection of Women* which, while sympathetic on several grounds, was ultimately unsupportive. The frequent appearance, however, of Frances Power Cobbe (with whom Froude himself was on quite friendly terms) did not persuade *Fraser's* to take an advanced view on women's rights.[19] Though he was later to repudiate it, *Fraser's* likewise pursued a balanced editorial line on the deeply divisive controversy over the conduct of Governor Eyre in Jamaica. A defence of Eyre signed 'by a late resident in the island' was prefaced by Froude with an appeal for an alternative view and a note strongly condemning Eyre's conduct in the execution of his principal native-born opponent, Mr Gordon. In the following issue the case against Eyre was duly published.[20]

On such divisive issues, considerations of competition, as well as the editor's own ambivalence, counselled caution. But on other matters, *Fraser's* in the 1860s was, if not noticeably radical, still quite abreast of reformist opinion. In regard to social and economic issues, the magazine was far from

17. Newman, 'The Duties of England to India', 'The Dangerous Glory of India', *Fraser's*, 64 (December 1861), 674–89; 90 (October 1874), 448–64; Stephen, 'Kaye's *History of the Indian Mutiny*', 70 (December, 1864) 757–74.
18. Mill, 'The Contest in America', 65 (February 1862), 258–68; Conway, 'President Lincoln', 'Virginia, First and Last', 'The Assassination of President Lincoln', 71 (January, March, June, 1865), 1–21, 277–94, 791–806; Fuller, 'North and South', 66 (September–November 1862), 299–318, 433–48, 647–62; 'Negroes and Slavery in the United States', 67 (February 1863), 192–204.
19. 'Women's Votes: A Dialogue', 77 (May, 1868), 577–90; Henry Taylor, 'Mr Mill on the Subjection of Women', 81 (February 1870), 143–65; Bertha Thomas, 'Latest Intelligence from the Planet Venus', 90 (December 1874), 763–6.
20. J. H. L Archer, 'Jamaica and the Recent Insurrection there', W. R. Greg, 'The Jamaica Problem', 73 (February–March, 1866), 161–79, 277–305. Froude's notes are on 161 and 177; he regretted his failure to be more active in the defence of Eyre in his *Thomas Carlyle: His Life in London*, ii, 329.

complacent. In the 1860s Froude commissioned several pieces concerning pauperism and the appalling state of the cities.[21] The magazine also published a sequence of articles on the condition of the urban working class by Thomas Wright, 'the journeyman engineer', and took a moderate view on trades unions: the rights of combination and bargaining were upheld, but the right to strike condemned.[22] *Fraser's* was an unambiguous champion of state-supported primary education, of a progressive income tax, of agricultural labourers, and of extensive reform of relations between landlords and tenants.[23]

Though critical both of Liberal *laissez faire* and Tory complacency, the political tone of the magazine was in general reformist. Froude not only published Mill and Henry Fawcett, but also gave space to the ideas of the radical franchise reformist Thomas Hare.[24] *Fraser's* principal political commentators were similarly critical of the status quo. Abraham Hayward, who was recruited by Froude in the early 1860s, was at heart a Tory radical, but with Froude's encouragement he nevertheless pursued a bitter campaign against Disraeli up to and beyond the 1868 election, and had many good things to say about the Liberals, especially Lord John Russell, and even about Gladstone.[25] The political economist Bonamy Price was more overtly conservative in both his political and economic articles; but he also refused to endorse the Tories, and frequently encouraged the Liberals, while Froude commissioned several articles on political and economic reform by the then radical economist J. E. Thorold Rogers.[26]

Throughout the 1860s, moreover, *Fraser's* was in the vanguard of arguments for the extension of the parliamentary franchise, raising the case long

21. F. P. Cobbe, 'The Indigent Class, their Schools and Dwellings', 73 (February, 1866), 143–60; Cobbe, 'The Philosophy of the Poor-Laws and the Report of the Committee on Poor Relief', 70 (September 1864), 373–92; 'Our Manufacturing Districts and Operative Classes', 66 (September 1862), 363–82; Thomas Wright, 'On the Condition of the Working Classes', NS 4 (October, 1871), 426–40.

22. 83 (June 1871), 751–61; 84 (July, October, 1871), 62–8, 426–40; 86 (November 1872), 641–50.

23. E. S., 'How may a Peace Income-Tax be Supplanted', 69 (April 1864), 507–20; 'The Duties of the State', NS 5 (June 1872), 737–50; T. E. Cliffe Leslie, 'The Land Tenure Question', 69 (March 1864), 357–77; Thorold Rogers, 'Capital–Labour–Profit', NS 1:4 (April 1870), 500–12; 'The Agricultural Labourer', NS 1 (April 1870), 427–43.

24. *Fraser's* published three essays by Hare arguing for extensive reform of political representation, 61 (February, April 1860), 188–204, 527–43; 68 (December 1863), 713–29.

25. Hayward contributed thirty articles to *Fraser's* under Froude's editorship. For his attacks on Disraeli, see 77 (April, May 1868), 525–44, 666–78; 78 (September 1868), 363–74.

26. Froude published three essays by Thorold Rogers; see especially 'Capital–Labour–Profit', 1:4 (April 1870), 500–12.

before it was again taken up by the parties, roundly criticising what it believed was Disraeli's indifference and cynicism in regard to the matter, and supporting the Liberals in the 1868 election. On the death of Prince Albert, Froude himself published a highly controversial piece against the sentimentalisation of the monarchy to which the eulogising of the consort was giving rise, which was regarded in some quarters as sheer republicanism.[27]

This increasing preoccupation with political and social issues which his tenure of *Fraser's* editorial chair necessarily entailed, did not imply a diminution of Froude's characteristic engagement with theological and moral questions. Unlike fiction and *belles lettres*, essays bearing upon religious and theological topics underwent no sharp decline under Froude's editorship. In his first months in the office he had on several occasions opened the pages of the journal both to the defenders of the embattled authors of that manifesto of religious heterodoxy, *Essays and Reviews* (1860).[28] Throughout the 1860s, moreover, he published several articles by Francis Newman, Fitzjames and Leslie Stephen, and several anonymous authors, excoriating the Church of England in general and the episcopal bench in particular.[29] 'Even strife and trouble are better than a sleeping acquiescence in falsehood', declared one unidentified author, 'when shall we be able to say that three-fourths of the English clergy belong to some shade of opinion?'[30] Other essays on developments in continental theology, on religious anthropology (including some by Friedrich Max Müller), and on the religious practices of the laity advanced a more oblique attack on the establishment.[31] Occasionally Froude even allowed a demand for outright disestablishment to be advanced without editorial disclaimer.[32]

Notwithstanding its attacks on the establishment, *Fraser's* was on guard, warning its readers against the seductive alternatives of 'Puseyism' and

27. 'The Late Prince Consort', 76 (September 1867), 269–83. Froude believed that the article kept him permanently out of favour with Queen Victoria; Froude to Sir Arthur Helps, n.d., Helps MSS, Duke University Library, Special Collections Department.

28. W. D. Watson, *Essays and Reviews*, 62 (August 1860), 228–42; 'Toleration within the Church of England', 63 (April 1861), 483–92; A. P. Stanley, 'Aids to Faith', 66 (August 1862), 200–6.

29. For example, Newman, 'The Future of the National Church', 67 (May, 1863), 549–62; Fitzjames Stephen, 'The Privy Council and the Church of England', 69 (May 1864), 521–37; 'The Present State of Religious Controversy', 80 (November 1869), 537–74; Leslie Stephen, 'Dr Pusey and Dr Temple', 80 (December 1869), 722–37; 'The Broad Church' and 'The Religious Difficulty', 81 (March, May 1870), 311–25, 623–34.

30. 'Theology in Holland', 67 (March, 1863) 359–70; the quotation is from 370.

31. Max Müller, 'Lectures on the Science of Religion', 81, 82 (April, July, 1870), 444–55, 100–12.

32. 'Fact and Phantasms on the Ecclesiastical Question', 78 (November 1868), 567–83.

'Romanism': Froude commissioned the redoubtable Fitzjames Stephen to write a series on the rise of ultramontanism, and it was he whom Froude chose to review (negatively, of course) Newman's *Apologia pro Vita Sua*, while reserving for himself the right of supplying a subtle but negative critique of *A Grammar of Assent*.[33]

Froude's own contributions to the religious controversies of the 1860s may be seen in part to be of a piece with those of the other free-thinking intellectuals of the decade. In his 'Plea for the Free Discussion of Theological Difficulties' and in its companion piece on 'Criticism and the Gospel history', Froude appeared to come to the defence of *Essays and Reviews*, advancing a case for toleration and debate which seemed to match John Stuart Mill's secular liberalism. The effects of the new biblical criticism, wrote Froude, could not be ignored by the defenders of the church. Condemnation and repression led only to cynicism and obscurantism in the worst minds and alienation in the best; it would never still the recurring waves of sincere and intelligent enquiry. Instead, a critical approach to the sacred texts, properly conducted and properly received, would issue in a renewed sense of the eternal significance of the Christian message to generation after generation and thus to a recurring regeneration of the human spirit. The state of the human soul was not so fragile as to be in need of stiffening by a rigid and unbending orthodoxy. 'The creed of eighteen centuries is not about to fade away like an exhalation.' Its continuing vigour was manifest not in the strident affirmations of 'its professed defenders, [but] in those many quiet humble men and women who in the light of it and the strength of it live holy, beautiful and self-denying lives', and so it will continue 'so long as the fruits of the Spirit continue to be visible in charity, in self-sacrifice, in those graces which raise human creatures above themselves and invest them with that beauty of holiness which only religion confers'.[34]

This was a considerably milder restatement of an argument which Froude had pressed with such urgency in the past, and it concluded, moreover, with a far more optimistic assessment of the state of affairs than the

33. 'Dr Pusey and the Court of Appeal', 70 (November 1864), 644–62; 'English Ultramontanism', 71, 72 (June, July, 1865), 671–87, 1–35; 'Dr Newman's *Apologia*', 70 (September 1864), 265–303; 'Father Newman, *The Grammar of Assent*', 81 (May 1870), 561–80, reprinted in *Short Studies*, II, 101–45.

34. The essays appeared in *Fraser's*, 68 (September 1863) and 69 (January 1864), 277–91, 49–63 respectively, and were reprinted in *Short Studies*, I, 202–40, 241–80, to which reference is made here. The quotation is from 'Plea', 217–18.

one which had motivated his writings in the 1840s and early 1850s. Its apparent calmness and moderation was partly a result of the significantly changed environment for religious debate in which the pieces were written. The fact that the lesson which he had sought to teach in such a solitary and afflicted way some dozen years previously had now been taken up and propagated by the brightest minds in Oxford and Cambridge may have been a source of limited satisfaction to him, and there is a distinct note of condescension in the somewhat cool manner in which, while coming to the defence of the 'Essayists', Froude appealed over their heads to 'humble men and women'.[35]

A more potent source of Froude's detachment from the issues that had once so passionately engaged him, however, was the conviction that he had long since moved beyond the position which the 'Essayists' had now reached by means of the powerful vehicle on which he was now concentrating so much of his energy: history. It is significant, therefore, that Froude's further interventions into the revived religious and theological debates of the 1860s were expressed not by additional contributions of a philosophical or speculative kind, but through the medium of history. This he did in a series of lectures and papers directed at a broader audience than those engaged in theological debates which were designed to supplement and popularise the message which he was gradually unfolding in his *History of England*.

III

In the first and slightest of these essays 'The Influence of the Reformation upon the Scottish Character', Froude put forth the case that the successful establishment of the Reformation in Scotland was the achievement not of the nobility or the clergy but of 'the Scottish commons ... the farmer, the peasant, the petty trades-man and the artisan'. Before the Reformation this was an amorphous body whose members had 'no political existence' outside their individual allegiance to their own lords and masters; but in its hour of crisis, it was the commons who had rallied to the Reformation's defence, and in doing so had created themselves as a distinctive and permanent

---

35. *Short Studies*, I, 218. A further note of condescension is discernible in Froude's reference to the *Essays* in 'The Science of History: A Lecture delivered at the Royal Institution, February 5, 1864', first printed in *Short Studies*, I, 1–38, at 17.

element within Scottish culture and the source 'of all that is greatest in the Scottish character.'[36] This was a polemical argument, designed to reinforce the view which Froude was propagating in the later volumes of his *History of England* that the tap-root of spiritual regeneration was to be found not among the clergy or the political elite, but in what he amorphously identified as 'the ordinary people'.[37] It is significant largely because it overtly asserts a dialectical principle in Froude's account of the process of Reformation which he had hitherto been content to leave implicit in the dense narrative of the *History*, according to which at a particular time and place, certain individuals or groups of people actively and decisively changed the course of history and in turn set the terms for shaping the character of individuals and peoples for generations thereafter.

First asserted in regard to the Reformation in Scotland, this was a principle on which Froude next elaborated in terms of the European Reformation as a whole in a series of lectures entitled 'The Times of Erasmus and Luther'.[38] Conceived as an exercise in popular history to be presented to a general audience, the lectures establish a contrast which seems rudimentary: the opposition between the man of intellect and the man of faith. Erasmus is the representative of 'the large-minded latitudinarian philosophers':

> ... men who have no confidence in the people, who have no passionate convictions; moderate men, tolerant men who trust to education, to general progress in knowledge and civilization, to forbearance, to endurance, to time— men who believe that all wholesome reforms proceed downwards from the educated to the multitudes ...

Luther, on the other hand, represents the men of faith who

> consider conscience more important than knowledge ... who are not contented with looking for what may be useful and pleasant to themselves ... [but] for what is good—for what is just.[39]

---

36. Lecture delivered at Edinburgh in November 1865, first printed in *Short Studies*, I, 154–87, esp. 174–5.
37. For a summary of modern interpretation on the nature of the Scottish Reformation, see the entry by Michael Lynch on 'Reformation', in Michael Lynch (ed.), *The Oxford Companion to Scottish History* (Oxford, 2007); also Jenny Wormald, *Court, Kirk and Community: Scotland 1470–1625* (London and Edinburgh, 1981), chs. 5–6.
38. Three lectures delivered to the Newcastle Literary and Philosophical Society in January 1867, first printed in *Short Studies*, I, 39–153.
39. *Short Studies*, I, 114–15.

A populist anti-intellectualism apparent in the essay on Scotland and his qualified defence of the 'Essayists' is also evident here. Confronted with the crisis of Christianity which the corruption of the once noble Catholic Church provoked, Erasmus, scholar and critic, retreated into an ironic superiority; but Luther stood up to bear witness to his times, knowing in his heart 'that his thoughts were the thoughts of thousands.'[40] It was this faith in the historical necessity of his protest that separated him irrevocably from Erasmus. Whereas to Erasmus the value of truth and justice was founded on reason which estimates the relativity of things, Luther's faith rested on the conviction of eternal truths which were constantly being obscured in history and which needed at certain times to be boldly asserted whatever the immediate consequences. It is history, Froude insists, which repeatedly presents the test of eternal faith against temporal reason; and while reason may help in developing and improving upon processes already in motion, it is faith alone that initiates all real historical change. The recurrence of such faith-inspired epochs, however, though inevitable, was never predictable. While it was true that the spirit of the Creation ensured that in the long run the good would be attained, the occasion, the pace, and the stability of such a process were altogether in the hands of men charged with the responsibility of seeing it through. Before this challenge, Luther, for all his faults, had risen magnificently, and Erasmus, for all his talents, had failed. It could easily have been otherwise. It was a matter of character.

Froude's concern here was not merely to celebrate and glorify the past achievements of Protestant pioneers, but to point a general moral. Though the philosophers and men of reason have often been responsible for genuine material progress, 'the spiritual progress of mankind has followed the opposite course. Each forward step has been made first among the people, and the last converts have been among the learned.' Implicated as they generally have been in the interests of 'the cultivated classes', the learned have traditionally been 'enlisted on the side of the existing order of things' and have used their abilities 'only to find arguments for believing what they wish to believe':

> Simpler men have less to lose; they come more in contact with the realities of life and they learn wisdom in the experience of suffering. Thus it was that when the learned and the wise turned away from Christianity, the fishermen of the Galilean lake listened, and a new life began for mankind.[41]

---

40. *Short Studies*, I, 97.   41. *Short Studies*, I, 153.

A final and most radical instalment of what might be considered Froude's popular history of the Protestant Reformation provides the clearest indication of the impulses which underlay his populist anti-intellectualism. In 'On the Condition and Prospects of Protestantism', Froude announced that the fate which had attended paganism, and medieval Catholicism, now awaited Protestantism.

> We are left face to face with a creed which tells us that God has created us without the power to keep the commandments—that He does not require us to keep them; yet at the same time that we are infinitely guilty in His eyes for not keeping them, and that we justly deserve to be tortured for ever and ever, to suffer, as we once heard an amiable excellent clergyman express it, '... the utmost pain which Omnipotence can inflict, and the Creature can endure, without annihilation'.[42]

This is the falling away from the true spirit of the Reformation which has given rise to so much discontent among Protestants: the mindless authoritarianism of the bishops, the pointless disputations of the divines, the silent drift of many toward agnosticism and indifference, and the hysterical return of many more to 'the worn-out idolatries' of Catholicism.

What has happened to Protestantism, Froude argues, was not mysterious, but a recurrent and recognisable historical process. Like all spiritual revivals in the history of mankind, the Reformation of the sixteenth century was a combination of two impulses—one positive, the other negative. The former represented a reaffirmation of the truth of all religions—'the obligation of obedience to the law of moral duty'. The latter was a powerful rebellion against the corruptions, hypocrisies, and delusions of the age.[43] Though, like all spiritual movements, it contained both components within itself, Protestantism, as the term itself declared, was deeply imbued with the latter force, which was at first its greatest strength, and afterwards its principal defect. Once Catholicism's power of oppression had been successfully challenged and Protestantism was established as an independent force, it soon

> showed a disposition to revive in its own favour the methods from which it had suffered, [and] the tide which had carried it to victory ceased to flow.[44]

42. *Fraser's Magazine*, 77 (January 1868), 56–70; *Short Studies*, II, 146–79; quote from 151.
43. *Short Studies*, II, 161–4.
44. *Short Studies*, II, 166.

This gradual loss of spiritual force had been evident is successive generations, and seemed now to have reached its nadir displayed in the flight to
Catholicism, the ritualism and elitism of the Established Church, the smugness of the evangelicals, and the pervasive but unspoken agnosticism of
everyday materialism.

Did any hope remain? Froude was doubtful. From the clergy, preoccupied with their petty doctrinal and liturgical wranglings, nothing could be
expected; and from the men of 'higher intellect' and learning little more was
forthcoming: their confidence in the nostrums of Benthamite political
economy or 'the will o'the wisp of Positivism' being in itself a symptom of
the current spiritual malaise. But Froude espied one glimmer, albeit 'but a
faint one'. It was

> that the laity who are neither divines or philosophers may take the matter into
> their own hands as they did at the Reformation ... For fixed opinions beyond
> our reach, we may yet exchange the certainties of human duty; and no longer
> trusting ourselves to so-called economic laws ... we may place practical reli-
> gion once more on the throne of society.[45]

The direction of England's future remained deeply uncertain; but whether
it led toward a continued decline into moral obloquy and social collapse, or
whether it would turn toward a new era of moral and spiritual regeneration,
lay in the hands of that large undifferentiated group which Froude called
'the laity'.

IV

But how was this to be achieved? How were the people who were to serve
as the agents of historical change to be reawakened to the role which imminently they were to be required to play? In the past, as we have seen, Froude's
conviction that he might have a part to play in such a process of renewal had
been expressed sometimes modestly in his audacious fictions, and sometimes less so as in the massive undertaking of his grand historical narrative.
Now, partly due to his consciousness of the limitations of those voices, but
more importantly because of his experience, earned in the editorial chair at
Fraser's, of the changing nature of the audience he must address, Froude

---

45. *Short Studies*, II, 179.

began to explore different ways of re-presenting himself to the public. The historical and autobiographical voices which had been so central to his earlier modes of address would not be abandoned, but their mood and their intended effect would be altered by a more direct engagement with the immediate interests and concerns of the expanding reading public of the 1860s whom his magazine and its competitors were already cultivating. Before long this would lead Froude to assume a committed and often controversial voice on public issues—on political reform, education, colonial policy, and on Ireland. Yet an underlying continuity between this new voice and his earlier ones can be found not only in the popular lectures and essays discussed above, but in an experiment in publication which appeared before the public even as the Reform Bill was being passed into law in the autumn of 1867, and which he entitled *Short Studies on Great Subjects*.[46]

The republication of selected occasional essays by journalists and *litterateurs* was by no means unknown when Froude set about preparing his own two-volume exercise in the form; and in accounting for its appearance, some commercial considerations no doubt applied. The repackaging of essays first published in the expensive higher journals in compact form and at a relatively economical price was clearly an attempt to cash in on the expanding market of a self-improving reading public.[47] The very title of the collection is in itself evidence of such an intent. Although the studies (running on average to more than 12,000 words each) were hardly short, and the topics covered not always recognisably great, the catchy title seems designed to recommend the book to a reader anxious to become abreast of subjects of major cultural importance. Yet if such an appeal to the self-improving was commercially attractive, it also accorded wholly with Froude's deep and enduring desire to find a voice which would most effectively stimulate in his readers the moral regeneration that he believed was urgently necessary.

Seen in this light, the selection and organisation of the pieces collected in *Short Studies* is revealing in several ways. First, Froude's exclusion of anything he had written before 1850 is confirmation of his opinion that, however sincere his intentions had been, his critical and philosophical essays of

---

46. Published in two volumes by Longman and Green, the essays were to be reissued in all subsequent editions in one volume as the 'First Series' of what would ultimately be a four-volume set.
47. Richard D. Altick, *The English Common Reader: A Social History of the Mass Reading Public, 1800–1900* (Chicago, 1957); Simon Eliot, 'The Business of Victorian Publishing', in Deirdre A. David (ed.), *The Cambridge Companion to the Victorian Novel* (Cambridge, 2000), 37–60.

the 1840s were no longer relevant in the 1860s. Next, his decision to exclude most of the essays dealing directly with English history which had established and spread his reputation in the 1850s and 1860s—he selected only two of a possible twenty-five—and to include some early essays which had appeared in relatively obscure journals, is also indicative of a distinctive purpose. This was not intended as a commercial enterprise recycling the early studies of a now famous historian. Froude had something more in mind.

The internal organisation of the collection is also worth examination. The sequencing of the essays is not chronological. The collection begins with three recent and hitherto unpublished pieces: a lecture on 'The Science of History', the sequence of lectures on Erasmus and Luther, and the lecture on the Scottish Reformation noted above. It then moves far back to an essay on 'The Philosophy of Christianity', here re-titled, without explanation, 'The Philosophy of Catholicism', which first appeared in 1850. There follow the two essays on the theological debates stimulated by *Essays and Reviews* in the 1860s which are succeeded by Froude's earlier essays on Job and Spinoza first published in 1853 and 1855 respectively. Next follow the two English history essays on 'The Dissolution of the Monasteries' and 'England's Forgotten Worthies' which first appeared in 1857 and 1852. Essays on 'Homer', 'The Lives of the Saints', and 'Representative Men', first published in 1852 and 1850, come next. Froude's disturbing 1852 piece on Reynard the Fox is the last formal essay in the collection, which concludes with a set of fables, 'The Cat's Pilgrimage' and four shorter pieces which were first published in *The Leader* in 1850.

Amidst this chronological muddle, a clear pattern of argument can, however, be discerned. Froude's keynote essay, 'The Science of History', has sometimes been seen as an expression of pure philosophical scepticism; for it is here that he introduces the notorious image of history as a pack of cards which the historians may shuffle at will while History with its passive irony will let them have their way. But such scepticism was merely preparatory. It was intended to dispel the attractive and popular notion that students of history could derive rules of development comparable to those of science, so that Froude might reassert the true purpose of historical writing and reflection which as in drama and poetry was interactive, imaginative, and liberating:

> In the anomalies of [historical] fortune we feel the mystery of our mortal existence, and in the companionship of the illustrious natures who have shaped

the fortunes of the world we escape the littleness which clings to the round of common life, and our minds are tuned in a higher and nobler key.[48]

The purpose of historical study, then, is ethical and aesthetic: it functions within our imagination in the same manner as poetry and drama. So it is with lines from Wordsworth's 'Ode on the Intimations of Immortality' that Froude chooses to conclude his argument. Although the theories of history of theological and post-theological scientific schools will come and go, there will remain, as long as human self-consciousness persists, 'those obstinate questionings [and] shadowy recollections ... which ... have the power to make our noisy years seem moments in the being of the eternal silence.'[49]

This opening thus sets the terms under which the critical and historical essays that follow are to be read. They are intended to demonstrate that it was such a transcendent vision into the essential nature of things in Creation, often vouchsafed to ordinary men—the Scottish commons, the English sea-dogs, and even Luther—that was the real motive force of change in history. More importantly, however, they taught that neither history nor poetry alone had ever been sufficient: action, inspired by the poet's (and the poetic historian's) vision, but carried out by the capable Reynards of the world, was what was always required.

The purpose of the concluding fables is to drive home this message in its universal form. It was the providential role of every creature, as the peregrinatory cat finally understood, to discover what their individual duty to the creative spirit was, and to fulfil it without envy or complaint.[50] It could not be evaded by a facile and all too human dependence upon received dogma and wisdom. Just as the sustaining 'breadfruit trees' of the next fable withered, these too were destined to lose their inspirational power and to decline amidst the inescapable processes of historical entropy. But while ideas, and the people who embodied them, were transitory, the universe through which they passed was not: and, as 'Compensation', the final fable in the sequence taught, each unit in that vast creation—animal, vegetable, and mineral—could do no more than fulfil its own distinctive role. The role reserved for humans, of course, was especially complex. Because our very consciousness of the processes of historical change entailed an obligation to

48. *Short Studies*, I, 37.
49. *Short Studies*, I, 38
50. See ch. 6.

further the advance of the creative spirit, lest by our ignorance, inaction, or indifference we served to obstruct and deflect it, it was not sufficient for philosophers, theologians, nor even ordinary people simply to interpret the world. For Froude, as for Marx, his exact and more famous coeval, the point was to change it.[51]

V

But how was the change to begin? For Marx, Mill, and the positivists, the answer lay in some form of mass education: the raising of class consciousness or the provision of better and longer state education. For Froude, historical idealist, an educational strategy was also an urgent necessity, and like many other cultural critics of the 1860s he was strongly in favour of increased state intervention in primary education through the extension of compulsory attendance, increased investment, and thoroughgoing overhaul of the curriculum and its text-books. But because it arose from principles quite opposed to those of the materialists and the positivists, it was inevitable that Froude's understanding of the need and purpose of educational reform should lead to very different proposals as to how it should be undertaken.

Thus in 1869, when Froude, as the distinguished author of the *History of England*, was elected to the honorary position of Rector of the University of St Andrews, he used the occasion of his inaugural lecture to take issue with the pedagogical views of his immediate predecessor in the rectorial chair, John Stuart Mill.[52] In his own address Mill had urged an extension of classical education to the masses, and a vast increase in the amount of general knowledge to be included in the syllabi of state schools.[53] Froude objected: 'General knowledge ... was general ignorance.' It was acquired by mindless cramming, and would be forgotten as soon as the pressure of a terminal examination was removed. More seriously, Mill's assumption that a broad education would encourage the naturally talented in all classes and pave the way for a career open to talent was dangerously misleading. On the

51. 'Compensation', in *Short Studies*, I, 660–2.
52. 'An Address delivered to the Students at St Andrews, 19 March 1869', first printed in *Short Studies*, II, 439–78.
53. J. S. Mill, *Inaugural Address delivered to the University of St Andrews, 1 February 1867* (London, 1867); see also A. J. Mill, 'The First Ornamental Rector at St Andrew's University: J. S. Mill', *The Scottish Historical Review*, 43 (October 1964), 131–44.

contrary, England was a country 'where each child that is born among us finds every acre of land appropriated, [and] a universal "Not yours" set upon the rich things with which he is surrounded'. Given the unlikely prospect that such conditions would be overthrown, and the unwillingness on the part of the liberal political economists to recommend that they should be overthrown, each child, Froude insisted, had 'a right to demand that he be given such teaching as shall enable him to ... take such a place in society as belongs to the faculties which he has brought with him'.[54]

Instead of hopeful platitudes about the benefits of a broad education, what was urgently required at primary level in particular was a reformed system of industrial education deliberately attuned to the probable futures of the youths under tuition. Thus, for those most probably destined for a career as tillers of the soil, an educational programme designed to acquaint them with the elementary rules of 'agricultural chemistry', the function and use of agricultural machinery, 'the laws of the economy of force, and the most curious problems of physiology' was to be devised. Similarly, a tailored curriculum ought to be devised for all categories of manual and skilled labour. The principle remained the same:

> Teach your boys subjects which they can learn only mechanically, and you teach them nothing which it is worth their while to know. Teach them facts and principles which they can apply and use in the work of their lives; and if the object be to give your clever working lives a chance of rising to become Presidents of the United States or millionaires ... the ascent into those blessed conditions will be easier and healthier along the track of an instructed industry.[55]

What was true of the primary and secondary level applied equally to university education. The universities' curricula ought likewise to be redesigned specifically to answer the needs of those intending to pursue a career in medicine, law, engineering, and even religion. For those determined to pursue what he conceded to be the higher callings of 'spiritual culture'—philosophy, literature, and history—Froude had a stern warning. Necessarily unproductive in a material sense, such endeavours were traditionally associated with a form of self-sacrifice—the poverty of the wandering scholar or the frugality of the poor clergyman. But in recent times, as literary and intellectual life has become professionalised, so the pressures of the market

54. 'Education', *Short Studies*, II, 455–6, 467.
55. *Short Studies*, II, 462.

have threatened to undermine the integrity of the writer and thinker in ways even worse than the corruptions of the lower occupations. In such circumstance Froude could offer only stark advice: either to reject the scholarly path as a wasteful and deluding vanity, or to embrace a life of isolation and poverty.[56]

Froude's views on education will strike many observers as contradictory, if not hypocritical. His contention that scholars and intellectuals should resign themselves to a life of seclusion and austerity will seem odd coming from a figure now comfortably ensconced at the heart of the London literary scene. Likewise, while his insistence on the importance of vocational education and the broadening of the university curriculum may appear to anticipate some of the most important pedagogic and academic reforms of the coming century, it seems also to bear traces of a more unsavoury corporatism. His Carlylean denunciation of the universal 'not yours' which confronted the propertyless in contemporary England has echoes of the agrarian radicalism which not infrequently made its appearance in *Fraser's* in the 1860s. But there is no hint that Froude, any more than the economists he opposed, had any intention of altering this situation. Finally, Froude's demand that education should be designed to fit the preordained social roles of its subjects must appear profoundly conservative, and directly contrary to his contemporaneous affirmation that real historical progress takes place only through the agency of the people. H. G. Wells's subsequent contemptuous dismissal of such an attitude as a proposal 'to educate the lower classes for employment on lower-class lines, with specially trained inferior teachers' must therefore seem strongly persuasive.[57]

But there is a significant passage in his rectorial address which separates Froude from many of the other contestants in the debate on educational reform. In the address Froude boldly contended that the principal aim of any such improvement in the provision of technical and vocational skills for the disadvantaged should be designed not to keep them in their place within England's class society; but to enable them to leave it altogether. The cumulative problems of rising population, growing unemployment, and increasing mechanisation in British industry were not about to disappear, nor to be

56. *Short Studies*, II, 463–5, 471–5, where Froude declares that 'if a son of mine told me that he wished to devote himself to intellectual pursuits, I would act as I should act if he wished to make an imprudent marriage.'
57. Wells, quoted in Briggs, *Victorian People*, 257.

resolved by the hypocritical palliatives of Liberal policy. They were economically and historically irresistible, and their very necessity made it more
urgent than ever to supply the country's labouring population with sufficient skills to enable them to make an independent living for themselves
elsewhere. This was a process which their emigration to the United States
was already making plain. Rather than passively tolerating their migration
to America, however, Froude urged that a positive policy of encouraging
such skilled labourers to emigrate to Britain's own colonies, where the
demand for such basic skills was as high as ever, would not only alleviate
social and economic pressures at home. More importantly, it would increase
the bonds of allegiance between the colonies and Britain, and in the longer
term prepare Britain for the competition with the other rising world powers which he believed to be inevitable.[58]

VI

Although he played a significant part in the debate on colonial policy which
arose in the late 1860s, Froude's intervention came comparatively late, and
from the beginning was of a noticeably individual nature. The sudden erup-
tion of the debate itself remains something of a puzzle.[59] In 1868, after several years of relative quiet, the refusal of Gladstone's Colonial Secretary, Lord
Granville, to respond positively to an appeal of the New Zealand colonists
for military support in their war of dispossession against the Maoris of the
North Island sparked a sudden protest against what was seen as the negligence of the Colonial Office and in some quarters as a secret design to rid
Britain of all its colonial holdings. Although criticism of the Colonial Office
had arisen sporadically in the periodical press in the 1860s, with *Macmillan's*
and the *Fortnightly* taking the lead, the extent to which *Fraser's* contributed
to such flurries was, in contrast to its role in earlier decades, quite limited.
Thus an anonymous piece on 'The Colonies', featured in May 1862, deplored
the lack of an active policy on the part of the Colonial Office, and asserted

58. *Short Studies*, II, 'Education', 467–9.
59. K. T. Hoppen, *The Mid-Victorian Generation, 1846–86* (Oxford, 1998), 221–36, and more especially,
    B. A. Knox, 'Reconsidering Mid-Victorian Imperialism', *Journal of Imperial and Commonwealth
    History*, 1 (1973), 155–72; W. P. Morrell, *British Colonial Policy in the Mid-Victorian Age: South Africa,
    New Zealand and the West Indies* (Oxford, 1969); A. J. Harrop, *England and the Maori Wars* (Melbourne,
    1937); C. A. Bodelsen, *Studies in Mid-Victorian Imperialism* (London, 1925).

the rights of the mother country, but without promoting specific policies in regard to any particular areas.[60] Similarly, a mild review of Goldwin Smith's provocative book *The Empire*, which proposed absolute severance, called simply for an explicit and consistent colonial policy of whatever hue.[61] As late as July 1866 Froude was prepared to publish the views of an anonymous author who affirmed that 'we might abandon our colonial empire and give up the allegiance of those natives who are subjects of England all over the world without any loss of real greatness'.[62] It is odd also that while the appearance of Charles Dilke's highly influential *Greater Britain* in 1868 drew forth lengthy reviews and commentaries in most of the monthlies and quarterlies, it received no notice in *Fraser's*.[63]

As the controversy provoked by the New Zealand appeal gathered strength elsewhere, *Fraser's* remained relatively detached. In January 1869 Froude published a mild piece by the distinguished Cape Colony administrator, John Robinson, which, while ignoring the New Zealand issue, entered a modest plea on behalf of colonists everywhere who were 'proud of their British origin and prouder yet of being British subjects.'[64] It was to be a further twelve months before Froude himself began to publish on the colonial question in *Fraser's*. Developed in a series of articles which appeared between January and September 1870, Froude's colonial argument contained the same fundamental elements which, though occasionally altered in the sequence of their appearance for rhetorical or polemical purposes, retained the same logical sequence. In all of them it is clear that for Froude the colonial debate was not primarily a question about the state of the colonies at all; it was the latest version of the familiar problem concerning 'the condition of England'.[65]

The social crisis which had threatened to engulf England in the late 1840s may have passed, but the fundamental forces which had provoked it,

---

60. 'The Colonies', *Fraser's Magazine* 65 (May 1862), 551–64.

61. 'England and her Colonies', *Fraser's Magazine* 68 (October, 1863), 454–70.

62. 'Ireland', 74 (July, 1866), 1–14.

63. Dilke, *Greater Britain: A Record of Travel in English-Speaking Countries during 1866 and 1867* (2 vols., London, 1868).

64. 'A Voice from the Colonies on the Colonial Question', *Fraser's Magazine* 79 (February 1869), 202–16.

65. 'England and her Colonies', 'The Merchant and his Wife: An Apologue for the Colonial Office', 81 (January, February, 1870), 1–16, 246–7; 'The Colonies Once More', 82 (September, 1870), 269–87, reprinted in *Short Studies*, II, 180–216, 348–50, 397–438, from which all subsequent quotations are taken. For a discussion of Froude in relation to other contributors to the debate on colonies, see Duncan Bell, *The Idea of a Greater Britain: Empire and the Future of World Order, 1860–1900* (Princeton, NJ, 2007), esp. 34–45, 143–9.

according to Froude, had not gone away. The depopulation of the country-side, caused by high rents, removal of commonage, and the consolidation of estates, has, he observes, continued to accelerate, depriving England of its solid class of tenant farmers and threatening to render the country unable to supply itself with basic necessities in the near future. Fostered by this flight from the country, the growth of large industrial cities has also continued unchecked. It is this growth in England's manufacturing sector that has been hailed by political economists as the cause of England's recovery from economic depression and the greatest hope for her continued prosperity. But it contains in itself—in the increasing impoverishment of the industrial labourers, in the foul state of the manufacturing towns and cities, in the scandals of shoddy and adulterated manufactured goods, and most importantly in the rise of militant trade unionism—the seeds of its own destruction.

On occasions Froude appeared to predict that such a collapse was imminent. England's advantage in world trade rested precariously on a price advantage secured by the suppression of wages; but organised labour is everywhere resisting wage restraint.

> The unions and the master employers are in a state of war ... every strike is a battle ... in which there is no glory to be gained and no victory to be won which does not widen the breach more irreparably, while the destruction of property and the resulting ruin and devastation are immediate and irreparable.[66]

Political reform, moreover, may have paved the way for revolution. Should the working classes choose to exert the power now being placed in their hands by taking control of parliament, they would, Froude predicted, use it to nationalise land and to impose a communist-style fixed wage rate 'where the idle and incapable shall share alike with the skilful and industrious'.[67]

On occasion Froude seems less apocalyptical. In one essay he allows for the sake of argument that the optimistic political economists may be right. If England's manufacturing continued to increase and her trade continued to expand without collapse or revolution, there would eventually come a time when, as wealth became concentrated into fewer hands and the great industrialists succeeded in reducing their wage costs through machinery and efficiency, the vast majority of its population would become superfluous,

66. *Short Studies*, II, 197–8.
67. *Short Studies*, II, 435.

driven into dissolution and poverty, or forced to emigrate. By the laws of political economy that were now in the ascendant, the latter is the option that would be most preferred: 'Emigration, like wages, prices, and profits, must be left to settle itself according to the laws of nature.' But under these conditions such a *laissez faire* attitude would be fatal, as the masses forced to emigrate would leave possessed of an undying hatred for the country which so abused them, as the Irish had left with a hatred for England in the years after the Great Famine. And, like the Irish, they would most probably emigrate to the United States of America.[68]

Thus Froude invokes yet another apocalyptic vision. The current tendencies of political development throughout the world were working in favour of greater territorial consolidation and against small states. In this process, one country had progressed far beyond others: the United States.

> We have no present quarrel with the Americans; we trust heartily that we may never be involved in any quarrel with them. But undoubtedly from the day they became independent from us, they became our rivals. They constitute the one great power whose interests and whose pretensions compete with our own … From the day that it is confessed that we are no longer equal to a conflict with her, if cause of rupture should unhappily arise, our sun has set: we shall sink as Holland has sunk into a community of harmless traders, and leave to others the place which we have once held …[69]

The signs that such an eventual conflict was far from unlikely were already present in two developments, for both of which Britain herself was responsible. The first, as Froude had already hinted, was the phenomenal growth in the influence of the anglophobic Irish in American political life which was already beginning to influence American politics at federal level. The second, no less pressing, concern was the prospect that Britain's own colonies, especially Canada, might seek a closer alliance and even union with the United States through their disillusion with the indifference, disregard, and annoyance shown to them by Britain herself.[70]

It was to forfend against all these future woes that an active colonial policy was imperative. The colonies were to be tied ever closer to their mother country through several measures suggested by Froude on various occasions, including the inauguration of a general confederation (the ancestor

68. *Short Studies*, II, 186–7.
69. *Short Studies*, II, 180.
70. *Short Studies*, II, 213.

of the Commonwealth), the establishment of an imperial assembly, the construction of a free-trade area along the lines of the Prussian Zollverein, and the development of an imperial army and navy. But all of these occasional propositions were overshadowed by the one major policy advocated by Froude in all his colonial writings: namely, the introduction of a major scheme of state-subsidised emigration which would undertake the movement of large numbers of British natives to the colonies, their education, training, and development in agriculture, crafts, trade, and services, and their settlement as independent citizens in the colonies through the provision of land or employment.[71]

Froude was by no means the only public figure to urge state-aided emigration as a solution to England's and the colonies' social problems.[72] But for one who was preoccupied with the problem of regenerating the historical spirit of the English people, a proposal which appeared at once to halt the current social and moral decline of the English masses, encourage England's colonial development, and help in the forthcoming struggle with the other emergent world powers had a unique and powerful resonance. For a while, within Britain itself, the prospects of the moral regeneration which was so desperately needed seemed further away than ever, the possibility that it might take shape amidst the countless possibilities of individual renewal held out by a new life in the expanding colonial world could not be denied. Froude, as we have seen, was convinced that the forces of historical change were immanent rather than external, and that they arose within a people at once conscious of their own identity but aware also of the injustices, hypocrisies, and general irresponsibility which was corrupting the world in which they held their place. From such principles there arose his further conviction that the seeds of a new moral reformation lay in the drive to transform England into the centre of a great global commonwealth in which all parts shared equally in pursuit of a common goal.

It was his distinctive understanding of the dynamic of historical progress that separated Froude from contemporary social commentators—not only in his approach to colonial policy, but to all of the issues arising from the effects of political reform and the inexorable advance of democracy. Thus the intensification of partisan politics and of the political manipulation of

---

71. *Short Studies*, II, 180–6, 211–15; *Short Studies*, II, 409–22.
72. By the close of the 1860s, three societies had founded to agitate in favour of the policy, in one of which Froude himself took an active role; and in March 1870 a Bill proposing such a scheme had been introduced in the Commons by the Liberal MP R. R. Torrens.

the newly enfranchised which, in common with so many other intellectuals, Froude saw as the inevitable consequence of franchise reform, did not lead him to withdraw from the political arena. It encouraged in him a tendency already present in his journalistic writings of the 1860s toward simpler and less demanding but no less provocative forms of address than he had essayed in the past.

By the close of the 1860s his experiences in that decade had convinced him that changes in his compositional and rhetorical strategies were not only required, but also attainable. His acceptance of the fact that the religious and moral questioning for which he had once suffered so much had at last become acceptable, and his recognition that for all its success his great *History* would not attain all of the effects he had hoped for, were compensated for by a corresponding awareness that a whole range of deeply related social and political issues had emerged through which he might continue his appointed task. Among these, the question of colonial policy loomed large. But so too did a related problem which could not be separated from the task of building a newly regenerated British Empire. This was the challenge of confronting England's unfinished business in post-Union and post-Famine Ireland.

9

The Challenge of England's
Future: Ireland, 1862–77

I

Froude's first re-engagement with Ireland and Irish affairs since the 1840s is commonly assumed to have occurred in the closing months of 1872. It was then that he delivered a hugely controversial programme of five lectures to audiences in New York, Boston, and Philadelphia tracing the course of Irish history from the coming of the Normans in the twelfth century to the present.[1] It was at that time also that the first instalment of his explosive three-volume history of *The English in Ireland in the Eighteenth Century* appeared.[2]

The central argument of Froude's American lecture programme is easily summarised. Throughout their history the native Irish had repeatedly proved themselves to be quite incapable of self-government. It was the barbaric state of the whole island in the twelfth century, its political and moral decline from the golden age of saints and scholars, to the degeneracy of the warring petty kingdoms and the virtual disappearance of the Christian Church that had induced Pope Adrian IV to set in train the conquest of Ireland for the salvation of its own people. Through the neglect of the English kings, however, the Irish were again left to their own devices in the later middle ages; and along with the descendants of their one-time conquerors, they once again descended into an anarchy which was to be suppressed only by the force of the Tudor conquest. Yet this opportunity was soon squandered by further neglect and corruption which was to suffer its

1. Versions of Froude's lectures appeared in *The Times*, 29 October, and 6, 7, 8, and 22 November 1872, and in *The New York Times*, 29 October, and 2, 21, and 22 November 1872.
2. 3 vols. London: Longmans, 1872–4; 2nd edn., 1881.

nemesis in the bloody rebellion of 1641. Only with the coming of Cromwell, the destruction of the old elites, and the initiation of a radical political, religious, and tenurial restructuring of the whole island did the promise of making Ireland at last capable of peaceful government seem possible. This brief experiment, however, was also quickly abandoned. By the end of the century the Irish were again in rebellion against England, and bloody repression was again required. The pattern of English rule repeated itself in the following century, until at its close the bloodiest repression of all was required.

Even in the nineteenth century the Irish capacity for rebellion had been shown at least twice, in 1848 and 1867. But the short-lived and feeble character of both of these efforts gave grounds, Froude affected to believe, for hope. The changes that had been brought about in the aftermath of the calamity of the Famine were, he argued, the primary causes for this change. The large-scale emigration of the underemployed peasantry, the ruin of idle and absentee landlords, the gradual development of a more economically sound approach to estate management, and the emergence on the part of the British government of a more responsible policy toward land tenure as evidenced in Gladstone's Land Act ('the most healing measure that has been devised for Ireland during two centuries at least') had all contributed to a fundamental change in Irish society and Irish attitudes toward England. Ireland, Froude concluded, had been given 'a fair start now':

> She has better laws than England has. Let her point to any other measure of practical advantage to her and no matter what interests are affected, she will not ask for it in vain'.[3]

But there was one exception: Ireland must never be conceded Home Rule. It had always been impossible, and now when so much was promised under a newly reconstructed Union, it was totally insupportable. Left to itself, Ireland would return rapidly to the cycles of corruption, poverty, division, and violence which had characterised all her previous history.

A brief digest of this same general interpretation of Anglo-Irish relations was supplied in the early pages of *The English in Ireland in the Eighteenth Century* (3 vols., 1872–74), preceded by a terse declaration of the axiomatic assumptions underpinning it. Geographical determinism is first asserted: when two countries are so close to each other it is inevitable that the stronger

3. 'Ireland under the Union', *Short Studies*, III, 553, 561.

one will determine the character of the weaker. Moral determinism is next pressed into service: as with individuals, so with communities, the state of liberty is not simply a given condition, to be passively accepted, but a fragile possession to be fought for and defended. The strength of each country is thus determined by each one's ability to assert and defend its liberty against all comers. Then history is at last invoked: this liberty England has manifestly achieved, and, with equal certainty, Ireland has not. Incapable either of main-taining its autonomy, or yet, like the Welsh and Scottish communities, of accepting a peaceful union and integration with their English neighbour, the Irish have remained in a chronically inchoate state. 'The incompleteness of their character', says Froude, 'is conspicuous in all that they do or have done, in their history, in their practical habits, in their arts and in their literature.' 'Unstable as water, the Irish temperament wanted [lacked] cohesiveness to bear shapes which were imprinted upon it.' This being so clearly the case the right of England to claim responsibility for the Irish, to govern them with firmness and justice, was incontestable; and the feeble resistance of the Irish, so painfully illustrated throughout their history, was just another telling sign of their continuing cultural immaturity. The absorption of Ireland within the United Kingdom of England, Scotland, and Wales was, therefore, neither a great political injustice nor an unfortunate accident; it was the necessary outcome of an inevitable historical process.[4]

All of this would have been familiar to readers of the published lectures. Gradually, however, as the narrative develops, a theme which had been of secondary importance in the lecture series acquires a greater and a sharper prominence within the narrowed chronological confines of the book. Having established both on *a priori* and on historical grounds the rights of the English to govern Ireland, Froude then embarks upon his long historical narrative of the years between 1690 and 1800, the detail of which appears fatally to undermine such claims. Alternating between total neglect, suscep-tibility to vested interest and simple greed, the English administration in Whitehall had inflicted innumerable injustices on Ireland since the begin-nings of its involvement there. Its authority once established, the English parliament proved itself even more selfish and greedy. In Dublin, the execu-tives of the Crown, with few honourable exceptions, showed themselves to be either stupid, corrupt, or vainglorious in their management of their charges. Most of all, the English settlers themselves, from the Normans

---

4. *The English in Ireland*, i, Book One, sections ii–iv; quotations at 20, 23.

down to the representatives of the so-called Protestant nation, had shown an irresponsibility, a viciousness, and a reckless divisiveness that repeatedly stifled any chance of bringing about just government in Ireland. In no other period had the English displayed all of the vices and defects characteristic of their rule than in the eighteenth century, during which all the advantages of history had actually been granted to them. Thus it was to the detailed revelation of their repeated misconduct in so many areas that Froude devoted the bulk of the book before arriving at a conclusion which appeared to deny the very premise from which he had started: 'It would have been better and happier by far had England never encompassed the rule of the Irish and never attempted to force upon them a landed gentry of alien blood.'[5]

The apparent perversity of this position provoked a veritable carnival of critical reaction, most especially in Ireland.[6] For Irish nationalists, Froude's intervention was in large part a godsend, revealing once again the real attitudes of contempt and superiority underlying all English attitudes, no matter how benign their declared intentions. Even better, the results of Froude's researches, his revelation of the corruption and weakness of the Protestant Ascendancy and the Church of Ireland, and his condemnation of absent and rack-renting landlords and their agents and the like, supplied them with powerful ammunition (from the least friendly and therefore most useful of sources) in their own polemic against English rule. Froude handed Irish nationalists the invaluable gift of being able to exploit his research while denouncing the assumptions which underpinned it.[7]

It was this gross irresponsibility which above all infuriated those who might otherwise have been expected to be at one with Froude: the pro-Union Anglo-Irish. And it was from this quarter that the most trenchant and most persuasive criticisms of his endeavour appeared, most notably in

---

5. For central passages developing this indictment, see *The English in Ireland*, i, 215–39, 371–95; ii, 84–122, 453–75; iii, 469–505; the quotation is at 462.

6. For a critical review of reviews, see Donal McCartney, 'James Anthony Froude and Ireland: A Historiographical Controversy of the Nineteenth Century', in T. D. Williams (ed.), *Historical Studies*, VIII (Dublin, 1971), 171–90.

7. For representative nationalist responses, see John Mitchel, 'Froude from the Standpoint of a Protestant Irishman' *The New York Times*, 21 December 1872; see also commentaries in *The New York Daily Journal*, 2, 4, and 14 November, and *The New York World*, 14, 15, 22, and 30 November; and the sequence of violent attacks by J. P. Prendergast in *Freeman's Journal*, 30–31 October, and 11, 19 20, 21, 29, and 30 November; *The Nation*, 2, 16, and 13 November; see also *The Cork Examiner*, 7 November. The publication of the second edition in 1883 had a similar effect on the Irish Home Rule leader, Charles Stewart Parnell, who claimed that Froude's book 'threw more light on the Irish question than any book he had seen'; quoted in Paul Bew, *Enigma: A New Life of Charles Stweart Parnell* (Dublin, 2012), 159.

devastating reviews by the historian W. E. H. Lecky and the political economist John Elliot Cairnes. Discounting at once the original nature of his
researches in the Irish and English archives, and largely ignoring his prejudices concerning the character of the native Irish (in part because they
shared them), they chose instead to argue that Froude's history amounted to
little more than a polemic against liberalism and reform, and a panegyric to
unyielding authority and brute force. Moreover, his ugly view of history was
made all the uglier by its manifest inaccuracy and inconsistency with reason
and fact. They not only pointed to Froude's innumerable factual inaccuracies, but also highlighted a large number of interpretative inconsistencies as,
for instance, his condemnation of absenteeism and his attack on the independent Irish parliament which had served as the principal defence against
it; or his justification of the penal code (though for Froude it was not harsh
enough) and his condemnation of those who exploited the laws in their
own personal interest. They noted that the same King George III whose
proposal for suppressing the Irish parliament in 1760 Froude lauded was the
very monarch whose similar response to the American crisis a decade later
Froude deplored. Moreover, they highlighted an apparently profound inconsistency concerning Froude's assessment of the native Irish: the Celtic race
whose anarchic and mercurial traits Froude regarded as incorrigible were
also those whom he was happy to grant were free from any indelible mark
of race: 'We lay the fault', Cairnes quoted Froude, 'on the intractability of
the race; but the modern Irishman is of no race, so blended now is the blood
of Celt and Dane and Saxon and Norman and English and French ... The
Irishman of the eighteenth century rose to his natural level whenever he
was removed from his own unfortunate country.' Having exposed Froude's
contradictions at length, Cairnes disposed of the book as beneath further
comment, while Lecky consigned its author as 'fit for a place in Bedlam'.[8]

It is perhaps ironic that within a decade, Froude as a defender of the
Union would be joined by most of his severest critics, including Lecky.[9] His

8. Lecky's reviews appeared in *Macmillan's Magazine*, 27 (January 1873), 246–64; 30 (June 1874) 166–
84; Cairnes, *Fortnightly Review*, 16 (August 1874), 171–91. Cairnes, who pursued Froude's interpretative inconsistencies even more than Lecky, was citing from *The English in Ireland*, ii, 127.

9. Ann Wyatt, 'Froude, Lecky and "the Humblest Irishman"', *Irish Historical Studies*, 19 (1975),
261–85; Norman Pilling, 'Lecky and Dicey: English and Irish Histories', *Éire-Ireland*, 16:3 (1981),
43–56. Cairnes died in 1875, but his strongly unionist views were made clear in his other controversialist writings; see T. A. Boylan and T. P. Foley, 'John Elliot Cairnes, J. S. Mill and Ireland',
Hermathena, 135 (1983), 96–118. On the hostility of British intellectuals in general to the campaign for Home Rule, see Tom Dunne, '*La trahison des clercs*: British Intellectuals and the First
Home-Rule Crisis', *Irish Historical Studies*, 23:90 (1982), 134–73.

distinctiveness, however, lay not only in the prescience with which in the early 1870s he had already perceived in the mild stirrings of political agitation in Ireland a looming threat to the unity and structure of the United Kingdom, nor even in his provocative mode of expression, or his uncompromising refusal of concession. Rather, it lay in the depth of his conviction that the maintenance of the union of Britain and Ireland was essential for reasons far greater than matters of political, strategic, or economic advantage, and bore directly on England's moral and metaphysical role in world history.

II

In contrast to the concerns of his contemporaries, Ireland had never moved far from the centre of Froude's moral consciousness. The importance of the island's early history in his intellectual maturation has already been seen. Ireland featured significantly in his private correspondence and in his fiction in the later 1840s, and several of the essays he published in the early 1850s contain passing references to the troubled nature of that island—to the manner in which its early spirituality had been lost, to the shameful way in which it had been governed by English agents, and to the recent catastrophe of the Famine, responsibility for which England could not evade.

More importantly, however, England's failure to establish total sovereignty over the island, through the neglect, cruelty, and selfishness of its agents there, was one of the darker themes stated at the outset and reiterated throughout his *History of England*. In composing the *History*, Froude, as has been noted already, devoted remarkable attention to Ireland in a manner which was wholly original for its time.[10] Integral to the overall design of the *History*, these Irish chapters were intended to serve a number of purposes. They added a further set of perspectives and a further opportunity for confusion and uncertainty which was a characteristic feature of the narrative. They helped underline also the unfinished business of the Elizabethan regime as Froude catalogued an unending series of English failures and follies in the island. The corruption of one governor, the tyranny of another, the duplicity of a third, the ignorance and pedantry of the churchmen, the rapacity of the soldiers, the careless indifference of the government at

10. See ch. 7.

Whitehall—all are itemised in a mounting indictment of English rule in Ireland which is to be left hanging on the edge of the great conflagration of the Nine Years War. But in the later chapters of the *History* a far darker theme which had hitherto been raised only intermittently—in regard to the savage suppression of the Cornish and the Northern rebels, and the privateers' treatment of enslaved black people—began to assume an especial prominence in his account of Ireland.[11]

This is the record of English atrocity. Beginning with the massacres of Sir Peter Carew in the 1560s, sequentially recounting those of Humphrey Gilbert in Munster, the 1st. Earl of Essex in Ulster, of Captains Hungerford and Agard in Leinster in the 1570s, and ending in the horrors of the Desmond rebellion, Froude records the slaughter of non-combatants, and especially of women and children, with undisguised disgust:

> The English nation was shuddering over the atrocities of the Duke of Alva, yet Alva's bloody sword never touched the young, the defenceless, or those whose sex even dogs can recognize and respect. [12]

He makes his judgement on them with high Swiftian irony:

> The Gilbert method of treatment has this disadvantage; that it must be carried out to the last extremity or it must not be tried at all. The dead do not come back and if mothers and babies are slaughtered with the men, the race gives no further trouble. But the work must be done thoroughly: partial and fitful cruelty lays up only a long debt of deserved and ever deepening hate ... In justice to the English soldiers, however, it must be said that it was no fault of theirs if any Irish child of that generation was allowed to live to manhood.[13]

An even lengthier and more gruesome account of atrocities perpetrated by the English on Rathlin Island follows. Though it was quickly passed over at the time and lay buried for three hundred years, says the historical moralist just up from the archives, 'the bloody stain comes back again, not in myth and legend, but in the original account of the nobleman by whose command the deed was done; and when the history of England's dealings with Ireland settles at last into its final shape that search among the caves at

11. Ciaran Brady, 'Offering Offence: James Anthony Froude, Moral Obligation and the Uses of Irish history', in Vincent Carey and Ute Lotz-Heuman (eds.), *Taking Sides: Colonial and Confessional Mentalités in Early Modern Ireland* (Dublin, 2004), 266–90; Froude, 'How Ireland was governed in the Sixteenth Century', *Fraser's Magazine,* 71 (March 1865), 312–15.

12. Froude, *History of England,* X, 508.

13. *History of England,* X, 509.

Rathlin will not be forgotten'.[14] After all this, Froude concludes with the first expression of that statement which he would repeat so provocatively in *The English in Ireland*, and which to his critics seemed to undermine his entire case for the Union: 'It cannot be said that England deserved to keep a country which it mismanaged so disastrously.'[15]

The phrase is also repeated in an essay for *Fraser's*, ironically entitled 'How Ireland was Governed in the Sixteenth Century', in which Froude presented his bitter indictment of English atrocities in condensed form.[16] Again summarising the principal English atrocities in Ireland, from slaughter on the grand scale of Rathlin Island to the small-scale but in some ways more chilling, casual, and sporting brutality of individual bands of soldiers, Froude focuses on a particular instance which aroused his intense revulsion. A troop of soldiers in search of rustled cattle was approached by an informer who indicated the location of the prey and presented them with a choice either to be led to the cattle or to the group who had stolen them: to have 'kine or killing'. Unhesitatingly the captains chose killing, slaughtering 'churls, women, and children' as they slept. 'Captain Hungerford and Lieutenant Parker prefer human game', Froude observed bitterly: 'The sport was excellent, just a single soldier hurt, and just sufficient danger to add piquancy to the amusement.' After instancing these and other casual occasions of killing, Froude concluded, (mis)quoting Tennyson in irony:

> In 'the stately days of great Elizabeth' the murder of women and children
> appears to have been the everyday occupation of the English police in Ireland;
> and accounts of atrocities to the full as bad as that at Glencoe, were sent in on
> half a sheet of letter paper, and were endorsed like any other document with
> a brevity which shows that such things were too common to deserve criticism
> or attract attention.[17]

This essay for *Fraser's* dealing with English policy in Ireland was by no means unique. For one of the features distinguishing *Fraser's* from its peers among the monthlies and quarterlies during the time of Froude's editorship was the magazine's sustained interest in Ireland. Though most of the heavyweight journals occasionally carried articles pertaining directly to Ireland,

14. *History of England*, XI, 185.
15. *History of England*, X, 517.
16. *Fraser's Magazine*, 71 (March 1865), 312–15.
17. 'How Ireland was governed in the Sixteenth Century', 315; the mis-reference is to 'the spacious days of great Elizabeth' in Tennyson's 'Florence Nightingale'.

and while the *Edinburgh*, *Macmillan's*, and (after 1865) the *Fortnightly Review* displayed a more regular interest, it was *Fraser's* above all that demonstrated a consistent and increasing concern with Irish affairs in the years between 1860 and 1874.

During Froude's first years as editor, Irish-related articles appeared in *Fraser's* at a frequency of about three per year; and as the decade wore on, *Fraser's* interest increased sharply. Between 1865 and 1869 some twenty-six contributions relating to Ireland were published, and in the final years of Froude's editorship from January 1870 to August 1874 no less than forty-two items bearing on the state of affairs in Ireland were presented to *Fraser's* readers.[18] These figures, moreover, exclude fiction: during the 1860s *Fraser's* published at least two serial novels relating to Irish affairs, and it was in several sequential issues of *Fraser's* also that William Allingham's famous novel-in-verse 'Laurence Bloomfield in Ireland' first made its appearance.[19] None of the competing journals at any time came close to this remarkable engagement.

Obscured by the dust-storm raised by Froude's later polemical and offensive writing on Ireland, the character of his prior journalistic interest, as revealed both by the essays he commissioned and those he himself wrote for *Fraser's* in the 1860s and early 1870s, has been largely ignored. But these earlier materials are in themselves of particular interest, as they reveal an attitude toward Ireland that seems far more liberal than the uncompromising views expressed with such *hauteur* in *The English in Ireland*.

One source of *Fraser's* early interest in Ireland was the question of ecclesiastical disestablishment. Long before the proposal of disestablishing the Church of Ireland had become the focus of political debate at Westminster, *Fraser's* had been campaigning strongly on the issue. Almost all of *Fraser's* regular political commentators, including A. V. Kirwan, Bonamy Price, and Abraham Hayward, wrote in support of it, and several essays made reference to it as an urgent necessity.[20] *Fraser's* targeting of the weak and politically

---

18. These statements are based on analysis of the material supplied in the Wellesley Index on-line edition.

19. Allingham's 'Bloomfield' appeared in Nos. 66 (November–December 1862), 67 (January–June 1863), 68 (July–November, 1863).

20. Henry Cunningham. 'The Irish Church', 70 (July 1864), 1–17; A. V. Kirwan, 'A Fortnight in Ireland in the Lent of 1863', 67 (May 1863), 670–83; Bonamy Price, 'The Political Temper of the Nation' 69 (February, 1864), 135–59; W. M Brady, 'Church Temporalities in Ireland', 73 (January 1866), 16–26; Anon., 'The Church and Land Question in Ireland', 76 (August, 1867), 121–36; Hayward, 'The Caucasian Administration and the Irish Difficulty', 77 (April, 1868), 525–71.

isolated Church of Ireland was in part a tactical manoeuvre designed to serve a role in Froude's larger campaign against the Church of England, but the magazine's concern with Ireland throughout the 1860s was considerably broader. Between them the essays commissioned by Froude from his Irish specialists—including William O'Connor Morris, James Lowry Whittle, Frances Power Cobbe, and T. E. Cliffe Leslie, along with contributions by Hayward, Froude himself, and Allingham's 'Laurence Bloomfield'—developed a remarkably coherent case which may be summarised as follows.[21]

The Famine of the 1840s had been a terrible calamity, the responsibility for which no parties could escape, but the unintended benefits which had arisen from it could also not be ignored. At long last the whole corrupt and degrading structure of Irish rural society which had been allowed to proliferate through the greed and selfishness of absentee landlords, the extortions of middlemen and agents, the improvidence of peasants, and the total indifference of successive British governments, had been destroyed. In its wake, the opportunity for a new beginning arose. For those who visited the country—and so many of *Fraser's* Irish essays were disguised in the form of light travel literature—the signs of such a renewal were everywhere to see. Those tenants who had hung on were now reaping the rewards of their industry, frugality, and self-reliance. They represented a profound change in the character of the Irish peasantry, and heralded the emergence of a stable, progressive, economically active class, the like of which had never before been seen among the Irish peasantry. Many landlords also had responded positively to the crisis, investing in their estates, instituting improvements, and reforming their rent rolls and leasing policies.[22]

These, however, were signs of a beginning only; and, as the experience of Allingham's Laurence Bloomfield warned, it was a beginning that could easily be stifled.[23] Much of the recovery, moreover, had been dependent on

---

21. W. O'Connor Morris, 'A Few Words on the Census of Ireland', 64 (September, 1861), 300–7; Whittle, 'The Last Instalment of Irish Policy, NS 3 (March, 1871), 273–85; F. P. Cobbe, 'Ireland and her Exhibition in 1865', 72 (October 1865), 403–22; Cliffe-Leslie, 'Political Economy and Emigration', 77 (May 1868), 611–24.

22. W. O'Connor Morris, 'A Few Words on the Census of Ireland', 64 (September, 1861), 300–7; A.V. Kirwan, 'A Fortnight in Ireland in the Lent of 1863', 67 (May 1863), 670–83; 'Ireland and the Irish Land Question', NS 1 (January, 1870), 121–42; Froude 'A Fortnight in Kerry' NS 1, 3 (April, 1870, January 1871), 513–30, 28–45; 'The New Irish Land Law', NS 5 (May 1872), 296–309.

23. On Allingham's 'Laurence Bloomfield', see Alan Warner, *William Allingham* (Cranberry, NJ, 1975), ch. 3; Matthew Campbell, 'Irish Poetry in the Union: William Allingham's *Laurence Bloomfield in Ireland*', *European Journal of English Studies*, 3 (1999), 298–313.

high levels of emigration which had persisted long after the crisis of the 1840s had passed. In the 1860s *Fraser's* writers expressed different opinions as to the necessity of continuing emigration from Ireland. Some of the journal's contributors argued that its continuance was no longer necessary, and that the state should now encourage the improvement schemes of landlords that were enabling tenants to make a living on their holdings, while others, including William O'Connor Morris and the editor himself, seemed to regard it as an inevitability for the present.[24] But all were agreed on two points. The first was that the chosen destination of the vast majority of those who left should be immediately redirected by all possible inducements away from the United States to Britain's own colonies. The second was that what was most urgently needed now was enlightened legislation regarding land law (which would further protect the interests of the tenants), taxation (which would offer relief to improving landlords), the reform of the Irish university system (including the reform of the governing structures of Trinity College Dublin), and an education act designed specifically for Irish needs.[25]

Fraser's, of course, was staunchly unionist, in the sense that it believed that all future progress in Ireland depended on continued direct rule from Westminster and regarded the demand for a return to a parliament in College Green as an historical anachronism. But it was conscious of the process by which grievance over any issue could suddenly be transformed in the volatile Irish atmosphere into a movement for independence. The urgency with which *Fraser's* under Froude pressed for further reform in Ireland was therefore influenced to some degree by its awareness of the revival of political agitation in the later 1860s—but only to a limited extent. *Fraser's* writers did not share in 'Fenian fever'. Froude himself was personally unimpressed with the Fenian dynamite campaign. 'A few attacks on handfuls of police or the blowing in of the walls of an English prison with the wanton destruction of innocent life may suffice', he wrote contemptuously, 'for a scene or two in a melodrama, but they will not overturn an Empire … Fanians, *Faineants*,

24. W. O'Connor Morris, 'A Few Words on the Census of Ireland', 64 (September, 1861), 300–7.
25. O'Connor Morris, 'The Irish Policy of the Disraeli Administration and its Results', 78 (August 1868), 143–58; Hayward, 'Ireland and the Irish Land Question', 81 (January, 1870), 121–42; R. A. Arnold, 'The Transfer of Land [in Ireland]', 87 (March, 1873), 265–78; James MacDonnell, 'The Proposed Catholic University for Ireland', 84 (October 1871), 481–91; Anon., 'A Policy for Ireland', 88 (September, 1873), 273–83; 'Primary Education in Ireland', 90, (December 1874), 728–40.

Do-Nothings!'[26] In addition, articles commissioned by Froude from the *soi-disant* ex-Fenian agent Gustave Cluseret did much to confirm the journal's general contention that the threat to England's security from that quarter was greatly exaggerated.[27]

Fraser's Irish writers were, however, sensitive to the broader and longer-term implications of Fenianism. Ineffective and disorganised in itself, the Irish Republican Brotherhood had drawn its principal strength from disaffected Irish immigrants in the United States; and despite its failures in 1867 and thereafter, it continued to draw sustenance from the same dangerous quarter. It was from this expanding reservoir of resentment in America, potentially available to serve any separatist group in Ireland, that the greatest threat to the Union lay in the long term, making even the mildest and most constitutional movement capable of acquiring a greater force than would otherwise have been conceivable.[28] It was, in fact, the revival of constitutional, rather than physical-force, agitation in the form of the Irish Home Government Association and Isaac Butt's propagation of the notion of federalism in 1870 that actually provoked more concern among *Fraser's* writers than the prospect of Fenian terrorism.[29]

At first, however, there was little sense of urgency. *Fraser's* was quite sympathetic (if a little condescending) to the Home Government Association in its early days, and to Butt himself. An early article on the Association 'by an Irishman who is not a federalist', while disagreeing with the movement's aims, was highly laudatory of Butt's good intentions, and argued that his initiative would do useful service in generating debate in Ireland among Catholics and Protestants on secular and non-sectarian grounds.[30] Earlier, Butt's own pamphlet on the land question had been positively noticed in *Fraser's*, while the editor published two articles roundly condemning the revived Orange Order as a vehicle of sectarian hatred and division.[31] This was entirely consistent with *Fraser's* line, according to which any

26. 'Ireland since the Union: Lecture delivered in the United States, October, November 1872', printed in *Short Studies*, II, 514–62; quote on 551.
27. Cluseret, 'My Connections with Fenianism', NS 6 (July, 1872), 31–46.
28. 'England and America', 77 (March 1868), 269–85; 'The New Rebellion in America', 76 (November 1867), 622–37.
29. 'Home Government for Ireland', NS 4 (July, 1871), 1–12.
30. 'The Federalist Movement in Ireland', NS 2 (December, 1870), 754–64; 'A Third Irish tourist', 80 (November, 1869), 575–96.
31. 'Ireland and the Irish Land Question', NS 1 (January, 1870), 121–42; 'The Orange Society' and 'Irish Orangeism', NS 3, 8 (February 1871, October, 1873) 246–58; 399–419.

extra-parliamentary agitation was a warning sign—an admonition to the British government that a repetition of the neglect to which Ireland had been historically accustomed would result in the recurrence of the characteristic Irish reaction: rebellion, bloodshed, and continuing hatred.

That *Fraser's* was at first an enthusiastic supporter of the Gladstone administration's Irish policy is, therefore, hardly surprising. It welcomed the disestablishment of the Church of Ireland in 1869 and the Land Act of 1870, and, while stoutly defending the latter against complaints of the landlords and estate managers, continued as late as 1872 to argue for a further extension of the operation of the act in order to realise its full potential.[32] Curiously, the issue which actually precipitated *Fraser's* disillusionment with the Liberal government was the comparatively less urgent issue of education.

In 1870 *Fraser's* had been disappointed with the concessions to denominational education extracted by religious interest groups in Forster's National Education Act.[33] Then, in the early 1870s, through its Irish contributors James Lowry Whittle and James MacDonnell, *Fraser's* began to grow increasingly anxious about the implications of such concessions for the future of education in Ireland.[34] Taken together with the implications of the broadening of the franchise, the Education Act would lead to the strengthening rather than the weakening of existing interest groups. The government's agreement to subsidise denominational schools would have the effect of further benefiting one interest that was already overwhelmingly influential in Irish society: the Roman Catholic Church.[35] Coinciding with the rise of ultramontanism within Roman Catholicism as a whole, the opportunity now being given to the Catholic Church in Ireland to consolidate and intensify its control over the Irish laity was little short of disastrous. It would increase sectarian division, hinder the advance of progressive policies, and suppress free discussion on political, social, and moral questions of all kinds. Most seriously of all, however, when such reactionary and sectarian impulses inevitably came into conflict with the liberal principles of the British state, the Catholic Church would become the principal force behind renewed

---

32. 'The New Irish Land Law', NS 5 (May 1872), 296–309.
33. 'The Religious Difficulty' NS 1 (May 1870), 623–34.
34. 'Primary Education in Ireland', NS 10 (December, 1874), 728–42.
35. 'The Irish Schoolmaster and the Irish Priest' NS 7 (March, 1873), 385–90; 'The Christian Brothers and their Lesson Books', NS 9 (February, 1874), 186–209; 'Papal Ireland' NS 4 (December, 1871), 776–92.

agitation for repeal of the Union and the establishment of an independent Catholic confessional state. The only way of meeting this challenge was through the creation in Ireland of a class hitherto missing from its history: a strong secular middle class. Such a class was to be developed only by a radical reform of third-level education which, either through state foundations or through the opening up of Trinity College Dublin as a non-sectarian institution, would generate a new elite of secular professionals sturdy enough to resist the intimidations of the clergy. The unexpected opposition in Ireland to Fawcett's bill abolishing Trinity College's religious entry tests, the continuance of government support to the denominational colleges, and, most importantly, the collapse of Gladstone's Irish University Bill, represented a profound disappointment of *Fraser's* hopes, and it was from then that the magazine began to assume its uncompromisingly anti-Liberal and specifically anti-Gladstone stand.[36]

It was in these circumstances specific to the debate on Irish policy that Froude, both as editor of *Fraser's* and independently as an historian, began to engage. Unsurprisingly, his earliest personal contributions were closely in line with *Fraser's* other Irish contributors. In two ostensibly light travel essays which appeared under the title 'A Fortnight in Kerry' in April 1870 and January 1871, Froude (disingenuously, given his long experience of the island) assumed the guise of an innocent but well-intentioned visitor to Ireland.[37] Much to his delight, he announced breezily, the character of the Irish had changed in the years since the Famine. Those who had survived the great trauma, and those who had succeeded them, were determined that the wretchedness into which their forefathers had sunk would never again be repeated. Henceforth their approach toward making and increasing their livings would be frugal, responsible, and shrewd. This, said the much encouraged visitor, was the time for England to respond to the needs of the new generation. The moderate tenurial reforms introduced by Gladstone in the recent Land Act (1870) were to be welcomed, and in time needed to be developed by practical adaptations and modifications. There should be more state investment in education of a practical or vocational kind; more younger

---

36. J. L. Whittle, 'The Last Instalment of Irish Policy', NS 3 (March, 1871), 273–83; 'The Irish University Question', NS 5 (January, 1872), 55–64; 'The Irish University Question: Recent Attempts at Legislation', NS 7 (April, 1873), 514–24.

37. 'A Fortnight in Kerry', parts I and II, NS 1, 3 (April, 1870, January 1871), 513–30, 28–45; reprinted in *Short Studies*, II, 217–307, to which reference is made hereafter; 'The New Irish Land Law', NS 5 (May 1872), 296–309.

sons of the peasantry should be given places in the public service, including the police; and those who could not make an honest living from their mea-gre tenancies or other employments should be granted state subsidies to emigrate to the growing British colonies in Canada, Australia, and New Zealand, where they could start anew. But amidst all this, England must be careful not to listen to the demands once again being raised by some self-appointed leaders in Ireland that the Union should be dissolved and Ireland should have self-rule.[38]

> England deserves what has come upon her; yet the two islands must remain where nature placed them. They are tied together like an ill-matched pair between whom no divorce is possible ... the fortunes of the two islands are inseparably linked. Ireland can never be independent of England, nor is it likely that a further measure of what is called freedom will make Irishmen acquiesce more graciously in their forced connection with us.[39]

For these reasons, while further reforms might be granted, and further investment both public and private encouraged, any movement toward even the smallest measure of self-government must be resisted and suppressed.[40]

But why should this be so? Given his insistence both in the *History of England* and in his essay in *Fraser's* of the abominable treatment meted out to the Irish by the English, on what moral basis could such a terrible fate be imposed upon the Irish? At this point Froude offered no explanation. Yet it was this paradoxical insistence on the absolute permanence of the Union, notwithstanding the ills which England had visited on Ireland, that he was to reiterate both in his American lectures and in *The English in Ireland* which followed from them. It is only at the close of the lecture series that he sup-plies some indication of the assumptions underlying this apparent paradox. His survey of Anglo-Irish relations had revealed repeated cycles of abuse, rebellion, and repression that had given rise to Ireland's undying hatred, but for which England's guilt remained as yet unaddressed. Now this hatred, transmuted by emigration to the level of a world-historical phenomenon, was on the point of visiting its deepest retribution on England:

> The Irish in America are our bitterest enemies. The Irish vote will be given unanimously for war with us if at any time any question between the two countries becomes critical, and their presence in America, and the presence

38. *Short Studies*, II, 304–7.   39. *Short Studies*, II, 305.   40. *Short Studies*, II, 306–7.

which they are supposed to possess there, is the immediate cause of the present humour of Ireland itself ... Those who went hated us because they were obliged to go. Those who stayed behind hate us because fathers have lost their sons and sisters brothers, and friends have been parted from friends. And now we have Fenianism upon us saying openly that we dare not put it down, for America will not allow us.[41]

Given Froude's dismissal, in the course of the same lectures, of the actual threat presented to the Union by the Fenians, and the unlikelihood of any imminent war between Britain and the United States, all of this sounds unnecessarily alarmist. But behind Froude's growing anxiety concerning the development of interest politics in America, there lay an even broader concern about the direction of world history. This was his alarm at what he saw as a hugely regressive and even perverse phenomenon: the revival and extension of the influence of Roman Catholicism across the Western world, in the United States, and in Ireland in particular.

This too, in historical retrospect, seems exaggerated; but Froude's fears concerning Catholicism ran deep. Several of his observations concerning the faith can appear, when taken out of context, as little more than the crudest bigotry, while other reflections seem to convey a genuine sympathy for Catholicism's spirituality. Underlying this seeming ambivalence, however, was a relatively simple historicism. Once a force of great spiritual energy, Catholicism, like all such phenomena, was of limited power and duration. It had replaced a moribund pagan stoicism in the first and second centuries, and had in turn declined, to be replaced by a resurgent Christianity which in the sixteenth century took the form of Protestantism. Thereafter it was the force of Protestantism which required careful examination and address. It was this which since the 1840s was Froude's principal preoccupation: the question as to how to ensure that a spiritual force which was manifestly on the decline could be revitalised or replaced by a new and vibrant one. The outcome of this issue was always in doubt. Defections to Rome, Puseyism, latitudinarianism, and the rise of a blatant scepticism among the educated, and the persistence of sentimentalism, sectarianism, and complacency among the evangelicals were continuing sources of concern. But the battle had not been lost. Carlyle continued (however wounded), and Froude's own moderate success as a figure of influence was not to be discounted either. As late as the close of the 1860s, despite the survival of the Oxford deserters and

---

41. 'England and Her Colonies', 'Fortnight', 184–5.

remarkable recovery in Newman's public reputation, Froude remained convinced that the most direct threat to spiritual renewal lay not in the recrudescence of Catholicism, but in the continuing degeneration of Protestantism. In his sensitive essay on *The Grammar of Assent* he remained certain that, while Newman was struggling to revive by 'galvanism', a spiritual entity long since dead, the real battle lay around the future of Protestantism.[42]

After 1870, however, things changed. Froude was among the first to realise that the unification of Italy and the suppression of the Papal States had yielded a highly paradoxical consequence. Far from dealing a death-blow to the pope's political and cultural influence, it had liberated the papacy from the petty intricacies of Italian politics, and enabled it to resume a role of far greater potential on the international stage. The present incumbent, Pius IX, had not been slow to seize the opportunity. He summoned a grand council to the Vatican—the first to be summoned by the papacy in three hundred years—and in a series of initiatives which included the declaration of papal infallibility as an article of faith he established the authority of the Roman Catholic Church as an international force. Though it was a blow to liberal and ecumenical Catholics everywhere, not least in England, this reactionary assertion of papal authority supplied a powerful fillip to conservative and politically marginalised elements among the laity, resulting in the emergence of well-organised, avowedly religious, and anti-liberal political movements in France, Germany, Austria, and Italy which, after the French version of the type, were generically referred to as 'Ultramontane'.[43]

Genuine 'ultramontanism', of course, posed no immediate threat in Protestant England, though there were warning signs aplenty in the assertiveness of the recently inaugurated Catholic Archbishop of Westminster (Froude's old Oxford acquaintance, Henry Edward Manning) and in the general silence with which the dogma of infallibility had been received by England's Catholics, even by Newman. But it was rapidly at work in Ireland, not only in the way the Catholic hierarchy and laity had combined to defeat Gladstone's university schemes, but even more sinisterly in the way in which Catholic clergy had intervened in a series of recent by-elections, withholding endorsement from candidates until a public statement of their allegiance to

---

42. 'Father Newman on *The Grammar of Assent*', *Fraser's*, NS 1 (May 1870), 561–80, reprinted in *Short Studies*, II, 101–45.
43. 'The Crisis in France', NS 3 (February, 1871), 256–72; G. Cluseret, 'The Religious Question in Switzerland', NS 9 (February, 1874), 249–58.

the aims of the church had been made.[44] In the United States the influence of the Catholic clergy, especially the Irish clergy, over politics at local, municipals and state level had already been obvious before the onset of ultramontanism.[45] It was this combination of Catholicism's worldwide revival, its particular strength among the anglophobe Irish in America, and its resurgence in Ireland, where it had never died out, that was, for Froude, the most alarming of all recent historical developments, making the future prospect of the much-feared conflict with Britain's only rival for world power seem all the more probable in the end.

Froude's alarm at the prospect of such a possible outcome was intensified by the conviction that it had been encouraged by a parallel decline in the spirit of Protestantism against which he had for so long been warning. The petty institutional wranglings of the Protestant churches, the scholastic squabbling of their theologians, the shallow and condescending tolerance of modern secular philosophers, and the widespread indifference and hypocrisy among those who outwardly professed to believe in them had induced disillusionment, fear, and despair among the most sensitive of souls for whom the certitudes of Catholicism appeared to be increasingly attractive.

For Froude, of course, this was a development that was altogether unacceptable. But it was also historically impossible. That Protestantism, as a vehicle for the expression of humanity's sense of the meaning of Creation, should decline as its predecessors had decayed was regrettable but inevitable; and the point, as Carlyle had taught, was to ensure that from its embers another more vital spiritual force should emerge. That history should now appear to be moving in reverse, moving past the failures of nineteenth-century Protestantism, and beyond its achievements three centuries before, to allow the resurrection of the long-expired spirit of Catholicism, was historically and philosophically absurd. Nothing that had happened since 1870 was sufficient to make him doubt this proposition: no galvanic experiments, he continued to believe, could 'make dead limbs ... move ... The life once gone does not come back again.'[46]

44. J. L. Whittle, 'How to Save Ireland from an Ultramontane University', 77 (April, 1868), 433–51; 'Papal Ireland', NS 4 (December, 1871), 776–92; 'Irish Politics and Irish Priests', NS 1 (April 1870), 491–8.
45. 'Practical Workings of the Ballot in the United States', NS 1 (March, 1870), 373–10; 'Causes of Friction between the United States and England', NS 7 (March, 1873), 293–303; Froude, 'England and her Colonies', NS 1 (1870), 1–16.
46. Froude, 'Romanism and the Irish Race in the United States, part ii', North American Review (January 1880), 31–50.

It was his sense of the very impossibility of these recent developments, and the conviction that they had been permitted only by the failure of the Protestant spirit, that encouraged Froude in the belief that something truly effective might be done in the time to hand. By timely intervention, a critical voice which, even if it did not possess the prophetic power of Carlyle, was not without its own resources as a writer, as editor of *Fraser's*, and as one with a special knowledge of English history, might bring about a crucial change of attitude, and, if not redirect history, at least help set it on its proper course once more.

Thus *Fraser's* took on an increasingly marked sectarian attitude. Essays on the dangers of 'ultramontanism', on the power of the Jesuits, on the dangers of Catholic education, and on the irresponsible sentimentality of High-Church ritualists made frequent appearances in its pages.[47] In 1871 Froude volunteered to present an unprecedented second rectorial address to the students at St Andrews. The topic he chose was 'Calvinism', in which, while deftly avoiding an endorsement of the teachings of Calvin himself, provided an analysis of the present spiritual malaise and called for a revival of the same militant spirit which had rescued the world from similar decadence three centuries earlier.[48] Having been 'accepted for two centuries in all Protestant countries', Calvinism, Froude told his audience, 'has come to be regarded . . . as a system of belief incredible in itself, dishonoring in its object, and as intolerable as it has itself been intolerant.' And now, 'the Catholics whom it overthrew take courage from the philosophers, and assail it on the same ground.'[49] In 'The Revival of Romanism'—an extended piece which he composed as he was writing *The English in Ireland*—Froude developed the theme at considerable length.[50] In no way due to its own intrinsic strength, the revival of Catholicism, as Froude analysed it, was the product of several different factors. The challenge of modern science and literature, the theological disarray and organisational weakness of so many Protestant churches

47. See, *inter alia*, 'The Present State of Religious Controversy', 80 (November, 1869), 537–74; 'Dr Pusey and Dr Temple', 80 (December, 1869), 722–37; 'Mr Voysey and Mr Purchas', NS 3 (April, 1871), 457–68; 'Papal Ireland', NS 4 (December 1871), 776–92; 'The Irish Roman Catholic Laity', NS 6 (October, 1872) 491–6; 'The Jesuits and their Expulsion from Germany', NS 7 (May 1873), 631–46; 'The Christian Brothers and their Lesson Books', NS 9 (February, 1874), 186–99.
48. First published in *Short Studies*, II, 1–59; the lecture is discussed at greater length in ch. 11.
49. *Short Studies*, II, 3.
50. First published in the second series of *Short Studies*, internal evidence suggests that, like several other essays in the collection, it was written around the time of the 1874 general election; reprinted in *Short Studies*, III, 130–206.

across Europe, Catholicism's sentimental attractions for weak-minded Protestants made uneasy by the state of their religion, and the increasing toleration of Romanism's claims all contributed to this astonishing phenomenon. Developments in Ireland and in the United State were curiously absent from this general survey. But the omission was deliberate, because for these two closely related areas Froude had proposed special treatment.

Thus it was from these same considerations that, when offered the prospect of a literary lecture tour in the United States, Froude chose to deliver his lectures not on the subject which had made him famous—the history of Tudor England—but instead to address his audience on the general history of Ireland; and that he determined to abandon his long engagement with English history in order to devote himself to the presentation of an exemplary case of Protestant England's failure to fulfil the historical role which had been assigned to it. This emblematic case was to be fully explored in *The English in Ireland in the Eighteenth Century*.

III

The English in Ireland was from the moment of its appearance an intensely controversial and inflammatory book, far exceeding the indignation provoked by Froude's *History of England*. The critical reaction which it attracted, however, has obscured the range and the depth of research upon which it was based. In addition to the printed sources of newspapers, pamphlets, parliamentary debates, statute books, and published correspondence, Froude, as in his *History of England*, probed deeply into manuscript materials in the Public Record Office, the British Museum, the Irish State Paper Office, and most especially the muniments of Dublin Castle, on a scale never before attempted by an historian of eighteenth-century Ireland. Froude used sources, addressed topics, developed themes, and posed problems which were to engage scholars of Irish history for decades to come.[51]

Yet for all that, the book was indeed, as his critics so frequently claimed, a polemic—though a polemic of a deliberate and often wholly transparent character. The narrative, for example, is not infrequently broken by comments

---

51. See the comments on Froude's contribution to the development of the subject by one of the leading Irish historians of the period, L. M. Cullen, in W. E. Vaughan (ed.), *A New History of Ireland: The Eighteenth Century* (Oxford, 1986), 123–30.

and digressions on the applicability of certain historical lessons to recent or
contemporary political debates. The account given of William III's initially
liberal and tolerant attitude toward the defeated Irish Catholics reads very
like the critique of Gladstone's ecclesiastical and educational policies voiced
elsewhere by Froude and other *Fraser's* contributors.[52] A chapter on cattle-
houghing, rape, and murder in eighteenth-century Ireland is sardonically
entitled 'Irish Ideas' in mocking allusion to Gladstone's declaration that Irish
policy should be shaped by ideas emanating from the island.[53] Leading
Whigs sympathetic to Catholic Emancipation, franchise reform, and a measure of constitutional independence for Ireland are frequently referred to
anachronistically but pointedly as 'the Liberal party'.[54] Grattan is called 'the
Liberator', the United Irishmen dubbed 'Young Ireland'. An unnecessarily
detailed account of the severe conduct of 'Governor' Eyre (he was in fact
Mayor) of Galway in suppressing popery in the city and his subsequent
abandonment by Whitehall is included, one surmises, because of its contemporary resonance.[55] Lest any of its countless allusions had been lost on
his readers, moreover, Froude included in the second edition of the book
(1881) a preface, a supplementary chapter, and scattered notes making the
contemporary relevance of his history to the current debate on Home Rule
altogether plain.[56]

The unashamedly referential character of the book obscures, however,
deeper impulses. Underpinning it is Froude's deep historicism: his contention that, while historical development could not be predicted or explained
through sociological laws, a cyclical pattern of the rise and decline of the
spirit within specific civilisations could be discerned by the perceptive, and
occasionally halted, by agents uniquely inspired. This conviction that such
an historical dynamic could be demonstrated by detailed historical research
legitimised, for Froude, the overt indication of contemporary analogies,
and allowed for the pronouncement of different, apparently contradictory
judgements depending upon the character and the stage of the cycle under
analysis. But it might also be understood to entail the dangerous assumption that whatever had happened was justified by its very happening, that
ultimately might was right. That neither Froude nor Carlyle subscribed to

---

52. Vol. I, bk, I, ch.i.
53. Vol. I, bk, III, ch.i.
54. For example, vol. I, 382, 389; vol. 3, 151, 266, 458, 528.
55. Vol. I, 327, 602–8.
56. 2nd edn., 1881, vol. I, v–vi, vol. 3, 556–85.

such a crude view has for long been understood, but their mode of expression and argumentation has frequently given rise to the impression that they did; and the grounds upon which they claimed freedom from mere determinism were often so peremptorily or obscurely stated that, most particularly in the case of Froude's offensive Irish history, they demand further clarification.

For Froude, as for Carlyle and so many of the Romantics, there existed beyond the level of finite and imperfect historical knowledge an eternal realm in which truth, justice, and beauty had an absolute meaning against which human perceptions of the same would ultimately be measured.[57] Intimations of such a realm were vouchsafed to the few, and occurred to the many only rarely and then fleetingly. Since the existence of this eternal reality was, they asserted, axiomatic (or else there was no significance at all in the world), it was the duty of all sentient beings to move toward it by all means possible, either as prophetic leaders or inspired followers. Whatever the success of each individual pilgrimage, all could be assured that ultimately—or even occasionally as in Froude's sixteenth century—truth would be revealed. The point was to commence the journey.

The arrogation by Carlyle and Froude of the role of prophetic guides in this process was steeped in risk. Carlyle's achievement in *The French Revolution*, however, and Froude's own success in his *History of England*, appeared to offer sufficient grounds to presume that, despite its dangers, prophetic history might be applied to the profound and urgent challenge ceaselessly presented to England by Ireland. It was with this bold conviction that Froude undertook the composition of *The English in Ireland*, shaping its subject, its structure, its argument, and its style to these higher concerns of inspiring English readers without regard for critical scholarly opinion in general, or Irish opinion—scholarly and otherwise—in particular.

It was his distinctive conception of the significance and place of Irish history in relation to the unstated priority of England's history that helps explain Froude's compositional decisions concerning topic and period that were otherwise curious. Though he had repeatedly claimed, for example, that the single most important event in modern Irish history was the rebellion of 1641, it seems strange that, having decided to write an Irish history,

---

57. See *inter alia*, Peter Allan Dale, *The Victorian Conception of History: Carlyle, Arnold and Pater* (Cambridge, MA, 1973), chs. 1–2; M. H. Abrams, *Natural Supernaturalism: Tradition and Revolution in Romantic Literature* (New York, 1973), esp. chs. 3 and 4.

he should have decided to place his emphasis elsewhere. It was hardly from lack of knowledge of the relevant sources. Froude was keenly aware of the rich materials contained in the large body of depositions concerning the events of 1641 preserved in the library of Trinity College Dublin. But for all his insistence upon their importance, he declined to investigate the events of 1641, arranging instead that the work be delegated to an unknown scholar—the talented but impecunious Mary Hickson, whom he persuaded his friend Lord Carnarvon to fund.[58]

No less intriguing than this decision *not* to write on the period which he declared to be the most significant in modern Irish history is the structure of the book he actually chose to write. In the preliminary section of *The English in Ireland* where Froude supplied a concise but strongly interpretative account of Irish history, he devoted less than twenty of two hundred and forty pages to the outbreak of the 1641 rebellion itself, and likewise, though he confidently asserted that the Cromwellian period represented the noblest epoch of English rule in Ireland, he gave little more than twenty pages to the 1650s, basing his account largely on Carlyle's *Cromwell,* and the far from congenial authority of J. P Prendergast.[59] Even more surprising is Froude's distribution of emphasis in the main body of the book dealing with the eighteenth century. Though his narrative builds steadily toward the grand climacteric of the rebellion of 1798 which is foreshadowed at several times in the text (and related to the two other great catastrophes that frame it: the 1641 rebellion, and the Great Famine), it is curious how little space is actually provided for it in the end: a mere one hundred pages in a history of some sixteen hundred pages.[60] If he had been concerned primarily with demonstrating the instability, treachery, and violence of the Irish and the need to reassert firm English rule over them, it is surely toward the 1798 rebellion that he might have been expected, as so many like-minded historians, to give the greatest emphasis in his narrative.[61]

58. M. A. Hickson, *Ireland in the Seventeenth Century; or The Irish Massacres of 1641–2, with a Preface by J. A. Froude* (London, 1884), published by Froude's publishers, Longmans. Froude offered to write the Preface, but at Hickson's request he agreed to make several changes to it. Hickson's 'Note' in *The English Historical Review,* 2 (1887), 527. On Froude's support for Hickson, see Froude to Lady Carnarvon, 18 August, 5 September 1885, British Library, Carnarvon MSS, Add MS 60799B, ff. 96–100.

59. Vol. 1, 109–19; 119–40.

60. Vol. 3, bk. X, ch. I, 358–457.

61. The primary example of this kind of history is Richard Musgrave, *History of the Rebellion in Ireland in the Year 1798* (Dublin, 1803); on which, see James Kelly, *Sir Richard Musgrave (1746–1818): Ultra-Protestant Ideologue* (Dublin, 2009).

That he elected instead to diminish its importance by allotting priority to the ceaseless bickerings of the Irish parliament, the restless changes of policy and personnel of the Dublin administration, and the recurrent surfacing of terror, crime, and vice in the country at large in the century between 1690 and 1790 (in over half of which he claimed Ireland was 'without a history') is clearly indicative of a deliberate choice of theme on Froude's part.[62] He had chosen, that is, to write neither about an Irish rebellion nor a failed attempt at an Irish revolution, but about something in between. His topic was an Irish *ancien régime*—a period of peace, apparent stability, and real paralysis sandwiched between the religious wars of the seventeenth century and the revolutionary wars of the end of the eighteenth century, in which historical opportunities were fatally squandered by neglect, complacency, and vice, and another blood-letting ineluctably set in train.

It was the motif of an *ancien régime* that determined both the content and the structure of Froude's Irish history. The familiar conventional components of such a period thus supply the principal elements in his narrative. An established church, corrupt at all levels, neglectful of its duties, and oppressive in its impositions on the ordinary people; a corrupt, weak, and vacillating government working to deepen the corruption of the representatives of property in parliament; an idle, dissolute, and absentee aristocracy; a coarse and grasping middle class in town and country; an abject and deeply impoverished peasantry driven in their desperation to cowardly acts of horrific cruelty: these are the main actors in Froude's historical tableau which seems remarkably similar in character to the continental (particularly French) *ancien régime*. The implication, made explicit at several points in the narrative, is that the same catastrophe which befell the continental model awaited Ireland's version.

To this Carlylean model, however, Froude adds two further opposing but integrally related factors which together rendered the Irish situation unique. The first was the deep attachment of the Irish to Catholicism, or more precisely (in Froude's term) to 'Romanism'—an international historical force whose drive was toward total domination. The second was the attachment of Britain itself to the principles of *laissez faire*—a misguided illusion which served to justify English selfish, neglectful, and oppressive attitudes toward

---

62. Vol. 1, xvii, 657–9: 'for the half century intervening between the duke of Grafton's government and the revolt of the American colonies, Ireland was without a history.'

the island for whose governance England had assumed responsibility. Ireland, therefore, was at the centre of a conflict between two world-historical forces, both destructive of each other and of humanity's fundamental needs. This was the challenge which in the eighteenth century the English in Ireland had confronted, which they had utterly failed to meet, and which yet remained to be faced.

Because it was primarily concerned with the delineation of such a massive conflict, it is scarcely surprising that, in contrast to his *History of England*, the role of individual character is given little space in Froude's Irish history. The major figures of the period—Flood, Grattan, and Tone—are, of course, prominent, but each is sketched largely as a representative type within a revolutionary era: Flood as the ambitious placeman, Grattan the vain and self-deluding idealist, Tone the sentimental 'Young Irelander'; while other major figures such as Swift, Berkeley, and King are mentioned only in passing. Lord Clare, the Irish Lord Chancellor in the 1790s, though anomalous in many respects, is the only exception to this pattern. He is selected by Froude as the only clear-sighted and courageous prophet of his epoch, the only figure to approximate to Cecil or Knox in the English *History*. Unlike them, however, Fitzgibbon was an historical failure: for all his insight and his bravery, 'the greatest statesman whom Ireland ever produced' was abandoned by England, left to die in solitary gloom, and 'his memory [left] to be trampled on lest [England] should offend the prejudices of later generations of patriots'.[63] Again, while lesser figures make repeated appearances in the narrative, they are given summary character assessments by Froude that are unfailingly in accord with his interpretation: General Lake (egregiously) is brave and humane, and Father Murphy is coarse and vulgar. It is not personalities or individuals who predominate in Froude's text, but interests, groups, and anonymous collective identities—the English parliament, the government, the parliamentary placemen, the 'patriots', the smugglers, the Dublin mob.[64]

It is, moreover, in accordance with the priority of tracing the interaction and conflict of such collectives and interests, rather than leading individuals, that the history as a whole is organised. Composed of a series of ten books, each divided into two or three chapters which are in turn subdivided into between five and ten sections each, *The English in Ireland* offers a reading

63. Vol. 3, 307.   64. Vol. 3, 281–4, 306, 456.

experience that is markedly different from that to be derived from reading the *History of England*. Running to no more than ten pages each, the sections can be scanned and absorbed with relative ease, and an entire chapter can thus be comprehended as a rounded totality, a further iteration of the continuing juxtaposition of contrasting set pieces covering a defined chronological period, or, occasionally, a specific theme. Moveover, though the content of these sections varies in regard to topic, location, and event, the nature of the contrast obtaining between them remains the same. This is the unchanging interdependency of neglect, selfishness, and weakness on the one hand, with vice, anarchy, and unrestrained violence on the other. The chief actors in this sustained interplay may vary. The weakness and indifference of the Irish viceroyalty is contrasted sometimes against the irresponsible avarice of the English parliament, sometimes against intrigues of Court politics, frequently against the corrupt place-seeking of the Irish parliament, and increasingly against the terror tactics and violent demands of agrarian and republican agitators. Other candidates not infrequently assume the dramatic role assigned to the viceroyalty. Thus the Irish parliament is shown to be weak and vacillating in face of political anarchy, high and low; and the Church of Ireland is excoriated for its greed and neglect in the time of its greatest opportunity to convert the Irish from popery. But roles are occasionally reversed, and the Irish parliament is sometimes presented as an innocent victim rendered powerless by a vicious or foolish administration. The desperate pleas of the Irish peasants (no longer a mass of agrarian terrorists), in face of rapidly deteriorating social and economic conditions, are drowned amidst the ceaseless and ineffective posturing and bickering of would-be reformers.

It is this interrelationship of irresponsibility and anarchy (wilful or inadvertent) which is the implicit motif of the entire work. Occasionally it is made formally explicit. Book III, for example, which is set between Froude's account of the gradual decline of anti-Jacobite spirit within the English government and the Irish parliament, and a section featuring the corruption and feebleness of Irish parliamentary politics, offers a social survey of anarchy: murder, rape, and terror.[65] The concluding chapter of Volume I is concerned with 'The Progress of Anarchy', and the title of the concluding chapter of Volume III, 'Whiteboys High and Low', reasserts Froude's organising conceit.[66]

---

65. Ch. i, 'Irish ideas'; ch. ii, 'The Smugglers'.
66. Vol. 1, bk. iv, ch.ii; vol. 2, bk. vii, ch. ii.

So essential to the very conception of the work, this sequence of contrasts is also the source of its innumerable inconsistencies mercilessly exposed by Froude's critics and cavalierly ignored by the author himself. More importantly, however, it is this same intrinsic motif that underpins the curious distribution of emphasis which Froude determined upon in designing the structure of the work as a whole. Beginning with unqualified pseudo-axiomatic assertions about the way in which nations and the relations between nations are determined by fundamental geographical, racial, and cultural forces, the book ends with an explosion of violent anarchy, atrocity, and unrestrained, and still unexpiated, blood-letting. In between, constituting the vast bulk of the book, is a detailed narrative of the petty follies, vanities, and selfishness of individuals and groups, seemingly inconsequential in themselves, but of fatal significance when viewed retrospectively in the light of the catastrophe to come. What Froude has been undertaking here, both in the broader design of the book and in the detailed organisation of its individual sections, is a particular demonstration of his understanding of the general processes of history as outlined in his earlier speculative essays, and embodied in his English *History* in which Ireland was seen to have exerted a fateful and inescapable effect on England's own place in world history.

That human history has a purpose, and that such a purpose must tend ultimately toward the good, must be, Froude had asserted, a starting assumption for anyone still believing in the existence of an eternal creative force. From this universal imperative it followed that laws governing the advance of history toward its purpose must in principle exist. The difficulty, of course, lay in the fact that the human agents on whom this advance depended, and through whom these laws must be working, were only dimly aware of, and more often totally blind to, the forces that were operating around them. The revelation and liberation of such forces was the task of the few—the Carlylean great men of heroic epochs. History's forces, however, were no less operative in unheroic eras, and their misperception or outright rejection by those charged with the obligation of acting under them had consequences no less momentous than in heroic ages—only in the opposite, negative direction. In place of spiritual progress and freedom, there occurred not only stagnation and retardation, but actual regression and a recrudescence of those destructive human impulses which are an inevitable consequence of a rejection of duty.

Europe's eighteenth century presented a classic instance of such an unheroic age. In France the irresponsibility and defiance of history's agents had led to the blood-letting of Carlyle's French Revolution; and in Ireland it had led inexorably to the horrors of 1798. But for several reasons Froude's readers could not turn their backs on Ireland's ordeal with the same equanimity with which they might close the pages of *The French Revolution*. England could not suddenly abandon a moral obligation it had for long assumed, long profited from, and long abused, without consequences of major historical significance for herself. More acutely, the moral responsibility for the neglect which had resulted in the bloody events of 1798 could not be denied—all the more so because it had by no means been the first instance of such misconduct. The brutalities detailed in Froude's account of the sixteenth century were inexcusable, and the atrocities of 1798 had since been compounded by the sustained irresponsibility and greed which in turn had issued in the terrible Famine. And now, amidst the continuance of this unexpiated guilt, unmistakable signs of another brutal conflict between the English and the Irish were again emerging in the form of militant Irish-America and the resurgence of agitation in Ireland which, no matter how it turned out, could serve only to deepen England's and Englishmen's historical obligations.

It is true, then, that as its critics charged, *The English in Ireland* was an intensely polemical work, designed to use an account of history to lend force to contemporary political and ideological objectives. But it was so in a rather more profound way than they appreciated. To Froude, such a distinction between past events and current concerns was one which he regarded as both false and irresponsibly misleading. The sons whose fathers' sins would inevitably return to curse them deserved at least to be alerted to the challenge that faced them and to be exhorted to prepare themselves for it. It is in this last prophetic respect that Froude's Irish history drew its inspiration not only from Carlyle, but from a much older commentator on Ireland who had also assumed upon himself the task of forewarning his fellow Englishmen of the historical challenge posed to them by Ireland. This was Edmund Spenser.

Froude's intimate knowledge of Spenser's Ireland as mediated through *The Faerie Queene* and the *View of the Present State of Ireland* is in no doubt. He had been steeped in the former since youth, and his familiarity with the latter is clear in several passages in the *History of England*.[67] Certain points of similarity in Froude's and Spenser's perception of Ireland are obvious. It is

---

67. See, for example, *History of England*, ii, 241, 247, 249; viii, 245; x, 586.

from Spenser, for instance, that Froude finds an authority for his assertions concerning the cultural incorrigibility of the native Irish; and Froude's insistence that English laws and customs inevitably become perverted when introduced innocently into Ireland is reflective of a classic Spenserian motif. Dissimilarities between the two minds are, of course, equally evident. Froude, unlike Spenser, had not in any way supported the mass starvation of the Irish, and indeed had continued to proclaim England's moral responsibility for the Famine.[68] The authority of Spenser's interventionist, Calvinist God, moreover, had long since lost the conviction of religiously speculative English minds, Froude's included. It would therefore be historically otiose to claim that Froude was simply reiterating Spenser's Elizabethan attitudes in Victorian form. Yet just as the influence of the moral aesthetic of Spenser's friend and contemporary, Sidney, can be seen acting upon Shelley, Coleridge, and the other Romantics, so the more subtle resonances of Spenserian Ireland may be seen at work on Froude's imagination.[69]

In this refracted light, some parallels between the two are particularly striking. For both Spenser and Froude, Ireland, the island of the natives, was a land without time, where in Spenser's case history had never happened, and in Froude's it had become paralysed in the eighteenth century. For both, Ireland was a location where processes of political and social interchange could be seen as ceaselessly repetitive, predictable, and without hope of progress—a stagnant state, Spenser's 'sink', which could be reinvigorated only by sustained, forceful action that was impervious to the temptation of hesitant moral scruple. 'The type of Irish agitation', Froude asserts at the beginning of his book, declaring its fundamentally, Spenserian thesis, 'is so unchanging that the disease at all times is obviously the same.'[70] In Spenser also Froude would have found a model for his own particular form of polemic. For the *View of the Present State of Ireland* was also a powerful polemic, whose purpose was not primarily to denounce the native Irish (whose degeneracy was taken as given), but to persuade the English to abandon their naïve and shallow belief that Ireland could be made governable by the application of English laws alone. The vehicle which Spenser

---

68. Froude, 'Romanism and the Irish Race in the United States' *North American Review*, 129 (December 1879), 519–37; 130 (January 1880), 31–51.
69. On the influence of Sidney over the Romantics and the Victorians, see M. H. Abrams, *The Mirror and the Lamp: Romantic Theory and the Critical Tradition* (New York, 1953), chs. iii–iv; Michael Mack, *Sidney's Poetics: Imitating Creation* (Washington, DC, 2005), ch. 1.
70. Vol. 1, vii.

had employed as a means of altering *bien-pensant* English opinion and rendering it willing to countenance extreme and repressive policies—a set-piece dialogue between a good English humanist and an experienced old Irish hand—was a formal and rhetorical strategy of little potency three centuries on. And Froude's intended audience was markedly different from Spenser's both in its social composition and in its moral and intellectual sensibilities. But as their strategic purpose was similar—the persuasion of a passive but well-meaning group to endorse ostensibly repugnant policies—it is unsurprising that Froude should have followed Spenser in the adoption of a quite different but equally manipulative rhetoric through the creation of a distinctive literary persona. In Froude's case this was the person of the narrative historian himself.

Though Froude the historian of Ireland shared with Froude the English historian, the moral essayist, the narrator of fictional tales, the same determination to intrude upon and reshape the moral consciousness of his audience, it is the distinctive features of his Irish voice that are of interest here. Among the most noticeable of such features is its uncompromisingly dogmatic tone which announces itself immediately in those of *a priori* assertions concerning geopolitical determinism, natural inequality, the conditions underlying national self-determination and individual liberty, and the necessity of coercive power with which the book opens. In the *History of England* Froude had occasionally interrupted his narrative with controversial *obiter dicta* ostensibly derived from his deep and intimate immersion in the sources; but in *The English in Ireland* the emphasis is reversed. The philosophy informing the historian is stated at the outset not as the result of his investigation of Irish history, but as its original determining assumptions. Thereafter, by numerous allusions back to these basic theses, his readers are left in no doubt that what Froude is undertaking is 'a scientific account of the past'.[71] Given Froude's several statements concerning the impossibility of establishing a scientific approach to historical investigation, this may be regarded as just another of the inconsistencies and contradictions which, when it came to writing about Ireland, he regarded with cool indifference. Its significance becomes clearer, however, when seen in relation to a second and even more disturbing feature of his Irish voice: its militant and unrepentant sectarianism.

The Protestant sympathies of the author of the *History of England* had, to be sure, long been familiar to his readers, even though they had been

---

71. *The English in Ireland*, i, vii.

moderated by his essays arguing for the 'Free Discussion of Theological Difficulties'.[72] But in the Irish history the author's concentration was not upon the celebration of the achievements of the Protestants (who hardly merit any credit whatsoever), but rather upon the justification of repression of the Catholics. In Irish Froude, religious repression and persecution were not to be justified in terms of the exigencies of the time but on absolute terms. Catholics deserved and continue to deserve penal laws:

> The Catholics ... had no right to complain. They, who had never professed toleration, had no right to demand it. To them the same measure only was meted out which they had allowed to others in England while the power was theirs, and which they continue to allow them in other countries, where the power was still theirs ... The suspicion attaching to the representatives of a creed which has dyed its garments in blood so deep as Romanism has done will only finally disappear when the heads of a church which sanctioned the atrocities of the Inquisition has with equal solemnity condemned them.[73]

The unforgiving tone of such assertions was made even more disturbing by the historian's determination to draw contemporary moral judgements:

> Catholic writers express neither regret nor astonishment at these severities [the persecutions of the Inquisition], and reserve their outcries for when they are themselves the victims of their own principles ... Earnest Catholics ... still refuse the acknowledgements which are due to the conscience of Europe; and rather than make frank confession of their fathers' sins, they take refuge in dishonest evasions or in audacious denials of the established truths of history[74]

In the face of this total lack of contrition, contemporary opinion has been grossly irresponsible.

> The modern Liberal finds excuses for the Catholic which he refuses to the Calvinist. He perceives, or thinks he perceives, that in all creeds there is both truth and error, that the essentials are to be found in each, that mistakes of opinion are venial; and he considers that the Protestant in claiming a right to think for himself ought in consistency to have allowed the same right to others.[75]

But this was a nefarious historical anachronism, especially in regard to Ireland—a country in which 'at the bottom of every rebellion ... since the Reformation were to be found the Catholic bishops and clergy,'[76] and in

72. See ch. 8.   73. Vol. 1, 276, 588.   74. Vol. 1, 209, 588.
75. Vol. 1, 209.   76. Vol. 1, 210

which at present witnessed 'the reduction of the viceroy into a registrar of the decrees of the Vatican and the boast of a cardinal that Irish nationality was the Catholic religion'.[77] It was against this illusion of the age that the historian of Ireland was determined to take his stand.

IV

It was in these unqualified assertions that the real purpose underlying Froude's decision to write Irish history and all of the compositional, organisational, and expressive decisions that followed from it at last becomes clear. Froude's *English in Ireland*, along with his course of general lectures, was to be his contribution to what he regarded as the greatest cultural and moral challenge of his day: the worldwide revival of Romanism.

The place occupied by Ireland within this appalling historical regression was central. A European country where Catholicism was at its strongest, it also harboured an undying enmity toward England—not only for ancient wrongs, but for the more immediate guilt of the Great Famine. Though the Famine had not been deliberately caused by England, it was, Froude insisted, English greed and neglect which had been largely responsible for its occurrence, its scale, and its duration; and through her continuing inaction England was now sowing dragon's teeth in the form of the massive numbers of profoundly hostile Irish who were now establishing themselves in America, determined to take revenge on England.[78] Moreover, those victims of England's sin who had survived through emigration were now, by an extraordinary turn of events, steadily increasing in their strength in their adoptive country. In recent decades the remarkable advance of Irish Catholicism in the United States could be registered in a number of alarming milestones: in the fervent support given to the Fenians throughout the

77. Vol. 1., Vol 2, 278. Froude's reference here is to Cardinal Paul Cullen, whose public pronouncements frequently led English and Anglo-Irish critics to charge that he aimed at Rome rule. Such a view, represented most recently in Desmond Bowen, *Paul Cullen and the Shaping of Modern Irish Catholicism* (Dublin, 1983), has been critically challenged by many other scholars.

78. Froude, 'Romanism and the Irish Race in the United States' *North American Review*, 129 (December 1879), 519–37; 130 (January 1880), 31–51; Brown, *Irish-American Nationalism*, chs. 5–6; also Edward T. O'Donnell, 'The Scattered Debris of the Irish Nation': The Famine Irish and New York City, 1845–1855', in Margaret Crawford (ed.), *The Hungry Stream: Emigration from Ireland during the Great Famine* (Belfast, 1997), 49–60.

north-eastern states, in the establishment of the Irish Catholic Benevolent Union in Ohio and of Clan na Gael as an openly revolutionary organisation in New York, in the establishment of a potent propagandist weapon, *The Irish World*, and most of all in the success of Catholic Irish machine politics in the big urban centres of the north-east as illustrated in the operations of the Tweed circle of Tammany Hall.[79]

Though these developments were not in themselves immediately threatening, they were nonetheless symptoms of more profound forces now converging in the United States. What made the threat from Irish-America alarming were the broader global implications of America's transformation of which it was merely a part. The triumph of the North in the Civil War had signalled the victory for populist democracy, party politics, special interest groups, kick-backs, and ballyhoo: in fact, all of the mechanisms which had allowed the politics of Irish-American Catholicism to survive and thrive. More importantly, however, its own internal contradictions having been resolved, the United States was now embarking on a course of development that had already enabled it to rival, and would soon enable it to overtake, Great Britain as the pre-eminent world power.

Although relations between the two countries remained amicable, the rivalry and the coming challenge, Froude knew, were inevitable.[80] In this confrontation the match between the rivals was profoundly uneven. While Britain with her *laissez-faire* economics was disastrously alienating countless numbers of her English, Scottish, and above all Irish subjects, and with her *laissez-faire* politics was happily considering the abandonment of all her colonies and the fatal release of Ireland under Home Rule, America was expanding both politically and economically, welcoming all the discontented of the world to aid her in the construction of an industrial and commercial empire which would soon surpass any in history.

---

79. See in general, Thomas N. Brown, *Irish-American Nationalism, 1870–1890* (Philadelphia, 1966); Steven P. Erie, *Rainbows End: Irish Americans and the Dilemmas of Urban Machine Politics, 1840–1985* (Berkeley, CA, 1988).

80. This is a frequent theme in Froude's correspondence with Charles Butler, his American stockbroker, Edinburgh University Library, Butler MSS E.87. 105. See *inter alia* Froude to Butler, 22 December 1877; 6 July 1878, 1 January 1892; see also Froude to Carnarvon, 7 July 1885: 'If we let them have independence we shall have to interfere in a year or two and perhaps get into a scrape with the United States in turn', British Library, Carnarvon MSS, Add MS 60799B, f.90. The nightmare scenario of a war between Britain and the United States is imagined in Froude's fantasy, 'A Sibylline Leaf', *Blackwood's Magazine*, 133 (April 1883), 573–92; see ch. 15.

It was this terrifying vision that inspired and shaped the character of Froude's unionist crusade. In embarking upon his American lecture tour, even as the first volume of *The English in Ireland* was in the press, Froude was taking his war to the frontiers of history, deliberately cultivating American support in his attempt to forestall or delay the integration of the Catholic Irish into the transformed American polity. The American tour was not a success either as a propagandist or a financial enterprise, its failure in itself a symptom of the power of Irish-American influence; and though Froude continued to hope for a further invitation, it never came.[81] But he did attempt to continue the frontier campaign by proxy. Two essays on 'Romanism and the Irish Race in the United States', which he published in the liberal Protestant *North American Review* in the late 1870s and early 1880s, continued the attempt to alert like-minded Americans to the mutually destructive conflict toward which such tolerance of Romanism in the United States was driving both nations.[82]

For all its strategic perspicacity the American side of the campaign remained, if only marginally, a secondary one. Because for Froude the recovery of Catholicism was and would ever be preposterous, its apparent success was only a symptom of the spiritual malaise of Protestantism to be seen in the intellectual weakness of Protestant theologians and preachers and the complacent toleration of the modern liberalism and the liberal states, most notably in England itself.[83] For this reason the campaign against Romanism must be fought not directly against the Pope, nor solely against the Irish-Americans nor the Irish themselves. Just as it had been for his Elizabethan predecessor, the principal target of address for Froude was neither troubled Americans nor guilty Anglo-Irish, but the complacent well-intentioned Englishmen of his day. It was to this audience specifically that Froude in *The English in Ireland* addressed himself in his bold, dogmatic, uncompromising manner. While its tone and mode of expression was strikingly different from that employed in the *History of England*, its central purpose was the same. This was to awaken his readers to the massive moral obligations bequeathed by history which, whether they

81. Froude to Mrs (Charles) Butler, 9 November 1873, Beinecke Library, Yale University, Hilles MSS, Box 9, Froude files; Froude to Charles Butler, 23 February, 1878, Butler MSS, Edinburgh University Library.
82. Froude, 'Romanism and the Irish Race in the United States', *North American Review*, 129 (December 1879), 519–37; 130 (January 1880), pp 31–51.
83. 'Revival of Romanism', *Short Studies*, III, 130–206.

acknowledged them, denied them, or evaded them, lay inescapably before them. Ineluctable and universal, these were obligations which Ireland represented in a peculiarly stark and painful form: the desire unilaterally to forget (and by implication to forgive) the unredressed wrongs of the past would not serve to exorcise England's sin. It would merely compound it.

10

The Challenge of England's Future: South Africa and Bulgaria, 1874–80

For all the intensity of his concern and the clarity of his vision concerning the role of Catholic Ireland in England's world-historical mission, Froude declined to become engaged directly in any actual political campaign against Home Rule for Ireland. Even during the heated period of the Home Rule election of 1886 he was careful to stand aloof. He wrote no pamphlets, published only a few short letters in the papers, and declined invitations to speak on the Unionist side. On one occasion only did he address a Conservative Party meeting, because it had been specially organised in his honour near his holiday home in Salcombe, and even then he told his audience that he came before them to speak as an historian not as a party supporter.[1]

Such abstention was in keeping with his general philosophical outlook. Because in all of his writing he had aimed at the collective moral regeneration of the English people as a whole, inspiring them to see into the true reality of their condition and voluntarily to act in accordance with that insight, Froude preferred to remain aloof from the machinations of party politics and to shun association with the policy of any particular administration.[2]

---

1. Froude gave one interview to *The New York Herald* in March 1886, and wrote a letter to *Lloyd's Weekly*, published on 27 June. Froude's address to the Conservative Association at Salcombe (1 July 1886) opened with the declaration that 'it was not his intention to deliver a political speech, but to give a short lecture', *The Times*, 3 July 1886, 6. Froude wrote to *The Times* on 6 November 1887: '*The English in Ireland* expresses so fully what I have to say about [the Irish question] that I have not considered it necessary to add my voice to the present clamour.'
2. Froude, 'Party Politics', 1874, first published in *Short Studies*, III, 429–76; also Froude to Carnarvon, 13 March 1874, British Library, Carnarvon Papers, Add MS 60799A, ff.3–4; and to Lady Derby, 3 April 1875, Dunn, *Froude*, II, 419.

To this general rule there was, however, one exception. For a brief period in the mid-1870s Froude became intensely engaged in shaping and implementing government policy in the Cape Colony and the neighbouring states of Southern Africa as agent and adviser of the Tory government's Colonial Secretary, Lord Carnarvon. Froude's South African adventure was ultimately to prove a painful failure, confirming him in his original decision to remain outside the arena of active political life. In addition to such a personal lesson, the episode also revealed some profound tensions in his self-appointed regenerative mission which he was never fully to resolve.

I

Although his trenchant views on Britain's relations with her colonies may have in some part prepared him for it, Froude's sudden and intense immersion in South African politics was far from being the necessary culmination of his literary propagandising.[3] The Cape Colony was hardly noticed in Froude's early colonialist essays, which were primarily concerned with reviving and tightening England's links with Australia, New Zealand, and Canada, and the issues with which he was to became intensely engaged with in the Cape—defence, international diplomacy, and the thorny problem of race relations—had likewise featured little in his earlier discussions. In fact, Froude's South African episode was the result of a combination of accidental circumstances.

The first was personal tragedy. On 12 February 1874, after a short and apparently mild illness, Froude's second wife, Henrietta, to whom he had been happily married for eleven years, died suddenly at the age of forty-nine. His wife's death devastated Froude. He went into a period of private grieving into which even his closest friends—Carlyle included—felt unwilling to intrude. *The English in Ireland* was finished under these circumstances—Froude noting a falling off in quality which he had feared reviewers would notice. After sending off the Irish book, however, Froude felt even more bereft; and it was in these circumstances that he decided to appeal to some powerful connections he had made in the course of the colonial debate to succour him in his trouble.[4]

3. See ch. 8.
4. Carlyle to John Carlyle, 14 February 1874; Dunn, *Froude*, II, 388; Froude to Skelton, 11 March, 1 April, 1874, *Table-Talk of Shirley*, ii, 152–3; Froude to Margaret Froude, 15 April 1874, Dunn, *Froude,* II, 390. Froude to Fanny Kingsley, 12 January (1875), Duke University, Special Collections Library, Froude MSS.

In the early 1870s Froude's essays railing against Liberal colonial policy had brought him to the attention of the opposition Tory leadership. He found himself being consulted by Tory grandees among whom was Henry Herbert Molyneux, fourth Earl of Carnarvon, shadow to the Earl of Kimberly on colonial policy between 1868 and 1874. Similar views on the colonies had already brought Froude and Carnarvon close, and their friendship was strengthened by Carnarvon's particular fondness for associating with intellectuals and men of letters in general.[5] Then, in February 1874, in the month of Froude's bereavement, the Tories swept to power, and in forming his second cabinet Prime Minister Disraeli indicated his commitment to a more assertive foreign and colonial policy by appointing Lord Derby as Foreign Secretary, Lord Salisbury as Secretary for India, and Carnarvon as Colonial Secretary. Within a month, seeking an escape from grief and loneliness, Froude wrote to Carnarvon, congratulating him (belatedly) on his elevation, informing him of his own unhappy condition and tentatively mentioning his as yet unconfirmed plan to undertake a tour of Britain's Australasian colonies with a view, perhaps, to writing a book as a contribution to the colonial debate.[6] At this point Froude had nothing more in mind than obtaining letters of introduction from the Colonial Secretary which would enable him to go directly to the most important and influential figures in the British colonies. Carnarvon was more than willing to oblige his friend, but he also had other more urgent priorities concerning which, he believed, Froude and his proposed colonial tour might be of particular use.

The most pressing political problem facing the Colonial Secretary on entering office lay not in Canada, where the difficulties of dominion status were now largely resolved, nor in Australasia. It arose in the Cape Colony in South Africa, where a series of murky and apparently independent developments seemed on the point of converging into a crisis of major proportions.[7] The first of these arose from the actions of Richard Southey, recently

5. A. H. Hardinge, *Life of Henry Herbert Molyneux, Fourth Earl of Carnarvon* (3 vols., London, 1925); Froude to Carnarvon, 9 September 1873, British Library Add MSS 60799A, f.1–2; on the Tories' courtship of Froude, see Froude to Skelton, 10 February 1870, *Table-Talk of Shirley*, 141.
6. Froude to Carnarvon, 4 March 1874, cited in Dunn, *Froude*, II, 390; Carnarvon to Froude, cited in Harding, *Carnarvon*, 176.
7. A useful general survey of developments in the years 1840 to 1880 may be found in Carolyn Hamilton *et al.* (eds.), *The Cambridge History of South Africa: (i) From Early Times to 1885* (Cambridge, 2010), ch. 7. A more detailed treatment of the context in which Froude found himself is in Richard Cope, *Ploughshare of War: The Origins of the Anglo-Zulu War of 1879* (Pietermaritzburg, 1999).

appointed Governor of Griqualand West. A long-time colonial servant at the Cape, Southey was also an avowed expansionist who was deeply hostile to the independent Dutch territories of the Transvaal (the South African Republic) and the Orange Free State. He had also severely exacerbated intercolonial relations through his role in the dubious acquisition by the Crown of a disputed border territory between the Cape and the Transvaal upon the discovery there of a substantial deposit of diamonds (and so named the Diamond Fields), and by his enlightened attitude toward the African tribes and individual black workers in the Diamond Fields and Griqualand West. Tensions provoked by Southey were exacerbated by a set of independent events concerning Langalibalele, a major native chieftain in the province of Natal.[8]

Though Langalibalele had been tolerant of increasing European settlement in the territory, by the early 1870s he was becoming unhappy with attempts of the British administration to discourage African customs.[9] In particular, he was disturbed by one particularly clumsy measure which imposed a tax on the native custom of polygamy, ostensibly to suppress the practice, but actually to raise a revenue. The tax was potentially a source of serious tension within the native dynasties, and Langalibalele had sought to defuse it simply by advising the young men of the leading kins to ignore it. This mild defiance was taken badly by the Secretary for Native Affairs in Natal, Sir Theophilus Shepstone, whose sensitivity regarding his authority was further fuelled by a second portent of potential African hostility, the widespread purchase of firearms in Natal which had been encouraged by Southey's permissive policies in the neighbouring settlements.[10] In common with other European settlements, the British authorities in Natal ordered that all guns purchased by Africans be registered with them. But then, in another extraordinarily short-sighted move, they confiscated such weapons as were brought in for registration. Guns therefore became the real flashpoint between natives and settlers, as attempts to collect unregistered

8. In general, see J. A. Benyon, *Proconsul and Paramountcy in South Africa: The High Commision, British Supremacy and the Sub-Continent, 1806–1910* (Pietermaritzburg, 1980). The most detailed account of the Diamond Fields affair remains J. A. I. Agar-Hamilton, *The Road to the North: South Africa, 1852–86* (London, 1937).

9. For a sympathetic contemporary account, see 'Langalibalele', in *Fraser's Magazine*, NS 11 (January 1875), 50–6; for a modern analysis, see Norman Etherington, 'Why Langalibalele Ran Away', *Journal of Natal and Zulu History*, 1 (1978), 1–25.

10. David Welsh, *The Roots of Segregation: Native Policy in Colonial Natal, 1845–1910* (Cape Town, London, 1971).

firearms led to several confrontations in which scores of African tribesmen were shot dead. Abruptly summoned by Shepstone, Langalibalele stood off and agreed to come in only if both sides met unarmed. Once again the authorities cheated: an attempted ambush of Langalibalele was botched, and more than two hundred of his followers were killed. And when Langalibalele was eventually captured, a veritable purge of his tribe was launched in which hundreds were slaughtered and thousands dispossessed. This was sufficient outrage in itself to concern the Colonial Office, and the need to respond was made more urgent by the powerful campaign for justice and redress being organised in Britain by the influential J. W. Colenso, Bishop of Natal. But the matter was made even more serious by the decision of Natal's neighbour, Cape Colony, to support its action against the tribesmen by accepting Langalibalele for indefinite incarceration on Robben Island without consulting the imperial government in London.[11]

This was the interrelated set of potentially serious problems with which Carnarvon was grappling when Froude made his request to have some quasi-official support for his tour of the colonies. Thus he responded to Froude with a proposal that, in addition to his plan to visit Australasia, Froude should first stop over at the Cape and, while presenting himself as a private individual, should let it be known that he was acting in an unofficial capacity as a special agent of the Colonial Secretary. This was not what Froude had anticipated—after all, he had no conscious intention of immersing himself in actual politics—but after some hesitation he agreed. The timetable of his departure was deferred, and over the summer of 1874 he attended a number of meetings at the Colonial Office and at Carnarvon's seat at Highclere in order to be briefed by officials and work out a series of policy options.[12]

It was at these meetings that a further issue which was independent of, and had a longer provenance than, the immediate crises now pending resurfaced. This was the prospect of colonial confederation. A confederation of the several South African settlements was an idea that had been considered on several occasions before the early 1870s.[13] But the difficulties

11. Bill Guest, *Langalibalele: The Crisis in Natal, 1873–1875* (Pietermaritzburg, 1976); Etherington, 'Why Langalibalele Ran Away', *Journal of Natal and Zulu History*, 1 (1978), 1–25.
12. Carnarvon to Froude; Froude to Carnarvon, 12 and 16 April 1874, British Library Add. MSS 60799A, ff. 5–7.
13. C. F Goodfellow, *Great Britain and South African Confederation, 1870–1881* (Cape Town and London, 1966), ch. 2.

involved in constructing even such a loose association of settlements with so many different ethnic elements had usually been sufficient to discourage initiatives of this kind. Indeed, recent trends of colonial policy had moved in the opposite direction through the recognition of the Dutch states' independence, and the granting of 'responsible government' (a form of Home Rule) to the Cape Colony. The idea revived again with the appointment of Carnarvon, who was determined to initiate a more active imperial policy from the centre than had been the case for several years. For Carnarvon, a binding together of the British and Dutch settlements on lines similar to the federation of the United States or Canada over which the imperial government would still exercise a formal influence in matters of territorial development and foreign policy was an attractive possibility which he looked forward to seeing at some point in the future. But it would be too much to say that Carnarvon (or Froude, who wholly shared the new Secretary's activist intentions) regarded confederation as anything more than an aspiration when Froude left for South Africa. Through a combination of circumstances, however, the idea that it lay at the heart of Carnarvon's approach to the colonies was soon to take hold in the Cape, with deeply troublesome consequences for the Secretary and for his agent.[14]

Confirmed by the cabinet, with the agreement that his expenses in the Cape should be funded from Secret Service funds, Froude embarked upon his mission to the South African settlements arriving there at the close of September 1874, still with the intention of continuing on to his primary objective of Australasia. His tour, however, which lasted until January 1875, passed off with such apparent success that he became convinced that an opportunity existed for a great advance in the resolution of all intercolonial problems under the aegis of the British government. Having in turn visited each of the colonial settlements, British and Dutch, and securing interviews with the leading figures in each, Froude had developed the highly encouraging impression that despite the resentments and fears provoked by recent events in the Diamond Fields and Natal, there remained a strong and sincere interest among all the colonies for a general resolution of all differences and

---

14. Goodfellow *Great Britain and South African Confederation*, ch. 4; Cope, *Ploughshare*, chs. 3 and 4; Froude's memoranda to Carnarvon, 16 April, 12 May 1874, British Library Add. MSS 60799A, ff.9–11, 16–23; Froude to Herbert, 9 July 1874, The National Archives (hereafter TNA) 30/6/49: Colonial Memoranda: South Africa, 3–21.

misunderstandings through the medium of a general conference which might be held under the auspices of the imperial government.[15]

This practical and apparently moderate proposal carried within it, however, several related ramifications whose complexity was gravely underestimated by both Froude and Carnarvon. There was, in the first instance, the question of the annexation of the Diamond Fields whose resolution entailed the humiliation of two of the imperial government's senior officials, Southey and Sir Henry Barkly, if the Dutch of the Transvaal were to be conciliated. Next there was the outrage of the Langalibalele affair in which British public opinion and Colonial Office sentiments were directly at odds with the unrepentant views dominant in both the British and Dutch colonies. Most difficult of all, there remained the question in the minds of all of the colonials as to what might be entailed by holding an intercolonial conference, given the strongly centralising views which Carnarvon and his emissary Froude were believed to espouse. Such ominous implications, however, bore little upon Froude at the close of his brief mission. Instead, buoyed up by his belief that he had found a way by means of a grand conference to resolve all outstanding disputes and to encourage further intercolonial cooperation, he abandoned his plans to travel to Australasia in order to return to London to prepare for this second and final stage of the mission.[16]

On the voyage home, Froude set out his strategic thinking in a series of closely reasoned memoranda.[17] The principal imperial objective, as he saw it, lay in the maintenance of the military base at Simonstown on the Cape Peninsula, which would be of central strategic importance in the event of some attack on British India. Given this priority, the imperial government should follow all means to ensure its preservation. Since the granting of responsible government to the Cape Colony in 1872, however, the existence of a substantial Dutch minority in the new Cape parliament indicated that good relations between the imperial government and Cape Colony was dependent on the continuance of friendly policies toward the independent

15. Carnarvon's summaries of Froude to Carnarvon, 23 September, 4 October, 19 November 1874, NA 30/6/49, 111, 117, 129; Froude to Carnarvon, 18 October 1874, Dunn, *Froude*, II, 402.
16. Notes by Carnarvon on Froude to Carnarvon, 10 November, 1 December, 15 December 1874, TNA 30/6/49, 125, 131, 135; Froude to Margaret Froude 3, 29 December 1874, Dunn, *Froude*, II, 408, 412.
17. Froude's memoranda to Carnarvon, 16 April, 12 May 1874, British Library Add. MSS 60799A, ff.9–11, 16–23; Froude to Herbert, 9 July 1874, NA 30/6/49: Colonial Memoranda: South Africa, 3–21; Carnarvon's notes on Froude to Carnarvon, 15 December 1874, NA 30/6/49, 135.

Dutch states. This in turn required reparation for damages inflicted by the British—most especially in regard to the Diamond Fields. It also required the development of a uniform approach to the management of relations with the native peoples along lines which did not seriously challenge the modes of control already formally in operation in the independent Dutch states. It therefore necessitated the 'putting on the shelf' of the embarrassing Langalibalele affair in a manner which did no damage to any of the British or Dutch interests concerned.[18]

With this set of diplomatic bargaining chips and underlying mutual interests, it seemed clear to Froude that the grounds for a conference were firm. On his return to England he felt free to speak openly about the probable holding of such a conference to discuss all such outstanding issues, and allowed himself to speculate publicly that such a conference might form the basis of the long-hoped-for confederation of British and Dutch states in the region which would forestall the likelihood of any similar misunderstandings arising in the future.[19]

That Froude enjoyed the official backing of the Colonial Office in expressing such views was made clear first by a number of complementary, if less unambiguous, speeches made by Carnarvon himself in the following months, and in the announcement at the end of May 1875 that Froude was to return as Carnarvon's official envoy for the organisation of a conference somewhere in the colonies in the near future. In private, moreover, Carnarvon had already held out to Froude the prospect of a permanent senior post within the colonial administration—a proposition which Froude was seriously considering.[20]

In the meantime, as Froude set sail, Carnarvon and his permanent Under Secretary, Sir Robert Herbert, sent an official despatch to Sir Henry Barkly, High Commissioner of the Cape Colony, instructing him to publish and support the proposal of a colonial conference. Barkly hesitated: he showed the despatch privately to the Cape premier, J. A. Molteno, who immediately presented it to the colonial assembly, denouncing it (to loud approval) as an

18. Goodfellow, *Confederation*, 66, 71. The proposal of shelving the Langalibalele affair came from Froude: Froude to Saul Solomon, 10 February 1875, quoted in W. E. G. Solomon, *Saul Solomon: The Member for Cape Town* (Cape Town and London, 1948), 166–7.

19. *The Times*, 27 March 1875, 12.

20. Goodfellow, *Confederation*, 63–6; Cope, *Ploughshare*, 81–103; Froude to Margaret Froude, 30 June 1875, indicating that an offer of a colonial governorship had been suggested, Dunn, *Froude*, II, 427–8.

intolerable presumption on the part of the imperial government which must at all costs be rejected. There would be no conference, and Carnarvon's agent, Mr Froude, had no business to do in the colony.[21]

This was the critical and wholly unexpected situation which greeted Froude on his arrival at the Cape on 21 June. He had been convinced by his earlier interviews with leading figures in Cape politics that both in the government and opposition there existed a genuine desire for a conference. He had also believed, on the basis of his earlier mission, that he had a personal assurance of support from Molteno. Thus, when he heard the news, he suspected bad faith. In fact, more creditable factors were at work behind this supposed reversal to which Froude (and Carnarvon) had been insufficiently attentive. First, there was the role of Barkly himself, who, whatever the outcome of the conference, stood to be discredited over his part in the seizure of the Diamond Fields. It was more than naïve to have presumed that the High Commissioner could be enlisted in the cause of his own disgrace; and when Molteno, in threatening to resign as Prime Minister should the Commissioner publish the despatch as instructed, added further to his trouble, he caved in to local pressure.[22]

Then there was the content of the despatch itself. Carnarvon had not only assumed the right to nominate the Cape delegates to the proposed conference; he presumed also to override existing geographical and factional divides in the colony by nominating John Paterson, a leader of the English settlers in certain parts of the colony, and Molteno's greatest rival, to serve as a fellow delegate. Unwisely, in the light of this high-handedness, the despatch also contained one passing reference in the very last paragraph to the idea of confederation. If all went as well as expected, the despatch concluded, the conference might form the basis of a further set of meetings to consider general confederation. This provided the opportunity for Molteno and his supporters to allege that what really lay behind the proposed conference was not a resolution of the Griqualand West and Diamond Fields difficulties, as Froude had pretended, but a secret policy of enforcing a new dominion of South Africa, if necessary by force.[23]

21. Original and printed drafts of the despatch are in TNA CO 48/477; on its reception in the Cape, Goodfellow, *Confederation*, 73–4.
22. Froude to Molteno, 21 June 1875, TNA, 30/6/84, 12–13; Froude to Carnarvon, 22/24 June, TNA 30/6/84, 11; Froude to Barkly, 23, 24 June 1875, TNA 30/6/32, 185–7, 188–9.
23. Goodfellow, *Confederation*, 73–8.

This was strategically shrewd on Molteno's part, in that it allowed him to show the Dutch both in and outside the Cape that he was no pawn of the imperialists. But it was also unfair. There was no secret stratagem: neither Froude nor Carnarvon were planning at this stage to press for a confederation,[24] but it was nonetheless clear that Froude had contributed to this impression in several ways. In several after-dinner speeches made during his first visit he had spoken loosely of a South African nation being formed at some future date under 'your own Confederate flag', and he had urged the English settlers to be sensitive to the needs and fears of their Dutch neighbours.[25] In his enthusiasm for the Boers, moreover, he allowed himself to be convinced that their leading representatives, President Burgers of the Transvaal and President Brand of the Orange Free State, were themselves highly responsive to such ideas. Moreover, his confidence in Dutch attitudes was at least partly responsible for encouraging Carnarvon and the Colonial Office tentatively to raise confederation in the despatch. At the same time, Froude's praise of the Dutch had led many English in the Cape and the other settlements to fear that he would sacrifice their interests in any future confederation, and that therefore any proposal for a closer union that emanated from him was to be greeted with deep suspicion.[26]

In the weeks immediately following his return to the Cape, Froude quickly compounded his unhappy reputation as an irresponsible interloper in South African politics through a second tour of the colonies in which he now undertook to present the Crown's case for the conference directly in opposition to the Cape ministry.[27] His conduct is understandable. There could be no doubt that the intentions of the Colonial Secretary had been grossly and deliberately misrepresented by Molteno; and yet with the outright rejection of the proposal by the Cape parliament, Froude was left with no formal means of rebutting Molteno's allegations, and was given no support from High Commissioner Barkly in his attempts to have the genuinely modest intentions of the imperial government fulfilled. He was obliged, therefore, to find an independent platform on which to put the government's case. Froude's actions provoked outrage in the Cape government: he was denounced by them as acting *ultra vires*, and was represented throughout the region as a deliberate controversialist. Yet his strategy, though costly, was

24. Report of Froude's address in *Cape Argus*, 22 June 1875, cited in Dunn, *Froude*, II, 424–6.
25. Froude to Margaret Froude, 3, 19 December 1874, Dunn, *Froude*, II, 406–12.
26. Extracts from Froude's addresses included in Dunn, *Froude*, II, 413–17.
27. Froude to Carnarvon, 26, 30 June, 3/5, 9, 13 July 1875, TNA 30/6/84, 16–17, 26–9.

by no means ineffective. By the autumn of 1875 his appearances at public meetings and his articles denouncing Molteno in selected opposition papers had promoted such a violent feeling among Molteno's opponents, in which, on occasion, government representatives were heckled and physically assaulted, that genuine concerns began to arise in Molteno's cabinet that Froude might actually succeed in bringing about a secession of the eastern province from the Cape itself. Even in the Dutch settlements within the Cape, he began to be referred to approvingly as 'de Rebel'.[28]

Froude's actions thus had the effect of producing a movement toward compromise in the Cape as both sides began to see the dangers of their mutual antagonism. Aided by Carnarvon's assurances, and the urgings of political moderates such as Saul Solomons, Molteno was persuaded to recall the Cape parliament to reconsider the Colonial Secretary's proposal. Froude was also somewhat discomfited by the success of his popular agitation, and disappointed once more in his expectation that the Dutch states would actually support a conference. Thus he was also in the mood for compromise. In discussions with the opposition he proposed that the conference should now be held not in South Africa at all, but in London. This would give both sides an opportunity for some face-saving, and allow the essence of the proposal to survive unchanged.[29]

At first Froude was confident that, from the point of view of the imperial government, such a compromise would be of cosmetic significance only. He believed he had sufficient support in the assembly to force Molteno either to accept a conference, or resign and hold elections which, it was generally believed, he would lose. But by the time the parliament actually met the distribution of influence had changed. Froude began to realise that the assembly members on whom he most counted were either cooler than he assumed, or insufficiently strong to carry the house with them. Molteno began to shift away from acceptance of the conference idea, and began to threaten that he would continue to defend his actions in the previous session by a further condemnation of the Colonial Secretary. This deeply alarmed Froude, and he was forced into the humiliation of proposing that a vote of censure should be passed on him for his agitation if the condemnation

28. Froude to Carnarvon, 10, 19 September 1875, TNA 30/6/84, 48, 56; C. J. Uys, *In the Era of Shepstone: A Study of British Expansion in South Africa* (Lovedale, SA, 1933), 114–15; Goodfellow, *Confederation*, 83.

29. Froude to Carnarvon, 10, 19, 23 September 1875, TNA 30/6/84, 48, 51, 55–9; Carnarvon to Froude, 12, 13 October, NA 30/6/84, 53–4.

was dropped and Molteno was prepared publicly to state his support for compensation to the Dutch states for the annexations of Griqualand West and the Diamond Fields. This Molteno was prepared to accept. But when Carnarvon's second conciliatory despatch, which ignored the previous mention of confederation and made only the vaguest reference to 'a meeting in this country', was tabled before the assembly, Molteno seized the opportunity to proclaim it as a complete withdrawal (rather than a modification) of the original despatch, and without any further discussion on the second proposed conference, put his motion vindicating his stance to the vote and kept his majority.[30]

This was a more demeaning result for the imperial government than Froude sought to pretend. His own stoical acceptance of public censure was probably genuine, and he was generously supported by Carnarvon in the matter. But it was clear that his role as a significant intermediary between the imperial government and the colonies was fatally damaged, and that, for all his good-will toward them, the leaders of the Dutch states had no confidence in him. He could claim that his crucial objectives had been attained. Cape Colony had agreed to recognise its responsibilities in regard to its territorial disputes with the Dutch, and a conference in which this matter and the equally important issue of development of a common policy toward the management of the native peoples would go ahead after all. On this basis, the original hope that moves toward a closer confederation under the Empire might develop was still, he thought with uncharacteristic optimism, very much alive.[31]

Again, however, the drift of colonial politics was moving hard against him. Originally Froude had assumed that the London conference would take place in the following spring, but a succession of difficulties and the continuing intrigues of Molteno enforced delay. In the meantime, President Brand of the Orange Free State was in London, anxious to secure a resolution of his border disputes with Griqualand West; and Froude, still at the centre of things, achieved the remarkable coup of persuading Brand to drop all further claims to territory in Griqualand and the Diamond Fields for a sum of £3,000 in compensation, to be paid for out of Griqualand's revenues.

---

30. Goodfellow, *Confederation*, 88–9.
31. For a full account of Froude's conduct during his second mission, and his own defence of his proceedings, see *Parliamentary Command Papers, 1876*, no. 1399, esp. Froude's report to Carnarvon, 18 April 1876, no. 59; also Froude to Carnarvon, 14 November 1875, TNA 30/6/84, 87, and 21 April 1876, Carnarvon MSS, British Library Add MSS 60799A, ff.28–9.

This was a significant advance toward closer cooperation, but it was at the same time an obstacle, as the deal had been done in a series of private meetings without reference to the Griqualand leaders, who were not even invited to the conference. Even more seriously, it had been struck without Premier Molteno's knowledge or consent (for which Froude had sacrificed so much in the previous October), and Molteno professed himself to be deeply offended by this further act of imperial high-handedness.[32]

Froude was also partly responsible for creating a second obstacle to Molteno's attendance. While the Colonial Office waited patiently for Molteno to make up his mind, uninvited 'delegates' from the Eastern Province, upon whom Froude had counted so much in his agitation of the previous year, presented themselves at the conference, and Molteno refused to give any decision on his own attendance until their status had been determined. Thus the stalemate continued until, without anyone from the Cape in attendance, and with President Burgers from the Transvaal excluding himself, the conference finally began at the Colonial Office on 3 August 1876.[33] On paper, the priorities outlined by Froude at the beginning of his mission remained in place. The most significant territorial disputes having been resolved, the conference was to concentrate on the development of a co-ordinated policy toward the native Africans either as external tribes or as residents and workers in the British and Dutch states. The actual discussions, however, revealed that there was little real enthusiasm for anything more substantial than an exchange of views on common problems. The issue thus identified by Froude as central to the advance of any form of confederation was calmly shelved. Moreover, Froude's own negligible influence as a contributor to the conference was painfully illustrated when his own favourite plan for the encouragement of 'habits of industry' among the Africans within the colonies by means of a state apprenticeship scheme was deferred until the final session of the conference and then killed by an empty resolution.[34]

The London conference virtually ended Froude's direct engagement with the policy-making process of any aspect of imperial and colonial affairs. Over the following years he continued to correspond frequently with Carnarvon, with his successor, Hicks Beach, and with the Foreign Secretary,

32. Goodfellow, *Confederation*, 97–102.
33. Goodfellow, *Confederation*, 103–10.
34. Froude, 'Memorandum' *c.* August 1876, TNA 30/6/48, 135–61; 'Minutes of the London Conference', August 1876, TNA CO 48/484.

Lord Derby, offering commentary and advice on colonial and foreign policy affairs, and he contributed a number of articles on South Africa in the heavyweight journals.[35] But in the innermost government circles his reputation as a significant colonial adviser was severely damaged. Disraeli unhesitatingly declared his missions to have been a catastrophe,[36] and when in 1877 Froude proposed to accompany Sir Bartle Frere, Barkly's replacement as the new Cape Governor and High Commissioner, on a third mission, Carnarvon politely but firmly declined the offer.[37]

Frere's appointment signalled, in fact, a major departure from the policies advocated by Froude. Against Froude's advice, Carnarvon had already determined upon the annexation of the Transvaal on the ground that the state could no longer maintain its independence in face of a major war with the Zulu chief, Cetawayo.[38] As Froude had warned, the annexation not only deeply antagonised the Dutch in all colonies, but dragged the imperial government into a proliferating series of bloody wars with the African tribes. As the situation deteriorated under Frere's rule, Carnarvon himself resigned suddenly on a matter quite unrelated to colonial policy, and Froude lost any chance of influencing a policy in whose development he had lost all confidence.

II

By the close of the 1870s Froude's disillusionment with direct experience of colonial politics was nearly complete, for he had seen same combination of personal interests, intellectual limitations, and moral weaknesses which had been the bane of contemporary domestic politics all combining in the Cape to ruin a far-seeing vision of future strength, prosperity, and peace. His analysis of events, and the lessons he derived from his experience, was

---

35. See, for example, the several letters from Froude to Carnarvon between 1878 and 1881 concerning South African affairs, in Carnarvon MSS, British Library, Add MSS 60799A and 60799B; to Sir Michael Hicks Beach, 27 December (1879), Hertfordshire Archive and Local Studies, DE/P/F587, 22; and in Derby MSS in the Liverpool Record Office. Froude's major published interventions are listed in n. 39 below.
36. Disraeli to Lady Bradford, 27 September 1878, in The Marquis of Zetland (ed.), *Letters of Disraeli to Lady Bradford and Lady Chesterfield* (London, 1929), 189; *Notes by Sir Bartle Frere on Mr Froude's Article in the 'Fortnightly Review'*, Colonial Office Papers, African, No. 212, February 1880.
37. Carnarvon to Froude, 5 January 1877, TNA 30/6/43, 347.
38. Now better known as Cetshwayo kaMpande.

expressed in a number of carefully considered articles and lectures which he published in 1879 and 1880.[39] The narrow self–interest of colonial politicians, such as Molteno, the weaknesses of some colonial administrators, such as Barkly, the brutality of others, such as Shepstone and Frere, the ambition and greed of others, such as Southey, the short-sighted suspicion of the Boer leadership and the timidity of the Colonial Office each played their part, Froude argued, in the sabotaging of a great enterprise. But behind it all, cultivating and accentuating each of these human vices, was, he continued, the dysfunctional political system in which all the players moved. The granting of responsible government to the Cape in 1872 had been the cause of so much mischief in South Africa, its operation at once stifling the freedom of the colony's most able politicians and administrators. Worse, it had stimulated the centrifugal tendencies of the settlements, intensifying the drive for entrepreneurial territorial expansion and encouraging even the smallest units to seek the autonomy it promised.

Not least among its mischiefs, Froude added, had been the opportunity it afforded for the enforcement of policies toward the native Africans that were favourable to the territorial interests and labour needs of the colonies and altogether independent of the protective and humanitarian concerns of the imperial government. But it was, after all, the imperial government which had brought such evils upon itself—first by the long-term neglect of the settlements, and then by the imposition of responsible government, when there had been no serious demand for it, simply to satisfy the precepts of liberal political economy. Finally, when the worst consequences of such irresponsibility and neglect had become apparent, the same home governments had proved themselves incapable of maintaining their resolution in face of opposition in the colonies and criticism at home. Confronted with such combined resistance in the colonial and imperial parliaments, the government had lost control over developments in the Cape completely. It could not save itself from becoming involved in a costly, bloody, and shameful war with the Basuto, the Swazi, and finally the Zulu, which served no interests other than those of the Dutch and rogue English speculators. It was not even capable of lending official support to the cherished

39. Froude's major published interventions are 'English Policy in South Africa', *Quarterly Review*, 143 (January 1877), 107–45; 'South Africa Once More', *Fortnightly Review*, 26 (October 1879), 449–73; 'Leaves from a South African Journal', *Short Studies*, III, 476–558; *Two Lectures on South Africa* (London, 1880).

scheme for state-sponsored child emigration for which Froude had so long fought.[40]

There was some self-exculpation in this account. It neglected, of course, Froude's own contribution to the debâcle, ignoring the manner in which he had dismissed the Colonial Office's caution in regard to initiatives from the metropolis, and discounting his serious misinterpretation of the attitude of the Cape's British politicians in mistaking their speculative and conditional openness toward confederation as support for imperial intervention. Even more seriously, it failed to notice the extent to which his uncritical admiration of the Boer farmers as the last representatives on earth of the Reformation spirit blinded him at once to the political stratagems of their leaders, all of whom in turn disappointed his expectations, and to the brutal manner in which they exploited the native people among whom they had established their settlements.

If Froude was unwilling to acknowledge such misjudgements, he was even less willing to confront other deeper contradictions which lay unresolved at the heart of his own imperial thinking. Though he shared with Carlyle and all the other upholders of republican virtue a contempt for party politics, his own active intervention in the debate, his association with Carnarvon, and his frequently expressed condemnation of Liberal colonial policy had inevitably made him a partisan.[41] While he made some efforts to be even-handed, however, his first public statements and essays on South Africa after his return in 1875 were little short of political propaganda on behalf of Carnarvon. More seriously, while at the Cape he had himself become shamelessly embroiled in local politics. His public appearances on his second tour were in effect a one-man political campaign against the sitting administration, and even before that he had assiduously courted the principal opposition leaders to Molteno's government at the Cape to place pressure on the Prime Minister.[42]

Froude's exploitation of party interests at the Cape represented more than a personal inconsistency between precept and practice. In contradicting the moral purposes for which, by his own account, the cultivation of the colonies was most greatly to be prized, it ran even deeper. For Froude, the

---

40. The injustices perpetrated against the Zulus and the Basuto are especially emphasised in 'South Africa Once More'.
41. On Froude's 'imperial republicanism', see Duncan Bell, 'Republican Imperialism: J. A. Froude and the Virtue of Empire', *History of Political Thought*, 30 (2009), 166–91.
42. See the reports in *Parliamentary Command Papers*, 1876, No. 1399.

development of an active colonial policy and the nurturing of concern for the colonies' welfare was to be assumed by Britain not primarily for immediate economic or strategic advantages, but as a mode of regenerating the entire culture of the British people, saving them from the worst consequences of social and economic changes in the homeland itself. A sharing of burdens and a fusion of interest which might in the short term involve benefactions and even sacrifices on all sides would result in the longer term in a deeper sense of unity and purpose across the British Empire. In playing the party game at the Cape and in London, Froude might have argued that the means was justified by the end. But on the record of his own performance he could hardly have claimed that the end of altruistic non-partisanship had been much advanced, or have denied indeed that its opposite had not been significantly reinforced.

The moral ambiguities underlying Froude's practice were further illustrated by two quite separate issues. The first concerned imperial defence. In his early writings, strategic issues had featured little; but once he had become involved in South Africa, the maintenance of the military and naval base at Simonstown Bay had immediately assumed the greatest importance for him (even greater, indeed, than it had for the permanent officials at the Colonial Office). At first it was the guarantee of this strategic necessity that Froude used to justify his strongly conciliatory attitude toward the Boers; but as the mission collapsed, it was to this old-fashioned, Hobbesian, and far from regenerative, priority that Froude held to as the fundamental aim of British policy in the region. *In extremis* he was even ready to envisage the abandonment of the whole of the British settlements in order to preserve it.[43]

An even more serious ambiguity arose in regard to Froude's attitude toward the Xhosa, the native peoples of Southern Africa, or 'the kaffirs', as he, in company with most other white observers, habitually referred to them. On two occasions Froude led a delegation of the Aborigines' Protection Society to the Colonial Office, protesting against the abuses perpetrated against the Zulu and the Basuto in the imperial territories.[44] He also argued strongly (if condescendingly) in favour of eventual integration:

43. Froude to Herbert, 9 July 1874, TNA 30/6/48, 3–21; Froude to Carnarvon, 15 January 1877, Add MS 60799A, f.67; Froude's 'Memorandum', *c.* August 1876, TNA 30/6/48, 135–61; Froude to General Bisset, 13 July (1877), Froude MSS, Duke University, Special Collections Library: 'Let England keep the Table Mountain perimeter, the only part of the country which is of imperial service, and let the rest take its chance.'
44. *The Times*, 28 May, 28 June, 19 November 1880.

The eagle will not breed in the cage. It may be the same with the wild races, to whom civilisation means captivity. It may be so, but we do not know that it is; for the attempt to civilize them has never been fairly made. The first result of contact has been too often to poison them with our worst vices, when at once they begin to die off. But be the case as it may with the Redskin and the Australian, it is certainly not so with the Negro. The Negro multiplies beside the white man. He can learn trades and handicrafts; he is the best of servants; he is faithful, brave and, in his natural state, honourable and true. The white man has risen to his present state of superiority through a hundred generations of cultivation; the Negro has not been cultivated at all; and what latent capacity may be in him is as yet uncertain. If we are to justify the violence by which we have become the[ir] masters ... we must do it by setting ourselves with all our energy to try whether they are capable of becoming civilised men. It is the least which they deserve at our hands.[45]

The argument that Froude advances here is tentative and conditional, but his comments at least show little sign of racist determinism. He was, however, addressing himself to the largely liberal readership of the *Fortnightly Review*, and before other audiences Froude could adopt a different tone. Addressing a dinner of 'merchants and other gentlemen connected with South Africa' in March 1875, Froude declared that the Zulus within the colonies were 'not an indigenous race and had no aboriginal claim on the land they occupied', but were 'a conquering race who had come south because they were driven thence by their stronger fellows. He was not and never had been an enthusiastic sympathiser with those who dwelt on the excessive wrongs in these latter days of the black races (Hear, hear).' The settlers of Natal were not to be blamed for the atrocities committed against the Zulu (which he was fulsomely to condemn in the *Fortnightly*), 'any more than people were to blame for typhus fever breaking out in their houses when the drains were out of order. These things must happen as a fire-damp must accumulate in an unventilated coal mine.'[46] While he was in the Cape itself he had urged Carnarvon to consider the case of following the Boer method of 'native management' by forced labour with such enthusiasm that

---

45. 'South Africa Once More', 455.
46. 'Mr Froude on South Africa', *The Times*, 22 March 1875, 12. Froude's comments on 'kaffirs' and 'niggers' during his missions to the Cape also jar uncomfortably with his later professions; see Froude to Margaret Froude, 3 December 1874: 'Why is it that some people are so crazy about niggers that while what would be a crime in other people appears in them a pretty sort of playfulness', Dunn, *Froude*, II, 408–9; and for contemporary witness of his attitude, Mrs Saul Solomon to Miss Robina Thomson, 25 March 1875, quoted in Solomon, *Saul Solomon*, 179–80.

even Carnarvon was concerned that he was advocating the re-establishment of slavery by another means.[47]

It is perhaps impossible to determine which of Froude's voices is the genuine one, though his private comments are perhaps a closer and more disturbing indication of his underlying attitudes.[48] But it is clear that, whether he was condemning or condoning English colonials' dealings with Africans, his position was related closely to a far more consistent theme in his position: the defence of the Boers.

Even more than the Africans, the Boers, in Froude's account, had been shamefully treated both by the English colonists and the Colonial Office. They had been cheated of their independence, land they had settled had been taken from them, treaties made with them had been broken, they were exposed to exploitation by unscrupulous British traders and prospectors, and they had been regarded by colonists and metropolitans alike as little better than savages.[49] Froude believed that a revolution in English attitudes toward the Boers was urgent. All outstanding border disputes (and there were several) should be immediately settled on terms favourable to them, and Boer policy toward the Africans within their territories which entailed the refusal of all political and most civil rights, and the imposition of forced labour, should no longer be threatened by reformist and humanitarian interventions by the imperial government.[50] Froude's primary purpose in this was diplomatic and strategic. He was keenly aware of the deep antagonism toward Britain which existed in the quasi-independent Boer territories and even in Cape Colony itself toward England. He feared that should another European power ever seek to meddle in South Africa, it would find ready allies in the Dutch, and Britain's vital control of the straits might be lost. More immediately, he was concerned that it might lead to a movement for independence within Cape Colony and the abandonment of the substantial English community there. It was such considerations that shaped Froude's ambivalent attitude toward confederation: highly desirable if it were organised within the Empire, with the Dutch (suitably appeased by

---

47. Carnarvon's notes on Froude to Carnarvon, 23 September, 4 October 1874, TNA 30/6/49, 111, 117; Carnarvon to Froude, 2 September 1875, TNA 30/6/84, 37.

48. See, for example, Froude to Sir Garnett Wolseley (n.d., 1892/4): 'Niggers multiply when they are not allowed to kill each other,' Hove Central Library, Brighton, Wolseley MSS, M3/1/47.

49. 'English Policy in South Africa' *Quarterly Review*, 143 (January, 1877), 105–45; *Two Lectures on South Africa* (London, 1880), 50–64; 'Leaves from a South African Journal', in *Short Studies*, III, 497–8.

50. *Short Studies*, III, 493–4.

concessions on land and labour) included as willing subjects, but insupportable on any other grounds. And it was such thinking that characterised his opinions on the treatment of the Africans. Though there is no reason to doubt the sincerity of Froude's indignation and distress over the oppressions and cruelties suffered by black people at the hands of the colonists, English and Dutch, the manner in which it was to be addressed was likewise of a conditional character. To the extent that an undischarged moral responsibility served as a means of energising British public opinion to support a more interventionist colonial policy, then it must be given primary emphasis; but insofar as humanitarian criticisms of the way in which they treated black workers further alienated the Boers, the urgency of the issue might be correspondingly diminished.

The broader implications of such unresolved and inconsistent attitudes toward the status and destiny of peoples whom he considered to be ethnically and culturally inferior are deeply troubling. Did the end of contributing to England's moral regeneration really justify the manipulation of moral issues in regard to other as yet 'uncivilised' peoples? How would the colonial strategy he had espoused as a means of bringing about such renewal function in circumstances where these peoples refused to be 'civilised'?

These were the risks attendant on Froude's plunge into political agitation, and which he seemed unable to address. Mercifully for him, however, the ethically fraught nature of his position was for the moment occluded by his share in the unexpected success of another avenue of political agitation which occurred even as he was fighting for a British South Africa. This was the rapid emergence, and rapid resolution, of the Bulgarian crisis.

III

The crisis that arose in British domestic politics between the summers of 1876 and 1878 was the consequence of the government's response to the Ottoman Empire's savage suppression of several insurrections which had occurred in its Slavic European provinces—most notably in Bulgaria.[51] Concerned by the prospect of progressive destabilisation throughout the Balkans should Russia chose to intervene independently on the side of

---

51. Richard Milman, *Britain and the Eastern Question, 1875–8* (Oxford, 1979).

brother Slavs, Bismarck and Andrassy, the German and Austrian ministers, sought to establish a united front under which a list of concessions to the Balkan provinces would be demanded from the Turks, underpinned by the threat of an agreed Russian intervention. This moderate, united approach was deeply mistrusted by the British Prime Minister, Disraeli—in part because it was an alliance from which Britain had been excluded, and in part because he wished to perpetuate 'the Crimean system' of containing Russia and protecting the Ottoman Empire which Britain had established at so much cost after 1856. Disraeli's refusal to support the new alliance, however, had the unexpected effect of encouraging the Turks to further acts of suppression and atrocity, and of compelling the Russians to go to war with the assent of the Germans and Austrians early in 1877.

By then, 'the Bulgarian atrocities' had provoked an unprecedented popular campaign of protest in Britain itself. The rapid success of the Russians and their imposition of an altogether more severe set of terms than had originally been agreed provided the opportunity for another grand European conference at Berlin in July 1878, at which Disraeli was able to escape from the ill-consequence of his misguided policy by claiming, quite without foundation, to have been the architect of this 'peace with honour'. In the meantime, however, he had been responsible for the forging of a wide and extraordinarily diverse coalition of ideological and political interests in union against him.[52]

Froude's participation in the debate, despite his current links with the Tory government, is not entirely surprising, for his credentials as a defender of Russia were particularly sound. In the mid-1850s he had been one of a very small group of public commentators who had stood out in opposition against the Crimean War. He had published in the *Westminster* a series of provocative articles denouncing Russophobia, and suggesting that since the other European powers were capable neither of destroying Russia nor of replacing her as the representative of European civilisation in the East, they had better defend rather than attack her.[53] But as the anti-Turkish campaign developed, Froude, who was still engaged in his South African negotiations, remained aloof. 'Violent passions which rise suddenly', he assured Lady Derby (wife of Disraeli's Foreign Secretary), 'generally sink as fast if there is no reason for them. It is impossible that the people will fail to recollect in a

52. R.T. Shannon, *Gladstone and the Bulgarian Agitation, 1876* (Hassocks, 1976).
53. See especially 'The Four Empires', *Westminster Review*, 68 (October 1857), 415–40.

little while that the reticence of which they complain is under the circumstances inevitable.'[54] At this stage he approved of the Prime Minister's refusal
to join the European alliance, and his first public intervention was a short
letter to *The Times* suggesting that the best thing the opposition might do
was to let the government carry on with its own policy.[55]

By the end of the year, however, as the failure of the South African conference was beginning to become plain, and as the Turkish repressions continued, he began to change his mind. He attended the great 'National
Conference on the Eastern Question', where he shared a platform with his
great literary enemy Freeman and his even greater *bête noire*, Gladstone himself. And he spoke. Britain, he feared, would be responsible for the loss of
one of the greatest opportunities 'to bring the Turk to his senses'.[56] This was
a temperate statement. But once Russia went to war, he was, in his private
correspondence, unqualified in defence of its actions. His public interventions, however, remained few. His one substantial contribution lay in the
encouragement and support that he lent to Olga Novikoff, a formidable
Russian of minor aristocratic status who was touring Britain on a personal
mission to explain Russia's aims and intentions, and he supplied a supportive preface to Madame Novikoff's pamphlet *Is Russia Wrong?* which appeared
at the close of 1877.[57]

Froude's discomfiture in entering once again the lists of political controversy may in part be attributed to his dislike of openly opposing a Tory
administration with which he had so recently been closely associated. The
indignity of occasionally being associated in public with Gladstone was
doubtless a consideration, particularly because he professed disgust with the
way in which Gladstone, having been initially cool toward the question of
international intervention, suddenly became an ardent advocate once he
espied the political advantage to be derived from it.[58] Reservation may also
have been prompted by awareness of some clear inconsistencies in his position. In supporting rebels against their legitimate government he was flying
in the face of principles which he had strongly expressed in regard to political obligations elsewhere—most particularly in regard to Ireland. In addition, his support for Russia's pan-Slavic intervention brought him close to

54. Froude to Lady Derby, 11 September 1876, Dunn, *Froude*, II, 447–8.
55. *The Times*, 3 January 1876.
56. *The Times*, 1 June 1877.
57. Olga Novikoff, *Is Russia Wrong?* (London, 1877), vi–xiv. The preface was regarded by Madame
    Novikoff and some of her friends as cold and disappointing.
58. Shannon, *Gladstone*, esp., 222–3.

endorsing the right of the United States to interfere on behalf of the oppressed relations of Irish-Americans in the home country.

From such considerations Froude's restrained involvement in the Bulgarian agitation arose. Yet his reservations notwithstanding, the remarkable outcome of the agitation had the effect of significantly restoring his belief in the possibility of resuming public action, if only in a revised version of the indirect manner in which he had sought to influence political opinion before his painful fall into actual politics. Though initially sceptical about the effect of the public agitation on Disraeli's policy, and resigned to the workings of 'jingoism', by the end of 1877 Froude had become agreeably surprised. Public refusal to rise to Disraeli's appeals encouraged him, and gradually he had begun to see (what later historians have confirmed) the significance of the agitation as a watershed in the emergence of a new form of political activity representing a newly empowered electorate. His voice thus gained in confidence. 'Happily', he wrote in the preface to Novikoff's pamphlet, 'there is a power which is stronger than even parliamentary majorities—in public opinion; and public opinion has, I trust, already decided that English bayonets shall not be stained in defence of Turkish tyranny.'[59]

Froude, however, was no zealous convert. He remained suspicious and pessimistic about the consequences of impending democracy. At the end of the campaign he wrote sneeringly to Novikoff about the self-satisfaction of popular opinion: 'We think that it is all settled; and that We have settled it.' He expected that public opinion would have forgotten all about it in a month.[60] But the extraordinary uprising of sentiment against war with Russia, so different to the war-mongering of the 1850s, had nevertheless to be registered. His briefly renewed association with radicalism, epitomised in his brief but successful collaboration with that radical tribune of the people W. T. Stead, was also, especially in the circumstances of his increasingly obvious failure in the corridors of power, encouraging.[61] The coming democracy, it appeared, for all it awful eventualities, brought with it at least the possibility that a new form of political argument equally distant from the demagoguery of the street orators and the cynical manipulations of party organisers might yet be made effective. The experience thus served to

59. *Is Russia Wrong?*, xiii–xiv.
60. Extracted in W. T Stead, *The MP for Russia* (London, 1909), I, 535–6.
61. J. O. Baylen and Gerald Walsh (eds.), 'The Froude–Stead correspondence', *Huntington Library Quarterly*, 30 (1967), 167–83.

encourage Froude in the view that, despite the slow progress being recorded in regard to Ireland and South Africa, direct political engagement might still be refused, and that a rhetoric more popular and less intellectually demanding than the detailed historical writing and dense philosophical argument toward which he had been moving since 1870 was after all worth persisting with. Whatever the risks, he felt willing to take them.

II

Heroes and Historical Change in the Modern and Ancient Worlds, 1871–80

Froude's intense engagement with politics and with political agitation in the 1870s did not result in any significant diminution of his literary and historical output. On the contrary, between the early 1870s and the early 1880s, when his work upon the great biography of Carlyle began to preoccupy him, Froude published more than twenty lengthy articles, three substantial books, one collection of public lectures, and a selected edition of his essays in the third instalment of *Short Studies on Great Subjects*.[1] Within this mass of material no distinct theme is immediately obvious. About a third—one book and seven articles—is devoted to a study of the late Roman Republic and early imperial Rome, and about two-thirds to historical and literary studies of late medieval and early modern England. But one characteristic is clear: most are concerned with the lives or the works of particular individuals—some of them, but by no means all, recognisable as 'great'. The books are studies of Thomas Becket, Julius Caesar, and John Bunyan, while several essays are devoted to an examination of such well-known classical figures as Augustus and Cicero, and less well-known such as Lucian, Euripides, Celsus, and Alexander of Abonotichus. From this it might be easy to conclude that there is nothing more of interest here than another instance of the typical Victorian—or Carlylean—preoccupation with the doings of great men. But a closer examination of Froude's selection of 'lives' uncovers more interesting currents.

---

1. The third series of *Short Studies* was published by Longmans in 1877.

I

Froude's study of Thomas Becket, serialised in the *The Nineteenth Century* in 1877 and published in book form in the following year, is a case in point.[2] Given his attraction to the lives of great men, and his especial respect for martyrs, Catholic and Protestant, it might have been expected that Froude's sympathies would lie with the murdered archbishop. But, much to the surprise of many readers and the indignation of some reviewers, *The Life and Times of Thomas Becket* is an unrelieved polemic against the reputation of the saint in which Froude emphasises the continuity of his subject's principal characteristics despite his apparently Pauline conversion. Discounting the martyred saint's principal hagiographers, Froude cites John of Salisbury's description of Becket while Lord Chancellor as 'a magnificent trifler, a scorner of law and the clergy, and given to scurrilous jesting at laymen's parties'. There was no change: Becket remained, Froude contends, as he had been in his disreputable youth, an ambitious, aggressive, courageous, and wilful spirit:

> He was still the self-willed violent chancellor with the dress of the saint upon him but not the nature. His cause was not the mission of the Church, but the privilege of the Church to control the civil government and dictate the law in virtue of magical powers which we now know to have been a dream and a delusion.[3]

Though his stand against Henry II was personally brave, it was made, Froude claimed, in a wider context of enormous abuses and even crimes being perpetrated by the English clergy against the king's long-suffering subjects which the archbishop chose to ignore. It was, moreover, not untouched by a kind of personal vanity which also underlay his well-known ascetic and pious practices, and indeed the very manner of his martyrdom. Even worse, that martyrdom served only to perpetuate clerical exploitation of popular fears and superstitions through the absurd and meretricious cult of St Thomas the healer and miracle-worker which proliferated over the next four centuries.[4]

It was not difficult for readers and critics to see the analogy that was being implicitly suggested. Here in the twelfth century was an anticipation

---

2. 'Life and Times of Thomas Becket', *Nineteenth Century*, 40 (June–November 1877), reprinted in *Short Studies*, IV, 1–230, to which reference is made here.
3. *Short Studies*, IV, 29, 153.
4. *Short Studies*, IV, 177–202.

of another great struggle between church and state, between another Henry and another martyred Thomas that was to take place—with, as Froude had so trenchantly demonstrated elsewhere, a very different outcome—four centuries later. Froude's obvious parallel irritated critics, and provoked the fury of his old enemy, Freeman, who went as far as to insinuate that the work had been a sneaky revenge on the ghost of Froude's brother Hurrell, who had been an avid proponent of the revival of the cult of St Thomas.[5] Freeman's invective struck home on this occasion, and Froude, who had largely ignored Freeman's virulent attacks on his *History of England*, was driven to defend himself with a further supply of documentary evidence in support of his case and with a dignified denial of Freeman's nasty imputations.[6] In this critical spat, Froude, by the manner of his reply, appeared to have won the sympathy of the majority of those interested.[7] But amidst the storm a further inconsistency which might have thrown light on Froude's other intentions in writing about Becket was ignored.

Several years earlier, in an essay for *Fraser's*, Froude had provided a sketch of St Hugo of Avalon—another twelfth-century priest who, like Becket, was an energetic ecclesiastic, jealous of the rights of his church and of his powers as Bishop of Lincoln.[8] As with Becket, his stance had placed him in opposition to Henry II, who, as in the case of Becket, had been instrumental to his elevation to the episcopal bench; and, again like Becket, St Hugo openly defied his patron on more than one occasion. After his death, moreover, his doings and sayings were preserved in an elaborate body of hagiography which became the basis of his popular recognition as a saint. But despite these obvious similarities, Froude's sketch of St Hugo was, in contrast to his polemic against Becket, warmly sympathetic; and far from dismissing the hagiographical materials surrounding him as mere superstitions, Froude exploited them to the full as the basis of his own highly positive account.

This, as Freeman might have contended, was just another of Froude's inconsistencies spawned by his reckless opportunism. But that Froude

---

5. E. A. Freeman, 'Mr Froude's "Life and Times of Thomas Becket"', *Contemporary Review*, 31 (March 1878), 821–42; 32 (April–June 1878), 116–39, 474–500; 33 (September 1878), 213–41. Froude's 'Becket' also received a very hostile review in *Dublin Review*, 30 (April, 1878), 292–327.

6. Froude, 'A Few Words on Mr Freeman', *Nineteenth Century*, 5 (April, 1879), 618–37; E. A. Freeman, 'Last Words on Mr Froude', *Contemporary Review*, 35 (May 1879), 214–36.

7. Ian Hesketh, *The Science of History in Victorian Britain*, 90–1.

8. 'A Bishop of the Twelfth Century', *Fraser's Magazine*, NS 1 (February 1870), reprinted in *Short Studies*, II, 60–100.

himself saw no inconsistency of treatment is evident from his decision to select both for inclusion in successive volumes of his *Short Studies on Great Subjects*. Closer examination reveals that to Froude, despite their superficial similarities which have been reinforced by retrospect, St Hugo and St Thomas actually represented two profoundly different historical types, occupying two closely adjacent but very different historical epochs. St Hugo came to England and assumed episcopal office more than a decade after Becket's murder, and so became active in the conditions determined by that terrible event. In working within these post-traumatic circumstances, his special traits of character were of inestimable value. Though steadfast in his defence of the rights of the church, he was also moderate, and ever open to reconciliation, first with Henry, then with Richard his successor, and even with the egregious King John. Unimpeachably pious, he was also humane, careful of his tenants and loyal to his monarch. He not only represented the best of the old Catholic Church that was later to be drowned amidst the coming conflict between church and state, but also, by his conduct and his sainted memory, he discharged a vital role in deferring that confrontation.[9]

In this lay his fundamental difference with his near-contemporary. Becket, though personally brave and clear-headed about the objectives for which he was fighting, was nevertheless the premature harbinger of that new world of struggle for supremacy in which the principal victims would be the poor folk, pawns of both princes and prelates, and ultimately the church itself. The epoch whose formation he was struggling to establish was unworthy of his courage and commitment, and the subsequent degeneration of his memory in the excesses of the cult of Canterbury was a terrible retribution for his historical misjudgement. From this implicit but clear contrast between the two figures, a more subtle element in Froude's understanding of historical greatness and of the emergence of 'great men' can be seen. Froude's great men were not Emerson's 'Representative Men'—individuals who embodied the most progressive forces of their own time.[10] Nor were they, as Carlyle's heroes were too often (mis)understood to be, powerful figures who laid hold of history's currents and reshaped them according to their will. They were, strictly, *re-formers*. Gifted not only with the ability of seeing back through the warped and faded cultural formulae of their times to the

9. *Short Studies*, II, 92–100.
10. Froude, 'Representative Men', *Eclectic Review*, 95 (1852), 568–82; reprinted in *Short Studies*, I, 576–601.

eternal truths that those formulae so weakly projected, they were also capable, by the force of their words and actions, of reformulating those truths
into modes of living that were fresh and charged with renewed energy. In
times of great historical crisis they appeared in the form of a Luther or a
Knox, but in other times what appeared to be similar characteristics such as
those embodied by Becket led only to failure, suffering, and neglect; while
the moderate, restorative qualities of a Hugo were the truly positive forces
in history.[11]

It was this concern to explore intimations of the human potential for
greatness in periods other than those of great epochal crisis that also lay
behind Froude's short book on *Bunyan* which he contributed to John
Morley's 'English Men of Letters' series.[12] Though his study did not appear
until 1880, Bunyan had been a central figure in Froude's intellectual and
psychological formation. A reading of *The Pilgrim's Progress* had been of
crucial importance in his recovery from the traumas of childhood; and
Christian's sufferings, temptations, and triumphs had been echoed repeatedly in his early fiction. In the early 1860s he had diverted himself from his
History of England to publish a heavily annotated edition of William Thomas's
The Pilgrim—not merely to employ it in defence of his interpretation, but
also to introduce it as a sixteenth-century anticipation of this great text of
English Protestant literature.[13] And the Pilgrim's journey is a principal
organising trope of Froude's late autobiography.

In *Bunyan*, however, Froude advanced an interpretation of his hero that was
in several respects idiosyncratic, controversial, and far from uncritical.[14] In
biographical terms alone, Froude took issue with orthodox opinion. In
addressing, for example, Bunyan's adolescent crisis—his haunting by demons

11. Froude's unchanging view of Luther is restated in this period in his essay in *Contemporary Review*, 44 (July–August 1883), 1–18, 183–202; reprinted as *Luther: A Short Biography* (London, 1884).
12. First published in 1880, the book went though several reprints in the 1880s and 1890s and was issued in a popular Pocket edition in 1909. It is to this most readily available edition that sub-sequent references are made.
13. William Thomas, *The Pilgrim: A Dialogue on the Life and Actions of Henry VIII* (ed. and with an introduction by J. A. Froude, London, 1861). On Froude's discovery of the text and his sense of its importance, see Froude to Mr Dean, 13 March (1860/61), Froude MSS, Duke University, Special Collections Library.
14. For surveys of Bunyan's reputation in the nineteenth century, see C. S. Finley, 'Bunyan among the Victorians: Macaulay, Froude, Ruskin', in *Literature and Theology*, 3 (1989), 77–94, and Emma Mason, 'The Victorians and Bunyan's Legacy' in Anne Dunan-Page (ed.), *The Cambridge Companion to Bunyan* (Cambridge, 2010), 150–61. For another discussion specifically on Froude's work, see Frans Korstens, 'Froude and Bunyan', *Neophilologus*, 77 (1973), 489–97.

and his acute conviction that he was destined for eternal damnation—which had conventionally been seen as evidence of a precocious spiritual vision, Froude, who knew enough himself about childhood terrors, preferred to favour routinely psychological causes. It was not a foretelling of saintliness to come, and Bunyan's persistent belief in the Devil as a personal force of evil in the world was, though understandable in his time, naïve.[15] Froude likewise challenged convention—and even Carlyle—in opposing the supposition that at the siege of Bedford in 1643 Bunyan had fought with the Roundheads: the evidence, if it suggested anything at all, indicated that he may actually have sided with the Royalists (though modern scholarship has proved him wrong).[16] Again Froude dealt brusquely with suppositions of Bunyan's suffering during his long confinement in the 1660s. There is no evidence to suggest that his conditions were particularly severe. He could have secured his release at any time by an undertaking to cease public preaching, and the authorities were glad to be shot of him. Finally, he did not end his days, as was so often assumed, under the shadow of renewed persecution, but died unmolested in his bed.

More significant than these revisionist biographical contentions was Froude's openly expressed distaste for several aspects of Bunyan's theological understanding, and in particular for his austere view of predestination that enabled him to regard with equanimity the consignment of the majority of humankind—including innocent children—to eternal damnation. He cites Bunyan on instructing young children in prayer:

> The better way [is] for people to tell their children betimes [early] what cursed creatures they are and how they are under the wrath of God by reason and actual sin; also to tell them the nature of God's wrath and the duration of misery ... The way that men learn to pray is by conviction of sin, and this is the way to make our 'sweet babes' do so too.[17]

This is too much for Froude, who comments caustically:

> 'Sweet babes' is unworthy of Bunyan. There is little sweetness in a state of things as stern as he conceives. He might have considered too that there was a danger of making children unreal in another and worse sense by teaching them doctrines which neither child nor man can comprehend. It may be true that a single sin may consign me to everlasting hell, but I cannot be made to acknowledge the justice of it.[18]

15. *Bunyan*, 3–6.
16. R. L. Greaves, 'John Bunyan', *Oxford Dictionary of National Biography*.
17. *Bunyan*, 59.   18. *Bunyan*, 59.

Bunyan's notion of an angry God was not only callous, it was philosoph-ically confused, in its suggestion that divine anger could be justified only in cases where there is deliberate misuse of free will:

> It is senseless and extravagant when pronounced against actions which men cannot help, when the faulty action is the necessary consequence of their nature, and the penalty the necessary consequence of the action.[19]

It is this metaphysical and theological naïvety which, according to Froude, vitiates so much of Bunyan's literary work. Thus Froude's judgement on Bunyan's *Holy War*—an allegory which had been composed long after the achievement of *Pilgrim's Progress*—is entirely negative. The attempt to use the myth of the great conflict between God and Lucifer as a means of mag-nitude of the struggle taking place in Creation had defeated even the sophis-ticated and metaphysically well-informed imagination of Milton. In Bunyan it produced total failure. Similarly, and more controversially, Froude dis-missed the entire second part of *Pilgrim's Progress* in a single paragraph as 'but a feeble reverberation of the first', shrouded 'in a tone of sentiment that is almost mawkish' and unworthy of the reader's attention.[20]

After all this it might reasonably be asked what it was that enabled Froude still to claim Bunyan as a figure of genuine greatness. For Froude, however, it was precisely in the fact that he appeared so thoroughly to embody the characteristic deficiencies of his particular historical culture (which we with gift of hindsight can so easily discern) and yet succeeded so supremely in transcending them as to communicate his essential vision to countless gen-erations that came after him that Bunyan's true historical significance lay.

This was in some part, Froude argues, because, for all the narrowness of his theology and the bleakness of his eschatology, his sensibility was profoundly humane, and it was this characteristic which kept 'his genius ... fresh and vigorous under the least promising conditions'.[21] Like Luther and St Hugo, he had a warm sense of humour, a genuine humility, and, despite the stric-tures to which his brand of theology had driven him to apply, he had, like both, a genuine and deeply felt affection for children. Thus having condemned

19. *Bunyan*, 59. Froude's considerably more sophisticated view of the challenges posed to free will by necessity and deficiency are discussed in chs. 4 and 5 above. The classic statement of his philosophical position is in his 'Spinoza', *Westminster Review*, OS 64 (July 1855); reprinted in *Short Studies*, I, 339–400.
20. *Bunyan*, 171.
21. *Bunyan*, 91.

Bunyan's abandonment of the 'sweet babes', Froude then goes on to quote approvingly from a sermon on the duties of parents:

> I tell you that if parents carry [their duties] lovingly towards their children, mixing their mercies with loving rebukes, and their loving rebukes with fatherly and motherly compassions, they are more likely to save their children than by being churlish and severe to them.[22]

'Whole volumes on education have said less', comments Froude, 'than these simple words. Unfortunately parents do not read Bunyan. He is left to children.' Moreover, Bunyan's Pilgrim 'though in a Puritan dress, is a genuine man. His experience is so truly human experience' that Christians and non-believers alike 'can recognize familiar footprints in Christian's journey'.[23]

Human warmth was not Bunyan's sole distinction. He was, 'though he disclaimed the name', a poet in every sense of the word. Thus, even as he dismissed certain of Bunyan's texts that had been commended by orthodoxy, Froude advanced a strong defence of his verse, conventionally discounted as doggerel, claiming that at its best it was as successful in its purpose 'as the best lines of [Francis] Quarles or George Herbert'.[24] It was this artistic talent that informed his best work, regardless of its crudely didactic intent. Thus *The Life and Death of Mr Badman* succeeds beyond its immediate purpose as a cautionary tale through several deft touches: its acute observation of life among the middling sort in a small English town, its Defoe-like creation of a detailed sense of individuality and experienced reality from entirely fictional materials, and its finely judged conclusion which makes the eternal fate of Mr Badman all the more terrible by the unremarkable manner of his passing away. And it is the supreme but hidden artistry of *The Pilgrim's Progress* that invests this simple allegory with such deep and universal resonances that no readers, whatever their own theological or philosophical position, will fail to be moved by the experience of reading it.

Yet, no less than his humanity, his sheer artistry provided insufficient grounds for Bunyan's greatness. Rather, it was the purposes to which in his hands both were put to serve. It was through his imagination that Bunyan saw through the limiting forms of his particular epoch to the eternal questions which in all ages and amidst the ever-changing circumstances of existence all sentient beings must confront:

22. *Bunyan*, 62.   23. *Bunyan*, 154–5.   24. *Bunyan*, 92–3.

What am I? What is this world in which I appear and disappear like a bubble?
Who made me? And what am I to do?[25]

As we have seen, these are the same questions that are posed by Froude's
other heroes, fictional and historical, and the recognition of their centrality
and a dedication to answering them is, for Froude, the necessary criterion
for admittance into the small pantheon of exceptional human creatures.[26]
This, he concludes, Bunyan achieved fleetingly and uncertainly in his verse
and other prose writings, but completely in *Pilgrim's Progress*:

> *Pilgrim's Progress* is and will remain unique of its kind—an imperishable mon-
> ument of the form in which the problem [of understanding man's place in
> Creation] presented itself to a person of singular truthfulness, simplicity and
> piety, who after many struggles accepted the Puritan creed as the adequate
> solution of it.[27]

There is some incongruity here, as Froude clearly did not regard the Puritan
solution as an adequate one. But it was precisely because it was possible for
Bunyan still to perceive eternal truths while operating within a framework
which all of us now regard as grossly misconceived that the especial value of
his work lies:

> It was composed exactly at a time when it was possible for such a book to
> come into being; the close of the period when the Puritan formula was a real
> belief, and was about to change from a living principle into an intellectual
> opinion.[28]

And so, in Froude's estimation, it was destined to inexorable decay. Flowering
just before this descent of Puritan sensibility into atrophy, Bunyan's writings
served as a means of preserving and on occasion regenerating that consciousness in its most vibrant state for successive waves of individual readers.
This 'Poet-apostle of the English middle classes ... had the key of their
thoughts and feelings in his own heart', and because of this his writings have
been able over and over to reawaken in them intuitions that had been
ossified into creeds and codes.[29] Therefore:

> Men of intelligence ... to whom life is not a theory, but a stern fact condi-
> tioned round with endless possibilities of wrong and suffering, though they

---

25. *Bunyan*, 152.   26. See ch.5.
27. *Bunyan*, 152.   28. *Bunyan*, 152.   29. *Bunyan*, 176.

may never adopt the letter of Bunyan's creed, will continue to see in conscience an authority for which culture is no substitute.[30]

The nature of Bunyan's greatness, therefore, lay not in its peculiarity, nor in some innate talent or acquired skill. It existed rather in his demonstration, verified by subsequent history, that the central truths of humanity's place within the scheme of Creation could be perceived and held forth for all of his readers to hear by the humblest and least educated of men in the most troubled and turbulent times.

II

Froude's explorations into the lives of great and less-than-great individuals suggest that, despite the assumption of his critics, his own understanding of the concept of greatness was considerably more complex and more refined than it was frequently taken to be. That great men such as Luther and Henry VIII had emerged in critical times was indeed certain, but while it was appropriate that historians should give prominence to such individuals, the assumption that this select group was in some way uniquely endowed was in several ways deceptive. In giving prominence to the periods of crisis and transformation in history, it inadvertently neglected the long-term processes that led up to those points, as well as the long processes that issued from them. Furthermore, it gave rise to the misleading impression that the great individual movers of history were singularly gifted, and that they might themselves be given credit for their achievements. But the capacity to see through the routine and flux of temporarily prevailing conditions to the truth of things was, rather, a gift which was spread throughout humanity of all sorts and in all times because it was inherent in the process of Creation itself. It was only the pressures of particular times that brought forth a small sample of such figures who in other eras would have lived obscure or modest lives. Finally, insofar as it suggested that greatness lay in representativeness, originality, or any other form of human progress, the conventional notion of the heroic was false. Historical greatness was neither novel nor (in the modern sense) revolutionary. On the contrary, it resided in the power to inspire and to effect a genuine return of consciousness to the unchanging eternal truths of the human condition.

30. *Bunyan*, 181.

Unwilling, perhaps, to challenge openly the misreadings of Carlyle's concept of the heroic which had been so influential, Froude elected not to offer
an explicit statement of his own understanding of greatness in one general
statement, and chose instead to allow it to be derived from the contemplation of his selected biographies. Several years before he undertook such
practical demonstrations, however, Froude, in his essay on 'Calvinism', noted
earlier, had given a sketch of the dialectical processes of revelation, alienation, and transcendence by which he believed history moved.[31]

Its title notwithstanding, Froude was not at all concerned in this essay
with the intricacies of Calvinist theology. Calvinism, as defined by Froude,
was one of those world-historical processes through which human consciousness of the eternal waxed and waned. Having tactfully distinguished
the inspirational energy of the Calvinist movement from the theological
arguments and doctrines of its founder, he proceeded to the main purpose
of the essay.[32] This was to supply an exposition of the philosophical principles underlying the concept of greatness which had informed all his
historical writings up to that point. At the core of his thinking was the
ancient opposition between the philosophical concepts of human freedom
and natural necessity. Concerning necessity, the arguments from logic and
experience were compelling; and, moving from entirely different premises,
Calvin, Spinoza, Buckle, and Mill had all subscribed to a form of it. Yet the
implications of necessitarianism in any form were also profoundly disturbing, as they implied an acceptance of human inequality (physical, intellectual, economic, moral, and so on) which was at once arbitrarily
distributed and quite insurmountable. As such, it suggested that there was
no such thing as natural justice, and, most awful of all, that there was, in
consequence, no point in moral behaviour.

Arising from a natural revulsion at these terrible implications, a powerful
countervailing impulse has been evident in the expressions of the human
psyche from the beginning. In primitive societies, and in pagan, Christian,
and non-Christian civilisations there has been evidence of 'a conviction that
there is in all human things a real order and purpose, notwithstanding the
chaos in which at times they seem to be involved'.[33] Whether it found

---

31. 'Calvinism: An Address to the Students at St Andrews, March 17, 1871', *Short Studies*, II, 1–59.
32. When it came to it, Froude was clear in withholding from Calvin himself the accolade of
greatness, allowing to him only the concession that 'for hard times hard men are needed', *Short
Studies*, II, 52.
33. *Short Studies*, II, 9.

expression in the Greek notion of destiny or the Old Testament poets' view of providence, or the Christian belief in redemption, this alternative vision of the human predicament did not deny the existence of predetermining natural or historical forces, but sought to see through them to the universal and eternal order. Science's discovery of the complex processes of nature (and here Froude alludes without much concern to Darwin and Tyndall) does not challenge the existence of such eternal laws. It merely confirms the imperfect nature of the human intellect's comprehension of the world, and as such it reaffirms the validity of other, non-intellectual ways of perceiving existence.

Of these, the most important and enduring has been the perennial sense, possessed by some men in all eras, of 'the distinction between the nobler and baser parts of their being'. Froude does not seek to establish the origin of this moral sense, whether it be 'by external revelation or natural insight'; he merely seeks to affirm its existence as an historical fact. Nor does he claim that it is equally powerful at all times. Rather, the encasement of this primal sense in formalised religion and thence into an empty idolatry is 'a state of things perpetually recurring'.[34]

As a case study of this pattern of regeneration and decay, Froude went on to compose a survey history of the abbey of St Alban's from its foundation in the eighth century to its dissolution in the sixteenth century.[35] Although it might be expected that Protestant Froude's account of the monastery's history would be one of unrelieved decline from the pure asceticism of the age of the founders to its degraded state on the eve of the Reformation, he takes a different tack. Excoriating those who see 'a worthless government tyrannising for generations, or an exploded creed continuing to mislead the world after every active mind has divined its falsehood', he offers a more complicated story.[36] Though there was indeed decline at work from early on, there were also periods of recovery and genuine holiness for which the actions and the inspiration of several good men were responsible. But the regenerations thus effected from within the institution were possible only so long as the spirit which informed the institution remained vital; and as Catholicism steadily lost its intrinsic force, so the possibility of such internal

---

34. *Short Studies*, II, 14–16.
35. 'Annals of an English Abbey', first published in *Scribner's Monthly* in November/December 1873 and January 1874; reprinted in *Short Studies*, III, 1–129.
36. 'Annals of an English Abbey', *Short Studies*, III, 30.

revivals diminished, until by the 1530s there was no force capable of saving it from within.

For Froude, the essential problem presented by history is that, while this falling away in human understanding is inexorable, the universal laws of which human insight is but an imperfect expression remain unchanged; and the divergence grows until the gap between the pretensions to morality of organised society and the practical immorality of that society becomes so gross that its very fabric begins to unravel. In these circumstances, either complete dissolution ensues, as was the case with the English monasteries and with Catholicism in general in the sixteenth century; or a figure emerges who grasps the meaning of what is happening around him, and acts accordingly.

At first this individual discovers for himself 'that he is living surrounded with falsehood, drinking lies like water, his conscience polluted, his intellect degraded by the abominations which envelope his existence'. He withdraws from the world, but steadily

> he becomes conscious of impulses toward something purer and higher than he has yet experienced ... He is too keenly aware of the selfish and cowardly thoughts which rise up to mar and thwart his noble aspirations to believe that they can possibly be his own ... and concludes, not in vanity, but in profound humiliation and self-abasement, that the infinite face of God is rescuing him from destruction ... and he resolves thenceforth to enlist himself as a soldier on the side of truth and right ... Like a soldier he abandons his freedom, desiring only like a soldier to act and speak no longer as of himself, but as commissioned from some supreme authority. In such a condition a man becomes magnetic.[37]

As in the case of Knox and the Scottish Commons, however, the effective power of the heroic individual is dependent on the responsiveness of the people:

> There are epidemics of nobleness as well as disease ... Even in the most corrupt ages there are always more persons than we suppose who in their hearts rebel against the prevailing fashions; one takes courage from another, one supports another; communities form themselves with higher principles of action ... As their numbers multiply they catch fire with a common idea and a common indignation, and ultimately burst out into open war with the lies and iniquities that surround them.[38]

37. *Short Studies*, II, 16–17.
38. *Short Studies*, II, 17–18.

The relationship of the hero to his contemporaries is, therefore, complex. Far from being an embodiment of 'the spirit of the age', he is in revolt against it. But his vision of a better world is dependent for its power on the capacity of increasing numbers of ordinary people to apprehend it and to act on that apprehension. Historical greatness is not, then, a singular attribute of the superman, but a potential which is latent in a large number of individuals and which is fulfilled only when specific critical conditions apply.

From this perception, important interpretative consequences follow for the historian of 'great men'. It follows that in times before some great epochal crisis has been reached, or at some time after it has been passed, there will be men whose capacity to act as prophets of the eternal truths of existence will subsist unlooked for and neglected by their own generation, or will function as historical intermediaries, like St Hugo or the revivalists at St Alban's, temporarily forestalling the inevitable advance of divergence. It is from such neglect and misapprehension that there has arisen the confusion, as grievous as it is understandable, that human genius is an historically or psychologically relative phenomenon, rather than an expression and a confirmation of the absolute laws of Creation.

Froude's concern to offer a more sophisticated account of his understanding of the relationship of singular individuals to the broad forces of historical change was in part intended to alleviate confusions concerning the nature and purpose of great men to which he had himself contributed in his *History of England*. But he had also a more forward-looking intent. By the close of the 1860s, as we have seen, Froude, in company with many other Victorian intellectuals, was becoming increasingly disappointed by, and fearful of, the immediate consequences of Disraeli's 'leap in the dark'.[39] Far from leading to rejuvenation of public debate on issues of genuine importance, the election of 1868 brought only an intensification of all the posturing, demagoguery, and cynicism that had characterised party politics in the previous thirty years. Far from being established as a new force in politics, the new electorate had shown itself to be as amenable to sectional, regional, and personal appeals as any previous privileged constituency. But for all that, the realities of the new political world could not be ignored; the inevitability of the further extension of democracy was not to be resisted, and the cultural and moral crisis likely to be produced by these developments required to be addressed.[40]

39. See ch.8.
40. Froude, 'Party Politics', *Fraser's Magazine*, NS 10 (July 1874), 1–18; reprinted in *Short Studies*, III, 429–76.

It was with this heightened awareness of the urgency and complexity of the task that lay before him, that at the close of the 1860s Froude undertook the radical series of strategic reorientations noted in earlier chapters: the abandonment of his English *History*, and the commencement of an intense engagement with the colonies and with the re-emergence of crisis in Ireland. It was this conviction that fuelled his brief excursion into active politics. But it was in these circumstances also that Froude found it intellectually necessary to advance a further elaboration of his concept of the dynamics of historical change and of the role of individuals within it in a manner that reflected his ambivalent attitude toward the contemporary social and cultural changes which he was witnessing.

The audience which he was seeking to address in this enterprise was not simply the undifferentiated mass of the aspiring under-educated. It retained that central element of the cultured and morally engaged to which he had first directed his attention in the 1840s, now immersed in the wider sea in which they too must again seek to find their bearings. Moreover, unlike Arnold, Lecky, Leslie Stephen and others, Froude's own understanding of history required him to allow the possibility that even from within the masses, individuals might emerge with the power to inspire their fellows toward a moral renewal, as Luther and Knox had done, and as Carlyle had attempted in his own time. To be genuinely effective, therefore, the modes of expression which Froude adopted in addressing this complex audience had to be attuned to nuances and unexpected possibilities. Thus, even as he spoke with the voice of the militant campaigner demanding urgent political action in regard to Ireland, South Africa, and the colonies, and even as he continued in his role as celebrant of the Protestant Reformation, he was also obliged to enlighten those potential revolutionaries among his audience as to the conditions and forces surrounding them in order to help them on their way.

This was at once an inescapable and a perilous undertaking, freighted with moral responsibility for total failure or, worse, imperfect success. In the 1880s and 1890s it would present Froude with challenges with which, as we shall see, he was to grapple, with very mixed results.[41] At the outset of his task, however, Froude believed that he had to hand a set of vehicles to enable him to carry on his enterprise. One was to be found in the critical study of some prominent and some obscure figures of English history. But

41. See chs. 13 and 14.

in addition, Froude now discovered that the study of ancient history provided him with a remarkable opportunity. A return to the world of antiquity not only enabled him to transcend the wranglings of controversy which his own writings on English history had produced; it allowed him to establish that the patterns of interaction between individuals and historical forces which he had been tracing were not unique to England. They were recurrent throughout history.

III

Froude's familiarity with the history of ancient Greece and Rome was deeply founded. Like any public schoolboy and graduate of Literae Humaniores, his mind had been thoroughly stocked with the writings of the great classical authors, but in addition his linguistic precocity and his independent mode of reading led him as a young man to venture far beyond the prescribed canon. After his abandonment of fiction and at the very beginning of his turn to history in the 1850s he had planned a study of 'the age of Tacitus' in which it was probable from his hints at the time that the dominant theme would have been the replacement of a once virtuous but now degenerate pagan culture by the inspiring spiritual vision of early Christianity. But when in the 1870s he again returned to ancient history, his focus of attention was somewhat earlier than the second century CE.

In less than three years in the later 1870s Froude published no less than six substantial essays and a large monograph on classical themes. In the autumn of 1876 he published two pieces in his old journal, *Fraser's*. The first was an essay on 'Society in Italy in the Last Days of the Roman Republic' in which he used Cicero's boastful account of his defence of the Roman noble Cluentius to illustrate the extent of political and moral corruption in the republic before Caesar's war. The second was a free translation, with a lengthy critical introduction, of one of the short dramatic dialogues of the Augustan satirist Lucian, to which Froude attached the resonant title 'The Twilight of the Gods'. In the following year, in a further issue of his collected *Short Studies*, he included a hitherto unpublished essay on 'Divus Caesar' which, beginning as a commentary on the 'Pharsalia', the powerful anti-imperial tract of the first-century poet Lucan, returned to the theme of republican decline and offered a more overt justification of Caesar's march on Rome. In 1878 he embarked upon a partial rehabilitation of the Roman

Epicurean philosopher Celsus which involved him in some scholarly debate. In 1879 he contributed an account of the second-century magician Alexander of Abonotichus to *The Nineteenth Century*. And finally, in the same year, he published his full-length study of *Caesar* on which he had been working enthusiastically since his return from South Africa.[42]

Of these compositions, the last was by far the most provocative and controversial. On its first appearance Froude's *Caesar* attracted adverse critical opinion for all the familiar reasons. It was frankly popular both in tone and appeal, and marked a sharp departure from Froude's earlier authorial presentation to his readers both in his English *History* and in his periodical articles. But it developed a voice first heard in *The English in Ireland*, and in its structure and in its style it anticipated several of the distinctive features of the later popular travel books with which he was to experiment in the 1880s. In terms of Froude's own literary history, it was, in short, a new departure.

Divided into twenty-eight short chapters and supplied with detailed chapter synopses, it was written in a plain and familiar style. The author gave little impression that he expected his readership to be familiar with his subject, still less with all the interpretative and evaluative disputes that had surrounded him; and despite the contested character of the language and sources upon which it depended, all quotations were supplied in translation, the Latin originals and further references being relegated to sparse footnotes.

The book was not only candidly popular in appeal; it was also openly polemical in intent. Thoroughly biased in favour of its hero, the book was little short of an apologia for Caesar, exonerating him from most of the charges frequently brought against him, and charging his enemies with the basest of motivations. Above all it was unashamedly present-minded in its approach, opening and closing with chapters in which contemporary parallels and their future implications were bluntly stated. Composed in the wake of his political campaign on behalf of the colonies and his mission to

---

42. 'Society in Italy in the Last Days of the Roman Republic', *Fraser's Magazine*, NS 14 (August 1876), 150–62, reprinted in *Short Studies*, III, 260–94; 'Lucian', *Fraser's Magazine*, NS 14 (October 1876), 419–37, reprinted in *Short Studies*, III, 295–334; 'Divus Caesar', *Short Studies*, III, 335–88; 'Origin and Celsus', and 'Three Letters on Origen and Celsus' (debate with F. W. Newman), *Fraser's Magazine*, NS 17 (February, May 1878), 142–67, 548–55; 'A Cagliostro of the Second Century', *Nineteenth Century*, 6 (September 1879), 551–70, reprinted in *Short Studies*, IV, 432–79; *Caesar: A Sketch* (Longmans, 1879).

South Africa, *Caesar* can readily be seen as a part of Froude's great propagandist effort on behalf of a new imperial policy.[43]

The parallels between the history of the ancient Romans and that of the modern British people were asserted even in the opening sentences of the book in an unmistakable fashion:

> The early Romans possessed the faculty of self-government beyond any people of whom we have historical knowledge, with the one exception of ourselves. In virtue of their temporal freedom they became the most powerful nation in the known world; and their liberties perished only when Rome became the mistress of conquered races, to whom she was unable or unwilling to extend her privileges. If England was similarly supreme, if all rival powers were eclipsed by her or laid under her feet, the imperial tendencies which are as strongly marked in us as our love of liberty, might lead us over the same course to the same end.[44]

The challenges of imperial expansion and the management of colonies also feature as a central interpretative theme. The rapid acquisition of colonial dependencies had brought the republic unprecedented wealth. But instead of reinvesting in further development, the Roman Senate had allowed its profits to be squandered at home through personal aggrandisement, political corruption, and through pandering to the mob. Loyal and would-be loyal colonists had been exploited, their pleas to be recognised as equal citizens ignored, until finally they had been alienated. As a consequence, the frontiers of the Empire had become vulnerable, and the depredations of Jugurtha and Mithridates, as well as the operations of countless pirates, provided ample evidence of Rome's weakness and decline. The implications for Britain's imperial policy were plain:

> From the time when Rome became an Empire, mistress of provinces to which she was unable to extend her own liberties, the days of her self-government were numbered. A homogeneous and vigorous people may manage their own affairs under a popular constitution so long as their personal characters remain undegenerate. Parliaments and Senates may represent the general will of the community ... but such bodies can preside successfully only among subjects who are directly represented in them. They are too ignorant, too selfish, too

---

43. While the book was being written, Froude told his friend Charles Butler that he intended it to serve 'as a commentary on the modern situation: there are many curious resemblances', Froude to Butler, 6 July 1878, Edinburgh University Library, Butler MSS, E 87.105.
44. *Caesar: A Sketch* (Longman's Silver Library edition), 1.

divided to govern others; and Imperial aspirations draw after them, by obvious necessity, an Imperial rule.[45]

This apparent invocation of a Caesarean dictatorship as a solution to Britain's imperial problems was chilling, and was made all the more disturbing by the analogies implied in Froude's account of the Roman Republic's domestic politics, which formed the other central theme of his book. Expansion had brought with it increased population and an increased demand for land. Far-seeing attempts to secure the foundations of the republic on a broad basis of yeoman freeholdership, such as those proposed by the Gracchi, were violently suppressed by a vicious combination of the old landed aristocracy and a new class of 'capitalists and contractors' who had different reasons for resisting the general distribution of property in Roman society. Competition within and between these groups for the spoils of Rome's expansionist campaigns had inevitably arisen, and, also inevitably, the more ambitious and irresponsible had risked appeals beyond their class to the landless but enfranchised plebeians in order to gain political power and office. In these circumstances, riots and assassinations stimulated by internecine conflict among the elite were not infrequent; but more importantly, political instability was chronic, as annual competitions for Rome's public offices became the occasions of reckless abuse of public funds, wild promises, and ceaseless demagoguery. As the republic entered the last century before the birth of Christ, the drift toward anarchy and dissolution seemed inexorable.

Again, the parallels with contemporary England would have been obvious to Froude's readers. The increasing inequality and deepening immiseration of the poor which had accompanied Britain's economic ádvance had remained a subject of major concern throughout the second half of the nineteenth century. The manner in which the modern political elite were seen by many critics to have evaded their responsibilities, opposed and suppressed measures of reform, and sought to maintain their privileged position by the manipulation of a socially and morally disadvantaged populace would all have seemed strikingly similar to the account of Roman politics supplied by Froude. And the implications which he wished his readers to draw from his *exemplum* were profoundly unsettling: that should it continue on its present course, the British constitution was doomed to dissolve into anarchy, or else to be saved from its fate by the emergence of a great man, in the guise of a modern Caesar.

45. *Caesar: A Sketch*, 193–4.

It was this disturbing implication, coupled with its forthrightly populist appeal, which provoked such hostile reactions from Froude's predominantly liberal and scholarly critics.[46] It is true that in private correspondence in the 1880s Froude commonly expressed his deep disillusion with the consequences of democratisation, and his pessimistic belief that the present party system, and with it the entire constitution, was destined to fall.[47] But the temptation to discern embryonic Fascist impulses in Froude's despair of democracy and in his apparent desire to see a great man emerge to govern the masses should not obscure important subtleties in his attitude and intent. Had Froude wished merely to prophesy the arrival of a saving man on horseback, he had many models other than Caesar to suggest. He might, of course, have looked to Napoleon, or to the more contemporary example of Napoleon III (who in the mid-1860s had published his own self-laudatory biography of Caesar as a great man); or, since it was almost forty years since the appearance of Carlyle's imperfect work, and given his own sense of the importance of Ireland's history, he might have chosen Cromwell. But Froude had never been an admirer of Bonaparte, and had nothing but contempt for his nephew, about whose overthrow in 1870 he had been jubilant; and despite his historical expertise, he never felt attracted to the idea of completing Carlyle's work with a full-scale biography of Oliver.[48] In fact, the only other 'great man' on whose life Froude was considering a book was the less than dictatorial and less than successful Emperor Charles V. The choice of Caesar must be seen, then, as considered and deliberate, and the motivations underlying it are all the more curious because of the problems which his subject's controversial historical reputation presented to him.

That Caesar was a deeply flawed character was a charge frequently levelled against him by his contemporaries and by later historians. He was, they claimed, sexually licentious, ruthless in dealing with opponents, profoundly duplicitous, and intensely ambitious. Froude did his best to exonerate his hero from many of the most serious allegations. The scandalous accusation

---

46. See *inter alia* reviews in *Saturday Review*, 47 (May, 1879), 677–8; *The Academy*, 15 (April, 1879), 361, and *The University Magazine*, 4 (August 1879), 202–5. Anthony Trollope's *Life of Cicero* (2 vols., London, 1880) contains several passages which can be seen as a direct rebuttal to Froude's *Caesar*; see Bradford A. Booth, 'Trollope on Froude's *Caesar*', *The Trollopian*, 1 (1946), 33–47.
47. See, for example, Froude to Charles Butler, 18 November 1876, 2 May 1877, 6 July 1878, Edinburgh University Library, Butler MSS, E 87.105.
48. Napoleon III's *Julius Caesar*, which glorified the Roman as a kind of super-man, received hostile notice in *Fraser's* during Froude's editorship; see Anon., 'Julius Caesar', *Fraser's Magazine*, 76 (July, 1867), 1–15.

that while on diplomatic service in Asia Minor he had become the lover of Nicomedes, King of Bithynia, was mere salacious gossip without a scrap of evidence, and the saucy bisexual implications of a song which Caesar's legionaries were reported to have chanted about their commander were hardly different from the terms in which British sailors had often spoken about their officers. 'Affection, when it expresses itself most emphatically', says Froude with bare-faced innocence, 'borrows the language of its opposites'.[49] Caesar's ruthless destruction of the German tribes, which included the massacre of thousands of non-combatants, is likewise justified on several counts: the Germans were themselves invaders of Gaul, they had reneged on their treaty, the denunciations of the Senate were politically motivated, and Caesar had customarily shown more clemency to defeated enemies than his contemporaries. Yet it is significant that, while he sought to undermine the validity of such attacks, Froude felt obliged to acknowledge them all the same. He was prepared even to add a few of his own: Caesar's relations with women were often without propriety, and the fact (if it was a fact) that Cleopatra was lodging in his house at the time of his assassination was at least an occasion for scandal, and a slight on his wife Calpurnia.[50] And though he respected the formularies of Roman religion, he was an avowed secularist who treated the auguries with contempt, and was possessed of no trace whatever of a religious sensibility.[51]

Significantly, the allegation against which Froude strove most vigorously to defend Caesar was that he had harboured dictatorial ambitions from the outset,

> that he went through ten years of desperate fighting, exposed to a thousand dangers from the sword ... that he banished himself from Rome, uncertain if he would ever return ... with no other object than that of controlling domestic politics ... A lunatic might have attempted such a scheme, but not a Caesar.[52]

Far from being a would-be dictator, driven from the beginning by an heroic vision and of his own unique capacity to fulfil it, Caesar was in fact a moderate man—'a reformer' who aimed to save the Roman constitution from decay by extending the franchise, by raising the position of liberated slaves, by providing for a more even distribution of land, and by incorporating

49. *Caesar*, 544.   50. *Caesar*, 545–6.
51. *Caesar*, 556.   52. *Caesar*, 378.

defeated peoples as equal members of the Empire. In all this he had been frustrated by the selfishness, factionalism, and sheer lack of foresight of the aristocracy and the Senate, who even as he brought unprecedented gains to the Empire sought to destroy him. The Senate's intransigence, its fear that in his second consulship Caesar might implement the only measures which might save the Roman constitution, had precipitated civil war:

> The obstinacy, the ferocity, the treachery of the aristocracy had compelled Caesar to crush them; and the more desperate their struggles, the more absolute the necessity became.[53]

In order to 'restore as much popular liberty as was consistent with the responsibilities such a government as the Empire required', Caesar was compelled to have himself proclaimed dictator for life. In desperation at the imminent loss of their privileges, the aristocrats had assassinated him, 'and in doing so had passed a final sentence on themselves'. If Caesar was the somewhat imperfect hero of Froude's account, there could be no mistaking its consummate villains: they were 'the Optimates' of the Roman Republic.[54]

The minatory character of Froude's address to the British political establishment was thus clear: reform your ways, assume your responsibilities, abandon selfish interests, or constitutional collapse and revolution will ensue.[55] This was presumptuous not only in its message but in its medium, for in writing directly to a popular audience over the heads of the establishment, Froude seemed to be indicating that he was not altogether unhappy about the prospects against which he was now warning. The offence which his tactics provoked was compounded by the concluding lines of the book which, in an apparently blasphemous apotheosis, seemed to compare Caesar to Christ himself:

> Each was denounced for making himself a king. Each was maligned as the friend of publicans and sinners; each was betrayed by those whom he had loved and cared for; each was put to death; and Caesar was also believed to have risen again and ascended into heaven and become a divine being.[56]

---

53. *Caesar*, 536.
54. *Caesar*, 411, 461, 515, 536.
55. Froude's admonitory intent is made even more explicit in a short fable he produced slightly later: 'A Sibylline Leaf', *Blackwood's Magazine*, 133 (April 1883), 573–92. This fable is discussed at greater length in ch.15.
56. Quoted from the first edition of *Caesar*, 555; it is excluded from the Silver Library edition.

This was an extravagance for which Froude was to be firmly rebuked by the critics, and in subsequent editions he chose to replace it with a milder formulation, quoting Portia from *The Merchant of Venice*, that 'earthly power doth then show lik'st God's/when mercy seasons justice'.

The indignation which Froude unnecessarily aroused by this flourish only obscured the real lesson that he was attempting to teach. Despite his celebration of Caesar, Froude did not regard him as a model for the future. Caesar was, after all, destroyed, and his proposed reforms were cancelled. The constitution which he had striven to save was suppressed by his avenger, Augustus, and his posthumous deification was a sign not of his triumph but a portent of the precipitate decline which was to issue in the profanation of the proclamation of the Emperor Nero as a God in his own lifetime. For Froude, the historical significance of Caesar's career lay not in his personal heroism, but in what the destruction of this epitome of the Roman virtues revealed about the degenerating condition of Roman society at the dawn of the Christian era:

> The Roman nation had grown as the oak grows, self-developed in severe morality, each citizen a law to himself and therefore capable of political freedom to an unexampled degree ... [but] the Constitution under which the Empire had sprung up was poisoned and brought to a violent end.[57]

Thus Caesar's world perished, and it was Christ who triumphed. Elsewhere, in the farthest corner of the Empire, a new life was about to dawn for mankind. Poetry, faith, and devotion were to spring again out of the seeds that were sleeping in the heart of humanity. And it was here primarily that the real but altogether secondary nature of Caesar's historical greatness lay.

> [Before] the Kingdom of Heaven could throw up its shoots, there was needed a kingdom of this world where the nations were neither torn in pieces by violence nor were rushing after false ideas and spurious ambitions. Such a kingdom was the Empire of the Caesars.[58]

Caesar's greatness was to be assessed, therefore, not in relation to his individual achievements, but in the broader context of the historical processes which both preceded and succeeded him. His intervention in the course of Roman history was decisive because he cut through the thick growths of political and social corruption of his time. This was the decadent society

57. *Caesar*, 536.   58. *Caesar*, 558.

detailed by Froude in his essay on 'Society in Italy in the Last Days of the Roman Republic' which, based on Cicero's *Pro Cluentio*, revealed not only the sordid goings-on of Oppianicus and his accomplices, but also the cynical and worldly-wise way in which Cicero himself reported them. In a further essay on 'Divus Caesar' (whose intellectual demands and literary allusions indicated that it was directed at an altogether more sophisticated audience than those addressed in *Caesar*) Froude elaborated on this theme of spiritual decay. Like other religious cultures before and after, the simple strengths of early Roman beliefs in their mythical deities had lost their force through the importation of foreign ideas, philosophical criticism, and sheer habituation. By the first century BC the loss of faith was pervasive, manifest in the scepticism and pessimism of the most cultivated intellects, such as Lucretius and Caesar's contemporary and rival, Cicero, on whose treatise 'On the Nature of Gods' Froude provided a detailed commentary in the body of the essay. It was this loss of a spiritual sense which lay at the root of the general immorality of the privileged elite, and which, incidentally, was the fatal flaw Cicero's character.[59]

The decay, moreover, was more than particular:

> All that mankind had gained from the beginning of recorded time, all that Greece had bequeathed of art and culture, all the fruits of the long struggles of Rome to coerce unwilling barbarians into obedience to law, was on the brink of perishing. The human race might have fallen back into primeval savagery.[60]

Then Caesar had

> taken anarchy by the throat and destroyed it ... Order and authority were established under a military empire, and the Roman dominion which had been on the edge of dissolution, received a new lease of existence ... Society in the last pangs of dissolution had been restored to life.[61]

In view of Froude's final assessment of Caesar, this seems quite contradictory; for did he not claim that Caesar had failed and that his subsequent deification was a symptom of that failure? But Froude's position is more subtle:

---

59. 'Divus Caesar', in *Short Studies*, III, 241–79.
60. 'Divus Caesar', 261.
61. 'Divus Caesar', 261, 266.

Order and law and decency are the body of society, but are a body without a soul; and, without a soul, the body, however vigorous its sinews, must die and go to corruption. Human improvement is from within outwards. A state which can endure must be composed of members who all in their way understand what duty means and endeavour to do it. Duty implies genuine belief in some sovereign spiritual power. Spiritual regeneration comes first, moral after it, political and social last.[62]

In restoring authority in the Roman world and in extending that order throughout the Middle East, Caesar created the conditions of political stability and cultural tolerance which 'enabled the Apostles to carry Christianity through the world and organise a Catholic Church'—even though he could do little to halt the spiritual degeneration of his own people.

Having escaped from this self-imposed predicament, Froude appears immediately to have embroiled himself in another by a further rumination on the Caesars. Although it rapidly became grotesque, the deification of the Caesars, Froude insists, had its origins in a genuine sense of gratitude to the founder of the imperial family, and saviour of the nation, who deserved an honour equal to Quirinus, the mythical founder of Rome. The impulse, therefore, was pure, and pregnant with significance for the future. In deifying Caesar the Romans had begun again to imagine a son of God who was himself God and who had been born upon earth of a human mother and a Divine Father, that he had reigned as a king, that he had established dominion over mankind, and that after his death he had gone back to heaven, from which he had descended, there to remain forever: 'The ways of providence are obscure and perplexing ... They had looked for a union of God with man. They thought they had found it in Caesar ... they found it at last in the Carpenter of Nazareth.'[63]

Having once again raised the disturbing insinuation that the real historical significance of Caesar is to be seen as an anticipation of the appearance of the Christ, Froude undermined the portentousness of such a phenomenon by explicitly relating it to the general regression into superstition, sorcery, and mere charlatanism which was a marked feature of the late Republic and early Empire. Objection was obvious: if this was the case, why should the Christian cult with its magic, its miracles, its myth of divine incarnation, resurrection after death, and everlasting life be seen as in any

---

62. 'Divus Caesar', 271–2.
63. 'Divus Caesar', 267–72.

way different from the myriad sects and movements that were proliferating throughout the Roman world around the same time?

Responding to the problem he had himself posed, Froude is devious. Such scepticism, he says, was precisely the attitude of the most engaged and serious minds among the ancients. In sympathetic expositions of Lucian, Lucretius, Celsus, and even Cicero, he gives full credit to the scepticism which they expressed in regard to early Christianity or any form of mono-thesism. Among these, the best of pagan critics, there was no bigotry or complacency but a deep concern about the nature of Creation and of humanity's place within it, and a determination not to be satisfied by super-ficial or sentimental explanations, among which (when they noticed it at all) they regarded Christianity as just another example.[64] Froude, however, was prepared to answer the reservations of the pagans—and, by extension, the modern sceptics—head on.

In his essay on 'Origen and Celsus', Froude launched his rebuttal. The essay opens with an appreciative reconstruction of Celsus's 'True Account'[65]—a late second-century critique of the claims of early Christians (which survives only through the prism of the polemical response made to it by the Christian apologist Origen). Froude concedes that intellectually Celsus clearly made the more persuasive arguments, and that on this level 'Origen is a child, contend-ing with a giant':

> In the 'True Account' we find the tone and almost the language of the calm, impartial thoughtful European ... Celsus was in advance of his age. He was on an elevation from which he could survey the past and current supersti-tions, and detect the origin of most of them in ignorance or credulity.[66]

The difference between the two minds was fundamental. Sceptical, critical, and self-critical, Celsus remained indifferent to, or at best (like his friend Lucian) impotently indignant about, the deep moral degeneration into which his community—and his fellow critical thinkers—had fallen. Furthermore, for all his critical acumen, he could not, any more than Cicero and his friends, offer an answer to the fundamental moral problem of human

---

64. See, for example, Froude's sympathetic account of Lucian's position in 'Lucian', *Short Studies*, III, 295–334; also, 'I wish more of us read Lucian now. He was the greatest man by far outside the Christian church in the second century', Froude, *Life and Letters of Erasmus* (London, 1896), 81.

65. This is Froude's rendering of the title as transmitted by Origen; but modern commentators generally prefer 'On the True Doctrine'.

66. 'Origen and Celsus', reprinted in *Short Studies*, IV, 361–424; the quotation is from 422.

existence which, as they all recognised, was at bottom the problem of evil. Why does wickedness flourish and goodness perish before nature's impassive indifference? It is this powerlessness when confronted with the inescapable evidence of experience that evil goes unchecked and unpunished in the world that reveals not only the ethical deficiencies of these particular philosophers but the ultimate inadequacy of philosophy itself; and it is in this that, for all his undisputed intellectual superiority, Celsus, like all rational thinkers, remains morally inferior to his innocent Christian adversary.

For Origen, his credulities and crudities notwithstanding, had subscribed to the essential Christian message of compassion, forgiveness, and self-abnegation. In place of the implacable law of nature, 'woe to the weak', the Christians had substituted 'the still soft voice of humanity' which acknowledged that 'the strong and the successful are not always the good; the miserable are not always the wicked; and even for the wicked pity claims to be heard in mitigation of punishment'.[67] In contrast to the unflinching rationalism of the Epicureans (of which Lucian and Celsus are the finest specimens) or even the deeper, studied austerity of the Stoics (for whom Froude shows an equal sympathy), the Christians embraced 'compassion for the weak, the divinest attribute of God' which at length began to control and limit the cruelty of nature:

> Conscience, accepting another law for itself, has been compelled by Christianity to submit to a higher rule of obligation.[68]

It was only through the voluntary assumption of duty and the suppression of self-interest that individual humans might seek to transcend the brutal meaninglessness of their natural existence. For this undertaking, real guidance was to be found not among the philosophers but among the visionaries and the artists. It was for this reason that, as a central part of his exploration of the moral history of the ancient world, Froude undertook a study of the Greek tragedians, and in particular of the deeply ambivalent figure of Euripides.[69]

Often marginalised within the classical canon because of his perceived nihilism and amoralism, Euripides, Froude argues, occupies a crucial place in the history of the ancient world's moral sensibility. Because of the cruel and arbitrary nature of his plots, his characterisation of the gods as vicious

---

67. 'Origen and Celsus', 426.
68. 'Origen and Celsus', 426.
69. 'Sea Studies', in *Fraser's Magazine*, NS 11 (May 1875), 541–60; subsequently reprinted in Froude, *Short Studies on Great Subjects* (London, 1896 edn.), III, 207–59.

and vulgar as well as capricious, his apparent agnosticism, and his refusal to offer any form of catharsis, he has been unfairly judged in comparison to his great predecessors. Above all, his preoccupation with human sacrifice was regarded as sensational and unsavoury.

Euripides, however, was writing at a different time, says Froude, and to a different audience. A loss of faith in religion being common to all, some had taken refuge in the consolations of magic and superstition, while others had ascended to the plane of detached rational scepticism. Challenging both, Euripides had affirmed that in times of loss of belief, when the frame of explanation had been breached by the tidal wave of knowledge, the only attitude which could help sustain humanity's sense of meaning in the universe was the abnegation of the self. His dramatic presentations of human sacrifice were not indulgences in gory sensationalism, but the rediscovery of the purer vision of primitive but vibrant cultures in order to reinvigorate the spirit of sophisticated and exhausted ones. Human sacrifice—'a manifestation of Satan under the most hideous of aspects'—became in the hands of the artist 'an expression and a symbol of the most profound of spiritual truths'. In art and in all life, 'the upward sweep of excellence is proportional with strictest accuracy, to oblivion of the self which is ascending':

> Every act of man which can be called good is an act of sacrifice, an act which the doer of it would have left undone, had he not preferred some person's benefit to his own, or the excellence of the work on which he was engaged to his personal pleasure or convenience.[70]

It is in this agnostic Greek insight concerning human sacrifice that, whatever its other roots in the preservative or despairing practices of primitive or decadent cultures, the central stem of the Christian idea of sacrifice was to be found. As humanity's spirit recovered under the new form of Christianity,

> the doctrine of human sacrifice which had exerted so strange and growing a fascination was to lose its horrors while retaining its ennobling influence. The emotions and the conscience were reconciled when God Himself became His own victim.[71]

By now, Froude has travelled a considerable distance from the celebration of Caesar, his heroic imperial achievements, and his anticipations of Christ. But in the essays on Lucian, Celsus, Cicero, the posturing of Alexander and

---

70. 'Sea Studies', reprinted in *Short Studies*, III, 238.
71. *Short Studies*, III, 259.

Apollonius, and the deification of the Caesars, Froude was consciously addressing a more specific and self-aware audience than that for whom his populist book was intended. This was the educated and intellectually culti-vated intellectual readership of the heavyweight journals, many of whom, having absorbed the powerful but hugely destructive scientific discoveries of the age, had withdrawn, like the Epicureans and the Stoics, into a know-ing and passive indifference.

To Froude, the adoption of such an attitude amidst the inexorable flux of cultural and material change was not only irresponsible, but impossible. The cynical, the apathetic, and the compliant would all alike be swept up by forces that they had done nothing to control, and from which, as long as injustice and cruelty remained the law of nature, either anarchy, tyranny, or unremitting bloodshed was likely to follow. From such terrible outcomes neither the extremes of detached intellectual excellence nor of cynical political manipulation could promise any relief. Rather, said Froude, prophet-like addressing his selected audience, it was requisite that reforma-tion must start from within:

> Desire first to be good men—true in word just in action, pure in spirit ... So out of men who have life in them shall grow a society that has life, and the kingdom of the world shall be made in truth a kingdom of God.[72]

But whether he was addressing the popular audience of *Caesar* or the more sophisticated readership toward whom his studies of Lucian and Euripides had been directed, the underlying intent was the same. It was not that his readers should be persuaded by his argument to change the world, but rather that by reflection they would first be moved to change themselves.

IV

Beneath its many surface tensions, therefore, an underlying coherence can nevertheless be seen in the drift of Froude's understanding of the role of individuals—greater and lesser—in history. That there was some dynamic in history under which civilisations and cultures emerged, flourished, and declined was, he believed, readily demonstrable. The impulse underlying this dynamic was to be traced to the unremitting but always imperfect

---

72. 'Divus Caesar', *Short Studies*, III, 388.

attempts of human intellects to make sense of the world into which they had been plunged, and the inevitable tendency of such explanations gradually to lose power as the mass of knowledge and experience gathered within them breached the limits of such explanatory frameworks. It was clear from history also that as such critical epochs dawned, the human imagination worked strenuously to find ways of accounting for phenomena and experiences that were now inexplicable. Philosophy, religion, magic, and law were all in their different ways engaged on the same project of making intelligible a world that was fast becoming incomprehensible. The appearance, then, of clear-headed thinkers, mystics, and powerful figures of authority was at once a symptom of the impending crisis but also a reaffirmation of the human determination to engage with the mysteries of Creation. But of themselves, all of these modes of understanding were doomed to fail, unless they were sustained by a prior conviction that humans were placed in existence for a purpose, and that they must fight to rediscover that purpose not merely by thought and prayer but by a self-denying commitment to others. The denial of the self was arduous, and ran contrary to nature. But it was not only consoling and liberating; it was in the deepest sense sanctioned by human history. It was to be found among the greatest achievements of human nature—of the heroic deeds of great men and ordinary men. It lay at the heart of the deepest human imaginings—in poetry, music, and art. But above all it was at the core of the single point of contact between the finite human world and eternity—in the myth of Jesus Christ.

Such a vision of the dynamics of world history would be, Froude hoped, inspiring. But the difficulties all returned as he moved from the level of edifying precept to the ground of practical engagement. Where were 'the best' whose current lack of conviction was to be overcome? In a series of accompanying essays Froude seemed to suggest, to their own comfort no doubt, that they were still to be found in the ranks of the landed gentry, in families like the Russells of Cheneys, in those who would rise above the pettiness of party politics.[73] But did social elitism really offer a means to virtue, and was there any reason why, as with the early Christians, the good could not be found among the ranks of the meek and the poor? As to the

---

73. 'On the uses of a landed gentry: address delivered at the Philosophical Institution of Edinburgh, November 6, 1876', *Short Studies*, III, 388–428; 'Party Politics', *Fraser's Magazine*, NS 10 (July 1874), 1–18, reprinted in *Short Studies*, III, 429–76; 'Cheneys and the House of Russell', *Fraser's Magazine*, NS 20 (September 1879), 360–85, reprinted in *Short Studies*, IV, 480–542.

worst, did not Froude's methods—his anti-intellectualism, his appeal to the emotions, his elevation of duty and action above careful reflection—not risk encouraging the 'passionate intensity' whose narcissism would be the very opposite of the self-abnegation which he so desired?

In the later 1870s, however, as the biographical and classical studies on which he had embarked appeared to yield so much, and as his literary influence and reputation stood at its highest, Froude perhaps had little occasion to entertain doubts about the risks he was running, even though in private correspondence he sometimes expressed less hope concerning the potential of the social elite in whom he publicly expressed such confidence.[74] But in the years immediately following the publication of *Caesar* he was to be confronted with a challenge not only to his standing as a shaper of public opinion, but more importantly to the validity of the deeply ambiguous strategy he had chosen to pursue. The challenge arose in the form of a commission to write the life of Carlyle.

74. See, for example, Froude to Lord Derby, 13 April (1880), Liverpool Record Office, Derby MSS; Froude to Charles Butler, 6 February 1882: 'I am more and more confident that the future of the Anglo-Saxon race lies with you and not with us,' Edinburgh University Library, Butler MSS.

12

Writing the (Auto)Biography of Carlyle, 1876–84

I

The commission to write the biography of Carlyle was not sudden. It was the product of a complex process which had developed slowly over the two decades before Carlyle's death, as Froude's personal relations with the great man steadily deepened. Like many of his generation, Froude had been an admirer of Carlyle from the mid-1840s when he looked to the sage of Cheyne Row as one voice among others indicating a possible resolution to the theological and moral problems of the decade other than the terrifying alternatives of silence, indifference, or the flight to Rome. Froude reviewed Carlyle's *Cromwell* favourably in the *Oxford and Cambridge Review* in 1845, and Carlyle is referred to positively but ambiguously in *The Nemesis of Faith*.[1] But it was only after the scandal provoked by that book and its personal consequences for Froude that in the summer of 1849 he actively sought an interview with the great man which he secured through the good offices of his close friends Arthur Hugh Clough and James Spedding.[2] Although the first encounter, which took place at a typical soirée in Chéyne Row, was uncomfortable, it was not entirely unsuccessful. Carlyle, recently returned from a visit to Ireland, was contemplating a book on the subject and was interested in Froude's peculiar Irish experience and his abandoned plans to write a study of St Patrick and the early Irish saints. But Carlyle's initial estimation of Froude was, according to Froude himself, not high: 'He

---

1. See ch. 5.
2. Carlyle to Jane Welsh Carlyle, 3 April 1849, K. J. Fielding *et al.* (eds.), *Collected Letters of Thomas and Jane Welsh Carlyle*, 24, 6–7.

had said of me that I ought to burn my own smoke and not to burden other people's nostrils with it.'[3] Yet Froude passed the interview at Cheyne Row and was invited to call without prior arrangement—an offer, he proudly recalls, of which he took full advantage during his regular research expeditions to the capital in the 1850s. By the mid-1850s Froude was already sufficiently accepted in Carlyle's inner circle as to be able to send him galley proofs of the first volumes of his *History of England*. Carlyle responded promptly, enthusiastically offering many suggestions for improvement and correction—many (but by no means all) of which Froude incorporated in the final text.[4]

It was when Froude moved to London in the autumn of 1860 to take up the editorship of *Fraser's* that his visits to Cheyne Row became more regular and the relationship between him and Carlyle began to become particularly close. Early in the following year Froude was surprised when Carlyle called unannounced at his own home in Clifton Place, requested in a quasi-formal manner that Froude should be an even more frequent visitor, and invited him to act as Carlyle's companion on his daily walks and horseback rides. This semi-formal visitation was by no means a common practice of Carlyle, and Froude may be pardoned the extravagance of seeing it as something of a call to discipleship. At any rate he answered the call. From then on Froude became a guest at Cheyne Row several times each week, and gradually assumed the role of guardian of the Carlyles' privacy, indicating to other would-be callers when a visit would be welcome or unwelcome. Carlyle's unique friendship with, and dependence on, Froude thus deepened over the 1860s; but it became even more intense in the weeks immediately after 21 April 1866 when, during Carlyle's absence in Edinburgh, Jane Welsh Carlyle (aged sixty-five) collapsed and died suddenly in a street near their home. Suffused with grief, and nurturing a deeply personal sense of guilt, Carlyle now withdrew almost completely from society, and Froude's companionship became more than ever necessary. In the early days of grieving Froude accompanied Carlyle on almost daily pilgrimages to the place where Jane had been found dead, Carlyle all the while confessing to Froude his feelings of guilt and self-reproach for his treatment of his companion during their many years together.[5]

3. Froude, *Thomas Carlyle: A History of His Life in London* (2 vols., London, 1884), i, 457–60.
4. Dunn, *Froude*, I, 244–51; *Table-Talk of Shirley*, 130, 160.
5. *Carlyle: Life in London*, ii, 254–60.

So the relationship persisted, with Froude acting as a kind of carer and guardian for the increasingly solitary Carlyle, until one day in June 1871, just as on the previous occasion a decade earlier, Carlyle again called unexpectedly on Froude, bearing with him a large collection of papers and imposing on his friend a terrible commission. 'Take these for my sake,' Froude recalled Carlyle's solemn pronouncement:

> They are yours to publish or not to publish as you please after I am gone. Do what you will. Read them and let me know whether you will take them on these terms ... I must judge. I must publish it, the whole or else destroy it all, if I thought it was the wiser things to do.[6]

To this momentous burden Carlyle then added a further grave responsibility. It was his deepest desire, he told Froude, that no biography of him should be written, and that the materials now given to him should be the only authoritative memorials of his life. If Froude decided they should be destroyed, he would be consigning Carlyle to posthumous obscurity.

The obvious biblical resonances of this astonishing episode seem to border on the blasphemous. Froude was invited to partake of Carlyle's life in the most intimate manner, and was also to be given the freedom to determine if (and the manner in which) others might be included in the invitation. But the choice of accepting the invitation and the degree to which it was to be extended to others was to be left entirely to him as a matter of his own free will, with all the consequences which such discretion entailed. It might appear that Carlyle was straining after a covenant with his people in the manner of the Judaeo-Christian deity, and the solemn manner in which Froude records the occasion suggests that to some extent he himself saw it thus. Merely to take it as such, however, would be to mistake the character and intensity of Carlyle's moral vision.

Even by the time of this second visitation it was clear that Carlyle's promise as a prophet for his times had faded markedly. He was being read less, his detractors were many and popular, and most importantly he was no longer writing. The question that Carlyle was presenting, then, was both deeply sincere and urgent. Was there anything of the prophet's visionary gleam that might still be conveyed by the representation of his own life despite his obvious failures in living it? And since Carlyle, in the midst of his inexorable

---

6. *Carlyle: Life in London*, ii, 408–9. For an appreciation of the portentousness of this event, see Elliot L. Gilbert, 'Rescuing Reality: Carlyle, Froude and Biographical Truth-Telling', *Victorian Studies*, 34 (Spring, 1991), 295–314.

decline (both public and private), believed himself incapable of undertaking a task which demanded the most sustained imaginative self-recreation and the most honest self-criticism, other means needed to be found. Thus it was left to his closest living companion to determine whether it was at all possible by some other means to compose the spiritual autobiography of which the prophet himself was incapable. If it was, he must then consider the manner in which it should be attempted. This was a truly awesome responsibility, but its rejection would have amounted on Froude's part not only to the admission of the failure of Carlyle's work (and the understanding of the experience of human existence that it sought to convey), but also to a revelation that the professions of those like Froude who had continued to affirm the truth of Carlyle's vision were self-deceiving and vapid.

The stakes of the Carlyle commission were thus set high; but Froude's understanding of the extent of its demands and the range of its possibilities was to be changed completely when he actually turned to read the materials with which Carlyle had presented him on that day in 1871.

> Their perusal was infinitely affecting. I saw at once the meaning of his passionate expressions of remorse, of his allusions to Johnson's penance, and of his repeated declaration that something like was due for himself. He had never properly understood till her [Jane's] death how much she had suffered, and how much he had himself to answer for.[7]

In his frequent visits to Cheyne Row, Froude had become increasingly aware of the strained and difficult nature of the Carlyles' marriage, and in the years following Jane's sudden death he had seen ample evidence of Carlyle's deep remorse concerning his conduct toward his wife. But before he surveyed the large collection of her letters Froude had little idea of the depth of Jane's unhappiness during her marriage or of the extent of Carlyle's erratic, abusive, and outrageously selfish behaviour which had been its cause.[8]

Yet it was only when he also saw the extraordinary care and honesty which Carlyle invested in his own editing and annotation of the letters that he fully grasped the depth of the widower's determination to expose his

---

7. *Carlyle: Life in London*, 409. The allusions to Johnson refer to Samuel Johnson's later remorse for his refusal as a young man to help his father at his bookstall in Uttoxeter, as a consequence of which he stood out in the rain for long periods in the town's market square in attempted expiation of his guilt.

8. Froude, *My Relations with Carlyle* (London, 1903), 3–11.

responsibility for his wife's sufferings. The commission which had been imposed on him was, Froude now understood, unfair and even, and as he said, 'cruel'.[9] At the same time he also apprehended the profound matter with which Carlyle himself was struggling. Carlyle had realised that it was imperative that the prophet who had preached of the intensely personal nature of moral obligation, and of the social and historical consequences of a rejection of that obligation, should enact in his own case the duty of truthfulness which he had enjoined upon others. It would also have been obvious to Froude why Carlyle felt himself unable to undertake the task in his own right. Were the prophet to have written his story alone, he would have risked distorting the central force of his message either by evoking a sentimental and undeserved forgiveness from his readers, or, conversely, of provoking condescending disgust at his conduct or at his confessional self-abasement.

Such moral tribulations were doubtless reinforced by Carlyle's habitual reservation concerning his audience's critical capacities; but even more important was the persistent mistrust which the author of *Sartor Resartus*, *The French Revolution*, and *Cromwell* felt about the single, retrospective, first-person narrative voice which, he believed, necessarily enforced a radical distortion on how events actually occurred and how experience was actually felt. Effectively to realise his central purpose—which was to give personal testimony in the most intense way to the principal obligation of every conscious and sentient being—it was necessary that the prophet's voice be mediated in ways comparable to, but altogether different from, the earlier rhetorical modes through which Carlyle had sought to inspire his readers. For this, the ultimate of tasks, a more complex medium than ever was required which would involve many components and many voices, within which a central but by no means dominant one would be that of the loyal and dependable but truthful and courageous biographer.

> The question before me was whether I was to say that the atonement ought not to be completed, and that the bravest action which I had ever heard of should be left unexecuted, or whether I was to bear the reproach, if the letters were given to the world, of having uncovered the errors of the best friend that I had ever had.[10]

---

9. Froude, *My Relations with Carlyle*, 13.
10. *Carlyle: Life in London*, 410.

Not unnaturally, Froude prevaricated. On first receiving the materials he asked for some weeks to consider his decision, and although Carlyle agreed, he began almost immediately badgering Froude for an answer. Would he accept or refuse the most serious challenge of his career?—until Froude, at last, consented on terms. With Carlyle he agreed a programme of publication. It was proper that the letters of Jane Welsh Carlyle should be published in the form in which Carlyle had prepared them without any deletion or extenuation. But if this were to be done, the letters were to be preceded by the memoir of Jane written by Carlyle shortly after Jane's death and which he had hitherto decided would remain unpublished. Carlyle agreed to lift the ban, and also gave assent to a further request from Froude that Carlyle's initial wish that the publication of his materials should take place only after a period of twenty years from his death should now be shortened to a period of ten years from that point in 1873. By 1873 neither Carlyle nor Froude was confident that the decrepit and depressed Carlyle was likely to survive for a further decade. But the prophet's death was not at that time imminently expected, and the change of schedule is a clear indication of both men's agreed understanding of the purposes of the publication project. The intent of making available the 'remains' of Thomas Carlyle's life and work was not to enhance his posthumous reputation to later generations. It was primarily to underline the profound urgency with which his vision of the world, and his own failure properly to embody it, was to be made available to the generation still living.[11]

The seriousness of their intent in agreeing on the timing and the sequence of the great man's remains is evidenced by a further requirement from Froude. This was his demand, also agreed to by Carlyle, that the materials and the plan for their publication should be sent to Carlyle's solicitor and proposed executor, John Forster. Whether he read them or not, Forster made no comment on the manuscripts or on Froude's and Carlyle's plans for the timing and sequence of their publication. Recognising the seriousness of what was in train, however, Forster urged Carlyle to make Froude's position clear in the form of a will. In February 1876 Carlyle complied, and in a new will formally named Froude as his literary executor, though he added confusion by the vagueness in which he described the nature of his commission to Froude.

---

11. *Carlyle: Life in London*, 411–14.

Having made the will, however, Carlyle almost immediately complicated Froude's position further by despatching to him another, far larger, instalment of papers which included his journals, correspondence, copies of letters sent, working notes, reminiscences, and other miscellaneous materials almost overwhelming in their abundance. Once again the delivery was accompanied by the now familiar injunction: 'Take them and do what you can with them. All I can say to you is "Burn Freely". If you have any affection for me the more you burn the better.'[12]

Taken in isolation these words seemed to offer, as Froude's earliest critics' bitterly alleged, little justification for the biography that Froude went on to write. Critical scholarship has long since disposed of the claim that Froude had been acting independently of Carlyle.[13] Taken against the broader context of Froude's deep involvement in Carlyle's plans for the representation and assessment of his life, Carlyle's painfully ambiguous statement may be seen as a symptom of his grudging and fearful acceptance of the fact that some form of biographical study would have to accompany the publication of his autobiographical materials.

By the time of this final visitation Carlyle was himself resigned to the fact that, despite his wishes, biographies of him would be written. Already in the late 1860s two short biographies had appeared in German, and it was also abundantly clear that other identifiable figures who had been given access to the great man were bent on composing an early biography.[14] In these circumstances Froude understood Carlyle's actions as indicating yet another stage in his commission. If biographies were to be written, it was necessary that the one which would carry forward the true purpose of commemorating the life of Carlyle was the one which would contain within it the full significance of his terrible private life and the way in which he was attempting to atone for it. Thus, in addition to the responsibility of seeing into print the fragments of Carlyle's voices which he had accepted in 1871, Froude

---

12. *Carlyle: Life in London*, 412–15; *My Relations with Carlyle*, 14–15.
13. The early stages of the controversy are surveyed in detail—in a manner which, though largely sympathetic to Froude, is thorough and painstaking—by Waldo Hilary Dunn, *Froude and Carlyle: A Study of the Froude–Carlyle Controversy* (London, 1930); later critical discussions are considered in Trev Lynn Broughton, *Men of Letters, Writing Lives: Masculinity and Literary Biography in the Late Victorian period* (London, 1999), chs. 3–5; G. B. Tennyson, 'The Carlyles', in David J. DeLaura (ed.), *Victorian Prose: A Guide to Research* (New York, 1973); K. J. Fielding, 'Froude and Carlyle: Some New Considerations', in K. J. Fielding and Roger L. Tarr (eds.), *Carlyle, Past and Present: A Collection of New Essays* (London, 1976), 239–69.
14. John Clubbe (ed.), *Two Reminiscences of Thomas Carlyle* (Durham, NC, 1974); Froude, *Thomas Carlyle: The History of the First Forty Years of his Life* (2 vols., London, 1881), i, 'Preface'.

around 1876 now accepted a further and far heavier responsibility of supplementing those inchoate and conflicting voices with a further one which
was of equal necessity to the project as any of the others which Carlyle had
previously set in train.

It was against this background that Froude reluctantly but decisively
accepted the last part of Carlyle's commission and undertook the preparation of a biography while Carlyle was still living.[15] Carlyle's own relative
passivity in the project may seem, in the light of the interminable and
painful wrangling in which they later embroiled Froude, to have added
unnecessarily to an already massive burden. The biographical, moral, and
literary conditions from which it arose, however, were understood by both
men in a manner that made Carlyle's reticence and withdrawal perfectly
justifiable. If the fundamental message of the prophet was to be commu-
nicated in its purest form, it must be done under the terms and conditions
laid down by the prophet himself in his careful and fastidious preparation
of his remains, and represented for him by the only other mind which was
truly in tune with it.

The commission granted to Froude was therefore an immensely difficult
but at the same time an extraordinarily privileged one: to be not simply the
guardian of the late great man's reputation, but, far more importantly, his
evangelist. In assuming it, however, Froude was to be confronted by one
deeply troubling issue which presented him with a profound moral dilemma
that was to shape the very manner in which he approached the composition
of his peculiar biography. This was a secret and intimate problem which lay
at the core of the great man's private life, which not only grew deeper and
more painful for Froude, as he worked through the materials supplied to
him, but also more unavoidable.

At the back of Carlyle's initial insistence that no biography should be
written for him was his acknowledgement 'that there was a secret connected with him unknown to his closest friends, that no one knew, no one
would know it, and that without a knowledge of it no true biography of
him was possible'.[16] In fact, far from being kept securely by Carlyle alone,
that 'secret' was well known at least to some of Jane's closest friends and
eventually to Froude himself. During his consultations with Forster about

15. Froude to Carlyle, 7 September (1879), National Library of Scotland, Carlyle MSS 666,
    no. 132; to Skelton, 13 March 1880, Skelton (ed.), *Table-Talk of Shirley*; Dunn; Froude, II, 471–82.
16. *My Relations with Carlyle*, 17.

his role as Carlyle's literary executor, Forster had impressed upon Froude the significance of Carlyle's close friendship with Harriet Baring (Lady Ashburton). Up to this, Froude had regarded the affair with mild amusement: 'Lady Ashburton was a great lady of the world. Carlyle ... had the manners to the last of an Annandale peasant.'[17] As he worked through the private material Carlyle had given him, Froude began to realise the extent of Carlyle's infatuation, his 'idolatrous homage', and the demeaning manner in which he had 'made himself the plaything of her caprices'.[18] This discovery supplied a partial explanation for the unhappy atmosphere which so often prevailed among the Carlyles; and as Froude began to become aware of the extreme suffering which Carlyle's conduct had inflicted upon Jane, and of Carlyle's own awareness of the misery for which he had been responsible, a further revelation from Jane Carlyle's closest friend, Geraldine Jewsbury, threw a grim and abhorrent light on the Ashburton affair and the chronic angers at Cheyne Row:

> Carlyle was one of those persons [she told Froude] who ought never to have married. Mrs Carlyle had at first endeavoured to make the best of the position in which she found herself. But his extraordinary temper was a consequence of his organization. As he grew older and more famous he had become more violent and more overbearing. She had longed for children, and children were denied her. This had been at the bottom of all the quarrels and all the unhappiness.[19]

Froude accepted Jewsbury's testimony, not only because he regarded her as someone whose honesty and integrity rendered her incapable of 'any light or ill considered gossip', or because she confirmed the revelation on her death-bed 'with many curious details',[20] but because she authenticated in the most compelling manner what so many others, Froude included, had long suspected. 'It was common knowledge among those who visited the Carlyles that their marriage remained unconsummated,' Froude told Annie Ireland bluntly. 'Mrs Carlyle ought to have been a wife and a mother. She was neither ... Instead there was only companionship.'[21] But it was through Geraldine Jewsbury that he first saw how Jane's realisation that she would

---

17. *My Relations with Carlyle*, 16.
18. *My Relations with Carlyle*, 18.
19. *My Relations with Carlyle*, 21.
20. *My Relations with Carlyle*, 23.
21. Froude to Annie Ireland, 11, 21 October 1890, Beinecke Library, Yale University, Hilles MSS, Box 9, Froude files.

never have a fully loving relationship and never have children had driven her to despair and, on one occasion at least, to the point of suicide.

Froude's dilemma was acute. Obviously, the complete exposure of Carlyle's 'constitutional defect' was not in itself a necessity, and indeed would have been regarded as altogether inappropriate by Froude and the majority of his readers. Therefore, despite some confidential ruminations about it with friends, he had determined from the beginning to make no direct mention about it in the biography. But the importance of this unstated fact—central to so much of the character and conduct of Carlyle both in public and in private—could not be entirely ignored. Nor could other aspects of his character whose origins must in some way have been related to this hidden affliction—his biliousness, his hypochondria, his fits of depression, malice, and bouts of violent temper—be likewise brushed aside. In particular, the marked contrast between Carlyle's chronically cold (and occasionally brutal) attitude toward his wife, as revealed in her correspondence, and his tenderness toward his mother, and later his infatuation with Lady Ashburton as revealed in his own materials, was so stark as to command attention.

It was therefore more than an irony that Froude should have been presented by Carlyle with evidence of his sexual immaturity. Questions of sexual continence and incontinence had, as we have seen, been a central theme which had engaged Froude in the fictions he had produced more than thirty years earlier.[22] Edward Fowler—Froude's first fictional creation—was a sexually underdeveloped man who, even in his generally successful struggle to overcome his congenital and accidental deficiencies, still remained unable to confront the natural sexual impulses which he saw at play all around him. The sexual incompleteness of Markham Sutherland, on the other hand, was one that left him incapable of accepting full responsibility for the consequences of the natural desire that led him to fall in love with Helen Leonard.

Carlyle did not much care for Froude's early fictions; but he knew them, and it is unlikely that he had failed to grasp the nature of the issues with which the young Froude was grappling.[23] Thus, in presenting himself as a further but real embodiment of the incomplete man—a figure who in his

22. See ch.5.
23. Carlyle to John Forster, April 1849, K. J. Fielding *et al.* (eds.), *Collected Letters of Thomas and Jane Welsh Carlyle*, 12–13, 24.

insight, his courage, and his achievements had been far greater than Froude's fictional creations but still shared their essential flaw—Carlyle was adducing the greatest possible reason why Froude—and Froude alone—*must* be his biographer, and must re-engage with a problem once confronted by him but evaded and left unresolved in Carlyle's own moral mission.

For Froude, therefore, the stakes of assuming the responsibility of writing Carlyle's life could hardly have been higher. To have refused it would have entailed not only a rejection of the greatest ethical challenge with which his moral leader and mentor had presented him. It would also have amounted to a dereliction of one of the most fundamental questions which had from the beginning shaped his own moral vision: that is, the responsibility of each individual to ensure that their natural weaknesses, if they could not be over-come, should be openly confronted in a way that did no harm and might possibly be put to the benefit of all.

II

It was this unique awareness of the nature of the task before him that shaped Froude's conception of the way he would reconstruct and interpret Carlyle's life, but it also determined his view on the manner in which the entire cor-pus of Carlyle's remains should be placed before the public. To begin with, he decided that the *Reminiscences* should appear first—not in the form they had been delivered to him, but giving especial prominence to Carlyle's lat-terly composed memoir of Jane.[24] Next Froude deviated from the original plan to publish a selected edition of Jane's letters. Instead, publication of these materials would be withheld until Froude himself had produced the first two volumes of his projected four-volume biography bringing Carlyle's life up to 1839. Rather than then publishing a selected edition, however,

---

24. Allegations that Froude altered the form and structure and mode of publication of Carlyle's *Reminiscences* for his own interests, financial and otherwise, have been discredited by critical scholarship; but Froude's violation of the original manuscript by extracting Carlyle's memoir of Jane from the second section of the text to its end is undisputed: Charles Eliot Norton, 'Recollections of Carlyle', *New Princeton Review*, 2 (July 1886), 1–19; Hyder E. Rollins, 'Charles Eliot Norton and Froude', *The Journal of English and Germanic Philology*, 57 (October, 1958); Ian Campbell, 'Froude, Moncure Conway and the American Edition of the *Reminiscences*', *Carlyle Newsletter*, 8 (1987), 71–9; and especially the editor's 'Note on the Text', in K. J. Fielding (ed.), *Thomas Carlyle: Reminiscences* (Oxford, 1997), xxii–xxv. Froude placed the memoir of Jane just before the appendices including memoirs of Southey and Wordsworth.

Froude would issue a much larger collection of the letters running to three substantial volumes, before placing the final two volumes of the life before the public.[25] In the interim also, Froude, as literary executor, gave permission for the independent publication of Carlyle's *Reminiscences of my Irish Journey in 1849* and supplied a short introduction to the text.[26] In these ten volumes, therefore, the entire body of Carlyle's remains would be presented to the reading public—not haphazardly, but as an integrated whole in a sequence deliberately designed by Carlyle's literary executor.

There was nothing implicit in this. From its first appearance readers were put on notice as to the deliberate nature of this sequence. In his introduction to the *Reminiscences* Froude unfolded what he asserted to be Carlyle's own plan of the manner in which his life was to be remembered and reconstructed—the centrality of the confessional personal reminiscences, and especially of the section on Jane, the biography which Carlyle had only lately and reluctantly commissioned, and finally the importance of putting Jane's own letters and memorials before the public.[27] For those seeking a genuinely Carlylean way of coming to grips with Carlyle's own life, this was the reading course that they must follow.

To underline the point, in the preface to the first volume of *Thomas Carlyle* Froude reminded his readers that what he was presenting to them was not a biography but rather 'the materials for a life' which it was their responsibility to construct for themselves as they worked their way through the massive amount of primary evidence he was to put before them.[28] This injunction that readers must actively engage with the text is made even plainer in the manner in which Froude produced *The Letters and Memorials of Jane Welsh Carlyle*. In contrast to the editorial style of the *Reminiscences* and also to the full commentary supplied in *Thomas Carlyle*, Froude's introductory comments to this very large compilation are surprisingly brief, and throughout the text the editorial comment is kept to a minimum. On opening the first pages of the second instalment of the biography, however, readers are made aware that the author has understood that they have already

25. Froude (ed.), *Letters and Memorials of Jane Welsh Carlyle, Prepared for Publication by Thomas Carlyle* (3 vols., London, 1883).
26. Thomas Carlyle, *Reminiscences of my Irish Journey in 1849*, ed. James Anthony Froude (London, 1882).
27. Froude (ed.), *Reminiscences of Thomas Carlyle* (2 vols., London, 1881), i, v–xi.
28. Froude, *Thomas Carlyle: The History of the First Forty Years of his Life* (2 vols., London, 1881), i, 'Preface', xv.

digested the materials concerned in the *Letters and Memorials* and have also become acquainted with the Irish journal.[29] In this way he reinforces the instruction already imposed in several ways that, for a serious audience, the means of coming to know Carlyle was not simply by reading about him. It required an arduous and disciplined journey of reading and reflection, just as Carlyle had demanded of his readers in *Sartor Resartus*, *The French Revolution*, and *Cromwell*, and which in his own way Froude had sought to encourage in his *History of England*. As with those works, this programme also held out the promise of a fully transformative experience once the obligation had been fulfilled.

It is against this very particular background that Froude's biography of Carlyle—its structure, its underlying themes, and above all its pervasive mood—must be seen. Because it was envisaged as merely one component in a complex reading project, the biography was not to be a free-standing comprehensive and conventional account setting the life of the great man against the great events of his time. It was, indeed, one of the most frequent criticisms levelled against Froude that in contrast to the great works of contemporary biography—such as Forster's *Life of Dickens*, Stanley's *Life of Thomas Arnold*, or even Carlyle's own *Life of John Sterling*—his account of Carlyle made little attempt at such broad contextualisation, and that when he did so, his approach was so authorially intrusive as to reinforce the narrow and claustrophobic atmosphere of the book as a whole. Remarkably, for one whose reputation as an historian lay in the extraordinary resourcefulness and energy with which he sought out his sources, the research base for his biography of Carlyle was unusually narrow. Drawing almost entirely on the archive Carlyle had left him, and his own personal reminiscences, Froude did not go in search of corroborative evidence. He did not consult alternative bodies of correspondence. He did not refer to published matter such as newspapers, journal reviews, or other people's books. The narrowing of perspective which his almost exclusive concentration on Carlyle's own archive produced can hardly be accounted for through some lack of energy or of imagination on Froude's part. Rather, it arose from a deep conviction as to what his subject's real purpose was in allowing his life to be written. This was Carlyle's determination to have the life, lived by one whose acute insight into the realities of existence and the obligations of human agency was matched by an equal awareness of his sins and deficiencies, portrayed in

---

29. *Carlyle: Life in London*, i, 6–7.

so unflinching a manner as to be an admonition and an exemplar to those who chose to absorb it.

III

The most striking feature of Froude's *Carlyle* is its sustained and almost unvaryingly narrow focus.[30] Despite its four volumes running to over 1,800 pages, the book is far from an exercise in the 'life and times' form of biography. It is instead cast in a form that would now (perhaps unhappily) be classified as 'an intimate biography'. Although in his early years in Scotland and later in London Carlyle had developed a rich social life, seeking the acquaintance of, forming opinions of, and in turn being assessed by most of the leading figures in the cultural and intellectual elite of early and mid-Victorian Britain, it is remarkable how few of these feature or even make an appearance in Froude's pages. John Stuart Mill—Carlyle's early benefactor and inadvertent destroyer of the manuscript of the first volume of *The French Revolution*—appears on a number of occasions, and is the subject of a fair-minded assessment by Froude on the occasion of his death. Ruskin features only as his friendship with the ageing Carlyle grew closer, though not before. But these are exceptions; and a host of correspondents, acquaintances, and frequent guests at Cheyne Row, such as Southey, Tennyson, Browning, Thackeray, Dickens, F. D. Maurice, Harriet Martineau, and Lecky make only fleeting appearances. Even Carlyle's long-term close friend John Forster is introduced only as a consultant to Froude on the matter of Carlyle's intentions in regard to his papers.[31]

Those public figures who receive more than passing consideration do so for specific reasons. Thus Carlyle's dealings with Francis Jeffrey of the *Edinburgh Review* is treated at some length by Froude in order to provide a corrective to

---

30. Among the most enlightening discussions of the biography are A. O. J. Cockshut, *Truth to Life: The Art of Biography in the Nineteenth Century* (London, 1974), ch. 5; Christopher Ricks, 'Froude's Carlyle', in *Essays in Appreciation* (Oxford, 1996), 146–71; Elliot L. Gilbert, 'Rescuing Reality: Carlyle, Froude and Biographical Truth-Telling', *Victorian Studies*, 34 (Spring, 1991), 295–314; and the editor's 'Introduction' to John Clubbe (ed.), *Froude's Life of Carlyle* (Columbus, OH, 1979), 1–60.

31. C. R. Sanders, *Carlyle's Friendships and Other Studies* (Durham, NC, 1977); also Thomas A. Kirby, 'Carlyle and Irving', *English Literary History*, 13 (March 1946), 59–63, and Michael Goldberg, *Carlyle and Dickens* (Atlanta, GA, 1972); James A. Davies' entry on 'John Forster', in Mark Cumming (ed.), *The Carlyle Encyclopedia* (Danvers, MA, 2004), 163–7, which also contains several other entries on members of the Carlyle circle.

the critical account given by Carlyle himself in the *Reminiscences*; and similarly in writing about the evangelical preacher Edward Irving, Froude is concerned to offer a complementary perspective to Carlyle's earlier sketch. Irving's relative prominence in the early phases of the biography, however, is due to the brief but deep influence which he exerted on the life of one of the very few principal characters around whom the biography is constructed: the woman who married Carlyle, Jane Welsh. During their stormy and uncertain courtship Jane Welsh had continued for some time to hope for a proposal from the charismatic, unstable Irving. It was only when she learned painfully of Irving's commitment to another, Froude records, that she accepted Carlyle.

Next to Carlyle himself, Jane Welsh Carlyle is a figure of such centrality in the biography that for long stretches of the book—extending before their marriage and for long after her death—it may be accounted almost a dual biography. Chronologically, however, Jane is not the first of this small cast of characters. This position was occupied by Carlyle's mother, Margaret. Extending to the first thirty pages or so, Carlyle's early life with his family is allotted in Froude's study a space that was largely conventional in biographies of the period. His father James remains a formidable but shadowy figure, and while his eight siblings are noted as being always central in this eldest son's affections, few receive any notice, and only John, whose career intersected with Carlyle's on several subsequent occasions, is given any considerable space. This too is not unexceptional, but what distinguishes Froude's biographical perspective from the Victorian norm is the extraordinary significance which he continues throughout the book to attribute to the influence of Margaret Carlyle on her eldest child.

'A severe Calvinist', Margaret Carlyle cared anxiously for all her children's spiritual welfare, 'her eldest boy's above all'. She hoped to see him a minister. Her 'solicitude for the eternal as well as temporal interests of her darling child' was indefatigable.[32] It was love reciprocated. To Carlyle, 'his mother's love was more precious ... than any other form of earthly consolation,' 'he thought always of his mother ... the strongest personal passion which he experienced through all his life was his affection for his mother ... seldom out of his thoughts as he was seldom out of hers ... [Carlyle regarded his mother with an affection] passing the love of sons with whom ... he had more in common, as he often said, than any other mortal.'[33] 'To

---

32. *Carlyle: First Forty Years*, i, 47, 59.
33. *Carlyle: First Forty Years*, i, 98, 232, 288; ii, 137, 337.

his mother ... he showed his real heart ... Like a boy out of school' on holidays at home, Carlyle and his mother drove in a gig together 'or wandered through the shrubberies, smoking their pipes together, like a pair of lovers—as indeed they were'.[34] Lest this disturbing innuendo was regarded as unintended, Froude, in epitomising Carlyle's love of his mother, quoted from *Hamlet*:

> To his mother Carlyle was so loving,
> *That he might not between them the winds of heaven*
> *Visit her face too roughly*
> This was love indeed—love that is lost in its object and thinks first and only how to guard and foster it.[35]

It is likely that intimations of Hamlet's or Oedipus's predicament were familiar enough to the educated readers of Froude's time. But it is striking that, well in advance of Freud, Froude seemed also to be aware of the condition's sexual implications. Although first introduced as an isolated relationship, Froude gradually introduced a series of juxtapositions between Carlyle's love for his mother and his feelings for Jane Welsh. Devoting an entire chapter to Jane and her family, Froude goes on in subsequent chapters to emphasise the unstable and unequal relationship between her and Carlyle.[36] Attracted to Irving, Jane at first regarded her friendship with Carlyle as Platonic or purely intellectual, but following her rejection she allowed herself gradually to become more emotionally engaged.[37] But there were, as the biographer warns on several occasions, obvious incompatibilities. Jane was independent-minded, quick, impatient of intellectual flaccidity, and sharp-tongued, and Carlyle was self-centred, hypochondriacal, and bad-tempered. Both were strong personalities, and as Froude (in a curious Freudian slip of his own) observed, 'Two diamonds do not easily form cup and socket.'[38]

Such conflicting characteristics, in themselves merely interesting, became intensely serious when placed in the context of the couple's very different attitude toward marriage. Once in love with Irving, Jane had a clear idea of the purpose of marriage. 'There would have been no tongues', Jane much

---

34. *Carlyle: First Forty Years*, ii, 166, 272.
35. *Carlyle: First Forty Years*, i, 231.
36. *Carlyle: First Forty Years*, i, ch. viii.
37. *Carlyle: First Forty Years*, i, 145.
38. *Carlyle: First Forty Years*, i, 182; the correct formulation is surely 'ball and socket'.

later confided to Froude, referring Irving's gradual descent into insanity, 'had Irving married me.'[39] Carlyle, however, his first love vouchsafed to his mother, was little possessed of such instinctive understanding.

> He admired Miss Welsh, he loved her in a certain sense; but, like Miss Welsh, he was not *in love* [Froude's italics] ... He had allowed her image to intertwine with all his thoughts and emotions; but with love his feelings for her had nothing in common but the name. There is not a hint anywhere that he had contemplated as a remote possibility the usual consequence of a marriage—a family of children. He thought of a wife as a companion to himself who would make life easier and brighter to him. But this was all, and the images in which he dressed out the workings of his mind served only to hide their real character from himself.[40]

There are hints here the import of which, however delicately put, was unmistakable. And in case the suggestion was lost, Froude presses on: 'There were some things which Carlyle was *constitutionally* incapable of apprehending [Froude's italics] ... on which men in general do not think as he thought.'[41] But in contrast his description of the wedding night is a model of discreet inference. Having quoted from one of Carlyle's notes to Jane declaring his demands concerning his travel and accommodation arrangements and his insistence that he should smoke three cigars before they retired to bed, the delicate biographer duly notes that his travel arrangements were met in full, and adds drily: 'Whether Carlyle did or did not smoke his three cigars remains unrecorded.'[42]

Whether the Carlyle marriage was unconsummated or not remains a matter of dispute among Carlyle scholars,[43] but it is clear that Froude was convinced that it was—and, moreover, that it was his duty to indicate the case to those willing to take the hint. Why Froude should have felt this to be an obligation is a question that has occasioned controversy about his motives ever since. Psychological speculations about his desire (conscious or unconscious) to besmirch the image of his master are as untestable as they once

---

39. *Carlyle: First Forty Years*, i, 162.
40. *Carlyle: First Forty Years*, i, 232–3.
41. *Carlyle: First Forty Years*, i, 272.
42. *Carlyle: First Forty Years*, i, 296–8.
43. For balanced discussions of the matter, see Rosemary Ashton, *Thomas and Jane Carlyle: Portrait of a Marriage* (London, 2002) esp. 120–2, and Fred Kaplan, *Thomas Carlyle: A Biography* (Ithaca, NY, 1983); see also Trev Lynn Broughton, *Men of Letters, Writing Lives: Masculinity and Literary Biography in the Late Victorian Period* (London, 1999), chs. 3 and 4, for a consideration of the way in which Froude's treatment differed from others.

were common.[44] Concentration on the Carlyles' sex-life, however, has distracted attention from the larger issue with which Froude was primarily concerned, and in regard to which Carlyle's putative sexual impotence was merely an aspect. This was his subject's intrinsic defectiveness as a human being. Carlyle's inability to establish a mature separation from his mother, and his related incapacity to form a mature relationship with his partner, were merely the leading symptoms of his inherently flawed nature as a human being, other aspects of which included his petulance, his hypochondria, his violent temper, his jealousy, his insensitivity to the feelings of others, and above all his astonishing selfishness in practical matters—all of which Froude, scandalising his first readers, scrupulously revealed on every available occasion. That Carlyle was, in his mother's phrase, frequently cited and slightly misquoted by Froude, 'gey ill to liv wi'', might be seen as the *leitmotif* of this intimate biography, but underlying it was the even more devastating charge which Froude made more explicit as the biography advanced—that Carlyle remained in many respects a child.

> No one who reads his letters to [Jane] can doubt of his perfect confidence in her, or of his childlike affection for her. She was the one person in the world besides his mother whose character he completely admired ... whose happiness he was most anxious to secure ... But he came home to drive her immediately distracted ... These were times when Carlyle was like a child, and like a very naughty one ... It was not easy to live with a husband subject to strange fits of passion and depression, often as unreasonable as a child ... With all his splendid gifts, moral and intellectual, Carlyle was a like a wayward child—a child in wilfulness, a child in the intensity of remorse.[45]

There is on the surface a disturbing resemblance between Froude's biographical portrait of Carlyle and the anti-heroes of his early fictions, Edward Fowler and Markham Sutherland—both acutely morally aware and intellectually able, but both unable, when challenged, to rise to the demands of mature adult relationships, and one of them (Fowler) sexually incapable. But such similarity was merely preliminary. Unlike Sutherland and far more than Fowler, Carlyle rose triumphantly above the defects etched on his character by nature and environment to see through to the greatest prospects and challenges facing humankind as a whole. Such a gift having been granted to him, he elected to

---

44. James Crichton-Browne, *The Nemesis of Froude* (London, 1903). For an entertainingly extreme statement of this view, see Marshall Kelly, *Froude: A Study of his Life and Character* (London, 1907).

45. *Carlyle, Life in London*, i, 328, 78; ii, 212.

devote his entire life to the revelation of such a vision to all of his fellow creatures with such unflinching courage, earnestness, and self-sacrifice as had transformed this ordinarily afflicted man into a truly great human being.

But he did even more. Rather than seeking to evade his defects—like Fowler—or collapsing under them altogether—like Sutherland—Carlyle determined to exploit them for his greater purposes. By having them mercilessly revealed without evasion or extenuation, he would show that the revelation that had been granted to him was not the product of some unique personal quality but was available to each and every individual, no matter what their faults. Further to that, he would demonstrate in himself the truth of the precept that remorse and attrition were at once the necessary but also the universally available attitudes and actions for those seeking liberation from their inherited conditions.

Carlyle's unexpected presentation to Froude of Jane's correspondence and of the section of the *Reminiscences* which he had devoted to her with the injunction either to publish or destroy the materials was 'something so beautiful, so unexampled in the whole history of literature' that despite the deeply painful nature of the lives they disclosed, Froude 'could not but admire it with all my heart ... In his heroic life there was nothing more heroic, more characteristic of him, more indicative at once of his humility and his intense truthfulness.'[46] But the decision to act on this *démarche*, Carlyle had left entirely to Froude. It was this intimate engagement which rendered it inescapable that the fourth main character in his biography should be the biographer himself.

IV

Though most of the major biographies of the late nineteenth century were written by close acquaintances of their subject—Forster on Dickens, Stanley on Thomas Arnold, Gaskell on Charlotte Brontë, Morley on Gladstone, Fanny Kingsley on her husband—in no case, even the last, were the levels of involvement so many and so intense as in Froude's bond with Carlyle.[47] Its

---

46. *Carlyle, Life in London*, ii, 410.
47. For critical discussions of such biographies, see A. O. J. Cockshut, *Truth to Life: The Art of Biography in the Nineteenth Century* (London, 1974); James A. Davies, *John Forster: A Literary Life* (Leicester, 1983), ch. 11; Linda H. Peterson, 'Elizabeth Gaskell's *The Life of Charlotte Brontë*', in Jill L. Matus (ed.), *The Cambridge Companion to Elizabeth Gaskell* (Cambridge, 2007), ch. 5.

special character is announced in the opening pages, which detail the complicated and changing circumstances out of which Froude's commission arose. How Carlyle had not wished to have his life recorded at all: 'No one, he said, was likely to understand a history, the secret of which was unknown to his closest friends.' And how, when it became clear that unauthorised lives would be written in any case, Carlyle commissioned Froude as his official biographer, but 'with unfettered discretion'. Froude had therefore to present Carlyle in whatever light he chose.[48]

> And if I had studied my own comfort or the pleasure of my immediate readers, I should have produced a portrait as agreeable, and at least as faithful, as those favoured saints in the Catholic calendar. But it would have been ... an ideal, or, in other words, an idol to be worshipped one day and thrown away the next ... [Carlyle] himself laid down the conditions under which a biographer must do his work, if he would do it honestly, without the fear of man before him; and in dealing with Carlyle's own memory, I have felt myself bound to conform to his own rule'.[49]

That Froude was clearly troubled by this role is clear, for he returned to a defence of his position as a special biographer several times in the book. He concluded the first two volumes of the set with a section of apologetic reflections entitled 'Lights and Shadows'. Although he reiterated the claim, less persuasive after all that has gone before, that Carlyle 'has been substantially his own biographer', he immediately qualified it on the grounds that Carlyle was not of a character 'to see the lights and shadows of his life precisely as others see them'. And then he expresses doubt: 'If in this part of my duty I have erred at all, I have erred in excess, not in defect. It is the nature of men to dwell on the thoughts of those who stand above them. They are comforted by perceiving that the person whom they have heard so much admired was but of common clay after all.'[50]

Froude goes on to qualify such self-questioning comments: 'The life of no man, authentically told, will ever be found free from fault.' Carlyle was battling bravely with the consequences of being a genius, isolated among men in a

---

48. *Carlyle, First Forty Years*, i, vii.
49. *Carlyle, First Forty Years*, i, vii–viii. Froude expressed the same conviction more frankly in private correspondence: Froude to Colonel Higginson, 9 October [1884/5]: 'I should be false to him and false to my duty if I was to make him as a painted idol for the mob to put in their Temples [*sic*] like their Christs and Virgins while, by "keeping the commandments", they think as little of either one or the other,' Pierpont Morgan Library, New York, Misc. English MSS, MA 4500.
50. *Carlyle: First Forty Years*, ii, 470.

generally unfeeling and indifferent world: 'He carried the scars from his wounds both on his mind and on his temper,' and for the life of such a man authentically to be recorded, the scars must be revealed withal.[51] Elsewhere, again under the pressure of doubt, Froude likens 'the functions of a biographer [to] the functions of a Greek chorus, occasionally at the important moments to throw in some moral remarks' relevant to the occasion.[52] Again, after revealing and commenting on a particularly disagreeable aspect of Carlyle's conduct toward Jane, he is partially and awkwardly contrite, alluding again to *Hamlet*: 'I, as if, feel in dwelling on his wilfulness "I did him wrong, being so majestical, to offer him the show of violence".' Once more the confession is immediately withdrawn: 'But I learnt my duty from himself: to keep back nothing and extenuate nothing. I never knew a man whose reputation, take him for all in all, would emerge less scathed from so hard a scrutiny.'[53]

Finally, in two extended passages toward the close of the biography, Froude—by then fully aware of the hostility with which his work was being met—offered a carefully sequential account of the emergence of this critical biographical voice. Having determined that he should indeed be Carlyle's authorised biographer, Froude had first proposed to interweave parts of some of Jane Carlyle's letters with Carlyle's own, 'in an ordinary narrative, passing lightly over the rest, and touching the dangerous places, only so far as unavoidable'. 'The evasion of this difficulty', Froude adds disarmingly, 'was perhaps cowardly, but it was not unnatural.'[54] Carlyle's insistence, however, that a full edition of Jane's letters be published rendered such a course impossible. Publication of the letters necessary implied publication of Carlyle's own remorseful account of their marriage as part of the *Reminiscences*, and that in turn required a change in tone of the biography. At first Froude protested. The publication of the letters would restrict his discretion, and he could no longer use them as he had originally envisaged. 'But [Carlyle] was so sorrowful and earnest—though still giving no positive order—that I could make no objection.' 'I was forced back into the straighter and better course.' 'My final conclusion may have been right or wrong, but the influence which turned the balance was Carlyle's persevering wish, and my own conviction that it was a wish supremely honourable to him.'[55]

51. *Carlyle: First Forty Years*, ii, 469–78.
52. *Carlyle: First Forty Years*, i, 284, and see also 347.
53. *Carlyle: First Forty Years*, i, 355–6.
54. *Carlyle: Life in London*, ii, 414–15.
55. *Carlyle: Life in London*, ii, 415, 466–7.

The voice of the troubled moral executor, however, is not the only one adopted by Froude in the course of the biography. He is in addition the close confidant, the ardent disciple, and the critic. Though Froude first met Carlyle when his subject was fifty-three years old, and came to know him more closely only when Carlyle was in his late sixties, readers of the biography are made aware from its opening pages of Froude's special relationship not only through the prefatory matter detailing the origins of the biography, but also through a series of interjections in which Froude related confidences shared with him both by Carlyle and by Jane. As the biography advances, autobiographical incidents which might in other exercises in the genre have been reserved to a preface or afterword are treated as significant events in the book. Thus Froude's first introduction to Carlyle's writings, his first meeting with the great man, and his increasing closeness to him in the 1860s, are each given extensive treatment. In recording the single most catastrophic event in Carlyle's life—the sudden death of Jane while he was absent in Scotland—Froude also deems it appropriate to inform his readers that he himself had been invited to dine with Jane at Cheyne Row on that very night. The concluding volume of the biography contains two extensive sections in which Froude recounts the impressions and recollections derived from his almost daily meetings with Carlyle late in life which, in addition to noting his literary and philosophical *obiter dicta*, included instances of Carlyle's inveterate charity toward the (often undeserving) poor, his love for animals, his love of riding and his inferior horsemanship, his knowing self-deprecation, and the mildly ridiculous figure which he cut on the top of a London omnibus.

There is nothing in these reminiscences, apart from their frequency, that would have been regarded as altogether inappropriate at the time, but such affectionate observations of a close companion sit somewhat uncomfortably with two further contrasting voices which Froude frequently assumes: that of the devoted disciple, and that of the discriminating literary critic.

Concerning the fervency of Froude's devotion to Carlyle, little further needs to be said here. It is avowed in statements of belief in Carlyle's unique genius and unparalleled nobility which are scattered throughout the book: 'From the time I became acquainted with his writings, [I] looked on him as my own guide and master ... If I wrote anything, I fancied myself writing it to him.'[56] The source of this fidelity is revealed in one of the most elo-

56. *Carlyle: Life in London*, ii, 179–80.

quent passages in the book, describing Carlyle's effect on the troubled young
generation of the 1840s, which deserves quotation at length:

> It was an era of new ideas, of swift if silent spiritual revolution ... All round
> us the intellectual lightships had broken from their moorings ... The present
> generation which has grown up in an open spiritual ocean ... will never
> know what it was to find the lights all drifting, the compasses all awry, and
> nothing left to steer by except the stars. In this condition the best and bravest
> of my own contemporaries determined to have done with insincerity, to find
> ground under their feet, to let the uncertain remain uncertain, but to learn
> how much and what we could honestly regard as true, and believe that and
> live by it. Tennyson became the voice of this feeling in poetry ... Carlyle
> stood beside him as a prophet and teacher; and the young, the generous, to
> anyone who took life seriously ... his words were like the morning reveille
> ... [his] voice was to the young generation of Englishmen like the sound of
> 'ten thousand trumpets' ... [Carlyle] was the first to make us see [God's]
> actual and active presence *now* in this working world, not in rhetoric and fine
> sentiments, not in problematic miracles ... but in clear letters of fire which all
> might read, written over the entire surface of human experience.[57]

Froude could scarcely have given a more sincere testimony of his devotion
to Carlyle than this; but critics could hardly be blamed for noticing that such
declarations appeared somewhat hollow when juxtaposed to the remorseless
revelations of Carlyle's bad behaviour, the sinister insinuations as to the psychological origins of such conduct, and the seemingly condescending tone
which he frequently took toward his subject's foibles and weaknesses.

Though it was only occasionally perceptible in the manner in which
Froude commented upon Carlyle's petty eccentricities, his superior tone
appears to become more marked when Froude offered a critical assessment
of Carlyle's scholarly abilities and writings. The former Oxford don does
not take long to tell readers that Carlyle's Scottish education left him a poor
classicist, who had been unacquainted directly with Plato and Aristotle until
well into his adult life.[58] Froude was not alone in concluding that Carlyle
had not a genuine talent for verse, but he nonetheless felt it necessary to
make the point explicit by providing examples of his subject's best efforts in
the genre.[59] Despite Carlyle's own confidence in his potential as a novelist,
Froude dissented:

---

57. *Carlyle: Life in London*, i, 290–3.
58. *Carlyle: First Forty Years*, i, 129–30; *Carlyle: Life in London*, ii, 31.
59. *Carlyle: First Forty Years*, i, 323–5.

He could not write a novel, any more than he could write poetry. He had no *invention* [Froude's italics]. His genius was for fact: to lay hold on truth with all his intellect and all his imagination. He could no more invent than he could lie.[60]

Froude is no less critically discriminating in regard to Carlyle's major works. Such critical observations as he made on Carlyle's writings were, in accordance with the conventions of the biographical form, relatively brief and laudatory. But it is possible to discern within the subtle nuances of Froude's prose a clear sense not only of his critical assessment of the relative success of the works in Carlyle's canon, but of their larger significance in regard to his central purpose. Most of Carlyle's published works are duly noted by Froude from his early biographical sketch of Schiller to his last letter to *The Times*; but some items are ignored—notably Carlyle's early essays on 'History'—and some are allotted greater space than others.

Concerning *Sartor Resartus*—often regarded as Carlyle's most enduring work—Froude has relatively little to say, and his judgement is ambivalent. The book was conceived in Carlyle's mental tumult; but

> With all his efforts in calmer times to give it artistic harmony, he could never fully succeed. 'There are but a few pages in it', he said to me, 'which are rightly done'. It is perhaps as well that he did not succeed ... If defective as a work of art, *Sartor* is for that very reason a revelation of Carlyle's individuality.[61]

Froude's assessment of *The French Revolution* was far more positive and more extensive: 'it is in many ways the most perfect of his writings ... It stands alone in artistic regularity and completeness ... It has been called an epic. It is rather an Aeschylean drama, composed of facts literally true, in which the Furies are seen once more walking on this prosaic earth and shaking their serpent hair.'[62]

Carlyle was a prophet for the times, struggling 'to tell the modern world that, destitute as its affairs seemed to be of Divine guidance, God or justice was still in the middle of it, sternly inexorable as ever; that modern nations were as entirely governed by God's law as the Israelites had been in Palestine'.[63] For Froude, however, *The French Revolution* was no conventional exercise in the genre that might be submitted to the normal modes of criticism and evaluation. It was a 'spectral' history:

60. *Carlyle: First Forty Years*, i, 370.
61. *Carlyle: First Forty Years*, ii, 130.
62. *Carlyle: Life in London*, i.
63. *Carlyle: Life in London*, i, 89.

> For the actors in it appear without their earthly clothes: men and women in their natural characters, but as in some vast phantasmagoria, with the supernatural shining through them, working in fancy their own wills or their own imagination, in reality the mere instruments of a superior power, infernal or divine, whose awful presence is felt while it is unseen.[64]

Curiously, given the effect it had on the establishment of Carlyle's career, Froude passes lightly over *On Heroes, Hero Worship and the Heroic in History*. He writes sensitively about the contemporary audacity of Carlyle's attack on the complacent nostrums of liberty and *laissez faire* in *Past and Present*; but 'the arrangement is awkward—as awkward as that of *Sartor* for indeed there is no arrangement at all'.[65]

By contrast, *The Letters and Speeches of Oliver Cromwell* is a recognisably more conventional historical exercise. It is, Froude declares with some self-deprecating authority, 'by far the most important contribution to English history which has been made in the present century. Carlyle was the first to break the crust which has overlaid the subject of Cromwell since the Restoration, and to make Cromwell and Cromwell's age again intelligible.'[66] Yet it is not without flaw:

> Contrary to his own rule that the historian should confine himself to the facts with the minimum of commentary, Carlyle breaks in repeatedly in his own person, pats his friends on the back, expands, applauds, criticises to an extent which most readers would wish more limited ... Perhaps he allowed too little for our ability to think for ourselves.[67]

Frederick the Great was another masterpiece—'the last and grandest of them'—and supplies the occasion for an extended excursus by Froude on the philosophy of history which he and Carlyle shared.[68] In its anticipation of the future of German and European history—it was completed six years before the battle of Sedan—it was proleptic. But to the English audience to whom it was primarily addressed, it was not a success.

> The English mind remains insular and is hard to interest supremely in any history but its own. The tone of Frederick nowhere harmonised with popular sentiment among us, and every page contained something to offend.[69]

64. *Carlyle: Life in London*, i, 90.
65. *Carlyle: Life in London*, i, 284.
66. *Carlyle: Life in London*, i, 356–7.
67. *Carlyle: Life in London*, i, 357.
68. *Carlyle: Life in London*, ii, 200–5.
69. *Carlyle: Life in London*, ii, 284–5.

Finally, though Froude mounts a robust defence of *Latter-Day Pamphlets*, he felt obliged to register the enormous reputational damage which followed their publication. 'Wrath' drove Carlyle into writing them. Although much of what he had said against the hypocrisies and hidden cruelties of the 'cant' of political economy had since been vindicated,

> he said it fiercely, scornfully, in the tone that could least conciliate attention ... The ferocity with which he struck right and left at honoured names, the contempt which he heaped on an amiable, if not a wise experiment [prison reform] gave an impression of his own character as false as it was unpleasant ... He had nourished some practical hope for those pamphlets, and had imagined that he might perhaps be himself invited to assist in carrying out some of the changes that he had there insisted on. Such hopes, if he had formed them ... were utterly groundless.[70]

If Froude had been writing a detached intellectual biography in the modern mode, none of these critical qualifications would be regarded as anything other than necessary or helpful. Yet not only were such critical reservations comparatively rare in the standard Victorian 'Life', combined with the relentless revelation of Carlyle's failings as a private individual, they also appeared to subvert the claim of the biographer/disciple that Carlyle was the greatest man he ever knew, and was indeed one of the greatest who ever lived. Seen in this light, it is easy to understand how those claiming to be the great man's true disciples then and since, including Charles Eliot Norton, David Wilson, and Alexander Carlyle, regarded Froude's claims to fidelity as at best self-delusional and at worst malicious.

Such imputations have long since lost force; and equally, any assumption that Froude was writing something as modern as the life of a public intellectual is also wide of the mark. Single-mindedly and with an acute understanding of its special requirements and challenges, Froude was himself clear about the nature of the work he had undertaken. He was not writing the life of a public intellectual, he was writing the life of a modern prophet; and it was not in regard to their value as critical studies, but in the degree to which they inspired their readers to become engaged with the issues they raised that Carlyle's published writings were most properly assessed.

---

70. *Carlyle: Life in London*, ii, 21, 24, 30, 56.

V

That Froude had consciously conceived his book as a portrait of a genuine prophet is declared at its very opening and at several points thereafter:

> He was a teacher and a prophet in the Jewish sense of the word. The prophecies of Isaiah and Jeremiah have become a part of the permanent spiritual inheritance of mankind because ... [t]hey had interpreted correctly the signs of their own times, and their prophecies were fulfilled. Carlyle ... believed that he had a special message to deliver to the present age ... If, like his great predecessors, he has read truly the tendencies of this modern age ... then Carlyle too will take his place among the inspired seers, and he will shine on, another fixed star in the intellectual sky.[71]

Thus asserted in the preface, this conviction forms the *leitmotif* of the entire book. 'Carlyle's mission was that of a prophet and teacher—and a prophet's lessons can only be driven home in prose.'[72] He was 'an Ishmaelite, his hand against everyman and everyman against his'; he was the 'prophet of a new religion', the Prophet of Cheyne Row.[73] Isolated in Edinburgh, Carlyle was 'a prophet ... not readily acknowledged in his own country'. *Past and Present* was a 'prophetic utterance'. Carlyle was the 'prophet and teacher' of Froude's generation.[74]

In the closing pages of the first set of volumes Froude reiterates at length the declaration of the preface:

> Men who fancy that they have a 'mission' in this world are usually intoxicated by vanity, and their ambition is in the inverse ratio of their strength to give effect to it. But in Carlyle the sense of having a mission was the growth of the actual presence in him of the necessary powers. Certain associations, certain aspects of human life and duty had forced themselves upon him as truths of immeasurable consequence which the world was forgetting. He was a *vates*, a seer. He perceived things which others did not see. He regarded himself as being charged actually and really with a message which he was to deliver to mankind, and, like other prophets, he was 'straitened' till his work was accomplished.[75]

---

71. *Carlyle: First Forty Years*, i, xv–xvi.
72. *Carlyle: First Forty Years*, ii, 370.
73. *Carlyle: Life in London*, i, 11, 248, 252.
74. *Carlyle: Life in London*, i, 286, 291. This was stated even more trenchantly in private correspondence: 'Carlyle', he told Colonel Higginson, 'saw deeper into the spiritual and moral condition of the modern world than any of the false prophets whom [the people] take as their practical guides', Pierpont Morgan Library, New York, Misc. English MSS, MA 4500.
75. *Carlyle: First Forty Years*, ii, 384.

It was this conviction that he had been charged to present the life of Carlyle as that of a prophet for the modern age that shaped Froude's conception of the biography at every level. It was this which rendered necessary the painful revelations and honest judgements which he felt obliged to make about Carlyle's private character, and above all about his treatment of his wife: 'No concealment is permissible about a man who could thus take on himself the character of a prophet and speak to it in so imperious a tone.'[76] But the exposure of Carlyle's personal flaws was obligatory, not merely a matter of scrupulousness. In recognising them, in seeking to overcome them, and finally in transcending them through one great act of attrition of publishing Jane's letters and his own self-accusing 'Reminiscence', he had succeeded at length in integrating them into his supreme mission to present the truth of its condition to humankind. The prophet disarmed was the prophet triumphant.

The representation of Carlyle as a prophet not only determined the manner in which Froude dealt with the details of his private life; it also shaped his approach toward the assessment of his subject's published work. In addressing them, Froude's aim was not to evaluate each of Carlyle's writings as contributions to one or other of the intellectual and cultural developments taking place at the time, but rather to estimate the degree to which they served his primary purpose of bringing his readers to a true understanding of their place in Creation. Thus, while Carlyle's *Life of John Sterling* was among his most accomplished pieces—'he was no longer censuring the world as a prophet, but delighting it as an artist'—it was not among his most significant.[77] By the standards to which Carlyle had committed himself, it was to *The French Revolution* that primary place was allotted because of its combination of artistry and prophecy, and a sliding scale of Carlyle's other published achievements might be constructed on the basis of Froude's commentary from *Cromwell* down to the repelling bile of *Latter-Day Pamphlets*.

But the evaluation of the collective or individual achievement of Carlyle's literary output was not Froude's primary concern. Just as he had expected readers to have made themselves familiar with the *Reminiscences* and the *Letters and Memorials* as they made their way through the biography, so he assumed that they would also have taken the trouble to read at least some of the readily available works. His intent was to supply the context of their

76. *Carlyle: Life in London*, i, 4.
77. *Carlyle: Life in London*, ii, 75.

gestation and completion through the provision of extensive extracts from
Carlyle's letters, journals, and notebooks, and to offer supplementary commentary sufficient to enable readers to return to those texts with renewed
and informed attention. In his function as the biographer of a prophet,
Froude's primary aim was to use these extracts from Carlyle's private papers
to trace the emergence and development of his sense of mission, of which
his published work was merely the end product. Thus it was that, juxtaposed
to the persistent theme that as a particular human being Carlyle was 'gey ill
to liv wi'', was the contrapuntal theme of the evolution of Carlyle's sense of
the unique vision that had been granted to him—a sense that was at heart
religious.

'The secret of a man's nature', Froude writes at the beginning of the
second volume of the biography, 'lies in his religion, in what he really
believes about the world, and his own place in it.'[78] He had already devoted
considerable space in the previous volume to Carlyle's early struggles in
regard to religion—his growing dissatisfaction with the narrow Calvinist
orthodoxies under which he had grown up, and the painful consequences
of his loss of faith.[79] But now, in one of his very few departures from strict
chronology in the whole course of the biography, Froude produces for his
readers a lengthy extract from an unfinished draft of an essay composed by
Carlyle more than twenty years later to illustrate the position which Carlyle
had reached by his early thirties. There was nothing disingenuous about this:
Froude indeed makes his decision to violate chronology perfectly plain. He
was concerned to provide the clearest statement possible of Carlyle's mature
spiritual beliefs as a platform on which all his subsequent expressions, published and private, might properly be understood, and Carlyle had assured
him that it contained a 'conviction that lay at the bottom of all his thoughts
about man and man's doings in this world'.[80]

Although it was left untitled by Carlyle, Froude silently supplies the title
'Spiritual Optics' for this late unfinished essay.[81] He derived it from Carlyle's
imaginative analogy between the revolution in the science of optics achieved
by Galileo and Newton which replaced the old Ptolemaic view that the

---

78. *Carlyle: First Forty Years*, ii, 1.
79. *Carlyle: First Forty Years*, i, ch. 5, also 101–7.
80. *Carlyle: First Forty Years*, ii, 13.
81. *Carlyle: First Forty Years*, ii, 8–14. For a critical edition and discussion of the original manuscript
    and a comparison with Froude's edited text, see Murray Baumgarten, 'Carlyle and "Spiritual
    Optics"', *Victorian Studies*, 11 (June 1968), 511–22.

earth was at the centre of the universe, and a revolution in man's view of himself in the universe. The unthinking assumption that man was at the centre of the divine plan was at the root, Carlyle claimed, of all the trouble afflicting conventional religions—from the bigoted intolerance of one era to the troubled agnostic doubts of the present. Only reverse the perspective, and see mankind not as the centre but as a mere component of a vast divine Creation, and all those difficulties disappear at once. Humanity, though nothing more than 'poor, insignificant transitory bipeds', has nevertheless a distinctive role to play, a role whose lineaments can be discerned in all it has done, in the things it has built and thought—in short, in its conscious history. Human history, rather than the Bible, thus becomes the true source of the revelation of God's plan, and the study of history becomes the means not only of discovering God's will but of discerning the particular role—or duty—allotted to each of us in bringing it to fulfilment. Thus all of humanity's doubts and troubles are resolved in a humble self-denying determination to act for God in the world.

Froude is surely right in claiming that the insight presented in condensed form in this relatively late essay had informed much of Carlyle's work from *Sartor Resartus* and *On Heroes, Hero Worship and the Heroic in History*, most effectively in *The French Revolution*, and can even be discerned underneath the corrosive invective of *Latter-Day Pamphlets*.[82] But it is an unfinished, unpolished draft, and there are several passages in the original manuscript displaying self-doubt and straining to overcome it by rhetorical force which Froude omitted from his extract.

There is no reason to read much into such silent editing. In most cases, as Murray Baumgarten's careful analysis has shown, Froude was primarily concerned with clarifying and presenting Carlyle's message in the simplest form.[83] He was more than ready also to reveal Carlyle's own perturbation concerning his apparent inability properly to convey this insight in his previous writings: 'Till lately I had vaguely supposed that everybody understood it or at least understood me to mean it, which it would appear that they don't at all.'[84]

---

82. Among many discussions, see Albert J. La Valley, *Carlyle and the Idea of the Modern: Studies in Carlyle's Prophetic Literature and its Relation to Blake, Nietzsche, Marx and Others* (New Haven, CT, 1968); also J. P. Vijn, *Carlyle and Jean Paul: Their Spiritual Optics* (Utrecht, 1982) pt. iii.
83. Baumgarten, 'Carlyle and "Spiritual Optics"'.
84. *Carlyle: First Forty Years*, ii, 9.

Far from seeking to conceal them, Froude allowed Carlyle's increasing doubts about his ability to communicate his fundamental message to his readers to become an important theme in the second half of the biography. In the early 1850s, around the time he had sketched 'Spiritual Optics', Froude reports Carlyle's intense struggles to find a new vehicle for the presentation of his religious views. *Exodus from Houndsditch* was a projected volume in which Carlyle was to provide the basis for a new post-Christian religion to address the crisis of modern agnosticism and materialism. But though he returned to it frequently, it was a book, Froude reports, that Carlyle found 'impossible' to write.

> The 'Hebrew old clothes' were attached so closely to pious natures that to tear off the wrapping would be to leave their souls to perish in spiritual nakedness; and were so bound up with the national moral convictions that the sense of duty could not be separated from the belief in the technical inspiration of the Bible. And yet Carlyle knew that it could do no good to anyone to believe what was untrue.[85]

So why did he fail in this prophetic commission? Because, Froude explains, there was nothing to replace the delusional religious practices but 'the Gospel of Progress which was falser even than they'. Having originally been convinced that the *Exodus from Houndsditch* would give effect to this spiritual revolution,

> He had come to see that it would be but an entry into a wilderness, the promised land lying still far away. His own opinions seemed to be taking no hold. He had cast his bread upon the waters and it was not returning to him, and the exodus appeared less entirely desirable.[86]

This is a painful revelation of the prophet's sense of his declining powers in or around his sixty-ninth year. His frustration was further exacerbated by his failure to come to terms with modern science, specifically with Darwin. In contrast to Newman and indeed to Froude himself—both of whom took an open-minded attitude toward the theory of natural selection and its ethical implications—Carlyle, Froude records, was nervously hostile.[87]

---

85. *Carlyle: Life in London*, i, 423,
86. *Carlyle: Life in London*, ii, 262.
87. Direct references to Darwin in Froude's writings are rare, but his discussion in 'Science and Theology, Ancient and Modern', in *The International Review*, 5 (May, July, 1878), 289–302, 492–506, reveals a qualified acceptance of the processes of natural selection.

He liked *ill*, men like Humboldt, Laplace and the author of the *Vestiges*. He refused Darwin's transmutation of the species as unproved; he fought against it, though I could see he dreaded that it might turn out true. If man, as explained by Science, was no more than a developed animal, and conscience and intellect but developments of the functions of animals, then God and religion were no more than inferences, and inferences which might be lawfully disputed. That the grandest achievements of human nature had sprung out of beliefs which might be mere illusions, Carlyle could not admit.[88]

His denials notwithstanding, anxieties concerning the discoveries of science ran deep. In one of his regular theological conversations with Carlyle shortly before his death, Froude had observed that he 'could only believe in a God which *did* something' [Froude's italics]. 'With a cry of pain which I shall never forget, he said, "He does nothing"'.[89]

There may seem to be something of a paradox in Froude's text between the prophet triumphing over his personal defects and the prophet gradually losing command over his public audience. But the incongruity is more apparent than real, for in the text of the biography Froude is not writing separately about different aspects of Carlyle. By continually interweaving its public and private dimensions, he is intent on presenting Carlyle's life in the most dramatic form as a continuing struggle against his own human defects, against the conventional wisdom of the age, against the temptations of success and the self-pity of neglect. His narrative had been cast in such a form, however, not primarily to underline Carlyle's heroism, but rather to make clear the struggle which will inevitably be entailed when any individual, more or less defective, elects to follow Carlyle's way.

VI

It is in this context that a final central character in this intimate biography finally emerges in the person of the readers themselves. From its very opening pages, Froude, like the author of *The French Revolution*, has invited his readers into a special relationship both with himself as biographer and with the subject of the biography from which it proves increasingly to be difficult to escape, short of a complete refusal of sympathy to both. All of those

88. *Carlyle: Life in London*, ii, 259.
89. *Carlyle: Life in London*, ii, 260.

revelations of the complicated circumstances out of which the biographical commission emerged, and which recur throughout the text, are accompanied by the admonition that the readers have been provided only with the materials of a life which they themselves must fashion from their reading. In encouraging them in this, Froude has supplied his readers not only with copious extracts from the most private letters and journals which form the central spine of the narrative, but also with a sustained commentary—on some occasions frankly judgemental, on others subtly inferential—designed to reinforce the book's central theme. This is the heroism and greatness of the ordinarily defective individual who strives to overcome his faults in order to fulfil the duty of prophecy which has been imposed on him.

This is the formal aspect of the lessons which readers are expected to absorb: an exemplary demonstration of the truth that real knowledge of the world requires constant action and constant struggle such as that performed by its most passionate proponent. But the substantive element of the message is of equal importance. The readership to whom Carlyle had addressed himself—or more properly to whom Froude's biography is addressed—is specifically English, and it is the main purpose of the biography to clarify, to reinvigorate, and if necessary to revive that message in a manner expressly pertinent to the English.

The significance of Carlyle's message to the English is made clear throughout the whole of the book both in a positive and a negative sense. At the outset, readers are informed by Carlyle's own words that this will not be a typical biography of an English man of letters: 'A Damocles' sword of *Respectability* hangs over the poor English lifewriter ... and reduces him to the verge of paralysis.'[90] But this was a reticence—an avoidance of truth—which Carlyle had challenged at every opportunity, and in this his biographer, and his biographer's readers, must follow.

At the opening of the second set of volumes Froude glosses this Carlylean injunction. To have written a 'respectable' biography would have been unjust not only to Carlyle but to his public:

> His writings are now spread over the whole English-speaking world. They are studied with eagerness and confidence by millions who have looked, and look to him not for amusement, but for moral guidance and those millions have a right to know what manner of man he really was.[91]

90. *Carlyle: First Forty Years*, i, ix.
91. *Carlyle: Life in London*, i, 4.

It had not always, of course, been so. Carlyle, as befits a prophet, was not at first recognised by the people among whom he came to preach. There was no place for a man of his genius among the English who 'hitherto had supposed that the Bible had contained everything which it was indispensable for a man to know'. 'But England was growing, growing it knew not into what, but visibly needing further help.' Carlyle saw this, and he knew that he had 'something of infinite importance' to say.[92]

> England, as he saw it, was saturated with cant, dosed to surfeit with doctrines half true only or not true at all, doctrines religious, doctrines moral, doctrines political, till the once noble, and at heart still noble, English character was losing its truth, its simplicity, its energy, its integrity. Between England as it was, and England as it might yet rouse itself to be, and as it once had been, there was to Carlyle visible an infinite difference ... The degradation of the once great English people, absorbed, all of them, in a rage for gold and pleasure, was itself sufficient to stir him to fury.[93]

And so Carlyle became immersed in this broadest possible version of 'the condition of England'.

All of Carlyle's writings, Froude asserts—his essays, his lectures, *The French Revolution,* his *Cromwell,* even his *Frederick the Great*—were to the same purpose and on the same text. Famine in Ireland, revolution in Europe, convinced him that 'an equal catastrophe lay over England itself if she did not mend her ways ... He did not believe in immediate convulsion in England; but he did believe that unless England took warning ... her turn would come.'[94] This prophecy drove him to the extremes of the *Latter-Day Pamphlets,* but he had failed: 'He had lifted up his voice, and no one would listen to him, and he was irritated, disappointed, and perhaps surprised at the impotence of his own admonitions.'[95] 'The world says now that I am this and that, and professes to admire me', Carlyle told Froude in private, 'but they do nothing which I have told them and they do not believe what I say'.[96]

Although disappointed, however, he never despaired. The great debate over the broadening of the franchise again called him forth. He could not resist it, but he believed that

92. *Carlyle: Life in London,* i, 189–91, 224.
93. *Carlyle: Life in London,* i, 224, 281.
94. *Carlyle: Life in London,* i, 406, 429.
95. *Carlyle: Life in London,* ii, 85.
96. Froude to Colonel Higginson, 9 October [1884/5], Pierpont Morgan Library, New York, Misc. English MSS, MA 4500.

> If the English nation had needed governing when they had a religious belief,
> now, when their belief had become conventional, they needed it ... infinitely
> more ... [But] he knew how many fine qualities the English still possessed.
> He did not believe that the majority were bent on themselves on these
> destructive courses. If the wisest and ablest would come forward with a clear
> and honourable profession of their true convictions, he had considered it at
> least possible that the best part of the nation would respond before it was too
> late.[97]

He continued in this confidence to the end, boldly intervening on behalf of
Governor Eyre besieged by *bien pensant* liberals, attacking with equal bold-
ness the Balkan policies of the Disraeli administration, but above all working in solitary self-abnegation to produce the materials for his finest literary
and moral work of which this biography was the final instalment. Until
with death

> [his] work for England had closed, and yet had not closed. It is perhaps rather
> in its infancy; for he, being dead, yet speaks to us as no other man in this cen-
> tury has spoken or is likely to speak ... In future years, in future centuries,
> strangers will come from ... every isle or continent where the English lan-
> guage is spoken to see the house where Carlyle was born.[98]

But, Froude concludes, no monument will be necessary, for a man who in
all his writing, but most especially in this final bold experiment in which he
used Froude as his final alternating voice, 'has made an eternal memorial for
himself in the hearts of all to whom truth is the dearest of possessions'.[99]

The sincerity of this belief is evidenced in the fidelity and pertinacity
with which Froude executed this extraordinary commission to write the
life of a modern prophet with the combination of celebration, edification,
criticism, and censure which such an undertaking necessarily required. That
such an original and radically ambitious enterprise should provoke bewilderment, anger, and a sense of betrayal among many who would be counted
as admirers of Carlyle was inevitable. That Froude himself expected and was
stoically prepared to suffer such reactions is abundantly clear from his private correspondence both during the preparation of the volumes and in the
long aftermath of their appearance. Froude's riposte to such criticism,
anticipated within the biography itself and repeated on several occasions

97. *Carlyle: Life in London*, ii, 348–9.
98. *Carlyle: Life in London*, ii, 471–3.
99. *Carlyle: Life in London*, 473–4.

thereafter, was remarkably consistent. He was acting in accord with Carlyle's wishes in everything he wrote, and the appropriateness of what he had done would be entirely vindicated in the future when the true significance of Carlyle's teaching was appreciated: 'The world will understand it all hereafter and will love him and admire him all the more for his truthfulness. I too shall get justice bye and bye.'[100]

There can be little doubt that Froude underestimated, and was overwhelmed by, the bitterness and violence of the response to the book. His private journals for the mid-1880s (as shown to Waldo Henry Dunn) and his testimony published posthumously as *My Relations with Carlyle* bear more than ample witness to the extent of his suffering:

> 25 Feb 1887: The Carlyle worry comes back on me sometimes. What, in the name of truth, ought I to have done? It was a tragedy, as truly and as terribly as Oedipus; nor was the character altogether unlike … Was I to hide all this when he had prepared his own indictment?

> 5 March 1887: Bad Carlyle fit on me. What my connexion with him has cost me … Then the ten years of worry before the book was finished, and the worry for the rest of my life.[101]

Invariably heartfelt expressions of personal regret such as these were followed by affirmations that both Carlyle and his biographer would ultimately be vindicated.

> A hundred years hence the world will better appreciate Carlyle's magnitude. The sense of his importance, in my opinion will increase with every generation. The unwillingness to look closely into his character will be exchanged for an earnest desire to know all which can be ascertained about him, and what I have written will then have value.[102]

This confidently anticipated vindication has not yet arrived; and even if it be said that the issues of personal moral obligation, truthfulness, and a defiant rejection of the falsehoods of the inherited world are more pertinent than ever, the use to which Carlyle has sometimes been put in the twentieth century has hardly advanced the process. So for all its artistic merit, Froude's

---

100. Froude to [unknown], 24 September (1884), Pierpont Morgan Library, New York, Misc. English MSS, MA 4500. For similar expressions, Froude to Ruskin, 29 May (1886), Viljoen, (ed.), *The Froude–Ruskin Friendship*, 48–9; Froude to Skelton, 1 November (1884), *Table-Talk of Shirley*, 186.

101. Dunn, *Froude*, II, 550.

102. Froude, *My Relations with Carlyle*, 40.

biography must, on its own very ambitious terms, so far be accounted a failure.

In the years immediately following the publication of the biography, however, as the storm of controversy continued to obscure Carlyle's call to the English of the urgent necessity of personal moral regeneration, Froude himself continued to shoulder the responsibility of cultivating the sensibilities of those most likely to respond to Carlyle's appeal which his acceptance of the biographical commission had imposed on him. In the final and remarkably productive decade of his life, this consciously accepted evangelical role was to result in some of the best, but also much of the worst, writing that he had ever committed to print.

13

Educating Carlyle's Orphans:
Space, 1884–88

Among the several marked changes in register in Froude's literary voice which occurred over his career, the final one which emerged almost immediately upon the completion of the Carlyle commission was the sharpest; and, short of a simple regression to speculations about his intellectual and physical exhaustion, it is also the most difficult to account for.

I

For those seeking support for the view that Froude did indeed feel exhausted, isolated, and increasingly out of sympathy with the temper of his times, there is ample evidence to be found in his private correspondence. The furious reaction which his biography of Carlyle had provoked bore heavily on him. The bitter legal wranglings of Carlyle's own relatives, and the public condemnations of former friends and major international critics, such as Charles Eliot Norton, hurt him deeply—far more than the outrage with which so many of his earlier works had provoked in certain quarters. Froude's suffering in regard to this book was no doubt made worse by the fact that he felt unable under the terms of Carlyle's commission to defend himself in public in any way. It was at this time also that he was compelled to cope with the suicide of his eldest and troubled son Pascoe (Grenny) in distant Cape Town.[1] Amidst all this, it is hardly surprising that his privately expressed thoughts should reveal signs of the recurrence of the melancholy

---

1. See ch.1.

and sense of futility that had afflicted him during his adolescence and upon the death of his second wife.[2]

It is important, however, to guard against reaching a conclusion based largely on a reading of Froude's private letters. On this occasion as on the others, Froude sought to transcend the depression which threatened him by vigorous action—by accepting public engagements, by travel, and by work. Almost immediately upon the completion of the Carlyle project, he set out upon a world tour, travelling eastward to the antipodes and returning by way of a crossing of the United States and the Atlantic. Hardly home, he set off again in 1886 to the West Indies for another six-month journey; and both in the intervening period and thereafter he engaged energetically in extensive sea-going voyages in his own yacht moored at Salcombe. Moreover, despite his notoriety in many quarters, he remained a public man, making speeches and public statements on several causes—against Home Rule, in favour of stronger copyright laws, and especially in support of the idea of a British Commonwealth. Most importantly, in 1892 (aged 74) he gracefully accepted Lord Salisbury's nomination to the Regius Chair of History at Oxford, despite the daunting lecturing loads which had deterred so many others.

His literary output during these years also shows little evidence of a loss of energy. Between 1884 and 1894 Froude produced no less than ten books, including two volumes of travel writing, four historical studies, two collections of essays, two short biographies, and a novel, as well as several lesser contributions to journals and magazines. This was hardly the record of a man tired of life and with nothing left to say.

The problem of Froude's work in this last phase, however, relates not to its quantity but its quality. While several of his productions were to enjoy a passing popularity, none was to be of lasting significance, several rapidly acquired an unsavoury reputation for intellectual weakness or dishonesty, and only a very few retain an interest for the literary and intellectual historian. Far from showing development, most of Froude's late historical studies,

---

2. Froude's private pessimism and sense of defeat is evident in his correspondence with Ruskin during these years; see Helen Gill Viljoen (ed.), *The Froude–Ruskin Friendship, as Represented through Letters*, for example, Froude to Ruskin, 13 November 1884: 'I am listless and hopeless, hopeless most of all about myself: for I see all through my life that when I have ever done what my reason and conscience tell me to be right—I have always done it in the wrong way' (29); also 32, 38–9, 44–5, 57. See also Froude's correspondence with Annie Ireland, Beinecke Library, Yale University, Hilles MSS Box 9, F, and to Mr Scooner, 29 March (1886/7); Osborne MSS 5542.

for instance, reveal merely a reiteration of old themes or a dreary defence of old arguments, and despite some glimmers of new perspectives and old strengths to be found in his posthumously published Oxford lectures on Erasmus and the Council of Trent, the grand project of writing a history of Europe in the reign of Charles V never materialised.[3] The novel *The Two Chiefs of Dunboy* is an historical romance, a weak imitation of the boy's adventure stories of Robert Louis Stevenson, and while it reveals interesting evidence of the deeper issues underlying Froude's attitude to Ireland, it shows nothing of the serious engagement with the adult issues of his earlier fictions. Above all, Froude's two volumes of travel literature project a persona whose opinions and prejudices have become all the more distasteful because of the disingenuous and insinuating manner in which they are presented to the readers.

II

The first of these two efforts—*Oceana: or England and her Colonies*—appeared in January 1886 as the outcome of a leisurely tour of the British colonies in Australasia and revisits to the Cape Colony and the United States which Froude, accompanied by his second son, Ashley, undertook between December 1884 and May 1885. Although Froude had occasionally experimented with travel writing in the past, in his two essays on Kerry which preceded his history of Ireland, and in his two essays on the Norwegian fjords which he published in the early 1880s, this was his first book-length exercise in the genre.[4]

As a book, however, it differed in significant ways from those he had produced before 1880. Unlike the big histories of England and Ireland, this was a relatively short, single-volume text which was reissued as a cheap popular

3. Froude to Ruskin, 10, 13 March 1886, *Froude –Ruskin Friendship*, 36, 38; Froude to Max Müller, 8 December 1881, Dunn, *Froude*, II, 491; entry from Froude's West Indian journal, 7 March 1887, Dunn, *Froude*, II, 550.
4. In 'A Fortnight in Kerry' *Fraser's Magazine*, NS. 1, 3 (April 1870, January 1871), 513–30, 28–45, Froude's persona as a traveller and the dynamic of reactive travel observation was subordinated to more sustained political, social, and historical commentary. The two essays on 'The Norway Fjords' and 'Norway Once More', *Longman's Magazine*, 1, 4 (December 1882, October 1884), 195–222, 588–608, with their occasional personal intimations and sprinklings of philosophical reflections, may more properly be seen as preliminary exercises in the genre which Froude was to explore on a larger canvas in the mid-1880s.

edition within three months of its first appearance. Adorned by a set of photographs and engraved sketches, its 340 pages were divided into twenty-one chapters averaging merely seventeen pages and rarely exceeding twenty pages in length. Its contents pages provided detailed chapter synopses which were repeated at the head of each chapter and reinforced by carefully indic-ative running headlines, but no index is supplied which might have enabled readers to consult, cross-check, or otherwise use the volume as a handbook or work of reference. *Oceana*, in short, was designed to appeal to a broad, unsophisticated, and largely uncritical audience, and to encourage a mode of reading as a leisurely rather than a scholarly exercise. As such, it marks a development of the compositional and expressive techniques first essayed in Froude's *Caesar* and a further departure from the demanding requirements imposed on the readers of the *History of England*, or of the publications con-cerning Carlyle. Despite such differences in tone and style, however, and its very different intended rhetorical appeal, it may be shown to have been deliberately conceived in a manner no less manipulative in its intent than any of Froude's previous writings.

That *Oceana*, like so much Victorian travel writing, was more or less deliberately conceived by Froude for political and ideological purposes was obvious from the time of its appearance,[5] and it is this aspect of the book that has attracted most critical comment ever since.[6] Froude, in fact, made no secret of his ideological motivations. Political issues are central, for instance, in chapters 3 and 4, where he provides a potted history of the British government's unhappy dealings with the colonies, and repeats his case for a sustained interventionist policy. They recur in chapters 10–13, in which Froude reports his conversations with Melbourne politicians and records their anxieties concerning their place in the Empire, their eagerness to prove their loyalty by sending troops to the Sudan, and the far-sighted imperial views of men such as Premier Dalley and the deputy governor, Sir Alfred Stephen.[7] The book is framed also by two chapters in which Froude

5. For perceptive reviews linking Froude's travel book to his earlier essays on the colonies, see *The Academy*, 29 (30 January 1886), 68–70; *The Edinburgh Review*, 163 (April 1886), 405–36; *Macmillan's Magazine*, 54 (August 1886), 261–5; *Nineteenth Century*, 20 (August 1886), 171–82.
6. For a recent analysis which emphasises the distinctiveness of Froude's 'civic imperialism', see Duncan Bell, 'Republican Imperialism: J. A. Froude and the Virtue of Empire', *History of Political Thought*, 30 (2009), 166–91, and Bell, *The Idea of a Greater Britain: Empire and the Future of World Order, 1860–1900* (Princeton, NJ, 2007), ch. 5.
7. *Oceana: or England and her Colonies* (London, Longman, 1886), chs. xi–xii. References are made here to the more accessible Silver Library edition (1898).

makes his own political preferences and ideological perspectives absolutely plain.[8]

In these chapters the by now familiar elements of the colonial argument are again rehearsed. The neglect of liberal politicians and political economists, the failure to alleviate the suffering of the poor (especially the children) in England, the disappointment and disillusion of the colonists, the imminence of imperial rivalries, and the loss of the best emigrants to America are again reviewed. In Whitehall the old notion persists 'that colonies exist only for the benefit of the mother country', as sources of raw materials, of revenue, of penal resort, or political patronage; and as these benefits have steadily diminished, the possibility of separation has been regarded with equanimity. One relatively novel point, however, is given special emphasis: colonial policy has remained 'in the hands of men of rank, or of men who aspire to rank' who have habitually regarded the colonists as 'socially their inferiors, out of their sphere, and without personal point of contact'.[9]

This pointed observation is supplemented by a personal note. As the historian of England's greatest era, Froude had sought to spread the message that another age of achievement might dawn if only England would look to her colonies. Yet 'my sermons [were] as useless as such compositions usually are'.[10] His frustrating experiences in South Africa followed, but in the interval Froude had discovered that there existed at home a far stronger, warmer sentiment for the maintenance of the tie with the colonies which he now sought to nourish. Since 1884, he contended, a new political force has arisen:

> The people are now sovereign, and officials of all ranks will obey their masters. It is with the people that the colonists feel a real relationship. Let the people give the officials to understand that the bond which holds the Empire together will not be weakened any more but is to be maintained and strengthened ... There are certain things which only Democracy can execute; and the unity of our Empire, all parts of which shall be free and yet inseparable, can only be brought about by the pronounced will of the majority ... If the colonies are to remain integral parts of Oceana, it will be through the will of the people.[11]

---

8. *Oceana*, chs. i, xxi. For a recent discussion of the place of *Oceana* in Froude's colonial writings as a whole, see Theodore Koditschek, *Liberalism, Imperialism and the Historical Imagination: Nineteenth Century Visions of a Greater Britain* (Cambridge, 2011), ch.4.

9. *Oceana*, 8, 12, 332–6.

10. *Oceana*, 14.   11. *Oceana*, 337.

This eulogy to democracy would have sounded hollow to those who were aware of Froude's recently published views on the effects of democratisation, not to mention those in receipt of his private correspondence.[12] His overtly populist appeal notwithstanding, Froude was frank in professing no great confidence in democracy as a permanent form of government. Unlike capitalism, it was not, he confidently predicted, destined to endure. Its real historical value was to serve as a means of reviving and strengthening the British Empire in much the same way as it had served in laying the foundations of the Roman Empire in the closing days of the Roman Republic.[13]

It was this sense that his England was at precisely this time undergoing a particular historical moment not unlike (though not identical with) one which it had previously experienced at a crucial time in the mid-seventeenth century that was the inspiration behind his choice of title. Froude took it from a treatise composed in the mid-seventeenth century by James Harrington, entitled *The Commonwealth of Oceana*.[14] A substantial exercise in political argument published in 1656 at the height of the English experiment in republicanism, Harrington's *Oceana* presented a utopian vision of a future England that was avowedly republican in its assumptions and radical in many of its proposals.[15] It had long since fallen into obscurity, surpassed in influence by Hobbes and Locke; and though noticed briefly by Burke and Coleridge and praised for its support of religious toleration by Lecky, at the time Froude wrote it remained a forgotten text.[16]

There were several reasons why Froude should have turned to Harrington. It was in Harrington that he found support for some of his own cherished proposals, including mandatory military service, disestablishmentarianism, the maintenance of property qualifications for office-holding, and above all state support for an expanding British Empire. For Harrington, the establishment and defence of British colonies in the world was not simply a means of extracting wealth or disposing of surplus population or surplus goods. It was key to the survival and growth of the commonwealth of England itself. Harrington's seaborne commonwealth looked west, to the settlements

---

12. Froude, 'A Lesson on Democracy', *Fortnightly Review*, NS 32 (December, 1882), 728–47.
13. *Oceana*, 338–41.
14. *The Commonwealth of Oceana [1656] and a System of Politics*, ed. J. G. A. Pocock (Cambridge, 1992).
15. For contrasting assessments of Harrington's intent, see R. H. Tawney, 'Harrington's Interpretation of his Age', *Proceedings of the British Academy*, 27 (1941), 199–233; and J. G. A. Pocock, *The Ancient Constitution and the Feudal Law* (2nd edn., Cambridge, 1987), ch. 6.
16. H. F. Russell Smith, *James Harrington and his Oceana* (Cambridge, 1914).

already thriving in North America and the Caribbean.[17] But the change of geographical direction was of little significance, and Froude was perhaps also taking advantage of the linguistic association between Harrington's title and the term currently being employed to encompass all the South Pacific islands and Australasia: 'Oceania'.[18]

Although he was groping toward a broader concept of the seaborne 'commonwealth', Harrington's interest in overseas colonies remained centred on England; and though it was presented in a more oblique way, England remained Froude's centre of gravity also.[19] Indeed, at several points in the text Froude directly confronts differences of opinion between metropolitans and colonials. For state-sponsored emigration to be paid for by the British taxpayer there was, for example, universal support among the colonists; but for reciprocal measures, such as the provision of places in the House of Lords for colonial representatives, there was generally no enthusiasm. 'General comprehensive schemes will almost certainly fail', Froude warned his English readers, 'they will assuredly fail if suggested from England.'[20] The point, however, was not to let the colonists have it all their own way, but to encourage them to develop their own demands on the imperial system and to create an atmosphere of public debate at home sufficiently receptive to make those demands effective.

If all of this seemed highly sympathetic to the colonials' interests, other sections—notably chapters 14 and 15 and a section of chapter 18, all of which deal with New Zealand—present a rather different evaluation. The British settlements there enjoyed as great a potential for development as anywhere else, but almost immediately this promise had been impaired by an anarchic political system and a prodigal attitude toward borrowing which had resulted in the accumulation of a massive public debt. Although a few wise heads in the colony were fully aware of the inescapable problems that lay in store, an air of unreality prevailed elsewhere. The New Zealanders were as loud in their professions of loyalty as any colonist, and were as

17. Pocock, *Ancient Constitution*, ch.6; David Armytage, *The Ideological Origins of the British Empire* (Cambridge, 2000), ch.5.
18. Froude began reading Harrington only after his return from his circumnavigation, Froude to [unknown], 19 May (1885), Duke University, Special Collections Library, Froude MSS.
19. Other fruitful points of comparison can be derived from Mark Goldie, 'The Civil Religion of James Harrington', in Anthony Pagden (ed.), *The Language of Political Thought in Early Modern Europe* (Cambridge, 1989), 197–224.
20. *Oceana*, 194.

anxious for a great imperial war with Russia (or anyone else) as any jingoist; but they were quite unwilling to take any responsibility for it. Theirs

> was a loyalty which implied that we were to do anything for them—protect their coasts, lend them money as long as they wanted it, and allow them to elect a governor who should be entirely independent of us ... but we were to bear the entire expense—every part of it. Let us do all this cheerfully and then they would see how attached they were to us.[21]

Froude's strictures on the New Zealanders were to embroil him in controversy with antipodean reviewers.[22] But, as ever, Froude's primary concern was with his *English* readers, and his sharply contrasting observations on Australia and New Zealand were of primary value in allowing him to assure his domestic readers that an open and generous attitude toward the colonies did not imply a total surrender to their demands. In Oceana, as in its Roman model, all constituents, metropolitans and colonials alike, would have equal rights.

This setting forth of a new area of debate in which both England and her colonies would have an equal voice, and in which the English side of the debate would be influenced by an aspiring and appropriately informed new electorate, was a principal intention of the overtly political sections of *Oceana*. But the largely non-political chapters which constitute the bulk of the book also give a clear indication of Froude's ideas as to how that vital but as yet immature electorate should be appropriately informed.

Froude's method of instruction in these sections is characteristically indirect. The sheer motion of the journey provides an apparently innocent frame of discussion, as chronological narrative had done in the histories. Beginning on 9 December 1884 and ending on the 16 May 1885 (Froude is consciously precise about his dating), the circumnavigation took just over six months to complete. Regarding the seaborne sections of the journey, Froude has no travellers' tales of disruption, delay, disaster, or even disappointment to report. All, in fact, ran smoothly, and the voyage was concluded 'brilliantly' by registering the fastest passage yet recorded for an Atlantic crossing. The message being conveyed here is unmistakable: the British Oceana is not only global in its extent; it is also easily accessible and easily traversed, and communication is becoming easier by the year.[23]

21. *Oceana*, 283–4.
22. See, for example, the responses in the *Auckland Weekly News*, 6 March 1886, and the *New Zealand Mail*, 19 March, 2 July 1886.
23. *Oceana*, 329.

As in the case of historical narrative, the motif of the journey also provided an opportunity for selective emphasis and digression. Among the most obvious of these was the encounter with fellow travellers and colonial residents. Although independent accounts of Froude's actual demeanour on the voyage out that have come down to us suggests that he was a far from sociable or inquisitive traveller, as an author he is careful to assure his readers that he is far more interested in meeting people than observing things.[24] The people he encounters are all, moreover, conveniently relevant to his concerns. Some he has deliberately sought out, such as the Cape Premier Thomas Upington and the dynamic, pro-imperial Prime Minister of New South Wales, William Dalley. Others, usually unnamed, serve convenient rhetorical purposes, such as the young Australian man whom Froude cited as representative of all that settlement's contradictory sentiments.[25] The Irish too feature significantly. His readers, for example, are introduced to the emigrating peasant who, having attained his 'fixity of tenure', was ruined by borrowing—'Thim banks was the ruin of me', he exclaims rather helpfully to Froude. 'I had rather had to do with the worst landlord that ever was in Ireland than with thim banks'—and also to a patriotic Irish priest, 'his coat … threadbare, his cheeks … lean, his eyes … eager and dreamy' with his optimistic vision of an Ireland that would be at once Catholic and religiously tolerant. The presentation of 'this new victim of the old illusion' enables Froude to remind his English readers in 1886 that the necessity of facing up to the challenges and dangers of Empire are more urgent and more immediate that they might assume.[26]

Other chance meetings serve different but equally instructive purposes—such as the contrast Froude sets up between the eager and naïve missionary who believed too much in everything he had been taught, and the cynical, clever, 'Mephistophelic sort of gentleman' who believed in nothing at all, both of whom he claims to have met in quick succession on the voyage out from Auckland, and both warning of the temptations of colonial experience and the need to temper commitment with pragmatism and *vice versa*.[27] Between both there is the quasi-Carlylean Scot who 'had been thrown into the arena of colonial life with thousands of others … [and] had made his

---

24. See the account by Fr F. P. Kavanagh of his onboard conversations with Froude, *Freeman's Journal*, Tuesday, 18 May 1886.

25. *Oceana*, 298–9.

26. *Oceana*, 23, 200–1.

27. *Oceana*, 290–8.

way to the front.' Although he had once been radical, he was now a Tory 'because he had property to lose, and did not wish to lie at the mercy of those who thought as he had once thought himself'.

> He did not believe in the permanence of any forms of government ... The English constitution he regarded as an accidental result of the struggle between the feudal and popular elements ... It had been elevated into a principle ... held up as an example for all mankind, but its time was nearly out ... It would fail when there were no longer two parties and the democracy was completely supreme ... The only progress worth speaking of was moral progress. All the rest was only change, and often a change for the worse.[28]

Carlyle, and perhaps the Cromwellian Harrington, *redux*.

Despite their obvious utility to his purposes, there is no need to suspect that Froude simply conjured up these encounters—the Irish priest identified himself, while dissociating himself from Froude's account—but readers are entirely dependent on Froude's discretion as to what these individuals actually said, and the context in which they said it. One figure who is at the same time real and also idealised is Sir George Grey.[29] An old colonial hand, Grey had been appointed Governor of New Zealand in the early 1850s during the last of the Maori wars, where his firm but just rule over the defeated Maoris had earned him the title of 'their white father'. Disillusioned with the colonial service and 'having failed in his attempt for a seat in the English parliament', this modern Prospero had retired to Kawau—an island in the Hauraki Gulf—and there constructed for himself a utopia in the midst of Oceana. On Kawau, all the beneficent effects of Froude's colonial fantasy were already, apparently, realities. The economy of the island flourished under Grey's innovative and imaginative management. Attracted by his enlightened tenurial policies, new settlers and natives alike prospered in this 'little kingdom', and on his own demesne, owner and labourers lived in harmony:

> Between him and them, though he and they were alike Republicans, there had grown up unconsciously a feudal relationship, and seemed to feel that they belonged to one another for life. In manners these men were gentlemen: courteous, many, deferential to Sir George ... but with him and everyone,

---

28. *Oceana*, 290–1.
29. *Oceana*, ch. xviii, *passim*; compare N. C. Pollock, 'Sir George Grey and Kawau Island, New Zealand', *Geographical Journal*, 139 (1973), 191–2.

frank open and sincere; contradicting him if necessary, and looking boldly in his face as they did so.[30]

Amidst all of this, surrounded by loyal servants and faithful retainers, and also by his books—for like Prospero, Sir George, Froude informs his readers, is a bibliophile—the old man has completed his withdrawal from the world.

But the fragility of this Prosperine idyll is deftly suggested by Froude in a number of ways. Grey has his own contradictions and peculiarities. He persists in his radical beliefs, even though his practices are soundly tradi- tional. He insists too on his theory that the Maori were Japanese by descent, though the evidence seems to confound him.[31] His solitude, moreover, is far from perfect, for to preserve it from the jealous and prying eyes of the main- landers he is compelled at regular intervals to permit shooting parties from Auckland to disport themselves, killing deer at his expense. Theoretically he allows one buck to each boat, 'but he added sorrowfully "They wound more than they kill"'. And lastly, Sir George is old and soon to die; and when he does, all of his achievements, Froude fears, will wither and be forgotten.[32]

To these ominous signs Froude adds a symbolic one. During his stay with Sir George he and his companions were themselves caught up in a tempest. The only significant travel adventure recorded in the book, the storm was also a relatively mild affair evaded by a prompt decision on Froude's part to seek shelter in a neighbouring island. But the experience was a jolt back to realities: Froude and his companions were charged the going rate for board and lodgings as they waited out the storm, and they returned to worldly, grasping Auckland to resume their tour.[33] Encompassing at once Froude's admiration of all that might be achieved by enlightened colonial- ism, and his recognition that such a potential was far from being realised in Britain's colonial possessions as a whole, Froude's account of Sir George's island is an epitome of his entire treatise. Such singular and iso- lated experiments like Kawau were never likely to achieve conversions by the strength of their example alone until the broader and deeper impera- tives which underlay them had been understood and endorsed by the majority of people both in England and in the colonies. It is toward the

---

30. *Oceana*, 270.   31. *Oceana*, 267–8.
32. *Oceana*, 272–3. Grey did not die until 1898, and was in attendance at Froude's funeral.
33. *Oceana*, 275–82.

development of this recognition of mutual dependence, responsibility, and obligation that *Oceana* is devoted.

In working toward this end, Froude introduces his readers to two other sets of characters quite different from those real or idealised individuals he encountered on tour. The first of these are the authors of classical antiquity. References to classical writers are scattered throughout *Oceana*, and are used to give support to whatever argument or observation he is making at that point. Thus Horace is esteemed as 'a true prophet' of the dangers now facing England which once threatened to engulf Rome; Ovid is condemned as an instance of the decadent despair those dangers had induced; and Virgil is revered as a poetic celebrant of the empire which arose triumphantly from them. Pindar is praised as the clear-eyed but uncompromising poet of humanity's potential for virtue; Pericles is cited on civic virtue. Ennius supplies the epigraph to the entire text—'Moribus antiquis res stat Romana virisque'—and throughout his narrative Homer's seafaring hero is never far from Froude's mind.[34]

These recurring references to the Classical canon serve several purposes. They confirm the narrator's status as an educated, reflective man whose opinions and observations should be taken seriously, and they may be seen as part of his educative programme for the new readership (with the exception of the epigraph, all the quotations are given in translation). But it is of greater significance still. The voices of antiquity, Froude recognises, are linked to us 'only by the identity of humanity'. But it is in this that their very strength lies; for despite scientific advance, despite progress, despite all of history, 'human nature remains as it was. Science grows but morality is stationary.' For this reason, the great Classical authors (excluding Ovid) are

> the immortal lights in the intellectual sky, and shine on unaffected by the wrecks of empires, or the changes of creeds. In them you find human nature the same yesterday, to-day and forever. These great ones are beyond the power of Fate, and no intellectual revolution can shake them from their thrones.[35]

This eulogy was more than an indulgence. What the great writers in every era have demonstrated is the eternal nature of moral truth, even in the midst of ceaseless flux and pervasive decay.

---

34. *Oceana*, 8, 9, 20–2, 91, 204–5, 306. Ennius's maxim may be translated idiomatically as 'The strength of Rome rests on ancient traditions and heroes.'
35. *Oceana*, 204.

This insistence on the eternal nature of moral truths even amidst the flux of history is reinforced by Froude through the second set of figures encountered on his travels. These are the over-arching but non-human entities who together supply the pervasive environment within which all of his narrative develops: the sea and the sky, or, more precisely, the stars. The ideological importance of the sea in the armoury of this imperialist Englishman has already been suggested. It serves as the medium of unity, commonality, and facility of travel and communication within the same cultural community. For the inhabitants of one small island claiming equality with or superiority over the great territorial empires of Russia and the United States, Froude's affirmation that the sea was 'the natural home of Englishmen' was a useful and persuasive rhetorical device.[36]

The symbolic significance of the sea is, however, deepened when it is paired with the other element with which in Froude it is commonly associated. Among the more puzzling (and for some critics more irritating) features of *Oceana* was the way in which this travel journal is interrupted by reflections on astronomical and universal phenomena which appear to run counter to the search for the particular and the exotic with which such a genre is characteristically concerned. The journey has hardly begun when Froude launches into speculations as to how scientific advance has fundamentally altered our understanding of the night sky, severing us from the imaginative visions of the ancients.[37] On arrival at Melbourne, the first public building he visits after Government House is the Observatory—two successive tours of which allow him an opportunity for further reflections on astronomical measurement and knowledge.[38] An unusually high sea serves as an occasion for a technical discussion in which Froude suggests that the earth may be possessed of a force resisting and countervailing the processes of entropy.[39] A visit to the volcanic district on New Zealand's North Island becomes an opportunity for speculation on the origins and possible future of the planet,[40]

---

36. *Oceana*, 16. On the symbolic role of the sea for Froude and other Victorians, see Cynthia F. Behrman, *Victorian Myths of the Sea* (Athens, OH, 1977).

37. *Oceana*, 22–8.

38. *Oceana*, 92–3, 99–100. The symbolic importance of an observatory as a means of glimpsing the universe is also employed by Froude in his near-contemporary fable 'A Sibylline Leaf', *Blackwood's Magazine*, 133 (April 1883), 573–92, discussed in ch. 15.

39. *Oceana*, 64–5.

40. *Oceana*, 227–9, 246–51. This section of Froude's journey has been perceptively analysed in Anne Maxwell, 'Oceana Revisited: J. A. Froude's 1884 Journey to New Zealand and the Pink and White Terraces', *Victorian Literature and Culture*, 37 (2009), 377–90.

and even less impressive occasions—such as New Year's Eve and the passing of the International Date Line—prompt yet more considerations on time and infinity. At one point, however, Froude makes clear the significance of this recurring reference upward. History is but an evanescent thing:

> The generations of man are but the hours of a season ... the memory of them is trampled on by the million feet of their successors ... But the stars which we see are the stars which they saw. Time has not dimmed their brilliance ... Time for them is not. They are themselves the measures and creators of time ... In the silent solitude of sea and sky the unanswerable questions thrust themselves upon one unasked: 'What is it all? What am I? What is anything?'[41]

This counterpointing of the eternal, the natural, and the historically ephemeral which recurs throughout the book is opened rather more directly in two condensed philosophical passages which occur near its opening. Philosophical idealists from Plato to Schopenhauer, Froude tells his readers, have claimed 'that nothing is of which no idea has been formed by some conscious being ... [and that] the material universe is created and sustained by spirit, and without spirit is nothing'. Idealism, he goes on to suggest, implies a certain form of determinism: 'The event, whatever it is to be, lies determined ... in the chain of causation.'[42] And if so, what is the point of assertive human action? But any one event, says Froude,

> is not more determined than all else which is to happen to us, and the determination does not make us sit still and wait till it comes. Among the causes are included our own exertions and each of us must do what he can, be it small or great, as this course or that seems right to him. If we work on the right side, coral insects as we are, we may contribute something not entirely useless to the general welfare.[43]

Here, in potted and digestible form, is the Spinozan view of Creation which Froude had addressed thirty years earlier. But now Froude invokes Kant as a means of investing these theoretical reflections with a practical effect. Kant is right, he concedes, in arguing that characters such as Ulysses, Julius Caesar, Christ, or Hamlet have acquired as real an existence in the minds of mankind whether they had actually lived or not. 'Historical truth is a question of space and time which does not touch on eternal

41. *Oceana*, 25–6.   42. *Oceana*, 15.   43. *Oceana*, 25–6.

verities ... [and] the spiritual truth of a doctrine or a mythology lies in the recognition which the mind gives to it as conforming to and representing universal experience.'[44]

This is both true and necessary. Yet there is more to be advanced, Froude argues, beyond such modest positions. Julius Caesar's claims on us are strengthened because of the probability that he had in fact lived; this is even more true of Jesus; and the stars are as real as ever they can be. So the proper quest for an answer to those vast and fundamental questions posed by our location between the sea and the sky is to be pursued neither in the realms of the purely ideal or the crudely real, but in the interrelationship between the two. This is the task undertaken by the narrator of *Oceana*, and by those readers who choose to follow him. The regeneration of an energetic, reformist, and purposeful attitude toward the colonies in England would not only address the real political, diplomatic, and economic problems presently facing the country. It could go far deeper: it could initiate a personal moral renewal in all those who, on the basis of the lessons pointed by Froude, committed themselves actively to the task, releasing them from the selfish individualism which has been the curse of contemporary life in public and in private.

> United we shall all be great and strong in the greatness and strength of our common empire, and the British nation will have a career more glorious than our glorious past ... Faith in a high course is the only basis of fine and noble action. 'Believe and ye shall be saved' is as true in politics as it is in religion, and belief in the superior principle of our corporate life is itself its own realization. Let it be understood among us ... that we are one—though the bond be but a spiritual one—that separation is treason and the suggestion of it misprision of treason, and all is done.[45]

As so often before, the high-blown rhetoric which Froude is employing here is clearly intended to evoke an emotional response among the bulk of the readers at whom the book is aimed. But for the more critical and speculative minds in his audience, Froude, as we have seen, also supplied in passages and clues scattered throughout the text glimpses of the philosophical and ethical foundations which underpin and justify this modulated mode of address. Whatever inequalities of intellect and character may exist among his readers, it was Froude's aspiration that each one could be induced by different paths to acquire a common, powerfully motivating conviction

44. *Oceana*, 27–8.   45. *Oceana*, 306–7.

encapsulated in its epigraph of the Roman Republican poet: that the survival of the British nation not only as a political entity but as a moral force in the world depended on the renewal of its ancient values in modern form by the present generation.

From the perspective of his own strongly held ethical convictions, there was nothing duplicitous or even condescending about this approach to writing. To Froude it was in their moral rather than in their economic, social, or intellectual standing that the true equality of human beings lay, and it was his responsibility as a writer to appeal to all on whatever level was most appropriate to each. Moreover, given the loss of Carlyle's prophetic voice and the confusing and painful hubbub that had surrounded his own attempts to reinvoke it, it was even more imperative that Froude should find an alternative means of carrying on Carlyle's mission to his abandoned children.

There were, of course, profound contradictions in this determination of a writer, convinced for personal reasons that he had acquired a special insight into the nature of Creation, to set about the conversion of others to that insight by all means available which Froude seemed quite unwilling to address. But in the short term he was saved from the perils of self-criticism by his book's extraordinary success. *Oceana* was by far the most popular of Froude's books. Selling over 3,500 copies on its first appearance, it was reprinted five times within the first three months, and sold over 100,000 copies in nine months.[46] Thereafter it was reproduced in a cheap, popular edition which remained in print for years after his death.

III

It was indeed the immediate success of *Oceana* that encouraged Froude directly to embark upon a companion volume which would repeat the same exercise in relation to a part of the Empire quite different from and more troubling than Australasia: the West Indies. But it was this attempt at a second popular success that would inadvertently expose the fundamental ethical problems of the entire experiment in popular travel writing and their ultimate intractability.

46. Figures quoted in *Birmingham Daily Post*, Thursday, 21 October 1886.

Based upon a similarly leisurely steam-boat tour of the Caribbean in 1886, and published early in 1888, *The English in the West Indies or, The Bow of Ulysses* was in many ways a replication of the formula devised in *Oceana*. Its 372 pages, divided into twenty-two short digestible chapters, came equipped with chapter synopses, running headlines, copious illustrations, and no index. It imitated the exemplar also in structure and style. Between opening and closing chapters formally restating the familiar colonial argument, Froude supplied what he called 'sandwiches ... of politics and local descriptions' supplemented by occasional metaphysical reflections, and developed his commentary through encounters with more conveniently articulate representative figures.[47]

Some deviations from the model occur, however. Of necessity, the trip to the Caribbean and back lacked the smoothness of the original circumnavigation. But the sense of discontinuity is increased by Froude's ceaseless island-hopping whose pattern (which includes several revisits) is left unexplained by the author. The authorial voice has also declined from the assurance of *Oceana*. In *The English in the West Indies* Froude seems to be straining hard after humour. He tells jokes—including some very unfunny Irish ones—makes occasional risqué comments, and relates 'funny' incidents, such as the occasion when his argument with a black man over the treatment of a woman is interrupted by his horse who, bored by the interchange, wilfully takes the hapless author off.[48] The disingenuous tone of informality of the authoritative man of letters, relatively controlled in *Oceana*, is now exposed as a patent desire to be found endearing. Froude's readers learned, for example, of the author's insomnia, his vulnerability to mosquitoes and all kinds of insects, his imprudent penchant for cocktails, his incompetence as a billiard player, and several other forms of mild eccentricity.[49] The rhetorical intent of such disarming confessions appears to have been to enhance the effect of the informal style which had proved so successful in *Oceana*, rendering the disturbing opinions that will soon be expressed all the more persuasive on account of the innocence of their author. But here Froude appears to have gone beyond the limits of his rhetorical capacity.

---

47. Froude was encouraged by the largely positive reviews with which, like *Oceana*, the book was initially greeted in England: 'There *is* a public', he wrote enthusiastically to Skelton, 'even for sentiments so extravagantly heterodox' (Froude's italics); *Table-Talk of Shirley*, 201.
48. *English in the West Indies*, 263–4; for Irish jokes, see 66, 162, 184.
49. For example, *English in the West Indies*, 25, 43, 66, 72, 138.

Such failures of tone are symptomatic of a more general loss of authorial control. The promised sandwich of politics and observation is the familiar unvaried fare, while topics which pertain specifically to the West Indian colonies—such as the potential threat posed by the proximity of the United States, or the appropriateness of the form of rule established in British India to the West Indies, though frequently adverted to—are never developed. On occasion the apparent openness to different views, which was a rhetorical strength in *Oceana*, degenerates into confusion. In one of his philosophical excursions, for example, Froude speculates that a recognition of the incapacity of materialism and empiricism to serve as alternative religions might yet lead to a reconciliation of the Christian churches.[50] But elsewhere he declares unconditionally that the Catholic Church has altogether lost the power to sustain conviction.[51] Froude's attitude toward the Spanish Empire is similarly ambivalent. Having stood against the Reformation, Spain was destroyed by the forces of world history which made England great, and would never recover. Spain's colonisation of the New World, however, was more intense and more thorough than England's, and despite her present degeneracy 'the print of her foot is stamped in the New World in characters which will not be effaced, and may be found to be as enduring as our own'.[52]

Other inconsistencies are more serious. One of the points repeatedly insisted on by Froude is the need to impose the same form of authoritarian rule in the West Indies as was applied in India after the 1857 mutiny.[53] But he finds it difficult to deal with the one notorious episode of authoritarian rule which occurred in the West Indies: Governor Eyre's resort to martial law and the drumhead executions in 1865. Though as editor of *Fraser's* he had taken a more dispassionate view of Eyre, Froude now attempts a partial exoneration of the governor on Carlylean grounds.[54] There was a general fear of conspiracy among the whites of Jamaica—a feeling they would be slaughtered in their beds as had been done in neighbouring Haiti—and, not being a Jamaican, Eyre was too dependent on local advice. He over-reacted, his bloody repression of the rioters was ultimately unjustified, and his execution of the opposition leader Gordon was even more so. But 'the fault was

---

50. *English in the West Indies*, 269–70.
51. *English in the West Indies*, 304–7.
52. *English in the West Indies*, 304.
53. *English in the West Indies*, 204–9, 286–7.
54. Ch. xvi, *passim*.

not in Mr Eyre, and was not in the unfortunate Gordon, but in those who insisted on applying a constitutional form of government to a country where the population is so unfavourably divided'.[55] The excesses of authoritarian government could be excused, that is to say, because such a form of government had not been permitted in the first place.

The logic and ethics of this position are contorted, to say the least, but Froude's treatment of the origins of West Indian social divisions in slavery and race is even more murky. The history of slavery presents Froude with a particularly awkward problem. He must, of course, condemn it, or risk losing the sympathy of the majority of the readers he is seeking to influence. But to leave the condemnation unqualified would be to undermine not only the legitimacy of the white West Indian planters who prospered under slavery, but also the right of the English Crown, which had introduced the institution into the islands in the first place. Thus he resorts to the familiar apologias:

> They would have been slaves in their own country if they had not been brought to ours, and at the worst had lost nothing by the change ... As life goes [the black man] has been a lucky mortal. He was taken away from Dahomey and Ashanti—to be a slave indeed, but a slave to a less cruel master than he would have found at home. He had a bad time of it occasionally, and the plantation whip and the branding iron are not all dreams. Yet his owner cared for him at least as much as he cared for his cows and his horses ... The negroes who were taken away out of Africa, as compared with those who were left at home were as 'the elect to salvation' who after a brief purgatory are secured an eternity of blessedness.[56]

To persuade his readers of this, Froude repeatedly describes the simple felicity of the freedmen:

> Under the rule of England in these islands, the two millions of these poor brothers-in-law of ours are the most perfectly contented specimens of the human race to be found upon the planet ... If happiness be the satisfaction of every conscious desire, theirs is a condition which admits of no improvement ... Under the beneficent despotism of English government which knows no difference of colour and permits no oppression, they can sleep, lounge, and laugh away their lives as they please, fearing no danger.[57]

---

55. *English in the West Indies*, 261.
56. *English in the West Indies*, 49, 80–1.
57. *English in the West Indies*, 79–80.

This is at once inexcusably condescending, and utterly implausible. That Froude expected these claims to be endorsed on faith by readers whom he was also hoping would apprehend the grand philosophical issues he was placing before them is a further indication of a remarkable loss of rhetorical power. But that he should go on to argue on the basis of this presumed universal contentment that there was no need to take seriously demands that representative government be reintroduced into colonies, and that the franchise be extended to black freeholders, was even more preposterous.

The suggestion that the black population was too happy to be interested in political rights, however, was intended to serve as a support for a far more hard-headed argument which Froude was concerned to advance against the introduction of constitutional reform. Throughout the British West Indies, Froude informs his readers, the demographic balance between whites and blacks (including mulattoes) was distinctly unfavourable to the former, and growing increasingly so by the year. In these circumstances the re-establishment of any form of responsible government (representative or not) would inevitably lead to dire consequences. Should the interests of the whites be protected by franchise qualifications, they would oppress the blacks unmercifully without the restraining hand of the British government. But representative government would give rise to 'a yet grosser anomaly' in which a black majority would oppress a minority who were their superiors in all qualities, moral and mental. Either way, a war of extermination would follow, and should the whites lose or, as was more likely, flee, Britain would be bereft of a crucial part of her empire.[58]

This desperate scenario is replete with obvious internal inconsistency. The good white planters who have done so much to liberate the blacks from savagery and slavery are now potential monsters of tyranny; and likewise, the happy black folk, so contented with their present lot, will soon show their ingrained hatred of the very whites who granted them power. An English governor with a black parliament and a black ministry would be so intolerable, Froude declares, that no Englishman could accept the position, and the black politicians would despise him if he did, an observation which bluntly contradicts his earlier account of Grenada in which a black property-owning majority was apparently living per-fectly at peace both with the British governor and the white minority. Finally, there was the fleeting admission that at the back of it all Froude

58. *English in the West Indies*, 68, 74, 88–91, 123–4, 361–2.

was not primarily concerned with the fate of the white colonists or the former slaves, but with that of the Empire.[59]

More serious than any of these contradictions is Froude's discomfort in discussing the fundamental reason for which he believed that only direct rule from Britain could keep order and prosperity in the West Indies: 'We have a population to deal with the enormous majority of whom are', Froude insists, 'of an inferior race.'[60] The qualification included in this awkward formulation is symptomatic of the general ambivalence which afflicted Froude's attitude toward the non-white population of the West Indies. In his attempt to establish the basis of black people's inferiority his rhetorical talents appear to have deserted him altogether, and the techniques which he employs are as repugnant as the purposes for which they are intended.

Occlusion—deliberate or otherwise—is an important weapon in this armoury. Thus, while he takes pains to record evidence of the suspicion and hostility prevailing between blacks, 'Asiatics', and mulattoes, and includes a 'funny' incident describing a passionate debate between two black women on the status of 'half-breeds', he nowhere draws attention to important ethnic differences existing within the descendants of different African peoples.[61] All blacks are ethnically undifferentiated in Froude's account. They are socially undifferentiated also. On occasion Froude notes as exceptions singularly successful black men, such as the unnamed rich and educated young man 'with little more sense than a monkey', whom he encountered on the voyage out, or the distinguished jurist, 'Chief Justice R of Barbadoes'.[62] But they are each portrayed as suffering from their very isolation. Of the young man, Froude observes, 'that being lifted above his own people, he had been taught to despise them. He was spoilt as a black and could not be made into a white ... the inevitable and invariable consequence whenever a superior Negro contrived to raise himself.'[63] This gloomy prophecy, as Froude's earliest critics were to point out, was founded simply on a complete neglect of the substantial black middle class constituted by merchants, lawyers, professionals, and gentleman farmers who already represented a substantial interest throughout the islands. Finally,

59. *English in the West Indies*, 124–5.
60. *English in the West Indies*, 286–7.
61. *English in the West Indies*, 154–5.
62. *English in the West Indies*, 24–5, 125–6. The figure referred to by Froude was Sir William Conrad Reeves (1821–1902), Attorney General of Barbados 1884–86, and Chief Justice 1886–1902.
63. *English in the West Indies*, 25.

Froude occludes history. Although he eventually addresses the crisis of the Morant Bay revolt of 1865, nowhere in his celebration of contemporary contentment does he notice the many instances of conflict and division which had arisen from the discriminatory conduct of white estate managers and magistrates in the years before the insurrection and which continued to be recorded by public enquiry in the following twenty years.[64]

Froude's myriad evasions, selections, and misrepresentations of fact were soon to be exposed by a formidable set of West Indian critics—most notably, J. J. Thomas, N. Darnell Davies, and C. S. Salmon.[65] But, as in the case of the outrage he had once provoked among the Irish, Froude remained unperturbed by their often devastating criticisms, and disdained to reply. Again, as in the case of Ireland, Froude was not addressing the inhabitants of the country about which he wrote, but rather a distinctly English readership, the bulk of whom would read no further than his text, and whom he had every confidence would be little influenced by his Caribbean critics. In regard to retaining his attractions for this particular audience, however, Froude was prepared to go even further in the rhetorical devices he had employed with such apparent success in *Oceana*.

Here the insinuating voice was of crucial importance. The kindly old traveller who loses at billiards, is persecuted by insects, and cannot hold cocktails is also the one who speaks plainly and honestly to us about what the blacks are really like. They are lazy, of course, but no more so, he extenuates, than many whites. They are also docile and easily abused. At Kingston, Froude observes a group of black migrant workers setting sail for labour on the Darien canal:

> I found the whole mass of them reduced to the condition of the pigs who used to occupy the foredeck in the Cork and Bristol packets. They were lying in a confused heap together, helpless, miserable, without consciousness

---

64. The nature of such divisions had already been clearly revealed in the 'Report of the Jamaica Royal Commission', *Parliamentary Papers: 1866 Colonies: West Indies 3683*, 30–1. For a modern analysis, see A. B. Bakan, *Ideology and Class Conflict in Jamaica: The Politics of Rebellion* (Kingston, Ontario, 1996).

65. For a critical survey of responses to Froude within the Caribbean, see Faith Smith, *Creole Recitations: John Jacob Thomas and Colonial Formation in the Late Nineteenth Century Caribbean* (Williamsburg, VA, 2002), esp. ch. 4; J. J. Thomas, *Froudacity: West Indian Fables by J. A. Froude* (Bermuda, 1888) was the most influential rebuttal; but N. Darnell Davies, *Mr Froude's Negrophobia: or Don Quixote as a Cook's Tourist* (Demerera, 1888), captures more than any other riposte the deviousness of Froude's mode of presentation. Some efforts were made to bring Froude's inaccuracies to the attention of his English readers; see the letter by W. G. Donovan in *Pall Mall Gazette*, 19 March 1888, 14.

apparently, save a sense in each that he was wretched. Unfortunate brothers-in-law! Following the laws of political economy, and carrying their labour to the dearest market, where before a year was out half of them were to die. They had souls too, some of them, and honest and kindly hearts.[66]

There is slyness here—contempt masquerading as sympathy. And there is evasion: why 'brothers-in-law', not the brothers of the famous abolitionist motto? Which of them do and do not have souls? But the superficial effect sought for here is one of kindness, tolerance, and open-mindedness. Froude's insinuations can also be nastier: 'The Wild African black is not filthy in his natural state. He washes much and, as wild animals do, at least tries to keep himself clear of vermin. The blacks in Jacmel appeared (like the same animals as soon as they are domesticated) to lose the sense which belongs to them in their wild condition [and so] their smell [is] unendurable'.[67] Similarly, black women are beautiful and graceful when young. But:

> Poor things! It cannot compensate for their colour which now that they are free is harder to bear than when they were slaves. Their prettiness, such as it is, is short-lived. They grow old early, and an old Negress is always hideous.[68]

As extracted here, this is plainly abhorrent, but the passage is embedded in an assuring and ingratiating narrative stream designed to intimate that the traveller is, after all, only confirming what his readers already feel. He has, readers are assured, no hatred or fear of black people, and he is touched by their good-natured and playful innocence: 'The curse is taken off from nature, and like Adam again they are under the covenant of innocence.' Being prelapsarians, however, they have no sense of sin or of morality either.

> They sin, but they sin only as animals, because there is no sense of doing wrong. They eat the forbidden fruit but it brings with it no knowledge of the difference between good and evil. They steal but if detected they fall back upon the Lord. It was de will of de Lord that they should do this or that. De Lord forbid that they should go against his holy pleasure. In fact these poor children have escaped the consequences of the Fall and must come of another stock after all.[69]

The sly shifts and deliberate confusions (animals, he knows, cannot sin) by which Froude insinuates a racial prejudice of the crudest sort under the guise of amused tolerance require no further comment.

---

66. *English in the West Indies*, 192.
67. *English in the West Indies*, 187–8.
68. *English in the West Indies*, 119.
69. *English in the West Indies*, 50.

But the furtive and nervous manner in which Froude presents his views on race, his ambivalent and jocose reference to polygenesis—a central element of the purely racist argument—raise an obvious but far from simple question. If Froude really wanted to assert the racial inferiority of black people, why did he not simply do so?[70] By the mid-1880s purely racist arguments based on anthropological, psychological, anatomical, and biological evidence had, though not unchallenged, acquired considerable currency and authority. From mid-century on, a very large body of pseudoscientific literature had been produced to which Froude might have appealed without forfeiting the confidence of the readership he sought to address.[71] Yet eschewing Knox, Hunt, Galton, Spencer, and the like, Froude not only ignores the possibilities of scientific racism, but denies them. He had long ago considered phrenological and physiognomic theories of race, he tells his readers, and remains unimpressed:

> Having heard the craniological and other objections to the supposed identity of the Negro and white races, I came to the opinion long ago, and have seen no reason to change it, that whether they are of one race or not, there is no original or congenital difference of capacity between them any more than there is between a black horse and a black dog and a white horse and a white dog. With the same chances and the same treatment, I believe that distinguished men would be produced equally by both races.[72]

Instead, Froude retreats to the historicist argument—more liberal in theory, though hardly less repressive in its practical applications. Civilisation was a recent development for all humankind, no more than six thousand years old. Even the Anglo-Norman race had become capable of self-government only after a thousand years of submission to higher spiritual and civil authorities. The black races have yet even to start upon the road to self-reliance and sovereignty; and though it is possible that their exposure to firm European government and instruction 'may shorten the probation period for the Negro' during which 'his natural tendencies are superseded by a higher instinct', any premature grant of liberty would be disastrous.

70. For a recent discussion with a slightly different emphasis, see Koditschek, *Liberalism, Imperialism and the Historical Imagination*, 193–205.
71. See, in general, Christine Bolt, *Victorian Attitudes to Race* (London, 1971); D. A. Lorimer, *Colour, Class and the Victorians: English Attitudes toward the Negro in the Mid-Nineteenth Century* (Leicester, 1978); Lorimer, 'Nature, Race and Victorian Science', *Canadian Journal of History*, 25 (1990), 369–85; J. W. Burrow, *Evolution and Society: a study in Victorian social theory* (Cambridge, 1966) Stephen Jay Gould, *The Mismeasure of Man* (New York, 1981).
72. *English in the West Indies*, 124.

They will slide back into their own condition, and the chance will be gone of lifting them to the level to which we have no right to say that they are incapable of rising.[73]

As an argument this is hardly satisfactory. Its apparent acknowledgement of cultural development is undermined by the animalistic metaphors through which it is expressed and which are employed by Froude to different effect elsewhere:

> A Negro can be attached to his employer at least as easily as a horse or a dog. The horse or dog requires kind treatment or he becomes indifferent or sullen; so it is with the Negro ... conscious of his own inferiority at the bottom of his heart [the free blackman will] attach himself to a rational white employer with at least as much fidelity as a spaniel.[74]

Even on its own terms, however, Froude's argument from history is replete with difficulty. It is not at all clear, for example, why an early concession of freedom will necessarily lead to such a calamity as he predicts, especially as he admits that the period of subordination may be shorter than for the English. If it is to be shorter, by how much, and for what reasons? How the Europeans who had been responsible for the enslavement and oppression of the Africans (or at least for their continuance) could be trusted with their eventual liberation is also left unanswered. Again, how the (unstated) natural tendencies are to be superseded by higher instincts (not acquired capabilities) is also obscure. And why the means by which, according to Froude himself, the Anglo-Normans won their liberty by revolution, first against church and then against state, should not also be available to the black races is a question he chooses not to address.

In any case, in the concluding pages of *Oceana* published only two years previously Froude had delivered himself of the quite opposite contention. Referring to the conditions prevailing in the Sandwich Islands where now, under the influence of the United States, black people had migrated, he had declared:

> It is the nigger only who entirely prospers under these new conditions. As a slave he could grow into an Uncle Tom; as a free citizen he carries his head as high as his late master, and laughs, works and earns his wages, and enjoys life as becomes a man and a brother. It was predicted of him that he, too, when he

---

73. *English in the West Indies*, 125; see also 56.
74. *English in the West Indies*, 106; see also 98.

was emancipated, would die off like the rest; but he shows no sign of any such intention. The modern system of things, whatever its defects, agrees certainly with the Negro constitution.[75]

The cumulative deficiencies and outright contradictions in Froude's approach to race appear, therefore, to be so enormous that we may wonder why he found it necessary to involve himself in such contortions in the first place, when an easier and popular dogmatism lay to hand.

Froude's refusal to embrace scientific racism is in itself revealing, for his difficulties with the question of race were prompted by considerations more fundamental than mere rhetorical presentation. An acceptance of some pseudoscientific model of biological difference would necessarily have entailed an endorsement of determinism and a denial of the historicism which had been central to his thought from the beginning. The challenge thus posed was philosophical. But it was more than that; for it was on the basis of his conviction that not only were human beings changed by history, but that they had the power also to change the way in which it moved that had shaped the course of his entire public career and indeed his very sense of his own self. But even more than personal failure was at stake here. As long as the evidence for biological determinism remained inconclusive, it was possible to see it as yet another manifestation of that propensity of the human intellect to misconstrue the real tendency of historical development. Froude's travel writing—conceived as it was for a broader audience than most of his previous compositions—had been designed to extend and reinforce his historicist message, but its displacement of the lessons of history and the passage of time in favour of the prospects of space, and the promise of the future, had inadvertently brought him close to the edge of open contradiction, a condition which in *The English in the West Indies*—the weakest of all his works—had been made painfully clear.

It is not surprising, then, that after that book, Froude abandoned travel writing in this form and turned again to history. With that same broadened readership in mind, however, he began not with history-writing proper, but with historical fiction, returning to a subject which had never been far from his historical imagination: Ireland.

75. *Oceana*, 302–3.

14

Educating Carlyle's Orphans:
Time, 1889–94

I

Although there is some evidence that Froude had considered writing a fiction to accompany his formal history while *The English in Ireland* was still being written, he only began sustained work on the novel that was to be entitled *The Two Chiefs of Dunboy, or An Irish Romance of the Last Century* only after his return from the West Indies tour; and when he did he worked with extraordinary concentration and speed.[1] The correspondences between the novel and the earlier history are several. It is set in the mid-eighteenth century—the centre of gravity of the history. Many of its main characters are representations of actual historical figures who are introduced in the history and bear the same names; while several others, such as Lord B— or Dr S—, are indicated in such a way as to be easily identified by readers of *The English in Ireland*. Several of the principal events in the novel are based upon verifiable historical evidence first supplied in the history, while one of the central themes in Froude's history—the pervasive and nefarious practice of duelling in Ireland—is converted into the central trope of the novel. Froude was cavalier in his treatment of the historical record as it suited him, and departures from truth were rigorously exposed by the novel's first reviewers.[2] Rather

---

1. *The Two Chiefs of Dunboy, or An Irish Romance of the Last Century*, 456 pp. (London, Longman, Green & Co, 1889). An early version of the plot appeared in Froude, 'Stories of the Irish Smugglers', *Scribner's Monthly*, 5 (December 1872), 221–33; for Froude's intense struggles with composition, see Froude to Lord Derby, 13 April (1889), Liverpool Record Office, Derby MSS, no. 7.
2. The Irish scholar A. J. Fetherstonhaugh published a detailed factual refutation in 'The True Story of the Two Chiefs of Dunboy: An Episode in Irish History', *Journal of the Royal Society of Antiquaries of Ireland*, Fifth Series, 4, No. 1 (March, 1894), 35–43, No. 2 (June, 1894), 139–49; see also the exchanges in *Notes and Queries*, 18 May and 8 June 1889.

than straining after a false verisimilitude, however, the exploitation of the genre of historical romance enabled Froude to address his readers in a different register, to reach a different audience, simplifying and making more explicit his deepest feelings about the historical role of Ireland that had been ignored or misapprehended by readers and critics of the history.

The plot of *The Two Chiefs of Dunboy* is as thin as the conventions of the genre allowed. Two men—one a brave, honourable, and determined Englishman, Colonel John Goring, the other a brave, honourable but impulsive Irishman, Morty Sullivan—are pitted against each other through the intertwining of their lives in a variety of circumstances. They had fought each other at Culloden; the Irishman had been captured by the Englishman but had escaped. The Englishman now occupied the patrimony of the exiled Jacobite. He was introducing English Protestant colonies there, suppressing the smuggling trade by which the natives had earned their crust, and to rub salt in the wound he had evicted the Irishman's sister from her tenancy for aiding the smugglers. A duel was therefore inevitable, but it is to prove frustratingly difficult for Morty to organise. On his first return to Dunboy his challenge to the interloper went sour: his own weapon misfired, and Goring, refusing to engage, fired over Morty's head. The duel is then suspended. On the second occasion, Morty, against his better judgement and his sense of honour, is goaded into having Goring brought to face him by a ruse. But again, the brave colonel refuses to honour the Irish outlaw by conniving in an act of lawlessness. He struggles to break free from the trap, wounds the Irishmen who attended upon Morty, and is shot dead by Morty. Morty is distraught by the outcome. This was not the honourable challenge he had sought, but a sordid intrigue in which his antagonist had been unfairly trapped and brutally done away with. Disgusted by his part in the shameful conspiracy, and even more contemptuous of those companions who had persuaded him to take part, he leaves, swearing never to return. But a short time later, again under pressure from his followers, he returns to take his sister and her son, the heir to the O'Sullivan lordship, out of Ireland for good. On arrival he is betrayed by a kinsman moved to hatred by the scorn which Morty had poured on him after the killing of Goring, and is killed while trying to escape.

The novel's characters are hardly more subtle than its plot. They are largely representative types. The English are almost invariably good: like Goring, they are noble, brave, and industrious. The Irish are almost invariably defective: cowards and traitors such as Sylvester O'Sullivan, or figures filled with rancour and bitterness, such as Morty's sister Ellen. Even Morty is fiery, erratic, too sensitive to his standing in other men's eyes.

Amidst all this, however, there are exceptions whose subtleties repay a little attention. Not all of the English are good. An interlude in Dublin which disrupts the main lines of plot development allows Froude the opportunity of etching an acid sketch of the Anglo-Irish establishment whose leading figures (chief among whom are Archbishop Stone, Speaker Ponsonby, Henry Flood, and Lord Chancellor Bowes) are presented as the very epitomes of cynicism, corruption, and irresponsibility. The degeneracy of this ruling class is symbolised by an evening which Goring spends with them at the baths run by Dr Achmet Borumborad—an enigmatic Turk who is a highly fashionable figure in Dublin society. In the middle of their drunken cavortings which involve throwing each other into the baths, Achmet is exposed as an imposter, a pretend foreigner, who proudly declares himself to be

> No Turk at all, at all. Sure it is Pat Joyce from Kilkenny I am—no less—and as good a Christian as the Pope of Rome[3]

The lesson is clear: amidst this fun and frivolity the papists are all around, deceptive and disguised, but proud and confident of their future, and all the while the irresponsible leaders of Protestant Ireland can do nothing but laugh at their own condition. Thus the heritage which Cromwell's virtuous republicans had bequeathed was being drowned (literally) in a luxury that was as corrosive as it was illusory.

The symbolism here is obvious; but other specimens of human nature in Froude's Dublin project more ambivalent images. One is a Mr Fitzherbert, a Fellow of Trinity College. Although he is introduced as Goring's cousin, Fitzherbert's ancestry is as ambiguous as his name: it suggests but does not confirm an Anglo-Norman origin, and we are given no first name to offer a further clue. Fitzherbert speaks of himself as Irish, but in a disturbing way:

> What we are today [he tells Goring] we have been for a thousand years neither worse nor better. If the English wanted order in Ireland, they should have

---

3. *Two Chiefs*, 304. This incident in the novel is derived directly from an anecdote related in the *Personal Sketches* of the eighteenth-century Irish memorialist Sir Jonah Barrington; but whereas in Barrington's story Joyce is reported to have claimed that he was 'as good a Christian as the archbishop [of Dublin]', Froude silently but significantly alters Joyce's allegiance to the Pope; see Hugh B. Staples (ed.), *The Ireland of Sir Jonah Barrington: Selections from his Personal Sketches* (London and Seattle, 1967), 166–7.

left none of us alive. We were but half a million when the Tudor princes began interfering. At that time they might have made a clean sweep, and the world would have been better for the want of us. We are a beggarly race wherever we go, and what you can't mend you had better end.[4]

Here is the very model of the self-hating Irishman (and a Trinity don into the bargain). But it should not be inferred that Froude presents Fitzherbert for unqualified approval. Goring strongly dissents from such opinions, and Froude offers his own reservations: 'A critic and man of the world ... he had not sought admittance to either of the learned professions ... had never invited the suffrages of a constituency, and had amused himself with watching the action from outside of the most corrupt assembly in the world.'[5] Such amused detachment was an attitude which Froude abhorred among his own contemporaries, and the defeatism of Fitzherbert's view of the Irish is directly contradicted at the outset of the novel where the wealthy, commanding figure of Patrick Blake is held up as 'an instance—one among many to be observed in that epoch—of what an Irishman could do when transplanted from the land of his birth.'[6] Fitzherbert's world-weary passivity, moreover, is contrasted with his cousin Goring's endeavours, in establishing a colony, mining for copper, and reforming the agricultural practices on his estate. He himself dimly perceives the contrast during his stay at Dunboy, but to the end he cannot fully abandon his lassitude.[7]

Fitzherbert's character is also set against that of another Englishman, the senior artillery officer General Vavasour. In addition to his military profession, the general is also an enthusiastic student of Irish antiquities, and his discovery of a set of engraved stones at an ancient site on Dursey Island provides Froude with the opportunity of revealing the strengths and limitations of the central characters. Fitzherbert is quite uninterested in the discovery, his curiosity piqued only by the general's innocent engagement. Goring is more respectful, but sees in the site only the remains of an old cattle pen which in medieval times the Gaelic chieftains had used to protect their cattle from rustlers or to house cattle they had rustled themselves. The general is prepared to allow this as a later function in degenerate times, but continues to maintain with the support of some mathematical and astronomical calculations (of which

4. *Two Chiefs*, 260.
5. *Two Chiefs*, 237.
6. *Two Chiefs*, 2; also 3–8.
7. Froude's self-denigrating disdain for the idle man of letters is most fully expressed in his 'Education', *Short Studies*, II, 439–78, esp. 464–7.

Fitzherbert, significantly, is ignorant) that the site provided evidence of the earlier settlement there of a sophisticated, learned and spiritually minded people. The debate ends inconclusively: the general goes silent, but does not withdraw from his views, while the others remain sceptical. But echoes of the young Froude's intense and disturbing experience of Ireland in the 1840s are audible here, and his readers may be expected to retain respect for the general's opinion by the way in which he then sets about the practical defence of the island in the face of an imminent pirate attack.[8]

More interesting is the fact that the general's metaphysical speculations are echoed in an adjacent chapter by those of Morty Sullivan himself. Strolling disconsolately along a nearby strand, his confidence in the possibility of raising a rebellion from the unpromising conspirators with whom he has come in contact declining rapidly, Morty muses on the ceaseless motion of historical change:

> For how many ages had the bay and the rocks and the mountains looked exactly the same as they were looking then? How many generations had played their part on the same stage, eager and impassioned as if it had been created only for them! The half-naked fisherman of forgotten centuries who had earned a scanty living there; the monks from the Skelligs who had come in on highdays in their coracles to say mass for them, baptize their children or bury their dead; the Celtic chief with saffron shirt and battle axe, driven from his richer lands by Norman or Saxon invaders … the Scandinavian pirates … these had all played their brief parts there and were gone, and as many more would follow in the cycles of the years that were to come, yet the scene itself was unchanged and would not change. The same soil had fed the departed … The same landscape had affected their imaginations with its beauty or awed them with its splendours; and each alike had yielded to the same delusion that the valley was theirs and was inseparably connected with themselves and their fortunes.[9]

Unlike Vavasour, Morty relates his own career to this ceaseless process of change. As a child he had played on the same beach, had 'kindled with enthusiasm at the tales which were told him of his forefathers', had fought 'in the holy cause'—and now was it all for nothing?

> What was he? What was anyone? To what purpose the ineffectual strivings of short-lived humanity? Man's life was but the shadow of a dream, and his work was but the heaping of sand which the next tide would level flat again.[10]

8. *Two Chiefs*, chs. xxiii–iv.
9. *Two Chiefs*, 366–7.   10. *Two Chiefs*, 368.

Morty's insight helps elevate him close to the level of those truly reflective men whom Froude has always admired, and it shows that even in his reduced condition Morty retains the vestiges of the spiritual nature of the people from whom he is descended. Unlike Fitzherbert, moreover, Morty is not paralysed by this desolating revelation. Rather, like Goring, he is a man of action who will go on to do his duty as he sees it in an adopted course that will end in both of their deaths.

The insight that is granted to Morty should dispel any notion that he is being portrayed by Froude as a wild and passionate primitive. Instead, from his first appearance, Morty is presented as a gentleman, a brave and noble soldier whose acute sense of honour makes the service he must do for the cause as a pirate on the high seas painfully disagreeable to him. Morty's position as a pirate in Froude's novel is curious. This adventurer on the high seas whose daring raids on British merchantmen and naval frigates made his name a terror in the Caribbean and elsewhere is simply re-enacting in the eighteenth century the achievements of Drake, Hawkins, and the other sea-dogs of the sixteenth century which Froude had celebrated in earlier historical writings. There is no likelihood that the eulogist of 'England's Forgotten Worthies' was unaware of the parallel. But the point was that the English privateers of the sixteenth century had contributed to a profound historical change which had made their own activities thereafter redundant and illegitimate. They had, in other words, saved the Protestant Reformation and helped establish Britain as the leader and guardian of that world-historical movement. In the wake of this epoch-making revolution, Morty's attempts to mount a counter-revolution were therefore not only too late by two centuries and doomed to failure; by extension they were also, as he himself is privately aware, as unjustified as the contemporary actions of the English pirates Morgan and Kidd.[11]

---

11. Froude, 'England's Forgotten Worthies', *Westminster Review*, July 1852; also ch.6 above. For a revelation of Froude's highly relativist attitude toward the Elizabethan privateers see Froude to [unknown], 6 October 1862, Beinecke Library, Yale University, Hilles MSS Box 9, file F. 'Sir Edward Horsey was one of a large number of young, daring, adventurous, and ultimately unscrupulous young men who in the first years of Elizabeth were found too useful to be discarded, who had been revolutionists under Mary, and afterwards were either pirates, privateers, or freebooters. They took service with the government as far as it suited their purpose. The Reformation had filled Europe and England with such men much as the revolution of 1848 has done in our time ... Their restlessness which before would most likely have gotten them hanged, caused them to act with authority and distinction.'

This was, of course, a distinctly self-serving theory of historical justification. Significantly, however, Froude was now willing to apply the implications of this form of argument beyond the plight of the historically arrested Irish. He applied them also to his English hero, John Goring, who was almost equally out of date in eighteenth-century Ireland. From the first, Goring is presented in historical terms. He had served at Culloden against the Jacobites, and he had come to the aid of Colonel Eyre in Galway, where Patrick Blake is told by one of his sea-captains:

> He was like one of Cromwell's troopers, the Lord confound them! With a sword in one hand and a pistol in the other, and the Bible on the lips of him.[12]

Always a religious man,

> Under Cromwell he would have been the most devoted of the Ironsides ... an Englishman of the old Puritan school.[13]

Inheriting Dunboy through the death of his brother, he regarded this run-down estate 'as a direction of Providence to him' to revive the spirit of the Protestant settlers of Cromwell's day. But his mission had not gone well. Even as he is being introduced, readers are made aware of the troubles surrounding him. Though just thirty-two, the same age as Morty, his hair has already begun to grey, 'as if life had brought anxieties, which were leaving their marks upon him'.[14] He is married, but his wife Elizabeth is a shadowy, passive figure, troubled by their settlement there. He is under threat of death. They have no children. His situation deteriorates steadily throughout the novel. Surrounded by hostile natives and unsupported by the other local gentry, his colonists grow anxious by the day and seek permission to leave. Goring's attempts to encourage them are everywhere frustrated. He builds a chapel for them and appoints a non-conformist clergyman to minister to them. But these actions, and the fact that he had occasionally preached to them himself, had been a scandal to the local Established clergy, and he had been publicly rebuked. Innocently, he travels to Dublin to seek a licence from the Primate and is curtly refused. Meanwhile, agrarian terror accelerates the decline of the colony which is already on the point of failure before Goring is killed. On his death, we are told, his estate will descend to the

12. *Two Chiefs*, 46.
13. *Two Chiefs*, 59.
14. *Two Chiefs*, ch. v.

sterile Fitzherbert. Like Morty, Goring is also an historical anachronism, of only a slightly later vintage, and his enterprise is as doomed to failure in the eighteenth century as is his enemy's. In this sense they have equal status as chiefs of Dunboy—that is, as principal representatives of integral, distinct, and mutually incompatible cultures whose time had passed.

Froude's historical romance casts important light on the fundamental concerns which had engaged him in all his previous writings on English and Irish history. Several of the themes first developed in the two histories are rehearsed again, but in a subtly modulated way. The inability of the native Irish to govern themselves adequately in the island is again asserted, but qualified now by the recognition that this had not always been the case, and that in other places it was not so now. Such historically based reservations deepened the responsibility of England. A politically more stable and militarily more powerful culture, England's geographical propinquity had made her conquest of Ireland inevitable. But this legitimate event had been rapidly succeeded by a series of historical developments of disastrous moral import. Not only had the conquest not resulted in the moral development of the weaker people through their integration with the stronger (as had supposedly been the case in England); their defects had actually become grossly accentuated in a process for which the conquerors themselves must assume responsibility. Set against the contrasting evidence of their advancement once they had emigrated, this was a devastating revelation of weaknesses and vices inherent in the conquerors themselves which required immediate and urgent address if the process of decay was not to work its natural effects on them also. Geographically and culturally determined, the destinies of Ireland and England had been inexorably intertwined in their histories. In the process, history had reshaped them as moral co-dependants in which the fate of the one was ineluctably bound to that of the other. As the moral vitality of English Protestantism had been sapped by its own internal exhaustion, and by the complacent culture of *laissez faire* which replaced it, the assertion of responsibility for the government of Ireland now presented a final trial for England's spiritual redemption.

In now restating his Irish argument in fictional form Froude was straining after an authorial voice slightly different from but hardly less accessible to the audience toward whom his popular but highly problematic travel writing had been addressed. The return to history from geography not only freed him from that drift toward determinism which had threatened his endeavours in that field; it allowed him also to resume as a narrator a greater authoritative status, as he unfolded the dynamic of historical change and underlined the urgent and immediate need for political regeneration. And by returning from the world at large to the neighbouring island of Ireland, Froude had a means of conveying powerfully to his readers the message that the grand issues of historical responsibility to which he was alerting them were neither speculative nor indefinitely postponed. They were to be met with immediately in everyday British political life.

Whatever the rhetorical subtlety of his intent, however, the effect of the book was limited. From those quarters where Froude and his Irish opinions were approved, reviews were in the main positive. But the simplicity of the genre and his own incapacity to exploit its possibilities ensured that its metaphysical and historicist dimensions were largely neglected.[15] Historically minded reviewers—especially Irish ones—were negative, but perhaps the most damning response, as far as Froude's intent was concerned, came from a critic, also Irish, who was less concerned with Froude's politics than his artistry. With tongue in cheek, Oscar Wilde observed that while Froude's novel contained all the seriousness of purpose associated with a parliamentary blue book, it lacked the charm and elegance of the genre.[16]

II

It was nevertheless his recognition of the power that remained in historically based discourse to minister to the imminent challenges of the present that persuaded Froude to accept an invitation to contribute to a series of contemporary political biographies. Conceived by the journalist Stuart Reid, *The Prime Ministers of Queen Victoria* (9 vols., 1890–95) was a series of short biographical studies intended for a politically engaged readership; and early on in the project Reid invited Froude to contribute the volume on the recently deceased Benjamin Disraeli, Earl of Beaconsfield. Given the Liberal sympathies of the editor and of several of the contributing team (which included Justin McCarthy on Peel, and George Saintsbury on the Earl of Derby), it is surprising that Froude, who had been lately in the habit of refusing all offers of commission, should have agreed. But he did so

---

15. See *inter alia*, *The Athenaeum*, 13 April 1889, 469–70; *The Nation*, 16 May 1889, 403–4; *The Saturday Review*, 20 April 1889, 474.
16. 'Mr Froude's Blue Book', *Pall Mall Gazette*, 13 April 1889, reprinted in Richard Ellman (ed.), *The Artist as Critic: Critical Writings of Oscar Wilde* (Chicago, 1968), 136–40.

enthusiastically, securing permissions from Disraeli's literary executors to examine his papers, interviewing several of his closest friends and associates, including his son Ralph, Baron Rothschild, Lord Salisbury, and Lord Derby, and completing the entire task in a year.[17]

Reid's decision to commission Froude to write on *The Earl of Beaconsfield* was appropriate on several levels.[18] Disraeli's lifelong opposition to unchecked *laissez faire*, his defence of religious orthodoxy, his concern for the urban and rural poor, his belated conversion to imperialism, his championing of the Copyright Act, and his literary talent all seemed likely to make Froude a sympathetic commentator. In many ways this was so; but Froude's book was hardly a eulogy. Although the series was aimed at a popular market, the voice Froude adopted here was, in marked contrast to the ingratiating author of the travel books and the historical romancer, detached and astringent. Readers are made aware from the outset that they are in the hands of a strong-minded, experienced judge who has formed a clear assessment of his subject on the basis of prolonged personal experience of politics. He had been offered, they are told (on p. 3) a safe parliamentary seat by Disraeli in 1874 which he had declined.[19] And throughout, Froude's text is peppered with indications of his personal knowledge of some of the most important events and issues in his subject's career. Complex political issues such as the struggle over the repeal of the Corn Laws, the origins of the 1867 franchise reform, and the Bulgarian crisis of 1876 are treated without oversimplification; while other controversies such as the debate over Darwin, the grounds for religious latitudinarianism, and the role of the universities are presented with magisterial assurance.

The message carried through this authoritative voice is, moreover, far from uncritical. Astonishingly, the book opens with one of the strongest negative judgements ever delivered on Disraeli by Froude's own prophet, Carlyle, denouncing the Prime Minister and those who followed him over the Reform Bill of 1867:

> A superlative Hebrew conjuror, spell-binding all the great lords, great parties, great interests of England to his hand ... and leading them by the nose like helpless mesmerised, somnambulist cattle to such issue![20]

17. Froude to Lady Derby, 14 September, 9 November 1889, and to Lord Derby, 27 July 1889, 19 September 1890, Liverpool Record Office, Derby MSS, nos. 20, 23; and to Skelton, 10 November 1889, *Table-Talk of Shirley*, 206–9.
18. J. A. Froude, *The Earl of Beaconsfield (Prime Ministers of Queen Victoria)* (London, Sampson Low, 1890); the edition cited hereafter.
19. *The Earl of Beaconsfield*, 3.
20. *The Earl of Beaconsfield*, 2.

While Froude, out of decorum, enters a mild reservation to Carlyle's philip-
pic, as a man to whom 'he had not done perfect justice', the prophet reappears at several times throughout the text as a standard against which Disraeli
and all the politicians of his day are to be measured.[21] Froude, moreover, has
serious criticisms of his own. As one who disagreed publicly with Disraeli's
conduct in the Bulgarian crisis he had little choice but to repeat his censures
now. Given his own strident views on Irish policy, Froude was similarly
required to register complaint. Here, however, his disapproval is qualified: as
a figure who had once shown an instinctive grasp of the Irish problem, the
sins of Disraeli—in contrast to the irresponsible conduct of his rival
Gladstone—were ones of omission and neglect.[22] Froude has strictures to
apply to Disraeli's character also. He was persistently careless with his personal finances. He was a social climber, and in regard to his relations with
women, Froude, unlike many later biographers, was prepared to hint to
those already in the know that Disraeli was not always above temptation.[23]

Above all, he was personally ambitious. Disraeli, for Froude, was the first
of a breed of public figures who, holding their own values and ideals in
private reserve, attached themselves to particular political movements at
particular times not out of loyalty to a party, but as a means of enabling them
to exercise power. He was, in short, a professional politician:

> He desired generally to go into parliament as a profession, as other men go to
> the Bar, to make his way to consequence and to fortune ... Politics was his
> profession, and as a young barrister aspires to be Lord Chancellor, Disraeli
> desired to rise in the State.[24]

This was the central characteristic of his public life which underlay all of his
actions from his early disloyalty to Peel, splitting of the Tories during the
Corn Law crisis, to his embrace of franchise reform in 1867, all of which
were taken as steps to the attainment of the ambition he had boldly declared
at the outset of his political career, to become Prime Minister. Having registered this well-known feature, Froude proceeds to qualify it. The first of
his qualifications is hardly generous to Disraeli himself. The people, he
observes, get the politicians they deserve. If Disraeli was indeed the unprincipled adventurer depicted by his critics, 'one has to ask ... what kind of

---

21. Further references to Carlyle are on 1–3, 55, 79–80, 92–5, 160, 252–3.
22. *The Earl of Beaconsfield*, 102–6, 136–8, 142, 200–11, 233–8, 260.
23. For example, *The Earl of Beaconsfield*, 50–5, 89–90, 178–82.
24. *The Earl of Beaconsfield*, 54, 236.

place the House of Commons must be when such a man can be selected by it as its foremost statesman'.[25] That an outsider without connections, constituency, or even a university education could by shrewd calculation, intrigue, and manipulation of others' interests climb to the top of the greasy pole was less a reflection on him than on the political system within which he worked. Here Froude is indulging his intense distaste for the machinations of party politics which he was convinced were undermining the prospects of genuine moral regeneration. But, though he knew well how to operate within it, Disraeli, precisely because of his status as an outsider, had never been captivated by it, and was supremely confident of his ability to transcend it.

Disraeli's was no 'commonplace' parliamentary ambition, however. It rose far above considerations of personal gain and resided in his extraordinary conviction that he knew the tendency of the times—their dangers and their opportunities—and that he was possessed of a singular ability to avoid the former and exploit the latter which justified all his stratagems to gain power. It was in this that his unqualified (though unreciprocated) admiration for Carlyle (twice noticed in the text) lay. That Disraeli himself accepted the standards that were being set was clear not only from his desire to see Carlyle honoured, but in his own literary work.

Although it is not surprising that Froude should have paid particular attention to Disraeli's fictions, the space he gives to their consideration is considerable. In addition to the 'silver fork' novels, readers are directed by Froude to three early 'light satires ... which with one exception are the most brilliant of all his writings', and which reveal, according to Froude, a perception of the condition of England as profound and as urgent as Carlyle's.[26] The themes raised in these gentle but acute satires are revisited in *Sybil*—a novel to which Froude gives considerable attention—but finally in *Lothair*, which he declares to be Disraeli's greatest literary achievement and to which he devotes an entire chapter. In *Lothair* (1872) Disraeli returned to the theme of the promise and danger of England's condition with greater urgency than ever, analysing the inner threats to her vitality through the hidden vices of its aristocratic elite—their susceptibility to greed and idleness, the emotional attractions of the Roman Catholic Church, and the intellectual vanities of secularism. Embodying as it did so many of Froude's

---

25. *The Earl of Beaconsfield*, 197.
26. *The Earl of Beaconsfield*, 25–6.

cherished convictions, as well as his prophetical and rhetorical commitments, *Lothair*, he concludes, was the greatest achievement of Disraeli's life.[27]

> The true value of the book is the perfect presentation of patrician society in England in the year which was then passing over; the full appreciation of all that was good and noble in it; yet the recognition, also, that it was a society without a purpose, with no claim to endurance ... like the full bloom of a flower that opens only to fade.[28]

In *Lothair* Disraeli had, far more than Carlyle or Froude, succeeded in perceiving and representing the real nature of the impending crisis of English society in a manner readily comprehensible to those in a position to do most to confront it. But his insight was rarely matched by his commitment:

> He might have led a nobler crusade than Coeur de Lion. But it was not in him to tread a thorny road with insufficient companionship ... He was contented to leave things as he found them, instead of reconstructing society to make himself prime minister.

In so doing he abandoned the real historical task that lay before him and left all of the great problems of his day unsolved. For this he could never be accounted a truly great figure. Yet, as 'Gulliver was a giant among the Lilliputians', so Disraeli was relatively great:

> His aims were always perhaps something higher than he professed ... He had a genuine anxiety to serve his party, and in serving his party to serve his country ... As a statesman there was none like him before, and will be none hereafter. His career was the result of a combination of a peculiar character with peculiar circumstances, which is not likely to recur.[29]

Conceived within nine years of his death, this was an estimate of Disraeli that was as acute as it was austere. Its measured judgement and sophisticated mode of expression reveal a marked contrast with the light authorial persona of the travel literature. The audience toward which it was directed was expected not only to appreciate the nuanced nature of Froude's assessment, but also to have had a clear grasp of the Carlylean standards against which this relatively great man was being judged. The work of keeping alive the flame of Carlyle's insight continued on more than one level.

27. *The Earl of Beaconsfield*, ch. xv.
28. *The Earl of Beaconsfield*, 231.
29. *The Earl of Beaconsfield*, 261–2.

III

The appearance within less than a year of the publication of *Beaconsfield* of an even more substantial historical study from Froude's pen may be seen to give the lie to any notion that his creative powers were waning. Yet *The Divorce of Catherine of Aragon* is among the least satisfactory of Froude's historical works. The origins of the project are revealing of its essential weakness. During the completion of the Carlyle biography (and in part as a means of supplementing its message) Froude had been planning a full-scale revised edition of his *History of England*, and had been refusing all invitations and commissions on that account.[30] At some time between 1888 and 1890, however, his plan changed and narrowed, and rather than commencing a systematic revision of the great work he turned instead to a much more focused defence of one of the most controversial aspects of the very earliest volumes of the *History*: that is, his assertion that in all his dealings regarding his putting away of his first wife Catherine and his marriage with Anne Boleyn, Henry VIII had been entirely justified in his actions.

Thus Froude secured the agreement of Longmans to publish a companion volume to the complete history. It would be designed in the same format and even with the same font as the cabinet edition, and was presumably intended to fit alongside as a final volume in the set.[31] The new book's attempt to reproduce the narrative complexity of the original model is evident. The cast of characters is similarly large and the connective tissue of events similarly dense. But with its 463 pages of text divided into twenty-four short chapters the experience of engaging with the book was far less arduous than that demanded of the *History*'s original readers. The authorial voice was also familiar, judgemental, and unapologetically polemical; but now it was also personal, defensive, and self-justifying. Whereas in the *History* Froude had set out with the ambition of awakening his readers from the moral corrosion of latitudinarian complacency, here he was concerned primarily with personal vindication. In contrast to the restraint or indifference

30. Froude to Lady Derby, (n.d.) May 1890, Liverpool Record Office, Derby MSS; to Skelton, 3 August 1890, Skelton (ed.), *Table-Talk of Shirley*, 211–12; to Annie Ireland, 21 July 1891, Beinecke Library, Yale University, Hilles MSS, Box 9, Froude files.
31. *The Divorce of Catherine of Aragon: The Story as Told by the Imperial Ambassadors Resident at the Court of Henry VIII* (Longmans: London; Scribners: New York, 1891); citations are from the Longman edition.

with which he had received earlier adverse criticism, now he was determined to reassert himself. Although

> published criticisms of my work were generally unfavourable … the public, however, took an interest in what I had to say. The book was read and continues to be read; at the close of my life, therefore I have to go once more over the ground; and as I am still substantially alone in maintaining an opinion considered heretical by orthodox historians, I am to decide in what condition I am to leave my work behind me.[32]

In the thirty-five years since he first published he had found 'nothing to withdraw in what I then wrote, and little to alter save in correcting some small errors of trivial moment; but on the other hand I find much to add'. Refusing 'to allow myself to be tempted into controversy with particular writers whose views disagree with my own', Froude, though he did 'not pretend to impartiality', would set about a reiteration of his deepest conviction:

> I believe the Reformation to have been the greatest incident in English history; the root and source of the expansive force which has spread the Anglo-Saxon race over the globe, and imprinted the English genius and character on the constitution of mankind.[33]

The call for internal moral regeneration which had been the central intent of the original work was now supplanted by a narrower, direct appeal to readers who had been attracted by *Oceana* or *The English in the West Indies* to sympathise with the brave and much-maligned author that is made explicit in the Latin tag which he insisted be added as a subtitle to the book: *in usum laicorum*.[34]

This attempt to engage a broader and newer audience with a project conceived originally as an address to the concerns of an earlier and more sophisticated reading generation posed a compositional challenge of considerable proportions. While there are occasions in the course of the narrative where the clarity and force of Froude's style comes close to attaining it, the tensions produced by the need to make close and technical arguments concerning canon law, parliamentary procedure, diplomatic negotiation,

---

32. *The Divorce of Catherine of Aragon*, 15.
33. *The Divorce of Catherine of Aragon*, 18.
34. An ironical and polemical reference at once to the Roman breviary and to Newman's debate with Peel over the Tamworth Reading Room, the phrase is also an unintended expression of Froude's profoundly unresolved address to a putative audience at once uninitiated and educated.

and the authenticity of particular documents palatable to an uninitiated readership ultimately prevented him from achieving it. In *Catherine of Aragon* the inconsistencies and contradictions with which Froude had been repeatedly and sometimes unfairly accused in the past are manifold. They could be discovered in the instability of his characterisations: Henry VIII as far-seeing national monarch and fickle lover; in Pope Clement, willing diplomatist and 'conjuror' of superstition; and in Catherine herself, brave and dignified but stubborn and obtuse. Above all, however, they are obvious in Froude's use of the Imperial ambassador, Eustace Chapuys, who appears throughout the text as an unscrupulous schemer, intriguer, and dupe, but who was nonetheless the figure from whom, in this book, Froude derived most of the new 'evidence' in defence of Henry and the promoters of the divorce.

These inconsistencies, along with Froude's occasional misrepresentations of texts and his numerous inaccuracies, were seized on by his scholarly critics as similar defects had been in the past—though now, in contrast to the heated invectives of Goldwin Smith and Freeman, the very restraint and detachment with which his errors and elisions were put on display by a new generation of academic historians added authority to their adverse judgement.[35] More seriously for Froude's popularising purposes, however, the response of newspaper reviewers was cool: *The Times* was non-committal, and the *Pall Mall Gazette*, which returned to the book on two occasions, was openly hostile.[36] Notices overall were few.

More deeply damaging to Froude's evangelical purposes, however, was his own faltering authorial voice, which, as was the case in *The English in the West Indies*, became most noticeable when he felt obliged to confront moral issues. At the outset of the book he appears to suggest that the best reason for accepting his case lay in a rejection of the unconscionable alternative that the English people had acquiesced in the will of an evil man.[37] This is hardly persuasive. But there are other occasions when the moral dubiety of

35. See, for example, the cool but highly informed and critical reviews by Nicholas Pocock and Augustus Jessopp in *Edinburgh Review*, 175 (January 1892), 201–31, and *English Historical Review*, 7 (April, 1892), 360–5; see also James Gairdner's comprehensive critique, 'New Lights on the Divorce of Henry VIII', *English Historical Review*, 11 (October 1896), 673–702. Modern scholarship has not overturned these judgements.
36. *The Times*, 21 October 1891; *Pall Mall Gazette*, 21 and 23 October 1891.
37. 'The king of England was king of a loyal nation who obeyed him with heart and mind as loyal and faithful subjects. This was the character borne in the world by the fathers of the generation whom popular historians have represented as having dishonoured themselves by subserviency to a bloodthirsty tyrant', 20.

his position becomes even more murky, as in his handling of Chapuys's report of Cromwell's consideration of the murder of Princess Mary, the trial and execution of Queen Anne and her associates, and most significantly in his justification of the execution of several hundred ordinary English people in the aftermath of the Pilgrimage of Grace.[38] Admitting that in the *History* he had understated the extent of the bloody repression of the Pilgrimage, Froude now conceded that around three hundred rebels had been hanged after their surrender. But 'a severe lesson was required to teach a superstitious world that ... priests who broke the law would suffer like common mortals'.

> It must be clearly understood that, if these men could have had their way, the hundreds who suffered would have been thousands, and the victims would have been the poor men who were looking for a purer faith in the pages of the New Testament.[39]

The special pleading resorted to here is little short of shrill. After the partial success of *Beaconsfield* and *The Two Chiefs of Dunboy*, *Catherine of Aragon* exposed once more the strains which Froude had imposed on himself in his determination to carry the message of moral regeneration to a wider public. More ominously still, the pressure seemed to be undermining his capability in the very genre in which he had once excelled. The limitations of the ageing author's ability to address the younger, broader public which he so much desired to attract was becoming increasingly apparent in everything he had attempted since the completion of the Carlyle biography.

Whether and how Froude would have responded to this emerging fault-line in his public style if left to himself is now a matter of little significance; for in March 1892, within six months of the appearance of *The Divorce of Catherine of Aragon*, he was suddenly presented with an altogether unexpected opportunity of escaping from the difficulties into which his exercises in popular writing had placed him while still maintaining his address to a post-Carlyle generation. It came in the form of a letter from Prime Minister Salisbury, seeking his consent to his nomination to the Regius Chair of History at Oxford, now made vacant by the death of his old antagonist, E. A. Freeman.[40]

---

38. *The Divorce of Catherine of Aragon,* chs. xvii; xxii, xxiv.
39. *The Divorce of Catherine of Aragon,* 462–3.
40. Salisbury to Froude, 1 March 1892, quoted in Dunn, *Froude,* II, 575.

IV

In his rapid and positive response to the offer (he had accepted in principle within a week), the pleasure of succeeding his old enemy Freeman may have counted for something with Froude; but he had never ruled out the resumption of an academic career. Even as he had determined to leave the university he had applied for a teaching post in the Royal University in Ireland. He was delighted to accept honorary readmission as a Fellow at Exeter in 1858, and immediately began making less than delicate enquiries about his suitability for the vacant Regius Chair of History.[41] He applied for the newly founded Chichele Chair in 1862, and thereafter continued to show a discreet interest in the Regius Chair of History when it became vacant.[42] It is hardly surprising, then, that once the offer had been made he responded enthusiastically.

The Oxford to which Froude now returned was in many ways more congenial than the one from which he departed in the crisis year of 1849. The religious tests against which he had made his passionate protest had been abolished since 1871, and many of the reforms in university and college government and in the management of the undergraduate curriculum for which he had argued in the 1850s had been attained and surpassed.[43] Oriel—his undergraduate college to which he now returned as a Fellow—had recovered somewhat from the sharp decline it had suffered during Froude's student days: its intake of undergraduates had almost doubled.[44] More importantly, the incorporation of history as an academic discipline within the university syllabus for which he had argued in the mid-1850s had long been established; and the teaching of English history through the statute book and the other records of the English constitution for which he had been a passionate advocate since his own conversion to history, had now been firmly placed at the core of the history curriculum—ironically by one of his severest critics, William Stubbs.[45]

41. Froude to J. P. Lightfoot (Rector of Exeter), 15 March 1858, quoted in Dunn, *Froude*, II, 273.
42. Dorothy M. Owen, 'The Chichele Professorship of Modern History, 1862', *Historical Research*, 34 (1961), 217–20; Froude to Margaret Froude, 13 April 1874, on the rumoured resignation of Stubbs from the Regius Chair: 'They ought to do something for me the wretches. But they won't unless I ask, and perhaps not then', Dunn, *Froude*, II, 389.
43. M. G. Brock and M. C. Curthoys (eds.), *The History of the University of Oxford: Nineteenth Century Oxford, Part 2*, chs. 1, 2, 4.
44. *The History of the University of Oxford*, 123.
45. *The History of the University of Oxford*, ch. 14; also, Reba N. Soffer, *Discipline and Power: The University, History and the making of an English Elite, 1870–1930* (Stanford, 1994), chs. 3–6.

Some aspects of the reformed university were not, however, entirely pleasing. Under the revised Statutes of the University (1882) the Regius Professor of History was required to give no fewer than forty-two lectures during the academic year. This gave Froude some cause for concern.[46] Freeman had been granted a derogation on grounds of ill-health, and Froude, who affirmed that any public lecture he had ever given had required two to three weeks' preparation, hoped that, given his seventy-two years, he might be offered similar relief. Officially the university did not yield, but the Vice Chancellor suggested a fudge under which Froude might be allowed to interpret the terms of the statute for himself without interference. 'Like much else here', Froude noted mordantly to Cowley Powles, 'things are ordered for show to take the world in'. On 16 June Queen Victoria signed his letter of appointment.[47]

Froude's anxieties arose from more than a fear of overwork. He knew that his nomination had been greeted with derision by some of the dons, and feared that he would be out of temper with the changes in curriculum and assessment that had taken place since his time.[48] Ironically, the major reforms had had the effect of strengthening the position of the College tutors in relation to the disciplinary professors.[49] In history the undergraduate preference for those offering guidance through the new demanding examination system to those reporting research in progress had given rise to considerable tensions between the tutors and Froude's predecessors in the Regius Chair. Characteristically, Stubbs had complained mildly and privately, while Freeman had assumed an attitude toward the tutors of unfriendly distance.[50] But by contrast, once he assumed office, Froude plunged into college life with surprising enthusiasm, and worked hard to put his new colleagues at ease: 'I do best here', he told Annie Ireland, 'with the very old and very young; the intermediate careerists are suspicious of a professor who had a position outside the university ... The young men who come about me are bright and ingenuous, and even the dons and

46. Froude to Joan Severn, 18 April 1892, in Viljoen (ed.) *The Froude–Ruskin Friendship*, 117–18.
47. Froude to the Vice Chancellor, 11 April 1892, quoted in Dunn, *Froude*, II, 576–7; to Max Müller, 18 April 1892, Dunn, *Froude*, II, 578–9; to Cowley Powles, 3 February 1893, Dunn, *Froude*, II, 582; Oxford's *University Gazette*, *1892–3, 1893–4* reveals that while Froude lectured in every term, the number of lectures delivered fell short of the statutory requirements by almost 50 per cent.
48. Froude to Joan Severn, 15 September, 1 October 1892, in Viljoen (ed.) *The Froude–Ruskin Friendship*, 119–21.
49. Brock and Curthoys (eds.), *The History of the University of Oxford: Nineteenth Century Oxford*, Part 2, ch. 4.
50. *The History of the University of Oxford*, ch. 14, 366–9; Soffer, *Discipline and Power*, 79–80, 100.

tutors are not more stupid than they used to be.'[51] He especially liked the undergraduates, holding individual tutorials and presenting small lectures in his parlour at Cherwell Edge, and even (though it was not a requirement of the post) marking essays.[52]

More importantly, he took his professorial and teaching responsibilities with the utmost seriousness. Almost immediately after the start of term he delivered his inaugural lecture before the Vice Chancellor and the university on 26 October 1892.[53] Gracious and gently humorous as presentations on such occasions were expected to be, the lecture nonetheless provided Froude with the opportunity of presenting his own distinctive views of the nature and purpose of historical teaching and writing. Flying in face of the established orthodoxies, and rehearsing the arguments he had first made in the 1860s, Froude denied that history could be regarded as a science: it could establish no laws; its hypotheses could not be tested by experiment; verification was ultimately impossible; the sources on which it depended, and the interpreters of those sources, were equally clouded by prejudice and ignorance. Above all, it did not move from the particular to the general, but in the opposite direction.

> The relative importance of the general and the particular is with man in the inverse ratio to the rest of nature. In poetry, in art, in religion, in action and life, the interest always centres on persons and personal character.[54]

Still less, he asserted, was history to be seen as the record of human progress. The claim that there had been genuinely material progress was itself disputable. Undoubtedly true for some, it was far less so for others, as readers of General Booth's *Darkest England* would be compelled to acknowledge; and in general 'the lot of the immense majority of mankind is not even now a

---

51. Froude to Annie Ireland, 1 May, 7 March 1893, Beinecke Library, Yale University, Hilles MSS, Box 9, Froude files.

52. For an intimate account of Froude's teaching of advanced undergraduates, see L. H. Jordan, 'James Anthony Froude', in *Canada Presbyterian*, 7 November 1894. Amidst more critical observations of Froude as an historian, H. A. L. Fisher makes some complimentary statements about Froude's success as a lecturer to undergraduates in 'Modern Historians and their Methods', *Fortnightly Review*, 56 (1894), 806–16; see also the accounts supplied by F. M. Powicke and Percy Allen, in Dunn, *Froude*, II, 583–5. An encouraging letter from Froude to a student regarding an essay has also survived, Froude to [?], 23 October [1892/3], Duke University, Special Collections Library, Froude MSS.

53. Several versions of Froude's (untitled) inaugural lecture were published; that printed in *Longman's Magazine*, 21 (December 1892), 140–62, is the authorised version.

54. *Longman's Magazine*, 21, 145.

delightful one'. What the celebrants of progress really intended by the general term 'progress' was a steady increase in the area of individual liberty which, they claimed, history manifested. But insofar as it is true, what, Froude asks, is the significance of this development?

> Does history show that in proportion as men are left to their own wills they become happier, truer, braver, simpler, more reverent of good, more afraid of evil?[55]

Clearly it did not; and at the root of this contradiction lay a profound misunderstanding of the nature of liberty. Freedom was not to be confused with mere licence, a negative freedom from interference; it was instead a positive acquisition:

> The workman became free of his craft when he had learnt under a master all that the master could teach him ... The artist acquires a free hand when he knows what ought to be done, and eye and hand work together to do it. The musician is not free while his fingers blunder over the notes.[56]

Freedom as an end in itself, Froude insisted, is a chimera—and a dangerous one at that. The only real freedom in regard to which genuine progress can be registered is moral freedom—a freedom which develops as we transcend the obstacles, defects, and challenges that prevent us from acting for the good.

But, as Froude happily admitted, this was the kind of progress that the study of history could do little to measure or explain. So if history was not a science, if it could produce no laws, provide no explanations for the things that were really important, if it was so riven with bias, ignorance, and misunderstanding, what was the point of studying it at all? On this, Froude had no doubts. The point of studying history was not to explain, but to understand; not to essay a judgement as to *why* things happened, but by forming an understanding as to *how* particular events unfolded to attain a deeper understanding of humanity at all times and places. History was not a great unfolding pattern whose meaning was becoming clearer as each generation succeeded the next. It was 'a stage on which the drama of humanity is played out by successive actors from age to age'.

> If the historian would represent truly, he must represent as the dramatist does ... he must show you the figures that he is talking about, faithfully delineated,

---

55. *Longman's Magazine*, 21, 149–50.
56. *Longman's Magazine*, 21, 150.

with all the circumstances that surround them completely perceived and made intelligible, and then let them unfold their characters in their actions with such insight as you can gain into their inner natures.[57]

History, for the incoming Regius Professor, was decidedly an art. It may, however, have soothed the disquiet of the Vice Chancellor and the assembled dons that in his concluding remarks he wrapped such an old-fashioned view in the conventions of methodological best practice: source-criticism, prioritisation of manuscript over printed materials, state and parliamentary sources over private memorials, critical distance from secondary commentary, and so on ... and he had reassurance to offer them also in his intended topics of study. He would teach the sixteenth century—an age of collision between mighty forces

> where the best men were uncertain of their duties, where foresight was impossible, and princes consulting their wisest advisers received answers the most obvious; worst of all where none knew whom to trust.[58]

What may have been less obvious to his assembled audience, and more disturbing had they seen it, however, was that Froude was not concerned to adjudicate between such conflicting forces, straining in the best modern way for the high ground of retrospective objectivity. He was seeking instead to re-create this complexity for his young audience as the essential human condition which threatened every generation and every individual with bewilderment, paralysis, and failure, and from which there was no escape but unflinching personal commitment and vigorous individual action.

This was no mere aspiration. Long before his inaugural address—indeed, within two weeks of Salisbury's offer—Froude had laid out detailed plans for a connected series of lecture courses on what he regarded as the hinge of modern history. He proposed

> to take as the centre of the subject the figures of Charles V and Philip II, the materials for the knowledge of these princes having been greatly increased by recent publications and by the opening of the Continental archives. Erasmus and Luther, the Council of Trent and the great English naval empire rising out of the struggle with Spain would form subsidiary branches.[59]

57. *Longman's Magazine*, 21, 157–8.
58. *Longman's Magazine*, 21, 161.
59. Froude to the Vice Chancellor, 11 April 1892, quoted in Dunn, *Froude*, II, 575–6.

The centre of gravity of this proposed programme of courses may come as a surprise to those for whom Froude has been identified as the quintessential insular *English* historian. But Froude, unlike Stubbs, had never been a simple Little Englander. For many years, indeed, he had been planning to write a history of Continental Europe to parallel his *History of England* through studies of its two leading political figures, Charles V and Philip II. As late as the mid-1880s, after his labours on *Carlyle* had been completed, he was still eager to commence work on a major study of Charles V which he hoped would be the crowning achievement of his career, and, long before the offer of the Regius Chair arose, he had already begun a series of preliminary studies in the history of sixteenth-century Spain.[60] By the autumn of 1892 the plan had altered a little. In his first lecture to undergraduates he informed his audience that he proposed to offer three consecutive courses in the coming year. The first would deal with the Council of Trent, the second would be taken up with a detailed study of Erasmus, and the final course would be devoted to Charles V.[61]

The European and Catholic emphasis of this programme, Froude assured his listeners, represented no departure from his earlier convictions about the centrality of the Protestant Reformation: it remained for him as it had been four decades before 'the hinge on which all modern history turns'. But his decision to look at the great convulsions of the sixteenth century from the point of view of the Reformation's most implacable opponents necessarily added a perspective and an ambiguity hitherto absent from his writings.

The character and purpose of this alternative perspective was apparent in some measure in his preliminary studies of the later 1880s, most of which he collected in his *The Spanish Story of the Armada and Other Essays*. The title essay of the collection which, running at more than a hundred closely printed pages, constituted a small book in itself was occasioned by the appearance of *La Armada Invencible*—a very large collection of correspondence and other documents edited from the originals in the Spanish archives at Simancas by the Spanish scholar Capitan Fernandez Duro.[62] Rather than presenting a review and assessment of Duro's materials, however, Froude used them to present a narrative of the event from the point of view of its Spanish participants with all of the drama and all of the sympathy which

60. Froude to Ruskin, 10, 13 March 1886, in Viljoen (ed.), *The Froude–Ruskin Friendship*, 36, 38; also Froude to Max Müller, 8 December 1881, quoted in Dunn, *Froude*, II, 491.
61. Froude, *Lectures on the Council of Trent*, 6–7.
62. Cesáreo Fernández Duro, *La Armada Invencible*, 2 vols. (Madrid, 1884–5).

had characterised his earlier account from the English side. Characteristically, Froude pronounces judgement. To the commander of the fleet, the Duke of Medina Sidonia, greatest blame is allotted. It was his incompetence and timidity that was primarily responsible for the catastrophe. But he is not a villain: 'He knew nothing of the work he was sent to do; that is probably the worst that can be said of him; and he had not sought an appointment for which he knew he was unfit.'[63] Philip II was next in line for adverse judgement. But here also Froude is moderate. Mostly Philip behaved as

> a responsible and sensible prince, but the smallest thing and the largest seemed to occupy him equally ... [His fault] as a king and statesman was a belief in his own ability to manage things. In sending out the Armada he had set in motion a mighty force, not intending it to be used mightily, but that he might accomplish with it what he regarded as a master-stroke of tame policy.[64]

But for the majority of the warriors—and most especially the squadron leaders—Froude expresses an admiration equal to that accorded to England's defenders. The battle

> was fought out between men on both sides of a signally gallant and noble nature; and when the asperities of theology shall have mellowed down at last, Spanish and English authorities together will furnish materials for a great epic poem.[65]

This may appear a surprising aspiration from one whose own contribution to 'theological asperities', especially in regard to Catholicism, was not insubstantial. But the sincerity of Froude's present disposition is confirmed by two of the essays that follow. The first—a critical examination of the notorious 'Relacion' of Philip's disgraced former secretary, Antonio Perez—was intended to exonerate the king from his image as 'the evil demon of Protestant tradition'[66] by defending (and questioning the extent of) his involvement in the palace murders of Juan de Escobedo and King Philip's own son Don Carlos, and by refuting the story of his affair with the Princess of Eboli.

More interesting than this, however, was the succeeding essay on St Teresa of Avila. Froude had already written on Teresa in an essay in *Fraser's* which,

---

63. Froude, *The Spanish Story of the Armada*, 102.
64. *The Spanish Story of the Armada*, 25, 99.
65. *The Spanish Story of the Armada*, 2, 35–6.
66. *The Spanish Story of the Armada*, 106.

while not unsympathetic, accounted for her experiences largely in terms of an abnormal or hypersensitive psychology.[67] But in this later essay (which was a revision of one first published in the *Quarterly Review* in 1882), while he did not ignore the workings of psychology, Froude had moved away from accounting for the origins of the saint's acute spiritual consciousness to a consideration of its broader significance. He quotes at length and with unqualified admiration from Teresa's own 'very beautiful' account of her spiritual development which he declares 'exhibits the spiritual enthusiasm of the Spanish nation in its noblest form'.[68] Protestants may have broken from Rome 'in the name of liberty'; but 'the Spaniards loved liberty' also:

> But it was the liberty of their country for which they had been fighting for centuries against the Infidel. As aristocrats they were instinctively on the side of authority. United among themselves, they believed in the union of Christendom, and they threw themselves into the struggle against heresy with the same enthusiasm with which they contended with the Crescent in the Mediterranean ... While some engaged with the enemy abroad, the finer spirits among them undertook the task of setting in order their known house ... They too required a Reformation if they were to be fit champions of a Holy Cause; and the instrument was a woman ... distinguished only in representing ... the vigorous instincts of the Spanish character.[69]

Thus Froude recognised Teresa's affinity with the other representative character of sixteenth-century Spain whose reputation and influence, like Teresa's, long outlasted the decline and fall of that world: the author of *Don Quixote*. Froude had already published a highly appreciative essay on Cervantes in 1886, seeking to rescue him, as he sought to rescue Philip II and St Teresa, not only from his detractors but from misguided admirers who either through sentimentalism or cynicism failed to see the underlying unity and seriousness of purpose of his satire.[70] Underneath all the absurdities and insanity, Cervantes 'touches the deepest fibres of the experience of every generous mind, and teaches us to love what is noble even in its wildest aberrations'.[71] He is, moreover, the chronicler of the external decline of Spanish spirituality, even as Teresa was the embodiment of its internal survival in individual cases. From their different positions—one intensely emotional,

---

67. 'Saint Teresa: A Psychological Study', *Fraser's Magazine*, 65 (January 1862), 59–74.
68. *The Spanish Story of the Armada*, 195, vii.
69. *The Spanish Story of the Armada*, 181–2.
70. 'Mr Ormsby's *Don Quixote*', *Quarterly Review*, 162 (January 1886), 43–79.
71. *Quarterly Review*, 162, 76.

the other coolly reflective—they provide a revelation of the essence of Spanish culture at the very point of its turn from excellence to its long and terminal decline. Theirs was the Spain

> which gave its life blood to preserve what could not be preserved—the supremacy in Europe of the Catholic Church. She failed, but she did not fail ignobly. Institutions, creeds, orders, organizations, empires, have their day, and then pass away. All things which have life carry in them the elements of dissolution. When their work is done and they are no more needed, they die. But the end is not certain till it comes. Those who resist change are as noble in their motives as those who push it forward. Each does its best, according to its conviction, and Providence, or organic development, if we prefer to call it so, turns the balance this way or that.[72]

V

From these preparatory explorations it is possible to discern the purpose underlying Froude's university lecture programme. In shifting attention from England to Europe, and in particular to Spain, and in depicting how over the course of the sixteenth century Spain moved from a position of unprecedented power and pre-eminence to one of inexorable decline through its opposition to the forces of historical change, Froude was not inviting his students to indulge in yet another spasm of chauvinist self-congratulation. He was pointing to a moral. The culture which collapsed into decay at the close of the sixteenth century was no less powerful, no less wealthy, no less confident, and no less noble than that which even its most extreme celebrant would ascribe to contemporary Britain. Nonetheless, it failed utterly before the challenge with which history confronted it. And so what now of Britain's future?

Thus it was that, despite the familiar cataloguing of the corruptions and abuses of the pre-Reformation church with which they opened, Froude's *Lectures on the Council of Trent* provided no mere rehearsal of the triumph of Reformation over the forces of reaction. In fact, Froude based his work almost entirely on Catholic sources, depending largely for his evidence on the papally inspired *Istoria del Concilio di Trento* (Rome, 1656–66) by the Jesuit Cardinal Pietro Sforza Pallavicino, occasionally preferring the work of

---

72. *Quarterly Review*, 162, 45.

Pallavicino's predecessor and literary enemy, Paolo Sarpi, and supplementing these central texts by his own research into Spanish diplomatic correspondence in Simancas. The narrative strategy of the lectures is also indicative. Froude is halfway through his story before the Council actually convenes, and he ends his account at the inconclusive adjournment of the Council in 1552 rather than its actual conclusion in 1563 when its dogmatic assertions of theological orthodoxy and ecclesiastical authority were finally promulgated. All of this suggests that, far from presenting an account of the origins of papalist reaction, a more appropriate title for his lectures might actually have been 'The collapse of Roman Christendom as seen by its greatest defenders.'

Froude's *Council of Trent* exhibits some of the finest characteristics of his historical technique. There are no real villains—even among the several popes—and, oddly, no Carlylean heroes: Luther is but a shadowy presence at the start of the book, and irrelevant thereafter. Instead, Froude plunges his readers into a dense web of political and diplomatic complexity in which all the principal figures occupy positions which are under intense challenge by others. There is first (and foremost) the predicament of the popes whose authority, political influence, and wealth are under threat by the majority of their own bishops and by the Emperor Charles. But the bishops are themselves threatened by the laity—most notably the kings and princes of Europe, resentful of their own power and wealth. And the kings and princes are also challengers to, and fearful of, the imperial claims of the house of Habsburg. Surrounding all these are the contentions of the religiously committed: the zealous reformers, and the equally fervent defenders of orthodoxy. Even within such groups there are divisions: between bishops and cardinals, between secular priests and religious orders, and between moderate and radical Protestants, papalists, imperialists, and nationalists.

All these forces are introduced and reconsidered in Froude's narrative with remarkable clarity and economy; and while Froude's assessments of motive and consequence have been challenged by subsequent generations of historians, all are presented as being founded upon relatively rational and pragmatic terms. Froude makes clear, however, that amidst this labyrinth of the ecclesiastical and secular politics of sixteenth-century Europe, a power struggle of world-historical importance was actually taking place. This was the battle for the unity of Christendom being fought, according to Froude, between two powerful antagonists—an emperor and a pope, both equally convinced of the justice of their position. Though neither a prophet nor a hero, Charles V was a sincere, reasonable man who believed that Christian unity could be preserved only through the reform of the clergy and the redress of the grievances of the laity; and Paul III was likewise certain that concession to any reforms would lead to the dissolution of the papal power and the ruin of the universal church. Though at first neither the emperor nor the pope's immediate predecessors had realised the enormity of the stakes for which they were playing, and though as the conflict developed both parties had sought some form of compromise, the forces driving European Christianity apart were in the end overwhelming.

In the short term the papacy won. The drive for internal reform was stemmed, or diverted from the laity; and the codification of doctrine which the papacy regarded as central, and which Froude regarded as at once nefarious and irrelevant, became the Council's primary achievement. Yet in the long term, everyone lost. The indeterminate theological and metaphysical niceties so irresponsibly ruled upon at Trent were to be the occasion of the bloody wars, cruel persecutions, and profound depressions of the human spirit that followed for centuries thereafter. Until, after so much suffering, relief had come at last: the power of the papacy and the clergy everywhere had been curtailed, and religious persecution and religious intolerance had ceased. There remained, however, the terrible lessons about how men behave in the midst of forces they do not comprehend and about how history repays men for their deliberate but ignorant actions.[73]

VI

The sibylline note struck in the *Lectures on the Council of Trent* was further developed in the set of lectures on the *Life and Letters of Erasmus* which, in accordance with his plan, Froude next presented to his Oxford audience.[74] Based on a close study and original translation of Jean Le Clerc's ten-volume edition of Erasmus's *Opera Omnia* (Leiden, 1703–06), Froude's course on Erasmus was as scholarly in its foundation as its predecessor on the Council of Trent. The study of Erasmus which Froude now presented was not only more learned than the sketch he had drawn as part of his comparative study

---

73. This central argument is summarised in the final lecture, which was originally delivered in a large public forum; Froude, *Lectures on the Council of Trent delivered at Oxford, 1892–3* (London, 1899), 282–305.
74. *Life and Letters of Erasmus: Lectures Delivered at Oxford, 1893–4* (London: Longmans, 1894).

with Luther almost thirty years previously; it was also considerably more sympathetic. As we have seen, in 1867 Froude's Erasmus was a rather sorry soul. Engaging, delightful, and intellectually brilliant, he was also weak, both intellectually and morally. Unlike Luther he was incapable of comprehending the massive historical forces which were gathering all around him, and so was destined, also unlike Luther, to become historically ineffective, displaced, and in some quarters despised.[75]

Froude's later Erasmus is, by contrast, an altogether more attractive individual, on several levels. The art of the advocate is very much at work here. Just as he had been concerned to exonerate Charles V, Philip II, and St Teresa from the denigration of Protestant mythology, so Froude is now determined to clear Erasmus from the charge that out of weakness he had abandoned and betrayed Luther. 'His conduct', Froude concedes, 'was not perhaps heroic, but heroism is not always wisdom.'[76] Assured in the belief that reform from within the church itself was imminent, he regarded Luther not as history would reveal him, but as 'an honest, and perhaps imprudent monk who had broken out single-handed on a noisy revolt' over the wrong issue—indulgences, which to Erasmus were merely a minor symptom of the greater malaise he was determined to cure by his own methods:

> What was Erasmus to do in the new element which had sprung out so suddenly? Turn against Luther he would not, for he knew that Luther's denunciation of the indulgences had been as right as it was brave. Declare for him he would not. He could not commit himself to a movement which he could not control, and which for all he could see might become an unguided insurrection.[77]

Time proved Erasmus wrong. Rome was not to be reformed from within, and violent rebellion alone became the only means of regenerating Christianity. 'But Erasmus was not to know it, and I think it rather to his credit that he met Luther's advances as favourably as he did.'[78]

In contrast to the confident dismissal delivered thirty years previously, this was a measured final judgement. But Froude's defence of Erasmus's attitude to Luther was secondary to his principal purpose of presenting Erasmus as a recognisably familiar human being. Ample quotation from his

75. 'Times of Erasmus and Luther', *Short Studies*, I, 37–153; also ch. 9 above.
76. *Life and Letters of Erasmus*, 237, 257.
77. *Life and Letters of Erasmus*, 214.
78. *Life and Letters of Erasmus*, 238.

letters in a free and informal translation (of which Froude's critics were soon to complain) emphasised Erasmus's engaging humanity: his love of fun, his appetite for life in all its forms, his petty frustrations, his grand ambitions, his constant worry about money and reputation, his pursuit of patronage, his shrewdness, his wisdom, and, above all, his care for his friends.[79] As a means of introducing an undergraduate audience to a figure so foreign in many ways, this was, no doubt, good pedagogical practice. And there are other features of the text—knowing references to sex and drink, and little jokes at the expense of Cambridge—that suggest that Froude was by no means insensitive to this aspect of the lecturer's craft.[80]

Erasmus, as presented by Froude, is not only recognisably human; he is remarkably similar in his character and career to Froude himself. The correspondences are several. Both were born gifted, both were intellectually precocious and challenging, and both suffered deeply for their precocity at the hands of brutal schoolmasters. Both found themselves trapped by the terrible consequences of taking holy orders under pressure; both found ways of overcoming them. Both in their youth were regarded by their elders as troublesome and even scandalous figures. Erasmus, according to Froude, was the probable author of a scandalous fiction exposing the moral abuses of the time of which he, like the pseudonymous author of *Shadows of the Clouds*, vehemently denied. They were both always (and unpredictably) provocative: it was the nature of Erasmus, says Froude, 'to heat the water wherever he was'.[81] Erasmus, likewise, was 'no stationary scholar confined to desk or closet. He was out in the world, travelling from city to city'.[82] Both achieved recognition, even fame, and both, though they believed themselves to be outside it, were co-opted into the establishment of their day. Both were harassed throughout their career by small-minded niggling critics seeking to expose their inaccuracies, inconsistencies, and errors, and both endured them, though not without pain. Both had a habit of not dating their

---

79. Perhaps anticipating restiveness in his audience after another digression on Erasmus's complaints about his physical suffering, Froude interjects: 'It is well to mention these things if I am to make you respect him, as I hope you will,' *Life and Letters of Erasmus*, 404.

80. Froude also employs the standard lecturer's technique of signposting the exciting things to come in the following lecture at the close of the present one.

81. *Life and Letters of Erasmus*, 195. This was a metaphor which Froude had occasionally applied to himself. See Froude to Mrs Butler, 21 October 1872, in regard to his American lecture tour: 'the water is warm now, I feel it will boil over after tonight, and there will be two lectures more', Beinecke Library Yale University, Hilles MSS, Box 9.

82. *Life and Letters of Erasmus*, 195, 227.

letters—in Erasmus's case, Froude says, because he did 'not foresee the interest that would one day attach to them'.[83]

These biographical parallels are so manifold that few of Froude's audience would not have caught some of them, and as though to prompt such
reflections Froude takes occasion here and there in the text to remind his
listeners that he had had a public career of some controversy before assuming his professorship at Oxford. It is true that Froude was in an autobiographical mood at this time; and there may be something of an interior
monologue taking place here.[84] While it would be misleading, however, to
suggest that Froude saw himself as a kind of latter-day Erasmus, this was not
the first occasion on which he had drawn on autobiographical modes for
rhetorical or expressive purposes. In the present circumstances the drawing
of parallels between the lecturer and his subject was particularly pertinent,
for in presenting himself to his audience as a distinguished if highly controversial intellectual discoursing on an earlier strikingly similar figure who,
like himself, had been working in times of great spiritual crisis, Froude was
reinforcing the central message of his lectures. A reiteration of the *leitmotif*
of his biography of Carlyle, this was Froude's insistence that the writings of
greater or lesser thinkers could not be separated from their lives and their
actions in the world, that thinking and writing were actions like any other,
for the effect and consequences of which their originators bore an inescapable responsibility.

It was for this reason that, though he occasionally discusses Erasmus's
published works, Froude's emphasis, as his title indicates, is altogether on
Erasmus's letters; for it is in the letters that, despite (or in fact because of) his
gifts as a scholar of matchless ability, Erasmus showed his true understanding of the limited role of intellectual speculation. To Erasmus such issues as free
will, predestination, the efficacy of grace, and the nature of the Trinity were
beyond ultimate determination by humans, and ought therefore to be left
alone to those individuals who cared to speculate about them. 'May not a
man', Froude paraphrases Erasmus, 'be a Christian who cannot explain
philosophically how the nativity of the Son differs from the procession of
the Holy Spirit?'

---

83. *Life and Letters of Erasmus*, 40.
84. It was around this time that he has composing the fragmentary autobiography on which so
    much of our knowledge concerning his early life depends; see chs. 1 and 2 above.

If I believe in the Trinity in Unity, I want no arguments. If I do not believe, I shall not be convinced by reason. The sum of religion is peace which can only be when definitions are as few as possible and opinion is left free on many subjects.[85]

For Erasmus, according to Froude, religion was not dogma,

but a rule of life, a perpetual reminder to mankind of their responsibility to their Maker, a spiritual authority under which individuals could learn their duties to God and to their neighbour ... To Erasmus religion meant purity and justice and mercy with the keeping of the moral commandments, and to him these Graces were not the privilege of any peculiar creed.[86]

This was a very modern Erasmus indeed. And though many scholars would now agree with Froude's contention that Erasmus believed that the purpose of his work was to promote practical reforms in the real world rather than to perpetuate scholarly debate, few would go as far as this.[87] Forever the moralist, Froude was less concerned with precisely identifying the nature of Erasmus's faith than in emphasising its continuing relevance. In presenting Erasmus's 'plea for the free discussion of theological difficulties', Froude was, however, being no more eirenic than he was when he wrote directly on the topic thirty years perviously. Precisely because such issues were essentially indeterminable by the human mind, and precisely because we deficient humans must nevertheless live and act in history, it was imperative that we must not cleave to artificial and transient dogmas, or withdraw into an irresponsible indifference. Rather, we must train ourselves to act for the good.

It was this conviction that compelled Froude to invest one work by Erasmus with particular significance. Composed as Erasmus's long-awaited (and long-demanded) reply to Luther, *De Libero Arbitrio* was at the time Froude wrote largely regarded as a deliberately obscure piece of metaphysical wrangling through which Erasmus had hoped to avoid open commitment. For Froude, however, it was a central piece in his entire *oeuvre*. Erasmus's fear of dogmatism (Catholic and Lutheran) rested, according to Froude, on his profound appreciation of the extent to which individuals are free to act is limited by congenital and environmental factors, all of them

---

85. *Life and Letters of Erasmus*, 304.
86. *Life and Letters of Erasmus*, 312, 401.
87. For a useful summary of modern views, see Bruce Mansfield, *Erasmus in the Twentieth Century* (Toronto, 2003); and for Mansfield's own assessment of Froude's *Erasmus* and its intellectual context, see his *Man on His Own: Interpretations of Erasmus, 1750–1920* (Toronto, 1992), ch. 8.

accidental and transitory. By itself, therefore, the will 'is not sufficient to direct and control conduct'.[88] Since the principles of living a virtuous life are not innate, they must be taught and learned in the same manner as all other skills and crafts. The results will not always be perfect: 'perfection, or even excellence, is rare in any art or occupation'. The congenital defects may never be fully overcome, but teachers and students of virtue must do the best they can.

> The pains which we take in training children; the allowances which we make ... for inherited vicious tendencies, for the environment of vice and igno-rance in which so many are brought up prove[s] that in practice ... we act on this hypothesis.[89]

It is here that the theological dogmatists depart from the rest of humanity, 'with an absolute rule of right, to which they insist that everyone, young and old, wise and ignorant is bound to conform'.[90] They realise, of course, that very few humans do, so they have resort to divine grace. Thus the Catholics claim that grace is mediated through the sacraments supplemented by a superfluity of merit earned by the real saints, while the Lutherans affirm that it is granted to individuals only through the mysterious will of God before whom poor humans can do nothing other than prostrate them-selves. Both are hideous perversions of the real human condition. The former leads to superstition, idolatry, and all manner of corruptions; the lat-ter to hypocrisy, complacency, despair, and the ethical horror of predestina-tion. What these gross reductions lacked was the insight granted to the wisest philosophers and mystics (Spinoza and Goethe, of course, but also Erasmus) that the conflict between free will and necessity was a conceptual confusion of the finite with the infinite, and that the Creator was working within all of the elements of Creation to bring about an ultimate union in eternity. For this reason the claim that individuals must exercise their skills as best they can to bring about the purpose of their Creator was neither a hopeless illusion nor an unnecessary burden. It was a responsibility—a duty—essential to that purpose.

In these pages of his *Erasmus* Froude comes closer than he had been for several years to a reiteration of the primary ethical impulses which had driven him in the 1840s. But in resetting his theme in history through the

88. *Life and Letters of Erasmus*, 329.
89. *Life and Letters of Erasmus*, 330.
90. *Life and Letters of Erasmus*, 330.

life of a figure commonly regarded by Froude's contemporaries as one of history's great failures, Froude was sounding a warning to his audience (in relation to which the autobiographical resonances may have added a further point). Erasmus's failure had not been accidental. It arose not only from his over-confidence in his own intelligence and ability to influence men of power, but also from his deep reluctance to countenance the prospect of violent struggle.

> Times come when rough measures alone will answer, and Erasmian education might have made slight impression upon the Scarlet Lady of Babylon … The Romish Church would have proved too strong for reason and moderation and could be encountered only by a spiritual force as aggressive as its own.[91]

This Luther had grasped instinctively, and history had rewarded him for it.

VII

It is this militant undertone, ever-present though muted in *Erasmus*, that offers some connection between that reflective work and the altogether different final course of lectures which as *English Seamen in the Sixteenth Century* was to be Froude's last, and most popular, publication.[92] The extraordinary contrast of theme, tone, and expression between this posthumously published work and the two lecture courses which had preceded it is in some part a matter of occasion. The lectures on Trent and Erasmus had been given to a small, select audience in Froude's home at Cherwell Edge, while those on the 'English Seamen' were delivered before a large public audience. Unlike the other two courses, this set of nine lectures was based on no recondite primary sources, but was largely a brief recycling of fairly well-known materials with which Froude had been familiar since the 1850s.

The stories which Froude now rehearsed were for long well known: the adventures of John Hawkins on the high seas, Drake's circumnavigation, the privateers' raiding expedition to the West Indies, the daring attack on Cadiz,

---

91. *Life and Letters of Erasmus*, 238, 334.
92. *English Seamen in the Sixteenth Century: Lectures Delivered at Oxford Easter Terms 1893–4* (London, Longmans, 1895). First published in March 1895, the book was reprinted six times before 1899 and in 1901 issued in Longman's Silver Library, under which imprint it was reissued ten times before the outbreak of World War I. It is to the Silver Library edition that references are made here.

and, of course, the defeat of the Spanish Armada. But Froude retells them in a terse, dramatic fashion. Crisp sentences abound, paragraphs are short, and the narrative line is simple. In contrast to the multiple forces which Froude depicted acting on Charles V or the subtle challenges being presented to Erasmus, the English seamen were simple, brave men who faced the hazards of their adventures and triumphed magnificently. On many occasions Froude's text reads less like a scholarly lecture and more like a boy's adventure story:

> Two gates were in front of Carlile, with a road to each leading through a jungle. At each gate was a cannon, and the jungle was lined with musketeers. He [Carlile] divided his men and attacked both together. One party he led in person. The cannon opened on him, and an Englishman next to him was killed. He dashed on leaving the Spaniards no time to reload, carried the gate at a rush and cut his way through the streets to the great square.[93]

In fact, it is the genre of the boy's adventure story which characterises the entire design of the book. Here is England, isolated and at war with a great power driven by fanatical ideological commitment to achieve world domination. Within there are traitors, conspirators, and their dupes—Jesuits and other dark plotters who mean to engineer the assassination of Elizabeth and to aid invasion, and their foolish idealist fellow travellers, irresponsibly, childishly, unforgivably innocent. In Whitehall, as this terrible threat gathers, there is complacency, cynicism, and the feebleness of old age. Left alone to 'save their country and their country's liberty', there were only a few good men, heroes all.[94] From Erskine Childers through A. E. W. Mason and John Buchan down to Ian Fleming and beyond, this has been the standard formula of the popular English political thriller. In addition to its form, Froude may also be credited with anticipating one of the essential tropes of the genre: the suspension under extraordinary pressures of the normal rules of ethical conduct and the privilege of a licence to kill.

In the second lecture of *English Seamen* Froude again confronts the uncomfortable fact of John Hawkins's involvement in the Atlantic slave trade. His tergiversations about the ontological status of black people and the moral status of race slavery are no less uncomfortable now than they were in *The English in the West Indies*: while, under the tutelage of the white

---

93. *English Seamen*, 189.
94. *English Seamen*, 309.

man, black people have since displayed 'high capacities of intellect and character', slavery itself was an historical experiment whose origins should not be judged 'by the censures which in its later developments it eventually came to deserve'.[95] In addressing it, however, Froude was less concerned with the sufferings of the enslaved than with defending those obliged to become slavers. Hawkins, Drake, and the rest were compelled to engage in the slave trade because the French, the Portuguese, the Africans themselves, but above all the Spanish were already deeply implicated; and since England was, to all intents, at war with Spain, fighting the Spaniards with all of the weapons they had at their disposal was entirely justifiable. It was on similar grounds that Froude not only defended but actually celebrated acts of violence on the part of the seamen—such as Drake's slaughter of civilians in the West Indies:

> Vandalism, atrocity, unheard among civilized nations, dishonour to the Protestant cause ... so indignant Liberalism shrieked, and has not ceased shrieking. Let it be remembered that for fifteen years the Spaniards had been burning English seamen whenever they could find them, plotting to kill the Queen and reduce England itself to the vassaldom of the Pope.[96]

Violence must be met by violence, cruelty by cruelty. When Drake sent a message by 'a negro boy' declaring his high terms for truce, the poor wretch was stabbed by a haughty Spanish officer. 'He ran back bleeding to the English lines and died at Drake's feet. Sir Francis was a dangerous man to provoke.' When at last the Spaniards surrendered, he demanded the death of the killer.

> The offender was surrendered. It was not enough. Drake insisted that they should do justice on him themselves. The Governor found it prudent to comply, and the too hasty officer was executed.[97]

And so on: the killings of civilians at Cadiz, the hasty execution of Mary Queen of Scots, the wholesale slaughter of Armada survivors by English officers in Ireland were all true; and all were justified by the conditions of ideological world war.

Unlike most of his successors in the genre, however, Froude was intent on explicitly defending the moral elitism of his heroes' conduct:

95. *English Seamen*, 49, 52.
96. *English Seamen*, 191–2.
97. *English Seamen*, 190–1.

I have often asked my Radical friends what is to be done if out of every hundred enlightened voters, two thirds will give their votes one way, but are afraid to fight, and the remaining third will not only vote, but will fight too if the poll goes against them? Which has the right to rule? ... The brave and resolute minority will rule ... It appears to me that the true right to rule lies with those who are best and bravest whether their numbers are large or small; and three centuries ago the best and brightest part of this English nation had determined, though they were but a third of it, that Pope and Spaniard should be no masters of theirs.[98]

The absolute superiority of passionate intensity over moderate consideration could hardly have been stated with more brutal finality than in these late words of Victorian England's self-appointed moralist.

Conceived simultaneously, and composed and delivered within weeks of each other, there can be no greater expression of the bifurcation of Froude's voice than in the contrasting moods and messages of *Erasmus* and *English Seamen*. An underlying consistency can, it is true, be uncovered in Froude's persistent demand for active engagement over detached speculation, which had been his great liberating conviction since his coming of age. But the unmistakable contradictions of temper, tone, and address in these final works are evidence of the pressures under which Froude had placed himself in his determination to retain the force of his original prophetic voice while appealing to an audience chronologically younger and sociologically broader than that which, following Carlyle, he had once so successfully engaged. Such strains had first begun to appear in the 1870s as Froude turned to write about contemporary politics and especially about Ireland. But they became evident in the contrast between his strenuously honest *Thomas Carlyle* and the speciously disarming travel books that immediately followed it. The late historical commissions offered some possibility of renewal. But, though he occasionally chose to avail of it—as in his studies of Disraeli, Erasmus, and the Council of Trent—Froude's own determination to persevere in this last prophetic endeavour, despite all its manifest intellectual and ethical risks, is evident to the end. That he should have persisted in striving toward this increasingly unattainable objective is evidence perhaps of intellectual and moral sclerosis, but proof also of the underlying sincerity and selflessness that had shaped his career from the start.

98. *English Seamen*, 201–2.

VIII

Given its potential for further elaboration of his own view of the manner in which European history had evolved, it may be regretted that Froude never lived to offer the final course of lectures on Emperor Charles V which, according to his long-term plan, might have added a final balance to the secondary and popular lectures on the English seamen. But there is little reason to suppose that his account would have differed in substance from the lines indicated in the essays on Spain and the lectures on the Council of Trent.

In any case, Froude had little opportunity to prepare the course. Although he left Oxford at the end of Trinity term 1894 for his summer residence at Salcombe Harbour in Devon, where for many years he had been accustomed to spend the summer months, he fully intended to return in the autumn with a new set of lectures Early in June, however, the abdominal irritation of which he had been complaining on and off since the mid-1880s worsened. He was forced to abandon plans for a further trip to Norway and the temptation to sail again to New Zealand.[99] By the end of June he had been diagnosed with a stomach cancer that his physician judged to be inoperable. His condition steadily deteriorated over the summer, and early in September, under the care of his daughter Margaret, he was moved from his upstairs bedroom to the downstairs library. Here he made a final will and testament in which he ordered that all his papers and correspondence be destroyed. On Thursday 18 October he lapsed from consciousness into coma, and died peacefully two days later.[100]

His final intelligible words were a quotation from Genesis 18:25: 'Shall not the judge of all the earth do right?' This was Abraham's challenge to Jehovah before the destruction of Sodom, demanding that the city be preserved so long as any element of the just and the good continued to reside within it. Insofar as it encapsulated his profound awareness of the inescapability of moral responsibility and his commensurate confidence in the ability of mankind to rise to its duty and contribute to the fulfilment of Creation, Froude could hardly have found a more fitting farewell. But it is no less apt, for one whose persistent efforts to fulfil his duty had entangled him in contradictions which became increasingly irreconcilable, that Froude's last utterance should also have been a question.

---

99. Froude to Skelton, 22 June 1894; *Table-Talk of Shirley*, 222–3.
100. Will; the details of his last days were supplied by Margaret Froude to Froude's first biographer Herbert Paul; Paul, *Life of Froude*, 414–15.

15

Sincerity, Prophecy, Responsibility

In a space of just over three years, while he was in his early sixties, Froude composed two of the most startlingly contrasting pieces ever to have issued from his pen. One was an engaging fable about the Last Judgement which in its own way promised salvation for all; the other a futuristic fantasy which is among the grimmest of dystopias. But despite their markedly apparent differences, both essays may be seen to be remarkably coherent in their underlying assumptions and intent, embodying in the most compact manner Froude's fundamental convictions regarding the purpose of his life and work, and revealing thereby their unresolved contradictions and their disturbing implications.

I

In 'A Siding at a Railway Station' Froude returned to the genre of fantasy and parable which he had explored at the beginning of his career in the 1840s and early 1850s.[1] Exploiting the allegorical possibilities of the railway, the story recounts, through the voice of a narrator who is clearly intended to be identified as Froude himself, the experience of a trainload of passengers who find themselves diverted from their destinations into a siding, where they are met by a mysterious station-master. Informed that the train's journey has been indefinitely deferred, they are ordered to disembark. On the platform everything changes. Social distinctions disappear and all classes

---

1. First published in *Fraser's Magazine*, 599 (November 1879), 622–33, the essay was included in *Short Studies*, IV, 543–72, to which reference is made hereafter, except in the case of significant departures from the original text.

are suddenly on a level. 'A beggar woman hustled the duchess.' The great and the good—politicians, bankers, aristocrats, and clergymen—protest that they have important business from which they could not be diverted: a bishop is on his way to a synod held to debate the crucial issue as to whether gas-light might be substituted for candles at the communion service. But the station-master rebuffs their protests and the passengers are ushered into a large waiting-room where their luggage is to be examined. This luggage turns out to be something entirely different from the possessions they had brought with them. The third-class passengers, whose actual baggage had been meagre, now had their names attached to large boxes, while 'a moderate heap stood where the second-class luggage should have been'. But for the first-class passengers there was nothing but 'a few shawls and cloaks'. On inspection, the boxes are revealed to contain samples of the work which the named individuals had done in their life. With the exception of a few cheats and idlers whose boxes are empty, the working people pass this first test in great numbers, to be sent on to a higher court; but toward the first-class travellers, whose boxes are scanty, the station-master is stern:

> You have been in the world where work is the condition of life ... Those who work deserve to eat; those who do not work deserve to starve. There are but three ways of living: by working, by stealing, or by begging. Those who have not lived by the first have lived by the other two. And no matter how superior you think yourselves, you shall not pass here till you have something of your own to produce.[2]

With this, 'the large majority of the saloon passengers' are dismissed. The duchess is sent to begin her life again in a labourer's cottage, the fine gentleman to be a ploughboy, the preachers to become mechanics or apprentices. 'A philosopher who, having had a good fortune, had insisted that the world was as good as could be made was to be born blind and paralytic, and to find his way through life under the new conditions.' 'They will be all here again in a few years', says the station-master, 'for my part I would put them out altogether ... Some of the worst I have known made at last into pigs and geese to be fatted up and eaten and made of use in that way.'

So far this has been a simple parable rehearsing the familiar Christian message that 'the first shall be last, and the last shall be first'. But a scene now develops where the remaining passengers are subjected to a further examination

---

2. *Short Studies*, IV, 533–4.

in which the quality of their achievement is assessed in the light of their capacity, their potential, and their motivation 'to see how far [each] had done his best'. In each case the effect of such interrogation was to diminish the inherent value of every action and achievement as each was shown to have been in some degree infected by mean or vain motives. Under such pressure, one 'impressive-looking' passenger exclaims that it was all true, and that he had known from the beginning that despite the development of his talents, his defects had grown even faster. 'In the so-called good actions with which he seemed to be credited, there was nothing that was really good'; and now, because of this self-knowledge, 'he abhorred himself' and believed he 'had no merit which could entitle him to look for favour'. Such self-abnegation is rendered less impressive, however, when Froude informs his readers that the speaker was an eminent divine who had gained a great reputation in championing and maintaining this bleak teaching. The examiner then reproves the speaker for taking such an extremely pes-simistic view: 'Only those who are themselves perfect can do anything perfectly'; and human beings, by definition, are imperfect. Some had been given great talents, some few, some had 'naturally good dispositions; some ... naturally bad dispositions'. What counted was how they managed with the limited and unbalanced capabilities which they had been granted. 'Idleness, wilfulness, selfishness, and deliberate preference of evil to good' were the only genuine faults. To this kindly sentiment another hopeful passenger—an archbishop—enthusiastically assents. But readers are informed that he had made such a case when he had been engaged in controversy with the other divine in the past. The infection of human vanity is incurable.

This interchange troubles narrator Froude. If moral strength and artistic genius were, as the examiner implied, products of natural dispositions, surely so also were 'idleness, wilfulness, selfishness, &, &', and if that were the case ... ? Such ruminations are interrupted by his own summons to examination. All his writings being spread out before him, a fluid is poured over all the pages,

> the effect of which was to obliterate entirely every untrue proposition, and to make every partially true proposition grow faint ... Alas! chapter after chapter vanished away, leaving the paper clean as if no compositor had ever laboured in setting type for it. Pale and illegible became the fine-sounding paragraphs on which I had secretly prided myself. A few passages survived here and there at long intervals. These were those on which I had laboured least and had

almost forgotten, or those, as I observed in one or two instances which had been selected for reprobation in the weekly journals.[3]

At the end of his ordeal, however, just when Froude feels that he is to be granted a narrow exoneration, the scene changes dramatically. A screen is pulled back and he finds himself confronted by 'an interminable vista of creatures ... which in the course of my life I had devoured, either in part or whole to sustain my unconscionable carcass'.

> There they stood in lines with solemn and reproachful faces—oxen and calves, sheep and lambs, deer, hares, rabbits, turkeys, ducks, chickens, pheasants, grouse ... out of the sea had come the trout and salmon, the soles and turbots, the ling and the cod ... They seemed to be in millions and I had eaten them all ... A stag spoke for the rest. 'We all', he said, 'were sacrificed to keep this cormorant in being, and to enable him to produce the miserable bits of printed paper which are all he has to show for himself ... If the person who stands here to answer for himself can affirm that his value in the universe was equivalent to the value of all of us who were sacrificed to feed him, we have no more to say ... But ... we have long watched him—him and his fellows— and we have failed to see in what the superiority of the human creature lies. We know him only as the most cunning, the most destructive, and, unhappily, the longest lived of all carnivorous beasts. His delight is in killing. Even when his hunger is satisfied, he kills us for his mere amusement.'[4]

At this Froude is devastated, his mild sense of exoneration obliterated. His success even in the first examination is declared a mistake, and he is to be sent back to take up his life where it had been interrupted, condemned to render a better account than had so far been offered. And, says the implacable examiner, 'if you can find any better employment for your remaining years than that of book-writing, I advise you to take it'.[5]

A piece so light will hardly bear intense analysis. But the 'A Siding at a Railway Station' does rehearse several of the central themes that had characterised Froude's writing from his earliest efforts. It is unapologetically moralistic; but it also revisits the dilemma which Froude (much to his cost) had confronted in his early fictions: that is, the injustice suffered by those without

---

3. *Short Studies*, IV, 568
4. *Short Studies*, IV, 569–70. In the original version in *Fraser's*, the animals' representative was 'an aged ox', and Froude's alteration to a stag—favourite victim of the hunting classes—may have been made to underline the needless and prodigal character of much animal-killing.
5. This is the conclusion of the version in *Fraser's*, 633; the version in *Short Studies* ends more lamely, with Froude's awakening from the dream which he had had in the course of an ordinary railway journey.

the gifts to be brave and virtuous, and the unfair advantage enjoyed by those who had such gifts in their common pursuit of the good. His admission that the vast bulk of his literary output had been worthless, while remarkable, given the hugely controversial nature of his contemporary reputation, is also redolent of his characteristic (and in this case literal) self-effacement in the interests of his message.[6] Equally clear is the persistence of Froude's conviction that the only value residing in his literary efforts lay in their capacity to reveal to his readers the nature of the challenge which living presented to them all. Finally, Froude's guilty carnivorousness, while echoing his other publicly and privately expressed sentiments about the propriety of hunting, is evidence of the continuing influence over his view of life of his earlier encounters with the Zenda Vesta and with the philosophy of Arthur Schopenhauer.

But carnivorism had an important role to play within the fantasy itself. If among the mass of suffering animals there was also located the final corporeal embodiment of the duchess, the idler, the cheat, and all the other sorry humans whose dispositions and actions had determined that their final fate was to be consumed by the unworthy man of letters, then a strange form of resolution to all the moral difficulties produced by the unfair, and heavily determined character of human existence seemed to emerge. This was the suggestion that, for all the helpless depravity and inescapable misery of human life, and transcending all of the injustices consequent upon historical, social, and moral inequality, there is to be found in this terrible cycle of opportunity, failure, and renewed opportunity, proof of the fundamental equality of all human beings, and the promise, consequently, of their ultimate redemption.

In its uncompromising assertion of fundamental ethical imperatives that is informed by an empathic recognition of indelible human weakness and of inescapable universal injustice, 'A Siding at a Railway Station' remains engagingly humane. Altogether different, however, both in tone and its apparent intent, is the second short fable which Froude published three years later. 'A Sibylline Leaf' provides a vision of the near future centred on a grand astronomical conference held in the English colony of Cape Town in the year 1950.[7] The conference is being held in the wake of a period of

---

6. Froude's playful references to critics in the weekly (such as *Saturday*) reviews were doubtless intended to place some limitation to the damage thus invited, while the little digression on the vain self-abnegation of 'the polemical divine' is also perhaps an indication that he had anticipated the more clever ripostes to which he had now made himself vulnerable.

7. *Blackwood's Magazine*, 133 (April 1883), 573–92.

great convulsion which had begun to afflict the entire world since the time
when, almost a century before, mankind had come to believe 'that in politics and religion, the most important and most difficult subjects of human
study, every individual was to be left to form his own opinion, and to give
effect to it by his vote'. The immediate effects of this triumph of democracy had been wonderful: 'population multiplied, wealth multiplied, pleasures multiplied'. But wealth and pleasure had not been equally distributed:
'the few had much; the many little', and before long the many began to
demand an equal share for all. The result had been terrible war:

> ... confusion, anarchy and broken heads—the thousand millions of mankind
> dissolved into integrated atoms each caring to save himself, careless of what
> came to the rest; and finally perhaps the worst condition mankind had ever
> known since Noah's deluge.[8]

Out of this catastrophe, order had emerged. 'Out of their exhaustion' the
people cried for leaders 'Who will find us any good? Let them find our wisest men and let them govern us.' The 'wise' men of authority duly arose
in every country, and order was thus established.

But even as all political liberty was suppressed, the wise had thought it
prudent to leave matters of religion free. As religion had, however, disappeared to all intents and purposes, the effect of this licence was simply to
confirm the majority in the confident assumption that there was no divine
maker of their world, and as they had been permitted to retain their private
judgements in regard to such theological and metaphysical questions as the
origin and purpose of the universe, 'the scissors-grinder and the brick-layer'
retained the conviction that their own view of such matters was every bit as
good as that of the most intelligent and most expert astronomers. So things
might have continued, and science might have been destroyed by the 'same
causes that had destroyed religion and government' were it not for the sudden appearance of a massive comet which appeared for a time to threaten
the very existence of the planet. Panic ensued, comparable to that which
had issued from the descent into political anarchy. Mysteriously, however,
the comet had passed close to the earth, though 'not close enough to affect the
earth, and passing in the daylight, its presence had been unobserved'. The
crisis had been sufficient to destroy this last remnant of speculative arrogance among the *demos*, for only the trained astronomers had any real idea

8. *Blackwood's Magazine*, 133 (April 1883), 575.

as to whence the comet came and why it went on its way. Yet even their knowledge of this was limited, and in the course of their anxious observations the expert astronomers had become aware of other threats to the planet arising from a gradual loss of gravitational pull.

It was for this purpose that the great international conference at Cape Town had been held. All the nations had been represented there: Europeans and Americans and 'even Arab faces could be discerned, and Indian and Chinese'. Progress had been made but no easy solutions reached. The astronomers, however, had a message for ordinary mankind: that they were no more than a small part of nature and exercised no influence upon it; that the individual might

> play his wise or foolish part: to be moderately happy if he obeyed the rules which his Maker had appointed for him; to sink unpitied and unhelped in miseries of his own creation, if he chose to go his own way in delirious dreams of liberty.[9]

With this austere message the conference is about to close, but for the final session the organisers had invited 'a distinguished historiographer' to address the assembly. Among the audience, made up of scientists and military men, were a professor of the Cape Town College and 'a naval officer of rank' whose conversation is overheard before entering the hall. The naval officer had just returned from a tour of the territory between Simonstown and the Cape, and was most agreeably surprised at the speed with which the country had recovered from the bloody war which had been necessary to recover it. 'I could almost have fancied myself in Ireland,' says the contented officer. But the professor protests that the comparison is unfair: the colonists have only recently begun to recover from the war, while

> in Ireland there has been order for half a century. It is fifty years I think since the last patriot was hanged at Cork.[10]

The 'distinguished historiographer' they are now to listen to bears a striking resemblance to Froude. 'He was a tall man, about sixty, thin and slightly stooping, with a large head, thick bushy grizzled hair ... His eyes were violet blue.'[11]

9. *Blackwood's Magazine*, 133 (April 1883), 580.
10. *Blackwood's Magazine*, 133 (April 1883), 581.
11. *Blackwood's Magazine*, 133 (April 1883), 581.

Like Froude, he is no great orator, and the audience has to gather close to hear his words, but when he speaks they are transfixed by his awful narrative. He recounts the recent history of England—how toward the close of the previous century the country had come under the sway of a great and powerful demagogue, named Callicles. Leader of the Liberal Party, he had seduced the masses by the promise of liberty and equality. He 'set trade free—free for rogues as for honest men'. He disestablished the church. He divested England of her colonies. And fatally, he set Ireland free.

Heedless of the strategic importance of Ireland as he was of that of the colonies, anxious to be seen to do good for Ireland, and concerned to retain the support of the Irish MPs for his government, Callicles had made it his mission to bring peace to Ireland. Being as ignorant of the Irish people as he was of their history, however, he had failed to understand that the Irish would not be grateful.

> They hated England—justly hated England. They had gained much—they saw a chance of gaining all, and of ridding themselves of England altogether.[12]

As their agitation increased, Callicles yielded: 'He gave up the Union. He left Ireland to govern herself [and] English authority was reduced only to a name.' But even then the Irish were not satisfied:

> There was fighting and then the Irish in America sent out their cruisers to gorge themselves on the plunder of the fat English merchants, and America herself at last stepped into the arena, and the end came.[13]

As to what that end was, the lecturer, however, is frustratingly vague. The colonies revolted, and English society dissolved into anarchy. Unable to feed themselves, the millions in the towns starved, and then 'turned justly, upon the false prophets who had been teaching the gospel of progress' and upon the parliament.[14]

With these utterances the great historian's voice, 'sounding through the hall like the voice of the cavern of doom' grew so deep as to no longer be heard, and the vision dissolved. No further indication is given as to how the Irish-American onslaught receded, how England recovered so quickly from this awful paroxysm—so quickly, indeed, as to have been able so promptly

---

12. *Blackwood's Magazine*, 133 (April 1883), 590.
13. *Blackwood's Magazine*, 133 (April 1883), 591.
14. *Blackwood's Magazine*, 133 (April 1883), 592.

to despatch the last Irish patriot. But they can have been left in no doubt that whatever unfolded involved a massive blood-letting.

It may seem hard on the face of it to reconcile this exultant invocation of apocalyptical violence with the gentler, self-critical sentiments of 'A Siding at a Railway Station'. As in the 'Siding', there is in the 'A Sibylline Leaf' an obvious element of whimsy. There is surely playfulness in Froude's self-referential vignette of the distinguished historiographer, and a similar know-ingness in the nomination of the wretched Callicles. Clearly intended as a caricature of Gladstone, Callicles is named after the cynical, amoral aristocrat in Plato's *Gorgias*, whose contempt for the *demos* is explicit, and who, far from being a persuasive orator, retreats into a sulky silence for most of the dialogue. The apparent contrast between the modern Callicles and the original would have been plain to an educated audience which would also have been in a position to understand the joke that, for all his self-deceiving claims to be a supporter of freedom, equality, and virtue, in his practical effects Gladstone was no different from this epitome of self-seeking amoralism.

The entire vision is, moreover, couched within a mock-serious meta-physical framework in which the authority of Kant is appealed to in order to claim that once we have 'allowed something to be possible, we have already conceded that it is a reality', and, following on from this, Leibniz is invoked in support of the view that as time and space are but imaginary concepts' pertaining only to humans, an infinite number of possible uni-verses might be conceived of 'equally real in themselves though unrealised in sensible shape' and that 'all possibilities were alike in the infinite mind in which they originated'. The brevity with which such high metaphysical speculations are treated is couched in levity. Under these terms, the dreadful Sextus Tarquinius, rapist and murderer, might, says Froude, following Leibniz's notorious example, in other worlds have been 'a loving husband, a happy father, a faithful friend, a noble and worthy citizen'.[15] Who is to say? And is it fair that, from no volition of his own, he was cast by destiny into the vile and wretched creature that he was? It is this reflection upon Leibniz's notion of 'infinite possibilities' that forms the basis for the imaginary vision of 1950 with which the rest of the essay is concerned; and at its close, as the voice of the Froudian professor dies away, Leibniz and Tarquin are teasingly brought to mind again in Froude's final remark that in regard to the urgent

---

15. *Blackwood's Magazine*, 133 (April 1883), 573. The case of Tarquin had been originally adduced and discussed by Leibniz in the closing section of his *Théodicée* (1710).

question as to whether the terrible events just imagined 'were fated to become an actuality ... the genius of Leibniz, less kind to me than to Tarquin, was pleased to leave unrevealed'.[16]

Froude, follower of Spinoza, had never been persuaded by what he saw as Leibniz's bland Panglossian theodicy. In contrast to him and to the other professors of a natural theology, Froude had long been convinced that sustained and enduring action toward the good on the part of ordinary individuals was integral to the fulfilment of the divine will.[17] His tone here is, therefore, archly ironic—an implicit admonition to the credulous that if we were to follow Leibnitz in his moral complacency, we risk invoking all the horrors of the future just sketched out.

This philosophical teasing is also an indication of the kind of audience at whom the essay was aimed: educated, assertive, and not prone to accept the futility of taking action in the world. Even more pointed was the title of the essay itself. The books of the Sibyl, from which this was an analogous leaf, were, as all students of Roman history would have known, dangerous works of prophecy foretelling the bloody fall of Rome at some point in the future. Once discovered they had been kept under the control of the Senate, guarded by a select committee of senators—not, however, because they were regarded as containing the truth of Rome's ineluctable destiny from which the populace were to be protected, but as a warning to the senators themselves of the grave nature of the obligation which rested constantly on them, and of the dire consequences which would ensue from neglect of their duty. Thus Froude's appeal in the essay was to the political elite of the day, or more specifically to the traditionally educated upholders of tradition whom he identified amidst the ranks of the landed gentry, and in the benches of the House of Lords now facing (in 1883) a further round of democratisation and even the emerging threat of abolition.

II

Neither 'A Siding' nor the 'Sibylline Leaf' was intended as serious philosophical enquiry. They were literary exercises which aimed to move readers

---

16. 'A Sibylline Leaf', 593.
17. Froude, 'Spinoza', *Westminster Review*, NS 8 (July 1855), 1–37; reprinted in *Short Studies*, I, 339–400; see also ch.5.

by rhetorical and stylistic techniques rather than to persuade them by force of argument. Underlying this artfulness, however, was an intent of the utmost seriousness. Running through both, three fundamental assumptions are clearly discernible which not only make the essays compatible with each other, but with the entire corpus of Froude's writing. The first is the conviction that there is a cosmological force at work throughout the universe to which we, like all products of Creation, are ineluctably bound. The second is that even though we only dimly perceive its existence and direction, our actions or inactions have an integral role to play in relation to the pace and course of this force, and that there will be no surcease until that role has been fully played out. But the third is the most important. This is that our necessary ignorance of the great energy at work around us and our inability ever fully to understand it is, along with the inequality of talents, abilities, and moral capacities which exist among us, not an unjust and arbitrary affliction. It is an essential feature of our special role whose eventual transcendence is vital to the fulfilment of the entire creative drive.

It is this recognition of humanity's imperfect but altogether vital role that, for Froude, gave particular urgency to the means by which those who have been granted a special insight into the conditions of Creation should present that vision to the rest, who must yet be awakened to it. Given the predetermined inadequacy of our intellect, it is not through philosophical argument or theological speculation that we can arrive at a clear knowledge of our place in Creation. It is, rather, imaginative language, of the type characteristically devised by the great poets, bravely attempted in prose by Carlyle, and falteringly essayed in his own modest way by Froude himself, that alone could serve to alert willing and responsive human spirits to the challenge confronting them. As a precept this is clear; but in practice it entailed deep and indeterminable questions. What were the best means to awaken these souls? And in this particular epoch, to what end? For Froude as for Carlyle, and as indeed for Newman, the end lay in action or, more precisely, in that sustained, self-critical, and combative engagement that the Victorians termed 'duty'. The means were to be determined by circumstances, opportunity, and the particular strengths of the individual prophetic voice.[18]

This position, however, was always less clear than the prophets of individual commitment assumed, and was becoming murkier with each decade.

---

18. For a still valuable exploration of the problem of presentation as perceived by the great Victorian thinkers, see John Holloway, *The Victorian Sage: Studies in Argument* (London, 1953).

How, in the light of our awareness of the frailty, selfishness, and vulnerability of the human life-force now made increasingly gloomy by the claims of the biological and social sciences, could it be expected that even the most willing of souls might be inspired sincerely and continually to do their duty? The voice of the prophet had hardly ever been more urgently in need. Prophets there had been in Newman and Carlyle, who had been granted a deep insight into the nature of the spiritual crisis emerging before them. But the prophets had failed. One in desperation had fled to the authority and conformity of a different epoch, praying that others might follow him in this abandonment of duty in favour of obedience. The other, afflicted by self-doubt and the curse of physical deficiency, had collapsed into incoherence and silence. Amidst such disappointments, moreover, the proportions of the challenge had not diminished. Under the pressure of unprecedented social, political, cultural, and scientific change, it had increased enormously. In such conditions, what did Froude, acolyte to one and foil to the other of these failed messengers, have to offer?

As we have seen, Froude himself believed he had one modest but distinctive qualification. This was the sincere and fearless nature of his self-understanding. From the brave self-explorations of his first fiction through the no less courageous critical exposure of Carlyle, through the overt humility of 'A Siding at a Railway Station' and the more implicit self-recognition in the late lectures on Erasmus to the final lapidary sentences of the autobiographical fragment, Froude's disclosure of his own self was a defining feature of his literary persona. His understanding of the nature and purpose of sincerity was neither self-deceiving nor intellectually naïve. The self which he exploited in these frequent presentations was afflicted with defects which were in part congenital and in part the consequence of the accidents of time and circumstance. But for Froude it was precisely the recognition and presentation of the intractable weakness of the self that was the essential starting point in all human explorations of existence. Embodying in each individual the Christian myth of the Fall, and offering thereby an intimate validation of its universal truth, this indelible human stain also supplied the basis for a far more positive vision of a shared human prospect. Entailed in the very consciousness of the defects of nature and circumstance was an obligation to seek to overcome them which, once accepted, promised to unite in a common bond all human beings not only to each other, but to the central force of Creation. A residual Calvinism in this outlook is as obvious in Froude as it is in Carlyle. But it is important to recognise that such bleak determinism as was implicit in Calvinism was in both cases overlaid by a far more energising conviction that, once the obligation had been freely acknowledged and pursued, mankind enjoyed in every generation a unique and incomparable capacity actively to contribute to the character and the pace of the great cosmic drama. It was this belief that was of central importance in Froude's entire world-view, profoundly shaping his understanding of the nature of the present, the significance of the past, and the prospect of the future in everything he wrote.

In regard to the present, it shaped his attitude toward contemporary political and social problems which has sometimes been described—but hardly explained—as his Tory radicalism. For most of his career Froude refused to be identified with any political party, and was in that sense only belatedly a Tory. It is clear, however, that it was his early conviction that, at any one time, society was made up of a collection of more or less defective individuals that underlay his violent rejection of the complacent self-deceiving nostrums of *laissez faire*. These, he saw, were no more than a vulgar justification of greed, selfishness, and meanness which were among the most common of human vices. Yet it was also this same belief that underlay his unwillingness to go far beyond promoting mild state interventions in relation to emigration, education, and tenurial reform, his continued insistence on the sanctity of private property, and, in contrast with his contemporaries, Ruskin, William Morris, and Thorold Rogers, his rejection of any form of socialism.[19]

This mode of rejecting the supposed extremes of socialism and unrestrained capitalism which critics, of course, might easily regard as merely convenient, nevertheless raised serious internal difficulties for anyone who had sincerely premised this position on the defective individual. If this were the case, were there any grounds for engaging in political or public argument at all? Even more pertinently, why should it be expected that any hearing should be given to a self-professed defective who was not prepared to commit to any of the more general political positions of the day?

The answer to this dilemma—astonishingly obvious once Carlyle had pointed it out—lay in history, which, both as the record of the past and as the occasion of self-critical contemplation, provided the surest guide to

---

19. Froude offers a succinct summary of his views on the moral necessity of the rights of property in his 'Liberty and Property' address to the Liberty and Property Defence League, 25 November 1887, *The Times*, 26 November, 7.

understanding and acting in the present. In the first place it supplied an admonitory register of those occasions when humanity, neglecting its duties toward the force that had created it, had visited such grievous woes and miseries upon itself. It had also produced, though rather less frequently, evidence of mankind's repeated capacity to confront and rise above its sorry condition and renew its vital spirit. Such occasions were neither accidental nor mysterious. They recurred in a pattern which, though not regular, was discernible and analysable. As the principal world-images, ideas, and values which had formed a culture and brought it to maturity gradually lost their capacity to account for humanity's ever-expanding perception of the great universe which it inhabited, decline set in in the form of hypocrisy, bigotry, obscurantism, cynicism, and fearful selfishness. Since the very origin of such imaginative clusters was itself evidence of humanity's desire and partial ability to understand the world, it was inevitable that at some point some individual or some group would revolt against such an unnatural state of affairs and release in a new form—Carlyle would have said a new set of clothes— that intrinsic and uniquely human creative drive.

The import of this profoundly Romantic message, therefore, was ultimately joyful. Mankind, for all its weaknesses and foibles, possessed within itself the potential for its own recurrent and final liberation. But the good news came at a price. The emergence of the 'some point' and some individuals or groups was in no way vouchsafed by some mechanical universal principle. It depended instead on the dedicated and sustained actions of such individuals or groups who were clearly aware of the nature of the historical moment they occupied. But how was this awareness to arise, and how was it to be nurtured and sustained? Traditionally this had been the task of the prophet: to work by his gifts of expression, exhortation, and provocation to make the insight which had been granted to him apprehensible to the people at large. But now, in times when the image of the single, patriarchal intervening God of the Judaic and Christian traditions had lost its power to move the spirit of humanity, the prophet must offer a revelation of humankind's own history as a means of showing the workings of the divine in the everyday temporal world, and therefore become an historian. The virtues required of the prophet-historian—no more than in the case of their Old Testament predecessors—were not those of saints, martyrs, or heroes. It was necessary only that they should be steadfast in the task presented to them, that they should seek no easy path, no compromise, and above all that they should never confuse the importance of the message they were bound to convey with their own authority, glory, or fame. It was, in short, only required that they be sincere and selfless.

In his elevation of the virtue of sincerity as one of the cardinal principles of literary practice, Froude was hardly alone among his contemporaries. His old rival G. H. Lewes had celebrated it similarly in one of the most influential guides to successful writing of the period.[20] But Froude's understanding of the concept ran deeper than that of mere honesty, plainness, and transparency. In part derived from Carlyle's conception as expounded in *On Heroes, Hero Worship and the Heroic in History*, but a product also of his own profound self-criticism, sincerity entailed such a ruthless abjuration of the natural human tendency to appeal to an audience's self-comforting prejudices through the employment of any one of the myriad rhetorical sleights-of-hand available as to amount to self-abnegation.[21] So it was that for Froude, his sincerity and genuine self-disregard became the grounds of accepting that he had a second qualification to serve his generation: he might, in so ever modest a fashion, act as their prophet. Concerning the modesty of his self-estimation for the task, there can be little doubt. Despite his continued admiration of Carlyle's especial gifts, Froude never sought to emulate him, to approximate his revolutionary ambitions, nor to attempt his audaciously experimental formal and expressive modes. Sounded repeatedly in his private correspondence, Froude's sense of the limited nature of his own aspiration and achievement is openly avowed in 'A Siding at a Railway Station'.

Modest though it was, Froude's prophetic ambition remained firm and unquestioned. His assurance was in part sustained by the unprecedented success which he enjoyed in his later years as a popular writer. Though *Caesar, Oceana*, and *The English in the West Indies* attracted the usual criticism, their sales appeared to vindicate the means by which Froude had sought to reach out to a wider audience. His nomination as Regius Professor of History offered further validation, and further opportunities. Thus, even as the deep internal contradictions of his missionary strategy began to surface in the cruder formularies of his later popular writings, the very success of those writings enabled him to recover from the doubts that had beset him in the years after the completion of his great *History*, and to evade confrontation

---

20. G. H. Lewes, *The Principles of Success in Literature* (London, 1869), ch. 4.

21. 'Whosoever may live in the shows of things, it is for him a necessity of nature to live in the very fact of things. A man once more, in earnest with the Universe, though all others were but toying with it. He is a Vates first of all, in virtue of being sincere,' Carlyle, *On Heroes, Hero Worship and the Heroic in History* (London, 1840), Lecture III.96. For Froude's insistence on the importantce of this form of sincerity to his own generation, see his *Carlyle: Life in London*, i, 291–2.

with those contradictions until the end of his life. And yet they remained—embodied in his very conception of the audience he was so determined to address, and in the mode through which he sought to address it.

The most glaring of these related to Froude's voices. It seems incongruous that one whose claims to be a prophet rested on his profound sincerity should have assumed the right to adopt a variety of artificial voices in order to increase the rhetorical appeal of his message. Against such a charge there was, of course, a Froudian (and a Carlylean) riposte. Since the defective self of the prophet was of no great significance, and since the real purpose of the prophet's work was to bring about regeneration in the world by moving those best placed to effect it, it was the understanding and the needs of his audience that must be privileged above those of the author. In principle, this was plausible enough, once the *bona fides* of the prophet as a disinterested messenger was accepted. But a more serious problem arose in relation to the audience to whom the prophet had chosen to make his address. Careless of this consideration, the demanding and increasingly disagreeable manner in which Carlyle had chosen his own mode of address had steadily lost him any audience. But Froude, sensitive to the English temper, and adept at selecting issues and adopting voices by which to engage it, had steadily increased his. Yet the very different modes of address which in practice he had chosen—from *Caesar* to 'Sea Studies', from 'A Siding at a Railway Station' to *The English in the West Indies*, from *Erasmus* to *English Seamen*—were a clear indication of Froude's own profound uncertainty concerning the readers to whom he was making his appeal.

On the surface Froude seemed confident that the audience whom he believed he was best equipped to address was also the one best placed to give effect to the moral, social, and political transformations he believed were urgent. This, as Belloc understood, was the educated, rural, professional, and commercial middle-class of his day—a group whose numbers had been augmented and position consolidated by all the major political, economic, and cultural changes of the later nineteenth century. But this was by no means an homogeneous or united group; rather, it was riven by social, sectoral, and cultural divisions which, as Froude knew all to well, made it so susceptible to the machinations of cynical party politicians.[22] But if it was vulnerable to external manipulation, it was also available for leadership from

22. Froude, 'Party Politics', *Short Studies*, III, 429–76.

within—and the sub-group to whom Froude looked to discharge this vital role was the county gentry.

Froude's confidence in the historical significance of the gentry as a force of transformative potential rested on several grounds. As a consequence of family and domestic customs, they were, for the most part, stable and secure in their sense of position and identity. They were also moderately well educated: dim or brilliant, they had been subjected to the same course of education at public school and university which ensured at least some acquaintance with the patterns of history (as illustrated in classical antiquity) and with the contemporary lessons they suggested. But above all they were, by virtue of their position, deeply acquainted with the concept of duty. Although some might repudiate it, and others consciously reject it, the reality of historical obligation everywhere surrounded them, in their domestic and family affairs, in their social and economic activities, and in their political, administrative responsibilities. Thus, given Froude's conviction that the moral regeneration which was so urgently needed could never arise from sources that were purely intellectual, but could only be bodied forth by action, it was the gentry who were especially suitable to his purpose.[23] In embarking upon their mission they would be inspired neither through intellectual argument nor political rhetoric of demagogues like Callicles, but rather by history-writing of an inspiring character, by biography, by travel-writing, and by fable—in short, through parables presented to them by a prophetic voice to accomplish their imaginative and moral transformation.

So, the process of moral manipulation was to be extended further, from the prophet himself to the select group upon whom he conferred a special privilege of moral leadership. This in itself was disturbing; but there remained an even deeper difficulty—one which Froude was never properly to address. The role for which he had specifically destined this property-owning elite was neither conservative nor defensive—attitudes which might have come naturally—but radical, transformative, and, when necessary, violent. These were the cohorts who were to drive back the sea of democracy, to assert England's role as a world power, and to suppress movements for independence from England by all means available, including war. That a traditionally

23. In his latter years Froude devoted a number of essays to the celebration of the traditional virtues and untapped potential of the English gentry, 'On the Uses of a Landed Gentry', *Fraser's Magazine*, NS 14 (December 1876), 671–85; reprinted in *Short Studies*, III, 389–428; 'Cheneys and the house of Russell', *Fraser's Magazine*, NS 20 (September 1879), 360–85; reprinted in *Short Studies*, IV, 480–542.

conservative group might be transformed into a radical force to regenerate the world was an assumption fraught with extraordinary risk; and that Froude, for all his sincerity and genuine self-denial, was willing to assume the role of visionary prophet for the rising generation of potentially revolutionary gentlemen, guiding and justifying their actions was an act of singular arrogance. 'You cannot tell people what to do; you can only tell them parables,' wrote Auden—a figure whose moral sensibilities were not entirely unlike Froude's. Unlike the cautious Auden, however, Froude believed that his parables could indeed move people to transform their world. In this confidence he was willing to take all the risks of encouraging a self-selecting elite to fight for a future in which the political rights of ordinary English people would be decisively abrogated, the civil rights of millions of non-white peoples indefinitely denied, and the last of Ireland's patriots hanged at Cork.

In this desperate gamble on such an unlikely group, Froude lost: the gentry did not respond, and in the century that followed the fortunes of that class were to be far more sorry than Froude could ever have envisaged. But in his failure to reconcile the contrasting and divergent voices which he had adopted, Froude lost more seriously still. In posterity the troubled admonitions of the moralist were to be drowned out by the brazen assurance of the imperialist; and in consequence, unlike so many of his sometime peers, Froude has now been cast into the obscurity of history's ash-heap.

His limitations and his mistakes notwithstanding, however, Froude's fate has been unjust. For the stakes for which he contended were not simply historical and reputational; they were, and remain, obstinately and enduringly moral. Moreover, the challenges of personal responsibility, recurring persistently amidst the inescapable facts of individual deficiency, general cognitive inadequacy, and the unceasing flux of inherited history which he so bravely confronted and so imperfectly addressed, have not disappeared with his failure.[24] And our own alternative palliatives of moral relativism, ideological sclerosis, or the self-exculpating strategies of hermeneutic suspicion may in time seem no more creditable than the contradictory and reckless, passionate and sincere impulses which compelled Froude to make his stand.

24. Angus MacIntyre, *After Virtue: A Study in Moral Theory* (3rd edn., Notre Dame, IN, 2007), and Charles Taylor, *The Secular Age* (Cambridge, MS, 2011) offer eloquent discussions of the persistence of these problems.

James Anthony Froude: A Brief Chronology

1818	23 April born, the last of five sons and three daughters of Robert Hurrell Froude and Margaret Froude (née Spedding).
1827–30	Attends Buckfastleigh Parish School.
1830	January, enters Westminster Public School; June, is advanced to 5th form dormitory.
1833	June, is withdrawn from Westminster by his father.
1836	Enters Oriel College, Oxford.
1838–9	Meets and falls in love with Harriet Bush; summer 1839, connection is severed by her father; suffers a nervous collapse.
1840	June, graduates B.A., 2nd Division.
1841	Travels to Ireland to take up a post as tutor to the children of Rev. Mr William Cleaver, rector of Delgany, Co. Wicklow; travels extensively in the south and west of Ireland; returns to Oxford to study for MA.
1842	April, takes MA.; June, is awarded the Chancellor's Prize; elected Fellow of Exeter College.
1844	Engages with J. H. Newman in the 'Lives of the English Saints' project.
1845	(before June), takes deacon's orders; June-September, visits Ireland to research a life of St Patrick; applies unsuccessfully for a post in Royal University of Ireland.
1847	(before May), *Shadows of the Clouds* published under the pseudonym 'Zeta'.
1848	Retires to Killarney, Co. Kerry, to write.
1849	February, publishes *The Nemesis of Faith*; resigns his Fellowship at Exeter; March, offer of teaching post in Tasmania withdrawn; June, first meeting with Carlyle; August/September, is employed as private tutor to the children of Samuel Darbishire, Manchester; 3 October, marries Charlotte, 5th daughter of Pascoe Grenfell, M.P.
1850	June, leaves Manchester for Plas Gwynant, North Wales, begins work as a freelance reviewer and essayist; September, first child, Georgina Margaret, born.
1852	May, birth of second child, Rose Mary.

1853   October, leaves Plas Gwynant for Babbicombe near Torquay; begins work on sixteenth-century English history.

1854   February, third child, Pascoe Grenfell, born.

1856   (before June), first two volumes of *History of England from the Fall of Wolsey to the Death of Elizabeth* published.

1858   March, Vols 3 and 4 of *History of England* published; applies for Regius Chair of Modern History at Oxford.

1860   February, Vols 5 and 6 of *History of England* published; 26 April, death of Charlotte Froude.

1861   Officially appointed editor of *Fraser's Magazine*; March–June, first visit to the Spanish archives at Simancas; September, moves to London, 6 Clifton Place; 12 September, marries Henrietta, daughter of John Ashley Warre.

1863   28 June, birth of Ashley Anthony Froude; November, Vols 7 and 8 of *History of England* published.

1866   September, Vols 9 and 10 of *History of England* published.

1867   February–May, further visit to Simancas.

1868   June, birth of Mary Caroline Froude; 28 November, elected Rector of St Andrews University, defeating Benjamin Disraeli.

1870   January, Vols 11 and 12 of *History of England* published.

1871   June, Carlyle delivers first set of his private papers to Froude.

1872   September–December, undertakes a lecture tour to Boston, New York and Philadelphia on 'The History of Ireland'.

1874   12 February, death of Froude's second wife, Henrietta; June, resigns as editor of *Fraser's Magazine*; August, commences first visit to the Cape Colony.

1875   January, returns to London from the Cape Colony; April, death of Rose Mary Froude; June, commences second mission to South Africa; December, returns to London.

1876   August–September, participates in London conference on South African affairs.

1879   29 November, death of Froude's eldest son, Pascoe Grenfell.

1881   February, death of Carlyle; May, publishes his edition of Carlyle's *Reminisences*.

1882   March, publishes *Thomas Carlyle: The First Forty Years*.

1883   March, publishes *Letters and Memorials of Jayne Welsh Carlyle*.

1884   October, publishes *Thomas Carlyle: His Life in London*; December, commences round-the-world voyage and major visit to Australasia.

1885   May, returns to London from round-the-world voyage.

1886   January, publishes *Oceana: or England and her Colonies*; December, commences his tour of the West Indies.

1887   April, returns to London from the West Indies.

1888   January, publishes *The English in the West Indies, or The Bow of Ulysses*

1892   16 June, appointed Regius Chair of Modern History at the University of Oxford.

1894   20 October, dies.

Bibliography of the Writings
of James Anthony Froude

1842 *The Influence of the Science of Political Economy on the Moral and Social Welfare of a Nation: A Prize Essay read in the Sheldonian Theatre, Oxford, June 8, 1842.*

1844 'A Legend of St Neot', in *The Lives of the English Saints, Vol. 3. Hermit Saints*, ed. J. H. Newman.

1845 'Preface' to *Tales from the Phantasus of Ludwig Tieck*, ed. J. C. Hare and J. A. Froude (London, 1845), i–xv.

1846 'Goethe's *Faust*', *Oxford and Cambridge Review*, 2 (January–June 1846), 1–23.

Review of J. H. Newman, *An Essay on the Development of Christian Doctrine*, *Oxford and Cambridge Review*, 2 (January–June 1846), 135–67.

Review of Thomas Carlyle, *Letters and Speeches of Oliver Cromwell*, *Oxford and Cambridge Review*, 2 (January–June, 1846), 225–41.

'Louisa Varden', *Oxford and Cambridge Review*, 2 (January–June, 1846), 349–66.

1847 *Shadows of the Clouds* [by Zeta] (London, 1847).

Review of 'Zeta', *Shadows of the Clouds*, *Oxford and Cambridge Review*, 5 (July–December, 1847), 256–60.

'The Life of Spinoza', *Oxford and Cambridge Review*, 5 (July–December, 1847) 387–427.

Sermon on Corinthians VII, 10 preached at St Mary's Church on the occasion of the funeral of the Rev. G. M. Coleridge, printed in Dunn, *Froude*, I, 106–7.

1848 'Confessio fidei', ed. F. L. Mulhauser, as 'An Unpublished Poem by James Anthony Froude', *English Language Notes*, 12 (1974), 26–30.

1849 'The Swedenborgian', *Fraser's Magazine*, 39 (January 1849), 64–78.

The Nemesis of Faith (London: 1st edn., February 1849; 2nd edn. with a preface, April 1849).

1850 'The Lions and the Oxen', *The Leader*, 30 March 1850, 18; reprinted in *Short Studies on Great Subjects*, first series.

'The Farmer and the Fox', *The Leader*, 6 and 13 April 1850, 42, 67; reprinted in *Short Studies on Great Subjects*, first series.

'The Parable of the Breadfruit Tree', *The Leader*, 20 April 1850, 91; reprinted in *Short Studies on Great Subjects*, first series.

'Compensation', *The Leader*, 22 June 1850, 307; reprinted in *Short Studies on Great Subjects*, first series.

'The Cat's Pilgrimage', *The Leader*, 29 June, 6, 13, and 20 July 1850, 332, 356, 381, 405; reprinted in *Short Studies on Great Subjects*, first series.

1851 'Materialism: Miss Martineau and Mr Atkinson', *Fraser's Magazine*, 43 (April 1851), 418–34.

'The University Commission', *The Eclectic Review*, 1 (June 1851), 699–717.

'Apuleius and the Second Century', *The Eclectic Review*, 2 (July 1851), 67–84.

'The Homeric Life', *Fraser's Magazine*, OS 44 (July 1851), 76–92; reprinted as 'Homer', in *Short Studies on Great Subjects*, first series.

'The Philosophy of Christianity', *The Leader*, 14 June 1851, 563–4; reprinted as 'The Philosophy of Catholicism', in *Short Studies on Great Subjects*, first series.

1852 'King Alfred', *Fraser's Magazine*, OS 45 (January 1852), 74–87.

'Mary Stuart', *Westminster Review*, 57 (January 1852), 96–142.

'The Lives of the Saints', *The Eclectic Review*, 95 (May 1852), 147–64; reprinted in *Short Studies on Great Subjects*, first series.

'Representative Men', *The Eclectic Review*, 95 (May 1852), 568–82; reprinted in *Short Studies on Great Subjects*, first series.

'England's Forgotten Worthies', *Westminster Review*, 58 (July 1852), 32–67; reprinted in *Short Studies on Great Subjects*, first series.

'Ethical Doubts concerning Reineke Fuchs', *Fraser's Magazine*, 46 (September 1852), 321–30; reprinted as 'Reynard the Fox' in *Short Studies on Great Subjects*, first series.

'The Oxford Commission', *Westminster Review*, 58 (October 1852), 317–48.

1853 'Mary Tudor', *Westminster Review*, 59 (January 1853), 1–34.

'Kircaldy of Grange: A Chapter out of Scottish History', *Fraser's Magazine* (May 1853), 533–48.

'John Knox', *Westminster Review*, 60 (July 1853), 1–50.

Review of J. H. Burton, *History of Scotland, from the Revolution to the Extinction of the Last Jacobite Insurrection*, *Fraser's Magazine*, 48 (August 1853), 129–42.

'Morals of Queen Elizabeth (Part I)', *Fraser's Magazine*, 48 (October 1853), 373–87.

'The Book of Job', *Westminster Review*, 60 (October 1853), 417–50; reprinted in *Short Studies on Great Subjects*, first series.

'Morals of Queen Elizabeth (Part II)', *Fraser's Magazine*, 4 (November 1853), 491–505.

1854 'Arnold's Poems', *Westminster Review*, 61 (January 1854) 146–59.

'Contemporary Literature', *Westminster Review*, 61 (January 1854), 233–54.

'Lord Campbell as a Writer of History', *Westminster Review*, 61 (April 1854), 446–79.

'Cardinal Wolsey', *Westminster Review*, 62 (July 1854), 1–48.

'History: Its Use and Meaning', *Westminster Review*, 62 (October 1854), 420–48.

Translation of *Elective Affinities, in Novels and Tales by Goethe ... Translated chiefly by R. D. Boylan Esq* (London, 1854).

1855 'Four Years at the Court of Henry VIII', *Fraser's Magazine*, 51 (April 1855), 441–54.

'Spinoza', *Westminster Review*, 64 (July 1855), 1–37; reprinted in *Short Studies on Great Subjects*, first series.

'Suggestions for the Best Means of Teaching History', in *Oxford Essays by Members of the University* (London, 1855), 47–79.

1856 'Poems by Edward Capern', *Fraser's Magazine*, 53 (April 1856), 489–93.

Review of J. L. Motley, *The Rise of the Dutch Republic*, *Westminster Review*, 65 (April 1856), 313–37.

'Contemporary Literature', *Westminster Review*, 65 (April 1856), 313–37.

'The Gowrie Conspiracy', *The National Review*, 6 (October 1856), 255–89.

History of England from the Fall of Wolsey to the Death of Elizabeth (vols. 1 and 2).

1857 'Gleanings from the Record Office (Part I): The Dissolution of the Monasteries', *Fraser's Magazine*, 55 (February 1857), 127–60; reprinted in *Short Studies on Great Subjects*, first series.

'German Love', *Fraser's Magazine*, 55 (April 1857), 396–9.

'Gleanings from the Record Office (Part II): Henry the Eighth and Mary Boleyn', *Fraser's Magazine*, 55 (June, 1857), 724–38.

'The Four Empires' [Russian, Turkish, English, and French], *Westminster Review*, 68 (October 1857), 415–40.

1858 'The Commonplace Book of Richard Hilles', *Fraser's Magazine*, 58 (August 1858), 127–44.

History of England from the Fall of Wolsey to the Death of Elizabeth (vols. 3 and 4).

'The Edinburgh Review and Mr Froude's History', *Fraser's Magazine*, 58 (September 1858), 359–78.

1860 *History of England from the Fall of Wolsey to the Death of Elizabeth* (vols. 5 and 6).

1861 Obituary of J. W. Parker, *Gentleman's Magazine* 55 (February 1861), 221–4.

'Queen Elizabeth, Lord Robert Dudley, and Amy Robsart: A Story from the Archives of Simancas', *Fraser's Magazine*, 63 (June, 1861), 659–69.

'A Few More Words from the Archives of Simancas', *Fraser's Magazine*, 64 (August 1861), 135–50.

Editor: *The Pilgrim: A Dialogue on the Life and Actions of King Henry VIII, by William Thomas, Clerk of the Council to Edward VI, Edited with Notes from the Archives at Paris and Brussels* (London, 1861).

1862 'Santa Teresa: A Psychological Study', *Fraser's Magazine*, 65 (January 1862), 59–74.

1863 'A Plea for the Free Discussion of Theological Difficulties', *Fraser's Magazine*, 68 (September 1863), 277–91; reprinted in *Short Studies on Great Subjects*, first series.

History of England from the Fall of Wolsey to the Death of Elizabeth (vols. 7 and 8; subtitled *The Reign of Elizabeth*, vols. 1 and 2, published by Longmans).

1864 'Criticism and the Gospel History', *Fraser's Magazine*, 69 (January 1864), 49–63; reprinted in *Short Studies on Great Subjects*, first series.

1865 'How Ireland was Governed in the Sixteenth Century', *Fraser's Magazine*, 71 (March 1865), 312–15.

The Influence of the Reformation on the Scottish Character:Address delivered before the Philosophical Institution of Edinburgh (Edinburgh, 1865).

1866 *History of England from the Fall of Wolsey to the Death of Elizabeth* (vols. 9 and 10; subtitled *The Reign of Elizabeth*, vols. 3 and 4, published by Longman).

'The Science of History' (paper delivered at the Royal Institution, London, 5 February 1864), *Hours at Home* (New York), 2 (February 1866), 321–30; reprinted in *Short Studies on Great Subjects*, first series.

1867 'The Late Prince Consort', *Fraser's Magazine*, 76 (September 1867), 269–83.

Short Studies on Great Subjects, first series, in addition to reprints of the items noted above, contains the first English printing of 'The Science of History' (paper delivered at the Royal Institution, London, 5 February 1864) and 'The Times of Erasmus and Luther' (three lectures given to the Newcastle Literary and Philosophical Society, 7–9 January 1867).

1868 'Conditions and Prospects of Protestantism', *Fraser's Magazine*, 77 (January 1868), 56–70; reprinted in *Short Studies on Great Subjects*, second series.

1869 *On Education: Inaugural Address delivered to the University of St Andrews, March 19, 1869* (London, 1869); reprinted in *Short Studies on Great Subjects*, second series.

1870 'England and her Colonies', *Fraser's Magazine*, NS 1 (January 1870), 1–16; reprinted in *Short Studies on Great Subjects*, second series.

'A Bishop of the Twelfth Century' [St Hugo of Avalon], *Fraser's Magazine*, NS 1 (February 1870), 220–36; reprinted in *Short Studies on Great Subjects*, second series.

'The Merchant and his Wife: An Apologue for the Colonial Office', *Fraser's Magazine*, NS 1 (February 1870), 246–7; reprinted in *Short Studies on Great Subjects*, second series.

'Reciprocal Duties of State and Subject', *Fraser's Magazine*, NS 1 (March 1870), 285–301; reprinted in *Short Studies on Great Subjects*, second series.

'A Fortnight in Kerry, Part I', *Fraser's Magazine*, NS 1 (April 1870), 513–30; reprinted in *Short Studies on Great Subjects*, second series.

'Father Newman, *The Grammar of Assent*', *Fraser's Magazine*, NS 1 (May 1870), 561–80; reprinted in *Short Studies on Great Subjects*, second series.

'Fresh Evidence about Anne Boleyn, Part I', *Fraser's Magazine*, NS 1 (June 1870), 731–48.

'Fresh Evidence about Anne Boleyn, Part II', *Fraser's Magazine*, NS 2 (July 1870), 44–65.

'After Salmon in Ireland', *Hours at Home* (New York) (July 1870), 275–80.

'The Colonies Once More', *Fraser's Magazine*, NS 2 (September 1870), 269–87; reprinted in *Short Studies on Great Subjects*, second series.

'On Progress', *Fraser's Magazine*, NS 2 (December 1870), 671–90; reprinted in *Short Studies on Great Subjects*, second series.

The Cat's Pilgrimage: with Six Illustrations by J. B[lackburn] (Edinburgh, 1870).

History of England from the Fall of Wolsey to the Defeat of the Spanish Armada (vols. 11 and 12; subtitled *The Reign of Elizabeth*, vols. 5 and 6, published by Longman).

1871 'A Fortnight in Kerry, Part II', *Fraser's Magazine*, NS 3 (January 1871), 28–45; reprinted in *Short Studies on Great Subjects*, second series.

'England's War', *Fraser's Magazine*, NS 3 (February 1871), 135–50 ; reprinted in *Short Studies on Great Subjects*, second series.

Calvinism: An Address delivered at St Andrew's, March 17, 1871 (London, 1871); reprinted in *Short Studies on Great Subjects*, second series.

Short Studies on Great Subjects, second series, in addition to the reprints noted above, contains the first printing of 'Scientific Method as Applied to History'.

1872 'Lectures on Irish History', *The Times*, 29 October, 6, 7, 8, and 22 November 1872.

'Stories from the Irish Smugglers', *Scribner's Monthly* (December 1872), 221–33.

The English in Ireland in the Eighteenth Century, vol. 1 (London, 1872).

1873 'Address by J. A. Froude delivered November 30, in the Association Hall, New York [in answer to Father Thomas N. Burke]', *Fraser's Magazine*, NS 7 (January 1873), 1–21.

'Annals of an English Abbey', *Scribner's Monthly* (November–December 1873), 91–120, 187, 216, 282–311; reprinted in *Short Studies on Great Subjects*, third series.

1874 'Party Politics', *Fraser's Magazine*, NS 10 (July 1874), 1–18; reprinted in *Short Studies on Great Subjects*, third series.

'Our Dependencies', *Dublin University Magazine*, 84 (December 1874), 657–61.

The English in Ireland in the Eighteenth Century, vols. 2 and 3 (London, 1874).

1875 'Euripides and Sea Studies', *Fraser's Magazine*, NS 11 (May 1875), 541–60; reprinted as 'Sea Studies', in *Short Studies on Great Subjects*, third series.

1876 'Lord Macaulay', *Fraser's Magazine*, NS 13 (June 1876), 675–94.

'Society in Italy in the Last Days of the Roman Republic', *Fraser's Magazine*, NS 14 (August 1876), 150–62; reprinted in *Short Studies on Great Subjects*, third series.

'Lucian', *Fraser's Magazine*, NS 14 (October 1876), 419–37; reprinted in *Short Studies on Great Subjects*, third series.

'On the Uses of a Landed Gentry', *Fraser's Magazine*, NS 14 (December 1876), 671–85; reprinted in *Short Studies on Great Subjects*, third series.

1877 'English Policy in South Africa', *Quarterly Review*, 143 (January 1877), 105–45.

'Life and Times of Thomas Becket' (Parts I–IV), *The Nineteenth Century*, 1 (June–July 1877), 548–62, 843–56; 2 (August–September 1877), 15–27, 217–29; reprinted in *Short Studies on Great Subjects*, fourth series.

Short Studies on Great Subjects, third series, in addition to the reprints noted above, contains the first printing of 'Divus Caesar', 'Leaves from a South African Journal', and 'Revival of Romanism'.

1878 'Life and Times of Thomas Becket' (Parts V–VI), *The Nineteenth Century*, 2 (October–November 1878), 389–410, 669–91; reprinted in *Short Studies on Great Subjects*, fourth series.

'Origen and Celsus', *Fraser's Magazine*, NS 17 (February 1878), 142–67; reprinted in *Short Studies on Great Subjects*, fourth series.

'Three Letters on Origen and Celsus' [with Francis Newman], *Fraser's Magazine*, NS 17 (May 1878), 548–55.

'Science and Theology: Ancient and Modern', *International Review* (Toronto) 5 (May–July 1878), 289–302; 492–506.

'The Copyright Commission', *Edinburgh Review*, 148 (October 1878), 295–343.

1879 'A Few Words on Mr Freeman', *The Nineteenth Century*, 5 (April 1879), 618–37.

'The South African Problem', *Quarterly Review*, 147 (April 1879), 552–84.

'A Cagliostro of the Second Century', *The Nineteenth Century*, 6 (September 1879), 551–70; reprinted in *Short Studies on Great Subjects*, fourth series.

'Cheneys and the House of Russell', *Fraser's Magazine*, NS 20 (September 1879), 360–85; reprinted in *Short Studies on Great Subjects*, fourth series.

'South Africa Once More', *Fortnightly Review*, NS 26 (October 1879), 449–73.

'A Siding at a Railway Station', *Fraser's Magazine*, NS 20 (November 1879), 622–33; reprinted in *Short Studies on Great Subjects*, fourth series.

Caesar: A Sketch (London, 1879).

'Romanism and the Irish Race in the United States, Part I', *North American Review*, 129 (December 1879), 519–37.

1880 'Romanism and the Irish Race in the United States, Part II', *North American Review* 130 (January 1880), 31–50.

'Ireland', *The Nineteenth Century*, 8 (September 1880), 341–69.

Bunyan (English Men of Letters) (London, 1880).

Two Lectures on South Africa: Delivered before the Philosophical Institute, Edinburgh, January 6 and 9, 1880 (London, 1880).

1881 'Reminiscences of the High Church Revival: Six Letters', *Good Words*, 22, 1–6 (January–July 1880), 18–23, 98–202, 162–67, 306–12, 409–15; reprinted as 'The Oxford Counter-Reformation', in *Short Studies on Great Subjects*, fourth series.

'The Early Life of Thomas Carlyle', *The Nineteenth Century*, 10 (July 1881), 1–42.

1882 'Gardiner's *Fall of the Monarchy of Charles I*', *Edinburgh Review*, 156 (October 1882), 295–346.

'A Lesson on Democracy', *Fortnightly Review*, NS 32 (December 1882), 728–47.

'The Norway Fjords', *Longman's Magazine*, 1 (December 1882), 195–222; reprinted in *The Spanish Story of the Armada and Other Essays*.

Thomas Carlyle: A History of the First Forty Years of His Life (2 vols., London, 1882).

Thomas Carlyle, Reminiscences of my Irish Journey in 1849, ed. J. A. Froude.

1883 'A Sibylline Leaf', *Blackwood's Magazine*, 133 (April 1883), 573–92.

'An Unsolved Historical Riddle' [Antonio Perez] *The Nineteenth Century*, 13 (April–May 1883), 635–52, 801–23; reprinted in *The Spanish Story of the Armada and Other Essays*.

'Luther', *Contemporary Review*, 44 (July–August 1883), 1–18, 183–202.

'A Leaf from the Real Life of Lord Byron', *The Nineteenth Century*, 14 (August 1883), 228–42.

'Saint Teresa', *Quarterly Review*, 156 (October 1883), 394–435; reprinted in *The Spanish Story of the Armada and Other Essays*.

Editor: *Letters and Memorials of Jane Welsh Carlyle* (3 vols., London, 1883).

1884 'Norway Once More', *Longman's Magazine*, 4 (October 1884), 588–608; reprinted in *The Spanish Story of the Armada and Other Essays*.

Thomas Carlyle: A History of his Life in London (2 vols., London, 1884).

1886 'Mr Ormsby's *Don Quixote*', *Quarterly Review*, 162 (January, 1886), 43–79.

Oceana: or England and her Colonies (London, 1886).

1888 *Liberty and Property: An Address delivered to the Liberty and Property Defence League, 25 Nov. 1887* (London, 1888).

The English in the West Indies or, The Bow of Ulysses (London, 1888).

1889 *The Two Chiefs of Dunboy, or An Irish Romance of the Last Century* (London, 1889).

1890 *The Earl of Beaconsfield* (The Prime Ministers of Queen Victoria) (London, 1890).

1891 'The Spanish Story of the Armada', *Longman's Magazine*, 18, 19 (September–November 1891), 478–503, 585–602, 25–42; reprinted in *The Spanish Story of the Armada and Other Essays*.

The Divorce of Catherine of Aragon: The Story as told by the Imperial Ambassadors Resident at the Court of Henry VIII (London, 1891).

1892 'Inaugural Lecture' [as Regius Chair of History at the University of Oxford], *Longman's Magazine*, 21 (December 1892), 140–62.

The Spanish Story of the Armada and Other Essays (London, 1892) [includes, in addition to the reprints noted above, the first English printing of 'The Templars'].

1893 'English Seamen of the Sixteenth Century', Parts I–IV, *Longman's Magazine*, 22 (July–October 1893), 218–32, 309–23, 422–36, 514–36.

1894 'English Seamen of the Sixteenth Century', Part V, *Longman's Magazine*, 25 (December 1894), 142–57.

Life and Letters of Erasmus: Lectures delivered at Oxford 1893–4 (London, 1894).

1895 'English Seamen in the Sixteenth Century', Parts VI–IX, *Longman's Magazine*, 25 (January–April 1895), 248–61, 360–73, 471–85, 580–96.

1896 *Lectures on the Council of Trent: delivered at Oxford, 1892–3* (London, 1896).

1903 *My Relations with Carlyle*, ed. Ashley and Margaret Froude (London, 1903).

Index

Note: JAF refers to James Anthony Froude.